studies and issues in
SMOKING BEHAVIOR

studies and issues in
SMOKING
BEHAVIOR

Salvatore V. Zagona
EDITOR

THE UNIVERSITY OF ARIZONA PRESS
Tucson, Arizona

ACKNOWLEDGMENTS

Costs for the 1966 National Research Conference on Smoking Behavior[1] and for the preparation of materials included in this volume were defrayed by USPHS Project Grant 03-02-A66. The planning and the conduct of the Conference were carried out with the help of Dr. Daniel Horn and Miss Cherry Tsutsumida, of the National Clearinghouse for Smoking and Health. Mrs. Ann Garrity assisted in editing the transcriptions and research reports. Special thanks are due to Mrs. Patricia Matheny, secretary to the Center for Research at Arizona on Smoking and Health, for handling the details of the Conference and for supervising the transcription of its proceedings and the typing of the manuscript. Appreciation goes also to The University of Arizona Press, under whose imprint publication has been effected.

---

[1] Held at the University of Arizona in Tucson on March 30, 31-April 1, 1966.

ABOUT THE CONTRIBUTORS

ALLEN, WILLIAM A., Director, Public Health Education, Philadelphia City Health Department, Philadelphia, Pennsylvania. Project Director, Philadelphia Smoking & Health Research Project. M.P.H., University of Minnesota, Minneapolis. Former Health Educator, Minnesota Department of Public Health. *Concern:* To modify smoking habits of elementary age children's parents, and investigating attitudes toward and motives for smoking.

ALTHAFER, CHARLES, Project Coordinator, San Diego Community Laboratory on Smoking & Health, San Diego, California. M.P.H., University of Michigan, Ann Arbor. 1960-66 Director, Health Education, Oregon Tuberculosis & Health Association. *Concern:* Psycho-social aspects of smoking with studies involving student educational programs. Presently responsible for developing community action programs plus comprehensive base-line study evaluating attitude and behavior change.

BARRON, FRANK, Research Psychologist, Institute of Personality Assessment and Research, University of California, Berkeley. M.A., University of Minnesota, Minneapolis; Ph.D., University of California, Berkeley. Former lecturer: Bryn Mawr College, Harvard University. *Concern:* Measurement of ego-strength and prediction of response to psychotherapy; also, the effects of alcohol and of psilocybin on fantasy. His work on ego-strength is probably most relevant to research on smoking behavior.

BARTLETT, NEIL R., 1958 — Head, Department of Psychology, University of Arizona, Tucson. Ph.D., Brown University, Providence, Rhode Island. 1944-1956, associated with the National Research Council Armed Forces Vision Committee; 1951-1957, the National Research Council Panel on Training of the Committee on Underseas Warfare; consultant to U.S. Air Force; summer visiting psychologist, U.S. Navy Electronics Laboratory. 1965-66, Research Fellow, National Institutes of Mental Health, University of Paris. *Concern:* Vision and visual perception; human factors in equipments and systems; temporal factors in sensory stimulation and motor skills.

BEAL, GEORGE M., Department of Sociology, Iowa State University, Ames. Advisor and consultant to major business industries. *Concern:* Adoption-diffusion, communication, social system and social power analysis and social action.

BERKOWITZ, LEONARD, Professor of Psychology, University of Wisconsin, Madison. Ph.D., University of Michigan. From 1951-55, Research Psychologist, Human Resources Center, Randolph Air Force Base, Texas. Editor of ADVANCES IN EXPERIMENTAL SOCIAL PSYCHOLOGY; Consulting Editor for several other journals in related disciplines. *Concern:* The psycho-social aspects of smoking as a special case of individual reactions to threat, plus research on the use of fear arousal as an attitude change technique.

BORGATTA, EDGAR F., Professor of Sociology, University of Wisconsin, Madison. Ph.D., New York University, New York City. Lecturer and research associate: 1959–61 Cornell University; 1956–59 New York University; 1951–54 Harvard University. *Concern:* Personality, intelligence test development, social work evaluation methods, sociological and psychological factors relating to smoking in college.

BOWERS, RAYMOND V., Head, Department of Sociology, University of Arizona, Tucson. Ph.D., University of Minnesota. *Concern:* Social change, research methods; impact of technological change on careers in large organizations.

BRADY, FREDERICK J., 1961 — Director, Pima County (Arizona) Health Department. Consultant, PHS Cancer Control Program. Former Program Officer, Bureau of State Services. *Concern:* Psycho-social aspects of smoking behavior, behavioral changes and consultant's role.

BREHM, HENRY P., Medical Sociologist, Research Consultant, Gerontology Branch, Division of Chronic Diseases, USPHS, Washington, D.C. *Concern:* Psycho-social aspects of illness-related smoking behavior.

BRINEY, KENNETH L., Director School Health, American Heart Association, Washington, D.C. *Concern:* Health as a motivator in behavior; the "change process."

COAN, RICHARD W., Professor, Psychology, University of Arizona, Tucson; Co-director (with S. V. Zagona), Center for Research at Arizona on Smoking & Health. Ph.D., University of Southern California, Los Angeles. 1955–57 Research Associate, Psychology, University of Illinois, Urbana (collaborated with Dr. R. B. Cattell: personality in middle childhood). *Concern:* Relationship between smoking habit and overall organization and integration of personality.

CORWIN, EMIL, Information Officer, National Clearinghouse for Smoking & Health, USPHS, Washington, D.C. Former National Press Chief, American Cancer Society, New York.

CRAWFORD, MARILYN, Professor of Health Education, Madison College, Harrisonburg, Virginia. Ed.D., Health & Physical Education, University of Texas, Austin. *Concern:* Health Education in terms of behavioral change; research in teaching methods which can best motivate health-related behavior.

DAVIS, ROY L., School & Youth Program Specialist, National Clearinghouse for Smoking & Health, USPHS, Washington, D.C. Former School Health Coordinator & Public Health Consultant. *Concern:* Influence of home and school environments on smoking knowledge, attitudes and practices.

DUBITZKY, MILDRED, Research Psychologist, Institute of Social and Personal Relations, Berkeley, California. Ph.D., University of California, Berkeley.

DUNN, DOROTHY F., Associate Professor, Health Science, University of Illinois, Urbana. Ph.D., Purdue University, Lafayette, Indiana. Former Associate: Illinois Department of Public Health, Chicago, and U.S. Department of Agriculture, Washington, D.C.

EDWARDS, WARD D., Professor, Psychology; 1963 — Head, Engineering Psychology Laboratory, Institute of Science and Technology, University of Michigan, Ann Arbor. Ph.D., Harvard University, Cambridge, Massachusetts. Former Instructor: Brooklyn College, Boston University, Harvard, Johns Hopkins University. *Concern:* Human information processing and decision making.

EVANS, ROBERT R., Associate Study Director & Ph.D. candidate under Professor Borgatta, University of Wisconsin, Madison. 1959: Research on alcoholism noted correlation of drinking and smoking. *Concern:* Changes in smoking habits among college freshmen.

FACKLER, WILLIAM A., Associate, Philadelphia Health Research Project, Philadelphia, Pennsylvania. M. A., Health and Physical Education, University of Maryland, Baltimore. *Concern:* Determining effectiveness of education and group discussion techniques in changing smoking attitudes and behavior of parents with elementary age children.

FILBEY, EDGAR E., Chief Investigator, Smoking Control Program, Indianapolis Methodist Hospital Graduate Medical Center, Indianapolis, Indiana. Former Chaplain, Riverside Hospital, Division Adolescent Narcotics Addicts, New York City. *Concern:* Addiction and habituation, specifically alcohol, drugs and tobacco.

GUILFORD, JOAN S., 1964–66 Program Director, American Institutes for Research, Los Angeles, California. Ph.D. University of Southern California, Los Angeles. *Concern:* Accident-prevention, smoking, alcoholism, drug addiction, and all facets of irrational and self-destructive human behavior; characteristics and motives of people "wasting" their lives in self-defeating or harmful activities.

HARTER, M. RUSSELL, Teaching and Research Assistant to Dr. Robert W. Lansing, University of Arizona, Tucson. Ph.D., University of Arizona. Former Research Assistant; San Diego State College, San Diego, California (under Dr. Robert G. Eason); Navy Electronics Laboratory, San Diego (under Dr. Carroll T. White). 1965–66 National Aeronautics & Space Administration Predoctoral Traineeship. *Concern:* Physiological and environmental factors in time perception; perceptual and other factors in attitude change.

HORN, DANIEL, Director, National Clearinghouse for Smoking & Health, USPHS, Washington, D.C. 1962 — Assistant Chief, Research, Cancer Control Program

USPHS. Ph.D., Psychology, Harvard University. 1957–62, Director, Progress Evaluation, American Cancer Society, New York. 1954–57 co-author, Hammond-Horn Reports *re* relationship of smoking to death rates; 1959–60 Director Teenage Smoking Study, Portland, Oregon. *Concern:* Coordinating smoking research programs throughout the country.

IKARD, FREDERICK F., Research Psychologist, National Clearinghouse for Smoking & Health, USPHS, Washinington, D.C. M.A., University of Arizona, Tucson. Former Research Assistant, Center for Research at Arizona on Smoking & Health, University of Arizona. *Concern:* Experimental social psychology, *re:* group conformity, values, attitudes, and personality development.

JAMES, WALTER G., Assistant Vice-President for Public Education, American Cancer Society, New York. M.A., Education, University of North Carolina, Chapel Hill. Formerly with National Tuberculosis Association on local, state, and national levels. *Concern:* Planning and conducting educational programs on the health risk involved in cigarette smoking.

JONES, RICHARD D., Research Assistant, Center for Research at Arizona on Smoking & Health, University of Arizona, Tucson. Assisted in study of 45 Papago Indian villages for environmental stress (Bureau of Ethnic Research, University of Arizona; Department of Epidemiology, University of North Carolina, Chapel Hill).

KATZ, JANE, Coordinator, two community laboratories on Smoking & Health, National Clearinghouse for Smoking & Health, USPHS, Washington, D.C. *Concern:* Potential application at the community level of psycho-social research to smoking behavior.

LAWRENCE, ROBERT, Psychology student, University of Arizona, Tucson; Research Assistant, Center for Research at Arizona on Smoking & Health, University of Arizona. *Concern:* Working toward medical degree in Psychiatry.

LEVENTHAL, HOWARD, Associate Professor, Psychology, Yale University, New Haven, Connecticut; also Associate Professor Graduate Faculty, Yale University School of Nursing, and Associate Research Director, John Slade Ely Center for Health Education Research. Ph.D., University of North Carolina, Chapel Hill. *Concern:* (1) Survey of public reactions to epidemic threats; and (2) Study of patient response to threat of surgery; effects of fear-arousing communications on attitudes and behavior.

MAUSNER, BERNARD, Chairman, Psychology Department, Beaver College, Glenside, Pennsylvania. Ph.D., Psychology, Columbia University, New York City. Former associations: New York University, University of Massachusetts, Graduate School of Public Health, University of Pittsburgh. *Concern:* Determinants of social interaction; factors determining attitude and opinion change; application of social psychology to public health.

MAUSNER, JUDITH S., Faculty, Woman's Medical College of Pennsylvania, Philadelphia. Specialized Training in Epidemiology. *Concern:* Training medical students in epidemiology and furthering their perception of smoking as a critical issue in preventive medicine.

MOSSER, DONN G., Associate, Northwestern Hospital, Minneapolis, Minnesota. M.D., University of Kansas, Lawrence. 1964, Advisory Committee, Cancer Control Program. *Concern:* For 15 years, involved with radiation treatments of patients with malignant disease, of whom substantial numbers were lung cancer victims; exploring smoking cessation with patients and their families.

MOYER, LAWRENCE N., Associate Professor, Sociology, University of Toledo, Toledo, Ohio. Ph.D., Ohio State University, Columbus. Former Chairman, Department of Sociology and Anthropology, University of North Dakota. *Concern:* Psychological adjustment of the disabled.

NYSWANDER, DOROTHY B., Associate, School of Public Health, University of California, Berkeley. *Concern:* Personality components of smokers, including their value systems.

OPPENHEIMER, EDWARD ANTHONY, Associate, Pima County Health Department, Tucson, Arizona. Cardio-pulmonary Laboratory, Tucson Medical Center, Tucson, Arizona. M.D., Columbia University, New York City. *Concern:* Community programs related to smoking as a health problem, as well as psycho-social and basic medical research aspects; pulmonary diseases; medical physiological research related to smoking and bronchopulmonary disease.

REED, KENNETH E., Director, Chaplaincy Service, Methodist Hospital, Indianapolis, Indiana. Ph.D., Psychology and Pastoral Counseling, Boston University, Boston, Massachusetts. *Concern:* Correlations between factors in smoking withdrawal and the identity crisis experienced by hospitalized persons.

ROSENBLATT, DANIEL, Associate Professor, Department of Environmental Medicine and Community Health, Downstate Medical Center, State University of New York, New York City. Ph.D., Social Relations, Harvard University, Cambridge, Massachusetts. Former Director of Social Science Research Program, New York City Department of Health. *Concern:* Risk-taking among adolescents; doctor-patient relationships; group interaction techniques to change smoking habits among college students.

ROSENSTOCK, IRWIN M. Associate Professor, Public Health Administration, University of Michigan. Ph.D., University of California, Berkeley. *Concern:* Social-psychological research in health behavior, including smoking.

ROSS, CHARLES A., Chief, Thoracic Surgery, Roswell Park Memorial Institute, Buffalo, New York; Assistant Clinical Professor of Surgery, State University of New York at the Buffalo School of Medicine. M.D., Columbia University College of Physicians and Surgeons, New York City. *Concern:* Establishment of smoking withdrawal research clinics.

SANFORD, NEVITT, Professor, Psychology and Education and Director, Institute for the Study of Human Problems, Stanford University, Stanford, California. Ph.D. Harvard University, Cambridge, Massachusetts. Former Associate, University of California; Fellow, Center for Advanced Study in the Behavioral Sciences. Former President, Society for the Psychological Study of Social Issues;

President, Division of Personality and Social Psychology of the American Psychological Association. Editor and author, Physique, Personality and Scholarship, The American College, and The Authoritarian Personality. *Concern:* Alcoholism and addiction.

SCHWARTZ, JEROME L., Research Director, Smoking Control Research Project, Institute of Social and Personal Relations, and Lecturer in Social Welfare, University of California, Berkeley. Previously: Research in alcoholism, California State Health Department; Research Associate, Behavioral Science Project, School of Public Health, University of California, Berkeley. *Concern:* Research methodology and experimental design, behavioral aspects of health care; psycho-social aspects of smoking behavior and factors influencing smoking cessation.

STANT, KENNETH, Statistician, National Clearinghouse for Smoking & Health, Division of Chronic Disease, USPHS, Washington, D.C.

STRAITS, BRUCE C., Acting Assistant Professor, Sociology, University of California, Santa Barbara. Candidate for Ph.D., Sociology, University of Chicago. Former Associate: Population Research and Training Center; Community and Family Study Center, National Institutes of Mental Health (training program in social psychology); Exchange Consultant *Seguro Social* branch of Mexican Government. *Concern:* Research methodology, demography, urban sociology, social psychology, and social personality determinants of smoking behavior.

TANNENBAUM, PERCY H., Director, Mass Communications Research Center, University of Wisconsin, Madison. Ph.D. University of Illinois, Urbana. *Concern:* Social psychology; emphasis on communication processes, including attitude formation and change; psycholinguistics; vicarious social learning and emotional experience.

TOMKINS, SILVAN S., Research Professor, City University of New York, Ph.D., University of Pennsylvania, Philadelphia. *Concern:* Cognition and affect, with investigations in stereoscopic rivalry, affective determinants of ideology, computer simulation, the moving picture analysis of facial expression, and the preparation of an affect dictionary for the computer study of historical records. His interest in smoking behavior is in connection with a general model of motivation.

TSUTSUMIDA, CHERRY YURIKO, Educational Consultant, Office of the Director of the National Clearinghouse for Smoking & Health, USPHS, Washington, D.C. Bachelor's and Master's degrees at University of California, Berkeley. Formerly Director of the Division of Health Education for the Arizona State Department of Health, Phoenix. *Concern:* Community action programs assisting states and local communities in developing interagency councils on smoking and health.

WAINGROW, SELWYN, Assistant to the Director, National Clearinghouse for Smoking & Health, USPHS, Washington, D.C. Training: City College of New York and Columbia University. Former Assistant Director, Program Evaluation, American Cancer Society, New York City. He has been responsible for collecting data from general and special populations, and has assisted in data analyses and program formulation and evaluation.

Concern: The dynamics of planned social change and national and community surveys of smoking.

WEIR, JOHN M., Social Research Analyst, California Department of Public Health; Graduate Student in Psychology, University of California, Berkeley. *Concern:* Psychological aspects of human cancer and psycho-social factors in preventive medical procedures, e.g., cervical screening, psycho-social aspects of smoking behavior and relation of smoking practices to the development, maintenance, and the change of smoking-related attitudes, beliefs, and perceptions.

WIEBE, GERHART D., 1962 — Dean, School of Public Communication, Boston University. Ph.D., Psychology, Ohio State University, Columbus. Former Research Psychologist and Assistant to the President of the Columbia Broadcasting System; former partner, Elmo Roper and Associates (opinion and marketing research). *Concern:* Public opinion, communication, propaganda.

ZAGONA, SALVATORE V., Associate Professor, Psychology, University of Arizona, Tucson. Ph.D., University of Arizona. Director, Center for Research at Arizona on Smoking & Health. *Concern:* Attitude change and group processes. Currently investigating cross-cultural comparisons of factors related to smoking attitudes and behavior.

ZURCHER, LOUIS A., JR., Research Psychologist, Menninger Foundation, Topeka, Kansas. Ph.D., Social Psychology, University of Arizona, Tucson. Former co-principal investigator with Dr. Zagona on study of cross-cultural aspects of smoking behavior. *Concern:* Personality-organization interaction, role theory, group dynamics, and cross-cultural research.

CONTENTS

PART III
CESSATION PROCESSES

PART IV
PERSONAL CHARACTERISTICS OF SMOKER

PART V
EVALUATION AND SUMMARY

REFERENCE MATERIALS

INTRODUCTION

The material in this volume has been drawn principally from symposia and research reported at the 1966 National Research Conference on Smoking Behavior, held at the University of Arizona in Tucson. Its purposes were to report research under way on behavioral aspects of smoking, to evaluate this research in terms of its theoretical, practical, and ethical implications, and to stimulate additional interest in research on behavioral aspects of smoking.

Serious scientific concern with the question of smoking and health is relatively recent. Soon following the 1959 Public Health Service assessment of evidence linking smoking to health (particularly the tie between cigarette smoking and lung cancer), much additional data began to be accumulated on the subject. This led Surgeon General Luther L. Terry to appoint a committee, made up of scientists from a number of different disciplines, to review and evaluate all available information on the effects of smoking to the health and well-being of those who smoke.

The project culminated in the publication, in January, 1964, of *Smoking and Health: A Report of the Advisory Committee to the Surgeon General of the Public Health Service*. Widespread concern was generated by the Report among educators, public health people, others in related fields, and the public at large.

Surveying three separate types of research evidence (experiments with animals, clinical and autopsy studies, and several prospective population studies), the advisory committee came to several conclusions, the general tone of which indicated that smoking could indeed have a deleterious effect upon the human body in terms of both curable and, at the moment, incurable diseases. The advisory committee also felt that its conclusions should be explained to the people at large in order to warn smokers and potential smokers of the possible effects of the smoking habit.

It seemed important to point out that, for example, cigarette smoking is associated with a seventy per cent increase in the age-specific death rate of males, and to a lesser (but still significant) extent among females. These and other pertinent conclusions (based on a variety of sources) appeared to be predicated upon the number of cigarettes smoked daily: up to 10 cigarettes a day evidenced a 40 per cent higher death rate among smokers than among non-smokers; 10 to 19 cigarettes connoted a death rate 70 per cent higher; 20 to 39 cigarettes indicated 90 per cent higher, and 40 cigarettes or more a day, upwards of two packs, indicated an increase in death rate of 120 per cent.

The age at which an individual commences to smoke also seemed to predict the risk he was incurring for later life. Men who had begun smoking before they were twenty years old had a substantially higher death rate potential than those who had begun after the age of twenty-five. Also, cigarette smokers who stopped smoking before enrolling in one of the program's seven studies had a death rate which was about 40 per cent higher than that of non-smokers, as against 70 percent higher for current cigarette smokers. Further, in comparison with non-smokers, the average male smoker has approximately a nine-to ten-fold risk of developing lung cancer, while for heavy smokers this figure rises to a twenty-fold risk.

While lung cancer illustrates most obviously the correlation between smoking and disease, other diseases have also been linked to smoking. Among these are oral cancer (pipe-smoking may cause lip cancer), cancer of the larynx, and chronic bronchopulmonary diseases, such as chronic bronchitis, where cigarettes seem to be a much more important cause than atmospheric pollution or occupational exposures.

Other diseases, too, show significant increases among those who smoke; but as yet there is insufficient evidence to attribute the cause to smoking. Among them are cancer of the esophagus, cancer of the urinary bladder, pulmonary emphysema, cardiovascular disease (male cigarette smokers have a higher death rate from coronary disease than non-smoking males), coronary artery disease, peptic ulcers, tobacco amblyopia (a dimness of vision that cannot be explained by an organic lesion), and cirrhosis of the liver.

In addition to the maladies suggested above, there is additional evidence to substantiate the findings of past research which has indicated that smoking among pregnant women definitely tends to lower the child's birth weight. There is also evidence that the largest cause of fires and some accidents can be traced to smoking, although the effect on traffic accidents has yet to be determined.

The general conclusions of the Report, published in part or in full by every major newspaper and publication in the country at the time of its release in 1964, gave as definite a correlation as had ever been acknowledged between smoking and disease. The impact of its disclosures led to the law passed by Congress in 1965 requiring all cigarette manufacturers to print on each package: "Caution: Cigarette Smoking May Be Hazardous To Your Health," but the impact of this admonition on the habits of the American smoking public has yet to be evaluated.

There is evidence, however, suggesting that some headway is being made in the campaign to educate Americans on the hazards of smoking. In a paper presented to the annual meeting of the American Public Health Association in November, 1966, Dr. E. Cuyler Hammond reported a sharp decline in cigarette smoking for more than a half-million men and women who have been followed in an American Cancer Society Study from 1959 to 1965. Among men who were current cigarette smokers in 1959, there was a decrease of more than 21 per cent, while among women the decrease was over 12 per cent. Hammond reported that while 45.8 per cent of the men in the sample were current cigarette smokers in 1959, only 35.8 per cent were so classified in 1965 — "an absolute decrease of 10 per cent or a relative decrease of 21.8 per cent." For women, 25.8 per cent were current cigarette smokers in 1959, with the proportion dropping to 22.6 per cent in 1965. This represented an absolute decrease of 3.2 per cent and a relative decrease of 12.4 per cent.

For each of the five-year age groups in the 1959 sample, there was a steady decline in cigarette consumption, from 59.1 per cent of the 30-34 year group to 8.5 per cent of the men in the 85-89 year group. While cigarette-smoking among adults in a particular age range would have been expected to increase between 1959 and 1965, there actually was a *decrease* of 6 per cent in current cigarette smoking among men 36-85 years of age. (However, among women of the same ages, there was an increase of 1 per cent in current cigarette smoking in the same six-year period.)

"With the passage of time," the report notes, "a certain proportion of adult smokers give up the habit because of ill health. A larger proportion give it up or reduce their consumption apparently for other reasons. Presumably, reports linking cigarette smoking to increased death rates from lung cancer, emphysema, heart disease, and certain other diseases had a major influence in this respect."[1]

In order for the research interest (and public concern) originally stimulated by the Surgeon General's Report to be maintained, it seems necessary to continue publishing the results of investigations into the various aspects of this challenging — indeed, frustrating — new problem area. Historically, the selection of topics for study in the social sciences has been largely determined by social need, rather than solely by the choice of scientists, although the latter have helped to identify and express these needs. The social demand for research on smoking behavior has not reached the stage where it can be viewed as overwhelming. Nor can it be expected to become so, as long as it can be considered threatening to the economic well-being of many Americans in a variety of occupations, and as long as millions — among them noted personalities and others with whom it is easy to identify — continue to be seen enjoying smoking cigarettes.

While only a small proportion of the pages of the Report (15/387, to be exact) describe "Psycho-social Aspects of Smoking," there was implied in these pages a call for more research activity — in acquiring more knowledge, and in taking steps to deal with the problem at various levels of intervention: from the school, the community, state, and Federal health agencies, to Congress itself. It was considered necessary to achieve a better understanding of the habits, attitudes, and beliefs of the public related to smoking. What are the personal and social forces that instigate the habit, or which may be used to encourage people to stop smoking, or to smoke less? What effective help can be provided to those who earnestly desire to shake the habit? How can the incidence of smoking among teenagers be reduced?

To deal with these problems, an improvement of communications was recommended between national and local forces active in smoking control programs. A National Clearinghouse for Smoking and Health, which, among other things, encourages and coordinates research and community programs, was established as a part of the United States Public Health Service; local and state inter-agency councils on smoking and health are being organized swiftly and effectively, and representatives from non-medical areas convene to discuss the implications of smoking control from the view of their own disciplines. A number of national agencies are coordinating smoking and health programs at the local level, while periodically, research conferences are called for the shar-

[1] Hammond, E. C., and Garfinkel, L. *Changes in Cigarette Smoking 1959–1965,* A paper presented at the 94th annual meeting of the American Public Health Association, San Francisco, California, November 2, 1966.

ing of knowledge, experience, and ideas, thus avoiding costly duplication of effort.

In his opening address to the 1966 Conference, Daniel Horn, Director of the National Clearinghouse for Smoking and Health, described the challenges faced by those active in behavior research on smoking as two-fold:

> One is that we are dealing with the very serious and very practical problem of trying to do something to reduce the death and disability that result from smoking. The other challenge is the one to behavioral science, because if ever there was a public health problem that depends on a behavioral approach for its solution, this is it. We have no injections, no magic treatment. It will be solved only by understanding human behavior and the changes in human behavior which are going to be necessary if this problem is to be solved. My own feeling is that by applying behavioral principles to this problem we will do more for the development of behavioral theory than by spending equivalent amounts of time and effort with the kinds of highly theoretical problems that so much of behavioral research has been engaged in in the past few years. Can we solve a problem of this kind? If so, what will its effect be on behavioral science? The challenge seems to lie in utilizing findings in this area to best advantage for bolstering and adding to the stature of a growing discipline.

The 1966 National Research Conference on Smoking Behavior was the second organized with essentially the same purposes. The first, held at Beaver College, Pennsylvania, in the Spring of 1965[2] proved to be an important stimulant to opening the area of behavioral aspects of smoking as a significant field of investigation in the social sciences. That Conference effectively merged both practical and theoretical considerations into an analysis of the following factors deemed to be essential to the study of smoking as a national phenomenon: mass communications; social and psychological factors involved in decision making; the dynamics of the cessation process; and a theoretical model proposed by Silvan Tomkins[3] which has served to provide the basis for considerable subsequent research on the dynamics of smoking.

The projects presented in this volume have been classified, for the purpose of convenience, under the following main headings: 1) *Communications;* 2) *Intervention Processes;* 3) *Cessation Processes* 4) *Personal Characteristics of Smoker.* Obviously, much overlap can be expected, so that a project reported in the section on Communications may also be concerned with one or more of the other headings.

The first of these, *Communications,* includes a number of projects investigating the various aspects of a communication which may influence its effectiveness, such as the characteristics of the communicator, the kind of medium used, the form of the message, and the nature of the target audience. These variables interact in such a complex way that prediction, or even analysis, for a given situation is extremely difficult. However, a number of projects are studying the ways in which public health messages, especially in the schools, can be made more effective by a better understanding of communications which may have as their goal either direct changes of behavior, or changes in attitude which may lead to changes in behavior.

Under *Intervention Processes* are included a number of project reports investigating processes which may intervene between the individual and his tendency to adopt smoking behavior. Many smoking and health campaigns in the schools assume that an important intervener between the individual and his likelihood to begin smoking is his knowledge of its consequences to his health.

The section *Cessation Processes* contains a series of reports dealing with the general problem of what happens as a smoker is engaged in shaking off the smoking habit, or, to use a more technical rubric, "Dynamics of the Cessation Process."

The final section deals with research investigating the personal characteristics of the smoker — that is, research exploring the possibility of systematic differences in personality or other psychosocial variables between smokers and non-smokers.[4]

Participating in the Conference, in addition to those formally engaged in the study of smoking, were a number of social scientists who were invited because of their concern for the humanistic and ethical aspects of scientific research, as well as for the insights they might provide in this relatively new problem area. They led symposia directed at defining the role of smoking research in the social sciences, and evaluating the ethical implications of this kind of research in the rather controversial

---

[2] Mausner, B., and Platt, Ellen S., "Behavioral Aspects of Smoking: A Conference Report," Health Education Monographs, Supplement No. 2, 1966.

[3] Professor Tomkins described the essential features of his theory at the Conference on Behavioral Aspects of Smoking at Beaver College in 1965. Based on this talk was the paper *A Psychological Model of Smoking Behavior,* which he presented at the annual meeting of the American Public Health Association in Chicago, Illinois, later that year.

[4] These research papers were bound and distributed to participants some time in advance of the conference, at which time each author briefly summarized his report and led the discussion which followed. Obviously, to make this volume feasible, some editing was necessary — both in the written presentations and in the discussions — for the sake of clarity, and to keep the text within manageable size. Consequently, a number of illustrations, figures, and tables which accompanied the reports have been omitted, as were certain appendix materials and technical descriptions of methodology and statistical analyses.

matter of the control of human behavior. Certainly no issues were resolved, although many points of view were expressed. The question of how proper it is for the social scientist to exercise his skills and experience in manipulating behavior away from smoking constituted a major theme of debate not only for this Conference but for its predecessor at Beaver College in 1965. It would be impossible briefly to summarize the broad range of viewpoints held by the discussants.

One end of this spectrum of opinion reflected a clear distaste for control, represented best by the declaration, "I would rather lead a short, autonomous life than a long, healthy, supine one in the hands of a group of behavioral scientists" (p. 193). An opposing view was that the social scientist indeed cannot seriously abridge the freedom of the individual to make a decision on the matter of smoking, because this freedom has already been restricted by the pressures of advertising, social conformity, and suggestion (p. 196). Of course, behavioral scientists recognize that the problem of the ethics of behavior control is not limited to the smoking withdrawal clinic. Psychological practice and research in general, and more particularly the areas of learning — as represented by operant procedures — and clinical psychology with the controls inherent there, are involved in the same kinds of soul-searching.

The role of smoking research in the social sciences was the theme of the discussion moderated by Nevitt Sanford. Among the questions raised was the matter of the timeliness of this kind of study in the historical perspective of psychology. It seemed to be generally agreed that theory and method in psychology have advanced sufficiently to deal with the kinds of human problem areas represented by smoking behavior. It was felt also

that a broader interdisciplinary approach to the problem should be made, that concepts in sociology, anthropology and related sciences should be brought to bear more vigorously.

In terms of future prospects, a promising result of the Conference centered about the appearance of better organized research and more carefully designed experiments. There is a clear progression from isolated and uncoordinated gropings for questionnaire data to more thoughtfully planned research programs. A better understanding of total personality structure, and improvements in measurement procedures, such as Richard Coan's suggestion that greater use be made of multivariate techniques, seem to be steps in this direction.

Further, no broad research program can be sustained indefinitely without a basic theoretical model to guide it, despite the protestations of certain learning theorists. One of the tests of such a model is the extent to which it generates research. It is encouraging to see studies such as that by Rosenblatt follow the lines suggested by the Horn-Waingrow paper. Moreover, national survey data are currently being gathered, testing formulations based on the Tomkins and Horn-Waingrow models. In addition to being supported by experimental and survey evidence, the models accommodate to statements from personality theory — particularly with reference to the relationship of affect and cognition (see Tomkins, S. S., *op. cit.*). As the models are modified and expanded, we expect them to suggest new hypotheses, the testing of which will lead to further organized study, and hopefully eventually to the development of effective action programs.

SALVATORE V. ZAGONA

PART I

**FACTORS CONTRIBUTING TO THE
EFFECTIVENESS OF COMMUNICATIONS**

Social and Psychological Concomitants of Smoking Among Entering College Students

E. F. BORGATTA and R. R. EVANS
The University of Wisconsin

This report presents in preliminary form data from two longitudinal studies of freshman classes entering the University of Wisconsin at Madison in 1964 and 1965. The information included here is as follows: (1) some social and psychological correlates of smoking behavior on entering college; (2) some hypotheses and the design of the main study of the aspects relating to smoking behavior; and (3) a factor analysis of a set of attitude and belief items derived from the Horn and Waingrow "Study on Behavior and Attitudes, Form A" (October, 1964).

CONCOMITANTS OF SMOKING BEHAVIOR, FRESHMEN ENTERING IN 1964

During the summer of 1964 (i.e., before arriving on campus), all entering freshmen at the University of Wisconsin were mailed a twelve-page questionnaire. This questionnaire included panels of items, henceforth referred to as the Student Orientations (Stu Orient), Work Orientations (WCS), and Values. Besides a set of traditional sociological background items, including socioeconomic variables, religion and others, also included were three short-form personality measures: the Behavior Self Rating (BSR) Form (Borgatta, 1964), the Self Identification (S-ident) Form (Borgatta, 1965), and a series of items especially designed to encompass the area of "dependency" called Social Orientations (SO).

Through a series of follow-up procedures, data were collected from 94 per cent of the students who actually enrolled. Their smoking behavior was assessed by a response to the single item: "Do you smoke cigarettes?" with the choice of answering: "No, never," "Occasionally," or "Regularly." Other data, including the students' performance in academic work and their scores on the Minnesota Multiphasic Personality Inventory (MMPI), were made available to us through the regular data collection procedures of the University.

The results led us to make some new speculations as well as to confirm some old ones. Based on previous reported research, for example, we had expected to find a number of concomitants of smoking behavior. Most of these have been defined as social, but a number are psychological. For example, there is substantial evidence that junior and senior high school smoking is heavier and more frequent among lower-class children, among those with poorer academic records, and among those in difficulty with authority. Smokers also consider smoking a lesser threat to their health than do non-smokers. Other findings indicate that youth are more likely to smoke if their parents, siblings, and friends do; that persons from urban areas smoke more than persons from rural areas; and that smokers are more likely to be outgoing, social, or "extraverted" than non-smokers. The data collected from the entering freshman class in 1964 should provide support or the basis for alternative generalizations.

Data were obtained in two forms, for males and females separately; first, means, cut on the trichotomous responses to the smoking question (Never, Occasionally, Regularly), and second, correlations of the scores or items with the trichotomous smoking variable (coded 0, 1, 2).

At the top of Table 1 the distribution of cases by smoking habits is indicated. *Seventy-one per cent of the male respondents and 65.8 per cent of the females indicated that they never smoked cigarettes.* Virtually the same proportion of males and females replied that they smoked *regularly;* the difference lay in the greater percentage of females who smoked *occasionally.* This is contrary to expectation, and appears to be a real change in smoking patterns. One explanation, that social maturity of girls tends to be in advance of that of boys, as is traditionally thought (and smoking behavior is likely to be a part of this concept), is hardly adequate now as it has not been in correspondence with the earlier facts.

Prior to this time, the explanation for less smoking among girls has been that social pressures were stronger on them not to smoke, as "Nice girls do not smoke." Historically this adage has weakened and more girls (and women) began smoking. However, since the great wave of information linking cancer and cigarette smoking, the pressure against smoking appears to have had the most impact on the more educated groups. If this is true, a strong attenuation may be occurring in the smoking behavior of young men (and in theory should also be influencing young women). The effect may not be reg-

TABLE 1

Concomitants of Smoking Behavior (Freshmen Entering the University of Wisconsin Class in 1964)

Do you smoke cigarettes?

	MALES				FEMALES			
	Never	Occas.	Reg.	Total	Never	Occas.	Reg.	Total
Number of cases	1316	337	198	1851	1195	424	196	1815
Per cent of cases	71.0	18.3	10.7	100.0	65.8	23.4	10.8	100.0
WORK ORIENTATIONS	Mean Scores			r	Mean Scores			r
WCS Potential for personal challenge and development	24.6	24.6	24.9	.03	25.9	26.2	26.1	.03
WCS Responsiveness to new demands	17.9	18.0	18.1	.02	18.0	19.1	19.1	.02
WCS Competitiveness desirability	22.6	22.6	23.1	.03	21.9	22.1	22.1	.01
WCS Tolerance for work pressure	14.6	14.4	15.0	.02	14.3	14.4	14.5	.03
WCS Conservative security	21.4	21.5	20.2	−.05	21.5	21.3	20.2	−.06
WCS Willingness to seek reward in spite of uncertainty vs. avoidance of uncertainty	17.8	17.4	17.2	−.04	18.4	18.9	18.6	.03
WCS Surround concern	25.4	25.6	24.9	−.03	26.2	25.6	25.3	−.09
SELF-IDENTIFICATION SCORES								
S-Ident Leadership	7.0	7.2	7.6	.08	7.0	7.5	7.6	.09
S-Ident Impulsivity	12.9	12.4	12.7	**.12**	11.9	12.5	12.8	**.12**
S-Ident Intellectual Orientation	11.8	12.4	12.6	.02	12.9	13.0	13.1	.03
S-Ident Aloofness	10.6	10.6	10.9	.03	9.9	9.9	10.0	.01
S-Ident Self Depreciation and Low Morale	15.6	16.1	16.0	.05	15.7	16.2	16.1	.06
S-Ident Lack of Tension	13.1	12.9	12.9	−.03	12.5	12.1	12.2	−.06
BACKGROUND VARIABLES*								
Educational aspiration (Some college, Finish college, Professional or graduate school; 0-2)	1.7	1.7	1.7	.00	1.5	1.5	1.5	.01
Expected peak income (Less than $5000, $5000-7499, $7500-9999, $10000-14999, $15000-25000, $25000+; 0-5)	3.5	3.6	3.7	.06	2.1	2.2	2.4	.10
Importance of financial success (Very . . . , Quite . . . , Some . . . , Little . . . ; 0-3)	1.3	1.2	1.2	−.04	1.5	1.5	1.5	−.02
Father's income (Less than $2500, $2500-4999, . . . $25000+; 0-9)	3.3	3.5	3.7	.08	3.6	4.0	4.5	.20
Father's occupation (big businessman, professional, small businessman, large farm, craftsman, sales, clerical, household, laborer, farm laborer; 0-9)	3.2	2.9	2.5	−.07	2.5	2.2	1.7	−.11
Father's education (Less than 5 years grammar school to Professional or graduate school; 0-6)	3.8	3.8	3.8	.01	4.1	4.2	4.4	.06
Mother's education (Less than 5 years grammar school to Professional or graduate school; 0-6)	3.6	3.6	3.7	.02	3.8	3.9	3.9	.04
Attends religious services (Never, Rarely, About once a month, About once a week or more; 0-3)	2.2	2.1	1.9	−.10	1.6	2.0	2.3	−.20
BEHAVIOR SELF-RATING SCORES								
BSR Assertiveness	14.8	15.1	14.9	.02	15.0	15.3	15.2	.03
BSR Likeability	19.5	19.9	19.5	.03	20.7	20.7	21.2	.04
BSR Manifest Intelligence	27.5	27.1	27.2	−.03	27.5	27.1	27.1	−.05
BSR Emotionality	15.4	16.3	17.0	.08	17.1	18.1	18.7	.08
BSR Responsibility	27.5	27.0	26.4	−.08	28.9	28.2	27.6	**−.10**
SOCIAL ORIENTATION SCORES								
SO Independence-autonomy	13.1	13.1	13.7	.05	13.1	13.4	13.8	.09
SO Social dependency	12.4	12.7	12.8	.05	13.6	13.7	14.0	.04
SO Directiveness	10.4	10.6	10.8	.04	9.5	9.8	9.7	.03
SO Sociability	11.1	11.5	11.5	.08	12.6	12.7	13.1	.06
VALUES								
Adherence to Authority	20.5	20.0	19.5	**−.12**	20.4	20.0	19.8	−.07
Need Authority	12.8	12.7	12.7	−.04	12.8	12.9	12.6	−.04
Conventional Religiosity	17.5	16.9	15.9	**−.12**	17.7	16.7	15.2	**−.18**
Adherence to Conventional Sex Role Structure	15.8	15.7	15.5	−.03	13.4	13.3	13.1	−.03
Government Laissez-Faire	11.0	10.8	10.8	−.03	10.7	10.2	10.1	−.09
Cynical Realism	14.0	14.0	14.2	.03	12.8	13.1	12.9	.03
Fatalism	13.0	13.1	12.9	.01	12.9	13.0	12.4	−.04
Civil Liberties Intolerance	15.7	15.7	15.2	−.05	15.2	15.1	14.9	−.03
Right to Free Choice	12.9	12.8	13.0	.01	12.6	12.5	12.7	.02
Non-Separation, Church-State	8.7	8.6	8.8	.02	8.7	8.8	9.2	.09
MMPI SCORES								
The Hypochondriasis Scale (Hs)	12.4	12.8	13.1	.06	13.3	13.5	13.4	.01
The Depression Scale (D)	19.5	19.3	19.2	−.02	21.0	21.1	20.4	−.02
The Hysteria Scale (Hy)	19.9	20.0	21.0	.07	21.7	22.2	22.1	.05
The Psychopathic Deviate Scale (Pd)	21.9	22.9	24.6	**.18**	21.1	22.1	22.6	**.13**
The Interest Scale (Mf)	25.9	25.7	26.7	.04	37.7	37.3	36.6	−.07
The Paranoia Scale (Pa)	10.0	9.9	10.1	.00	9.9	10.2	9.9	.03
The Psychasthenia Scale (Pt)	27.4	28.0	27.1	.00	28.7	29.2	28.4	.00
The Schizophrenia Scale (Sc)	27.4	27.6	28.4	.05	26.9	27.9	27.6	.06
The Hypomania Scale (Ma)	20.2	21.1	22.3	**.15**	19.8	21.1	21.8	**.18**
The Social I.E. Scale (Si)	28.1	26.1	25.0	**−.12**	27.8	25.5	24.1	**−.15**
The Question Score (?)	2.8	2.9	3.5	.03	3.1	3.0	4.7	.04
The Lie Score (L)	3.3	3.0	2.8	**−.10**	3.6	3.2	3.2	**−.10**
The Validity Score (F)	5.0	5.4	6.6	**.13**	4.0	4.6	5.0	**.11**
The K Score (K)	14.1	14.1	13.6	−.03	14.8	14.1	13.9	−.08

Note: With $\alpha = .05$, two tailed tests for 1,800 cases, $|\tau| > .048$ would be judged statistically significant. Values of .10 or greater are bold face. Sample sizes arbitrarily determined by all cases for which all sets of data were completed (including MMPI's) as of Jan., 1966.

*Ranges of response categories and applied numerical code ranges are given in parentheses.

ular, however, as there is some *misinformation* asserting that the danger of cancer from smoking is more prevalent among men than women. Also, to continue this speculation, it may be, too, that smoking behavior has become a permissible way for young ladies to declare "independence" which is of greater importance to them than to young men, since the double-standard mores of our society do not provide women the same alternatives as men for showing independence. Such forces may have somewhat equalized the pressures on young people to smoke or not to smoke. However, there is still the possibility that young women tend to smoke earlier than young men since they are likely to date older boys and would therefore be more likely to respond to their norms. The proportion of cigarette smokers does correlate with age for the crescive period, according to most relevant research reports. The age differential may be attenuated in part in high school because the tendency to date within the class is strong. Exceptions exist because high school girls occasionally date college boys, but high school boys rarely date college girls. The age differential factor would be expected to be visible after the freshmen have been in college for some time. On the basis of these speculations, then, our prediction is that in spite of earlier evidence that more males tend to smoke than do females, some new data for testing the age differential hypothesis may indeed show a reversal of the earlier pattern. These data will be forthcoming in our future research, and the appropriateness of our predictions will be reported in subsequent publications.

Personality and Values. Although the many different aspects of student backgrounds and behaviors were examined regarding smoking, only values and personality data are examined here. Sometimes this type of evidence is more interesting than evidence of association, i.e., showing that people who are in contact with smokers, be they friend or family, have a higher probability of being smokers.

It should be pointed out that the relationships in Table 1 are very slight; also, that statistical significances in smoking behavior can be attributed only to relationships involving less than one per cent of explained variation. Thus, it is probably reasonable to assert (since many social and psychological aspects are involved) that they are pervasively but *slightly* related to smoking behavior. It may be of some interest that the indicators of "outgoing" behavior, implying leadership and sociability, *do not* have the largest relationships. Rather, if a profile of the average college freshman smoker were constructed, "rejection of conventional norms" might show up as the most relevant characteristic. For example, the S-ident Impulsivity score ran higher than scores of Leadership and Lack of aloofness; the MMPI Pd involved one of the

largest sets of correlations; and there was an alignment of values scores. Obviously, some relationships consistent with the extraversion-cigarette smoking hypothesis persisted; but in these data they did not dominate to the extent that might have been expected on the basis of past research. Our evidence suggests that some shift may be occurring in the relationship of personality and social values to cigarette smoking behavior.

SMOKING CHANGE AMONG FRESHMEN ENTERING IN 1965

Again the next year, all entering freshmen were sent questionnaires. These had two full pages of questions about the smoking behavior of the students and selected other persons, and two pages of items dealing with educational and health aspirations. The addition of these materials, however, meant reducing or deleting some of the panels of items in the 1964 form. The 1965 form included the Student Orientation items *in toto,* the Work Orientations and Values items comprising scales developed from a factor analysis of the 1964 data, plus all standard background items and the S-ident form. To compensate for the omitted information and to measure the effects of the condensed scales, one-third of the males were given instead the 1964 form plus a supplement containing all of the additional materials on smoking, health, and education.

The first follow-up questionnaire, administered two weeks after the beginning of the second semester of the freshman year, was an abbreviate of the initial questionnaire but contained additional items such as questions on campus social behavior. (No attempt was made to follow up persons who had left the campus.) The second follow-up and final questionnaire is scheduled to be administered at about the same point of the second semester of the sophomore year (1967).

While our research will be concentrated on this 1965 cohort, data from the freshmen entering in 1964 provided guidance for the 1965 design as well as information of a slightly different nature. Although the research questions for the 1965 study involved a more broadly based set of smoking behavior characteristics, the follow-up questionnaire will enable us to examine behavior change over the first two years of college. Our over-riding concern is the patterns of change which might develop following an anti-smoking campaign. This campaign used educational literature and advertising-style gimmickry only.

Since approximately four-fifths of the freshmen reside in university dormitories scattered about the campus, it was possible to set up a quasi-experimental situation. The dormitories are formed into complexes, each of which has a central commons, or eating and studying facility, where it was felt the greatest diffusion of materials might take place. Therefore, a saturation campaign by direct mail was aimed at alternate complexes of dormitories each housing approximately an equal number of males and females. The control dormitory complexes represent a parallel distribution of students across the campus. The mailings were packaged in individually addressed envelopes and delivered to the dormitory mailrooms. The first three mailings included various pamphlets and summaries such as those published by American Cancer Society and Roswell Park Memorial Institute. The fourth mailing included some novelty items. In addition, a fifth mailing including additional novelty items went to approximately half of the experimental sample. Distribution of these items began two weeks after the students enrolled on the campus; the last mailing was delivered shortly before Christmas vacation.

Utilizing the data from these three questionnaires principally, a study of change in smoking behavior of the respondents will be made, although changes in other variables and additional variables added at each phase will also be examined. With the exception of the analysis of attitude items which is described in Part III herein, no analyses of the materials from the class entering in 1965 has been completed.

ATTITUDES TOWARD CIGARETTE SMOKING

In the study of factors related to smoking behavior, knowledge about the attitudes that people have toward smoking is crucial. When this study, involving the 1965 entering freshmen at Wisconsin, attempted to assess the students' favorable-versus-unfavorable attitudes toward smoking, it included 15 items from the Horn-Waingrow "Study on Behavior and Attitudes, Form A" (October, 1964). The selection of a small segment of the many questions used by them was guided by four considerations. *First,* whether the question had been used for a considerable period of time and in a number of studies, and whether some knowledge of group differences based on it appeared useful. *Second,* whether the question could act as a single indicator of attitude toward cigarette smoking — although most of the information did not indicate that this would indeed be the case. Therefore, we had to give some attention to the inclusiveness of content and degrees of acceptance or rejection of smoking implied by the statement itself. Any indirect indicators of attitudes toward smoking were avoided, e.g., most doctors who have smoked cigarettes have neither quit nor cut down. In other words, the more "projective" or subtle items were not included; the emphasis was on a more direct reflection of smoking acceptance or rejection on a continuum of good to bad. *Third,* whether the question indicated any rationalization of avoiding smoking cessation. For example, the following item was included specifically for this purpose: "If a person has already smoked a lot, he might as well keep on smoking." Of

TABLE 2

Factor Loadings for SBA Items, Form A

FACTOR I

	Male	Female
h. There is nothing wrong with smoking as long as a person smokes moderately.	.58	.64
j. The whole problem of cigarette smoking and health is a very minor one.	.58	.61
e. If a person has already smoked a lot, he might as well keep on smoking.	.55	.58
k. Cigarette manufacturers should be required to put on the outside package a warning label like, "Caution: cigarette smoking may be hazardous to your health."	−.54	−.23
i. Cigarette smoking is not as dangerous as many common health hazards.	.41	.58
b. Cigarettes do more good for a person than harm.	.35	.39
l. There is no association between cigarette smoking and a higher death rate from heart disease.	.32	.31
d. Smoking cigarettes is harmful to health.	−.30	.25
a. Cigarettes are pleasurable.	.25	.53
n. A cigarette smoker can always quit later in life in plenty of time to avoid any bad effects.	.21	.53

FACTOR II

	Male	Female
a. Cigarettes are pleasurable.	.59	.56
c. Smoking costs more than the pleasure is worth.	−.58	−.58

FACTOR III

	Male	Female
d. Smoking cigarettes is harmful to health.	−.49	.68
m. Cigarette smoking is a major cause of chronic bronchitis.	−.42	−.04
g. Cigarette smoking is a major cause of lung cancer.	−.39	.58
j. The whole problem of cigarette smoking and health is a very minor one.	.38	.34
k. Cigarette manufacturers should be required to put on the outside package a warning label like, "Caution: cigarette smoking may be hazardous to your health."	−.06	.30

FACTOR IV

	Male	Female
n. A cigarette smoker can always quit later in life in plenty of time to avoid any bad effects.	−.46	−.04
o. Cigarette smoking is more dangerous for men than women.	−.39	−.41
l. There is no association between cigarette smoking and a higher death rate from heart disease.	−.03	.39
m. Cigarette smoking is a major cause of chronic bronchitis.		−.34

FACTOR V

	Male	Female
g. Cigarette smoking is a major cause of lung cancer.	−.42	.02
i. Cigarette smoking is not as dangerous as many common health hazards.	.36	.18
f. A person should have the right to decide for himself whether or not to smoke cigarettes.	.34	.18
l. There is no association between cigarette smoking and a higher death rate from heart disease.	.32	.06
b. Cigarettes do more good for a person than harm.	.05	−.31

course, it was understood that refusal to see cigarette smoking as a health hazard may reflect rationalization, but we were interested in the fatalistic connotation of the above question in contrast to the connotation of straight denial. Finally, some items were selected for inclusion because they emphasized an acceptance or rejection of the fact that cigarette smoking is harmful to health. Since the experimental design of the study included selective questions about anti-smoking information and propaganda, it was expected that questions of acceptance in these two areas would be important for subsequent analyses.

Preliminary analysis. In preparation for the follow-up questionnaire in the second stage of this research and to anticipate the more general analysis of the study, the panel of 15 Horn-Waingrow items was subjected to factor analysis, using two separate sub-samples of 300 males and 300 females, selected at random from the student respondents. The factor analysis, which was carried out twice using alternate extraction and rotation procedures, yielded only five factors for each analysis with loadings as large as .40 (see Table 2).

The structure of relationships among the variables is quite similar for the two analyses by sex, with the first three factors clearly parallel. Some variation is apparent. Although an explanation for this variation is not undertaken here, it is a fact that society's attitude toward smoking by men is not the same as that toward smoking by women; the corollary being that the smoking behavior of men differs from that of women. It is thus not surprising to find differences in the structure or strength of attitudes toward smoking when comparing male and female responses.

TABLE 3

Simplex Arrangement of Selected Smoking Attitude Items

	a	h	i	j	(–)g	(–)d
a	......	.42	.34	.17	.15	.14
h	.47	....	.50	.36	.27	.22
i	.28	.42	......	.35	.30	.21
j	.27	.42	.40	......	.34	.39
(–)g	–.03	.13	.23	.34	......	.33
(–)d	.11	.22	.20	.37	.44	......

Note: Male data are above the diagonal; female data are below the diagonal. N = 300 for each sample.

In terms of the factor analysis: Factor I relates to items dealing with cigarette smoking as a health hazard. Apparent differences between the male and the female data are as follows: the male data suggest that those who do not view cigarette smoking as a health hazard are more likely to resist requiring cigarette manufacturers to put a warning label on cigarette packages. On the other hand, the female data suggest a stronger tendency to see cigarettes as pleasurable if one denies that smoking is a health hazard, and similarly, accepting the "rationalization" that a smoker can always quit later and in plenty of time to avoid illness.

Factor II is defined primarily by items which identify cigarette smoking as pleasurable.

Factor III is defined by items which appear to be the more definitive or extreme statements on the harmfulness of smoking. Factor IV is not well defined. The item on differential reaction of males and females appears in the factor for the male and the female data, but an interpretation is virtually impossible, since the concomitants are quite different for the two cases. In the male data the largest loading for the factor is on item "h," which is the "rationalization" item indicating that a cigarette smoker can always quit later. In the female data there was a negative association between believing that cigarette smoking is more dangerous for men than for women and believing that there is no association between cigarette smoking and a higher death rate from heart disease. It should be emphasized, however, that neither definition was strong. Similarly, the situation with Factor V is of poor definition, and no interpretation was attempted.

The analysis of the factors suggested the utility of returning to the correlation matrices and examining the first order correlation coefficients. At best, three interpretable factors result from the analysis. Clearly, however, there is no single factor underlying the variables which places smokers on a continuum of favorable versus negative attitudes toward smoking. Arrangement of the first order correlations, based on the factor analysis, suggested a simplex-type arrangement. It will be noted in examining the factor tables that, although there is no dominant first factor, Factors II and III are defined by items that have joint loadings in Factor I, even though the loadings are not large. Therefore, pivoting on Factor I, a simplex was constructed that utilizes variable "a" and variable "(-)d" at the extremes of the simplex. This arrangement, and the trial-and-error involved in testing the additional items to fit the simplex, suggested that actually a two-factor system provides a good fit to the data, the poles of which are viewing smoking as pleasurable (or not pleasurable) and viewing smoking as a health hazard (or not).

In preparing the follow-ups for the second stages of research, decisions were required on whether to retain the same panel of attitudes-toward-smoking items. After analysis, four items ("b," "c," "f" and "k") were dropped because of a lack of empirical or interpretive clarity, and two items were added to the Horn-Waingrow series to emphasize the derived factors. The first was to emphasize the pleasurable aspect of smoking:

"Cigarette smoking helps people relax"; the second to emphasize the health hazard involved: "Cigarette smoking will shorten a person's life." In addition, an item was added assessing the validity of the Surgeon General's Report.

DISCUSSION

Percy Tannenbaum: On the follow-up, what is the dependent variable — whether they quit smoking or not?

Edgar Borgatta: That is one of the major dependent variables; that is, we expect that in the process of becoming college students, they will be exposed to many influences which will cause their behavior to change in many areas. One practical and relatively specific measurable area is smoking behavior. Drinking behavior patterns are also expected to change. One odd piece of incidental — yet significant — information is that the "arrival rate" of smoking is relatively low at the University of Wisconsin. That is, in terms of the question which asks for a distinction among "No, never smoking," "Occasionally smoking," and "Usually smoking," the last group (regular smokers) comprise only 11 per cent of both the males and the females. The other interesting fact is that among those who answer "No never," the percentage is higher in males than it is in the females. I suspect that this is a relatively new phenomenon.

Selwyn Waingrow: How is the control group defined? What built-in devices are there for measuring the possible contamination between experimental and control groups?

Edgar Borgatta: There are several controls, actually,

or several comparison groups which are available. The campus housing units are divided geographically. Essentially, we selected housing units built around "commons," that is, the eating and recreation areas which are associated with the housing units, which are detached. We would ordinarily expect the students to throw the material we mailed them away — in their rooms, in their commons or some such place. They don't eat with other student groups, so they are likely not to carry the material around too much. We tried to time the questionnaires in such a way as to avoid diffusion effect. We do ask questions on diffusion and contact in our follow-ups; on examining the questionnaires themselves, rather than the tabulated data, we do get a fair distinction on information. We have a problem of contamination which is more general; that is, that our control subjects do have access to information from other sources besides the University and the experimental group. The newspaper stories, for example, that break during the period sometimes make us a little nervous because we don't know how these will affect reactions to the questionnaires as well as to the mailed materials. But we certainly do get an indication of the diffusion effects from our follow-up data.

REFERENCES

Borgatta, Edgar F. A very short test of personality: The behavorial self-rating (BSR) form. *Psychological Reports,* 1964, 14, 275–284.

————, A short test of personality: The S-ident form. *Journal of Educational Research,* 1965, 58, 453–456.

Smoking Behavior Change

DANIEL HORN and SELWYN WAINGROW[1]
National Clearinghouse for
Smoking and Health

I.   DIMENSIONS OF CHANGE

In an earlier paper (1965) we have described four dimensions considered essential in the construction of any comprehensive model of smoking behavior change. They are:

A. The motivation for change.

B. The perception of the threat.

C. The development and use of alternative psychological mechanisms.

D. Factors facilitating or inhibiting continuing reinforcement.

To elaborate on these:

A. The Motivation for Change

In the light of current knowledge of the effects of cigarette smoking on death and disability, a tendency is to think of health as the *only* factor in determining whether or not an individual tries to give up smoking. However, at least four other broad classes of reasons can be identified which contribute to, precipitate, or are even primary in providing the motivation for this attempt at behavior change.

1. *The Exemplar Role:* This is typified by the parent who gives up cigarettes in order to set a good example for his children, the teacher for his stustudents, and the physician who does so because it puts him in a better position to influence his patients. Even here, however, the health factor may be basic to the desire to influence the other person's behavior.

2. *Economics:* The direct cost of cigarettes is not trivial for many people, particularly as the taxes on cigarettes continue to escalate. For some, cigarette burns in a favorite dress, a comfortable chair, or on the surface of a handsome table represent an economic loss that may precipitate smoking cessation. But again, the threat of death or disability to economic security may serve as an even more powerful motivation.

3. *Esthetics:* The unpleasant aspects of smoking can also become factors for change. On the positive side, the sentient pleasures of good health as reflected in the common experience that "food tastes better, the air smells sweeter," can again make health a part of this underlying motivation for change.

4. *Mastery:* The recognition that one is unable to control the habit of smoking that sometimes accompanies unsuccessful attempts to give up smoking can be an ego-shattering experience. For some individuals this inability to exert intellectual control is more threatening than the danger of death and disability which led to the attempt to give up smoking in the first place.

Nevertheless, it is scientific information on the effects on health of cigarette smoking accumulated over the last fifteen years (analyzed and summarized so effectively in the Surgeon General's Report in 1964) — scientific information that continues to pour forth from ongoing research in this field — that makes the problem of giving up smoking somewhat different from what it was in the past.

B. The Perception of the Threat

Whatever the stated reasons for anyone's trying to give up smoking at the present time, it would be difficult to ignore the health threat. However, a number of questions need to be raised. For example, how is the threat perceived? What are the conditions that are necessary or sufficient for different individuals to adopt self-protective behavior in the face of the threat?

One suggestion, for example, emerging from studies of giving up smoking is that the cessation of smoking might best be considered *not* as a single event in time but rather as a process that continues over a period of time and requires greater or lesser continuing expenditures of effort. Leaning heavily on the Hochbaum behavior model (1958), developed originally to provide a theoretical base underlying participation in a mass x-ray screening program, later modified by Hochbaum (1960), Rosen-

[1] Dr. Horn is Director and Mr. Waingrow is Special Assistant to the Director, National Clearinghouse for Smoking and Health, Division of Chronic Diseases, U.S. Public Health Service, Washington, D. C.

stock and others (1960), and still in the process of refinement, we suggest that there are at least four necessary conditions for engaging in self-protective health behavior in general, and that their applicability to the specific problem of attempting to quit cigarette smoking is as a part of the dimension we called "the perception of the threat." These conditions are:

1. An awareness of the threat.
2. The acceptance of the importance of the threat.
3. The relevance of the threat.
4. The susceptibility of the threat to intervention.

These conditions can be rephrased in the following more personal terms: 1) "Is there *really* a threat?" 2) "Is it *important enough* for me to *do anything* about it?" 3) "Is this threatening to *me?*" 4) "Can I *do anything* about it?" Unfortunately, although all of these appear to be necessary conditions for self-protective action, the absence of any one can serve to inhibit action. Furthermore, even the presence of all four conditions does not insure successful action, since there are many facilitating or reinforcing conditions which contribute to a successful outcome and which we shall shortly discuss. The second part of this paper presents data pertaining to this dimension for our October, 1964, National Survey on Smoking and Health Behavior.[2]

C. The Development and Use of Alternative Psychological Mechanisms

This dimension has been discussed from a theoretical point of view by Tomkins (1965) who distinguishes between smoking to increase positive affect, smoking to reduce negative affect, smoking with no affect, and addictive forms of smoking behavior. Tomkins states:

. . . Smoking can be learned to relieve any negative affect and to evoke any positive affect. So we may learn to pick up a cigarette to make us feel less afraid, less angry, less ashamed, less disgusted. We may also learn to pick up a cigarette to give us a positive affective lift of excitement.

Tomkins goes on to define and describe these four types of smoking behavior as follows:

In habitual smoking the individual originally may have smoked to reduce his negative affect or to experience positive affect but he has long since ceased to do so. He may hardly be aware that he has a cigarette in his mouth.

The second type is positive affect smoking behavior. Here we have distinguished two sub-types, smoking as a stimulant, to experience the positive affect of excitement, and smoking as a relaxant, to experience the positive affect of enjoyment. . . . (It has been suggested that there is) another type of positive affect smoking — that associated with the sensori-motor aspects of smoking, i.e., what one does with one's hands and the positive affect which some smokers report about watching the smoke as it leaves their lips. . . .

The third type is negative affect smoking behavior which we have labelled *sedative* smoking. In this the individual smokes primarily to reduce his feelings of distress, or his fear, or his shame, or his disgust, or any combination of these. He is trying to sedate himself rather than to stimulate or relax himself . . . . We have distinguished two sub-types of sedative smoker — the partial sedative and the complete sedative smoker. In partial sedation the smoker uses smoking as an assist in reducing his negative feeling enough so that he can face his problems and solve them. In the complete sedative smoker, smoking is relied upon exclusively to reduce negative affect and there is no confrontation of the source of his suffering.

In the fourth, the addictive type of smoker, there is *both* smoking for positive affect and for the reduction of negative affect organized in such a way that there is psychological addiction. In psychological addiction to smoking behavior, first, the smoker is always aware of the fact that he is not smoking whenever this occurs. Second, such awareness of not smoking invariably evokes negative affect. Third, he thinks that only a cigarette will reduce his suffering. Fourth, only smoking will evoke positive affects. Fifth, it is expected and it happens that his negative affect will increase in intensity until it is intolerable, so long as he cannot smoke. It is this steep gradient of accelerating negative affect which so often defeats the effort of the psychologically addicted smoker to break his dependence. Sixth, his expectations that smoking will both reduce his suffering and evoke positive affect are invariably confirmed.

Tomkins then goes on to discuss some modalities of intervention based upon this smoking behavior typology that he developed:

If there are these varieties of smoking behaviors, then clearly attempts to control them must be designed in the light of these differences. We can only sketch some general directions of such differences. In the case of habitual smoking the major effort must be directed at increasing the degree of awareness of the act so that it again becomes possible for the individual to choose whether and when to smoke. In the case of stimulant and relaxant smoking the individual must be directed to alternative substitute sources of positive excitement and enjoyment. In the case of sedative smoking, either an attack must be made on the sources of negative affect, to reduce their frequency and severity, or the individual must be taught alternative ways of making himself feel better on such occasions, or to more directly confront and solve his problems rather than to sedate himself. In the case of addictive smoking there are two major possible strategies. One is to interfere with the first link in the long chain, i.e., so to arrange his life that he ceases to

---

[2] The sample for this study has been constructed using area probability techniques and stratification both by type of population and by geographic area. A random sample of adults was interviewed, and then all other current smokers and former smokers in the sample households were also interviewed. Thus, all current and former smokers in sample households were interviewed, but only a sample of those who had never smoked. This "never smoked" group was weighted in such a manner as to bring all three groups into balance. The weighting procedure, as well as the basic design of the study, sampling and interview techniques, and results in tabular form, are provided in detail in Appendices A and B, *Smoking Behavior Change*, by the same authors, in Vol. II, *Research Reports*, National Research Conference on Smoking Behavior, The University of Arizona, April, 1966.

become aware of the fact that he is not smoking when he is not smoking. The other major strategy is to intensify the cold turkey method so that the crisis of deprivation affect is reached more quickly and with more intensity so that the individual can learn that the apparently intolerable is in fact tolerable — to produce in effect the prototype of true mourning in which the bereaved thinks and feels that he cannot live without the beloved lost one, but painfully learns he can.

We mention the development and use of alternative psychological mechanisms here and have quoted Tomkins extensively in the strong belief that whether or not attempts at giving up smoking succeed is *partially* dependent upon (a) the adequacy of the techniques used to satisfy whatever psychological conditions are operative, and (b) the ability to motivate people to apply the appropriate techniques designed for them.

This assumes that such psychological conditions are empirically definable and that specific and appropriate intervention techniques have been or can be devised through systematic research to produce change.

Research is continuing in these areas but it appears that much more work needs to be done from both theoretical and operational points of view.

That some smokers have obviously tried and discovered certain things for themselves is indicated by the following facts. In our already mentioned 1964 national study of adults, two-thirds of those who had ever been cigarette smokers reported that they had made at least one effort to quit in their lifetime. Effort is frequently rewarded with success since of those who had ever tried to quit, 38 per cent were not smoking at the time of the interview. This 38 per cent represents 31 per cent who had been off cigarettes for at least a year (so that one would expect most of them to continue off cigarettes), and 7 per cent who had been off less than a year (of whom an appreciable portion could be expected to return to smoking). The proportion of successes is probably in the neighborhood of one-third, representing one group at least that, happily, has no need to await further research. It is these "successes" that we are studying intensively, as well as the "failures" and the "never tried's."

D. Factors Facilitating or Inhibiting Continuing Reinforcement

What are the conditions which make it easier for the individual to take on and to continue the self-protective behavior of trying to give up smoking? It was suggested earlier that the giving up of smoking is probably a process, not an event. *Social forces* play a primary role in either *inhibiting* or *facilitating* this process. Also playing a role are interpersonal influences (family, friends, co-workers), the mass media (particularly television), the behavior and attitudes of certain key groups (government health workers, physicians), and the level of "social acceptability" of any behavior at a given time. The *current* general climate of acceptability of smoking is probably one of the strong counter-influences to those factors which would otherwise facilitate the cessation of smoking. Restrictions on the places and conditions in which smoking is permitted, and reduction in the influence of cigarette advertising might be two mechanisms for changing this climate.

However, acceptability, being a social phenomenon, is subject to social change. The sharp reduction in physician smoking during the past fifteen years has been accompanied by a diminished acceptability of smoking in physician groups. A similar reduction in the general population might lead to the same kind of self-generating reinforcement, or "band-wagon effect." On a smaller scale, the same kind of process can take place within small social units such as families, circles of friends, clubs, or work groups.

The third part of this paper presents data on this dimension of a model for smoking behavior change.

II. THE PERCEPTION OF THE THREAT

Our basic approach has been that of applying epidemiological methods to the study of behavior change in smoking. As a first step we employed the retrospective or case-history method to identify the characteristics which distinguished those who took up smoking from those who did not; continuing smokers from those who quit; those who have attempted to quit and have been unsuccessful from those who have been successful; and those who have thought about quitting and tried it, from those who have thought about it and not tried it, from those who have not even considered it.

We have selected a number of questions asked of our 1964 national sample which fit into the four aspects of the perception of the threat which seem to be of importance. From these items we have developed composite measures of (a) awareness, (b) importance, (c) relevance, and (d) susceptibility to intervention of the threat. At first the data represented a retrospective analysis, but during April, 1966 we began to re-interview some 3000 persons with a history of cigarette smoking who were interviewed about 18 months earlier in the retrospective study. This permitted us to test whether those factors which distinguished ex-smokers from continuing smokers on a retrospective basis were, in fact, predictors of subsequent change in smoking behavior. This is an important question, for, although there are many statistically significant differences between attitudes and beliefs of smokers and former smokers, we do not know which of these are results of changed behavior and which are either determinants of it, or, at least, predictive of change.

A. Awareness of the Threat

The following three items were combined to provide a measure of awareness of the threat:

1. Item 34 E. "There is nothing wrong with smoking." (This was one of a series of statements to which the respondent answered "strongly agree, mildly agree, mildly disagree or strongly disagree.") Sharp differences between continuing smokers and former smokers in response to this statement were noted, especially in the category of response indicating strong disagreement. One point was scored for either a "mildly disagree" or "strongly disagree" response.
2. Item 34 K, "Smoking cigarettes is harmful to health." Sharp differences were noted here also between continuing and former smokers. One point was scored for either a "strongly agree" or "mildly agree" response.
3. Items 18-22, all of which questioned the respondent's awareness of the Surgeon General's Report on Smoking and Health. The first question raised in the interview regarding smoking and health was q. 18, "Can you think of any event you heard or read about in connection with the topic of smoking and health?" After several probes to elicit more than one response, if there was no clearcut reference to the Surgeon General's Report, q. 22 was asked: "The Surgeon General put out a report on smoking and health. Do you remember reading or hearing anything about it?"

One point was assigned for either spontaneous mention or aided recall of the Report.

Thirty per cent of current smokers scored all 3 points; 31% 2 points; another 30%, only 1 point; and 9% scored zero on this measure.

B. Importance of the Threat

This index was prepared from the following:

1. Item 34 L: "People have enough problems without adding to them by trying to give up smoking cigarettes." A "disagree" response was scored one point toward this index.
2. Item 170 G: "The chances of getting lung cancer from smoking cigarettes are so small that it's foolish to worry about it." A "disagree" response was scored one point toward this index.
3. Item 170 O: "The whole problem of cigarette smoking and health is a very minor one." A "disagree" response was scored one point toward this index.

Thirty per cent of current smokers scored 3 points on this index; 28%, 2 points; 18%, 1 point; and 24% scored zero.

C. Personal Relevance of the Threat

This index was prepared from the responses to items in which all current cigarette smokers were asked, "Are you in any way concerned about the possible effects of cigarette smoking on your own health?" Those who said "yes" were then asked, "Would you say you were only slightly concerned, fairly concerned, or very concerned?" A "very concerned" response scored 3; "fairly concerned," 2; "slightly concerned," 1; and not concerned scored zero.

Fifty per cent of the continuing cigarette smokers expressed no concern (score, 0); 19% were slightly concerned (score, 1); 18% were fairly concerned (score, 2), and 13% were very concerned (score, 3).

D. Susceptibility to Intervention

This index was prepared from the following 3 items, the first (34q) representing the belief that cessation of smoking could reduce the hazard, and the last two (168, 169) indicating that the respondent considered himself capable of changing his own smoking behavior.

1. Item 34q: "If a person has already smoked a lot he might as well keep on smoking." A disagree response scored one point on this index.
2. Item 168: "How hard do you think it would be for you to cut down to *half* the number of cigarettes you now smoke? Do you think it would be very easy, fairly easy, fairly hard, or very hard?"

A response of either "very easy," or "fairly easy" to this question scored one point on this index.

3. Item 169: "How hard do you think it would be for *you* to *give up* smoking cigarettes? Do you think it would be very easy, fairly easy, fairly hard, or very hard? A response of either "very easy" or "fairly easy" to this question scored one point on this index.

Seventeen per cent of current smokers scored 3 on this index; 23% scored 2; 36% scored 1, and 24% scored zero.

A first approach to the patterning of these four measures was obtained by dichotomizing each distribution:

a. Awareness: + for scores of 3 or 2 (61%)
                 − for scores of 1 or 0 (39%)
b. Importance: + for scores of 3 or 2 (58%)
                 − for scores of 1 or 0 (42%)
c. Personal Relevance:
                 + for scores of 3, 2, or 1 (50%)
                 − for score of 0   (50%)
d. Susceptibility to Intervention:
                 + for scores of 3 or 2 (40%)
                 − for scores of 1 or 0 (60%)

The following frequency distribution of the 16 possible patterns was obtained:

TABLE 1.

Distribution of Patterns of Perception of the Threat

	Aware-ness	Impor-tance	Personal Relevance	Suscepti-bility	Frequency
no plusses (12.2%)	−	−	−	−	12.2%
1 plus (20.4%)	−	−	−	+	5.5%
	−	−	+	−	4.2%
	−	+	−	−	2.5%
	+	−	−	−	8.2%
2 plusses (25.2%)	−	−	+	+	1.2%
	−	+	−	+	3.2%
	+	−	−	+	4.1%
	−	+	+	−	6.0%
	+	−	+	−	4.2%
	+	+	−	−	6.5%
3 plusses (29.9%)	−	+	+	+	3.9%
	+	−	+	+	2.1%
	+	+	−	+	7.9%
	+	+	+	−	16.0%
4 plusses	+	+	+	+	12.4%

By these definitions, about 1 smoker in 8 has all the requisites of the perception of the threat necessary for action — aware, impressed, relevant and susceptible. An equal proportion fall at the other extreme — unaware, unimpressed, irrelevant, and unsusceptible to change. The remaining three-quarters fall in between, lacking one or more important requisites for action. Where these are present, the absence of the susceptibility factor is most common. Some of these smokers have given up smoking or have made other significant changes in their smoking behavior in the 18 months since they were interviewed. The question for our prospective study is, do these indexes predict future changes?

III. SOCIAL FACILITATORS AND INHIBITORS OF CHANGE

In Part I, section D, above, we listed a number of conditions related to the adoption and continuance of the behaviors involved in giving up smoking. Among these are (a) social forces, (b) interpersonal influences, (c) mass media, (d) behaviors and attitudes of certain key groups, and (e) the general level of acceptability of the behavior that exists at a given time. Success in behavior change was seen as a partial function of the presence of facilitators or the absence of inhibitors.

As in Part II, we selected a number of questions asked of our 1964 national sample which reflected the five factors mentioned above. For each of these, we obtained data indicating the distribution of responses for both men and women according to whether they never took up cigarette smoking, are continuing cigarette smokers, or are former cigarette smokers, except for those questions which were meaningful only to those who had *ever* been cigarette smokers.

Unlike those items in Part II, these items and factors are considered more or less equivalent in their relation to behavior change; that is, each of them has a validity of its own in its role in helping produce behavior change. Since these items may not be interrelated, they are presented in this part of the paper as small items. It is our intention, however, to examine further the data on these and other items to determine whether (as in Part II) they can be combined into composite measures for each of the five areas presented. We may then be able to develop these five measures into some overall index of social and interpersonal influence. The item analysis may yield data on how many and for what kinds of smokers is only a single item correlated with smoking behavior change and for how many other respondents is change correlated only with a composite or patterning of a variety of social and interpersonal influences.

The data represent a retrospective analysis, but the results of re-interviews of those who were current and former cigarette smokers when interviewed in October, 1964, will give us an opportunity to test whether those factors and items which distinguish current from former smokers on a retrospective basis are predictive of subsequent change in smoking behavior.

A. Social Forces

The following three items were selected to reflect certain aspects of this factor:

1. Item 36a: "At present, is there a rule against smoking at the place where you work?" Distributions by sex and their classes of smoking history were obtained; most people do not report the existence of such a rule. On re-interview, the phrase "rule against smoking" has been expanded to allow for the distinction between prohibition and restriction. Little or no difference is evident in the rate of giving up smoking among those who answer "yes" as against those who answer "no."

2. Item 26b: "At present is there a rule against smoking in your home?" Most people do not report rules against smoking in their home (usually, less than 1 out of 20). Although the numbers are small, the data suggest that the giving up of smoking is highest among those who report such a rule.

3. Item 36c: "At present, is there a rule against smoking imposed by your religion?" Among men, the giving up of smoking is more common among those who report such a rule against smoking imposed by their religion than among those who don't. This does not seem to be the case among women. Most people report there are no such rules.

B. Interpersonal Influences

The following items were selected to reflect certain aspects of this factor.

1. Item 33: In general, what do *most* of the people you know think about the connection between smoking and health? Would you say most of them think smoking is: "Definitely harmful, probably harmful, probably not harmful, definitely not harmful, or that most of them have no opinion either way?" The giving up of smoking is more common among men who report most of the people they know think smoking is definitely harmful than among those who don't. This is not the case among women.

2. Item 36d: "At present is there a rule against smoking imposed by your doctor?" The giving up of smoking is more common among those reporting the existence of such a rule than among those who don't.

3. Items 125, 207: "Did anyone ever try to get *you* to *cut down or quit* smoking cigarettes?"

4. Items 126, 208: "Who?"

Among women, the giving up of smoking is *less* common among those who report such an attempt at influencing their behavior than among those who do not report such an attempt. Among men, there are no differences between the two groups in the reported rate of giving up of smoking. No class of reported influencers appears to be particularly effective. For women, although the numbers involved in the categories are relatively small, the data suggest that children are *less* effective change-agents than some other groups. For men, this is so in the case of a son, while daughters appear to be about average in their relative effectiveness.

C. Mass Media

The following items were selected to reflect certain aspects of this factor.

1. Item 261c: "The advertising of cigarettes should not be controlled or limited." This was one of a series of statements to which the respondent answered strongly agree, mildly agree, mildly disagree, or strongly disagree. The giving up of smoking is most common among those strongly or mildly disagreeing with the statement and in that order.

2. Item 216o: "Cigarette advertising or commercials should *not* be required to carry a warning statement to the effect that smoking may be harmful to health." There are, again, differences on a retrospective basis between continuing and former smokers. The giving up of smoking is more common among those who strongly disagree with this statement.

3. Item 216r: "Cigarette advertising should be stopped completely." The giving up of smoking is more common among those who strongly or mildly agree with the statement, particularly among males.

D. The Behavior and Attitudes of Certain Key Groups

The following items were selected to reflect certain aspects of this factor:

1. Items 62, 100, 170m: "Most doctors who've smoked cigarettes have *neither* quit *nor* cut down." This was also one of a series of statements to which the respondent answered strongly agree, mildly agree, mildly disagree, or strongly disagree. The giving up of smoking is most common among those who strongly or mildly disagree with this statement and least common among those who strongly agree.

2. Items 68, 127, 209: "Have you ever talked with a doctor or has a doctor ever talked with you about cigarette smoking and health?" Items 69, 128, 210: "Did he say that cigarette smoking was: Harmful; Not harmful; Good for a person; or did he say that he didn't know one way or the other?" Giving up smoking is more common among men who report talking to a doctor who said it was harmful. Among women, those reporting a physician having said this are not any more likely than usual to give up smoking but are even less likely to do so if any other answer is provided.

3. Items 70, 132, 214: "Is your present family doctor now a cigarette smoker?" Among males, the giving up of smoking is most common among those whose family doctor doesn't smoke now. Among women, no such distribution exists.

4. Items 129, 211: "Did any doctor ever advise you to quit, cut down, or continue cigarette smoking?" The giving up of smoking is highest among those who were told to quit and lowest among those who were told by a doctor only to cut down.

E. General Level of Acceptability of the Behavior that Exists at a Given Time

The following three items were selected to reflect certain aspects of this factor:

1. Item 35: "Thinking about all of the people you know, out of the *twenty* you know *best*, about what *number* would you say used to smoke cigarettes but don't any more; what *number* were never cigarette smokers as far as you know; and what *number* would you say are now cigarette smokers?" Current smokers are more likely to know more people who now smoke among the

twenty they know best than do either former smokers or those who never smoked; former smokers are more likely to number people who used to smoke among the twenty they know best than are either current smokers or those who never smoked; while those who never smoked cigarettes are more likely to number these kinds of people among the twenty they know best than are either current or former smokers.

2. Items 62, 100, 170p: "A person should have the right to decide for himself whether or not to smoke cigarettes." This was also one of a series of statements to which the respondent answers strongly agree, mildly agree, mildly disagree, or strongly disagree. The giving up of smoking is lowest among those who strongly agree with this statement.

3. Item 216d: "The smoking of cigarettes should be allowed in fewer places than it is now." Another statement of the above mentioned series. The giving up of smoking is most likely among those who strongly agree or mildly agree with this statement, and in that order.

The question that remains is, do the differences reported here predict future change? Data obtained in this study indicated the extent to which these measures distinguish between continuing cigarette smokers and former cigarette smokers. We are now engaged in a discriminant function analysis of differences between a greater variety of sub-classes of both smokers and former smokers. Patterns of factors as developed from analysis of the earlier survey will be tested both for their applicability to a new independent sample and for their predictive value in identifying behavior change. The hypotheses built into the original survey thus become subject to testing both on a retrospective and prospective basis.

SUMMARY

Four dimensions of a model for smoking behavior change were considered: (A) The motivation for change; (B) The perception of the threat; (C) The development and use of alternative psychological mechanisms; and, (D) Factors facilitating or inhibiting continuing reinforcement. Data on the second and fourth of these dimensions were presented from a National Survey conducted in the fall of 1964.

Four different factors in the perception of smoking as a health threat are viewed as necessary conditions before attempts to change smoking behavior will be made: 1) an awareness of the threat; 2) the acceptance of the importance of the threat; 3) the relevance of the threat; and, 4) the susceptibility of the threat to intervention. Responses to interview questions used to measure these factors were presented and an index of each was described, as well as their patterning.

Success in behavior change is seen as a partial function of the presence of facilitators (or the absence of inhibitors) to encourage such action and to provide periodic or continuing reinforcement. Social forces, interpersonal influences, the mass media, the behavior and attitudes of key groups, and the general level of acceptability of the behavior were considered, as well as such entities as official and voluntary agencies, legislative bodies, television, health workers, physicians, family, friends, acquaintances, people at work, friendship groups, and clubs. Data from the survey on some of these points were obtained, showing many differences between ex-smokers and continuing smokers. Reference was made to a prospective study now underway to determine the predictive value of these interview responses.

REFERENCES

Hochbaum, G. M. *Public Participation in Medical Screening Programs*, Public Health Service Publication No. 572, Government Printing Office, Washington, D. C., 1958.

————. *Behavior in Response to Health Threats*, Paper presented at the Annual Meeting of the American Psychological Association, Chicago, Illinois, 1960.

Horn, D., and Waingrow, S. *Some Dimensions of a Model for Behavior Change*, Paper presented at the Annual Meeting of the American Public Health Association, Chicago, Illinois, 1965.

Rosenstock, I. M., Hochbaum, G. M., and Kegeles, S. S. *Determinants of Health Behavior,* White House Conference on Children and Youth, Washington, D. C., 1960.

Tomkins, S. S. *A Psychological Model of Smoking Behavior,* Paper presented at the Annual Meeting of the American Public Health Association, Chicago, Illinois, 1965. Based on a talk given at the Conference on Behavioral Aspects of Smoking, Beaver College, Glenside, Pennsylvania, 1965.

Effect of Fear Communications in the Acceptance Of Preventive Health Practices[1]

HOWARD LEVENTHAL
Yale University

There are many points of mutual interest in the goals of psychologists, physicians, and health educators; there are also many differences in emphasis. The health educator *evaluates* behavior in terms of its effects upon the health of the actor; the psychologist instead is intent upon a description of it in relation to its determining conditions. The conditions and phenomena of interest to me and my co-workers are those that affect a person's acceptance of health information. (The term *acceptance* here means that the person not only *learns* the information, but shows somehow that it has changed his attitudes and behavior.) (Hovland, Janis and Kelley, 1953.) More specifically, we have concerned ourselves with the question, "How can information be presented for it to have a maximal effect on attitudes and behavior?"

One assumption is that some form of arousal, or drive, is necessary for this effect, such as is involved in the response *away* from an unpleasant stimulus, or *toward* a rewarding one. We need more, in other words, than providing information on how properly to brush one's teeth, for example, to expect people to change their tooth-brushing behavior accordingly. In this instance, positive (approach) drives can be introduced in terms of the value of clean teeth (social and sexual advantages); an aversive drive can be introduced by arousing fear of the consequences of dental neglect.

Because of their effectiveness in health crises, we decided to undertake a detailed investigation of the effects of negative drives upon the acceptance of health recommendations. While fear is obviously unpleasant, it is less clear how it affects a person's willingness to undertake a recommended course of action. A person may avoid getting a physical check-up "because he was afraid" to see his doctor; yet, he may get one, finally, for the very reason that he *is* afraid. Common-sense interpretations of every day events provide numerous examples of such inconsistencies. The goal of our study was to determine the conditions under which fear facilitates or interferes with the acceptance of recommendations.

EARLY FINDINGS

Attracted by just such questions, Janis and Feshbach (1953) performed one of the early and well-known experiments in this area. They compared the effectiveness of fear-arousing and non-fear-arousing communications in generating acceptance of dental hygiene recommendations. They presented a common set of recommendations about the care of teeth to each of three groups of high school students. The High-fear group received slides of bleeding gums and rotted teeth, which provided a vivid account of the dangers of improper dental care. The Mild-fear group received a similar though far less vivid communication, and the Low-fear group received a very mild communication. The students had reported their attitudes and actions regarding dental hygiene practices on a questionnaire collected one week prior to the experiment. Immediately after the communication, questions were asked pertaining to the feelings aroused by the message. The previous questionnaire on attitude and behavior was repeated one week after the communication. The results showed that the highest fear level was associated with the lowest degree of acceptance of the recommendations.

While this finding fits one form of common sense, the results are puzzling, since they do not agree with the previous example of avoidance learning in rats. Rats learned to press a lever not only to avoid shock, but to escape from any cues that had been associated with shock. Janis and Feshbach suggest that their subjects also made strenuous efforts to escape the fear-producing message and did so by *denying* to themselves the relevance of the message. Under those conditions, where the communicator's recomendation cannot be immediately executed, an unrelieved state of tension will persist, motivating defensive avoidance. Supporting data for the defensive avoidance hypothesis are presented in a second study (Janis and Terwilliger, 1963) showing that subjects exposed to a fearful communication on smoking and lung cancer were more critical of the communication than were subjects exposed to a less fearful message. This study, however, fails to present evidence that criticalness is associated with resistance to stopping smoking.

[1]Adapted from a paper of the same title by Howard Leventhal which appeared in the *Bulletin of the New York Academy of Medicine*, vol. 41, No. 11, November, 1965. This investigation was supported in part by Public Health Service Research Grants MH 06719–01 from the National Institute of Mental Health and CH 00077–02 from the Division of Community Health Services, Bethesda, Md.

In their earlier discussion Janis and Feshbach state that under certain conditions, e.g., where action can be taken immediately, a fear-arousing communication could be more effective than a bland appeal. However, other sources have ignored such qualifications and concluded that fear-arousing communications produce less attitude change than non-fearful mesasges (Berelson and Steiner, 1964; Krech, Crutchfield and Ballachey, 1962; Health Education Monographs, Supplement No. 1, 1963). Given one misstatement of the findings, we undertook to determine whether fear would enhance acceptance of an immediately available action and interfere with acceptance of a long-range decision (Leventhal and Niles, 1964).

Our experiment was conducted at the New York Health Exposition, New York City Coliseum, August 1961). The participants included any visitor to the fair who was interested in seeing a motion picture. Each person was assigned to one of three conditions: High-fear, Mild-fear, and a Control condition. The control group read a pamphlet giving statistical data on the relationship of smoking to lung cancer. These people were also advised to stop smoking and have a chest x-ray at the mobile unit located within the exposition hall, thus giving us a direct record of x-ray behavior. People in the Mild-fear and High-fear conditions read the booklets, were given identical recommendations, and in addition were exposed to portions of a film on smoking and cancer. The portion of the film shown the Mild-fear group related the diagnosis, hospitalization, and preparation for surgery of a young man suffering from lung cancer. The High-fear group was exposed to the same information and to an additional 10-minute film, with the camera focused directly on the patient's chest, showing the highlights of the surgical procedure. The entire film was in color and the vivid surgical scenes were obviously disturbing to a large portion of the audience.

After viewing the film everyone completed a questionnaire asking for the amount of fear experienced, and the intentions to take x-rays and stop smoking. While the communications were highly successful in arousing fear the subjects in the Control group expressed stronger intentions to give up smoking than did the Mild-fear or High-fear groups. While this could suggest that fear produced resistance to change, it is important to note that the High-fear group was just as willing to give up smoking as those in the Mild-fear group despite the fact that the former reported much greater fear.

There was no significant difference between the groups regarding intentions to take x-rays. A count of people having them (based on those who had not had an x-ray in the last six months) also showed no differences. The greater proportion of x-rays taken by the experimental groups in comparison to the control groups was also not significant; although a greater proportion of x-rays were taken by people exposed to the films than by people not viewing any of the experimental programs.

The negligible differences between the Fear groups could suggest that different levels of fear have no effect upon attitudes and behavior. On the other hand, it is possible that it does affect them, but that the effects vary so widely from person to person that *group* differences are unobtainable. An examination of the data revealed that in each group people varied both in reported fear and intentions. Therefore, correlations were computed between these measures in each condition. The arousal of fear may have elicited two reactions to smoking and taking x-rays: 1) if you quit smoking, you don't need an x-ray, or 2) if you take an x-ray, you don't need to quit smoking. If so, we might expect negative correlations between these intentions among the High-fear group, which would also have eliminated any possible treatment differences between high and mild fear. The results show that people who wanted to take x-rays also wanted to stop smoking, and that people who reported the greatest amount of fear reported the strongest intentions to take x-rays and to stop smoking. These relationships were the same in *both* High-fear and Mild-fear conditions, disconfirming the notion of an inverse relationship. Moreover, the level of reported fear and desire to quit smoking was higher among x-ray takers than among nontakers.

The analyses did suggest a positive relationship between the intensity of fear reported after a communication, and the desire to take either of the two preventive measures. However, the relationship is an imperfect one,

TABLE I

Response to Fear-Arousing Communications[1]

Variables	Condition		
	High fear	Medium fear	Low fear
Reported fear	4.25 (175)	3.24 (204)	1.59 (34)
Intentions to			
a) stop smoking (smokers only)	2.4 (62)	2.2 (58)	3.2 (13)
b) take x-rays (eligible Ss only)	2.55 (68)	2.28 (89)	2.14 (14)
Correlations between (smokers only)			
a) fear and intentions to stop smoking	.40** (61)	.47** (57)	
b) fear and intentions to take x-rays (eligible Ss only)	.42* (24)	.34 (22)	
c) intentions to stop smoking and intentions to take x-rays	.46* (24)	.55* (20)	

Note: scores are for smokers and non-smokers, unless otherwise specified.

[1] Leventhal and Niles, 1964

*p< .05
**p< .01

and it is clear that not all people showed increased acceptance when they were made increasingly fearful. That we did not find any overall superiority for the High-fear groups suggests that a sizable portion of the subjects, though frightened, were less willing to accept the recommendations.

The study also provided evidence on the validity of questionnaires. People who stated that they had a very strong desire to take an x-ray were far more likely to do so (75 per cent) than those who said they had a moderate desire (42 per cent) or no desire (5 per cent). Experiments to be reported later suggest that under certain conditions intentions and actions are less clearly related. In the present case the relationship appears to depend upon the availability of action immediately after the communication. Whether this is the crucial factor is, at this moment, less important than the fact that few people appear motivated to please the experimenter by stating they will act when they really do not intend to do so.

NEUROTIC ANXIETY VERSUS REALISTIC FEAR

If we could specify the personality factors responsible for these differences, they might suggest environmental conditions that could be used to overcome the resistances. One possible way of approaching this problem would be to elaborate upon a distinction made by Freud (1927) and other writers (Goldstein, 1939; May, 1950; Janis, 1958; Janis and Leventhal, in press) between realistic fear and neurotic anxiety. In neurotic anxiety, inner conflicts and past fantasies are projected upon the current environment, and the individual alleviates his tension by recourse to various defense mechanisms, such as repression, denial, reaction formation, aggression, and the like. These reactions reduce fear by eliminating thoughts about danger, although this has no effect upon the danger. On the other hand, the following six characteristics would seem to apply to the individual and his situation for reflective or reality-based fear: 1) the appearance of the fear response depends upon the onset of external stimuli; 2) the intensity of the fear response is proportional to the magnitude of the danger; 3) the individual is alert or vigilant for environmental cues signaling changes in the behavior of the threat agent; 4) active efforts are made to seek information or reassurance against the danger; 5) changes are introduced (and expected to be made by others) to minimize or avoid impact with the danger; and 6) upon completion of protective action, or upon receipt of authoritative information signaling the removal of the danger, there is a reduction in the fear response.

When a fear reaction does not show these characteristics, either because of persisting personality characteristics of the subject, or because a particular feature of the environment prevents one or another of these things from taking place, we can expect neurotic and defensive behavior, e.g., panic, chronic anxiety, or other maladaptive responses, such as denial, repression, or anger. For example, in the previously discussed experiment by Janis and Feshbach (1954) the authors subsequently divided their subjects on the basis of their scores on a test of neurotic anxiety and found that only the predispositionally anxious students were resistant to the high-fear message and highly accepting of the mild-threat message. Nonanxious students were equally accepting of both messages. In another study on dental hygiene, Goldstein (1958) has reported a similar effect where subjects classified as *copers* (those who make active efforts to recognize and deal with impulses and dangers) were equally accepting of recommendations under high and low fear, while those classified as *avoiders* (those who deny dangers) resisted the fear-provoking message. Thus if a person lacks the personality traits to cope with or recognize the outer event determining fear, or is in a situation that prevents him from reacting with realistic fear, we should predict resistance to protective recommendations.

EVIDENCE OF SOURCES OF RESISTANCE TO FEAR COMMUNICATIONS

A series of experiments has been completed that provide considerable empirical evidence on the conditions for neurotic anxiety versus action-oriented or realistic fear. In a second experiment on smoking and lung cancer, a graduate student working in our research unit demonstrated the significance of prior beliefs in vulnerability to disease upon the acceptance of recommendations (Niles, 1964). Prior research had indicated that subjects who believe they are vulnerable to disease threats are very likely to take preventive health actions when given relatively mild warnings (Hochbaum, 1958; Leventhal et al., 1960; Kegeles, 1963). Niles reasoned that if a person is so sensitized that mild warnings arouse considerable fear, then strong danger signals will arouse a disproportionately intense amount of fear, i.e., a kind of neurotic anxiety reaction, which would inhibit acceptance. Thus subjects high in beliefs of personal vulnerability should be increasingly persuaded as fear increases from very low to mild levels and then decreasingly persuaded as fear becomes more intense. On the other hand, people low in vulnerability beliefs may be non-responsive to moderate increases in fear but become increasingly accepting under intense arousal.

Identical recommendations about x-rays and smoking were delivered to three treatment groups, high-, mild-, and low-fear. Prior to the communications the subjects, Yale students (all smokers), were given both the anxiety scale used by Janis and Feshbach (1954) and a seven-question attitude scale on susceptibility to illness. On the post-communication questionnaires, subjects high in vulnerability beliefs stated the strongest desires to take x-rays and to stop smoking in the mild-fear condition. Low-vulnerability belief subjects indicated strongest desires to act under the high-fear stimulus. Despite the resistance to change for high-vulnerability subjects with high fear, the increased acceptance for low-vulnerability subjects was so great that the overall effectiveness of the high-fear communication exceeded that for either the mild- or low-fear message.

The vulnerable subjects in the high-fear condition reported less confidence in x-rays and surgery as cures for cancer, e.g., they said they would get lung cancer even if they stopped smoking. Thus, their resistance to the high-fear message did not seem to stem from denial of vulnerability, but from a strengthening of vulnerability feelings that led to beliefs in the ineffectiveness of protective action. These results also suggest that our failure to find an overall superiority of high-fear in the New York Exposition study (Leventhal and Niles, 1964) occurred because the sample included more people who regarded themselves as susceptible to disease.

Because the Niles (1964) study used students and omitted a behavioral measure, a third experiment was undertaken (Leventhal and Watts, 1966). Leventhal and Watts developed a brief version of the vulnerability-beliefs scale that was suitable for a non-student population. Subjects rating themselves as vulnerable to disease were expected to feel the threat to be more relevant and to report more fear when exposed to the communications than those who did not rate themselves as vulnerable. Because the threat is more relevant to smokers than non-smokers, it was expected that smokers would report more fear than non-smokers. However, it was also hypothesized that heavy smokers, the group most directly in danger, would show relatively strong resistances to admitting fear if they believed themselves to be invulnerable. Thus feelings of invulnerability will inoculate a person against fear, and these beliefs are likely to be especially strong if one is highly committed to behaviors that are alleged to lead to danger.

The three smoking groups, light smokers, heavy smokers, and non-smokers, were divided into those who believed they were vulnerable to disease and those who believed they were not; a total of six sub-groups. These measures were obtained immediately before exposure to a smoking communication. The experiment was conducted at the New York State Fair, and the films comprising the communications were shown in a theatre located in a pavilion called the Hall of Health. A free mobile x-ray unit was at one of the pavilion entrances, and both were at the center of the fair ground. Three experimental treatments, high, mild, and low fear, were used.

The amount of *fear* reported by subjects followed predictions closely (Fig. 1). Most striking was the fact that light smokers with high vulnerability beliefs reported considerable fear even when exposed to the low-fear film

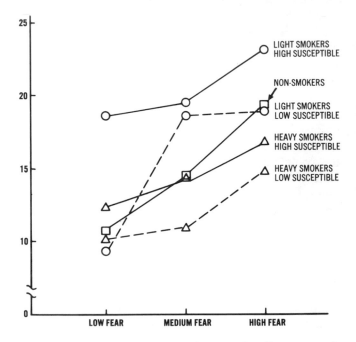

Fig. 1. Emotional response to fear-arousing films on smoking and lung cancer (Leventhal and Watts, 1966).

that contained only statistics and charts on the relationship of smoking to cancer. On the other hand, heavy smokers who had previously rated themselves as invulnerable to disease reported the least fear in each of the three conditions.

The questionnaire measures of intention were disappointing. As in the first study by Leventhal and Niles (1964), there were no statistically significant effects between the fear treatments or between the vulnerability and smoking groupings for acceptance of either the recommendation to stop smoking or to take x-rays (Table II). However, there were positive correlations between fear and acceptance within the conditions. An examination of the frequency of x-ray taking for *eligible smokers* showed a highly significant decrease in x-rays going from the *low- to the high-fear* condition! Fear had apparently produced resistance to x-ray taking. However, many people in the high-fear condition indicated they would prefer to go to their doctors for an x-ray rather than take one at the mobile unit. This would be plausible if they thought something could really be amiss with themselves. Therefore a follow-up questionnaire was mailed to the participants five months later to check on the subsequent taking of x-rays and, at the same time, to determine how many people cut down or stopped smoking.

TABLE II

Reactions of Health Education Visitors to Fear Communications on Smoking[1]

	Communication		
Reaction of Smokers	High fear	Medium fear	Low fear
1) Strength of negative emotion (fear, nausea, etc.)	18.2 (61)	16.2 (47)	12.1 (71)
2) Intention to			
a) stop smoking	3.7 (55)	3.7 (45)	3.4 (61)
b) take x-ray	5.5 (60)	5.1 (51)	5.1 (71)
3) Took x-ray at exposition	6% (17)	44% (16)	53% (19)
4) Stopped or decreased smoking	73% (23)	57% (30)	57% (29)
5) Correlations between			
a) fear and intentions to decrease smoking	.40*	—.08	.11
b) fear and intentions to take x-rays	.37*	.32*	.28*
c) belief in effectiveness of stopping smoking and intentions to decrease smoking	—.03	.05	.30*
d) belief in effectiveness of x-rays and intentions to take an x-ray	.09	.34*	.51*
e) fear and belief in effectiveness of stopping smoking	.25*	.26	.18
f) fear and belief in effectiveness of taking x-rays	.15	.28*	.06

[1] Leventhal and Watts, 1966
*$p < .05$

Because only 45 per cent of the subjects returned their questionnaires, the data may be biased and must be interpreted with caution. However, two factors suggest that the returns were representative of the original sample: 1) the proportion of returns was not significantly different for each of the three conditions, and 2) people who had taken x-rays at the fair stated this on the questionnaire. Few new x-rays were reported, and the greatest number of x-rays remained in the low-fear condition. However, for smoking, the proportions attempting to stop were the same across the fear groups, but significantly more subjects in the high-fear condition reported *success* in stopping.

The above results are opposed to the hypothesis initially stated by Leventhal and Niles (1964), that fear will enhance immediately available actions, e.g., x-ray taking, and interfere with long-range actions, e.g., stopping smoking. Yet if we realize that the threat is not only death through lung cancer, but death through surgery, the result of decreased x-ray taking for smokers makes good sense (the rate of x-ray taking for non-smokers was equivalent across the fear conditions).[2] An x-ray as a necessary precursor to surgery leads *to* threat as well as away from threat. Stopping smoking, though it may entail deprivation, is not a step toward threat. Thus

where escape was possible (for smoking) the subjects showed realistic fear, and where they were "trapped" (x-rays) they showed neurotic or unrealistic fear.

Since plausibility is an insufficient criterion for accepting a hypothesis, evidence for this new assumption was sought by computing correlations between the responses given by subjects within each condition. In the low-fear condition, desire to conform to protective recommendations was correlated with beliefs in their effectiveness. As the communication became more fearful, desire to act was increasingly correlated with fear, and the correlations between desires to take x-rays and beliefs in effectiveness became zero. Thus with a threatening recommendation, fear rather than beliefs in the effectiveness of the recommendation appeared to be the primary motive for acceptance. This result confirms Niles' (1964) earlier conclusion that the arousal of fear increases acceptance unless the recommended actions appear inadequate to protect oneself from danger. In the Niles study the recommendations were seen to be inadequate only among students high in vulnerability beliefs. For smokers in the present population (older, from less well-to-do homes, probably less accustomed to seeing themselves as able to fend off environmental threats than Niles' [1964] Yale subjects) the fear communication produced an overall decrease in acceptance regardless of the subjects' vulnerability beliefs. Since beliefs in the effectiveness of stopping smoking remain correlated with fear it would appear that effectiveness beliefs for smoking were somewhat less shaken by the fear message. Moreover, as quitting smoking probably occurred later in time than the x-ray taking, the fear could have dissipated, permitting confidence in the action to return to normal. Whatever the process, the threat message induced realistic fear and action with regard to smoking.

Several parallels exist between the reactions described in the previous experiments and responses observed during times of extreme danger. For example, as with heavy smokers who believe themselves invulnerable to disease, people adapted so rapidly and thoroughly to the threat of aerial bombardment during World War II that they ceased to follow authoritative warnings of danger. Few people left cities such as London during even the most severe phases of the blitz (Glover, 1942; Schmideberg, 1942). The same types of reactions have been observed in response to natural disasters such as the Kansas City flood and threats of mine cave-ins (Logan, Killian and Marrs, 1952). As discussed in detail by

[2] In the Leventhal and Niles (1964) study, the results reported for x-ray taking combine smokers and non-smokers. There were relatively few smokers in that sample who were eligible for x-rays, and their behavior did not differ from that of the non-smoking group.

Janis (1958) and Janis and Leventhal (in press), invulnerability defenses develop under conditions where warnings are repeated without the approach of danger. But when a powerful warning occurs (e.g., similar to high-fear communications), it may break through invulnerability beliefs, arouse fear, and motivate protective behavior. Severe breaks in invulnerability defenses are vividly illustrated by near-miss experiences in disasters, e.g., where people are helpless against the threat, trapped in wreckage, thrown by blast, but uninjured. Such experiences often produce chronic sensitivity to threat analogous to the hyper-vigilant behavior seen in people with high beliefs in vulnerability. High levels of fear are readily stimulated in these people, and the fear does not lead to a meaningful pattern of escape behavior.

FEAR AND HIGH-EFFECTIVENESS RECOMMENDATIONS

Unlike cancer or heart disease, many danger situations pose less risk to the organism or offer far greater possibility for controlling the threat agent. For example, preventives or cures are now available for a number of otherwise fatal infectious diseases. In a recent study on acceptance of warning communications, Leventhal, Singer and Jones (1965) made use of an issue high in threat and high in preventability. For their high-threat communication the authors used a booklet that presented a case history of a patient who died from tetanus. Color photographs illustrated various aspects of treatment, e.g., tracheotomy wounds, drainage tubes, etc., and the language of the booklet was vivid and frightening. For a low-fear message the booklets gave the same information about the disease but substituted innocuous black and white photographs for the color pictures, and used bland instead of emotional language. A recommendation was made to *all* subjects (college students) to get a free tetanus shot at the University Health Service. Half the students in each fear group also received a map of the campus with the Student Health Service clearly circled. Detailed suggestions were also given for planning a trip to the Health Service. For example, explicit mention was made of several class changes, routes to the library, etc., that would bring the student near the Health Service. Two control groups were also included. One received only the detailed instructions on how to get a tetanus shot. The other was a randomly drawn sample unexposed to any messages and whose shot-taking behavior was also recorded. Thus, there were four experimental groups, high-fear with and without specific instructions and low-fear with and without instructions, and the two controls.

On the questionnaire given immediately after the communication, subjects exposed to the high-fear booklets (specific and nonspecific) reported significantly greater tension, fear, and nausea, more favorable atti-

TABLE III

Reactions to Tetanus Communications[1]

	Communication		
Response measure	A. High fear	Low fear	No fear
	Specific and nonspecific recommendation	Specific and nonspecific specific recommendation	Specific recommendation only
Reported fear	9.2 (30)	4.5 (29)	3.0 (29)
Belief in the importance of shots	11.6 (30)	10.2 (29)	8.8 (29)
Strong intentions to get shots	60% (30)	31% (29)	18% (29)

	B. High and Low fear	High and Low fear	No fear	No fear
	Specific recommendation	Nonspecific recommendation	Specific recommendation	No recommendation
Took shots	28% (29)	3% (30)	0% (30)	0% (60)

[1] Leventhal, Singer and Jones, 1965.

tudes toward inoculation, and stronger intentions to take shots than subjects exposed to the low-fear booklet (Table III). The control group exposed only to specific recommendations reported considerably less favorable attitudes toward shots and less desire for inoculation than either the high-fear or low-fear groups. When a count was made of subjects getting shots, it was found that students who received the specific recommendations along with either fear communication were significantly more likely to get tetanus inoculations than those not receiving the instructions (specific and fear, 28 per cent; nonspecific and fear, 3 per cent). But while specific instructions were necessary for behavior, the high-fear group receiving specific instructions showed no greater proportion of shot takers than the comparable low-fear group. Neither information alone nor fear alone was sufficient for behavior. It should be emphasized that all of the students were seniors and all knew the location of the Health Service.

It may be seen that while some level of fear was necessary for behavior, the highest level of fear was successful in creating further increases in attitude change but not in behavior. However, this failure of the attitude change to carry over to action may be more apparent than real. The increased verbal acceptance for high-fear relative to low-fear was measured *immediately after* exposure. All shot-taking behaviors occurred three days to three weeks later. As time passes both fear about contracting tetanus and favorable attitudes or intentions toward getting shots should return to their pre-exposure level. Thus, an equal proportion of shots might be expected in both high-fear and low-fear groups when the behavior is measured after a delay.

To verify that both attitudes and fear decay over time, Leventhal and Niles (1965) measured attitudes at four points in time (immediately, 1 to 2 hours, 1 day, and 1 week) after exposure of one to four different durations (8, 16, 24, or 32 minutes) of fearful motion pictures of automotive accidents. Concern about accidents, and the desire to drive safely were significantly stronger for people exposed to the longer films. However, the increased effectiveness of long exposures was noticeable for groups measured very near to the time of exposure. For people whose attitudes were recorded a day or week afterward, the differences were largely absent.

While the automotive accident study (Leventhal and Niles, 1965) verifies the hypothesis that both changes in attitude and feelings of fear dissipate with time, it does not account for the fact that fear *combined* with specific recommendations produced a lasting change. In the auto study, attitudes and behaviors of people exposed to any of the four durations returned, in time, to the positions held by subjects who were *unexposed* to messages on driving. Although a delayed attitude measure is lacking in the tetanus study (Leventhal, Singer and Jones, 1965), the subjects given *specific* information in the high-fear and low-fear groups took many more shots than those in the no-fear controls (28 per cent versus 0 per cent). Thus, combining some amount of fear with specific recommendations caused a "permanent" change for a significant proportion of subjects but the level of fear (high or low) did not differentially affect this change. However, it must be remembered that a tetanus shot is a single act (or two- to three-visit affair at most), while safe driving is a day by-day affair. In the accident study, driving practices may have changed temporarily and then gradually reverted to their earlier state. There is no way of detecting reversion to early practices for shot taking. In addition, there are likely to be many more factors sustaining present driving practices and thereby resisting change than there are factors in favor of not taking tetanus shots.

Three conclusions seem warranted from the two studies. First, when the actions recommended are clearly effective, attitude and behavior change is more likely to take place than if doubts exist about response effectiveness. Second, the effects of fear communications are subject to dissipation over time, though the loss of effectiveness is less likely when specific recommendations are given and/or when the behavior recommended is a simple one-shot measure.[3] Third, when specific instructions for action accompany a fear message, it is doubtful whether there is any long-range gain in acceptance once fear is raised above some "adequate" threshold.

[3] In a just-completed study on smoking, it appears that specific instructions are the critical factor in maintaining and *increasing* behavior change.

REPLICATIONS AND EXTENSION OF FINDINGS TO DENTAL HYGIENE

The only health topic where the research reviewed in this paper exclusively supports the hypothesis that high-fear generates less acceptance than low-fear is dental hygiene. Since it is possible that the original result obtained by Janis and Feshbach (1953) is more readily replicated with this issue, Leventhal and Singer (1965) undertook a new study comparing the effectiveness of fear-arousing and nonfear-arousing communications for the acceptance of dental hygiene practices. An effort was also made in this experiment to assess the importance of the reduction of the fear drive for the acceptance of specific reassurances (see also Miller, 1963). To manipulate the association of recommendations with fear arousal and fear reductions, Leventhal and Singer used several groups to vary the order of presentation of the fear and recommendation stimuli (see also Aronfreed, 1964; Cohen, 1957; Moltz and Thistlethwaite, 1955). It was predicted that presenting the recommendations *after* the fear stimuli would result in pairing the recommendations with the greatest reduction of fear, and lead to the greatest acceptance. But recommendations given prior to the fear communications (where there is no fear to be reduced) are less likely to be recalled and used to reassure oneself (Cohen, 1957). A third group was used with recommendations intermixed with the fear material. This replicated the Janis and Feshbach order and was predicted to be less effective than the fear followed by recommendations, yet more effective than recommendations followed by fear. A fourth group, where fear stimuli were given without reassuring recommendations, provided the condition for unrealistic fear and the very lowest acceptance. (Four groups such as these were run for both the high-fear and low-fear messages.) Two control groups, one exposed only to recommendations, the other to neither fear nor recommendations, were also used.

The tape-recorded communications and slides were presented to small groups of people attending the New York State Fair. The data, consisting entirely of questionnaire responses given immediately after the communication, showed that the groups exposed to the high-fear communications were more fearful, more accepting of the recommendations (intending to carry out the recommended practices) and more convinced of the effectiveness of the recommendations than were those given the less fearful messages (Table IV). To see if increased acceptance depends upon fear reduction, the fear measures and the acceptance scores were compared for the different orders among the high-fear groups. As predicted, the position of the recommendations did affect level of fear, with the level of reported fear among the High-fear treatments increasing as follows: 1) recommendations after

TABLE IV

Reactions to Dental Hygiene Communications by Health Exposition Visitors [1] and by High School Students [2]

Variables	High fear				Low fear	Rec. only	Base
	Fear only	Rec.-fear	Mixed	Fear-rec.			
A) Exposition vistors							
1) Fear arousal (1-35)	21.03	19.79	17.12	15.47	10.51	11.10	10.47
2) Intentions (acceptance)	27.87	29.11	28.24	30.03	26.15	27.68	25.24
3) Effectiveness	34.31	35.55	35.12	35.47	32.51	34.06	33.87
N	35	41	35	32	36	30	35
B) High school students (college-prep course)							
1) Fear (1-7)			3.72	3.17	1.35	1.42	
2) Intentions			28.97	28.39	28.26	28.16	
3) Effectiveness			35.49	34.46	35.13	30.77	
4) Toothbrush taking			88%	80%	79%	61%	
N			41	35	38	23	
C) High school students (general course)							
1) Fear (1-7)			4.29	3.90	2.01	2.12	
2) Intentions			29.15	29.65	27.12	25.77	
3) Effectiveness			37.89	35.90	35.76	31.79	
4) Toothbrush taking			84%	84%	81%	70%	
N			38	25	27	20	

[1] Leventhal and Singer, 1965
[2] Singer, 1965.

fear arousal, 2) recommendations and fear arousal intermixed, 3) recommendations prior to fear arousal, and 4) fear arousal without reassuring recommendations. However, there were no significant differences between these groups in their intentions to follow the recommendations.

It is possible that the superiority of the fear-recommendation sequence in generating attitude change will appear only after some lapse of time, i.e., over time the acceptance induced by fear will dissipate in those high-fear conditions where all of the fear has not been reduced by the recommendations. Since all measures were obtained immediately after the communication in the Leventhal and Singer study, Singer (1965) conducted a second study to investigate the persistence of the effects. The study was conducted in two high schools that drew their students from highly similar ethnic and social backgrounds. All of the ninth-grade classes in each school were assigned to one of the four conditions, high-fear followed by recommendations, high-fear or low-fear intermixed with recommendations, or a control group receiving only the recommendations. Groups using intermixed recommendations were designed to follow the procedure of the Janis and Feshbach (1953) study. The effects upon acceptance of differences in fear reduction were to be tested by a delayed (two weeks) comparison of high-fear-intermixed with high-fear followed by recommendations.

Because he was working with high-school students, Singer was able to obtain measures of anxiety, dental attitudes, and reports of current dental-hygiene practices two weeks prior to the communication. Immediately after the communication, measures were taken of fear and of intentions to carry out the recommendations. The measure of attitudes and a second report on dental-hygiene practices were obtained two weeks later. In one of the schools the students were given the opportunity to obtain a free toothbrush at any time during a three-day period following the communication. The same opportunity was given in the other school but two weeks later in time, when the second measure was made of dental practices.

The results replicated the findings of the Leventhal and Singer study in showing that intentions to engage in proper dental-hygiene practices, as measured immediately after the film, are strongest in the high-fear group, next in the low-fear group, and weakest in the recommendations-only control. The results were weaker but basically the same for the behavioral response of getting toothbrushes during the three days following the communication. However, 80 per cent of the students obtained toothbrushes, and it is clear that the action was much simpler and less threatening than x-ray taking, stopping smoking, or taking tetanus inoculations. Two weeks after the communication there were essentially *no* differences between the groups. Thus, the Janis and Feshbach (1953) finding of the superiority of low-fear to high-fear was *not* repeated for the reported practices measure.[4] The absence of a differential effect for the fear treatments on the delayed measures of attitude and behavior parallel our earlier findings from the automotive (Leventhal and Niles, 1965) and tetanus (Leventhal, Singer and Jones, 1965) experiments.[5] In fact, as the rate of toothbrush taking was almost as high two weeks after the communication (78 per cent) as it was immediately afterwards (80 per cent), one might conclude that, as in the tetanus study, there was retention of the communications effects over the delay period. However, it seems more reasonable to assume that many of the factors that maintained a high level of motivation for free toothbrushes had little to do with the communications.

---

[4] Janis and Feshbach (1953) found no differences between groups for their attitude measures.

[5] It is possible that a delayed difference would have resulted if a high-fear-only group had been run. However, the automotive results (Leventhal and Niles, 1965) suggest that this may not be true.

Singer's data also revealed effects highly suggestive of social class differences. The immediate increase in intentions that was caused by fear was much stronger for students registered in the *non-college* preparatory program. Those in the college preparatory program were equally accepting under low and high levels of fear. It is worth noting that the basic findings of both the Leventhal and Singer (1965) and the Singer (1965) studies have been independently replicated by Haefner (1964) at the University of Michigan. Haefner reports high-fear to be more effective than low-fear in motivating subjects to obtain a dental hygiene booklet but finds no differences between his fear groups in later reports of adherence to recommended dental practices. His fear effects are also stronger among students in lower socio-economic groupings.

The dental studies both reinforce and add to our earlier discussion by suggesting that: 1) the added strength given to a recommended attitude or related behavior by a fear-arousing communication, in comparison to a non-fear arousing communication, is greatest at the time of the communication and decreases thereafter; 2) fear strengthens acceptance when beliefs in the adequacy of recommended actions are either undisturbed or strengthened by the fearful communication; 3) while a minimal level of fear arousal seems to be necessary for acceptance, increases in fear to higher levels seem unlikely to facilitate acceptance, especially for subjects from upper socio-economic groups.

It should also be noted that we have recorded long-term behavioral influences in only two instances, success in stopping smoking (Leventhal and Niles, 1964) and receiving tetanus inoculations (Leventhal, Singer and Jones, 1965). In the tetanus study, specific recommendations produced more tetanus shots regardless of the fear level, as long as some fear-arousing material was presented along with the recommendations. Because of the questions that can be raised regarding the loss of subjects in the smoking study, one must conclude that the evidence is still unclear as to whether the maintenance of influence over time depends upon the specific nature of the tetanus recommendations (i.e., suggestions on when and how to carry them out) or upon the fact that the recommended response can be performed on a single occasion versus one requiring repetitive action.

At present, our evidence for changes in more complex responses, such as driving habits and dental care, is restricted to changes in verbal intention and attitudes. However, these acts might have shown change if the reports of behaviors (direct observation was not used) were taken on the day(s) immediately after the communication. It should be pointed out that difficulty in sustaining change is not unique to attitude studies using communications. The difficulty is also reported by investigators using intensive group methods in smoking clinics (Ross, 1965). It may be that success in producing change is closely related to the "magnitude" of the change that is required, i.e., whether we are simply *inhibiting* an old reaction or requiring the acquisition of a new and complex habit, and to the degree to which the investigator can maximize transfer by creating realistic conditions for practice.

At the outset, I took special pains to justify focusing on a particular problem. Now the strength and weaknesses of focusing are apparent. While we know a fair amount about a small problem, we are plagued by unanswered questions. For example, we have not compared acceptance produced by fear-arousing messages with that produced by messages arousing other affects, such as joy, shame, disgust, and other emotions. Such comparisons are difficult to make because it is difficult to vary the emotions provoked by different messages while holding communication content constant. Thus, it is conceivable that any form of arousal is adequate to generate acceptance and that the results are not specific to fear. Moreover, it is not clear that emotion is directly responsible for the effects that have been recorded. It is possible that the "fear message" is effective by virtue of presenting a more adequate picture of the threat. If so, one could presumably generate acceptance by using this manipulation under conditions where the fear itself was minimized.

Clearly many questions remain to be answered regarding the relationship of "emotion" to measures of acceptance. In addition, the manifest difficulty in maintaining the changes that have been produced suggests the need to investigate the relationship of emotion-provoking communications to various factors that are known to maintain action, e.g., public commitment (Lewin, 1943), or group norms (Festinger *et al.*, 1960). However, knowing what we now do about fear and acceptance, we are ready to extend our efforts in answering these questions and in providing ways of constructing effective techniques for influencing health actions.

REFERENCES

Aronfreed, J. Origin of self-criticism, *Psychol. Rev.* 71:193, 1964.

Berelson, B. and Steiner, G. A. *Human Behavior*. New York, Harcourt Brace, 1964.

Cohen, A. R. Need for cognition and order of communication as determinants of opinion change. In: Hovland, ed., *Order of Presentation*. New Haven, Yale Univ. Press, 1957.

Festinger, L. *et al.* The operation of group standards. In: Cartwright, D. and Zander, A. F., eds. *Group Dynamics, Research and Theory*, 2nd. ed., Evanston, Row Peterson, 1960, p. 241.

Freud, S. *Inhibitions, Symptoms and Anxiety.* J. Strachey ed., London, Hogarth Press and Institute Psycho-Analysis, 1961.

Glover, E. Notes on the psychological effects of war conditions on the civil population: Part 3, the blitz, *Int. J. Psychoanal.* 23:17, 1942.

Goldstein, K. *The Organism, a Holistic Approach to Biology,* New York, Amer. Book, 1939.

————. Relationship between coping and avoiding behavior and response to fear arousing propaganda, *J. Abnorm. Soc. Psychol.* 58: 247, 1959.

Haefner, D. Use of fear arousal in dental health education. Paper read at the 92nd Annual Meeting of the American Public Health Association, Dental Health Section, October 7, 1964.

Hochbaum, G. M. Public participation in medical screening programs: a socio-psychological study. Washington, D. C., Public Health Service Publication No. 572, Government Printing Office, 1958.

Hovland, C. I., Janis, I. L. and Kelley, H. H. *Communication and Persuasion.* New Haven, Yale Univ. Press, 1953.

Janis, I. L. *Psychological Stress.* New York, Wiley, 1958.

Janis, I. L. and Feshbach, S. Effects of fear-arousing communications, *J. Abnorm. Soc. Psychol.* 48:78, 1953.

Janis, I. L. and Feshbach, S. Personality differences associated with responsiveness to fear-arousing communications, *J. Personality,* 23:154, 1954.

Janis, I. L. and Leventhal, H. Human reactions to stress. In: Borgatta, E. and Lambert, W., eds., *Handbook of Personality Theory and Research.* Boston. Rand McNally. In press.

Janis, I. L. and Leventhal, H. Psychological aspects of physical illness and hospital care. In: Wollman, B. ed., *Handbook of Clinical Psychology.* New York, McGraw-Hill. In press.

Janis, I. L. and Terwilliger, R. An experimental study of psychological resistances to fear-arousing communication, *J. Abnorm. Soc. Psychol.* 65:403, 1962.

Kegeles, S. S. Some motives for seeking preventive dental care, *J. Amer. Dent. Ass.* 67:110, 1963.

Krech, D., Crutchfield, R. S. and Ballachey, E. L. *Individual in Society.* New York, McGraw-Hill, 1962.

Leventhal, H. *et al.* The impact of the 1957 epidemic of influenza upon the general population in two cities. Washington, D. C., U.S. Dept. Health, Educ. Welfare, 1960.

Leventhal, H. and Niles, P. A field experiment on fear arousal with data on the validity of questionnaire measures, *J. Personality,* 32:459, 1964.

————. Persistence of influence for varying durations of exposure to threat stimuli, *Psychol. Rep.* 16:223, 1965.

Leventhal, H., Singer, R. P. and Jones, S. H. The effects of fear and specificity of recommendation, *J. Pers. Soc. Psychol.* 2:20, 1965.

Leventhal, H. and Singer, R. P. Order of affect arousal and recommendations as determinants of attitude change, mimeo copy, 1965.

Leventhal, H. and Watts, J. Sources of resistance to fear-arousing communication, *J. Personality,* 34: 155–75 June 1966.

Lewin, K. Psychological ecology. In: Cartwright, D., ed., *Field Theory in Social Science,* New York, Harper, 1951.

Logan, L., Killian, L. M. and Marrs, W. A study of the effect of catastrophe on social disorganization. Chevy Chase, Md. Operations Research Office, 1952.

May, R. *The Meaning of Anxiety.* New York, Ronald Press, 1950.

Miller, N. E. Some reflections on the law of effect produce a new alternative to drive reduction. In: Jones, M. R., ed., *Nebraska Symposium on Motivation.* Lincoln, Univ. Nebraska Press, 1963, 65–112.

Moltz, H. and Thistlethwaite, D. Attitude modification and anxiety reduction, *J. Abnom. Soc. Psychol.* 50:231, 1955.

Niles, P. The relationship of susceptibility and anxiety to acceptance of fear-arousing communications. Unpublished doctoral dissertation, Yale Univ., 1964.

Ross, C. Roswell Park Smoking Clinic. Paper read at the Connecticut Conference on Smoking Behavior, January 1965.

Schmideberg, M. Some observations on individual reactions to air raids, *Int. J. Psychoanal.* 23:146, 1942.

Singer, R. P. The effects of fear-arousing communications on attitude change and behavior. Unpublished doctoral dissertation, Univ. Conn., 1965.

Young, M., DiCicco, L., Paul, A. and Skiff, A. Methods and materials in health education (communication). Section 3 in: Review of research related to health education practice, *Health Educ. Monog., suppl. No. 1,* 1963.

DISCUSSION

Howard Leventhal: I'd like to make a point, for those of us who are theoretically interested, concerning these data and all others that have been gathered on this topic. There is actually no evidence in any of the studies, although theory assumes it, that the arousal of fear is a necessary condition for getting changes in either attitudes or behavior. All we know is that when people change their attitude they are also behaving in a fearful manner. Our latest theoretical paradigm asserts that when a person is confronted with some danger or threat, that danger or threat is very likely to make the person fearful. In addition, the danger or threat is likely to make the person attempt some adaptive responses. The two types of responses, while they may interact with one another, don't necessarily have any causal relationship with one another. They can be parallel rather than serially arranged reactions. If they are serially arranged, the fear response is a necessary precursor to making an adaptive reaction.

I feel it is important to state this because the studies that we have conducted are beginning to point in this direction. Moreover, because of this change we are focusing now on three kinds of problems. The first concerns how a person decides that he is in danger; how does he evaluate symptoms, changes within his body, within the environment, such that they mean to him, "The flag is up, it's time to run!" In our latest study, we are finding that there are specific strategies which people apply to their own bodies, specific tests in search operations.

The second focus will be to understand how an individual converts attitudes into behavior. This type of investigation follows from our specificity findings and will explore what it means to have a man rehearse a response, to be aware of the situation, the precise cue in time when he ought to make the response.

The third area concerns a "simple" but very complicated question to work on respecting the function of fear. Why do people become frightened, or what function does fear have for the human organism? We feel that if we study it carefully, we would likely find that the function of fear varies, depending upon the age and intelligence of the organism. We also suspect its function in fact is largely communicative in nature, telling others to "lay off me," rather than having any directly motivating effect upon the individual's own behavior.

Bernard Mausner: There may be a class gradient involved in this. In our own work we found opposite relationships between anxiety arousal and attitude change between middle class and working class subjects, and last night I heard of two other researches that seemed to find the same kind of relationship; that is, among working class subjects, high anxiety seemed to be related to attitude change and in middle class subjects it was the other

way. It may be that the key to the whole matter is to ask, as you have, in just what way is anxiety or fear instrumental? That may lead to some very interesting research.

Howard Leventhal: It is also a matter of defining what fear responses are. Perhaps the word should be thrown out. When we talk about fear, instead of describing the facial, postural, and autonomic responses that a person makes in a tight situation it is like a meteorologist talking about overcoat weather or raincoat weather.

Irwin Rosenstock: Under the best of all your experimental conditions, what is the maximum proportion of subjects you were able to persuade to follow some recomended practice?

Howard Leventhal: Between 30 and 45 per cent. The tetanus shots ran about 30 per cent. For smoking it depended upon the measures used to determine smoking reduction. We scored people as successfully reducing if they had dropped more than the median amount for their group; e.g., heavy smokers (averaging 17 cigarettes a day) had to cut by at least seven cigarettes, and light smokers had to drop by four to be qualified as successful. Successfuls numbered about 46 per cent of the group that received both a fear communication and specific instructions, and it was maintained for a three-month period.

Credibility of Source and Recipient's Attitude: Factors in the Perception and Retention of Information on Smoking Behavior[1]

SALVATORE V. ZAGONA and
M. RUSSELL HARTER
The University of Arizona

INTRODUCTION

A considerable amount of interest has been directed toward investigating the effects of source and recipient variables on communication effectiveness (Anderson & Clevenger, 1963; Petrie, 1963). Credibility of source and recipient's attitude are two such variables which have been studied extensively in relation to attitude change and the learning of information. In light of the practical implications of such studies, it is unfortunate that their findings have been in part inconclusive, especially in the area of learning. The purposes of the present report were, first, to review past studies in this area in order to identify some possible causes of conflicting results, and second, to evaluate further the effects of credibility of source, and recipient's attitude on reactions to and retention of a given body of information. (How S reacts to the message, i.e., his perception of it as "agreeable" or "disagreeable" to his belief-disbelief system, or his perception of it as biased or unbiased, trustworthy or untrustworthy, is referred to as his "perception" of the message.)

In reviewing related research, studies may be divided into the following two groups depending on the variables under investigation: first, studies concerned with the effects of credibility of source on learning and attitude change; and second, studies concerned with the effects of recipient attitude on learning and attitude change.

Effects of Credibility of Source on Learning and Attitude Change. Information attributed to sources of high credibility has been shown to be more effective in producing attitude change than information attributed to sources of low credibility. This has been demonstrated by attributing identical bodies of information to different sources assumed to vary in credibility. Kelman and Hovland (1953) varied source credibility by introducing speakers as a judge (source of high credibility), a juvenile delinquent (source of low credibility), and a person selected at random (neutral source). All three speakers presented the same information on juvenile delinquency. An atti-

tude questionnaire administered immediately after the speeches indicated that the recipients tended to agree more with the source of high credibility than with the source of low credibility, although agreement was higher for the two extreme sources than for the neutral source. Bonato (1962) found similar changes in opinion in the direction advocated by sources of both high and low prestige, although the change was greater with the high source.

Fine (1957) varied source credibility in a similar manner with negative results. Recipients read an article on biological warfare attributed to the *New York Times* (high credibility source) and the *Daily Worker* (low credibility source). No significant difference was found in opinion changes between groups reading the article from the sources of high and low credibility. This lack of significance may be attributed to the possibility that credibility was not varied since the sources were selected intuitively and no objective measure of perceived credibility was employed.

Weiss, Buchanan, and Pasamanick (1964) employed a somewhat more objective and quantitative method of varying credibility of source by use of the communicator consensus technique. Arguments were claimed to be advocated by "all the experts" (source of high credibility) and by "half the experts" (source of low credibility). The high consensus source led to greater agreement with the source of information than did the low consensus source.

A number of Es have investigated the effects of credibility of source on opinion change and measured retention of the presented information (Hovland & Weiss, 1951; Paulson, 1954; Tompkins & Samovar, 1964; Weiss, 1953). In these studies, tests of content were administered immediately after the information, attributed to various sources, was presented. The general results of these studies indicated: (1) greater opinion change when information was attributed to a source of high credibility than to the source of low credibility; (2) retention was not significantly related to credibility of source; and (3) retention was significantly greater when the recipient agreed with the speech content than when he disagreed with it.

---

[1]Reprinted by permission from *Perceptual and Motor Skills,* 1966, 23, 155–168. Copyright 1966, Southern Universities Press.

Effects of Recipient's Attitude on Learning and Attitude Change. Subject variables, mainly attitudes toward the speaker and his speech content, similarly influence effectiveness of communication. This was demonstrated by the effects of differences between communicator and recipient attitude (communicator-recipient discrepancy) on attitude change. Brehm and Lipsher (1959) presented anonymous opinion statements on current events to high school students while systematically varying the degree of discrepancy between the stand taken by the students and by the statements. Perceived trustworthiness was measured after each communication. When the position taken in the communication had no supporting content, moderate increases in discrepancy resulted in a decrease in perceived trustworthiness. With extreme discrepancy, however, the communications were perceived as very trustworthy.

Whittaker (1963) similarly investigated the effects of communicator-recipient discrepancy on several issues and on judgment of autokinetic movement. A curvilinear relationship obtained between discrepancy size and attitude change, the latter being greatest with intermediate discrepancy as compared to either small or large discrepancy.

The apparent logical inconsistency between the above findings — moderate discrepancy resulting in both increased distrust and attitude change — may be explained by considering attitude change in terms of an interaction between perceived trustworthiness and the amount of change possible. It is evident that discrepancy is necessary before attitude change can occur. Therefore, it may be assumed that some degree of mistrust is tolerable during attitude change. With extreme discrepancy, perhaps *S* completely rejects the information, although a greater amount of attitude change toward the communication is possible.

The effect of the recipient's attitude on learning information has been demonstrated in a number of studies. Investigators have presented *Ss,* known or assumed to take a particular stand on an issue, with information both for and against the issue (Gilkinson, Paulson, & Sikkink, 1953; Levine & Murphy, 1943; Weiss, 1953). These studies consistently show that learning and retention were greater for information congruent with *Ss'* attitudes.

Postman and Murphy (1943) demonstrated a similar relationship between *Ss'* attitudes and associative memory. When children learned noun-adjective word pairs, e.g., Nazi-honest, American-good, retention was greater for word pairs compatible with *Ss'* attitude toward the subject matter than those which were incompatible. That is, American children learned and retained, for example, the word association American-good better than Nazi-honest.

In contrast, Berlo and Gulley (1957) found that learning was not significantly affected by *Ss'* prior attitude toward the learned information. Five stimulus messages were presented to *Ss* having either favorable or unfavorable attitudes toward the content of the messages. *Ss* with various prior attitudes toward the messages did not differ significantly in their ability to recall the five stimulus messages. The authors suggest that possibly the lack of significant results may be attributed to the restricted sensitivity of both attitude and learning measures utilized.

Paulson (1954) investigated the effects of prior attitude on both retention and attitude change. Attitude before and after speeches on voting was measured as well as retention of speech content. The retention measure was the score on a fifty-item test. The findings were: (1) the percentage shift varied according to the initial attitudes of the listeners, those initially undecided showing the largest percentage shift, those initially favorable next largest percentage shift, and those opposed showing the least percentage shift; (2) mean retention scores differed significantly between *Ss* who were initially favorable to the speech content and those who were initially opposed, the former having the higher retention scores. These results obtained when the speeches included one- and two-sided arguments.

The few studies investigating the interaction of credibility of source and recipient's attitude on attitude change have provided inconclusive results. Aronson, Turner, and Carlsmith (1963) attributed communications concerning poetry to T. S. Eliot (source of high credibility) and a college student (source of low credibility). When the communication was attributed to the source of high credibility, attitude change increased as a function of discrepancy between position taken by *Ss* and the communication. In contrast, when the communication was attributed to the source of low credibility, attitude change increased with increasing discrepancy to a point, with further increases in discrepancy resulting in a decrease in attitude change. Similar results were obtained by Bergin (1962) for self-ratings of masculinity-femininity which varied in discrepancy with ratings of the sources of high and low credibility. When *Ss'* ratings were discrepant with the ratings of the source of high credibility, attitude change increased as a function of discrepancy; when the ratings were discrepant with the source of low credibility, attitude change decreased with discrepancy.

In contrast, Choo (1964) found no interaction between source credibility and communication discrepancy on attitude change. Opinion toward there being a causal relation between smoking and lung cancer was measured after *Ss* read communications attributed to sources of varying credibility (American Tobacco Company, National Cancer Institute, and Public Health

Service). Although opinion change increased with increases in credibility and discrepancy, the interaction of these two variables was not significant.

The results of the above studies may be generally summarized as follows: (1) with the exception of one study (Fine, 1957), greater positive opinion change occurred when a communication was identified with sources of high credibility than with sources of low credibility; (2) acquisition of information was not significantly related to the credibility of the source of information; (3) there was an optimal level of discrepancy between communicator-recipient opinion for opinion change — too little or too much discrepancy resulting in less change than moderate levels of discrepancy; (4) with the exception of one study (Berlo & Gulley, 1957), retention of information was greater when the information was compatible with the recipient's attitude than when the information was incompatible; and (5) with the exception of one study (Choo, 1964), an interaction effect was found between credibility of source and recipient attitude, greater attitude change resulting from discrepancy between communicator-recipient attitude when information was attributed to a high source than a low source of credibility.

The exceptions to the general findings and the lack of apparent relationship between credibility of source and learning in the studies reviewed may, in part, be explained in terms of low degree of sensitivity of the measures and by factors which reduced the effects of credibility of source on learning. Sensitivity was reduced due to a number of factors. First, sources were chosen intuitively and assumed to have a certain level of credibility in all except four of nine studies reviewed (Bonato, 1962; Choo, 1964; Hovland & Weiss, 1951; Tompkins & Samovar, 1964). Therefore, no means were available for knowing whether credibility of source was varied. Second, sources were either "high" or "low" in credibility which limited the investigation of possible effects of intermediate credibilty levels in all except two of the ten studies (Choo, 1964; Tompkins & Samovar, 1964). Third, retention was measured by means of tests with eight items or fewer in four of the eight studies. Unless the effects of credibility of source on learning were very great, such tests would not be sufficiently sensitive to measure differences of learning. Finally, past research has not been systematic in exploring the possible interaction between credibility of source and recipient's attitude on learning.

Two factors may possibly have attenuated the effect of credibility of source on learning in the reviewed studies: failure to identify the communication with the source and presence of other factors which encouraged a high level of learning regardless of source. In the above studies, the source was related to the communication either before or after the communication. In no studies were Ss reminded of the source within the communicaion. Furthermore, the effects of credibility of source on learning were excluded in two studies since the source was not known to Ss until after the communication was presented (Hovland & Weiss, 1951; Weiss, 1953).

Variables other than credibility of source which encouraged a high degree of learning were necessarily present in all experimental studies reviewed. For example, students were used as Ss in all studies cited. Possibly students are practiced in attending to information on which they may be tested, regardless of their attitude toward the source. Ss were cued to a possible test situation either by direct verbal instruction or by a preliminary questionnaire. Therefore, the effect of credibility of source as a factor in directing attention may have been reduced.

In view of the above observations, a number of steps were taken in the present study to maximize the influence of credibility of source and to increase sensitivity of measurement while investigating the effects of credibility of source and recipient's attitude on the perception and retention of information. First, credibility of source was determined by means of a preliminary rating questionnaire administered to Ss three weeks prior to the experiment proper. This ensured the relative credibility of the sources employed and reduced the chance of cueing Ss to a possible test situation. Second, sources of high, intermediate, and low credibility were associated with the communication in order to expand the range of levels of credibility under investigation. Third, a fourteen-item factual multiple-choice test on the communication content was used as a measure of retention. Fourth, the sources were identified with the communication both before and during its presentation. And fifth, a number of precautions were taken not to direct Ss' attention to the content of the communication. The communication was presented in as unstructured a situation as possible, so that Ss could direct as much time and attention to the communication as they wished.

Finally, a number of investigators have effectively utilized the theory of cognitive dissonance, or modifications thereof, to predict the effect of source credibility and recipient attitude on attitude change (Aronson, Turner & Carlsmith, 1963; Bergin, 1962; Berlo & Gulley, 1957; Bettinghaus, 1961; Brehm & Lipsher, 1959; Osgood and Tannenbaum, 1955). This theory essentially asserts that when an individual's perceptions, attitudes, beliefs, expectancies, and other cognitions conflict with one another or with behavorial tendencies, he is motivated to change them in order to reduce this conflict. In that retention and perception are related to cognitive structure, the following hypotheses were made on the basis of cognitive theory: (1) a greater amount of information will be retained when the perceived information is attributed to a high as compared to a low source of credibility; (2) a greater amount of information will be retained which is consistent with the recipient's expectations and attitudes than information which is inconsistent with his expectations and attitudes; and (3) information will be perceived by the recipient in a manner consistent with his expectations and beliefs about the information source.

METHOD

Subjects

Fifty-seven *Ss* of both sexes, recruited from introductory psychology courses at the University of Arizona, were given a passage discussing the effects of smoking on health and the role of smoking in a social situation. Although the material was identical for all *Ss,* it was ascribed to a source of high credibility to a randomly selected one-third (*n*=19) of *Ss;* to a moderately credible source to another third, and to a source of low credibility to the remainder. The passage was identified with the source in the written instructions preceding each passage and in the text of the message itself.

The level of credibility of each information source had been previously determined as follows. A preliminary questionnaire was given to *Ss* three weeks prior to the experimental session. *Ss* were asked to select a high credibility source ("trustworthy and reliable"), a moderate credibility source ("you would read it but not swear by it"), and a low credibility source ("untrustworthy and unreliable") from nine different sources presented to them. The selected high, moderate, and low sources were, respectively, *Surgeon General's Report on Smoking and Health, Life Magazine,* and an advertisement by American Tobacco Company.

All *Ss* were able to identify accurately the ascribed source in the questionnaire administered following the information presentation.

Information

The information was presented in printed form and was concerned with the effects of smoking on health and with the role of smoking in social situations. It was altered to eliminate effects of past learning on this topic and it discussed both positive and negative aspects of smoking (smoking is related to poor health but not causally, smoking is enjoyable and releases tension, etc.).

Attitude Groups

The three experimental groups were divided into subgroups on the basis of existing attitudes toward the presented information and on the basis of whether *Ss*

were smokers (those who smoke at all) or non-smokers (those who never smoke). Recipient attitude toward the presented information was measured in terms of agreement, perceived trustworthiness, and perceived position (as being "for" or "against" smoking).

To measure retention and recipient attitude, an eighteen-item multiple choice test was given immediately after *Ss* had read the information on smoking. Two of these items were five-category Likert-type questions on the recipients' agreement with the information and its perceived trustworthiness. One question measured *Ss* smoking habits and another whether *Ss* saw the information as being "for" or "against" smoking. The remaining fourteen items were questions tapping facts of the presented information and were used as a measure of retention.

Procedure

All fifty-seven *Ss* were asked to read the printed instructions accompanying the information on smoking carefully and to note the source of the communication. *Ss* were then given the printed smoking information and asked to answer the accompanying question indicating their general agreement or disagreement. This question gave *Ss* a reason for looking over the passage. They were *not* told to read the passage and they were not told that later they would be tested on its contents. After each *S* answered the question, he was requested to raise his hand so that the information sheet could be collected and the questionnaire handed out. No time limit was imposed.

RESULTS

Four variance analyses (one for each attitude measure) were performed to test the effects of credibility of source and recipient's attitude on retention. A factorial design for unequal cell frequencies, utilizing the least squares method (Winer, 1962, pp. 375–76) was employed. Individual means were compared orthogonally. Chi squares and contingency coefficients were used to measure the effects of credibility of source and smoking habits on frequency of favorable and unfavorable responses to the information.

Effects of Credibility of Source and Recipient's Attitude on Retention

The effects of credibility of source and recipient's smoking habits on retention of the smoking information are indicated in Fig. 1. An orthogonal comparison indicated that the groups receiving information from either a high or low credibility source learned the material significantly better (P<.05) than the group receiving the information from the intermediate source. Groups with

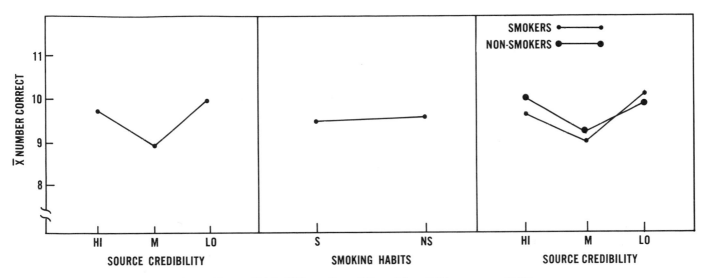

Fig. 1. Effects of high (HI), medium (M), and low (LO) source credibility
and smoking (S) and nonsmoking (NS) groups on retention.

sources of high and low credibility did not differ significantly (P>.05) in retention. The effects of smoking
habits and the interaction between credibility of source
and smoking habits were not significant (P>.05).

Recipient's perception of the communication was
related to retention (Fig. 2). Of the three measures of

attitude obtained (agreement, trustworthiness, position),
only judged position of information (as "for" or
"against" smoking) showed significant effects (P<.05).
The groups that perceived the information as being
against smoking performed more poorly than the group
who perceived it as being neutral toward smoking (P<

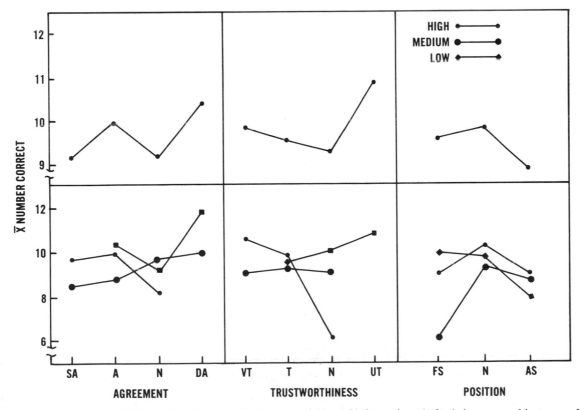

Fig. 2. Effects of source credibility and recipient attitude on acquisition of information. Attitude is expressed in terms of agreement
(strongly agree, agree, neither agree nor disagree), trustworthiness (very trustworthy, trustworthy, neither trustworthy nor untrustworthy, untrustworthy), and position (for smoking, neither for nor against smoking, against smoking).

.05). The group which perceived the information as being for smoking also performed more poorly than the neutral group, although the difference was not significant (P>.05).

Although credibility of source did not interact significantly with perceived trustworthiness and position of the information (P>.05), a definite trend in the data was indicated (Fig. 2). Ss in the high credibility group who perceived the information as trustworthy and who were neither for nor against smoking retained more than those who perceived the information as neither trustworthy nor untrustworthy and were for or against smoking. Ss in the low credibility groups who perceived the information as untrustworthy and were for smoking retained more than those who perceived the information as trustworthy or against smoking.

Effects of Credibility of Source and Recipient's Attitude on Perception

The effects of credibility of source on the percentage of Ss who had favorable and unfavorable reactions to the information (in terms of agreement and trustworthiness) are illustrated in Fig. 2. Significant chi squares were obtained for all of these relationships (P<.05).

The resulting contingency coefficients indicating the degree of correlation between credibility of source and agreement and trustworthiness were .42 and .38, respectively. As credibility of source decreased, the percentage of Ss who agreed with the information and found it trustworthy decreased and the percentage of Ss who disagreed with it and found it untrustworthy increased.

The relationship between credibility of source and perceived position of the information on smoking is illustrated in Fig. 3. A significant chi square (P<.001) and contingency coefficient (C=.51) were obtained for this relationship. As credibility of source decreased, the percentage of Ss who stated the information was "for smoking" inceased and the percentage of Ss who stated the information was "against smoking" decreased.

Although no significant relationships between smoking habits and frequency of favorable and unfavorable responses to the presented information were indicated, some trends were evident (see Fig. 3). Smokers tended to agree with the information and perceive it as trustworthy. Moreover, non-smokers tended to perceive the information as either "for" or "against" smoking, whereas smokers tended to perceive it as being neither for nor against smoking.

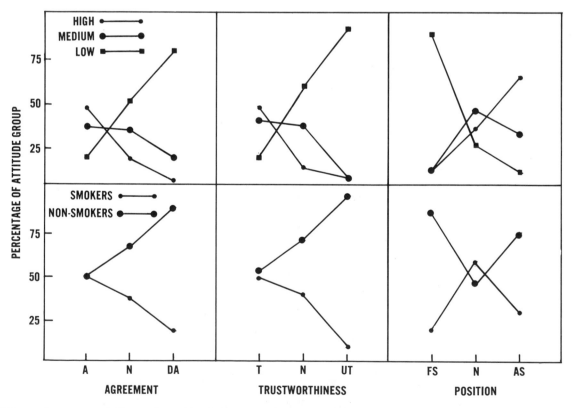

Fig. 3. Effects of source credibility and smoking habits on attitude toward the presented information. Attitude is expressed in terms of agreement (agree, neither agree nor disagree, disagree), trustworthiness (trustworthy, neither trustworthy nor untrustworthy, untrustworthy), and position (for smoking, neither for nor against smoking, against smoking). Note.— The data are expressed as the percentage of each attitude group.

DISCUSSION

Effects of Credibility of Source and Recipient's Attitude on Learning

In the introduction, it was hypothesized that credibility of source would affect retention of information, in that information attributed to a source of high credibility would be retained better than that attributed to a source of low credibility. The results partially support this hypothesis. Credibility of source affected retention of information, but information attributed to sources of high and low credibility was learned better than that attributed to the source of moderate credibility.

These results differ from those of past studies which concluded that credibility of source did not affect learning of contents of the communication (Hovland & Weiss, 1951; Kelman & Hovland, 1953). This apparent inconsistency is in the conclusions drawn, not in the data collected. As stated in the introduction, most studies investigated only the effects of sources of high and low credibility on learning and attitude change. (Since, in this study, a measure of retention was obtained so soon after Ss' exposure to the communication, no distinction can or need be made as to whether we are dealing with a problem in effectiveness of learning or retention.) The effects of moderate credibility on learning were not investigated. Therefore, their data did not differ from those of the present experiment where the effects of extreme sources also did not differ. Although Kelman and Hovland (1953) investigated the effects of sources of high, low, and neutral credibility (as determined by an introductory statement) on learning, they did not have a source of *moderate* credibility condition. Learning, as indicated by an open-end questionnaire, was not affected by the conditions of credibility.

In light of the above results, the effects of credibility of source on attitude change require further study. Traditionally, the effects of credibility of source have been evaluated in terms of the acceptance or rejection of information with little attention directed toward the learning of information. The effects of learning have been assumed to be of minor significance. In that past studies have investigated conditions where learning was not differentially affected by credibility of source (high and low levels of credibility), further research is necessary to investigate conditions under which credibility of source may influence learning, i.e., when information is attributed to a source of moderate credibility. The prediction may be made that attitude change would be less for the moderate than for the high or low sources of credibility in that the recipients would not attend to or learn the information and therefore not be exposed to its influence. The importance of learning would be greatest for long-term attitude change, since the recipient tends to disassociate information from its source over time (Hovland & Weiss, 1951) and base his opinion primarily on content. Therefore, it is the opinion of the present authors that the effects of credibility of source on attitude change are a function of both the learning and acceptance of information.

The suggested relationships between credibility of source and recipient's reactions to the presented information tend to support the prediction that learning would be greatest when expectations and perceptions are consonant. Ss receiving information from the source of high credibility (in this instance the *Surgeon General's Report,* a source thought to be trustworthy and unbiased by Ss on the basis of their preliminary questionnaire responses) learned more facts when they perceived the information as very trustworthy and neutral in position (unbiased) than when they perceived it as neutral in trustworthiness and biased in position. Similarly, Ss receiving the information from the source of low credibility or advertisement by the American Tobacco Company (a source thought by Ss to be untrustworthy and biased) learned more facts when they perceived the information as very untrustworthy and biased for smoking than when they perceived it as trustworthy and against smoking. In groups both with the high and low sources of credibility, learning was greater when the recipients' expectations of and reactions to the information were consonant.

Past studies investigating the effects of attitudinal variables on learning support this interpretation. In addition to the Postman and Murphy (1943) study mentioned earlier, demonstrating the more effective learning of "compatible" word-pairs of children, Levine and Murphy (1943) found that it was more gratifying (tension reducing) to learn and retain material congruent with one's attitudes than other types of material. Similar results were found in a number of other studies (Ager & Dawes, 1965; Gilkinson, Paulson, & Sikkink, 1953).

The relationship between perceived bias of information for or against smoking and the learning of this information is of particular interest. Although prior studies have investigated the effects of communicator sidedness on attitude change (Brehm & Lipsher, 1959; Fine, 1957), they have not related such effects to learning. The above results suggest that learning is greater for information which is perceived as unbiased than for information which is perceived as biased.

Effects of Credibility of Source and Recipient's Attitude on Perception

The hypothesis that the recipient will perceive information as being consistent with his expectations and attitudes was strongly supported by the results. In agreement with past studies (Choo, 1964; Bonato, 1962; Hovland & Weiss, 1951; Kelman & Hovland, 1953; Paulson, 1954; Tompkins & Samovar, 1964), the recipients tended to concur with information attributed to a source of high credibility and disagree with information attributed to a source of low credibility. Similarly, the recipients tended to perceive the information as trustworthy when attributed to the source of high credibility and untrustworthy when attributed to the source of low credibility. Brehm and Lipsher (1959) obtained similar results, reporting that perceived trustworthiness of information was a function of communicator-recipient discrepancy, the greater the discrepancy in position the less the perceived trustworthiness.

The proportion of Ss who perceived the information as biased for or against smoking or neither for nor against smoking similarly was a function of the expected position of the source. When the information was attributed to the Surgeon General's Report (a report emphasizing the negative effects of smoking on health), recipients tended to perceive the information as being against smoking. Similarly, when the information was attributed to an advertisement by the American Tobacco Company (an organization promoting smoking) and to Life Magazine (no known stand on issue), the recipients tended to perceive the information as being for and neither for nor against smoking, respectively.

The effects of Ss' smoking habits on the perception of information can also be interpreted in terms of the theory of cognitive consistency. In that the information suggested no causal relationship between smoking and diseases, possibly smokers tended to agree with the information and perceive it as trustworthy and unbiased; non-smokers tended to disagree with the information and perceive it as untrustworthy and biased (either for or against smoking).

The data derived from the present investigation tend to indicate that the learning and perception of information is a complex function of characteristics of communicator and recipient. Furthermore, the efficiency of a communication in facilitating learning and change in attitude appears predictable on the basis of the cognitive consistency between the recipients' expectations and beliefs. Such an interpretation appears to apply for both the perception and retention of information.

SUMMARY

The effects of credibility of source (high, medium, and low) and Ss' smoking habits (smoker and non-smoker) on how Ss react to and retain information contained in a printed passage on smoking were investigated. The credibility of the various sources and Ss' smoking habits were determined by preliminary questionnaires given to Ss earlier. The high, medium, and low credibility sources selected were the Surgeon General's Report on Smoking and Health, Life Magazine, and an advertisement by the American Tobacco Company, respectively. Each of these sources was identified with the smoking information both verbally and in the information content. Then the printed information was given to 57 male and female introductory psychology students to read; a group of 19 Ss received the printed information from one of the three sources. Immediately, retention was determined on an eighteen-item test, their reactions in terms of their stated agreement or disagreement with the source, and whether they considered it trustworthy or biased. Statistically significant results indicated that: (1) Ss receiving the information attributed to sources of high and low credibility retained more information than those receiving the information attributed to a source of medium credibility; (2) Ss who perceived the information as unbiased retained more than those who perceived it as biased; and (3) as credibility of the source increased, the percentage of Ss who agreed with the information and perceived it as trustworthy also increased. Results were interpreted in terms of the cognitive consistency of Ss' attitudes toward the source and content of information.

REFERENCES

Ager, J. W., and Dawes, R. M. Effect of judges' attitudes on judgment. J. Pers. Soc. Psychol., 1965, 1, 533–538.

Andersen, K., and Clevenger, T. A summary of experimental research in ethos. Speech Monogr., 1963, 30, 59–78.

Aronson, E., Turner, J. A., and Carlsmith, J. M. Communicator credibility and communication discrepancy as determinants of opinion change. J. Abnorm. Soc. Psychol., 1963, 67, 31–36.

Bergin, A. E. The effect of dissonant persuasive communications upon changes in a self-referring attitude. J. Pers., 1962, 30, 423–438.

Berlo, D., and Gulley, H. E. Some determinants of the effect of oral communication in producing attitude change and learning. Speech Monogr., 1957, 24, 10–20.

Bettinghaus, E. P. The operation of congruity in an oral communication situation. Speech Monogr., 1961, 28, 131–142.

Bonato, R. The effect of source credibility and amount of information on opinion change. Dissertation Abstr., 1962, 22, 2895.

Brehm, J. W., and Lipsher, D. Communicator-communicatee discrepancy and perceived communicator trustworthiness. J. Pers., 1959, 27, 352–361.

Choo, T. H. Communicator credibility and communication discrepancy as determinants of opinion change. J. Soc. Psychol., 1964, 64, 65–76.

Fine, B. J. Conclusion-drawing, communicator credibility, and anxiety as factors in opinion change. J. Abnorm. Soc. Psychol., 1957, 54, 369–374.

Gilkinson, H., Paulson, S. F., and Sikkink, D. E. Conditions affecting the communication of controversial statements in connected discourse: forms of presentation and the political frame of reference of the listener. *Speech Monogr.*, 1953, 20, 253–260.

Hovland, C. I., and Weiss, W. The influence of source credibility on communication effectiveness. *Publ. Opin. Quart.*, 1951, 15, 635–650.

Kelman, H. C., and Hovland, C. I. "Reinstatement" of the communicator in delayed measurement of opinion change. *J. Abnorm. Soc. Psychol.*, 1953, 48, 327–335.

Levine, J. M., and Murphy, G. The learning and forgetting of controversial material. *J. Abnorm. Soc. Psychol.*, 1943, 38, 507–517.

Osgood, C. E., and Tannenbaum, P. The principle of congruity in the prediction of attitude change. *Psychol. Rev.*, 1955, 62, 42–55.

Paulson, S. F. The effects of the prestige of the speaker and acknowledgment of opposing arguments on audience retention and shift of opinion. *Speech Monogr.*, 1954, 21, 267–271.

Petrie, C. R. Informative speaking: a summary and bibliography of related research. *Speech Monogr.*, 1963, 30, 79–91.

Postman, L., and Murphy, G. The factor of attitude in associative memory. *J. Exp. Psychol.*, 1943, 33, 228–238.

Tompkins, R. K., and Samovar, L. A. An experimental study of the effects of credibility on the comprehension of content. *Speech Monogr.*, 1964, 31, 120–123.

Weiss, R. F., Buchanan, W., and Pasamanick, B. Social consensus in persuasive communication. *Psychol. Rep.*, 1964, 14, 95–98.

Weiss, W. A "sleeper" effect in opinion change. *J. Abnorm. Soc. Psychol.*, 1953, 48, 173–180.

Whittaker, J. O. Opinion change as a function of communication-attitude discrepancy. *Psychol. Rep.*, 1963, 13, 763–772.

Winer, B. J. *Statistical principles in experimental design.* New York: McGraw-Hill, 1962.

SYMPOSIUM:

Factors Contributing to the Effectiveness of Communications — Theoretical and Practical Implications of Reported Research

Moderator
PERCY H. TANNENBAUM

Discussants

LEONARD BERKOWITZ   IRWIN ROSENSTOCK
WARD EDWARDS   SILVAN TOMKINS
DONN MOSSER   GERHART D. WIEBE

SUMMARY

Ward Edwards presents a decision-making model as it applies to smoking; he also comments on the usefulness of small but statistically significant relationships ("micromelodies") obtained in research. Silvan Tomkins describes his theory of the role of perception and motivation in the decision-making process; cautions against the use of fear in communications on the hazards of smoking: "The individual becomes more concerned about reducing fear than about reducing what produced the fear." Howard Leventhal's rebuttal. Cites experimental studies of subjects' adaptive reactions to their perception *of fear. Frank Barron discusses decision-making in terms of gambling odds and the "risk of ruin." Edgar Borgatta: a critique of the Edwards decision-making model as laboratory-bound, inapplicable to "manipulation-in-the-field" work; defends research which produces small ("micromelodic") amounts of predictable variance. Frank Barron: a hedonic model of smoking behavior. Howard Leventhal and Bernard Mausner make a plea for recognizing the utility of various models as non-competitive, accounting for smoking at various behavorial and research levels. Gerhart Wiebe: how to fashion communications to "modify behavior most effectively." More discussion on the role of fear as a motivating influence. Threat* distinguished from fear. *The use of the fear approach vs. the "straight appeal of rational information." Effectiveness of teachers and other adults who participate in smoking communication programs as "models for identification." Daniel Horn speaks against classifying "smoking" behavior in moral terms, favoring, instead, research on personality dynamics that will clarify the processes relevant to starting and stopping smoking. Percy Tannenbaum, overview: an analysis of the communications process; the problem of selection; competing information; redundancy; the role of information in bringing about changes in attitudes and behavior.*

Robert Lawrence advocates using personal appeals on television by members of stricken families. Gerhart Wiebe, drawing from radio experience during World War II, recommends against the use of the "scare technique" on the grounds that audiences simply tune out. Suggests the spot announcement instead. Points to the enormous potential in the millions of transistors being used, and the audience interest shown in public service programs on the subject of smoking. Dr. Mosser cites the success of the taped telephone message. The power of television as an "example-setting" device is discussed, and proposals to establish smoking "lobbies" among the networks is considered. The effectiveness of the humorous (satiric) approach is debated. The use of mass communications to change the "social milieu" and the problem of evaluating the effects of "mass education" are considered.

Ward Edwards: Two issues are always involved in every decision. One is, "What's in it for me?" In the technical language of decision theory, this asks, "What pay-off will result from a combination of the act I choose and the state of the world that it will obtain?" The other is, "What are the odds?" This asks, what is the probability of occurrence for each of the various possible consequences? By probability is meant how likely one *thinks* it is, not how many times in a thousand it has occurred in the past, although, of course, this may influence one's thinking.

Applying this partitioning of the decision process to smoking, there should be a sharp distinction between the impact of communications on utilities, values, and the what's-in-it-for-me kind of question, and the impact of communications on changing the probabilities of consequences. In more abstract research on decision processes this latter emphasis has been indispensable; but perhaps the same distinction should be made about the object of the communication's impact. Dr. Leventhal, for instance (pp. 17 ff.), is concerned with communicating a number of changes to people, among which is, "What courses of action are in fact available to me?" This question quite obviously must be answered before the question "What's in it for me?" For example, if one tells an individual he can do something, maybe he will; but first he must have some reason why it might be worthwhile.

One of my professors in graduate school was engaged in the study of what was called micromelodies. Micromelodies are tunes not in our ordinary chromatic scale but in a scale of music whose adjacent notes differ from one another by only a few cycles per second. At first hearing they sound like nothing on earth; but if one listens to them long enough, they start sounding like serious melodies. A research paper can have a major conclusion based on the difference between 9.9 correct responses and 9 correct responses. The authors are unwilling to reject the hyopthesis that the true difference is statistically insignificant; on the other hand, we must concede that there isn't very much of a difference between 9 and 9.9. An example of a micromelodic effect is where a correlation coefficient of .40 is accepted as a conclusive relationship even though only 16 per cent of the variance is accounted for between the variables studied. Since my own work is with much less complex material, I have difficulty adjusting to micromelodies. If we are concerned with having a major impact on social phenomena, it really would be nice to get bigger differences, bigger effects.

Leonard Berkowitz: Although he is not a social psychologist, Dr. Edwards is actually very much in tune with contemporary social psychology in emphasizing the importance of the decision-making processes affecting behavior. However, as a social psychologist, I'd like to take a non-social psychological approach and suggest that contemporary theorizing has over-emphasized the decision-making processes. There is an interesting discrepancy between the findings of Leventhal (pp. 17 ff.) and those of field surveys, which tend to emphasize rationalistic, decision-making aspects of behavior. Dr. Horn has also suggested that smoking, too, is not always affected by any kind of rationalistic decision making. Many acts are governed by the stimuli in a given situation to which an individual more or less automatically responds; couldn't this be true also in smoking? Our research on aggression, for instance, has led over and over again to the conclusion that the stimulus properties of the target influence the magnitude of the attack. In these cases, the actions probably did not involve decision-making but merely automatic responses which might have been facilitated by fear or anger.

Bernard Mausner: This issue was discussed at length during the 1965 Conference,[1] and my colleagues and I have been thinking about it since then, in interpreting our own data. I have a feeling that the word *decision* is given certain surplus meanings by people who think in dictionary terms. If one thinks of the word *decision* as implying a casting up of odds with numbers in little boxes as a verbal process, then Dr. Berkowitz's comments are justified. But if one uses the word *decision* purely as a construct, as a conceptualization of the variables which

one might consider in order to determine behavior at choice points, then it is not necessary to worry about the fact that there are non-rational considerations. Obviously, non-rational considerations go into determining expectancy and also go into determining value.

We are not discussing making choices, but behavior which goes this way or that way. I talked about choice *points,* not choice *ends.* This becomes a valid exercise in trying to lay out the variables which determine behavior at choice points even if we don't assume that what the individual is experiencing is something that can be verbalized, which is called making a choice. There is no question that under some circumstances he may make a choice, like the subject who walks out of an experiment on attitude change, or the patient who walks out of a conference with his doctor. Take the case of the girl in the taxicab who said to her friend, "If we're going to quit, let's quit now." She then grabbed the package of cigarettes and threw them out the window, to the horror of the cab driver. This was her choice point. Granted, it won't always work that way; it probably very rarely does, but this should not prevent us from using all sides of decision theory, complicated though they may be. One of the things we have emphasized in this section of papers is the necessity for bringing into play considerations beyond those used for analyzing any behavior; but still the direction is a valid one if one faces squarely the fact that he is not referring to choices which lend themselves to verbal description.

Silvan Tomkins: I would like to present a model slightly different in organization within personality which is specifically related to it. I was disturbed by some parts of Howard Leventhal's paper.

First, I would distinguish very sharply the stimulus which evokes an affect from the awareness of that stimulus; that is, one can have an affect evoked and not know exactly (or be mistaken about) what it was that triggered it.

My second point concerns the option in strategy of attempting to reduce that affect, once it has been evoked. That is, "I want to get rid of this fear" *per se,* without any regard to what produced that fear. I may not *know* what produced it; I may wake up in the morning with free-floating anxiety, and say, "This is for the birds, I don't want to feel like this; I'm going to try to stop it."

So there are critical distinctions among the stimulus which *evokes* an affect, the *awareness* of that stimulus, and the motivating power of the affect once aroused — i.e., the individual is not necessarily pushed in the direction of instrumental behavior to modify that affect. He may say, "That's the way I feel; I don't feel good today, I feel sad." But there it stops; that's the end of it. I would agree, then, that there is in a sense no more motivating power there. It just goes no further. That is a theoretical

[1] Mausner, Bernard and Platt, Ellen S. Proceedings of the Conference on Behavioral Aspects of Smoking. Glenside, Pa.: Beaver College (September, 1965).

possibility. That doesn't happen too often, but it does happen. Often the perception of the stimulus is tied very tightly to the affect which it evokes, and the strategy for reducing the negative affect is, in fact, also a strategy for reducing what is presumed to have produced it. That often happens and gives rise to this kind of model of motivation — that is, "I feel this way, and that produced it; let me do that which will reduce both of them." There is no question in the individual's mind as to what has taken place: he is fully aware.

More typically, however, there are organizations which I have called "habitual skills," in which the motivational aspect is what I define as an "as if" one. A simple example is crossing the street every day. Most of us don't have anxiety attacks when we cross the street; nonetheless, there was a time when this did create some fear and caused us to be cautious — we looked up and down, and so on. Now if we can evolve a program which has compressed information in it and which can be expanded with minimal decision (and here we come to the decision point), once that program has been forged and a trace of it laid down, it can be run off a thousand times with decisions varying in terms of what I call "density of monitoring." The more habitual a thing is, the smaller number of readings the individual has to take to analyze what he's doing, should be doing, or whether he should do it differently.

We come finally to organizations where an individual really has no awareness of what he is doing. The behavior appears unmotivated, although it is not, since one usually will not cross the street without a little sampling to see if things are in order. But he can be conversing with someone at the same time; the behavior places minimal drain on the channel. If a car should suddenly swerve out toward him, however, the rules are changed. He now goes back into decision strategies: full awareness of all the contingencies, what it is that is making him feel anxious, and how to avoid the car. Then we have the phenomenon of the delayed affective response, where he is almost hit by the car and two minutes later he becomes afraid. He didn't have the channel capacity at that time to talk about reducing fear; he had to get out of the way of the car. So we have many degrees of freedom here in the organization of affect, the perceived activators, and the strategies for reducing them. What I really objected to was the notion that the motivating power of fear would be judged by a particular linkage; whereas, in fact, when fear becomes too intense, people will frequently do anything to reduce that fear, including letting themselves be killed. The same is true with animals. Horses that are panic-stricken in fires run into the flames and are destroyed because they become crazed with fear and want to do something to get rid of that fear. But in doing so, they perform the act that kills them. It reduces their fear, but does not deal with the things that aroused it. I agree that we should be cautious about using fear in this kind of campaign, because if the individual becomes more concerned about reducing fear than about reducing what produced the fear, a failure in strategy will result.

Howard Leventhal: It is important to distinguish between fear as a necessary motivator, i.e., a link in a chain, that must be aroused before the behavior adaptations appear and fear as a response which is caused by a stimulus and is parallel to other responses. The second paradigm says there's an awareness of the stimulus and that this may lead to fear reactions and to adaptive reactions. Obviously, at a later point in time, the subject can be aware of both the stimulus, his fear response, and his adaptive reactions. Where the danger stimulus is exceedingly clear we feel the subject is primarily attentive to the danger, and in fact he attempts to cope with the danger and doesn't pay any attention (indeed, may never even be aware of) his fear reaction. If in fact the subject has a complex past history in the area in which he's functioning, he may not even experience the fear. He may be so busy behaving in other channels that fear doesn't have time to develop. It seems to be necessary to recognize the independence between the two types of responses especially under special situations where their independence is especially clear. For example, patients with neurological damage escape dangers but don't experience fear; or the research on perceptual defense, in which it has been found that both verbal statements and autonomic GSR changes are correlated with the presence of a shock word in a tachistoscope but are correlated independently with the stimulus. Thus, when the stimulus is very weak, then the verbal and autonomic systems can track the stimulus independently. Of course, when the stimulus is strong, both responses usually appear simultaneously. Obviously, though, when danger is ambiguous or unclear, then the only sign that the subject may have about the presence of the threat is in fact his own fear reaction.

Silvan Tomkins: Your position is that if the danger is clear, you may assume that the individual will perceive it as a salient one. He sees the threat and attempts some adaptive behavior. But one doesn't know, I would suggest, the specific weightings given to these two things. I think that we have a great tendency to simplify the instability of psychological fields. This can be clearly demonstrated with a stereoscope. Put two stimuli on the two eyes and watch what happens. The nervous system is just going back and forth madly between these two sources of information, fusing them, first suppressing one, and then the other. One gets the picture of an extraordinarily labile mechanism. I would suggest that that be introduced into this kind of theory construction. While it would be more comfortable to have variables that stayed put, the mechanism we're discussing isn't like that. An individual, let's say, begins to talk about probabilities at T-1, but at T-2, there's a sudden rush of fear and the question of probability is suddenly blanched. But at T-3 the probability thing returns.

Of course, we do not *know* that the probability is blanched; this is just an analogy. All I know is that if I pay attention to people, if I listen to them in situations where there is what I call an "ideo-affective pool" — that is, there are many affective responses — there are many information sources; these things bounce around like water in a bucket, and to conceptualize this is extraordinarily difficult. I can give an example in dissonance work with the latter-day business of regret. If one looked at pre-decision closely he would find regret and dissonance competing with each other frequently very wildly *before* a decision is reached, and the picking up of regret twenty minutes later is a very special case. It just doesn't have that stability. To come back to micromelodies, what I'm arguing for here is a microview of psychological processes. These vary quickly in time and complexity with varying weights being assigned from moment to moment to information, to affect, to action strategies, and so on.

Selwyn Waingrow: However, even at this stage, if there are differences between two points in time in the total population, can you assume, without knowing which individuals are doing what or at what stage you have caught this labileness, that the phenomenon is randomly dispersed at both points in time and you are, therefore, still measuring meaningful total change in your entire population?

Silvan Tomkins: I would say one can experiment. It's very hard to make inferences from data, but one can still set up the experiment to heighten one variable or another from time to time, at *varying* times.

Howard Leventhal: You can't study everything at once, and certainly there is some value in conducting experiments at a point in time when one can attempt to assess the contributions of emotional and other informational factors to consequent behavior. For example, we are now attempting a study in which we increase or decrease the subject's fear by techniques which are irrelevant to the communication issue. We want to see if in fact there is any relationship between intensifying emotional response and later adjustment behavior. Schachter has data like this which he has misinterpreted. He found that people who were exposed to a humorous film after being given epinephrine laughed more than people who saw the same movie after taking chlorpromazine. He reports that the people who took epinephrine thought the movie was funnier. Well, they didn't think that at all. His own data showed that they didn't think it was funnier, and that they said things such as, "I couldn't understand

why I was laughing so much, because it was not that funny a movie." Here is a condition where there is a clear stimulus and where in fact you can vary the intensity of the expressive aspects of the subject's affective behavior and it has no effect on his evaluation of the stimulus. On the other hand, others have tried to show that when you manipulate affective behavior so that the subject attributes it to the stimulus, his evaluation of it is changed.

Research into processes which fluctuate widely often requires a shift in strategy to simple experimental studies. You may also stop "experimenting" at stages where you are trying to invent or infer new variables. For example, in some interviewing studies we are doing, we present the subjects with problems, such as his suddenly coughing up blood, and ask him, "What do you do? What do you think? What do you feel?" And he starts feeling himself and he starts doing things. He searches for antecedents. He relocates the symptom. He sees if he can make a change by doing things for himself, and we get some idea of his various strategic operations. He may "symmetry test," i.e., see if lumps are on both sides, whether they are an intrinsic part of him or not, and we get some idea as to what variables are involved in his deciding if he is in danger.

It's too early from my point of view to apply a formal decisional model for this process because I don't know yet how the individual goes out looking for information and what kind of strategy he's going to adopt in coming to a decision. But I think this procedure gets closer to the temporal processes that Silvan Tomkins is talking about. Obviously we're going to be inventing new methodology to go into this further with less articulate subjects and it is also obvious that at some point we'll do more "true" experiments.

Frank Barron: One variable that is important in gambling systems as a basis for deciding how to behave in betting is "the risk of ruin." Risk of ruin is a function of the amount bet, the proportion that amount is to one's total capital, and the expectation of gain, or "the odds." The amount that one bets every time he smokes is always very small, of course. One is bound to lose but he's not going to lose very much on any given smoking occasion. At some point, however, the risk of ruin begins to increase rapidly. The signs that the risk of ruin is increasing are the kinds of things you've been mentioning. I'm not sure what relevance this has, but possibly it could lead to a way of presenting to people the rational basis for deciding to stop. Of course, rationality has hardly ever convinced any gambler.

Edgar Borgatta: The decision-making model suggested by Ward Edwards is a reasonable one when examined in terms of a laboratory situation, but not necessarily so in terms of the kind of changes which we are trying to effect in the field because of the intrusion of other variables. In what terms does one value pay off, for example? Is it simply in terms of whether I die or do not die, or whether I have other options to pick up in this regard? Do I enjoy it, for example? (This latter consideration may be an alternate pay off.) Perhaps the problem in terms of Silvan Tomkins' suggestion is that one doesn't make such a decision once, but all the time. If I understand Dr. Tomkins correctly he has said that an individual's decision for a particular action is conditioned by his subjective perception of the situation he is in; he will therefore be influenced only by those stimuli which fit into this perception. This leads to the kind of problem that occurs in reproducing an experiment in the laboratory by what we call "manipulation in the field." While we can account for 60 per cent of the variance in the laboratory situation we may not be able to account for more than 1.4 per cent in the field study. Fortunately, in our current work (pp. 3 ff.) we have a sample size of over 8,000, so that we can attribute statistical significance to these small differences. It is a frustrating realization, but I think we are dealing with a concern of the heart rather than of science; for in real life there are few things that are very predictable. The term "What predicts," for example, goes flat quickly when we try to account for the performance of school children. Adding new variables doesn't help much, either. Thus, a small amount of predictable variance may be all that's available. This means that we cannot and do not discount any finding simply because it predicts only 2 per cent above chance. We have also learned that small differences may be vitally important; the difference of one per cent in terms of the number of smokers, for instance, will be about a million people.

Leonard Berkowitz: The Air Force personnel selection program illustrated the same point. Their addition of new tasks to their qualifications tests did not significantly increase the predictability; but working with small levels was found to be most profitable.

Ward Edwards: I'm sure that what you're saying is that I should learn to listen to micromelodies. I agree.

Frank Barron: It might be worthwhile to try to construct a hedonic model of smoking behavior — c.g., what are the factors that give pleasure, what are the factors that produce pain, and what factors might be replaced by some other kinds of behaviors? Consider the use of alcohol, for instance. There are three major motives that one can see: the alleviation of anxiety, the release of inhibitions, and an alteration of consciousness in which philosophic meanings are emphasized. If one can meet these needs in other ways, then one can more easily give up drinking. A similar analysis might be used in respect to cigarette smoking. Substitutes for the factors within it must be found.

Howard Leventhal (after a lengthy discussion of the role of models in clarifying the dynamics of the decision-making process): These theoretical models do not necessarily compete with one another; they have somewhat different purposes. The level at which one operates in the laboratory concerning predicting the effects of a specific stimulus variable upon consequent behavior is perfectly legitimate. That model clearly omits or may omit the model which considers more prolonged sequences of behavior. I would hope that rather than seeing these models as competitors for our hearts, that they would turn out to be jointly acceptable to us so that efforts will be made to integrate the properties of both models. Then we could account for both the dependency of the response upon the external stimulus as well as its dependency upon prior responses that the subject has made.

Bernard Mausner: I should like to make a plea for the ecumenical spirit, also. The problem of smoking is a complex one that covers a wide variety of people. There is no single "most appropriate" research strategy, and every study can be criticized for neglecting some important variable. But the fact remains that in the real world we must slice the results one way or another in order to interpret them meaningfully. I agree that the "social interaction" approach is important; but the "behavioral change" model is equally important. Experimental laboratory conditions, while they are of necessity contrived, still seem to provide worthwhile results in clarifying the problem area. Some of the results may prove extremely valuable, because certain kinds of stimulus controls and response specifications are possible in the laboratory that would not be possible under "natural" circumstances. Such research will not solve all the problems of behavior, but its usefulness should not be underestimated.

Gerhart Wiebe: Presumably, the purpose of developing research programs is to investigate problems that cannot be easily solved without them; yet often the practical and obvious kinds of things (by which behavior may be changed) are not dealt with first, thereby leaving too much debris, so to speak, which can obscure the fundamental problems which really require the research.

In terms of how to fashion communications to modify behavior most effectively, several points should be considered. We must continually remind ourselves that a mere dissemination of facts does not yet constitute communication. If we don't put the facts into the right media, they won't get to the audience. First, a fact which is distributed but not perceived is certainly not communicated.

Secondly, in addition to the basic information that needs to be distributed, we should look to see whether we are doing the workman-like job of getting these messages into the most appropriate media for reaching the audiences for whom they are intended. A third point is that of the importance of "ego ideals," influential leaders who will endorse a point of view which we think it is desirable to propagate. Teachers, athletes, those who are particularly bright and so are presumably well able to regulate their behavior in terms of rational input — these people should be special targets so that those who tend to be followers rather than leaders will see ego ideal acting in a particular way and will find it rewarding in terms of style, in terms of ego rewards, to modify behavior in the desired direction.

Dorothy Nyswander: It would seem that representatives of target audiences should be more widely used to interpret material in a given medium — films, for example. They, not the professor, the teacher, or the expert, should be making the interpretation back to their own group. There will always be the problem of social distance between the intervener and the group. There is the need for additional research, particularly with groups other than those which have already received research attention. I'm afraid we may be developing theories of intervention based on studies of artificially formed groups which are not representative of the real world — a world made up of great, changing societies.

Irwin Rosenstock: There has been some considerable confusion over this problem of fear as a motivating influence. Dr. Leventhal has succeeded nicely in confusing us. In early times we believed fear was good; later we believed fear was bad; then we believed it was good; now we don't know what to believe. We have talked about the possibilities of using different kinds of appeals to persuade teenagers, especially, of the dangers of smoking. One of the points that occurred to me is the question of whether we could not link smoking to more proximate effects than mortality or diseases, which occur only 40, 50, 60 years later. It seems that the answer to this question would have some practical implications.

Howard Leventhal: I apologize for the confusion; but it is reasonably clear that there is a positive correlation between how fearful people are and how favorable their attitudes are, and a less clear relationship between their fear and their behavior. The issue is really a theoretical one as to whether a paradigm that deals with fear as responses is an appropriate basis for theory versus a paradigm which says that fear is in a parallel to attitude and other responses. In terms of the real world either one of these models may not be discriminable in many natural settings. We may see things and interpret what we feel in terms of either paradigm. However, some special situations may be of specific interest to the person testing a theory as he needs to discriminate the accuracy of the two views. So I think that it is unrealistic to expect that every aspect of a theory will necessarily have immediate pay-off.

With respect to Dr. Rosenstock's second remark about proximal cues, I can report that a student of mine did a study of communications which generated a lot of concern about immediate events in the body. She found that when she did this, she stimulated a lot of resistance against the communication. It was as though when focusing on the self, people started closing out and saying it didn't matter.

John Weir: It seems appropriate here to recall the old one-liner about the man who was reading so much about the evils of smoking he decided to quit — reading, that is.

Edgar Filbey: It seems important to note that the Horn-Waingrow study of threat dealt primarily with cognitive functioning, whereas other studies of fear have dealt with affect and other aspects.

Donn Mosser: I do clinical cancer work; I have seen many patients and have spoken to many lay audiences. It has impressed me that situations with fear have much less effect upon behavior than might be expected. Can it be an effective deterrent, particularly in families of lung cancer patients which still include heavy smokers? I would certainly not deprecate the productivity of research that doesn't have an obvious, immediate practical application. Quite clearly some of the research described at this Conference has substantial significance. But we in medicine who are trying to deal with the problem (and we're fairly new at this) would like to avoid the kind of thing we have encountered in many aspects of medical research today, the great gap between research and the patient's bedside. We need your help in looking at some of these problems.

The discussion at this point turned to the use of threat in fear arousal. The question was raised as to how threat and fear are related.

Irwin Rosenstock: We have used the term "threat" in some of our research in the past, although we were then really talking about a more cognitive thing, an awareness of potential danger. We were not specifically thinking of the emotional concomitants of the perception of danger. Most experimental studies of fear-arousal try to raise the level of emotionality. I'm not sure what the relationship is between the kinds of fear studied in the laboratory and the term "threat" as we have used it in some of our earlier surveys.

Daniel Horn: In this whole discussion of threat we are referring to something that is truly cognitive, with a minimal *affective* component. I was intrigued with Leventhal's (p. 25) off-hand suggestion that fear might not have caused the changes, but that *any* emotion could have caused them.

Irwin Rosenstock: Leventhal has suggested that the perception of danger leads simultaneously to the arousal of fear and to the adaptive response, at least under certain circumstances. The trick is, how do you get people to perceive the danger? Perhaps the main function of some of this fear arousal material is simply to attract attention.

William Allen: From a practical point of view, the threat may be effective with an older person, one with a heart disease or some other health problem. We at the Philadelphia Project have had difficulty reaching the younger parents and the youths themselves. Fear is not a factor because the consequences to health seem so remote to them.

Irwin Rosenstock: Are you suggesting that the arousal of fear would not be effective with young people or that it's more difficult to arouse real fear?

William Allen: It is more difficult to arouse real fear.

Gerhart Wiebe: Dr. Mosser has been arguing that we have neglected the straight appeal of rational information. The information included in the Surgeon General's Report has been given tremendous circulation, but I wonder what proportion of high school students have even a vague idea of what these studies have shown? We have not done one of the basic jobs that advertisers have learned to do — to hammer away at the essential facts, eliminating all of the side issues, getting right down to the central kernel and then repeating it almost *ad nauseum* until you penetrate the consciousness of the people with it.

Daniel Horn: We often get side-tracked when we start talking about the effects of fearful messages. It may be a mistake to use fear as the only negatively valenced end-result. Aren't we actually too concerned with the negative aspect of fear as a consequence of smoking? Whether this fear is *aroused* fear, or guilt, or shame, it still has a negative effect which may be less significant than accepting it merely as a step toward a level where alternatives can be considered. We get into problems when we concern ourselves with only one particular kind of emotion-arousing communication, in this case fear, since one of its functions is to make cigarette smoking undesirable. By employing it as a method, the smoker arrives at a point of deciding whether to stop smoking because the consequences are undesirable. Based on the premise of fear arousal alone, is an individual capable of arriving at the decision to quit?

Irwin Rosenstock: Are the channels of information used to disseminate smoking-health information the same as those used by the intended targets? The question has been asked whether teenagers are aware of the nature and specifics of the Surgeon General's Report. I can readily imagine that they would not be, since it has been transmitted mainly through channels that I think they don't frequently use. This is beyond what the school itself may be trying to do in the way of providing information. That's a topic on which more information is needed.

Donn Mosser: One of the real road blocks encountered in distributing smoking-health information in the high school is the high level of smoking among teachers, particularly female teachers. In many instances, they merely give lip service to the information. One of the most insincere things a teacher can do is to teach about smoking problems in a health class while her students can easily tell by smell that she's a smoker. This is the kind of non-rational behavior that a lot of teachers who are the leaders of these youngsters are following. They constitute a major and continuous channel of information for years in a child's life.

Gerhart Wiebe: Several relevant points can be summarized: *First,* that Dr. Mosser has just made, is that people in positions of leadership, such as teachers, should provide good examples. *Second,* we have reason to feel that young people in this generation *do* take pride in intellectual competence, and in the ability to evaluate information and act in terms of it. We ought to be very sure that they have the information which presumably would lead them away from smoking. *Third,* the distribution of information should be made through appropriate channels for the intended audience. For unless the message is received by the target audience you are simply not communicating.

Mildred Dubitzky: Dr. Mosser speaks about factors that influence attitude and behavior change among teenagers and school children and the important influences they are exposed to by means of identification with teachers and people they are faced with as models for identification. I would agree that young people are probably not influenced much by the fear of dying from disease, especially when they seem healthy at the time. On the other hand, young people *are* influenced by identification models. They want to identify with people who embody traits that they wish to emulate. From this come a number of points.

First of all, there is the problem of social class. Some of the programs described in this section deal with disseminating information of various kinds of credibility, bias, and so forth. It is a matter of trustworthiness at the source. Is the Surgeon General's Report, for instance, coming from the government and Public Health Service equally trustworthy and valued by children of all social classes who have had nothing but bad dealings with the government, or don't really feel that government has done much for them? The same for teachers. Many young people don't really care so much about teachers as they do about people in their own peer groups. What should be done about teachers who smoke and tell children not to smoke? Should they be dismissed, told not to teach anti-smoking, or what? Should you increase their conflict by chiding them for preaching against smoking while continuing to engage in the habit? Or would it be more practical to have teachers admit they smoke, and say, "I continue to smoke but I've been doing this for so long that I can't stop now. I could have been so much better if I hadn't smoked — you can be better than I am." Instead of setting a teacher up as an example in all fields of teenager education, perhaps they could be a little more honest about it, admit they may have weaknesses, thereby enhancing their trustworthiness and value in the eyes of teenagers from all classes.

Donn Mosser: I have been asked this question by teachers who say they cannot stop smoking. I have told them that anyone who is a smoker would be better off not teaching anything about smoking, because I think a teacher who says, "I'm weak, I can't stop; these are the facts; you can be stronger than I," leaves the student with more or less undesirable conclusions about the teacher. Students do look up to teachers.

Daniel Horn: Since people obviously behave in terms of their own pattern of goals and personality structure, it seems to be our job to understand these patterns and then try dealing with them. I think we make a great mistake using the terms like "super-irrational" and so on, regarding people's behavior. By doing so we imply that there is some inferior kind of organization involved in behavior and that others are stupid but can be changed to be as smart as we are. This implies a moral judgment, which doesn't belong to our examination. It is true that we have certain end results in mind, but they should be sought in the framework of trying to understand why and how people behave rather than in classifying their behavior in moral terms.

Donn Mosser: We are talking about doing something now with goal-directed behavior where the objective is far down the road. There were two great epidemics of polio in Minnesota — some three or four thousand cases — many of them fatal. This was during the period when the Sister Kenny Institute was providing much local information about polio. Yet in Minneapolis when the the polio vaccine was offered on a free basis, only half the people in the entire city took it. I don't think that people are stupid, it's just a matter of *how* do we approach them to modify behavior in a given direction?

Gerhart Wiebe: This comes back to Dr. Leventhal's point: People must be given specific instructions: walk down the street, take the third right, go in and give them your name, and sit down in a line of chairs; then they come and hand you a little thing to drink. It has been found in various settings that this kind of specific instruction is necessary. We're awfully groovy, you know. We get into ruts and we stay there.

Percy Tannenbaum: We are concerned with the communication of facts, with the effects of messages or treatments on individuals or groups to bring about change. It can be a change in attitude, in level of information, or a change, ultimately, in behavior. One theory implies that "if you know more, and if you have the appropriate atti-

tudes, you will also behave in an appropriate manner." Generally, we are concerned with two sets of variables influencing the effectiveness of any communication message: 1) variables within the message itself, and 2) variables relating to a description of the recipients of the message. The first includes such considerations as to how the message is structured, how it is presented, the relative fear or non-fear appeal, and so forth. The second deals with the wide variety of differences among people and their reactions to messages. Generally speaking, the first question we can put to the situation is, "Do different messages directed at the same person have different effects?" The second question is, "Does the same message directed at different people have different effects?" There seems to be a concern with both of these questions in the field of smoking research. The fear-appeal study best exemplifies the message-characteristic variable, and from what I heard about the Berkeley project (Schwartz pp. 115 ff.), there is also group-versus-individual counseling versus no counseling, and so on, all of which can be included in a communication frame as well. It seems that the audience characteristics are being defined largely in terms of the old demographic variables, although there seems to be an intention of going into some individual personality data as well. Of course, the main distinctions in the audience are smokers at present, ex-smokers, non-smokers — that is a division of the target audience on the basis of their actual behavior on the central issue involved.

An important problem that doesn't seem to be receiving sufficient attention is that of selection. In mass-communications we are faced with the problem of a large variety of messages, all competing for the individual's attention — far more at a given time than we can possibly attend to. He accepts some things and rejects others. The critical variables governing what he accepts and what he rejects are somewhat vague. The selective-exposure postulate emerging most clearly from dissonance theory is that people will tend to expose themselves to information consonant with their existing viewpoints and will actively avoid — and this is a most critical factor as far as cigarette smokers are concerned — will *actively* avoid information that is contrary or dissonant to their views. If this is the case, if they won't expose themselves, the message cannot possibly achieve any effect. The experimental evidence on this is not conclusive, but does suggest that we can do little more than make the material available to those people, and that it's up to them to receive it. There has been some research on such selective exposure on the cigarette issue, but I think there should be more. In the laboratory situations, we can govern exposure, but it is almost like force-feeding the information. In the public situation, however, where the actual applications must be made, advertising-type messages must reach the people by their own choices, not ours. Factors governing such selection will have to be investigated thoroughly before a truly effective program can be developed.

The appeals featuring the dangers of smoking remind me of the legal phrase, "a clear and present danger." But it may be quite remote to the individual. Most of us who have continued smoking feel this way: the statistics apply to somebody else. It would appear that the threat would have to be present and clear for them if the appropriate motivation for change is to occur. It is probably unethical to do this kind of study, but I wonder if we could try an experiment where instead of just giving the subject information, we send him to a doctor who tells him he has a heart condition and *then* see if there is a reduction of smoking consumption. Perhaps this is the way we will have to start manipulating some of these variables to see how much this kind of information means to a person in his individual setting, as opposed to abstract statistics from which he can readily divorce himself. It is also where the difference of the more abstract models and the social interaction models become involved.

There is also a related problem of *competing* information on the same topic for a given individual. While a lot of information is being made available on the ill effects of smoking, there is also a concerted effort on the part of the tobacco industry to represent the other side of the debate. Apparently, the tobacco industry is recognized, by college students, at least, as a low-credibility source for such information as the study done here at Arizona shows. But I wonder about the effectiveness of this information in competition. Consider the recent controversy over the Department of Agriculture film on the glories of smoking, ostensibly for dissemination abroad, to help our tobacco industry. There are other such inconsistencies within our own country. Congress authorizes placing warning labels on cigarette packages, while at the same time subsidizing tobacco-raising farmers. Again, what are the effects on the individual of such competing information continuing to bombard us from both sides?

A great degree of redundancy of information exists on both sides. The same kinds of things are being said constantly. I would tend to disagree with the statement by Dr. Wiebe (if I read him correctly) to the effect that the young people don't know the plain facts about the evils of smoking. I don't know what the plain facts are myself, but there is probably a fairly high level of awareness by the people of possible negative by-products (including death) of cigarette smoking. I maintain that the information is generally known, if not felt. I would like to know whether there is any evidence to the contrary.

Donn Mosser: How aware people are of the dangers of smoking becomes apparent when speaking to groups like Rotary, Kiwanis and other businessmen. They invariably comment, "Yes, we knew cigarette smoking was dangerous, but weren't aware of these specific facts — the total number of cancer deaths, for instance." I relate the figures to the automobile-accident death rate. This means something to people, whereas quoting the statistic "48,000 deaths" apparently means nothing.

Percy Tannenbaum: Is it important for them to know the relative mortality rates from automobile accidents and cigarette smoking or the fact that they are both very dangerous? I don't think it's a matter of which is more dangerous.

Donn Mosser: It is, if someone relates it for them. They don't relate it because they don't know what this many deaths means in a population of 200 million. They can divorce themselves from this fact just as much as they can from something else.

Daniel Horn: Among cigarette smokers, very roughly speaking about 75 per cent are aware that a threat exists; about 70 per cent accept it as being of sufficient magnitude to warrant doing something about it; about 50 per cent express personal concern, and about 40 per cent think that intervention is either possible or desirable.

Percy Tannenbaum: Assuming that there is a substantial level of awareness, but not a perception of a clear and present danger, I wonder about the effectiveness of the public media of communication and the Advertising Council public-service type of appeal. For one thing, communication almost by definition is an indirect, vicarious way of getting results. It is remote. I wonder whether some work shouldn't be undertaken, not so much on showing the relative effectiveness of individual versus mass-communication appeals (which is being done) but more away from the mass-communication situation, more toward different kinds of appeals on the individual level or on that of small groups. My guess is that from what we already know about the mass communication avenues of persuasion those media are not going to be the most effective. They can help create the aura for effectiveness; they can help get some of the superficial information across — which I think has already gotten across — but in the actual specific details they are required to offer a very bland menu, almost by definition; and you are now talking about the kind of rich diet these people are going to need in order to take the appropriate action. I don't think the mass media are the appropriate means of doing this, which puts more pressure on schools and other informal communication situations.

Robert Lawrence: But television seems to be a medium through which we could fight fire with fire. Since this is where we get the seductive cigarette commercials, this is where we could retaliate. Of course, nationwide television coverage costs thousands of dollars a minute. But even at that rate, what would we do with our minute once we bought it? As Dr. Horn has pointed out, we must consider the dynamics of the smoking change process; for example, we probably couldn't expect a lot of change if we just cited statistics about how likely you are to get sick or die if you smoke. But if we really posed a threat by showing, for instance, a person who has been told by his doctor that he has lung cancer and that he has six months to live — showing him walking with his family, then having him appeal directly to the camera, to the people, saying, "I am going to die because I smoke; don't smoke, please." The person watching in his home might say, "I can't let this happen to me and my family — I'm going to quit." This sort of television message should have a tremendous impact.

Gerhart Wiebe: I was with one of the major networks during the early part of World War II. We developed a series of broadcasts aimed at giving the people a realistic appreciation of what the boys were going through on the fighting front. I learned a lesson then that I will never forget about mass communication in a free society: get too rough, people just turn the button. It's that simple. Advertisers are aware of this, and very seldom use appeals of a threatening nature. As Daniel Horn has suggested, however, we must proceed toward community-wide or society-wide techniques, using a *style* orientation, to make it very easy *not* to smoke and a little uncomfortable to smoke. The problem certainly represents a big challenge, and one in which we fail. The mass media have worked in selling things; there is no reason why they should not succeed in providing different orientations to things. In any case, I would question the effectiveness of a tough "scare" approach.

We should also keep radio in mind, as well as television. There are about seven million television sets in the country today, but counting the sets in cars and transistor portables, there are over 120 million radios. I recently listened to a public-service program on the subject of smoking and health. Although it was on from one to two a.m., when you wouldn't think too many people would be listening, the program drew over 700 telephone calls from listeners. Thousands of people were reached this way, many of whom requested and were mailed literature on the subject. There are indeed many opportunities afforded by the mass media, keeping in mind radio as well as television. . . . But if we begin using the mass media in competition, so to speak, with advertising for smoking, we are going to have to be realistic in the measure of effort and patience that will be required. It is highly doubtful that we can generate as much as 10 per cent of the budget that is used on the other side. And we are only beginning, where they have forty years of momentum. These points should be considered when we begin evaluating our effectiveness in this new area.

The suggestion was made that the huge response may have come from those who need "treatment" least; non-smokers or successful quitters. At exhibits, for example, those who showed an interest in materials and literature were the non-smokers. Dr. Wiebe pointed out that the strategy of advertising is based on "getting in with a message, and getting out before the non-believers leave you."

Donn Mosser: One technique for getting out information is the taped telephone message. The Cancer Society has used it in Washington, D. C., and our group have in Minneapolis. A spot announcement can be put on radio and television to dial a particular number and listen to it. "Cancer Answers" is the expression that has been used locally. We have had four of these installed. I did one on smoking and health hazards; it ran for two minutes. There were times during the day when all four lines were tied up for long periods. It would be interesting to learn whether it was the smoker or the non-smoker who was calling.

Dorothy Nyswander: The same problem applies here that applied with war-bond appeals. Who came to the theater to see the films promoting the sale of bonds? Mostly people who were buying war bonds! Likewise, people who listen to programs on smoking are non-smokers, rather than smokers. The people who ask for literature at fair exhibits are non-smokers, rather than smokers. These practical problems enter the picture when we think of supplementing some of our visual aids and mass material.

Kenneth Reed: We had ten consecutive messages in Indianapolis on a program like that, which is still functioning. Initially there was good response, but it tapered off. We have maintained these messages because we continue to get support for them. The group that made the tapes and put them on was the Seventh-day Adventists, with their Five-Day Program. However, the second time they went for a radio spot announcement, the radio people turned them down because they had gotten some kick-back from their advertisers, who wouldn't permit this kind of thing to jeopardize their accounts.

Asked whether the Seventh-day Adventists protested the refusal to sell them time, Dr. Reed indicated that the time was not sold; it had formerly been donated by the station. But when the group offered to buy it, they were refused.

Gerhart Wiebe: Of course, if stations contribute the time, I guess they can choose to whom they give it. But if they offered to buy and were turned down, then I think that a protest ought to have been made to test the station's right to refuse to sell time.

It was suggested that instead of concentrating on half-hour fact programs over the mass media, our resources could more effectively be used in trying to persuade people who are seen on television not to smoke while they are on the air. Unfortunately, people who are famous and highly educated can be seen smoking on television as well as those who are not. Smoking is not exclusively a lower class behavior.

Gerhart Wiebe: This is a parallel to that suggestion in the case of the major religions, which have their lobbies working around the major television-production centers. They have no coercive power and they don't claim to, but they try to cultivate acquaintance. They become friendly enough to be allowed to see the scripts, and they guard the interests of their own religions. They prevail upon the producers, directors, and continuity-acceptance people not to put on a particular scene, or to take out a certain line, and so forth. Working at low key, they are fairly effective. This kind of campaign of moral persuasion may be used with some success against cigarettes and in favor of pipes or cigars or some other substitute.

The question of the use of satire was discussed; it was agreed that in terms of getting and keeping the attention of audiences, particularly those comprising adolescents, the humorous approach seems to be effective. Whether attitudes or behavior are changed as a consequence of their use, however, is questionable.

The device of having children write essays was also questioned, since many children writing on themes such as "Why Teen-agers Shouldn't Smoke," simply say what they know their teachers expect to hear. Children who are not concerned with the problem simply "tune out," go through the motions, and either passively or aggressively do not conform to expectations. It was suggested that this may also be true of adult smokers who are passive-aggressive and go along with the doctor in entering smoking projects; they only want to defeat the doctor and prove nobody can help them so they can go on smoking.

Mildred Dubitzky: It is surprising — and unfortunate — that we do not apply more of what research has already brought to light, even in further research. Studies have shown how different ethnic groups, for instance, have different values and how teen-agers value certain recklessness and adventurousness in keeping with their age-sex development and their role behavior. This should not surprise us. Why don't we try to explain to them that it's not really smart or adventurous to smoke, that they are being taken in by the advertisers, and that other people are laughing at them? We agree that it should be made easier for people not to smoke. This involves changing the social milieu, which takes a long time. But the impression can be given that the social milieu *is* different now, with smokers being non-conforming, instead of the other way around.

Dr. Mosser suggested that simple experiments could be built into high-school biology classes, where children could, for example, paint extract of nicotine on mice and observe the results. Dr. Ross said that his group has developed a small pamphlet containing a series of experiments that can be done in the classroom, relating to pulse rate and to the effects of nicotine on goldfish in a bowl. It even shows students how to collect their own tobacco tar and paint it on mice (see p. 255).

The discussion returned to the problem of evaluating the effectiveness of the mass media in presenting information on the hazards of smoking. How can the various components of a message be analyzed on a large scale to measure their effects?

Selwyn Waingrow: There are plans for follow-ups of the inputs in some community settings. Whether plans exist to isolate and measure the components separately, I don't know, but there will be an attempt to toss in everything but the kitchen sink in terms of community effort in order to measure the total interaction effect.

Percy Tannenbaum: Are you throwing them in in such a way that you can pull them out again? I become worried about the kitchen sink, because once it gets in, there's a lot of plumbing to contend with. It can be argued that we ought to let all efforts go forward — different theories, different methodologies and so on — it can't hurt. We have heard this, but it can be argued that on methodological grounds, if no other, we need much more selectivity, focusing on a set of identified, specific problems, doing one study at a time instead of a combination of many thrown together.

PART II

INTERVENTION PROCESSES

Relation of Knowledge of Effects of Cigarette Smoking to the Practice of Smoking Among High School Seniors

KENNETH L. BRINEY
American Heart Association

Various educational programs, particularly in the schools, have been directed at providing the "facts" about the health effects of cigarette smoking. The intent obviously is to deter smoking by providing knowledge of its deleterious effects on the individual's health. The assumption apparently is that health knowledge is an important determinant of related behavior. This study attempts to assess the relationship between knowledge and behavior in regard to cigarette smoking.

The school selected for testing is in a predominantly middle-class suburb of San Francisco. The test sample consisted of all high school seniors present on a given day in May, 1963. The data were collected prior to the publicity which subsequently surrounded the Surgeon General's Report. No "anti-smoking drives" had yet been conducted in this school.

The instrument developed for this study was made up of two sections: (1) a nine-item smoking practice scale and (2) a 66-item multiple-choice test on the knowledge of the effects of smoking. All data were anonymously furnished.

Of the 348 completed answer sheets analyzed, 156 were for boys and 192 for girls.

Table 1 summarizes incidence data by sex:

TABLE 1

Students' Self-Reported Cigarette Smoking Practice By Sex According to "Smokers" or "Non-Smokers"

Smoking Practice	BOYS No.	BOYS %	GIRLS No.	GIRLS %	TOTAL No.	TOTAL %
"Smokers"	72	48.6	69	36.7	141	42.0
"Non-smokers"	76	51.4	119	63.3	195	58.0
Total	148	100.0	188	100.0	336	100.0

These data compare with those provided by Horn et al. (1959) who reported 39.8 per cent of senior boys as "smokers" and 30.7 per cent of senior girls as "smokers" (in the Portland Study). Salber et al. (1962) reported the following as smokers among high school seniors in Newton, Massachusetts: boys, 45.5 per cent; girls, 54.7 per cent.

Thus in this study more boys are classified as smokers than in Newton or Portland, using the same definition of "smoker." A greater percentage of girls were found to be "smokers" in this study than in the Portland Study but less than those in Newton.

Scores for knowledge of effects of smoking are summarized in Table 2.

TABLE 2

Summary of Test Results on Knowledge of Effects of Smoking by Sex

ITEM	BOYS	GIRLS	TOTAL
Number of Questions	66	66	66
Range of Scores	14–52	15–50	14–52
Median Score	33	34	34
Modal Score	36	35	36
Mean Score	32.9	34.1	33.5
Reliability	.79	.67	.74

Chi-square comparisons of students' reported smoking practice and their achievement test score were tested according to several different groupings of test scores and smoking practice categories in order to confirm the direction of the relationship.

Boys. The simplest breakdown demonstrates the relationship found for boys. Table 3 indicates the procedures used in testing the relationships.

TABLE 3

Calculation of Relationship Between Knowledge Test Score and Smoking Practice for Boys

Knowledge Test Score	Reported Smoking Practice Categories		
	"Smokers"	"Non-Smokers"	Total
2. Mean (33) & Higher	37	45	82
1. Below Mean	35	31	66
Total	72	76	148

Knowledge Test Score	Reported Smoking Practice				Total d2/E
	"Smokers"		"Non-Smokers"		
0 (E)	37	(40)	45	(42)	
2. Above Median Mean d		3		3	
d²		9		9	
d²/E	9/40=.23		9/42=.21		.44
0 (E)	35	(32)	31	(34)	
1. Below Mean d		3		3	
d²		9		9	
d²/E	9/32=.28		9/34=.26		.54
				Chi Square Value	.98

Girls. For girls quite different results are found. A comparison of "smokers" and "non-smokers" by their scoring "above the mean" and "below the mean" is shown in Table 4.

The chi-square values obtained between girls' smoking practices and knowledge score yield levels of significance of .01 in both cases. (The value 6.635 would have been sufficient for a .01 level of significance to be reached.) It is concluded that chance would account for

TABLE 4

Calculation of Relationship Between Achievement Test Score and Smoking Practice for Girls

Knowledge Test Score	Reported Smoking Practice Category		
	"Smokers"	"Non-Smokers"	Total
2. Mean (34) & Higher	26	75	101
1. Below Mean	43	44	87
Total	69	119	188

Knowledge Test Score	Reported Smoking Practice				Total d2/E
	"Smokers"		"Non-Smokers"		
0 (E)	26	(37)	75	(64)	
d		11		11	
d²		121		121	
d²/E		3.27		3.27	6.54
0 (E)	43	(32)	44	(55)	
d		11		11	
d²		121		121	
d²/E		3.78		2.20	5.98
				Chi Square Value	12.52

the relationship found here in far fewer than one out of a hundred cases.

DISCUSSION

Data obtained in this study on the smoking practices of high school seniors substantially agree with those of other studies. Although they differ notably in cigarette smoking practice, boys and girls differ little in their level of knowledge about the effects of smoking, as indicated by test scores.

Had a strong relationship been found between level of knowledge and smoking practice, it would have provided a good argument for the continuance of current "information campaigns" in the schools. A complete absence of such a relationship would make the wisdom of continuing these campaigns seriously questionable. Since the results of this study show a major difference between the sexes for the relationship in question, the implications are somewhat ambiguous, calling, certainly, for additional research with different samples and measurement techniques. If these differences are reliable, obviously they must be noted in the development of smoking-health programs.

Numerous questions are raised by these results, principally concerning sexual differences in the perception of smoking as a threat to health, in the degree to which boys and girls differ in being guided in their behavior by health information, and, in general, the role that smoking plays in the personal and social lives of boys and girls.

Several reports (Beckerman 1963; Cartwright, Martin, Thomson 1960; Jeffereys, Westway 1961) have been published describing educational campaigns in schools designed to deter cigarette smoking by providing information about the harmful effects of smoking on health. Each of these studies reports that the campaign was not effective in influencing smoking practices of students. It has often been observed in this connection that knowledge alone is not sufficient to motivate behavior; the individual may know, without really believing or accepting the information as a basis for his action.

SUMMARY

Anti-smoking programs appear to be based upon the premise that persons possessing factual knowledge about the ill effects of smoking will tend not to smoke.

The present study, conducted with high school seniors in California, was designed to determine the relationship between knowledge of effects of smoking and smoking practice.

An instrument was developed which included the two areas of study, i.e., smoking practice (behavior) and knowledge of effects of smoking. Validity for the items on factual knowledge was established through use of a panel of health experts experienced in the subject of the effects of cigarette smoking. Reliability was established through the split-half method. Three hundred forty-eight completed questionnaires were analyzed.

The relationship between knowledge of effects of smoking — as measured by total test score — and smoking practices was tested by the chi-square method. The results varied by sex. For boys it was determined that chances were greater than five in a hundred that chance alone could have accounted for the relationship. For girls, on the other hand, it was determined that chances were less than one in a hundred that chance alone could have accounted for the relationship. Using .01 as an arbitrary level of significance, then, this study showed a lack of significant relationship between knowledge and behavior in regard to cigarette smoking for boys but a positive relationship for girls, i.e., girls who have higher knowledge scores about effects of smoking are less likely to be smokers than those with low knowledge scores.

REFERENCES

Beckerman, Stanley C. "Report of an Educational Program Regarding Cigarette Smoking Among High School Students," *Journal of the Maine Medical Association* (March 1963). Reprint.

Cartwright, Ann, Martin, F. M., and Thomson, J. G. "Efficacy of an Anti-Smoking Campaign," *Lancet* (February 1960), 327–329.

Horn, D., Courts, F. A., Taylor, R. M., and Solomon, E. S. "Cigarette Smoking Among High School Students," *American Journal of Public Health,* XLIX (November 1959), p. 1498.

Jeffereys, Margot and Westway, W. R. "Catch Them Before They Start," *Health Education Journal,* XIX (1961), 3–17.

Salber, Eva J., MacMahon, B., and Welsh, Barbara. "Smoking Habits of High School Students Related to Intelligence and Achievement," *Pediatrics,* CXXIX (May 1962), p. 780.

DISCUSSION

Asked if there have been any twin studies on the variability of the tendency to like to smoke tobacco, Dr. Briney referred the question to Dr. Guilford, whose research is more appropriately related.

Joan Guilford: Twin studies I know of that have been done, have been done in Europe exclusively, and they have demonstrated that monozygotic twins are much more alike in their smoking habits than dizygotic twins, and the same applies to the dizygotic comparisons of siblings; but there have been no American replications and nobody is sure what this means yet, and nobody has checked to find out whether the constitutional hypothesis holds for parents and children.

Selwyn Waingrow (To Dr. Briney): Can you speculate on this sex difference?

Kenneth Briney: I'd be happy to because I think that there are many implications which require further discussion. Smoking is probably a very different device for boys than it is for girls. We have not sufficiently investigated these sexual differences. Perhaps, for different age levels, and for different children, smoking represents a pattern of accepted behavior. We already have some information on the beginning of smoking in children — for example that boys begin before girls do, although we know that physiologically girls are more mature at a given age. There are also many social factors involved here. My hunch would also be that the matter of knowledge of effects is not a determinant for girls; rather, it may be something that is related to a determinant on whether or not these girls smoke. Extending the problem to the field of education, the question becomes, "With this much discrepancy, should boys and girls be taught separately and differently about smoking?"

The Relative Effects of Selected Teaching Methods In Influencing Smoking Patterns Among College Women[1]

MARILYN CRAWFORD
Madison College

The primary purpose of this study (covering only the first year of a two-year project) was to investigate the relative effectiveness of various teaching methods on the smoking habits, attitudes and knowledge of college women. The subjects were 339 women students at Madison College in Harrisonburg, Virginia, who were enrolled in a required two-semester-hour Personal and Community Health course — for which biology was a prerequisite; therefore, none of the participants was an entering freshman.

Two separate procedures were involved. The first was the administration of a smoking questionnaire at the beginning and end of the semester and again several months later. It was designed to measure information concerning smoking behavior and attitudes of the respondents, their parents and friends, as well as other knowledge of the effects of smoking. It was evaluated and judged to be quite valid and reliable after several trial periods, including a test-retest pattern administered to fifty-one summer school students.

The second procedure involved four separate teaching methods which were incorporated into different class sections of the health course in the area of tobacco education. (An attempt was made to have equal numbers of students taught by each method; otherwise, the methods were randomly assigned.) The course enrollment consisted of about one-third second-semester freshmen, one-third sophomores and one-third juniors, of whom 41 per cent smoked cigarettes, 6 per cent were ex-smokers, and 180, or 53 per cent, did not smoke at all. Of those stating they smoked at all, 10 per cent claimed they smoked one to six cigarettes weekly; 56 per cent allowed one to ten cigarettes daily; 27 per cent smoked one-half to one pack daily, and 8 per cent smoked more than one pack daily. Sixty-four per cent of the smokers had been smoking less than three years and over 80 per cent said they smoked when they were nervous, relaxing, or studying. Only 6

per cent stated they did not inhale. Over half of the non-smokers gave one or more of the following reasons for not smoking: "I don't see any point in it" (83 per cent), "I don't like it" (66 per cent), "Health reasons" (55 per cent), and "Too expensive" (52 per cent).

There were three teachers involved in the study, each of whom used one or more of the following teaching methods: 1) *The Neutral Approach.* The most important effects of smoking were presented by the teacher as objectively as possible in the manner of, "Here are the facts; the decision of whether or not to smoke is entirely up to you." 2) *The Committed Approach.* This teaching method differed from the neutral approach only in terms of the teacher's attitude. She acknowledged her conviction that smoking was harmful and that she was concerned about the students' health: "Here are the facts: although many people smoke, the evidence clearly indicates that smoking is injurious to health." 3) *The Incidental Method.* This teaching method consisted of approximately five "incidents" (each five to fifteen minutes in length) which correlated the effects of smoking with other topics of study covered by the health course. A variety of teaching aids were used and one "incident" (such as an example of the hazards of smoking) was included in the teacher's lecture about every three weeks during the semester. (One incident, for instance, was introduced in a discussion of health in pregnancy, another in a discussion of cardiovascular diseases.) 4) *The Control Group.* There was no presentation made about smoking, although direct questions were answered.

Two additional individually oriented teaching methods were used, although these are not included in this analysis. 1) *The Performance Approach.* As a topic for a term paper, a student conducted research and submitted a written documented report on smoking. 2) *The Authoritarian Approach.* As a semester project, a student elected to stop smoking. This action was voluntary, but once committed, it required the student's cessation of smoking by mid-semester — approximately seven weeks. If the commitment was not fulfilled the student received a failing grade on the project, which in turn affected his final grade in the course.

[1] Sponsored by Public Health Service Community Cancer Demonstration Project Grant No. 4907B64. This report is based on data obtained during the first year of a two-year project being conducted at Madison College, Harrisonburg, Virginia.

TABLE 1

Mean Changes in Attitude Scores[1]

| | Behavior | Teaching Method | | | | F Ratio | Signif. |
		Neutral	Committed	Incidental	Control		
Beginning	NS	−1.53	−1.08	− .32	.00	.82	
to End of	S	+ .53	−2.31	+ .78	+1.67	3.30	.05
Semester	Total	− .84	−1.63	+ .11	+ .63	2.55	
Beginning of	NS	+ .76	− .35	+1.16	+2.89	2.17	
Semester	S	+ .90	− .47	+ .34	+ .93	.42	
to Follow-up	Total	+ .82	− .41	+ .81	+2.05	2.14	

[1] A decrease in score indicates a more negative feeling toward smoking.

The *homogeneity of the classes* was investigated in terms of demographic information, smoking habits, attitude scores, and knowledge scores. No great differences were observed in the demographic information (classification, age, major, marriage, sorority, and work status), when data were grouped according to individual classes, teaching methods, or teacher. The chi-square statistic was used in investigating non-smokers and smokers, classified according to teaching methods, and teacher; the significance in each situation was greater than the .70 level, thus indicating the probable independence of these variables. Analysis of variance was applied to the attitude and knowledge scores. No significant (.05 level or smaller) F-ratios were obtained when data were grouped according to classs, teaching methods, or teachers; non-smokers, smokers, and combined scores were investigated. This indicated that the non-smokers, the smokers and the combined scores, grouped according to individual classes, teaching methods, or teachers could probably be considered homogeneous at the beginning of the study.

The results for the four teaching groups were evaluated in terms of the changes in smoking habits which might have occurred, the changes in individual attitude toward smoking between the beginning and the end of the semester and between the beginning of the semester and the follow-up evaluation. In studying the changes in behavior among these different groups, no significant relationships were revealed. It did not make any difference which teaching group the students were in; some started to smoke and some stopped smoking, with all of the groups changing little.

The mean changes in attitude scores are presented in Table 1. The committed approach was the only teaching method in which cigarette smokers developed decreased attitudes toward smoking. Although lacking statistical significance, the data presented in Table 1 indicate that the only students (smokers [S] and non-smokers [NS]) who maintained more negative feelings toward smoking over a period of months were those in the committed teaching group. Although the neutral group resulted in more immediate desirable changes in attitudes than the incidental group, the follow-up evaluation found a close similarity of changes between these two groups. Students who received no instruction developed more positive attitudes toward smoking than students who received instruction in the effects of smoking.

In summary, no teaching method appeared to be superior to others in changing behaviors. However, significant relationships were obtained between behaviors (smokers and non-smokers) and attitude scores and knowledge scores. Based on the changes which occurred in attitudes and knowledge scores, the committed method proved to be most effective in bringing about desirable changes; this was followed, in rank order, by the neutral approach, the incidental approach, and the control group.

Mean changes in knowledge scores are presented in Table 2. By the end of the semester the changes in knowledge scores among students in the neutral and committed groups were significantly higher (.01 level) than those in the incidental and control groups. Mean scores among these two teaching methods were also higher at the end of the follow-up period, although only the committed teaching method maintained a significant relationship to the two lowest groups. Only smokers in the committed group recorded an increase in mean scores at the end of the follow-up period. Students in the control group recorded a slightly larger increase in scores than did students in the incidental group.

The relative effectiveness of the three teachers was studied in the same manner as the teaching methods, although no statistically significant relationship was found between the teacher and smoking behaviors or attitude scores. While three teachers were involved in the project only one taught all four teaching groups; the second teacher had three of the four groups. They all ranked about equal in the final results in terms of effectiveness, and there were no significant differences obtained from the follow-up. In terms of knowledge scores, however, a

TABLE 2

Mean Changes in Knowledge Scores[1]

	Behavior	Teaching Method				F Ratio	Signif.
		Neutral	Committed	Incidental	Control		
Beginning	NS	2.53	2.92	1.22	.72	6.74	.01
to End of	S	2.19	2.64	.31	1.15	5.77	.01
Semester	Total	2.42	2.80	.87	.89	11.58	.01
Beginning of	NS	1.84	1.45	.72	.33	3.52	.05
Semester	S	.70	2.78	.03	.64	5.55	.01
to Follow-up	Total	1.34	2.06	.42	.47	6.29	.01

[1] All scores carry a plus value.

significantly greater increase in scores was made among the non-smokers taught by the first teacher, who also taught all four groups, than by the others. (This first teacher taught seven classes as versus five and two, respectively, for the others.) It was also obvious at the end of the follow-up period that the students taught by the committed approach had the greatest increase in scores. Students taught by the neutral approach had the second-best increase with the control group third and the incidental group fourth. Everyone's scores increased, however, and that in itself was gratifying.

We also tried to assess whether there was any correlation between attitude, knowledge, and behavior and whether behavior can be grouped in terms of non-smokers and smokers. The data turned up a significant relationship between the smoking behaviors and the attitude scores at the one per cent level of confidence where the non-smokers had a more negative feeling toward smoking than did the smokers. As would be expected, non-smokers made significantly higher knowledge scores than did smokers.

A couple of other things have appeared during this first year of the project. Among the class students, for instance, there is some indication of a progressive increase in the percentage of students who smoke. At the beginning of the first semester, 37 per cent of the women students smoked; at the beginning of the second semester, 44 per cent smoked and at the beginning of the last semester, 52 per cent of them were smoking. Although it is perhaps not too relevant, certainly not to our own program, it was interesting to learn that the number of entering freshmen who have never smoked seems to be on the increase.

Our hope is that an additional year of study will give us more comparative results as well as significant statistical findings which will give some indication as to whether one teaching method is preferable over another, one type of teacher over another, and a general consensus as to whether our questionnaire is accurately cov-

ering and signifying the information we are trying to gather.

SUMMARY

The primary purpose of this study was to investigate the effects of selected teaching methods upon the smoking habits, attitudes, and knowledge of college women. The subjects were 339 students enrolled in a required health course at Madison College. A Smoking Inventory was administered at the beginning and end of the semester and again several months later.

The teaching methods used were as follows:

1. *Neutral.* The effects of cigarette smoking were presented in an unbiased way.
2. *Committed.* This was similar to the neutral approach, but the teacher expressed the belief that cigarette smoking is harmful.
3. *Incidental.* The effects of smoking were presented in five short "incidents."
4. *Control.* The topic of smoking was avoided.

Measured in terms of changes which occurred between the beginning of the semester and the follow-up evaluation, no teaching method was found to be more effective in the changing of smoking habits. The committed method resulted in the most desirable changes in attitude scores; this was followed in order by the neutral approach, the incidental method, and the control group. These findings were not statistically significant. Among changes in knowledge scores, the committed and neutral groups scored significantly greater increases than the incidental group; the control group scored only slightly higher than the incidental method. Thus, when measured in terms of smoking habits, attitudes, and knowledge, the committed method was found to be most effective; this was followed in rank order by the neutral approach, the incidental method, and the control group. When the data were studied according to the three teachers, no significant differences were found.

An Analysis of Selected Socio-Economic Characteristics as Related to the Smoking Habits of University Freshmen

DOROTHY F. DUNN
University of Illinois

Since the purpose of this study was to understand the smoking situation on a university campus, the first step necessary was making an appraisal of present practices. Unfortunately, the University of Illinois in Urbana kept no smoking histories of students. (Actually, student health records are kept for long periods of time by few universities; among these are Harvard University and the University of Pennsylvania.) In the absence of this backlog, information was selected from the student data system and questionnaires which were administered in January 1965 to 3,567 students who were at the end of the first semester of their freshman year. Running the study after Christmas vacation afforded the opportunity of querying immediately after most students had been under some parental influence. Also, at this point in time, the Report of the Surgeon General's Committee on Smoking and Health had been out for twelve months, which gave the opportunity of ascertaining how influential it had been on student smoking behavior. In addition, if the student reports could be adjudged valid, the timing offered some insight into the smoking habits of parents.

The study yielded data on 102 variables on selected demographic, socioeconomic, attitudinal and academic characteristics and smoking habits. Although the results have not been fully tabulated, they appear to conform to the findings of other studies dealing with college populations. Of the total group involved in the study, 70 per cent were males, of whom 43.3 per cent smoked, while 35.7 per cent of the girls smoked. Of those who had been smoking twelve months previously, 56 per cent had increased the number of cigarettes smoked per day (50 per cent of the men and 69 per cent of the girls), and 43 per cent indicated a desire to stop smoking. Most freshmen believed that teenage smoking is a major public health problem, possibly because some 95 per cent of those queried had started smoking some time before they were eighteen. This gained rather startling significance when the data also revealed that eight out of ten freshmen believed students were adequately informed regarding the potential dangers of cigarettes and nine out of ten believed that the cigarette smoker had a greater chance of developing lung cancer than the non-smoker.

Since the University's enrollment consists of many students from rural backgrounds, we examined this factor to determine the influence of city-versus-country rearing as an atmosphere for conditioning a child to begin the habit. Approximately one in five of the students had grown up in rural areas. Twenty-six and two-tenths per cent of this group smoked, while the number of smokers coming from the Chicago area, for instance, was substantially larger at 46.4 per cent. Further study might reveal some of the influence and characteristics of urban life which serve as pre-conditioners to an acceptance of smoking. It is not a new theory that country life seems to be a favorable atmosphere in which to produce non-smoking adults.

It was also found that students with higher academic achievements did not smoke as much as other students. For instance, only 20.3 per cent of those who had been valedictorians in high school smoked. There appeared to be an inverse association between grade average and smoking. Of those students with an "A" average, only 16.7 per cent smoked, while 59.1 per cent of the "E"-average students smoked. Also, more than half of those who did not return to the university smoked. While it is perhaps unfair to measure college grades so early in the adjustment to college curriculum, it would probably be worthwhile to follow up on the less than 30 per cent who consistently showed up as non-smokers among those who had chosen the more technical courses of study.

The findings also showed that those involved in campus activities where leadership and organization ability were involved smoked considerably less (by around 15 per cent) than did their counterparts, who belonged to no school or community organizations. It might be interesting to run separate studies, one for student leaders and another for unparticipating students, and compare the results in terms of smoking behavior. More than eight of every ten students had held membership in school and community organizations during the past 12 months. Of these, 39.2 per cent were smokers, while 47.4 per cent of the non-member group smoked. One in two of those with organization membership held an elective office, and of this group only one in three smoked.

If student reporting about their parents' smoking habits is reliable, it would appear that the Surgeon General's Report had had a definite impact on them; the findings indicated that between January 1964, the time of the report, and January 1965, many parents had decreased the number of cigarettes smoked per day. Significantly, this number was greater for the fathers than for the mothers. If one parent smoked it appeared to have the same effect on the student, however, as if both parents smoked. There was also a positive relationship between the smoking behavior of the parents, prior to the publication of the report, and that of their smoking offspring. At the time of the survey, 37.1 per cent of the parent group were reported by their children to be non-smokers. Of the balance who smoked, 31.2 per cent smoked cigarettes only, with the others smoking pipes or cigars. Of cigarette-smoking fathers, almost 43 per cent of their children smoked. These parental habits did not quite jibe with parental attitudes: only 2.3 per cent of the non-smoking students and 4 per cent of the smoking ones reported that their parents approved of their smoking and the majority of students with older brothers or sisters regarded their parents as being indifferent to their smoking. In reference to parental education: increased amount of schooling for the parents was associated with a decrease in the amount of smoking among their children. For those who had only attended elementary school, the percentage of smokers among their children was almost 44 per cent; for those parents who had received post-graduate training, the number reduced to around 35 per cent.

A student's living accommodations seemed to be importantly related to his smoking habits. The study showed that housing played an important part as far as smoking habits of the freshman and his roommate were concerned, particularly in an increase in the number of cigarettes smoked per day over the 12-month period. When the roommate smoked and shared a room with a student who smoked, the increase in 12 months was greater than when the roommate did not smoke; when three people shared a room the increase in smoking was least if one person smoked and two did not. Of smokers whose roommates did not smoke, almost 48 per cent increased the number of cigarettes smoked per day. But when the roommates also smoked, the proportion of those who increasingly smoked more rose to almost 61 per cent.

For reasons which as yet are undetermined, the University cooperatives for both men and women had by far the lowest percentages of smokers and climbed to its highest in sororities and off-campus facilities. For some inexplicable reason the curve showed a sharp rise to 60 per cent for those students living in trailers.

It appears that the majority of the students may be more ready for tightening the limitations on smoking areas than the adult population in the campus community. There was statistical significance at the 0.001 level of probability in this study for the following variables: freshman approval of teenage smoking, academic achievement, organization membership and use of leisure time, belief that lung cancer is more likely to develop in smokers than in non-smokers, smoking habits of parents, place of residence when in high school, smoking habits of roommates and belief that teenage smoking is a public health problem.

In general the study revealed the following opinions held by student smokers: smoking is very bad for a person, but enjoyable; quitting is no trouble, can quit "when going home"; smoking is not the best thing for anyone to do, but it is better than munching and nibbling on food; smoking makes one nervous instead of calm; would probably stop smoking if left college; death of father from lung cancer direct cause of strong recent dislike for smoking; smoke only on week-ends because smoking impairs studying. Non-smokers in general voiced the following: smoking is a great waste of money and a social problem; to smoke or not is a question to be resolved by the individual; smokers are resented for infringing on right of non-smokers who find it difficult to breathe in smoke-filled rooms; smokers should be more considerate of non-smokers — they should not just light up whenever the urge hits them because others might be inconvenienced; most teenagers smoke mainly because they are pressured by their friends to start smoking; younger people smoke to go along with the crowd, to prove their maturity; at college smoking seems to be the thing to do; smoking is highly offensive, would rather roommate did not smoke.

In conclusion, a profile for an Illinois freshman who smoked one or more packs of cigarettes a day (27.7 per cent of those who smoked) would read as follows: Half of them had been smoking one or more packs a day 12 months previously; over 95 per cent of them inhaled smoke into the lungs; about 75 per cent smoked three-fourths (or less) of the tobacco portion; about 25 per cent smoked more than three-fourths of the tobacco portion; about 75 per cent smoked cigarettes with a filter; over 60 per cent who increased the number of cigarettes during the year had a roommate who approved of smoking; over 75 per cent had increased their smoking during the last 12 months, and half of that group had increased from one-half to one pack a day; most smoked anywhere unless smoking was prohibited; over 75 per cent dated persons who approved freshmen smoking; about half had a father and one third had a mother who also smoked one or more packs a day; and over one fourth had tried four or more times to stop smoking.

An Exploratory Survey and Smoking Control Program Conducted Among Parents of Philadelphia School Children[1]

WILLIAM A. ALLEN and
WILLIAM A. FACKLER
Philadelphia Smoking and
Health Research Project

The problem of smoking and health resolves itself, as do almost all health problems, into the two basic problems of cure and prevention. Obviously, illnesses and premature deaths resulting from cigarette smoking can be reduced or minimized by cessation or reduction in cigarette consumption among current smokers. They can also be eliminated altogether by preventive measures, which should be aimed principally at those who have not yet contracted the cigarette habit. The basic research of the Philadelphia Smoking Project may be characterized as a two-pronged study, involving both cure and prevention, inasmuch as it is directed at parents of elementary-school children. A successful program geared toward parents, pointing out the various hazards of cigarette smoking, could conceivably result in a modification of their own smoking behavior, with consequent benefits to their health. It could also arouse such concern for the future health of their children as potential cigarette smokers as to lead them to exert a stronger influence, either by admonition, or example, or both, on their future smoking behavior. The utilization of parents as subjects for study in the Philadelphia Project was considered promising from the point of view of this two-fold approach to the dual problems of cure and prevention. Studies have shown that only half as many children smoked cigarettes in families where parents were not smokers. Additionally, the motivation of setting a good example to offspring seemed to offer an added success factor for parents in their attempts to give up or cut down on their smoking. This led to the major goal of the research project, which was to determine how effective education and group discussion can be in changing the smoking behavior of young parents. It should also be noted here that the major goal led to the distribution of some 30,000 questionnaires, which afforded much base-line data for the project staff.

The procedure for the project was as follows. The city of Philadelphia has a population of about 2,000,000; it is divided into eight separate school districts, with clearly defined geographical boundaries. District No. 7, located in the lower northeast section of the city, represents a cross-section of the socio-economic range of the entire city, and for this reason it was chosen as a suitable testing ground for the research of the Philadelphia smoking-and-health project.

School District No. 7 houses a total of 27 public elementary schools and 23 parochial elementary schools, with a student enrollment of some 36,000 in grades one to six. Some 15,000 mothers and 15,000 fathers with youngsters attending grades one to six of the elementary schools received the four-page smoking-and-health questionnaires. Students in grades one to six attending the participating schools were asked to carry questionnaires home to their parents. (Arrangements for this had previously been made with the Health and Physical Education Department of the school district of Philadelphia and the Associate Superintendent of the Archdiocesan Schools of Philadelphia.) The questionnaire was designed to ascertain the habits and attitudes of parents towards smoking, the extent of their knowledge of smoking as a health problem, and the possible interest of the smoking parents in joining a Smokers' Withdrawal Clinic. Each youngster was given two questionnaires, one for each parent, with instructions to return the completed questionnaire to the school within one week. From the completed questionnaires the following response was obtained: 30,796 questionnaires were distributed; of this number, 21,553 (70 per cent) were returned. This broke down as follows: 6,596 had never smoked, 3,548 were former smokers, and 11,409 were current smokers.

The questionnaire included the item, "Would you be interested in quitting if a smokers' clinic were organized?" Responses were as follows: Yes, 4,775 (indicating that they were interested in attending a clinic); No, 6,045; Did not answer, 589. The parents who had indicated interest in quitting were then asked to attend a meeting which would discuss the relationship of smoking and health and the possibility of participating in a smokers' clinic. Of the 11,409 current smokers, 4,775 indicated an interest in attending a smoking clinic. A mass meeting was then scheduled, but only 257 persons attended. The number attending clinics that were then set up was 150.

[1] This research was supported by USPHS Project Grant No. 4017-B-65.

At the end of the ten-week discussion groups, which were made up in the clinics, 64 people had stopped smoking; at the end of six months 56 were still not smoking, and at the end of a year 35 were still off the habit. This result raised the question of the desirability of modifying the procedure for the next phase of the project.

In August of 1965 a meeting was arranged to explore possibilities of involving large numbers of Philadelphia parents in a research project. Held in Philadelphia, the meeting was attended by the Philadelphia Committee on Smoking and Health (which serves as an advisory committee to the project) and representatives of the United States Public Health Service. The meeting resulted in a recommendation that in the next phase of the Philadelphia Research Project the research team emphasize the involvement of parents in meetings, on the basis of their concern for the smoking problem among school children. It was also suggested that the lack of response in earlier parental meetings may have indicated some resistance to an obvious attempt at recruitment of clinic participants. The committee felt that more parents would participate in meetings if the smokers' clinics were not mentioned while the educational discussion sessions of smoking among school children were given emphasis. If at the meetings the parents themselves suggested or requested a smokers' clinic, the staff would then follow up by providing one. It is hoped that the meetings discussing the problems of smoking among school children will provide sufficient motivation for the parents to give up cigarettes, without the necessity of a smokers' clinic. It is further hoped that this new approach will have a greater impact on their future smoking behavior and on that of their youngsters. Time will tell whether this will prove to be the case.

SUMMARY

Some 30,000 parents having youngsters attending elementary school in School District No. 7 (Philadelphia) were contacted via a questionnaire in order to determine demographic data, present smoking habits, and attitudes toward smoking. Smokers' cessation clinics were then organized for the currently smoking parental respondents, using a combination of mass education and small-group discussions in the clinic format. Since the clinic participants were all mothers and fathers, emphasis was also placed on pointing out the role of parents as exemplars. As a result of the questionnaire survey and the subsequent smokers' clinics, the following findings and conclusions are reported:

Of the 21,000 parents responding, 30.6 per cent never smoked, 16.5 per cent formerly smoked cigarettes, and 52.9 per cent were currently smoking cigarettes.

Former smokers smoked less than their currently smoking counterparts and did not inhale as deeply. The largest group of current smokers (24.7 per cent) smoked a little over a pack a day with some 41 per cent of the currently smoking parents smoking over twelve years and 84.3 per cent smoking more than eight years. Some 55 per cent of the smokers began before age 18 with 38.7 per cent beginning specifically between 15-17. Over 60 per cent of the smokers draw the smoke into their lungs with only 3 per cent reporting that they just puff. No significant differences were found between parochial and public school parental smoking habits nor between the demographic variables for these groups.

Some 4800 currently smoking parents indicated that they wanted to quit at a clinic, but when contacted only 257 parents (5.4 per cent) attended meetings designed to give information and 150 (3.1 per cent) actually attended a clinic, with 56 participants successfully quitting for at least six months. Based on the data accumulated for School District No. 7 it would appear that other ways of approaching parents who smoke will have to be devised if significant inroads are to be made on their smoking habits.

DISCUSSION

Donn Mosser: In this process, had you done anything by way of educating the students, inviting them to carry home some of the information and needle their parents a little?

William Allen: I think the students did that to some extent. Although most of the questionnaires were filled out very completely, there was some indication that some had been filled out — perhaps just because of needling — rather hurriedly. In general, however, the questionnaires were well completed. We also invited the students to accompany their parents to one of the meetings, in the hope that they would do some further needling. In the revamping of the project we will probably try to do more of this and set aside at least part of the meeting for the students themselves.

Dorothy Nyswander: I just wonder how much parents like to be needled about a personal habit by their children.

Donn Mosser: High-school audiences have frequently asked me, "How do I get my father or my mother to stop smoking?"

William Allen: We have also been asked that question by school groups. Students have told us that they are very worried about their parents' smoking and asked what can they do. It seems to be a matter of serious concern to them. They want to know what they can do to help, because they are worried about their folks.

Dorothy Nyswander: Since you had a whole school

district — representing a cross section of the city — I was wondering about the people who did show up for the first meeting. What social class did they come from?

William Allen: I think they were mostly from the upper socio-economic end of the scale.

Dorothy Nyswander: In terms of what I call administrative studies or administrative process research, I am concerned about this gap between the number of people who said they were interested, and the number that finally showed up. Is it possible that there are a number of factors which intervened between the two steps that need examination? Something might have gone wrong there.

Selwyn Waingrow: Will there be any analysis of the "shows" and "don't shows"? Is that to be included in the project?

William Allen: As we go into the next phase we will try to work along those lines.

Selwyn Waingrow: What I meant was an analysis of differences between those who say, "Yes, I'd like to come," and then don't show up as against those who say, "Yes, I'd like to come," and *do* show up. For example, one might ask if there are attitudinal, belief, and demo-graphic differences between these two groups, as well as behavioral differences.

Dorothy Nyswander: Another problem is that people may not have wanted to go to the designated meeting place.

This certainly was an extensive project. When you think of the great numbers of people who were originally involved and the work that was required at each level, only to find in the last stage that a mere handful are refraining from smoking, it certainly gives reason to wonder about methods of intervention.

One of the problems, I think, that we often have in discussion groups is that of who is involved in the discussion. We speak about using "group process," or "group work," and we refer to "group decision"; sometimes we just call it a group meeting. For experimental purposes, however, "group methods" must be defined quite carefully, so that practitioners will know exactly what has taken place. I have heard "group process" methods very strongly criticized for the kinds of results that followed, but I have observed that what was called group process was *not* group process. It was just group instruction, and there's quite a difference.

Attitudes, Information and Behavior of College Students Related to Smoking and Smoking Cessation[1]

DANIEL ROSENBLATT,
BERNARD ROSEN
and HARVEY ALLEN
New York City Health Department

The data presented in this paper are from a broader study intended to demonstrate whether or not it is feasible to use group interaction techniques as a means of changing smoking habits, and to evaluate the different power of traditional techniques such as films, literature, and lectures as opposed to the technique of group interaction, among college students.

As a first step toward assembling experimental groups, college freshmen were administered a questionnaire which dealt with their smoking habits, those of their friends and families, their attitudes toward smoking, their knowledge of its effects, their motives for wishing to continue to smoke or desire to stop, etc.

For purposes of this paper, we have chosen to focus on the "dimensions of a model for smoking behavior change" as presented by Daniel Horn and Selwyn Waingrow (1965). These authors have proposed four dimensions which they consider essential to "the construction of any comprehensive model of smoking behavior change." They are:

1. The motivation for change

2. The perception of the threat

3. The development and use of alternative psychological mechanisms

4. Factors facilitating or inhibiting continuing reinforcement

The aim of this paper is to determine how fruitful this model can be in the analysis of data collected from a college population. A description of our results will proceed along the lines indicated by their model. It should be pointed out that the following data are not applicable to the section on alternative psychological mechanisms, although it is hoped that the work in the group sessions will provide fruitful material for a later discussion of this important area of working through the problem of becoming an ex-smoker.

PROCEDURE

A smoking behavior questionnaire administered to 1466 students at Queens College (New York) revealed the following about their smoking habits:

Smoking History	No.	Percentage of Respondents
Non-smokers	728	50
Regular cigarette smokers*	307	21
Occasional cigarette smokers**	261	18
Cigarette smokers who have stopped	139	9
Cigarette smokers who switched to pipe or cigar	11	1
Regular pipe or cigar smokers	21	1
Total	1466	100

*more than one pack per week
**less than one pack per week

Thus, of the total population, 59 per cent were non-smokers, while 41 per cent smoked cigars, cigarettes or pipes.

Twenty-seven students volunteered to participate in group discussion as a means of changing their smoking habits. In addition, a sample was selected for analysis which included 100 non-smokers, 100 ex-smokers, and 200 smokers. The 200 smokers included 66 "heavy" smokers (those who smoked over ten cigarettes per day) and 134 "light" smokers (those who smoked ten cigarettes or less per day).[2]

This sample was selected for homogeneity on the basis of age, sex, marital status, academic class, and social class.

---

[1] This investigation was supported by the Division of Chronic Diseases, Public Health Service, under contract CD 00104. The funds were administered by the Medical and Health Research Association of New York City, Inc.

[2] These definitions of "heavy" and "light" smokers are slightly different from those ordinarily used for an adult population because college students smoke less than the average population of the same age, and because at this age, smoking has not as yet become so deeply entrenched as a habit. The number of cigarettes smoked per day rises for the next two age decades.

FACTORS FACILITATING OR INHIBITING CONTINUING REINFORCEMENT

Horn and Waingrow suggest that the decision not to smoke or to give up smoking is part of a continuing process and not a single event. In order to tap various dimensions of the factors which facilitate or inhibit smoking, they suggest examining the role of primary groups, major institutional groups, and the mass media. The present study examines the role of the first two agents: primary groups and major institutions.

Influence of Primary Groups

The students were asked about the smoking habits of their parents, their older siblings, their friends, and their steady dates or spouses.

With regard to *parents,* the smoking habits of neither mother nor father currently appear influential in the behavior of their late adolescent offspring. Chi-square comparisons for each (mother 9.78, and father, 6.02) proved to be not significant. However, it should be noted that the highest percentages recorded for parents who do not smoke or who have stopped smoking are located among the student group who also do not smoke or who have stopped smoking. Thus, although the role of the parents as exemplars appears weaker than might have been anticipated, there is a trend in the expected direction. It is possible for this group of late adolescents that while the importance of parents as exemplars is diminished, that of the older sibling or the peer group is increased.

With regard to *older siblings,* the exemplar role appears more pertinent. Significantly more (p < .05) of the heavy smokers indicate that their older siblings also smoke (67 per cent) than is true of those who have never smoked (40 per cent) or those who have stopped smoking (51 per cent). This relationship becomes more evident with regard to *friends.* Among non-smokers, 53 per cent report that their friends do not smoke, while only 4 per cent of the heavy smokers indicate that most of their friends do not smoke. The light smokers and those students who have given up smoking represent an intermediate group with 15 per cent and 27 per cent respectively, indicating that most of their friends smoke. (These relationships are significant at p < .001.)

It would therefore appear that for a group of college students, the influence of the smoking behavior of the parents assumes less importance than that of the older sibling and, more importantly, that of the peer group. It is possible, however, that the relative importance of parents and peers is related to a developmental sequence. In the upper levels of grade school and among secondary school students, the exemplar role of parents is possibly of great importance. With the shift toward greater inde-

pendence and maturity that ordinarily accompanies college attendance, the peer group assumes primacy as the group to emulate (Salber, MacMahon, Harrison 1963).

We were also interested in learning about the relationship of the smoking habits of the *steady date or spouse* and the various student groups. Within the freshman class, the smoking habits of steady dates and spouses appear to have little influence on their partners ($\chi^2 = 8.83$, p = not significant). Nevertheless, as with the parents, the highest percentage was recorded among those steady dates and spouses who do not smoke and those students who do not smoke (59 per cent). Once again, on a developmental level, the smoking habits of the steady date and the spouse may assume greater importance at a later stage, perhaps during the senior year or the early post-graduate years.

It is also worth pointing out the special nature of the Volunteer Group with regard to the role of interpersonal forces on the continuation of smoking. The Volunteer group reports minimal congruence between their decision to attempt to stop smoking and the behavior of their family or peers. Among the Volunteer Group, 73 per cent of the fathers smoke, 70 per cent of the mothers smoke, and 72 per cent of the siblings smoke. At the same time, they report that 96 per cent of their friends also smoke. This group is, therefore, under the greatest social pressure from their immediate environment to continue smoking. It may be that one of the reasons for volunteers to join groups is that they received so little additional support from their friends and families that they feel the need to seek outside affiliation and reinforcement. It should also be noted that the smoking habits of steady dates and spouses of the Volunteer group resemble most the pattern of the non-smokers and ex-smokers. Additional research is needed to determine the significance of this sex group as an important source of strength in stopping smoking.

Smoking and Sex Roles

To determine the relationship between smoking and attitudes toward masculinity and femininity, we asked students to agree or disagree with these two items: "Smoking makes a man appear *more* masculine," and "Smoking makes a woman appear *less* feminine."[3]

There was significantly more (p < .01) agreement among non-smokers and ex-smokers than for any of the other groups that smoking makes a woman appear less feminine. Non-smokers and ex-smokers also disagreed

---

[3] On all of the attitude items, students were asked to respond in terms of the extent to which they either agreed or disagreed with its content. Responses ranged from strongly agree to strongly disagree on a five-point scale. In all cases, a high score represents a negative attitude toward smoking and a low score represents a positive attitude.

most (p < .05) that smoking makes a man appear more masculine. Thus it appears that both non-smokers and quitters perceive "non-smoking" to be related to sexual attractiveness. The question as to whether this attitude motivated their decision either not to smoke or to stop smoking remains to be answered. It is possible that if smokers perceive smoking as offering reinforcement for sex roles, this may be one of the means by which they also experience tension release (see section on Motivation for Change).

Governmental and Legal Supports

We also checked students' attitudes toward legal restrictions against smoking. We asked them to indicate the extent of their agreement or disagreement with the statements, "The Government should be doing more to discourage cigarette smoking," and "Strong legal action should be taken against vendors who sell cigarettes to minors." For the statement about the Government's discouraging of cigarette smoking, the rank order of the means indicates that subjects most in agreement were those who had never smoked, followed by those who had stopped smoking, and then those who volunteered to join a group. Those least in agreement were the heavy and light smokers (p < .05). Almost identical results were obtained with the statement about taking action against vendors who sell cigarettes to minors. The rank order of the means indicates that the students in strongest agreement were those who had never smoked, followed by the volunteers and those who had stopped smoking. Those in least agreement were the light and heavy smokers. However, in this instance, the differences between the groups were demonstrated by trend only; statistical significance was not reached.

It would appear, then, that in terms of official governmental and legal agencies, there is a consistency between the attitude expressed and the smoking behavior of the student group. Should the Government take a more active role in discouraging smoking, it might be influential in helping change the attitude of smokers, although our data suggest such official actions would be most effective where least necessary: among non-smokers, ex-smokers and volunteers.

It thus appears that the non-smokers and ex-smokers inhabit a different world from the light and heavy smokers in terms of relevant social factors. The non-smoker and ex-smoker tend to come from families where parents and older siblings do not smoke; they have fewer friends and steady dates who smoke, and they believe more in governmental and legal action aimed to discourage smoking. They also tend to disagree with smoking as a means of reinforcing sex roles. The opposite findings tend to be true for the light and heavy smoker, with the volunteer group falling between the smokers and the ex-smokers.

In terms of future action programs, it is important to think of means by which the resolve of volunteers to give up smoking can be strengthened. Our own project of using groups as one such technique appears to have the difficulty of not enlisting enough volunteers on a college campus to make this technique workable enough.

THE MOTIVATION FOR CHANGE

We attempted to learn about the motivation for change in two different ways. First, we asked smokers why they started to smoke and, second, why they continue to smoke. We also asked ex-smokers why they started to smoke and why they stopped smoking. Finally, we asked non-smokers why they never began to smoke. Since we assume that many motives are present in deciding to smoke, to continue smoking, to stop smoking, or not to begin to smoke, students were permitted to indicate more than one choice. For this reason, the percentages add up to more than 100 per cent, and we cannot determine the single most important motive for a specific individual. However, we can infer hierarchies of importance of motives as a result of the frequency with which a motive is selected.

In addition, we attempted to determine the exemplar role as well as the importance of economics, esthetics and mastery by including one question from each of these areas.

The Process of Deciding to Smoke

Among smokers, 60 per cent indicated that they started because of "novelty or curiosity." Forty per cent stated that smoking "helped me to relax and release tension." Almost as many indicated "most of my friends smoke" (39 per cent), and a fourth category was composed of individuals concerned with their status ("to feel grown-up and independent," 31 per cent; "to impress others," 22 per cent; "to feel more self-confident," 21 per cent). Only 20 per cent indicated that they "enjoyed the taste and/or smell of cigarettes." Only 11 per cent stated as a motive for beginning to smoke that "most members of my family smoke." The five most chosen motives are, therefore: novelty, relaxation, enjoyment of taste-smell of cigarettes, and that friends smoke or else it makes one feel self-confident, grown-up, or impresses others.

The same frequencies are noted among the different groups who started smoking, with the following exceptions: 30 per cent of the *heavy smokers* mention the taste and/or smell of cigarettes in contrast with 21 per cent, 22 per cent and 13 per cent of the other groups; ex-smokers, only 22 per cent started in order to relax in contrast with 56 per cent, 45 per cent and 44 per cent of the other groups, and 28 per cent of the ex-smokers started in order to impress others — a motive which should lose its strength with time.

The Process of Continuing to Smoke

Among the smokers, novelty and curiosity obviously lose their effect as a motive for continuing to smoke. Instead, 72 per cent of the smokers indicate that relaxation and tension-release are reasons they now smoke; only 40 per cent gave this as a motive for beginning to smoke. Originally, 20 per cent claimed that the taste and smell of cigarettes was a factor in smoking; 32 per cent indicated that it is a reason for continuing to smoke. Nearly 40 per cent stated that they began to smoke because most of their friends smoked, but only 9 per cent mention their friends as a factor in their current behavior. "To feel grown up" and "to impress others" were chosen by 31 per cent and 22 per cent of those who began to smoke, but only 9 per cent and 3 per cent continue to list these as reasons.

Thus, it is clear that whatever the original motive to begin smoking may have been, other factors begin to exert an important influence. Most significantly, continuing smokers note that they feel more relaxed and that they enjoy the taste and smell of cigarettes. This would suggest that smoking has positive values for those who remain smokers — that they receive two major sources of pleasure from it: relaxation and sensual gratification. If smokers are to be led toward non-smoking, then it is likely that some alternative means of gratification must be substituted or else the psychological mechanisms by which non-smoking can be promoted must be perfected beyond our current knowledge. Initial work by Tomkins (1965) in this direction is promising.

The Process of Deciding to Stop Smoking

Among those who decided to stop smoking, 54 per cent indicate that they "no longer enjoy it"; 37 per cent that they have stopped smoking because of "fear of bad effects on my health," and nearly as many, 34 per cent, state that it is "too expensive." Only 7 per cent indicate "messiness or dirtiness" as a motive for stopping, just as among this young population, only 5 per cent indicate "doctor's advice" or the presence of "symptoms such as coughing, wheezing, etc." (15 per cent).

Just as the decision to continue to smoke appeared to be related to the positive benefits of smoking, such as enjoyment or relaxation, so the most frequently selected reason for quitting smoking is that it is no longer a pleasurable activity. It would be important to know more about how this re-definition of the activity is accomplished. The fact that it is now perceived as too expensive or too messy reflects the part of the Horn-Waingrow model dealing with economics and esthetics, but neither

of these motives appears particularly impressive in terms of frequency chosen, although additional data presented below may suggest otherwise. Unfortunately, the "fear of bad effects on my health" is something that is so far in the future for most college freshmen that it is unlikely that this motive can be strengthened significantly.

The Decision Not to Smoke

The non-smokers were asked to indicate the major reasons for their abstinence. Almost the entire group (94 per cent) selected the statement, "I don't see any point in it." This is not particularly revealing, but it does suggest a generalized immunization process which needs closer investigation. The other reasons provide a little additional enlightenment. Slightly more than half (51 per cent) gave health reasons; another 21 per cent indicated cigarettes were "too expensive" and 19 per cent stated that "My parents asked me not to." Thus, the exemplar role of the parents and the cost of cigarettes appear to have some weight as motives for those who do not begin to smoke.

Exemplars, Esthetics and Mastery

We have already indicated the actual behavior of parents and older siblings of the students with regard to smoking. We also asked the students to indicate what their wishes were for the future regarding children they may have later. They were asked to agree or disagree with the statement, "If I have children, I hope they will not smoke cigarettes." Non-smokers, ex-smokers and volunteers agree most with the statement in that order, and light and heavy smokers are in least agreement. (This difference is significant at p < .001.) Just as non-smokers and ex-smokers tend to come from families with a pattern of non-smoking, or little smoking, so they also hope to continue such a tradition in their future families to a greater degree than smokers.

Students were also given an opportunity to agree or disagree with the statement, "Cigarette smoking is a dirty habit." The non-smokers agree most strongly with the statement, followed in rank order by the ex-smokers, the volunteers, the heavy and light smokers (p < .01). With the exception of the non-smokers, there is a fairly low range of agreement that smoking is a dirty habit, with small differences between the remaining groups. Just as the previous data indicated this was not a major motive for stopping smoking, so this attitude question also supports the point of view that the esthetic approach is limited in its appeal as a motivation for change.

As a means of learning more about the mastery dimension, we asked students to agree or disagree with the statement, "Anyone who wants to quit smoking can do so without outside help." Ex-smokers disagree with the statement more than any of the other groups (p < .05), probably because they have the most experience and know how much additional outside help is necessary. They are followed by the volunteer group who also have some inkling of the difficulties involved in stopping smoking. It should also be noted that both classes of present smokers were found to be in most agreement.

Unfortunately, in terms of motivation for change, these three attitude questions indicate that the heavy smokers (those whom one would be most interested in reaching) seem least susceptible, in terms of an appeal to act as a future exemplar, to be concerned over the esthetics of cigarette smoking, and to be involved in a realistic fashion with the problem of mastery. Of course, these data present only one item for each aspect of the motivation for change, and additional research is necessary. Nevertheless, the heavy smoker appears as a hard-core individual whom it will be difficult to reach on an attitude level quite apart from the health message.

THE PERCEPTION OF THREAT

Under their discussion of The Perception of Threat, Horn and Waingrow (1965) indicate "four necessary conditions for engaging in self-protective health behavior." These are (1) an awareness of the threat, (2) the acceptance of the importance of the threat, (3) the relevance of the threat, and (4) the susceptibility of the threat to intervention. To learn more about the perception of threat along these various dimensions among our student groups, we asked our subjects to agree or disagree with the following statements:

a. Cigarette smoking is harmful to health.
b. A person has to die from something so it might as well be from smoking.
c. A cigarette smoker can always quit later in life in plenty of time to avoid any bad effects.

In addition, we asked the subjects to indicate from among 10 different diseases those to which heavy smoking was related.

a. "Cigarette smoking is harmful to health." Non-smokers and ex-smokers have greater awareness of the threat as measured by this question (p < .001). Heavy smokers are least aware.

b. "A person has to die from something so it might as well be from smoking." According to Horn and Waingrow (1965), the acceptance of the importance of the threat can be rephrased by the question, "Is it important enough for me to do anything about it?" Non-smokers and ex-smokers disagree most with the statement as we phrased it, and heavy smokers are in greatest agreement. Thus, heavy smokers are least accepting of the importance of the threat.

c. "A cigarette smoker can always quit later in life in plenty of time to avoid any bad effects." In this question, we are dealing with the relevance of the threat, or, rephrased, as the question, "Is this threatening to me?" Once more, it is clear that the non-smokers and ex-smokers agree with the statement, and the heavy and light smokers tend to disagree. The threat does not appear to be as relevant to the smoking groups, just as they were less aware of the threat and less accepting of the importance of the threat.

Students were asked to indicate which diseases were statistically related to heavy cigarette smoking. The three correct answers were cancer, heart disease and emphysema. None of the heavy smokers checked all three, in contrast with 20 per cent of the non-smokers. It is also worth pointing out that it is the non-smokers and the ex-smokers who are most aware of the threat of cancer only (38 per cent and 42 per cent), in contrast with the light and heavy smokers (33 per cent and 32 per cent). Thus, in terms of knowledge about the dangers of heavy smoking, the heavy smokers seem to be the most insulated group, and the non-smokers and ex-smokers the most aware group, although these differences are not statistically significant.

SUMMARY

On every level, then, whether it be information concerning, awareness of, relevance, or acceptance, the heavy smokers are least responsive to the perception of threat and the non-smokers and ex-smokers are most responsive.

In an analysis of the combined mean of all the attitude items, the same rank order is preserved. Those most opposed to smoking in terms of expressed attitude are the non-smokers, followed by the ex-smokers and then the volunteers. Those most in agreement with attitude toward smoking are heavy smokers, followed by light smokers.

A considerable advantage of the Horn-Waingrow model for dealing with smoking behavior change is that it can be utilized in a practical attempt to describe a general college population. By isolating the conditions for smoking behavior change as clearly as they have, future researchers may experiment with individual factors or combinations of factors, and note their effects. It is also clear from a utilization of their model that heavy smokers have the lowest motivation for change, are least able to perceive the threat and are least accessible to factors facilitating reinforcement. At the same time, the Volunteer Group appears to be attempting to shift toward the non-smoking and ex-smoking groups. Perhaps the best hope for future success lies in experiments focusing upon this group in order to develop means by which such attempts might be furthered.

REFERENCES

Horn, D., and Waingrow, S. "Some Dimensions of a Model for Smoking Behavior Change," paper presented at the 93rd Annual Meeting of the American Public Health Association in Chicago, Illinois, October 20, 1965.

Salber, Eva, MacMahon, B., and Harrison, S., "Influence of Siblings on Student Smoking Patterns," *Pediatrics*, Vol. 31, No. 4, 1963, pp. 570–71.

Tomkins, Silvan. "A Psychological Model of Smoking Behavior," paper presented at the 93rd Annual Meeting of the American Public Health Association, Chicago, Illinois, October, 1965.

DISCUSSION

Dorothy Nyswander: One wonders how early these educational programs should begin, whether college isn't too late — or even high school. One study reports children younger than nine years of age starting to smoke. I am thinking about the entire problem, too, of group support. You're finding that the family is not too much of a support. One of the studies included older brothers. Were they a support?

Daniel Rosenblatt: It isn't that the family wasn't a support; it's just that these are college freshmen, and at their age the peer group is perhaps more important than it ever will be again; so the influence of the parents would certainly be more important at an earlier developmental level.

Dorothy Nyswander: This matter of finding peer groups seems to me a problem.

Selwyn Waingrow: I wonder what this yes-and-no pattern means in terms of the function of saying "yes" and not showing up, as against those who say "no" and don't show up? What is the difference between these two groups? There has been some theoretical discussion about the significance of this. The question to be raised is, "If they're not going to come to some place when they say 'yes,' what does this 'yes' mean?" What function does saying "yes" serve in relation to the number and type of anxieties they have about the problem; are they "buying" something by saying "yes"?

Daniel Rosenblatt: In our study, it was interesting to observe that the volunteer group was in the middle between the light and heavy smokers, and the ex-smokers and the non-smokers. On different items they tended to be closer to one or the other. They seem to be precariously poised in this way. They are really not sure yet. One of the ways they indicate this uncertainty is when they say, "I want to give it up"; then when it comes right down to it, they don't. We also know from bitter experience that those who *do* come don't give it up either. During the 1965 Conference the question was raised as to what constitutes a good predictor (of success). How can you tell who is serious about quitting? And we concluded that it was the person himself, who states, "I think I will be able to give up smoking." The conscious, rational prediction was the best one. What we do is ask people to throw away their cigarettes. It is quite clear that the ones who do not will not give up smoking. They have come to the clinic because they feel they ought to. Some people feel guilty about smoking, and make "attempts" to quit merely for the social reinforcement associated with making the gesture. But if you ask them to give you their package of cigarettes right at that point, they will not. They're saying quite clearly, at that moment, "I'm here, but I'll be damned if you're going to get me." And my answer is, "I'm not." On the other hand there are the people who say, on the first day, "I'm going to give up smoking." These are your best prospects. The others are there for different motives.

Bernard Mausner: One problem with all the studies of this kind — and this one is, I think, certainly one of the most sophisticated ones — is that there are various *kinds* of college students or even high-school students. In fact we're not dealing with people who come to the problem fresh. Like most other schools, we at Beaver College run anti-smoking programs. We assemble our students in the gymnasium, we show them those Mickey-Mouse slides, and we tell them all about emphysema. The last time I did it I asked if many of them had been through this before. They all shouted "Yes." I asked them if many are tuning out. And they all shouted "Yes!" From conversation afterwards, it was pretty clear that there wasn't a soul there who hadn't been through a ritual like this at least five times, starting with the seventh grade; so that by this time I don't think we were going to be able to do an experiment, contrasting various ways of imparting the same kind of information, with populations that are already quite ready to "tune out" what is being offered.

Daniel Rosenblatt: The New York City Public School system insists that at least two class periods per year be devoted to the smoking question. So if as you say, students are long exposed to this kind of message, maybe one of the reasons I got such good results was that attitudes had had a chance to come alive.

Dorothy Nyswander: A great many children are being saturated with information, and this includes some of the lower-economic groups, which I think have not received enough attention in smoking research. Our problem becomes one of methodology — of channels — of getting *closer* to the problem than we are at the present time. In a great many of our health services and university studies we are a long way from the value systems of the people we are trying to cure — a long, long way. We're giving the same lecture over and over. They know that just as well as we do, and they're always so polite, they listen, and one doesn't know how ineffective his health program is.

Resume of the Chicago Study of Smoking Behavior[1]

BRUCE C. STRAITS
University of California, Santa Barbara

Despite a series of announcements referring to a possible link between smoking and lung cancer in recent years, the apparent effect on smokers has been slight as reflected by average cigarette consumption per capita in the United States. The negligible impact of this anxiety-arousing information could be because current smokers are unaware of the reports, disbelieve them, are not motivated to give up smoking, or are unable to translate their motivation into action. Thus for conceptual purposes, the discontinuation process may be broken down into several stages.[2]

	Heard?	Believe?	Should Quit?	Quit?
Uninformed	no	no	no	no
Unbelieving	yes	no	no	no
Unmotivated	yes	yes	no	no
Unable	yes	yes	yes	no
Quitter	yes	yes	yes	yes

This study was initiated to study the latter two categories in the above typology: smokers who have tried to quit but were unsuccessful (unables), and ex-smokers who were able to quit (quitters). Later, the study was expanded to include two additional groups — smokers who have never attempted to quit smoking and non-smokers. These additional groups enabled us to take a cursory although incomplete look at the other categories in the discontinuation typology (uninformed, unbelieving, and unmotivated), and to explore some of the factors which may be related to the adoption of smoking.

THEORETICAL BACKGROUND

Explicit in Festinger's theory of cognitive dissonance is the belief that "the human organism tries to establish internal harmony, consistency, or congruity among his opinions, attitudes, and values."[3] For cigarette smokers, there are two common ways that inconsistency may arise. First, they may acquire information which is dissonant with their present behavior, namely, the reports linking smoking with lung cancer. Secondly, their opinions, attitudes, and values relating to smoking may not correspond with those of their friends and intimates. In the first instance, studies of personal influence have shown that a person faced with conflicting messages from the mass media (such as smoking-health questions) is likely to turn to his cohorts for their perception of the situation.[4] When a person's opinions, attitudes, and values conflict with those of his friends, tension is usually produced which induces restoration of cognitive balance (consistency).[5] Because of the strains (imbalance) produced when only one member of a social group of current smokers quits (e.g., husband-wife) and the tendency of individuals to turn to others for their perception of an ambiguous situation such as smoking-health questions, we expected to find those who are able to give up smoking in interpersonal environments characterized by a larger proportion of non-smokers and/or quitters than those unable to quit.

A formal decision model was developed which conceptualizes the basic elements of the "quit-smoking" decision process (perceived harm, perceived probability of the harm occurring, and subjective utility attached to each possible outcome). The solution to the model assumed that individuals will act to maximize expected

---

[1] This is a summary of the author's report, "Sociological and Psychological Correlates of Adoption and Discontinuation of Cigarette Smoking," Chicago: Department of Sociology, University of Chicago, 1965 (Mimeographed). The research design evolved from ideas outlined in a research proposal by Elihu Katz and Jacob Feldman. Financial support was provided by the Council for Tobacco Research U.S.A.

[2] These categories are very similar to the stages of adoption of new farm practices as formulated by rural sociologists. See Herbert F. Lionberger, *Adoption of New Ideas and Practices* (Ames, Iowa: The Iowa State University Press, 1960).

[3] Leon Festinger, *A Theory of Cognitive Dissonance* (Stanford, California: Stanford University Press, 1958).

[4] For example, Elihu Katz and Paul F. Lazarsfeld, *Personal Influence* (Glencoe, Illinois: The Free Press, 1955); Lionberger, *loc. cit.*; and Paul F. Lazarsfeld, Bernard Berelson, and Hazel Gaudet, *The People's Choice* (New York: Columbia University Press, 1948).

[5] See especially F. Heider, *The Psychology of Interpersonal Relations* (New York: John Wiley, 1958); Dorwin Cartwright and Frank Harary, "Structural Balance: A Generalization of Heider's Theory," *Group Dynamics*, ed. Dorwin Cartwright and Alvin Zander (Evanston, Ill.: Row, Peterson, and Co., 1960), pp. 705–726; Robert P. Abelson and Milton J. Rosenberg, "Symbolic Psychologic: A Model of Attitudinal Cognition," *Behavioral Science*, III (January, 1958), pp. 1–13; and Charles E. Osgood, "Cognitive Dynamics in the Conduct of Human Affairs," *Public Opinion Quarterly*, XXIV (Summer, 1960), pp. 341–365.

utility. It was hoped that smoking patterns (rate of smoking, number of years smoked, perception of the health controversy, etc.) and elements relating to the decision to discontinue smoking would help explain why some people succeed in stopping and others do not. For instance, we hypothesized that the greater the immediate presence of the perceived harm (e.g., having "smoker's cough" is more immediate than fear of incurring lung cancer), the less difficulty will a smoker have in quitting. Other factors which may relate to discontinuation of smoking were selected after reviewing findings from previous studies of smoking behavior. We hypothesized that quitters will have social-psychological characteristics more similar to non-smokers than to smokers.

HOW THE DATA WERE COLLECTED

The study is based on personal interviews with four groups of males: 100 smokers who have never made a serious attempt to give up smoking, 50 smokers who have made such an attempt but were unsuccessful, 50 ex-smokers who were able to quit, and 100 non-smokers. These four groups will be referred to as "smokers," "unables," "quitters," and "non-smokers," respectively.[6]

Interpersonal environments were examined by asking the respondents to describe the smoking habits of

---

[6] Because of the relatively small proportion of quitters in the general population in 1962, telephone screening (with numbers picked at random from the Chicago City Telephone Directory) was selected as a practical method of locating respondents, although this biased the sample since those with unlisted numbers, those without phones, and those not usually at home were excluded from the sample. In all, slightly over two thousand completed telephone calls were required to secure an adequate number of quitters and unables. This screening was conducted during the day by female interviewers with any adult member of the household, most often the housewife. This technique of asking a member of the household about the smoking behavior of the males in the family and eventually confirming this report with the respondent gave us a double check on the honesty of the reported data. Despite numerous sources of bias inherent in this procedure, the proportion of smokers in the screening (49.0 percent) closely corresponds to the proportion of regular cigarette smokers (50.2 percent) among men in urbanized areas of a million or more found in a national sample in 1955. Source: William Haenszel, Michael B. Shimkin, and Herman P. Miller, "Tobacco Smoking Patterns in the United States," Public Health Monograph No. 45 (Washington, D.C.: U.S. Public Health Service, 1956).

Since there was so much variability in individual smoking behavior, it was necessary to establish arbitrary benchmarks to define smokers, unables, quitters and non-smokers. Unables were defined as current smokers who had made an attempt to quit smoking *for as long as two weeks* within the last 8½ years (since the first major announcement of the possible link between smoking and lung cancer in December, 1953) *and* were trying to give up smoking completely when they tried to quit. This last restriction excludes those who intended only to give up smoking temporarily (such as for Lent). Anyone who had not smoked for the last six months but had been an active smoker within the last 8½ years was classified as a quitter. Smokers qualified if they smoked more than 10 cigarettes daily, had done so for as long as three months, and had *never* tried to stop smoking. Non-smokers are those who have never smoked cigarettes at all on a regular basis. Although these definitions are mutually exclusive, they are not collectively exhaustive. Since these definitions are arbitrary, they were set on the conservative side (for example, attempting to quit for as long as two weeks).

their parents and current associates: (1) their closest relative (usually the wife), (2) their closest friend at work, (3) their closest friend away from work, and (4) their family doctor. Also, the respondents were asked if they had ever discussed the smoking-lung cancer controversy with these associates.

To the associates named by the respondents were administered short "snowball" interviews over the telephone or in person.[7] The snowball interview involved questions concerned with the associates' smoking behavior and health fears. Many of these were the same questions asked of the respondents in order to compare responses.

A Word of Caution

Before we review the main findings, it is pertinent to warn that this study is only exploratory; the sample sizes are too small to make generalizations about the area sampled (male adults in Chicago), let alone to the larger proportion of smokers in the United States. Even if the sampling plan had been more representative, it is difficult to trace the direction of causal relationships in surveys of this type.

This, of course, is not sufficient reason to reject the survey approach in favor of the artificial (but more controllable) atmosphere of the laboratory. However, findings from surveys should be treated with caution, and, when possible, validated by other research approaches. For instance, we observed a statistical relationship between the smoking habits of the respondents and their closest relatives. A different research design is necessary to test whether these differences are attributed to interpersonal influence or to a selective process of mate selection or to both.

Since this study is exploratory, the findings are treated in a speculative manner rather than rigidly rejecting trends which are not statistically significant in the small sample.[8] The best confirmation of these hypotheses is not an expansion of the same methodological procedure and operational definitions to a larger sample, but rather replication in a slightly different context using different methodological procedures and operational definitions of the variables.

PROFILE OF A QUITTER

The man who had successfully given up smoking was a very rare occurrence in Chicago of 1962. A preliminary screening survey (of over 2000 households) disclosed

---

[7] This name is commonly applied to interviews conducted with people whose names were given by other respondents.

[8] In exploratory research, much more concern should be placed on avoiding a Type II error (accepting the null hypothesis when in fact it is false) than a Type I error (rejection of the null hypothesis when in fact it is true), since rejected hypotheses are not likely to be investigated in subsequent research.

that less than 13 per cent of the males surveyed had made a serious attempt to give up smoking since the first major announcement (1953) of a possible link between smoking and lung cancer. Moreover, only one out of *every three* respondents who attempted to quit was successful.[9]

Since quitters are such an exclusive club of individuals, one might expect these individuals to be exceptionally different from other people, especially unables and current smokers. This is not the case. Factors such as education, military experience, smoking behavior of parents, income, coffee consumption, brand usage, religion, etc., are not significantly different among quitters, unables, or smokers.

What do set quitters apart from current smokers, and to a lesser extent unables, are their reasons for attempting to give up smoking. A higher proportion (82 per cent) of quitters mentioned specific health ailments (for example, a chronic cough, heart trouble, shortness of breath) and/or advice from a doctor than did the unables (60 per cent) or smokers (37 per cent), who mentioned less immediate threats or weaker reasons such as "waste of money" or "test of will power" more frequently.

Health fears relating to the future (like lung cancer) were mentioned by only 11 per cent of the quitters and unables. Although individuals do not always give the real reasons for their actions, we have other bits of evidence which indicate that present physical ailments played a more important role in the discontinuation of smoking than health fears for the future. One might expect certain ailments like coughs and nasal conditions (including emphysema) to increase with age and also with heavier tobacco consumption. The quitters were found to be older and heavier consumers than the unables.[10]

Discontinuation of smoking was also related to inter-personal environments. Quitters were more likely to have wives who were non-smokers (43 per cent had never smoked) than were the unables (26 per cent). If the husband had made an attempt to give up smoking or was a non-smoker, the wife was more likely to have made a similar attempt to stop smoking.

In general, the findings portray the quitter as a man who is likely to be older, a heavier smoker, more likely to have present physical ailments, and in inter-personal environments less supportive to smoking than those unable to quit.

PROFILE OF AN UNABLE

We have reviewed the various characteristics which distinguish unables from quitters. Now how do unables differ from smokers who have never tried to quit smoking? One important factor has already been mentioned — the presence of physical ailments. There is some evidence that fear of lung cancer and other future health fears are important motivating factors in the decision to try giving up smoking, although not strongly related to the successful implementation of this decision. Unables and quitters were more likely than current smokers to believe in a relationship between smoking and lung cancer. That a higher proportion of quitters believe this relationship cannot be explained solely as dissonance reduction, since unables are also more likely to believe this relationship than regular smokers. Additional indirect evidence of the impact of health fears can be inferred from the lower chance orientation (less fatalistic outlook) scores of unables and quitters as compared to smokers.

Another scale, which measures attitudes toward smoking (Horn's attitude scale), sharply discriminated between unables and quitters on the one hand, and smokers on the other. If this scale is a fairly good measure of values existing at the time of the original decision to quit, which was indirectly inferred from analysis of data,[11] an unfavorable attitude toward smoking is likely to precipitate or support the decision to quit smoking.[12]

---

[9] Furthermore, since a very strict operational definition of an unsuccessful quitter (current smokers who had tried to quit for as long as two weeks) was employed, the ratio of ex-smokers to smokers who made any type of an attempt to stop smoking would be very much lower than one-third.

[10] Furthermore, the combination of having a present health ailment related to smoking and being in the late forties or older has a slightly greater effect on the discontinuation of smoking than one might expect on the basis of the combined additive effects of the two variables. An analysis of variance comparison between additive and interactive regression models revealed that joint functions of health (present ailment/other reasons given for quitting) and age, and consumption and age accounted for a higher proportion of the variance on a dichotomous dependent variable (unable/quitter) than did other single and joint independent variables.

[11] Cross-classification of parental smoking behavior by Horn's attitude scale revealed that for both smokers and non-smokers, an increasingly favorable attitude toward smoking accompanies a greater likelihood that the respondent's parents smoked. Consequently, attitudes toward smoking may be formed in early life in response to parental behavior and may persist relatively unchanged throughout life. Such persistence in attitudes results from the avoidance of information incompatible to them (selective exposure) or the denial of conflicting evidence to awareness.

[12] Although the relationship between discontinuation and attitude toward smoking sounds self-evident, its significance is more apparent when one realizes that attitudes toward smoking do not necessarily correlate strongly with benefits or pleasures of smoking. It is helpful to examine the items which comprise this scale:
  a) Smoking costs more than the pleasure is worth. Do you strongly agree, slightly agree, don't agree or disagree, slightly disagree, or strongly disagree with this staatement?
  b) When I have children, I hope that they never smoke. Do you strongly agree . . .?
  c) There is nothing wrong with smoking. Do you . . .?
  d) Smoking is a dirty habit. Do you . . .?
  e) There is nothing wrong with smoking as long as a person smokes moderately. Do you . . .?
As New Year's resolution makers know, one can receive much pleasure from behavior that one also believes is wrong from a moral or health standpoint. The things which please one's *id* are not always the same things which please the *superego*. Thus, a person with a heavy investment in smoking can still wish that his children will not take it up.

A factor that was not measured in this study, and indeed would be difficult to measure, is the question of addiction. If there is any truth in the addiction theory, the difficulty of quitting should increase with rate of smoking. The study data support this conclusion: among quitters, a higher proportion (71 per cent) of lighter smokers (under 30 cigarettes per day) were able to quit smoking the first time they tried, compared to a lower proportion (52 per cent) of heavier consumers (more than 30 cigarettes per day). In the same way among the unables, a lower proportion (53 per cent) of the lighter consumers reported more than one attempt to stop smoking than did the heavier consumers (75 per cent). Consequently, heavier smokers are *more likely to attempt* but *less likely to succeed* in quitting than are lighter consumers.

In summary, the unable (as opposed to the current smoker) appears to be a person suffering from physical ailments, especially those easily connected with smoking. He has a relatively unfavorable attitude toward smoking and a nonfatalistic outlook on life.

CURRENT SMOKERS

We have seen that very few individuals fall into the unable category, and still fewer in the quitter category. Consequently, the majority of current smokers must fall into the uninformed, unbelieving, or unmotivated categories of our discontinuation typology.

Although the present study was not specifically designed to study the uninformed, the unbelievers, and the unmotivated, we do have some evidence concerning the prevalence of these various stages. First, data from this and other studies indicate that very few persons are uninformed about the smoking and health questions.[13] Contrary to expectations from early dissonance theory, current smokers are very well informed, in fact, probably better informed about this topic than non-smokers.

Current smokers are less likely to believe in a relationship between smoking and lung cancer (52 per cent believed) than non-smokers (80 per cent), unables (68 per cent), or quitters (68 per cent). Yet, over half of the smokers professed to believe in a link between smoking and cancer. Thus, a large number of smokers — perhaps as many as three-fourths — are maintaining a high degree of dissonance between their actions and beliefs.

We posited one explanation as to why such a large number of smokers fall into the unmotivated category — many current smokers have a chance-oriented, fatalistic outlook on life, which renders them less vulnerable to anti-smoking propaganda based on health threats. Whether or not this is an important factor remains to be established by further research. Other means by which these people are tolerating a high degree of dissonance between their beliefs and actions, such as rationalization, should also be an important area for further research.

Adoption of Smoking

A proper study of factors related to the adoption of smoking would require a longitudinal approach: a set of measurements (psychological, sociological, and physiological) to be taken before and after a sample of individuals pass through the critical adoption years (for example, between ages 15 and 21). Otherwise, we are not certain whether or not observed differences between smokers and non-smokers actually existed at the time of adoption (or non-adpotion).

Nevertheless, we have drawn some speculative conclusions from the Chicago data concerning the adoption process. First, let us examine social influences, which have frequently been cited as important determinants of smoking behavior.[14] Contrary to the findings of some studies, adoption of smoking did not relate to parental smoking habits. This fact and secondary analysis of other data suggest that the importance of parental smoking may be limited mainly to determining *when* an individual adopts smoking and not *whether* he eventually smokes or not. Although parental smoking behavior has an initial effect on children's orientation toward smoking, influences outside the home gradually eradicate these original differences. Military service, for example, has a profound effect on the conversion of non-smokers to smokers. In this study, 67 per cent of the smokers and 41 per cent of the non-smokers served in the military.[15] Educational

---

[13] See N. T. Feather, "Cognitive Dissonance, Sensitivity, and Evaluation," *Journal of Abnormal and Social Psychology*, LXVI (1963), 157–163; and Lawrence A. Pervin and Raymond J. Yatko, "Cigarette Smoking and Alternative Methods of Reducing Dissonance," *Journal of Personality and Social Psychology*, II (1965), 30–36.

[14] For example, the report to the U.S. Surgeon General on smoking and health mentioned that "the overwhelming evidence points to the conclusion that smoking — its beginning, habituation and occasional discontinuation — is to a large extent psychologically and socially determined." (Source: "Excerpts from Report on Smoking, Health," *Wall Street Journal*, January 13, 1964, p. 6.)

[15] Because respondents are not a random sample of veterans, it could be misleading to run the percentages in the other direction — that is, the percentage of veterans, or veterans who served in combat, who are smokers. Some of this variance might be explained by a selective process: individuals who smoke may be more likely than non-smokers to volunteer and more likely to be drafted into the army. However, data on cigarette-smoking histories and previous military service of men surveyed in a national study conducted by the Bureau of the Census refute the selec-

institutions are another opportunity for influences outside of the family of orientation to affect smoking behavior. Although the impact of schooling on smoking may be limited to extra-curricular friendships and cliques, there may be some institutions whose norms with regard to smoking are more strongly followed than others. For example, a study of Portland, Oregon, public and Catholic high schools revealed marked differences by type of school: the percentage of smokers was highest in the parochial schools, intermediate in the city public schools, and lowest in the suburban public schools.[16] Whether or not these differences may be attributed to the normative milieu of these types of schools or to systematic differences in the composition of the student bodies (for example, social-economic differences) remains a question for further research.

We found stronger evidence of inter-personal influence when we examined the smoking behavior of the closest relatives (usually the wife) of our respondents. Nearly twice as many smokers as non-smokers had close relatives who smoked. However, approximately a third of the non-smokers and half of the smokers were not in balanced (i.e., both smokers or both non-smokers) husband-wife dyads. In addition, husband-wife attitudes toward smoking and lung cancer, their brand preferences, and consumption patterns exhibited a low level of balance.

Perceived smoking behavior exhibits a higher degree of balance than does actual behavior. Unables, and to a lesser extent smokers, were more likely to perceive non-smokers among their closest associates as smokers than were quitters and non-smokers. A hypothesis that closest associates are employed as vehicles to obtain social support for continuing to smoke was neither strongly supported nor disproved.

The similarity between the smoking habits of respondents and their associates may alternately be explained as a selective process — "birds of a feather flock together." Non-smokers differ in occupational preferences from smokers, which may partly explain why smokers have a higher proportion of smokers among on-job friends than do non-smokers.[17] In addition, non-smokers may have more in common with other non-smokers and may choose these people as friends and mates. If the moderate degree of uniformity of smoking behavior observed between husband and wife is due to social influence, and not to selective mate selection, one would expect to find an increase in the extent of balance in husband-wife dyads over time. An attempt was made to explore this hypothesis with data gathered by Ernest W. Burgess on the smoking patterns of engaged couples during the engagement period (around 1939) and the early years of marriage (about 1942).[18] The Burgess data suggest that a very large proportion of the observed similarity of smoking patterns within husband-wife dyads is due to mate selection as the degree of balance for engaged couples closely corresponds to the figures for married couples in the present study.[19] Furthermore, the degree of balance did not improve over time; the proportion of couples reporting similar smoking behavior (65 per cent of the couples were both smokers or both non-smokers) remained unchanged between the 1939 and 1942 interviews.[20]

---

tive hypothesis; cumulative percentage curves for veterans and non-veterans (in five age groups) according to age at which smoking was first started do not show a significantly higher rate of smoking among veterans *until after* the age of probable entrance into the military service. (Source: William Haenszel, Michael B. Shimkin, and Herman P. Miller, "Tobacco Smoking Patterns in the United States," Public Health Monograph No. 45, Washington: U.S. Public Health Service, 1956.)

Rather, it seems more plausible that in military life where individuals live under great stress, have less freedom of activity, and often a paucity of amusements, the pressures toward adoption of smoking will be greater. That conditions of stress would encourage the adoption of smoking is supported by the finding that 46 per cent of the smokers as against 24 per cent of the non-smokers in this study had served in combat duty. Clearly, the conditions of military life which foster adoption of smoking can not be separated from the prevailing social climate, especially group norms toward cigarette smoking.

[16] Daniel Horn, Frederick A. Courts, Robert Taylor, and Erwin S. Solomon, "Cigarette Smoking Among High School Students," *American Journal of Public Health*, XLIX (November, 1959), p. 1505.

[17] Charles McArthur, Ellen Waldron, and John Dickinson, "The Psychology of Smoking," *The Journal of Abnormal and Social Psychology*, LVI (March, 1958), pp. 267–275.

[18] I wish to thank Donald J. Bogue, Director of the Community and Family Study Center, for permission to use these data. For a more complete description of this study see Ernest W. Burgess and Paul Wallin, *Engagement and Marriage* (New York: Lippincott, 1953).

[19] Among the males interviewed during the engagement period, 55 per cent of the smokers and 20 per cent of the non-smokers had fiancèes who were smokers. In the Chicago study, 53 per cent of the smokers and 27 per cent of the non-smokers reported that their wives were smokers.

[20] Although the net balance remained unchanged during the first few years of marriage, slightly over one-fourth of the couples shifted smoking behavior; a substantial increase in the number of dyads where both parties smoked was offset by a decrease in the number of strictly non-smoking dyads.

We do not believe that these data strongly support or disprove a balance-theory model in respect to husband-wife smoking behavior. One reason is that the period between the two interviews was very short — three or four years. And the possibility still remains that some of this consensus in respect to smoking behavior may have been achieved earlier in the courtship before the engaged couples were interviewed. For instance, the husband may have introduced his wife to the smoking habit during their courtship. Since most (78 per cent) of the shifts were due to one or both partners adopting smoking, it is possible that forces acting toward restoration of balance may be more effective at a later date when a greater proportion of the shifts will involve quitting smoking, especially when the spouse is also confronted with the smoking-health controversy.

A theory implicit in many smoking studies is that there are underlying psycho-physiological and sociological factors which are similarly related to (1) the adoption of smoking, (2) rate of smoking, and (3) discontinuation of smoking. We could not adequately test this theory, which would have required a representative sample of psycho-physiological and sociological variables. We did compare 21 available measures[21] to see if they displayed a similar pattern (direction of correlation) to adoption and discontinuation of smoking, and rate of smoking. A similar, but weak, relation was observed between these measures and the adoption and discontinuation of smoking, but not to the rate (average daily consumption) of smoking.

---

[21] Number of years smoked; average daily consumption; mention of a specific ailment and/or doctor's advice as a reason for quitting smoking; smoking behavior of father, mother, closest relative, closest friend at work, closest friend away from work, and family doctor; belief in relationship between smoking and cancer; military record; age; education; income; age when started smoking regularly; chance orientation, extroversion, and neuroticism scores; regular coffee drinker; consumption of beer, wine or whiskey; and Horn's attitude-toward-smoking scale.

SUMMARY

In order to examine the process of forgoing cigarette smoking, personal interviews were conducted with four groups of males: non-smokers, ex-smokers, current smokers who tried but were unable to quit smoking, and current smokers who have never made a serious attempt to stop smoking. In addition, brief interviews were conducted with the current associates (closest relative [usually the wife], closest friend at work, closest friend away from work, and family doctor) of the respondents in order to examine interpersonal environments. An attempt to stop smoking was associated with the presence of physical ailments (especially those easily connected with smoking), heavier tobacco consumption, less supportive interpersonal environments (particularly if the wife was a non-smoker or an ex-smoker), a relatively unfavorable attitude toward smoking, and a non-fatalistic outlook on life. Successful quitters tended to be older and to have the above-mentioned characteristics (with the exception of fatalism) to a greater extent than those unable to stop.

The Discontinuation of Cigarette Smoking: A Multiple Discriminant Analysis[1]

BRUCE C. STRAITS

Until recent advances in computer technology, analyses of survey data typically have been confined to cross-tabulation tables and allied measures of association. While few would doubt the merits of the traditional method, which is best exemplified by Lazarsfeld's scheme of "elaboration," some have questioned its efficiency.[2] Even a mediocre elaboration is time-consuming and expensive; moreover, a very large sample is required to analyze three or more variables simultaneously.

One new approach to survey analysis has been the application of multivariate statistical techniques, such as multiple regression and sequential models based on analysis of variance. Although various procedures have been tried, with some success, to adapt ordinal and nominal independent variables for use in regression and sequential analyses, the dependent variable must be measured on an interval or ratio scale. This paper describes multiple discriminant analysis, a technique which permits analysis of categorical dependent variables. The technique is applied to analyze the relationship between a smoking discontinuation typology (smokers, smokers who have been unable to quit, and quitters) and eleven psychological and sociological factors theoretically related to smoking behavior.[3]

Implicit in many smoking studies is the theory that there are underlying psycho-physiological and sociological factors which are related to the adoption of smoking, the amount smoked, and cessation of the habit.[4] If it is assumed that the eleven variables listed in Table 1 approximately represent the psychological and sociolog-

ical factors related to discontinuance of smoking, the process of discontinuance may be conceived as an eleven-dimensional space in which each group (smokers, unables, and quitters) occupies a given position. Several hypotheses follow from this conceptualization: for example, two or more groups may occupy similar positions within this space; they may occupy different but collinear positions, and they may be equally spaced

TABLE 1

List of Independent Variables[a][b]

#2 Average daily cigarette consumption (current or when last smoked)

#3 Mention of specific present health ailment (e.g., emphysema) and/or doctor's advice as a reason for quitting smoking (Coded "1"; coded "0" if only other reasons for stopping were given)[c]

#4 Smoking behavior of wife (coded "1" if smoked, otherwise "2")

#5 Age (coded by five-year age groups)

#6 Education (Coded by last grade of school completed)

#7 Age when started smoking regularly (actual age coded)

#8 Chance orientation score (a higher numerical score indicates a more fatalistic outlook on life)[d]

#9 Extraversion score (a higher score indicates greater extraversion)[e]

#10 Neuroticism score (a higher score indicates greater neuroticism)[e]

#11 Consumption of beer, wine, or whiskey (coded as number of days per average week when the respondent has a drink)

#12 Horn's attitude-toward-smoking scale (a higher numerical score indicates a more favorable attitude toward smoking)[f]

[a] Missing data were replaced by group averages.

[b] This paper will be limited to the discussion of statistical relationships; no attempt will be made to defend the selection of variables or their causal sequence.

[c] Unables and quitters were asked the open-ended question, "Why did you want to stop smoking?" Smokers were asked "What reasons might you have for giving up smoking?"

[d] Source: W. H. James, "Internal Versus External Control of Reinforcement as a Basic Variable in Learning Theory," unpublished doctoral dissertation, The Ohio State University, 1957. See also Bruce C. Straits and Lee Sechrest, "Further Support of Some Findings About the Characteristics of Smokers and Non-smokers," *Journal of Consulting Psychology,* XXVII (June, 1963), 282.

[e] Source: H. J. Eysenck, *et al.* "Smoking and Personality," *British Medical Journal* (May 14, 1960), 1456–60. The neuroticism scale was shortened from Eysenck's 12 questions to 5 questions in this study.

[f] This scale, which was developed by Dr. Daniel Horn, and the item weights, were generously provided by Professor Bernard Mausner, Department of Psychology, Beaver College.

[1] Adapted from a paper presented at the 1966 annual meeting of the American Sociological Association. Computations were subsidized and performed at the Western Data Processing Center, University of California at Los Angeles.

[2] For example, see James N. Morgan and John A. Sonquist, "Problems in the Analysis of Survey Data, and a Proposal," *American Statistical Association Journal* (June, 1963), pp. 115–25.

[3] The data reported here are from a larger research project, "Sociological and Psychological Correlates of Adoption and Discontinuation of Cigarette Smoking," supported by the Council for Tobacco Research U.S.A.

[4] Obviously, we cannot test this theory adequately since we do not have a representative sample of psycho-physiological and sociological variables.

apart. In other words, are the given explanatory variables related in the same fashion (magnitude and direction) to the decision to give up smoking as to the successful implementation of this decision?

AN OVERVIEW OF TYPES OF DISCRIMINANT ANALYSES

Textbook discussions of multiple discriminant analysis usually focus on the fact that the discriminant function has the property of discriminating between two populations better than any other *linear function of the independent variables*. Of more importance to the behavioral scientist, however, is the fact that group membership may be employed as a dependent variable without arbitrarily scaling the groups in some manner along an ordered continuum.[5]

The two-group discriminant function proposed by R. A. Fisher in 1936 is obtained by maximizing the ratio of between-groups to within-groups sums of squares.[6] This has the "effect of spreading the means of the groups apart while simultaneously reducing the scatter of the individual points about their respective means."[7] In more than two groups, one may restrict the analysis to a single discriminant function (which results in some loss of discriminatory power if the group-means are not collinear), fit orthogonal functions to the residuals of the preceding functions (as will be done here), or achieve optimal discrimination by computing a maximum likelihood function for each group.[8] The second approach was selected for the present analysis in order to study group configurations in the predictor space. On the other hand, the likelihood ratio method is more appropriate if one is using discriminant analysis to predict the behavior of unclassified individuals rather than as a tool of data analysis.

Application of the regression model is valid in instances where the values of the independent variables are decided before the sample is drawn (as in categorical survey questions) and need not represent an underlying normal universe, provided that the dependent variable is normally distributed about the regression function. The converse applies in the discriminant model: the dependent variable may be predetermined (group membership), while the independent variables must be normally distributed with equal covariance matrices for each group. Although one rarely encounters normal multivariate distributions in the behavioral sciences, the practice has been to employ a discriminant function if prediction is satisfactory.

RESULTS

On the basis of multivariate tests of significance, four of the eleven independent variables (the age when smoking started, neuroticism, extraversion, and level of education) were eliminated from the analysis.[9] If the seven remaining variables bear the same relationship to the decision to try to quit smoking as to the successful implementation of this decision, a single discriminant function (linear combination of the variables) would be sufficient to account for the essential variation between groups (i.e., smokers, unables, and quitters) in the seven-dimensional space described by the independent variables. Conversely, if the three groups do not lie along a straight line within this space, a second discriminant function, orthogonal to the first, may be taken. Although a second function was extracted in the present analysis, the group configuration is nearly linear: slightly over 83 per cent of the total discriminable variance was contained in the first discriminant function, leaving only 17 per cent for the second function.[10]

Table 2 presents the coefficients (discriminant weights) of the seven variables for the two discriminant functions. In scaled form, these coefficients indicate the relative contribution of each variable to the corresponding discriminant function; in this sense they are analogous to Beta coefficients in regression analysis.

[5] If use had been made of multiple regression analysis, the more common method of analyzing multivariate populations, it would have been necessary to scale the three groups in some arbitrary fashion, perhaps by assigning a value of "1" to quitters, "2" to unables, and "3" to smokers. The multiple discriminant model thus retains information which could be lost in a regression analysis by the assumption that the three groups may be positioned on an unidimensional scale.

[6] R. A. Fisher, "The Use of Multiple Measurements in Taxonomic Problems," *Annals of Eugenics,* VII (1936), pp. 179–188.

[7] David V. Tiedeman, "The Utility of the Discriminant Function in Psychological and Guidance Investigations," *Harvard Educational Review,* XXI (1951), 75.

[8] The reader is referred for examples of these three approaches to William F. Massy, "On Methods: Discriminant Analysis of Audience Characteristics," *Journal of Advertising Research,* V (March, 1965); M. G. Kendall, *A Course in Multivariate Analysis* (London: Charles Griffin & Company, Limited, 1957); and Salomon Rettig, "Multiple Discriminant Analysis: An Illustration," *American Sociological Review,* XXIX (June, 1964), pp. 398–402.

[9] Since it is not very practical to compute discriminant functions for every possible combination of independent variables, an exploratory stepwise analysis was performed to determine which independent variables should be retained in the analysis. The procedure for testing the significance of adding a variable to a set of predictors (independent variables) after removing the effect of the previously entered variables by covariance analysis is described in *Biomedical Computer Programs,* ed. W. J. Dixon (Los Angeles: Health Sciences Computing Facility, Department of Preventive Medicine and Public Health, School of Medicine, University of California, Los Angeles, 1965), pp. 594–95. As in regression analysis, a stepwise procedure may not always yield the most efficient set of predictors. However, the results from the stepwise analysis agree essentially with previous exploratory analyses using the likelihood ratio approach to discriminant analysis.

[10] The proportion of variance absorbed by the first function (83.2%) was not significantly changed by including the 11 original variables in the discriminant model (81.9% was absorbed in the latter instance).

TABLE 2

Coefficients of the Discriminant Functions in Raw-Score and Scaled Form

	Coefficients in raw score form [a]		Scaled coefficients [b]	
	Function I	Function II	Function I	Function II
#2 Consumption	0.14	−0.48	0.27	−0.55
#3 Health	0.95	−0.15	0.66	−0.06
#4 Wife Smokes	0.24	−0.83	0.18	−0.38
#5 Age	0.00	−0.04	0.08	−0.48
#8 Chance orientation	−0.14	−0.15	−0.33	−0.23
#11 Alcohol	−0.04	−0.19	−0.15	−0.44
#12 Horn's attitude	−0.04	−0.03	−0.57	−0.26

[a] These are the characteristic vectors v of the matrix equation $(W^{-1} A - \lambda I) v = O$ where W^{-1} in the inverse of the within-groups covariance-variance matrix and A is the corresponding between-groups covariance-variance (dispersion) matrix. The weights for each vector have been normalized (ie., $\Sigma v_j^2 = 1.00$).

[b] The scaled coefficients are obtained by normalizing the products of the v vector weights and the square roots of corresponding diagonal elements of the W matrix. The computer programs employed are described in Kenneth J. Jones, *The Multivariate Statistical Analyzer* (Cambridge, Massachusetts: Harvard University, 1964), pp. 101-117.

A composite mean score may be calculated for each group on each discriminant function by summing the products of discriminant coefficients and group-means across the independent variables. These composite group-means may be used to examine the configuration of the groups in the reduced two-dimensional discriminant space as shown in Figure 1. Along the first discriminant dimension, the maximum separation occurs between the smokers and the quitters, with the unables occupying an intermediate position. That the first function serves mainly to distinguish quitters from smokers is also confirmed by classification errors: the first discriminant function correctly classified only 4 per cent of the unables, whereas the inclusion of the second discriminant function brought this proportion up to 40 per cent.

The scaled coefficients for the first function indicate that the probability of classification as a quitter rather than as a smoker increases with the presence of the following variables: health ailments related to smoking (variable #3), an unfavorable attitude toward smoking

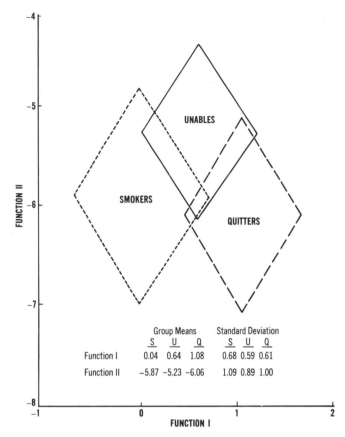

	Group Means			Standard Deviation		
	S	U	Q	S	U	Q
Function I	0.04	0.64	1.08	0.68	0.59	0.61
Function II	−5.87	−5.23	−6.06	1.09	0.89	1.00

Figure 1. Configuration of the groups in the discriminant space (drawn approximately to scale by enclosing the four points lying plus or minus on standard deviation from the group-means along the discriminant axes).

(#12), a non-fatalistic outlook on life (#8), a high rate of smoking (#2), and a non-smoking wife (#4). With the exception of fatalism, the same characteristics contribute to the separation of quitters from unables. The scaled coefficients for the second function reveal that unables as compared to the quitters, tended to be younger (#5), lighter consumers of both alcoholic beverages (#11) and cigarettes (#2), and more likely to have a wife who also smoked (#4). Of course, the causal relationship may work both ways; for instance, a person with poor health may have to give up both smoking and drinking.

SYMPOSIUM:
Intervention Processes — Theoretical and Practical Implications of Reported Research

Moderator
DOROTHY NYSWANDER
Discussants
GEORGE BEAL   DANIEL HORN
EDGAR BORGATTA   NEVITT SANFORD

SUMMARY

Edgar Borgatta stresses the need for understanding the nature of predictor variables in the study of smoking behavior ("explanations cannot be made on the basis of a single source"); uses the concept of social desirability as an example. The problem of reliability of criterion and predictor variables. Howard Leventhal's distinction between determinants of behavior and contemporary correlates. Selwyn Waingrow: the complexity of the "psychological context" of communications on intervention. Selection and identification of concepts for measurement (e.g., sociability, attitude toward death). Borgatta distinguishes between change *forces and those used to* maintain *changed behavior. Nevitt Sanford suggests that the tremendous diversity of conditions shown to be related to smoking or not smoking indicates an equally great variety of possibilities for intervention and provides examples. Selwyn Waingrow cites the possible goals of intervention; the question of* reducing *smoking or delaying its onset rather than* eliminating *it are discussed along with other intermediate goals for intervention programs. Again the question of the effectiveness of presenting information as an inducement to change was argued; Ward Edwards, applying learning theory and his model of decision-making, contends that information alone would be insufficient to effect change in smoking. Nevitt Sanford prescribes more effective techniques of providing "smoking education" to high school students. It was decided that the nature of such group differences as age, social status, and sex, call for different intervention procedures, and that programs involving youngsters themselves are more successful than the method of authoritarian control. Marilyn Crawford, citing her own research, stresses the importance of the teacher's attitude for the success of school programs. Daniel Horn urges that research finding on social influences in the schools be translated to control programs to modify the "social climate" re smoking; Gerhart Wiebe recommends a study of the "hierarchy of influence" among adolescents to achieve the same end. Daniel Horn cites the Philadelphia study as evidence for the futility of the "frontal assault" on adult smoking; recommends group discussion of the problem as a more effective device than attempts at direct intervention. The increased "social acceptability" of cigarette smoking as a substitute for tobacco chewing is traced since the appearance of the cigarette in 1910.*

Edgar Borgatta points to the need of developing flexible models of intervention, in view of the changing nature of society ("we are dealing with a generational problem"). Nevitt Sanford cautions against using harsh intervention methods, especially with children; substitute behavior may be worse. Summary remarks by Daniel Horn and Dorothy Nyswander.

Edgar Borgatta: If we try to explain smoking behavior in terms of the mechanisms that are involved, we must in time come to grips with related problems. If it is decision-making, we will want to understand the decision-making process, why a person makes a decision to smoke or not to smoke. But will this type of model become explanatory for the class of behavior with which we are concerned? One of the common contentions made, at least in the sociological arena, is that explanations cannot be made on the basis of a single factor or a single source. This creates the problem of applying the notions of a model — learning theory, for instance — in the laboratory. The problem is of translating all those factors into the single medium of cost, or payoff, or however one wants to phrase it. It turns out that these variables aren't so easily translated. We develop very interesting experiences about them. An example is the developing of scales without taking into account the balancing of social desirability. An entire literature exists in the area of social desirability. It appears to have relevance, but turns out not to when you start building tests, nor does it have relevance in a very specific and well-known area, despite what Dr. Edwards says. If social desirability item sets are factor analyzed, multiple-factor structures result. If sets of items which are socially desirable and equally balanced are built into tests of the type that Dr. Edwards proposes where items are balanced on social desirability, but ostensibly are of a different content, the resulting responses are not balanced. The reason for this is the matter of saliency associated with the factors involved operating quite independently of what may be called social desirability of response.

In connection with the smoking project at Wisconsin (pp. 3 ff.), I have the problem of predicting behavior at either the initiation or cessation stage of smoking. We require much more complex theories to deal with the various types of behavior involved. Perhaps we should find and examine new kinds of variables that would improve our predictions. Unfortunately the operative model must contend with the under-reliability of criteria as well as the under-reliability of predictors. In fact, some classes of predictors are often gross and account for little more than the subtle social and psychological predictors involved. The whole concept presents a complex problem, particularly since the stability of the findings depends upon the nature of the populations used. I would only add that if predicting behavior can be made more complex, it should be, although I also believe it is inappropriate to isolate smoking behavior from other behavior involving decision-making. Students, for example, are constantly bombarded with pressures to succeed academically, to participate in various group activities, to date, and so forth. All of these behaviors require the making of decisions, some of which correlate with the smoking decision. For instance, the best single indicator we have to gauge whether people are going to smoke or not is their answer to the question: "Do you drink?" Thus if you want to explain smoking behavior, perhaps you must also explain other types of behavior.

Howard Leventhal: I don't understand your notion of explaining behavior. It seems to me that a response can be controlled by n conditions, and that as times change and history changes there are changes in the determinants of the responses. I don't fully understand what you mean by going backwards from the variance in response to look for those things which "explain" it. They may be contemporary correlates, but certainly not determinants.

Edgar Borgatta: The model is of explanation in terms of historical sequence. It is highly complex, certainly; I won't argue that point. There is the problem of having the correlates of time one, with the correlates of time two; they are inter-wound. There often develops what can be called an attrition model in terms of predictive efficiency as you go from time one to time two, and time three to time four. The question of how much can be explained in that sense is an interesting one. The simplest model we have of this type of example is essentially that of intelligence, where essentially we can predict from time one to time two with high efficiency. The further you get from time one the lower the efficiency. You can draw a simplex which runs from time one all the way to time n, where you have high predictions in the immediate periods. But you have correlates to this, such as socio-economic status

of the parents and things of this sort. Surely this is not a simple model, and I am not sure that it is wholly explanatory because of its apparent circularity.

Selwyn Waingrow: This is part of what I meant earlier in the context of communications. This could include, for example, the psychological context within which the communication content is received; it could also include the sociological context, as well as the spatial, geographical, and physical contexts.

There are also the problems of complexity and context in terms of deciding where you intervene in research. Where is the payoff? Where, when, how, and on whom can research time, effort, and money be spent most effectively? These are decisions that must be made. One might, for example, suggest using college populations; but in what kinds of social and psychological contexts should they be investigated?

On the basis of some of these research reports, there are indications that we are at a stage where there is a need for more sophistication in the kinds of concepts used in working with these populations for a better understanding of the observed phenomena. What sort of concepts might we look at? Sociability is one; value systems is another; career choices, anxiety about Vietnam or the worsening international situation are others that have been suggested. How, if at all, are they related to each other and, more importantly, how are they related to smoking?

Howard Leventhal: My concern is with the product of a model that has an historical aspiration. Since it is conceivable that the determinants of behavior shift year by year, it could be a never-ending search. The intelligence issue may be different, although that is debatable; in that case, the determinants are more stable across times and populations.

Edgar Borgatta: We have access to a knowledge of the mechanisms that are operative; but not the input variables. Yet we haven't accomplished very much. There is the problem that our manipulation of the system is limited. If we are to predict futures in a systems kind of way, certainly we will not do so by avoiding the task. We probably have more options, in terms of experimental manipulation and comparative study, than we have utilized; that is, we have access to more than most people want to consider. But very often the manipulations are gross; there is no question about this. A certain amount of sensitivity has to be reserved.

The point is that the mechanisms that we sometimes select and proceed to test are not the most sophisticated or the most appropriate ones. For example, in terms of our populations, we make no pretense that we will change the behavior of the masses of committed smokers at this stage, certainly not this year. We may as a cumulative process, however, and if we are concerned with cumulative processes, then small changes that we can gauge are of relative importance. If we think of it in terms of the cycling of generations, then we may be concerned with what happens progressively with children. We can deal with some of the manipulations that we have in the social systems which are more restrictive — the school systems, community systems, and the like — in an intelligent manner. We may find that some things which are manipulated as variables, as particular kinds of pressures, are operative and are recurrent. All culture is located in a place and time. We can't avoid this in any of our social and psychological research at this level. If we are going to manipulate systems, we will have to do some research at the system level as well.

George Beal: Because most of us are scientifically oriented, when we go from the realm of definition to that of operational process, or to specific measure, we sometimes lose sight of the concept we originally wanted to measure. In terms of sociability, for instance, in some of the smoking research we have found a general disposition toward innovation or change-orientation. This is quite general, but in it may lie a useful concept for various specific behaviors, including smoking.

We might also consider one's attitude toward science. How much does an individual really trust science and consider what science can do for him? If we have consistent findings in one field, we may be able to broaden the levels of generality and predictability for them. There is a need for specific, empirical measures of the phenomena with which we are dealing; but we need to get these concepts and measures from higher levels. The broader concepts will then allow for generalization.

Selwyn Waingrow: I'm glad you raised that point, and I would add another: the whole aura surrounding various concepts and attitudes toward death, which are often repressed and which raise problems, particularly from a governmental point of view, when one attempts to investigate them. More research is needed here, as well as in such other public health problem areas as drinking, automobile accidents, and the like, where this would be involved.

Edgar Borgatta: But there are corollary and additional kinds of notions. For example, we say we are concerned with changing behavior, when actually we may be concerned with those forces which can be used to *maintain* a class of behavior. Our younger people who are coming through the generations, for example, are generally not smokers at ages 12, 13, or 14, although certainly some are. We are concerned essentially with establishing the conditions under which change does *not* occur. The *change* forces are those which are associated with advertising media, those who want to sell tobacco. We can actually reverse the whole view with which we tackle the problem at this level.

Nevitt Sanford: In the study of smoking, we generally deal with a bit of behavior which can and does get connected with almost everything in the person's life at one time or another. In terms of intervention this is probably a blessing, because it suggests that smoking can be modified by a great diversity of little devices that are applicable to the great mass of the population. The fact that smoking depends on such factors as number of roommates, number of smokers in the group, smoking habits of the parents, and so on, means, I should think, that one can actually modify smoking by such devices as the placement of vending machines, and the control of prices. A little change can make an enormous difference if one is talking about a population of a few million people.

This seems to be very different from the smoker who has quite a habit going and who has somehow connected the thing with personal problems of one sort or another. Examples would be the children for whom smoking might indeed be connected with whatever it is that makes them get venereal disease before the age of 17, or these nice girls who learn faster than anybody else all the facts and who also tend to be non-smokers; the good, well-behaved girls who both learn well and who don't learn. This is a different kind of non-smoker, I suppose, than is to be found in other connections.

When it comes to the person, there is quite a diversity of conditions associated with smoking and also with non-smoking. It would be worthwhile knowing some of the personality types found in non-smoking, some of the underlying motives for being a non-smoker. Some people, non-smokers for example, are very mean to people who smoke. They make quite a point of it. And some youngsters are extremely cruel in dealing with their parents because the parents smoke and the young people have been told that they must not. In a general way it seems that strategy should be taken along the lines suggested by Frank Barron: an overall scheme of gains and losses to be associated with a given policy about smoking. The fact is that not smoking, or giving up smoking, may have its drawbacks as well as its benefits. Some people who give up smoking get fat right away, which may be more dangerous to their health than smoking; others become mean and hard to live with. The losses should be considered, as well as the gains.

There is also a practical matter to be considered by those engaged in smoking withdrawal research. Is it possible to conceive of gradations of advantage in this area? Must it be smoking or not smoking, or can some of the education be directed to smoking in some less undesirable way?

Selwyn Waingrow: There are at least five possible goals of intervention — ways to change smoking behavior: prohibition, and voluntary or involuntary cessation or reduction. A researchable question in terms of strategy is, to what extent when you try for reduction do you get nothing, as against trying to get people to quit and at least, for example, achieving *some* reduction?

Nevitt Sanford: This is a practical point that seems to be critical. If a great deal of education and counter-propaganda are used, must they be almost entirely directed toward not smoking at all, relying on the belief that once one starts he cannot stop — which may be more of a fiction than we would like to think? Or should our energies be directed toward smoking less, not inhaling, smoking pipes and cigars rather than cigarettes, or starting to smoke as late in life as possible? We might have a better chance of achieving some degree of success with these more moderate goals than with trying to stop smoking altogether. Of course, the ultimate criterion of success of any of these goals, from a program point of view, is whether they bring about a reduction in mortality.

Cherry Tsutsumida: Perhaps in trying to make changes in behavior for which the public is not ready we may be defeating our purposes. If we cannot persuade people to have the same goals as we do, we will not succeed.

Ward Edwards: It has often been implied that telling people smoking is bad for their health ought to create in them a desire not to smoke. Somehow there is supposed to be a linkage between that kind of information and that kind of resulting behavior. There seems to be some surprise expressed at the general lack of success produced by any kind of informative communication of that sort. I'd like to ask the experimenters why they expect success. I don't know how anyone can expect that telling people not to smoke will produce any change in their smoking behavior.

Louis Zurcher: In the Arizona study this decision wasn't expected for some of the groups. It was expected that males in the Mexican-American group, for example, because of their cultural valuation for *machismo* — the masculine strength needed to overcome fear — might react in the opposite direction to a smoking-health communication which could induce fear. Actually, in calling smoking a fearsome thing, you might be saying to these boys, "If you do smoke, you will be showing that you're overcoming another kind of fear." Some of the early results are tending to substantiate this point. In fact with one of the communications we presented, smoking was reinforced rather than changed as intended.

Bernard Mausner: It seems that smoking should be viewed in terms of degree of risk. If someone is told there is a gun pointed at his head and that every single chamber has a bullet in it, he will not pull the trigger if he values living. But if you tell him he has several million chambers and only three or four have bullets, and he enjoys the idea of pulling the trigger, maybe he will take the chance. The general issue of whether information about risk does or does not lead to change of behavior seems irrelevant here. The question we have been asking all along concerns the degree to which people perceive a risk and adopt various methods for reducing it.

Ward Edwards: I don't think that was relevant to the question I was asking, which simply is, why do you expect that giving people information about the fact that smoking is harmful should make them quit smoking?

Cherry Tsutsumida: I should like to ask Dr. Edwards: is the type of information included in smoking programs redundant, already well-known by the people and therefore ineffective, or are you suggesting that people simply do not respond to information anyway?

Ward Edwards: I don't think I'm saying either of those things. Rather, that the information being communicated will affect behavior only if it has a direct bearing on one of two issues: one is, "What's in it for me?" and the other is, "How good are the chances of getting what's in it for me?" Information presented abstractly about a remote eventuality which is improbable in any case doesn't seem to have enough connection to lead to any effect. While I think many studies are trying to find out what will make people want to quit smoking, it is interesting to compare the way researchers try to get people to change their smoking behavior and the way in which the animal psychologist, for example, trains animals to press a bar. One of the things he will emphasize most is the *immediate* temporal contingency between the response that he is interested in and the resulting consequences. The other thing he will emphasize is the *"repetition* of these very close temporal contingencies. In practical animal-training problems, issues of immediacy turn out to be the crucial ones. I think issues of immediacy are also important to people. Those studies which have involved using gory lung operation movies, for instance, illustrated that movies at least have immediate impact.

Edgar Borgatta: I agree with the point but question whether the manipulations which an animal psychologist might use are available to use for influencing smoking behavior. Is it a matter of developing controlled experimental conditions where we can almost certainly effect changes, or is it a matter of finding natural conditions where almost any relationship will be influential? Maybe this means merely manipulating changes in practical areas. It certainly means that changes will only be made slowly and gradually; they will be cumulative and possibly unimpressive to any psychologist who expects to find direct or immediate results.

Nevitt Sanford: I thought there was enough information provided us today to permit a suggestion concerning smoking education. Practically all of the education that has been described so far has been focused on smoking and health or on the dangers of smoking. The reports in this section suggest that it would be a pretty good thing if youngsters were taught about the relationships that turn up in these researches. Why not discuss with them the various kinds of motives for smoking that have been pointed to and the kinds of smoking cultures that exist? One might speak directly about the problems of the youngster whose family does not want him to smoke but whose companions are all smoking. We must reach them where they live. If they become increasingly conscious of actions and their implications, they are helped to behave in a more reasonable way with respect to smoking; whether it would make them stop altogether, I don't know. But in the meanwhile, we can be pretty sure that this kind of discussion with youngsters about smoking would probably be helpful to them in a variety of other ways at the same time.

Daniel Rosenblatt: Someone has remarked about the growing concern school children have over their parents' smoking. I believe that children are concerned, but not over the matter of cigarettes — it is a diffuse anxiety with respect to their parents and their relationship with them. When the school-age child pressures his parents not to smoke, it is not with an adult recognition of the causes and effects of smoking; it is a child-like response to the meaning his parents have for him, his dependence upon their protection, and his fear of what would happen if they were to be lost. I would rather not encourage the child to think along these lines. Of course, I'm not talking about high-school students but about younger children: seven-, eight-, and nine-year-olds who are given question-naires to take home, and who are asked to talk to their parents about not smoking.

Daniel Horn: I know a mother of a seven-year-old child who opened a package of cigarettes and discovered that the child had cut all her cigarettes into shreds because he was panicky. He thought that when she lighted a cigarette she would drop dead.

It was brought out that studies have indicated a "delay factor" for children from families where the parents had a higher education, but that eventually they smoked at about the same rate. These same studies showed that children who started smoking earlier were more likely to come from parents with less education. Daniel Horn mentioned that his (1957) study confirmed this relationship not only for education, but for other socio-economic measures; however, the relationship did not hold for parental smoking habits. Of course, moving into a college population involves working with a selected population, so that the differences in smoking habits are those of a population of parents whose children are in college. Kenneth Briney's (pp. 53 ff.) experience with children of various ages led him to the conclusion that there seems to be a "correct" age to begin smoking for groups represent-ing each of the socio-economic levels; it is "all right" for

the 12-year-old girl to smoke from one group, but it was "not nice" for a 12-year-old girl from another group to smoke. He believed that the area of social support should be examined more carefully, with less emphasis placed upon the distribution of information about health effects.

Daniel Horn suggested that one method of control might be to make some attempt, not at eliminating smoking, but at delaying the time of onset. He pointed out that all available data show that the earlier people begin smoking, the more heavily they become committed to it, the more difficult they find it to give it up, and the more disease results from it.

Kenneth Briney: Our schools provide smoking-health instruction at a given grade level, but my hunch is that we should be providing different kinds of instruction for boys and for girls, for different socio-economic levels, as well as for different age groups.

In answer to a question, Dorothy Dunn said that at Illinois, more boys smoke than do girls, and that the higher the education level of the parents, the less their children smoke.

Daniel Rosenblatt: I don't think that's uniformly true. Some studies have shown, for instance, that there are more male college students who have never smoked at all than there are females, to whom smoking means a kind of sophistication and sexual attractiveness. My college population included girls who smoke more than the men, and begin smoking earlier. Smoking has a different meaning for girls and goes along developmentally with dating, in the sense that the cigarette has a meaning of "I'm ready to date." To turn to your comment about not making it accessible to smoke at a younger age, one of the things that cuts across all these other discussions is the continuum of middle-class to lower-class. Someone has said that the material on the role of exemplars does not particularly apply to the lower classes. They don't emulate their parents particularly; they don't emulate their teachers. My data indicate that the parents of lower-class children may object to their smoking, but it doesn't make any difference. It's just one more area in which the parents are ineffectual. Who is going to control their smoking? If the parents can't keep them from delinquency, skipping school, dropping out and other deviant behaviors, of which smoking is a minor phase, how is anyone else going to reach this much larger group which starts smoking earliest and goes on smoking heaviest?

Jerome Schwartz: It is clear that intervention methods now under way are insufficient: physicians' influence with patients, providing information to school children by way of films and slides, etc. Authoritarian demands by teachers that children *don't* smoke, that they *don't* drive fast, are not really effective. Other ways must be found of approaching them. Perhaps school leaders — not necessarily the athletic leaders — could be identified through sociometric techniques. The health educator could then work through them. It could then be determined whether this method is an improvement over the method of authoritarian control.

A number of participants agreed that "programs involving youngsters themselves in the education process" were more successful in actual behavior change, but those which depended upon children having a "teaching program foisted upon them" showed relatively little —or no — change. It was suggested that the "involvement" could also include student participation in surveys and research, giving reports, etc.

The problem of reaching children through organizations such as Boy Scouts, 4 H and other after-school clubs, was considered impractical with "lower class" youngsters, who are thought to be notorious non-joiners.

Charles Ross: Our group was invited to work in a small, isolated community because the people felt they had a serious problem with smoking. We worked with students in advanced biology who comprised the upper ten per cent of the classes — irrespective of social class. It was very easy to work with them, but they were an essentially non-smoking group; children interested in the natural sciences tend to be non-smokers.

Marilyn Crawford: I was impressed with one of the things that came up in our study, in that teaching is still at least to some degree, a person-to-person relationship between the teacher and the student. Some students come to our college because they are tired of being a number in a very large university. We were impressed with the influence of the instructor who has concern for the student, and the benefit derived from that concern. Our data indicated that there was no relationship between the smoking habits of the parents and those of the older students. The teacher seems to take the place of the parents. Students are still looking for authority, which the teacher gives them, even on the college level. The person-to-person relationship can provide this, but I doubt that an impersonal relationship can. Somehow in this climate in which the student feels the teacher does care about him and is concerned about him as an individual, the teacher's attitude toward smoking *does* influence the students' decision whether to smoke or not.

Daniel Horn: That's putting a burden on the teacher, asking him to engage in a process that may even be in conflict with his own behavior. How do you handle that?

Daniel Rosenblatt: We assume a prior commitment on the part of the teacher, owing to his role as an authority. The psychoanalytic model may be applied here: if the therapist insists that the patient change his behavior, the patient may do it to please the therapist, but once therapy is over he may revert to his previous behavior. The teacher is full of fire and converts students. Once the relationship ends, the influence disappears. Of course, in psychoanalytic therapy the process of identification carries with it a high degree of internalization; the patient really matures.

It was proposed that the individual therapy implied by the psychoanalytic method has limited applicability to the problem of working with groups — peer groups, or groups of ex-smokers, who are developing into a new sub-culture in our society, where quitting smoking is becoming the thing to do. When it was argued that teaching in the school atmosphere has limited value in comparison with other methods (in terms of behavior change) Marilyn Crawford disagreed.

Daniel Horn: But in terms of potential application, what kind of action program could one undertake? We have discussed the school setting at the school level and the lower grades, but what about colleges? Again and again I keep hearing and reading of all the social pressures and social influences that exist, the effect of one room-mate on the other, the effect of living in a dormitory or in a fraternity house, where no smoking is allowed. How does one translate that into some kind of a control program? How do you change the social climate? That's what we're going to have to do.

Gerhart Wiebe: A study should be undertaken to identify the hierarchy of influence among college people, not only within a single college, but for the nation. For example, music styles sweeping through the nation, make song writers and singers rather important for high-school and college-age people. They listen to radio a lot; who are the heroes of the transistor air-waves? Adolescents are great copiers. We all know how fads sweep through dress, manner of speech, hair styles, and so forth. There ought to be a serious attempt to identify the leadership hierarchy for these young people, to find out what in their social structure is *out* and not *in?*

Another thought on this matter: Dr. Dunn has suggested the possibility of eliminating vending machines, a practical suggestion which I think should be considered. It may or may not be a good thing to do, but if the taste for cigarettes is not really habitual yet, then it makes it easier to smoke less if cigarettes are not so easily available. Taking the vending machines out of colleges might have a good impact in terms of amount of smoking. On the other hand, it might boomerang. People might say, "They're trying to take this away from us," and make a thing about buying them by the carton instead of the pack.

Jerome Schwartz: The general availability of cigarettes, which encourages their use, will continue to be a problem. Whatever small attempt is made at reducing this availability, such as the removal of cigarette vending machines from college dormitories, is offset by the army's practice of providing them "automatically" in every duffel bag, and by the custom of free distribution by service groups. On most airline flights, they are furnished with meals. Why should the airlines stop if the Government won't? The Government is spending the money for research, but beyond requiring the printing of a few weak words on cigarette packages, it is doing a lot of talking and not enough producing.

Daniel Rosenblatt: Is it possible to identify for college students some of the specific things that lead one toward the smoking habit, to show them how much money is spent on advertising and the powerful interests at work? A college-age group would seem to be most responsive to an understanding of the influences at work, wanting not to let themselves be led by them. At least they would be able to see where they are being "taken." They enjoy laughing at Hollywood movies to show that they are superior to them; they like to indicate that they're grown up and sophisticated.

Daniel Horn: There seems to be a very strong implication in the report of the Philadelphia study (pp. 63 ff.) that in trying to work with adults in the changing of smoking habits or even in getting people to the point of thinking about change, a direct frontal assault is simply uncalled for and is going to lead to difficulty. In that case, the original sample is 30,000 people. Of the 11,000 smokers, 4,800 show an interest in coming to a meeting, 257 turn up, 150 go on, and 56 make some change. There's a diminution of effect that shows that something is wrong.

There followed a discussion of the difficulties of arranging large meetings: transportation difficulties, time and place convenience, and so forth. Mr. Allen indicated that his project had decided to change its meeting schedule to a series pattern (six or eight), rather than single mass meetings.

Daniel Horn: The key to this whole problem is that the (Philadelphia) questionnaire was directed toward saying, "Are you interested in quitting smoking? Do you want to come and try to quit smoking? Do you want to come and talk about your quitting smoking?" One of the experiences that came out of the study that's going on with the blue collar group from Hammond, Indiana, was that you could not get participation at that level, but you could get participation in group discussion, if you restricted it to, "Well, let's get together and talk about the problems of smoking, not talk about *your* smoking and whether or not you want to quit, just to talk about the problem of smoking." Orient the discussion toward the problem of smoking by children, rather than to their own smoking, and it becomes more acceptable. It is almost as if people wrap their arms around themselves to protect themselves against your trying to encroach upon their personal behavior.

It was suggested that perhaps the only solution to the problem is for people voluntarily to give up smoking. Yet in other areas of public health some of the greatest gains have been made through control of the environment. Relatively little has been done in terms of getting the people to volunteer to behave in different ways. What would be the implications of a "prohibition" of cigarettes away from at least certain groups of people, perhaps people under 21, people over 60, people with heart conditions and so on. It could be taken off the market on the basis that it is a dangerous drug.

Another approach would be to restrict further the places and conditions under which it is permissible to smoke: to have, for example, dormitories for those who want to smoke; the same for dining rooms, and so forth.

Daniel Horn: With regard to the matter of acceptability of using tobacco at certain times and places, consider the per capita consumption of chewing tobacco in the U.S. since 1880. It grew from three pounds per person at that time to a maximum in 1894 of four and quarter pounds per person. Then it began to go down. It took a really sharp turn around 1910, and has continued to slide until it is now down to a fourth of a pound per person. It has taken 60 to 70 years for that drop to take place. A tremendous change took place in the use of tobacco during this period. Aesthetic factors are involved — such as the aesthetic objection to spitting all over the place, health factors, such as the TB campaigns against spitting; legal restrictions against spitting on the sidewalk or other public places, and so on. A good many factors converged in producing that, such as the appearance, in 1910, of a substitute, the cheap and attractive cigarette. But the substitution was brought about by a new population, a new cohort, rather than by people switching from chewing tobacco to smoking cigarettes.

Edgar Borgatta: In problems of prediction and explanation of smoking behavior, the concern is not with a single phenomenon, but with one phenomenon among many. And if in dealing with a generational problem, it is in a social system which is continually changing. Generations grow; they run through particular types of sequences, so that consistently effective models of intervention cannot be deveolped. Models of intervention must utilize gross types of entering stimuli. There is also the problem of providing information toward no single criterion, such as smoking behavior, but toward other classes of behavior as well. Someone has observed that in considering these other classes of behavior, we may be dealing with *concomitants* rather than with *causal* factors. But this does not alter the fact that an influence can be exerted somewhere in this circular system.

Ward Edwards has asked why we should expect that giving persons information would change their behavior, since in many experimental situations it has been shown that immediacy of reward and immediacy of salience of the action may influence whether or not behavior changes in a particular way. A possible answer to this question is that in society you often may not use those manipulations which would be sure to work quite effectively, so that the classes of measures that you have to deal with sometimes bear little relevance to efficient change in society itself.

There is also the question of the goals of behavioral change. Should those goals be selected which are the ultimate goals for the behavior considered to be the relevant point for change, or are there *intermediate* goals which could be more effectively put into play?

Nevitt Sanford: Although we believe that smoking has so many diverse possible determinants that we don't know where to intervene, we can still do things which *might* be effective with respect to smoking and which we are quite sure will do no harm. When we talk about interventions of this kind we tend to focus on some particular kind of behavior that we are quite sure we want to prevent and then act in such a way as to favor its prevention. In using such a narrow conception, we must take care lest we do things that are harmful. I am not convinced, for example, that lecturing high-school children about the extreme dangers of smoking is necessarily a good thing, particularly since we know that most of them are going to smoke anyway. We might merely disturb them without changing their behavior. On the other hand, I think that there is absolutely nothing to be lost in explaining to young persons the reasons why people smoke in our society and how the manner of one's smoking — when he begins and how and where he does it — is determined by the sub-culture to which he belongs. Education designed to modify some of the stereotypes of what is masculine and what is feminine, for example, would be all to the good. It might favor more reasonable approaches to smoking, and it might in fact be helpful in various other ways at the same time.

Smoking education programs seem not to be taking full advantage of what is actually known. Most educational devices are focusing on the ill-health implications of smoking when, as a matter of fact, much information is available which ought to be presented immediately to high-school youth. I think they would find it quite interesting and would participate with some interest in discussions about smoking and related phenomena.

Experience in alcohol education can be cited in this connection. Nobody has ever been able to demonstrate that teaching facts about alcohol or preaching against alcohol has ever had much effect on drinking behavior. It would be somewhat regrettable if those of us who are interested in smoking were to make the same mistakes that were made in the past in that area.

The comment was made that if physicians were to recommend against smoking to particular patients, the behavior may be supplanted by something worse. Dr. Sanford was asked if he knew of any studies demonstrating that people who have quit smoking have made other kinds of adjustments.

Nevitt Sanford: I don't know of such studies, but I do know of individual cases of people who gave up smoking, put on weight, and were gone pretty soon. We know this about alcohol: if one gives up drinking, after drinking for 25 years, he has to be very careful. For one thing, cholesterol level may go up very fast. What are the physiological implications of suddenly quitting smoking after smoking for 25 years?

Dorothy Nyswander: My daughter, who is a psychoanalyst, periodically stops smoking for about two weeks. She says she cannot have patients during that period; she simply leaves the city. She is a wreck. When she returns and starts smoking again, she can go back to work. I was present on one such occasion; it was terrible.

We don't use the word "addict" in smoking research, de we? I have observed that Mr. Straits (see pp. 73 ff.) does not use that word; he uses the rather gentle term, "unables."

Daniel Horn: In terms of practical actions, we have discussed the three different basic population groups that were presented in the research in this section: school children, college students, and adults. In the school-children discussion, we were concerned about any attempts to increase anxiety in children with regard to their own parents. This is apparently one of the concomitants of so-called smoking education, of preaching about the hazards of smoking, particularly with young children. This may very well be an example of the kind of consequence of a smoking program in which the cure may be worse than the disease.

The question was raised about the problem of the age at which it is considered all right to smoke, and how this varies from group to group. For example, girls begin to smoke about one year later than boys. Within various sub-groups in the population it must vary tremendously. Certainly it is earlier for the lower-class groups than it is for the middle-class groups, and lower for the middle-class groups than it is for the higher-class groups. We have considered also whether it is worth trying to delay smoking, rather than having the prevention of smoking as the primary aim. From medical and psychological data we do know that people who do start smoking young are the ones who become the heavier smokers; it is they who find it more difficult to give it up (a lower proportion do give it up), and harmful effects are greatest in this group. A number of studies have shown fairly consistent differences in this. We don't know whether these are selective factors, in terms of those who take it up early, or whether we are dealing with an accumulated dosage response.

It has been suggested that different smoking programs be developed for boys and girls because of the differences in the way they seem to be reacting to the information on smoking. Going beyond this, the proposal was made for a greater refinement of groups, making more use of sociometric techniques to identify significant group clusters within the school population, and to try to get involvement of the students themselves in activities which are appropriate to the groups of which they are members. This raised the point that it would be necessary to use non-school groups if there was to be any opportunity for getting at many of the lower-class children, where participation in the school groups is at such an extremely low level. With the college population, the caution was expressed that, in the first place, college populations are a selection of the total population in that particular age group, and therefore, phenomena that occur in a grade-school or in a high-school population may not continue to the college group, either because of selective factors, differences in age, or both.

Teaching is a person-to-person process, and the finding that the feeling and concern of the instructor communicates itself to students is a valuable one, because it indicates the importance of the teacher in the effectiveness of the teaching process. The implication certainly is that the preparation of a good educational school program on smoking is more than just a production of materials and a curriculum guide for the teacher; it also requires some kind of process with the teacher himself, in order to improve the quality of the instruction and the participation of the teacher.

An identification of the hierarchy of influence among college students was recommended. What are the determinants of fads and fashions for that population? How could you persuade folk singers of the day to communicate to college students, and help to make "out" things "in" and "in" things "out"? An emphasis also on the degree to which students are manipulated by vested interests was proposed as a possible area for utilization that would have special appeal to the college student, who carries with his idealism a certain amount of cynicism as to vested interests and what they can do to him. Perhaps the concern about this kind of external manipu-

lation may be a significant factor encouraging him to resist being one of the vassals of the habit. The provision of alternative gratifications was also proposed, although it led to some difficulties. Certainly the proposal to have dormitories for those who smoke and dormitories for those who don't smoke implies that there be dormitories for those who drink and dormitories for those who don't drink, and, of course, houses for those who engage in sex and houses for those who don't.

With reference to educational programs for the adult group, the primary concern was the question of the direct attack versus the indirect attack. In one study, the implication was made that inviting people to come and participate in a program to get them to give up smoking was much less attractive and acceptable than merely inviting them to come and talk about the problem of cigarette smoking. The direct attack, in which you move in and show very clearly that you are trying to change somebody's behavior in what he considers to be an area of personal property and his own concern, is a threatening one and certainly is not as productive as one that is indirect and tries to get the individual to contribute towards the solution of a general problem.

Legislative or regulatory actions which reduce the possibility of smoking were also considered in terms of their contribution to any kind of an adult program: any action which would make for a lowered acceptability of smoking and a reduction of the places and conditions under which people could smoke should operate in the direction of providing a reduction in the hold that cigarette smoking has on the adult population. Perhaps the key to change of smoking behavior in our adult population is the key to change in some problems of mental-hygiene. This may very well contribute to the development of insight into one's own behavior.

At this point a participant expressed apprehension about the possibility of "prohibition" of cigarette manufacture and sale, recalling the situation with liquor: "We had a whole new underworld develop; I'm frightened of prohibition and black markets and what-not."

Daniel Horn: I don't think anybody has seriously proposed prohibition in this issue. We were referring to the placing of controls and restrictions: "Here are places and conditions under which it is permissible to smoke, and here are places and conditions under which it is not permissible." As these restrictions increase, as you narrow the life space within which one can smoke, you are in effect reflecting the overall social acceptability or unacceptability of smoking.

Dorothy Nyswander: That wasn't done with prohibition of liquor a few decades ago. It would be strange to have speakeasies for cigarettes, wouldn't it?

It has been interesting to realize that the practitioner, the change agent, is a person who must first make some kind of diagnosis. We call it an *educational* diagnosis as distinguished from *medical* diagnoses. It is to the behavorial scientists that we go for this diagnosis. Two types of help have been provided here. One type is that of a diagnosis as to the nature of the smoker, which I don't think we have explored sufficiently in comparison with the other groups. But what data have been gathered are beginning to be helpful. We need to know much more about the nature of the smoker — his value systems as they are developing, and some of his personality dynamics.

A second effort being made that may prove helpful is in the area of the influences affecting the smoker. If peer groups and friends are shown to be important, then much more work should be done identifying and working with these groups. Additional experimental work is needed to determine if it is important that girls and boys be taught separately with different content and different methods. We can't set our objectives until we know more about the nature of the learner and the nature of the situation. Out of these come our objectives for the practical program of bringing about change. We often look to the social scientists for clues as to methodology, and I think he is quite right when he says, "Look, that's your job, you're the practitioner. You ought to be able to work on the methods." While the need for more research continues, we should avoid gathering the same kind of data over and over. I think of the dozens of studies that have been made in India on the attitudes of families toward the ideal number of children in the family. There have been so many that you can just rattle off the numbers and they will come out just about the same, practically anywhere. In smoking, there seems to be a paucity of data for the lower socio-economic groups, a lack of data for the "rebels." The modern university "rebel" seems to represent a different kind of person. What is he like? Would he be interested in listening to lectures on smoking at this time? He has big problems he is interested in, and I'm not sure how much credence he would give to the Surgeon General's Report if it signifies Government. If government can be fallible in one area, does its fallibility carry over to other areas?

PART III

CESSATION PROCESSES

Sex Differences Between Successful and Unsuccessful Abstainers From Smoking[1]

JOAN S. GUILFORD
American Institutes for Research

Despite the fact that the behavorial aspects of smoking have been subjected to a great deal of research, little attention has been paid to characteristics which discriminate between smokers and non-smokers or between smokers who break the habit and smokers who try to abstain but fail when these differences are a function of sex differences. The two major studies which reveal the most about ex-smokers apply only to males (McArthur, Waldron & Dickinson, 1958; Straits, 1965) although studies of teen-age smokers, non-smokers and ex-smokers were done by Salber, Welsh and Taylor (1963) and Salber and Rochman (1964) in such a way as to differentiate between boys and girls. As Straits (1965) says, "Attention should also be directed at female smoking behavior, a neglected area of research" (p. 105).

The study reported here was originally designed (1) to evaluate the effectiveness of a group-treatment program (the Seventh-day Adventist Five-Day Plan) as opposed to a self-initiated, self-sustained regimen of abstinence, and (2) to attempt to describe the relevant characteristics of those who successfully gave up smoking for six months when compared with those who after six months were smoking as much as (or more than) they were at the time of their decision to quit. Relevant characteristics consisted of personal-situational variables; smoking patterns; motives for starting, continuing and terminating the habit; knowledge concerning the facts about smoking and health hazards; attitudes toward smoking and smokers; temperament; beliefs; self-perceptions; needs; techniques used to aid in abstinence; subjective changes or symptoms experienced during initial abstinence; and reasons for success or failure in the attempt.

PROBLEM

Although the "Aided" group (those who took part in the Five-Day Plan) was matched to the "Unaided" group with respect to sex, age, marital status, occupation level, education and intensity of habit (number of cigarettes smoked per day), an examination of success rates by sex revealed that the superiority of the group treatment at three months was attributable to women but not to men. Although the success rates of Aided and Unaided smokers were not significantly different after six months, the success rate for Aided women was still significantly higher than was the success rate for Unaided women. These findings appear in Table 1. It should also be noted that when men and women attend the group treatment program, their success and failure rates are virtually the same at each period; but when they do *not* attend a program, the men maintain the same success and failure rates as if they had been part of the program while the women have markedly lower success and markedly higher failure rates. This finding might lead one to ask: "Are the men essentially giving up smoking on their own whether they take part in the program or not?" and "Do the women need the support of such a program in order to achieve the success which men would have without it?" One way to determine the answer to this question would be to discover to what extent males and females actually participated in the program when they attended it.

These discrepancies led the investigator to conclude that gross comparisons between successful abstainers and unsuccessful abstainers would be less fruitful than comparisons between male successes and male failures on the one hand and female successes and female failures on the other. Combining the sexes for comparison purposes would even mask true differences if it should happen that differentiating characteristics were reversed for the two sexes. The problem, then, was to see which characteristics differentiated *Successes* from *Failures* within sex categories.

[1] Data presented in this paper represent selected findings from a study supported in whole by the U.S. Public Health Service, Research Grant Number CD 00149-02 from the Division of Chronic Diseases, Bureau of State Services. Further information can be obtained in Guilford, Joan S., *Factors related to successful abstinence from smoking: an interim report of three-month follow-up of the clinic group.* Los Angeles: American Institutes for Research, 1965, AIR-E17-3/65-Tr.

TABLE 1

Success and Failure Rates of Aided and Unaided Male and Female Smokers at Three and Six Months with Tests of Significance

Criterion Group	Sex	Aided	Unaided	χ^2	Sig. Level
Success (3 Months)	Males	32%	33%	0	n.s.
	Females	35%	15%	8.00	<.01
Success (6 Months)	Males	27%	23%	.60	n.s.
	Females	29%	12%	6.24	<.05
Failure (3 Months)	Males	28%	20%	1.33	
	Females	21%	45%	8.73	<.01
Failure (6 Months)	Males	26%	27%	0	n.s.
	Females	25%	46%	6.21	<.05

METHOD

Subjects

The Aided subjects were chosen from among those volunteers who, in response to a city-wide publicity campaign, enrolled in the Five-Day Plan sponsored by the Glendale Hospital and Sanitarium, a Seventh-day Adventist hospital. To obtain a sufficiently large sample, two programs were used. Attrition was approximately 50 per cent when failure to attend the program, failure to return questionnaire forms, and inaccessibility on follow-up were considered. The final Aided group used for analysis consisted of 173 subjects, 82 of which were men and 91 of which were women. The Unaided group consisted of 175 subjects in the general population, solicited by advertising, and selected to match the Aided group with respect to sex, age, marital status, education, occupation level and number of cigarettes smoked. The total sample of Unaided subjects consisted of 75 men and 100 women. An analysis of the characteristics differentiating these two groups, apart from the matching variables, revealed few differences. For the comparisons between males and females it was necessary to combine the Aided and Unaided groups to obtain large enough samples of Successes and Failures for analysis.

No pretense is made that the samples employed in this study are representative of any population of smokers. They are representative only of smokers who volunteer to stop smoking. Both samples are well above the population norms with respect to education and occupational level (or socio-economic status). They are also somewhat older than the average smoker. These characteristics are consistent with the research findings of other investigators and with the experience of those who conduct anti-smoking treatment programs.

Experimental Treatments

Both Aided and Unaided subjects were contacted and interviewed before the formal decision to stop smoking was made. A battery of questionnaires designed to assess the many variables included in the study was administered in the subjects' homes. The Aided subjects subsequently attended the Five-Day Program where they received a "decision" card to sign stating that they would stop smoking. The Unaided subjects were given identical decision cards by their interviewers and signed, dated, and returned them to A.I.R. along with a record of experiences during their first five days of abstinence. Upon receipt of his materials each subject received a $5 stipend. Dates on decision cards determined the lapse of time required for three- and six-month follow-up. Unaided subjects were given no materials, suggestions or help in abstaining. Aided subjects received the treatment included in the Five-Day Plan, a detailed description of which appears in Guilford (1965). In brief, it consists of films, printed materials, lectures, prescribed changes in routine, the "buddy" system, and testimonials by ex-smokers. In addition, a telephone service was made available for smokers who needed further support in their effort of abstain.

Follow-up of both groups was done by telephone. The first follow-up was scheduled after a three-month interval, the second after a six-month interval. Subjects were asked how many cigarettes they were currently smoking. After six months they were also asked why they thought they had failed if they were still smoking and to what they attributed their success if they were not.

Criteria

Criteria of success were defined in terms of reduction in consumption of cigarettes. Those who had reduced their intake more than 90 per cent were termed "Successes" and those who had reduced it less than 10 per cent were termed "Failures." Reduction in intake was computed on the basis of a comparison between the number of cigarettes smoked at the time of the interview and the number smoked at the time of the follow-up. When these criteria were applied, it was found that after six months there were 47 men (24 per cent of the total males) and 38 women (20 per cent of the total females) who had been successful in their efforts to abstain and 41 men (26 per cent of the total males) and 69 women (36 per cent of the total females) who had failed.

Data Analysis

For each of the comparisons the significance of the difference between the success group and the failure group was computed. In most cases the statistic used was χ^2 because responses to questionnaire items were dichotomous or in discrete categories. For comparisons based on continuous variables, t ratios were used. In the tables which appear in this paper data are presented in terms of percentages of groups. In most cases these percentages will not add to 100 per cent because only those findings which are of major interest are given. Where subcategory percentages are given they represent the per cent of the group in the major category responding in the manner described.

RESULTS

Demographic Variables

The results of the comparisons indicate that age is differentiating for both sexes with the Failures in each case being younger than the Successes. Education does not differentiate for males but Female Successes seem slightly better educated than Female Failures. Marital status differentiates between Female Successes and Failures with the failures being more likely to be married. Although the difference is not significant, single and widowed women seem to have a better chance of succeeding in giving up smoking. Occupation level does not differentiate for either group. Occupation levels for women were based on husband's occupation if the woman was married and her own occupation if single. Having children does not seem to affect either men or women. The proportion in each group having children represents the proportion of the "ever married" group in each case.

Information

It has been suggested by many experts in the field of smoking research that the theory of cognitive dissonance implies a tendency of smokers who do not want to give up the habit to reject information concerning its dangers. Included in the questionnaires used in this study was a 50-item test of knowledge concerning the facts about smoking as set forth in the U.S. Surgeon General's Report. The average difficulty level of the items in this test was close to .50 for both samples (Aided and Unaided). The scores (corrected for chance) for Successes and Failures were quite low. Male Successes obtained a mean score of 11.9; Male Failures scored 13.9. This difference was not significant. Female Successes had a mean score of 14.7 while Female Failures scored 10.3. This difference was significant beyond the .01 level of confidence. In the male subgroups, then, the Failures were slightly more familiar with the facts than were the Successes while in the female subgroup, the Successes were significantly more familiar with them. Whether this may be interpreted as meaning that dissonance is more motivating for women than for men is a question which cannot be answered here.

Attitudes

A large number of items designed to measure attitudes toward smoking and smokers were included in the same questionnaire as were the information items so that subjects would not realize that a portion of this question-naire was a "test." There were 40 of these items and none of them differentiated between the criterion groups.

Initiation of Smoking

The circumstances surrounding the smoker at the time he or she started smoking and the reasons for initiating the habit were obtained by questionnaire responses. Women were shown to have started to smoke at a later age than the men. For both sexes the first smoking trial, the age at which smoking was adopted as a habit, and the age at which the smoker became aware that it was a habit were slightly younger for the Failures than for the Successes, lending support to the hypothesis that the longer a person has smoked, the harder it is to give it up. For the men, age of awareness of habit is significantly higher for the Successes than the Failures. For the women, the age at which they had their first cigarette is significantly higher for the Successes than for the Failures.

The only differentiating motive for starting to smoke is the sub-category "for a thrill" which seems to be characteristic of Male Successes. It is interesting to note, however, that for both males and females, "being like others" is slightly more characteristic of Failures while "being different" is slightly more characteristic of Successes.

Grade placement at the time of initiating the habit is not significantly different for either success or failure group although there seems to be a tendency for female failures to have been behind their normal grade placement at the time.

The influence of family and friends in starting to smoke is negligible except that the Male Success significantly more often had a best friend who smoked when he started. It is true of both males and females that their best friends of the same sex were smokers and that members of their social group smoked. There is a slight tendency for Successes in either sex group to have started smoking more frequently with parents than did Failures. There is also a slight tendency for Male Failures to have older siblings who smoked than was characteristic of Male Successes. Parental smoking habits do not seem to have affected the success or failure of either males or females significantly but maternal smoking and having both parents smoke is more characteristic of Male Failures than Male Successes and the differences approach significance. The women, on the other hand, seem unaffected by their mothers' smoking habits but might, in a larger sample, be influenced by their fathers. Perhaps initiation of smoking is more a matter of Oedipal attachments than identification.

The only other differentiating responses indicate that Male Failures found that smoking made them feel sophisticated and at the same time they felt guilty the first time they had a cigarette.

Continuation of Smoking

Only one of the satisfactions derived from smoking differentiates between any of the groups. Female Successes more often state that smoking quiets their hunger pangs. The only other difference which seems interesting enough to comment on is the tendency for Failures (especially Males) to feel that smoking helps in social situations more frequently than Successes do.

When subjects are free to mention any motives for smoking that come to their mind, the only significant difference appears to be between Male Successes who smoke to keep their weight down and Male Failures who do not mention this motive. There is also a tendency for Successes to smoke as "something to do" and this is more true of Female Successes than Male.

It is important to note that the males and females smoke the same amount of cigarettes per day (approximately 30) and, further, that "amount smoked" does not differentiate between Successes and Failures for either group. Both Successes and Failures regardless of sex, are what might be called "moderate to heavy smokers." Furthermore, data obtained on the Aided and Unaided groups as a whole in a preliminary analysis showed that the mean consumption for the Aided group was 32 per day and for the Unaided, 30 per day. Thus, the Successes and Failures in each group (i.e., the extremes) consume cigarettes at the same rate as the groups as a whole do. The same holds true for the number of puffs taken on each cigarette which is virtually the same across all four subgroups.

Smoking after every meal is significantly more characteristic of Female Failures than Successes but does not differentiate between Male criterion groups. Smoking more while drinking liquor (while with other people rather than alone) and while relaxing (rather than working) is more characteristic of Male Failures than Male Successes. Females do not correspond to males with respect to liquor or smoking alone; in fact, they tend to be more successful if they smoke alone. They do correspond when it comes to smoking more while relaxing as a possible predictor of success and women in general smoke more while relaxing while men smoke more while working. Male Failures more often start the day with a cigarrette and have one just before going to sleep but the differences between them and Male Successes in these respects are not significant. Inhaling deeply is more characteristic of Failures in both sexes but does not differentiate. The only kind of cigarette which seems to make a difference between Successes and Failures is the mentholated type, smoked more often by Female Failures. Most of the subjects, whether male or female, smoke king-size filtered cigarettes. Failures, particularly males, seem to succumb to advertising in choosing brands to smoke

although the difference is not significant. Male Failures would smoke leftover stubs if they ran out of cigarettes but Female Successes, strangely enough, seem prone to this behavior. Unconscious smoking (finding a cigarette in the hand without any memory of having lit it and lighting another cigarette while one is still burning) is behavior which characterizes Male Failures and to a lesser extent Female Failures. Male Failures would smoke a distasteful cigarette rather than go without significantly more often than would Male Successes but this is not true of women. Male Failures would go out at night to buy cigarettes and so would Female Successes. This may be more a function of sex differences in willingness to go out at night than differences in willingness to expend effort to get cigarettes. It is interesting to note that almost everybody in each group has made some previous attempt to stop smoking and that such former attempts are not prognostic of success in *this* attempt.

The interpersonal environment of the smoker does not seem to have much effect on his or her ability to give up the habit. About half of each criterion group lives with a smoker and for those who do live with one, it is a husband or wife in the majority of cases. Having someone in the family disapprove of their smoking is significantly more characteristic of Female Failures than Female Successes and of those with a disapproving relative, it is the disapproval of a child that seems to contribute most to failure. Both Male and Female Failures are more often surrounded by friends who smoke than are Successes in either group but the differences are not large enough to be significant.

Giving Up Smoking

Why do smokers try to break the habit, how do they go about it, and what effect do motives and techniques have upon success or failure in the attempt? Among the motives mentioned by the Successes and Failures (Male and Female) in the study, the only differentiating items indicate that Male Successes are *less* inclined to mention the Surgeon General's Report and the dangers of smoking than are the Failures, and the Failures mention "dropped ashes" more often than the Successes. Male Failures are slightly more inclined to have respiratory problems and sore throats than are Male Successes. It would seem that those who are less concerned about the smoking problem have an easier time giving up the habit.

When it comes to techniques, the most differentiating item has to do with the Five-Day Plan in which the Aided group participated. This was only one subcategory of the major category called "Change routine" but it discriminated perfectly for Female Successes and Failures. This result, combined with the evidence that neither of the Male groups mentioned following the Five-Day Plan to any extent, suggests that for the males the program was irrelevant while for those women who participated in it, it was helpful. It should be noted that these techniques were solicited in an "open-end" fashion so that failure to mention the program did not imply non-attendance. It would only imply that the respondent did not consider it important enough to list as an aid to abstinence. Cutting down on smoking rather than "quitting cold" differentiated between Female Failures (who cut down) and Female Successes who did not mention this technique. The other differentiating item was the use of commercial drugs, characteristic of Female Failures and, to a much lesser extent, of Male Failures. It might also be noted that Male Successes more often used oral substitutes (in the form of gum, candy, food, etc.) than did Male Failures but that for women there was no such difference.

The only distinctly differentiating symptom was "impairment of concentration" which was much more characteristic of Male Failures during the first four days of the five-day record period. Males seemed to be more drowsy if they were Failures, and Females were drowsier if they were Successes. Successful women also had headaches more often during the entire five days than did women who failed. Women who failed were slightly more anxious than Female Successes. None of the symptoms discriminated between Female Successes and Failures to a statistically significant extent.

Behaviors and attitudes during the initial five days of abstinence were by far the most discriminating characteristics for Successes and Failures, particularly for females. Whether or not the subject smoked on the fifth day was predictive of long-term success for both males and females and smoking on the first four days was predictive for females. During the first four days almost everybody craved cigarettes but by the fifth day the differential was so great for females as to be significant beyond the .001 level. Eating more than usual became differentiating on the fifth day for males with the Successes engaging in extra eating. Confidence in ability to stop smoking is a major determiner of success for both males and females, particularly by the fifth day. It is, of course, highly correlated with progress in quitting as is the attitude of pride in accomplishment which also differentiates between Successes and Failures in both groups by the fifth day.

Reasons for Failure

The reasons given for failure by those who fail are as follows: (1) Lack of will power (e.g., succumbed to temptation; didn't try hard enough); (2) Enjoy smoking and don't want to give it up; (3) Boredom; (4) Nervousness (e.g., some change in life situation, personal problem, pressure at work or at home, illness, death in the family); (5) Neurotic reasons (e.g., loneliness, need for a psychological crutch, have to have a cigarette while

drinking liquor); (6) Weight gain; (7) Addiction (e.g., can't quit or withdrawal symptoms too painful); (8) Social pressure (e.g., live with a smoker, friends smoke, need it as a social crutch, advertising influenced behavior); and (9) Blame cast on either the Five-Day Program or A.I.R. No analysis has been made of these rationalizations as yet.

Reasons for Success

The reasons given for succeeding by the Successes are in line with the techniques used in giving up the habit. Will power, quitting "cold," talking oneself into it, attending the Five-Day Program, using substitutes such as other tobacco or chewing gum, and medication are all given by successful subjects. It was interesting to see in another analysis that the "Aided" Successes attributed their achievement to the Five-Day Program and its suggestions while the "Unaided" Successes attributed theirs to "Will power." No analysis of male-female differences with respect to this variable has been made as yet.

Self-Concepts

In response to incomplete sentences about themselves, Male Successes tend to make the following statements significantly more frequently than do Male Failures: (1) Most people think of me as being . . . cheerful, friendly, sociable; (2) My chief goal in life is to . . . serve others and to be secure; (3) Bad habits are . . . annoying; smoking; (4) I most admire . . . success or successful people; (5) I am lost without . . . money; (6) I feel superior when . . . I impress other people or other people show they care for me; (7) A person's health is . . . important; (8) Making sacrifices is . . . difficult; (9) If I have a personal problem, I . . . get help (usually from my wife); (10) The person I most want to please in this world is . . . my wife. Male Failures, on the other hand, respond as follows: (1) If I failed at something, I would . . . find out why and try again; (2) My chief goal in life is to . . . change myself or to further my personal development; (3) A person's health is . . . the most important thing he has; (4) I feel superior when . . . I accomplish something; (5) Making sacrifices is . . . worthwhile; good. It would seem that the man who succeeds in giving up smoking is more sociable, dependent, unselfish, success-oriented and outer-directed than the man who fails. Furthermore, he is less concerned about his health. The Failure is very concerned with his health and with his own personal development.

The picture presented by the women who succeed, when compared with the women who fail, is somewhat different. Female Successes, more often than Female Failures, complete their sentences as follows: (1) Most people think of me as being . . . successful or talented;

(2) If I failed at something I would . . . try again; (3) My chief goal in life is to . . . be healthy; (4) When I am in trouble I . . . try to get out of it; (5) The most difficult thing to do is . . . something disagreeable or unpleasant; (6) I am lost without . . . something to read; (7) I feel superior when . . . I accomplish something; (8) I feel proud of myself when . . . I do something unselfish; (9) In a room full of strangers I . . . feel alone or lost; (10) I most admire . . . mentally healthy people (people who are well-adjusted, calm, happy) or non-smokers. Female Failures complete their sentences, more often than Female Successes, as follows: (1) My chief goal in life is to . . . change myself or further my personal development; (2) Bad habits are . . . annoying or frustrating; (3) I feel superior when . . . I impress others (with my knowledge) or when I am gratifying my own needs; (4) A person's health is . . . important; (5) Making sacrifices is . . . difficult; (6) People who smoke are . . . addicted. Contrary to the Male Successes who are sociable and outgoing, the Female Successes like to read and are ill at ease in strange social situations. Male and Female Successes are alike in having unselfish goals. Male Successes and Female Failures are alike in finding bad habits annoying and sacrifices difficult. Both Male and Female Failures are concerned with the importance of health and both are interested in their own personal development. Male Failures and Female Successes would try again if they failed at something. It is evident that the two sexes are similar in some ways and different in others. It is interesting that out of over 200 coded responses to the 20 items, the same ones repeatedly seem to discriminate Successes from Failures but not always in the same direction for both sexes.

Personal Characteristics

A 200-item questionnaire was administered to all subjects. Of these 200 items, one would expect to find 20 significantly discriminating beyond the .10 level of confidence, 10 beyond the .05 level and 2 beyond the .01 level. For men, 25 reached .10, 14 reached .05 and only 1 reached the .01 level of confidence. For women, 21 reached .10, 11 reached .05 and only one reached .01. It is justifiable to speculate that the differences found arose by chance and to assume that they might disappear on cross-validation. No interpretation of the results will be made here but the characteristics described by the differential responses are interesting and, consequently, are described below.

Male Successes more often said that they believed their home life was as pleasant as most people's. They felt that few obstacles would stand in the way of their reaching their goals. They would rather be leaders than followers and usually expected to succeed in the things

they did. They tended more often to go to church every week. They start new projects with enthusiasm. They rarely daydream and they dislike people who are indecisive. The Male Failures, on the other hand, endorsed the statement "At times you think you are no good at all" (which differentiated them from Successes beyond the .001 level of confidence). They said they had nervous habits such as nail-biting and pencil-chewing and that they preferred chewy candies to other kinds. They more often become bored with routine and they suffer keenly from feelings of inferiority. They sometimes crave something intensely without knowing what it is and they often have trouble sleeping at night. Criticism or scolding hurts them terribly and they are sure they get a "raw deal" from life. They have had to give up plans often because they couldn't carry them out. They need encouragement in order to keep on with their work. They have difficulty starting to do things and think the future is too uncertain to make plans. They have trouble expressing themselves in conversation. They often resist doing what they are told to do and they sometimes feel that they are about to go to pieces. The picture of the Successes is one of confidence and a realistic outlook on life. The Failures seem to be neurotic. They are nervous, hypersensitive, lacking in self-confidence, and probably self-defeating.

The picture for the women is not so clear-cut. In fact, it is confusing. Successful female abstainers become irritated over little annoyances and tend to procrastinate more than Failures do. They also suffer from gastrointestinal problems when emotionally upset, are more inclined to have headaches than Failures, and feel that there is little love and companionship in their family. When something unexpected comes up they are often at a loss as to what to do. They are normally underweight and are quick in their actions. The only positive things which can be said about them are that they accept suffering as a normal part of life and they like themselves rather well. Female Failures are not interested in going out at night but prefer to stay home. They are terribly hurt by criticism and consider themselves to be nervous. They shrink from facing any crisis or difficulty. They are seldom short of breath and don't have headaches but they have been hospitalized more than three times (excluding childbirth). They seem rather dependent, stating that their conduct is largely controlled by other people's behavior and that their parents' ideas of right and wrong have always been best. They have more difficulty in expressing themselves in conversations than the Successes do and they were toilet-trained at an unusually early age. The picture of the Female Success seems to be one of a thin, energetic, irritable and unhappy martyr with a nervous stomach. The Female Failure is dependent, hypersensitive, fearful and a "home body."

DISCUSSION

From the results of an exploratory study of the characteristics of males and females who try to stop smoking and either succeed or fail, we have attempted to discover sex differences which might account for the differential effects of a group treatment program. The results of this attempt provide possible hypotheses for further research but because of the restricted size of the subsamples of male and female successes and failures, the differences found are of questionable reliability in many cases. We do not intend to draw any conclusions on the basis of this report but we feel that it does demonstrate rather clearly that men and women are different in their social orientation and their personality dynamics, particularly when it comes to the exercise of self-discipline. Because of these differences it would seem self-evident that further studies should either confine themselves to one of the sexes or differentiate between them. It is also suggested that if women are to stop smoking they may have a greater need for the kind of support offered by the Five-Day Plan or a similar group treatment.

SUMMARY

In a major research project, a portion of which is contained in this report, it was found that men and women responded differently to a group-treatment program designed to help smokers abstain from the habit. Men were equally successful in abstaining whether or not they participated in the program. Women who participated succeeded as well as men but women who did not participate had a success rate half as high and a failure rate twice as high as those who did. Curiosity concerning this phenomenon led to analyses of data by sex. Four criterion groups were established: (1) Male Successes; (2) Male Failures; (3) Female Successes; (4) Female Failures. The criterion for success was 90 per cent or better reduction in smoking; the criterion for failure was 10 per cent or less reduction. The abstinence period was six months. Prior to the decision to stop smoking, all subjects were interviewed to obtain data on a wide variety of personal-situational and psychological variables. The results of comparisons between Male Successes and Male Failures on the one hand, and Female Successes and Female Failures on the other, indicated that the differentiating characteristics were by no means the same for the two sexes and it was suggested that future studies take these sex differences into account and that treatment programs consider the possibility of differential approaches to male and female smokers based upon what can be found in more intensive comparative study.

REFERENCES

Guilford, Joan S. *Factors related to successful abstinence from smoking: an interim report of results of three-month follow-up of the clinic group.* Los Angeles: American Institutes for Research, 1965, AIR-E17-3/65-TR.

McArthur, C., Waldron, Ellen and Dickinson, J. The psychology of smoking. *Journal of Abnormal and Social Psychology,* 1958, *56,* 267–275.

Salber, Eva, Welsh, B., and Taylor, S. V. Reasons for smoking given by secondary school children. *Journal of Health and Human Behavior,* 1963, *4,* 118–129.

Salber, Eva, and Rochman, J. Personality differences between smokers and non-smokers. *Archives of Environmental Health.* 1964, *8,* 459–465.

Straits, B. C. *Sociological and psychological correlates of adoption and discontinuation of cigarette smoking: a report to the Council for Tobacco Research U.S.A.* Chicago: The University of Chicago, 1965.

DISCUSSION

Joan Guilford: There is what may be called an epilogue to the study: observations that did not appear in the report. After a year, I did a follow-up on these people and found that the success rate for people who attended the clinic was about 16 per cent, and for the people who did not attend it was about 10 per cent, which, although discouraging, is in line with general findings.

Since the men and the women turned out to have such different success rates, we decided to compare them on all of the variables that we were interested in. There were about 2,000 of these variables, which of course I cannot dwell upon here. The things that differentiate male successes from male failures are generally in line with previously published research findings. But the factors that differentiate between female successes and failures are rather strange and sometimes in the opposite direction from those that differentiate the males. This leads us to wonder what it is about women that makes them so different. We find, for example, that the men who succeed are much less neurotic, much more self-confident, much more goal-directed, success-oriented, practical, and so forth, while the men who fail are indeed quite neurotic, with strong feelings of inferiority. But this does not hold for the women: the women who succeed are extremely neurotic, but so are the women who fail. Now, whether or not all the women in the group were neurotic we don't know, since we didn't obtain that kind of information for them.

We found some interesting things that differentiated men and women. When we gave an information test based on the *Surgeon General's Report,* consisting of fifty factual items concerning the dangers of smoking, we found that the male *failures* more often, although not significantly more often, had more information about the dangers of smoking than did the male successes; whereas, it was the female *successes* who had more information about the dangers of smoking. This supports Kenneth Briney's findings of differences between smokers and non-smokers, with respect to the matter of information (see pp. 53 ff.).

We examined such things as why they started smoking (at a very superficial level) by asking them why they started, why they continued to smoke, what satisfactions they derived, why they had decided to give up smoking, what techniques they had used before when they tried to stop smoking. We found that attitudes toward smoking didn't differentiate at all. We had something like forty attitude items, with perhaps three of those showing significant differences, which is less than a chance probability.

We found also that the *failures* in our study had *more* reasons for quitting, that their reasons were more immediate, and yet they failed. This is a negative result if Straits' study (pp. 73 ff.) is considered, because he found immediacy of reason to be probably the best predictor of whether or not they at least tried to quit, and whether or not they were successful.

We found, as most others have, that those who were successful in quitting were older than those not successful, that they had been smoking for a shorter length of time, and that they started smoking at a later age; these are fairly consistent with previous findings. We did not find anything, however, with respect to the amount of cigarettes smoked. Interestingly, we found that our females smoked as many cigarettes as our males did, with the mean for all groups — successes and failures, male and female — being approximately thirty cigarettes per day. We will shortly examine extremes to determine whether there are any differences among heavy, medium and light smokers, when these three groups are compared with one another.

Howard Leventhal: Could you tell what you mean by "immediacy"? You said those who had more immediate reasons for quitting, did so. Just what are these reasons?

Joan Guilford: I meant those reasons having to do with current conditions, for instance, bronchitis, smoker's cough, emphysema, being told by the doctor that they ought to stop smoking, and so forth. Something painful was occurring to them as a function of smoking, and they were well aware that it was a problem for them right now.

Howard Leventhal: Did you use any potent communication stimuli with the groups?

Joan Guilford: Well, those who went to the clinic did receive potent stimuli. Those who stayed home got absolutely nothing except our questionnaire, which was also given to the other people. As a matter of fact, we very carefully avoided offering any suggestions on how they might quit, and when they asked we just said, "You're on your own."

Howard Leventhal: Then your finding replicates that of a dissertation by one of my students. He found that those who were given many immediate reasons under threat conditions were the ones who showed failure.

Joan Guilford: I see many indications here (although I hesitate to make any generalizations because the differences are not significant) that the people who really are the most highly motivated have the worst time trying to give up the habit. Whether this has implications for self-destruction or suicidal impulses or something I really don't know. It looks that way.

Daniel Horn: It seems to me that this is a selective problem because the people who have a strong immediate reason for giving up smoking simply give it up and are completely successful. We never get them because they never come in to talk to people about their smoking; it's no problem for them. They certainly don't seek help.

Joan Guilford: That's true. Most of our people (I would say about 85 to 90 per cent) had tried at least once before to give up smoking, and most of them had tried to give it up many times. These are people who have a history of failure, which does make them a very special group.

Bernard Mausner: Do you have any data differentiating those who succeeded because they went to the clinic and those who succeeded on their own?

Joan Guilford: Yes, we do, but it isn't in the study. Also, we thought it would be interesting to know whether the men who attended the clinic didn't really *participate* in the clinic. For example, they didn't follow the directions, which are considerable. The Five-Day Plan is very complex, but we thought that the women who attended did follow it. We found this to be true: none of the techniques which were prescribed by the clinics were used to any significant extent by the men. They were used by the women, and when we called them and asked the people who succeeded their reasons for succeeding in quitting smoking, the large majority of women attributed success to the clinic: "Because I went to the clinic"; "Because I joined the group"; "Because I followed the Five-Day Plan." The men, on the other hand, almost never mentioned the clinic at all, even though they had attended.

The Influence of A Physician on the Smoking Behavior of His Patients[1]

BERNARD MAUSNER
Beaver College, Pennsylvania

JUDITH S. MAUSNER
and WILLIAM Y. RIAL
Women's Medical College of Pennsylvania

Our interest in the use of informational messages to get people to change their attitudes and, we hoped, their behavior in smoking began in 1962 and was based on the notion that if people *really* understood the facts, they woud act on them.

In our first program we studied the effect of information on attitudes towards smoking (Mausner and Platt, 1964) and found that subjects who intensively learned the facts about the deleterious effects of smoking from programmed materials developed opinions consonant with their newly acquired information. We also found that their feelings toward smoking were less likely to change than their opinions about the cause of lung cancer. Unfortunately, although both opinions and feelings did change in many subjects, smoking behavior was affected little if at all. Learning did not even lead to a decision to try to limit smoking. (However, we did obtain some interesting data on the differences between the appeal of a programmed message based on statistical evidence and one based on a citation of authority, although I don't think our findings have important implications for practice.)

Our next step was to look for some way of getting people to make a commitment to change, because we became very interested in the problem of the interrelationship between attitudinal change and what we have been loosely calling decisional processes or commitment. We felt that it would be useful from a practical point of view. Subsequently we applied common sense as well as the findings of sociologists who had studied "influence processes" and discovered that a relevant, personally-known authority, an influencing figure, is the most useful means for getting people to change their behavior.

For example, one of the most thorough sociological studies of personal influence (Katz and Lazarsfeld, 1955) concluded that the most potent influence comes from individuals who are both authoritative and involved in personal interaction with the person to be influenced. The applicability of this finding was dramatically confirmed by Bass and Wilson (1964), who found that telephone messages from a "safety organization" and letters from pediatricians were relatively ineffective in influencing people to purchase seat belts for their automobiles. What *was* effective was a brief recommendation about seat belts from the pediatrician during a routine office visit. A follow-up study showed that a significantly higher proportion installed seat belts as compared to those in control groups who did not talk to the doctor.

Since the most obvious relevant authority in their findings was the physician, we first approached two physicians and asked them to cooperate in a study. One of the physicians was designated for the experimental group, the other for the control group. The design for the study was very simple: All patients coming to see the two doctors were given our pre-test questionnaire by the receptionist before they had any contact with their doctor. The questionnaire asked for a report on the amount each subject usually smoked and on his life-time smoking history in a format developed by Ravenhold and Applegate (1965). In addition, everyone was asked to furnish several items of personal information. The experimental physician then told each patient who smoked that he ought to do something about his smoking. He offered him a Nicoban pastille (a cigarette substitute in pill form) and a pamphlet (describing hints to assist in cessation of smoking) to those patients who indicated any interest. There was no attempt to explain the ill effects of smoking in detail or, indeed, to argue the point. The control physician said nothing to his patients.

Several days after the office visit we conducted a telephone interview with the patients and roughly six months later we conducted a second post-test. As we had done previously, all the patients we could contact were asked about their smoking behavior during the past day and on the average during the preceding month. Questions were also asked about their recollections of the visit to the doctor and the degree to which it influenced their smoking behavior.

Four hundred forty-one people who came to the office during the period of the study filled out questionnaires. Most of these were patients of the two doctors, although a few people were there to accompany a patient.

[1] The work reported here was carried out under Grant CD 00039 from the United States Public Health Service, Bernard Mausner, principal investigator.

TABLE 1

Decision to Change Smoking Habits
(Follow-up I)

Group	Change	Not to Change	Totals
Experimental	51 (42%)	70 (58%)	121
Control	14 (39%)	22 (61%)	36
TOTAL	65	92	157

TABLE 2

Decision to Change Related to Actual Change
in Smoking Behavior
(Follow-up I)

Group	Actual Behavior	Decision Change	Decision Not to Change
Experimental	Change	42	12
	No Change	9	58
Control	Change	6	3
	No Change	8	19

TABLE 3

Number of Subjects Changing or Not Changing Smoking Behavior
in Experimental and Control Groups
(Follow-up II)

Group	Change	No Change	Totals
Experimental	31 (33%)	62 (67%)	93
Control	3 (10%)	29 (90%)	32
TOTAL	34	91	125

$\chi^2 = 6.90$, df $= 1$, p $< .01$

TABLE 4

Change on Follow-up I vs. Change on Follow-up II
Experimental Group

		Follow-up I Change	Follow-up I No Change	Totals
Follow-up II	Change	21 (68%)	10 (32%)	31
	No Change	23 (37%)	39 (63%)	62
	TOTAL	44	49	93

$\chi^2 = 7.79$, df $= 1$; p $< .01$

Of the 441, 253 were non-smokers or ex-smokers; 31 could not be used because they submitted incomplete questionnaires or could not be reached for the first telephone interview. This left 157 persons: 121 in the experimental group and 36 in the control group.

About 40 per cent of those in both groups (the experimental and the control) made an initial commitment on the questionnaire to do something about smoking. This was a little disconcerting, because we really hadn't wanted the control-group subjects to respond so positively; but we realized afterwards that if one goes into a doctor's office and is given a questionnaire about smoking, it may be even more significant if nothing were to happen after that. It may start some concern about smoking. But if someone telephones you and says, "I am from the Department of Preventive Medicine, Women's Medical College; what about smoking?" The answer is likely to be, "Sure, I really ought to quit." It is also probably relevant that the physician for the control group selected was well known to his patients and in the community as being opposed to smoking; in fact, he had NO SMOKING signs on his office walls. The difference in the effect of the two physicians may lie in the actual expression *to each patient* of a concern with smoking and the offer of a drug may legitimize the notion that smoking is itself a disease to be cured.

On the initial follow-up a fairly high proportion, 80 per cent of those in the experimental group, who committed themselves to curtail or at least reduce their smoking actually did report some smoking reduction, as compared to only 30 per cent of those in the control group.

The differences between the experimental and control groups were much more marked after six months. At this juncture we were able to reach and include in the analyses 93 of the subjects in the experimental group and 32 of those in the control group (see table 3). The subjects included 68 per cent women and 32 per cent men. In large part they were from clerical, sales, or skilled craft occupations. There was a sizeable minority of professional and technical people; their educational levels were consonant with the distribution of occupations. Over a third of the experimental subjects at this time reported either a cut of one-half pack or more in their smoking or complete cessation; fewer than 10 per cent of the control group showed similar change. A "success" was (by our criterion) one who reported a smoking level of a half-pack or more lower on the six-months follow-up than he had initially reported. (It should be emphasized that our statistics do not involve quitting necessarily, but only cutting down.) It is incidental but interesting that of the nine married couples in our experimental group not one of the husbands or wives changed.

Most previous studies have found that light smokers are more likely to reduce or stop than heavy smokers. By contrast, in our study those who changed were heavy smokers at the time of their initial interview. They had also a heavier life-time burden of smoking. One could posit that the difference could be accounted for by differences in sex distribution, since men smoke more heavily than women. We tested this possibility and found that there was a tendency, although only of borderline significance, for proportionately more of the men to change than the women. However, within each sex it was the heavier smokers who changed. In addition the possibility exists that the smokers with a heavier life-time burden have a greater tendency to reduce their smoking because of symptoms such as coughs or shortness of breath which made the physician's warning meaningful. It was this "life-time burden" which was the significant differential between changers and non-changers. There were no significant differences in age, in age of starting to smoke, or in the number of years of smoking.

Although the information on smoking patterns was limited by the brief telephone interview, several findings of note emerged. The changers did not use filter cigarettes more frequently than non-changers, nor did they reduce the length of the butt. They did report a tendency to diminish the amount they inhaled, but the use of the Nicoban was insignificant.

In the first follow-up, in answer to the question of whether they preferred to smoke alone or in social situations, a significantly higher proportion of non-changers than changers was found among those for whom smoking is largely social. Another question dealt with the affective importance of smoking. Thirty-seven per cent of the changers were in the highest two groups on the rating of emotional factors in smoking; only 25 per cent of the non-changers were in these groups.

Unfortunately, the relationship between decision and actual change is obscure. Of those who changed only half had been in the group who initially reported a decision to change. But there was a significant tendency for those who reduced their consumption of cigarettes immediately after seeing the doctor to persist and thus be included among the changers.

In summary it appears that the use of the physician's influence represents a potent way of altering smoking behavior. It cannot be sufficiently stressed that the study was not conducted with volunteers who came to a smoking clinic because of a previously developed decision to change their smoking behavior. The subjects were an unselected group of patients who came to a doctor's office during an eight-week period. We succeeded, with just a 35-40 second message from the physician, in creating significant change — *not* in a group of volunteers, *not* in a group who came in response to an advertisement. Of course, they were not randomly selected from the total population of smokers since, for one reason or another, they came to seek medical help for themselves or their families and were, therefore, more aware of health than a random sample of the population would be.

The fact that change occurred in large part in those whose smoking habits were not bound up with social relations was not predicted. It is quite logical to assume, however, that if contact with the doctor changes something in the patient's own pattern of mediating responses to the cues which arouse a tendency to smoke, the likelihood that this change could be maintained is greater if smoking is not continually reinforced by external, predominantly social cues.

The experiences of the research staff in conducting the study may be of interest to physicians who are considering the risk of making nuisances of themselves over smoking. In no instance did a patient in the experiment refuse to be interviewed; in fact the mention of the doctor's name led to 100 per cent cooperation among those subjects with whom subsequent contact was made. There was no indication that the experiment aroused any negative feelings.

Our findings raise the possibility of experimenting with several variables. First of all, it would be interesting, theoretically, to know about the *sequence of events*. If we had provided the information message *after* the commitment, the results might have been more significant. (It would also have been interesting to try providing the information *before* the commitment.) Second, and perhaps more important, we have been experimenting with the factors which determine decision. It would be interesting to note what it is in the contact with the physician that changes people. Does their evaluation of various possibilities, various outcomes, change? Is it the level of expectation of this outcome that changes? Or, as we are beginning to suspect, is it merely that contact with the physician forces people to "tally up the odds" in a way that they normally don't as they go through life? It may be that we will discover no real change in their decisional matrices, if we can get at them; but we will discover that the change lies in their willingness to act, or perhaps even in their actual thinking in terms of a decisional matrix. The findings appear to hold out possibilities for investigating the dynamics of change rather well.

Another area for investigation could be the on-going characteristics of smokers. On the basis of data from a smoking clinic we conducted, we developed a three-dimensional model for the characteristics of smokers, on the assumption that there were three probably independent (although we don't have evidence for this) kinds of rewards related to smoking. One of these has to do with the social interrelationships of smoking, the degree to which smoking is part of the cement that ties together social groups. This is an important part of smoking. The second concerns affective factors, which include smoking as a pacifier and tension-releaser, for both externally caused tension and the personal misery of not having a cigarette. The third dimension, which may be more important in young people than in older ones, is the *act* of smoking — the actual gestures of smoking and also its symbolic characteristics as part of the behavior which defines an individual's role to himself and to others.

It might be interesting to look at the differences in the characteristics of hospital or doctors' patients who are and are not affected when they change their smoking habits. We were able to do this in the current study in a minor way. There isn't much you can accomplish by a telephone interview, but we asked several questions to ascertain what people derive from smoking. We were able, rather crudely, to spread people out among two of our three dimensions. We discovered that to a minor but still interesting degree, people who cut down were primarily those for whom smoking was related to affective factors. Oddly enough it was the men, the heavier smokers, who cut down; with them smoking was bound up with intrapersonal concerns. Those who reported that they tended to smoke with people, that it was a *social* rather than intrapersonal behavior, tended to be unaffected by the doctor. And, of course, it makes sense. If smoking is a private business, then you would expect that an influence at one point in time could maintain its effect through a long period of time. On the other hand, if smoking is heavily reinforced by ongoing social relations it is not surprising that an influence at one point in time has relatively little continuing effect.

SUMMARY

This is a study of the influence of two physicians on the smoking habits of their patients. After an initial questionnaire in the doctor's office, there were two follow-ups by telephone: one after seven days, the second in six months. The results revealed that a respected authority can have significant effects upon the smoking habits of individuals.

REFERENCES

Bass, L. W., and Wilson, T. R. The pediatrician's influence in private practice measured by controlled seat belt study. *Pediatrics,* 1964, 33, 700-704.

Katz, E., and Lazarsfeld, P. *Personal Influence.* Free Press: Glencoe, Ill., 1955.

Mausner, B., and Platt, Ellen. *Changing attitudes toward cigarettes and lung cancer,* Beaver College, 1964.

Ravenholt, R. T. and Applegate, J. R. Measurement of smoking experience. *New Eng. J. Med.,* 272, 789-790, Apr. 15, 1965.

DISCUSSION

Jerome Schwartz: What did you do about the occasional smokers who smoke only one to five cigarettes a day? Were they included? Also, I wonder about this whole definition of a "success." I was hoping that there would be a small group of say five or six people at this conference who would get together to try to figure out what we mean by "success," so that we could use the same criterion around the country. For example, take someone who smokes sixty cigarettes a day who cuts down a half a pack. My table shows that's 16 per cent success. If a person starts out smoking forty a day cuts down a half a pack, that's 25 per cent success. This isn't much success.

Bernard Mausner: We had a rather small group of subjects after all, and as I remember it the smoking level in this group is not terribly high; I don't think there were any three-pack-a-day smokers in the group at all. We did not include people who only smoked a couple of cigarettes a day, or who smoked only occasionally. Five to seven cigarettes a day was the minimum to be included in the group we considered as smokers, but they did have to smoke regularly. The half-pack criterion was one of these quick, look-at-the-distribution things. It might have been more elegant to use a relative-change criterion, but as I think about the data, I doubt whether more than one or two of our subjects would have changed over from one group to another if we had applied that kind of criterion. If we do a more eleborate study, we may have to be more rigorous about our criteria of change.

Daniel Horn: It might be rather useful to take Jerome Schwartz's suggestion that we try to set out what the different criteria of success have been for people working in this field, and come to some kind of practical solution.

Smoking Control With an In-Patient General Hospital Population

KENNETH REED
Methodist Hospital, Indianapolis

This study is based upon the phenomenological assumption that a person responds to his world in terms of how he views himself in relation to it. The concept of the self is formed by a combination of many social, psychological, constitutional, and cultural forces. Personality becomes rather firmly established over a period of time, with an increasing resistance to change, and any serious attempt to modify it is likely to produce anxiety and defensive behavior. It is assumed, also, that the hospitalized person, already anxious and fearful by reason of illness, is more amenable to attempts at modifying his smoking behavior than he would otherwise be. Some change in self-image might be demanded anyway, particularly if the patient undergoes surgery or is successfully to manage a medical condition after his discharge from the hospital. In other words, if he is forced to make any change in his self-concept because of illness or hospitalization, this change must be integrated into his total self-concept in order for him to make an adequate adjustment and recovery. So much for our presuppositions.

In March, 1965, we surveyed 1,721 adult patients over 16 years old admitted to the hospital by first asking them, upon admission, whether they smoked. We are presently accumulating follow-up data on these persons. This was the only time they were questioned about their smoking behavior while they were in the hospital. Of these, 44.6 per cent listed themselves as cigarette smokers, including 51.6 per cent of the males and 40.7 per cent of the females. (It should be noted that some patients stopped smoking shortly before admission on their doctor's advice, or voluntarily because of illness. Upon admission, therefore, they sometimes reported themselves as non-smokers.)

The procedure that we have been following in working with patients is getting a selected group of physicians to refer all of their patients to us. They ask us to see all of them and ascertain whether they are smokers or non-smokers. The patients are told that we are there at the request of the physician. With the support of the hospital as well as the smoking-control project personnel in Indianapolis we attempted to evolve a full change in identity, from that of smoker to ex-smoker. It must be kept in mind that many of those interviewed were not always strongly motivated to change their smoking behavior even when it had been medically recommended. In some instances a patient was openly hostile. Many of them had never tried, nor even seriously considered, attempting to control their smoking; others had tried several times to stop with varying degrees of success.

A member of the project staff obtained a "smoking history" for each of the patients involved in the study who was able to be interviewed at bedside. On the basis of these data, we could adjudge an individual's degree of exposure to tobacco, his pattern of smoking, his attitude toward the use of cigarettes, and his knowledge of the relationship between smoking and health. From this we evaluated whether he had any motivation for changing his smoking behavior. We also provided each patient with material about smoking when it seemed appropriate to do so, and invited him to attend the group sessions which were held in the hospital.

We tried to promote these group sessions, in which we showed films and discussed smoking behavior as well as related psychological and sociological factors such as motivation, learning and so forth. However, for a variety of reasons, we did not have a great deal of success getting patients to respond: rarely did anyone attend more than once or twice.

Of the original 1,721 on whom we are in the process of follow-up, there were 263 patients from whom we obtained smoking histories at the end of January. (Of these, 68 were inactivated for various reasons: 40 addresses unknown, 15 died and 13 were inappropriate to be included in the study — they were cigar smokers, or had quit before referral to the hospital, were uncommunicable or uncooperative.) For 93 we had no usable follow-up data.

We divided the balance of 102 into the following categories: 1) whether or not the patient had quit smoking, and 2) whether or not he had cut down by more than 50 per cent, cut down by less than 50 per cent, switched to a pipe, had not changed or had increased his smoking. Our results were these: 26 per cent had quit smoking completely at the time of discharge from the hospital; 15 per cent had cut down their smoking by more than half; 4 per cent by less than half; 2 per cent

TABLE 1

Change in Smoking Behavior, During And After Hospitalization, For Selected Patients At Methodist Hospital of Indiana

The following table is a breakdown of the population (N=102) for whom we have smoking histories and current follow-up data.

A. Represents patients attending at least one group session (N=40)

B. Represents patients interviewed but not attending group sessions (N=62)

C. Represents the total patients interviewed who responded to a letter or phone follow-up as of January 31, 1966 (N=102)

Proportion of patients who changed amount smoked daily:

	Pt. Quit	Cut down 50%+	Cut down less than 50%	Switched to pipe	No change	Smoking increased	Total* No. of Persons
In hospital at the time of interview							
A.	11 (27%)	5 (12%)	2 (5%)	2 (5%)	20 (50%)	0 (0%)	40
B.	16 (26%)	10 (16%)	2 (3%)	0 (0%)	30 (48%)	4 (6%)	62
C.	27 (26%)	15 (15%)	4 (4%)	2 (2%)	50 (49%)	4 (4%)	102
2 Weeks after discharge							
A.	12 (30%)	11 (27%)	6 (15%)	1 (3%)	6 (15%)	4 (10%)	40
B.	17 (27%)	11 (18%)	10 (16%)	0 (0%)	19 (31%)	5 (9%)	62
C.	29 (28%)	22 (22%)	15 (15%)	1 (1%)	25 (25%)	9 (9%)	102
1 Month after discharge							
A.	10 (30%)	7 (21%)	7 (21%)	1 (3%)	4 (12%)	4 (12%)	33
B.	14 (27%)	11 (21%)	9 (17%)	0 (0%)	15 (28%)	5 (9%)	54
C.	24 (28%)	18 (21%)	16 (18%)	1 (2%)	19 (22%)	9 (10%)	87
2 Months after discharge							
A.	7 (41%)	4 (24%)	3 (18%)	0 (0%)	2 (12%)	1 (6%)	17
B.	9 (21%)	9 (21%)	9 (21%)	0 (0%)	11 (26%)	4 (10%)	42
C.	16 (27%)	13 (22%)	12 (20%)	0 (0%)	13 (22%)	5 (8%)	59

*Rounding errors will account for 1% error in some categories if percents are totaled.

had switched to a pipe; and in 49 per cent there was no change. By telephone interview two weeks later, we learned that 28 per cent had quit smoking (an increase of two persons who had quit after discharge from the hospital), 22 per cent had cut down more than half (an increase of 7 persons from the time of discharge), and 15 per cent had cut down less than half (11 more than at the time of discharge). (See Table 1.)

One smoker, for example, told us that she quit only as a result of our initial contact. While it is likely that other forces were operating, this illustrates the dynamics at work in hospitalization on which we are attempting to capitalize in order to bring about sustained reduction in smoking. It also points to the problem of establishing an appropriate control group for this study.

Originally the group of 102 was also divided into 2 groups: Group A, consisting of 40 patients, attended at least one group session. Group B, consisting of 62 patients, for various reasons did not attend a group session. From one day to the next, the number of patients able to attend group sessions varied for several reasons: 1) the physical condition of the patient, 2) the ther-apeutic procedures which were scheduled at the same time, 3) a conflict of the meeting with visiting hours and 4) a patient's rejection of the idea of attending such a session.

In other ways, the two groups are generally comparable. Both had been exposed to the smoking project services through at least an initial contact and a half-hour interview. The project staff members made supplementary visits to many patients in both groups to provide them with information, and encourage participation with the follow-up program.

In the table it will be noted that Groups A and B are comparable in terms of the *proportion of patients* who quit or reduced their smoking upon hospitalization; 50 per cent for Group A and 46 per cent for Group B. For the two-week, one-month and two-month follow-up periods, both groups maintained or increased the degree of withdrawal from cigarette smoking. For both groups, the drop in the number of cigarettes consumed daily upon entering the hospital is statistically significant, and amounts to about one half of a pack. The discrepancy between the number smoked while in the hospital and one month after discharge is *not statistically significant.* Therefore, for the group as a whole, the decrease in smoking upon hospitalization was sustained.

This sustained drop, and the slight decrease after discharge, reflect additional gains in withdrawal made by patients after exposure to the smoking project services, or could be an artifact of this particular population since our numbers are still modest. Our data for the periods beyond one month are still too small to treat statistically with confidence.

We are attempting to form a control group that will minimize distortions from even the superficial contact which our program may introduce. Unfortunately, control group data are not yet available. All of the comparisons with data being presented in this report will have to come temporarily from those populations studied in different situations and be reported elsewhere.

It will be interesting to compare those results with the ones cited above. It occurred to us that those patients who were unsuccessful in achieving control of their smoking would be less likely to return follow-up forms, thereby skewing the results toward a "successful" picture. With this particular sample we made at least one phone call to persons who had not responded by mail. There was no apparent difference in distribution between mail and telephone return with regard to those people who "succeeded" or "failed." It seems, however, that this should be more carefully investigated.

It also occurred to us that attendance at group sessions may be based on motivation, or various personal characteristics of the patient, and that the group becomes a selection factor rather than a causative agent in determining the success in smoking control. This is possible, since group attendance is somewhat moderate, and for reasons already discussed, the majority of patients only get to one or two sessions before they are discharged. When more data are available we may be able to study this possibility more closely, and also determine to what degree success in smoking control might be related to various aspects of our project or the patients' situation.

In any case, work with hospitalized patients seems to be a fruitful avenue for learning about, and implementing, smoking control. Additional data are now beginning to confirm our original findings, namely, that more people are smoking less after they leave the hospital, many more than we originally thought there would be. We attribute this largely to the fact that strong motivation is probably the reason for quitting; although long-range cessation of smoking probably reflects a change in identity.

SUMMARY

This was a project to study the feasibility of a smoking withdrawal program at an in-patient general hospital. Its purpose was to demonstrate that smokers tend to establish their own particular level and pattern of tobacco consumption, to which they are likely to return after that pattern is interrupted. There was also an attempt to find out whether permanent withdrawal may be expected to relate to a sustained strong motivation over-riding the urge to smoke, *or* whether it relates to a change in identity. It was discovered that smoking control does enhance the total treatment program and contribute to long range health goals of hospital patients for whom the relationship of smoking to health is often particularly pertinent. The conscious effort of participating in their own therapy can become, for some, a tension-reducing activity to supplant the tension-reducing behavior of smoking.

Smoking Withdrawal Research Clinics

CHARLES A. ROSS
Roswell Park Memorial Institute
Buffalo, N. Y.

In September 1963, Smoking Withdrawal Research Clinics were started at the Roswell Park Memorial Institute in Buffalo, New York. The purposes of the Clinics were (a) to develop a format which would reach large numbers of people in an uncomplicated fashion in order to influence their smoking habits, and (b) to determine whether a drug or combination of drugs would be of any assistance in withdrawing from cigarettes.

The participants in these clinics, of which there have been twenty-seven held to date, were all volunteers from the community whom we attracted by a simple notice in the newspaper which announced that such clinics were going to be held.

After our first announcement, some 1500 people called and volunteered. We contacted personally about 100 of these people for each clinic. Of these, an average of somewhere between 70 and 75 actually attended. However, at the end of the first week, only 50 per cent of this number were returning for the second session, a rather significant drop-out. It was with those who stayed beyond the second week that we had any measure of success. It is important to note that our volunteer sample probably does not represent a cross-section of the cigarette smoking population. They are, for the most part, people who say they wish to stop smoking, but feel they cannot do it on their own, or people who try to stop and fail. The mere fact that they attend such a clinic does not necessarily mean they are well motivated. Many attend out of curiosity or to occupy an evening.

In the early stages, we experimented to get the most efficient and well-timed meetings. One attempt involved holding the clinics one evening a week for two consecutive weeks. The first of these sessions involved a lecture outlining the relationship of smoking to disease, a brief medical examination, the distribution of pertinent literature and medication. Each participant was given forms to fill out which asked about his smoking and medical history as well as his general background. We also queried the reactions to the idea of smoking withdrawal, medication, etc. The second evening involved answering questions about withdrawal symptoms and other reactions to smoking withdrawal. The participants then openly discussed the various phases of smoking withdrawal and additional medication was passed out. After the first few clinics it became obvious that the course was not sufficiently intense. Many of the participants said they felt abandoned after the second meeting. Others said they felt they would not have smoked again after quitting if they had had an additional program to look forward to. The program format was therefore changed so that meetings were held on five consecutive evenings. This was followed by a three-week period during which there was only one meeting a week. Our results were not much more successful with this procedure, as five evenings were far more than most volunteers were willing to allow: at the end of the first week, only about one-third of the starting group were still in attendance.

The clinics were then changed to one evening per week for four consecutive weeks, followed by monthly meetings on an indefinite basis. People from various clinics attended the monthly meetings.

At the four weekly meetings, a member of the professional staff led discussion and question-and-answer periods for up to one hour. This was followed by a movie, either a documentary or a satire. The clinics were further refined by mailing the forms, to be filled out and collected at the first meeting, to the participants a week in advance. This allowed for more actual participation time during their attendance at the clinic.

Three of the clinics were conduced in a non-educational manner so as to determine how important this aspect was in helping people stop smoking. One such attempt was accomplished by having the participants receive forms and have the medication passed out to them at the pharmacy window. This, however, did not create a clinic suitable for comparison, since they did not meet as a group. Therefore, two other clinics were held in which there were discussions of the medication, and of reactions to smoking withdrawal, but no discussion of the relationship of smoking to disease. Also, the formal educational material and documentary films were withheld. These non-education clinics were highly unsuccessful as compared to the regular clinics.

We used the medication Lobeline, which we manufactured ourselves. We employed it on a double-blind, randomized basis; we did not know who received the

Lobeline and they did not know. In most cases randomization included a placebo. It became necessary to set up a separate randomization for couples since they often would try each other's medication. As it turned out, Lobeline did have some initial effect in helping people give up cigarettes, but it had no long-term effect. As a matter of fact, we found it impossible to continue medication to help people stop smoking beyond a month, and at the end of six months those who had received the active drug were not smoking less than those who had received the placebo. (It was understood by the people who were attending these clinics that some of them would receive placebos.)

I might mention that we did give some of our people nicotine. There was considerable discussion of this by a number of my colleagues, who said that since nicotine was a poison you could not go around giving it to people. But I replied that if the tobacco companies could do it we could do it, too. And so we did give people nicotine in the same amount that they would get from a cigarette, telling them to take one of the capsules of nicotine at any time they wished a cigarette. The only statement that we can make is that nicotine is not a complete substitute for a cigarette. About a third of the people receiving nicotine said that every time they took a capsule they

TABLE 1
Long Term Success, 7th Day Success and Duration Of Long Term Follow-up by Clinic

Clinic Number	Total Clinic Patients	7th Day N	7th Day % Quit*	Long Term N	Long Term % Quit*	No Answer Long Term Follow-up	Number Weeks Long Term Follow-up
2	51	32	62.74	14	27.45	0	56.8
3	57	31	54.38	11	19.29	1	52.8
4	49	20	40.81	8	16.32	0	48.6
5	52	17	32.69	11	21.15	2	46.8
6	49	26	53.06	10	20.40	1	43.5
7	60	27	45.00	9	15.00	0	38.8
8**	63	19	30.15	4	6.34	3	37.8
9	38	15	39.47	8	21.05	2	33.8
10	65	8	12.30	11	16.92	6	28.8
11	63	17	26.98	8	12.69	5	25.0
12	69	22	31.88	4	5.79	2	20.0
13	56	18	32.14	8	14.28	3	16.0
14	32	7	21.87	2	6.25	1	43.6
15	53	20	37.73	11	20.75	0	39.6
16	68	37	54.41	8	11.76	0	27.3
17	67	21	31.34	14	20.89	0	25.3
18	60	15	25.00	16	26.66	0	22.1
19**	86	18	20.93	10	11.62	0	21.4
20**	86	16	18.60	5	5.81	1	20.8
21	89	38	42.69	18	20.22	0	17.7
22	82	30	36.58	18	21.95	0	17.5
23	82	28	34.14	17	20.73	0	14.4
24	95	32	33.68	19	20.00	1	10.4
Total	1472	514	34.91	244	16.57	28	30.82

*No answer to 7 Day (238 cases) and long term follow-up (28 cases) were counted as failures.
**"No education" clinics.

TABLE 2
7th Day Success by Sex and Medication

Medication*	Males Stopped Total	N	%	Females Stopped Total	N	%	Total Stopped Total	N	%
5 mg. Lobeline plus 8 mg. Amphetamine	210	97	46.19	223	73	32.73	433	170	39.26
5 mg. Lobeline plus Amphetamine Placebo	59	19	32.20	64	14	21.87	123	33	26.82
8 mg. Amphetamine plus Lobeline Placebo	56	20	35.71	64	16	25.00	120	36	30.00
Lobeline Placebo plus Amphetamine Placebo	209	78	37.32	205	53	25.85	414	131	31.64
5 mg. Nicotine plus 8 mg. Amphetamine	15	4	26.66	21	3	14.28	36	7	19.44
10 mg. Methamphetamine plus 60 mg. Pentobarbital	24	12	50.00	21	9	42.85	45	21	46.66
10 mg. Methamphetamine	20	5	25.00	23	11	47.82	43	16	37.20
8 mg. Amphetamine no Lobeline Placebo	18	8	44.44	23	9	39.13	41	17	41.46
Amphetamine Placebo only	24	7	29.16	17	6	35.29	41	13	31.70
0.5 mg. Lobeline lozenges	53	21	39.62	44	12	27.27	97	33	34.02
Lobeline Placebo lozenges	40	18	45.00	40	9	22.50	80	27	33.75
	728	289	39.69	745	215	28.85	1473	504	34.21

*Dosage: 5 mg. Lobeline — Twice a day, morning and evening

8 mg. Amphetamine — Once a day, on arising

5 mg. Nicotine — Twice a day, morning and evening

10 mg. Methamphetamine with or without 60 mg. Pentobarbital — Once a day on arising

0.5 mg. Lobeline — As needed

wanted a cigarette more. So there must be other things in cigarettes that make people want to smoke.

The results of these clinics may be found in Tables 1 and 2. While various factors appear to influence the ability to stop smoking, an understanding of the relationship between smoking and disease appeared to be the most important.

SUMMARY

Smoking withdrawal research clinics have been held at Roswell Park Memorial Institute, Buffalo, New York, since September, 1963. Clinics consist of 50 to 100 volunteers from the community and are held in the evening, once weekly, for four consecutive weeks. Educational material is presented and audience participation encouraged. Approximately 35 per cent immediately stopped smoking and over the long term the withdrawal was approximately 20 per cent. An appreciation of the relationship between cigarette smoking and disease appeared to be the most significant factor relating to successful withdrawal.

DISCUSSION

Charles Ross: I would like to point out also that we were very much interested in determining whether an authoritative medical approach to the relationship between smoking and disease would make any difference in the success of people in quitting. So we held two clinics in which this approach was not used. We discussed with them their withdrawal symptoms; we discussed with them any kinds of reactions that they might have to the medication they received or to smoking withdrawal, but refrained from drawing any correlation whatsoever between smoking and disease. At these clinics there was only a 5 per cent success rate; but in the clinics in which there was presented a rather authoritative explanation of the relationship between smoking and disease, the success rate was between 16 and 20 per cent.

In all of the clinics the men appeared to be uniformly more successful than the women in giving up cigarettes. Married men did almost twice as well as single men; but married women did no better in giving up cigarettes completely than did single women.

The fact that they felt that they should stop smoking for medical reasons did not influence the success rate at all. About a third of the people had indicated medical reasons among those for wanting to quit. The success rate for them was 16 per cent, which was roughly the average of the success rate for other groups.

We have not as yet put together all of our data concerning those things which seemed to help people while they were in the process of giving up smoking. Also, we have only had brief opportunity to interpret the psychological materials yielded by our study. Again, it appears that those who are the most stable emotionally are the ones who are most successful in giving up cigarettes, and those who are least stable actually smoked more cigarettes as a result of attending the clinics, rather than quitting.

Success in giving up smoking on a long-term basis appears to be cued to initial success. Those who have not been able to quit by the seventh day have almost uniformly been unable to give up smoking beyond that time. (I should like to emphasize that our 16 to 20 per cent success rate includes only those people who are not smoking at all after six months or more.)

Joan Guilford: Our project people kept a five-day record; we also found that the over-all best predictor of success was success in the first five days. If they didn't make it by then, they were very unlikely ever to bother to try again.

Charles Ross: It should be pointed out that we tried to call personally about 100 people for each clinic. Somewhere between 70 and 75 of those who said they would come did show up. After the first week, an average of 50 per cent returned for the second meeting. So there is a rather rapid drop-out, and it is only among those that stay with us beyond the second week that we have any measure of success.

Daniel Horn: Here we have two cases where initial success is the predictor of future success. We conducted a study using two groups of 165 each. We used an entirely different approach, in which we tried to get people to keep on smoking during the course and engage in all sorts of de-conditioning, re-learning processes. Only about three per cent were off smoking at the end of the course, but by the end of the year it had gone up to 15 per cent. That's a long-term process! So the finding that initial success is a predictor of eventual success is conditioned by the fact that this was the intent of the course and these people were doing what they were told to do. With a different set of expectations, it can work in the opposite direction.

Kenneth Reed: In our study at the hospital (pp. 107 ff.) the same data are beginning to turn up: that results in time tend to get better; more people are smoking less after they leave the hospital than we originally thought there would be. We attribute this to a kind of softsell, that in the case of initial success the factor of continued strong motivation is probably the reason for quitting; but in long-range discontinuance it may be a change in identity.

Percy Tannenbaum: Dr. Ross, did the group who received the nicotine pills know they were getting nicotine pills?

Charles Ross: They were told they were getting nicotine, yes.

Daniel Horn: You didn't use nicotine injections?

Charles Ross: No, we did not.

Bruce Straits: You said it didn't work because one-third of the group on nicotine indicated they still desired cigarettes, but what about the other two-thirds?

Charles Ross: Some of them said it helped, that after taking a capsule of nicotine it reduced the desire for cigarettes. About a third said it had no effect at all, and about a third said that it increased their desire.

Bruce Straits: Can you compare this with the other groups to determine whether this was just a placebo effect?

Charles Ross: Well, the whole purpose in giving the nicotine was to try to answer, if possible, the question that has been brought up by many; that is, is it the nicotine in the cigarette that people are addicted to? My results have convinced me that, although there is something about nicotine that produces a physiological response, making it one of the reasons why people smoke, that it is not the *only* reason why people smoke.

Methodology of the Smoking Control Research Project[1]

JEROME L. SCHWARTZ
and MILDRED DUBITZKY
The Institute of Social and
Personal Relations
Berkeley, California

INTRODUCTION

During the 1965 National Conference on the Behavioral Aspects of Smoking, the methodology of previous smoking control studies was subjected to critical analysis (Mausner, B. and Platt, Ellen S., 1965). Among the deficiencies noted were the use of subjects from a single age group, too few subjects to permit meaningful comparisons, and the use of inappropriate controls. Specifically, many investigators recruited *students* as subjects instead of members of the general adult population. Although it is certainly important to study the smoking habits of younger people and to help them quit, methods tested among students may not apply to an adult population with different social and demographic characteristics, and different smoking habits.

It is often difficult to attract large numbers of adult volunteers for smoking control programs. Furthermore, even among adult groups, people who *volunteer* for such procedures may be different from other smokers in significant ways. Therefore, the characteristics of the population from which the study sample is drawn must be investigated.

Another problem inherent in smoking studies is that of securing adequate control groups. For example, subjects who *refuse* to participate in a control effort, or *fail* to show up for a scheduled meeting, are sometimes used as controls. A "control" subject, in the true experimental sense, comes from the *same population* as experimental subjects, meets the same selection criteria, and has undergone the same procedures *prior* to the start of the treat-

ment (Group for the Advancement of Psychiatry, 1959; Mainland, D., 1958; Kish, L., 1959). Furthermore, control subjects should be randomly assigned *at the same time* that experimental subjects are selected.

In smoking control studies dealing with the general population, it is unrealistic to attribute the subject's success or failure to the *treatment method alone,* without considering current environmental or situational factors. The ecological setting, including attitudes of the family, pressures on the subject, and events that occur during the treatment period, may significantly affect the outcome of the change effort.

The Smoking Control Research Project, which began in July, 1964, has attempted to solve some of these problems in research design. It represents an experimental effort to evaluate three methods of helping smokers to break the habit. The study was designed as rigorously as possible. For example, large numbers of adult smokers were recruited for treatment methods and matched controls were carefully chosen. Provisions were also made to examine the possible effect of environmental factors which lay outside the scope of the treatment methods.

Aims of the Study

The study is organized to answer the following questions:

1. What are the smoking habits and general characteristics of the population from which the subjects participating in smoking control methods are drawn?
2. What differences (if any) exist among smokers, ex-smokers, and those who have never smoked?
3. What differences exist between smokers who are *willing* and those *unwilling* to participate in smoking control methods?
4. Are there different types or classes of smokers?
5. What factors sustain the cigarette-smoking habit?
6. Do certain specified methods help people to stop smoking?
7. What is the nature of the change process itself?
8. What socio-psychological factors influence the ability to give up smoking and to resist recidivism?

[1] Dr. Schwartz is Project Director and Dr. Dubitzky is Research Psychologist for the smoking Control Research Project. Dr. Schwartz is also lecturer in Social Welfare, University of California, Berkeley. The study is sponsored jointly by the Institute of Social and Personal Relations, Berkeley, and by the Permanente Medical Group-Kaiser Foundation Health Plan, Walnut Creek, California. Neil E. Anderson, M.D., Medical Director for the Project and Frederick A. Pellegrin, M.D., consultant, represent The Permanente Medical Group on the Project Committee.

This project is supported by Cancer Demonstration Grant No. 05–15–C66 from the Division of Chronic Diseases, United States Public Health Service, Department of Health, Education and Welfare.

Study Population

The study population consists of all male members of the Kaiser Foundation Health Plan-Permanente Medical Group, 25-44 years of age, living in central or eastern Contra Costa County, California. The Kaiser Foundation Health Plan is a large prepaid group practice plan with a broad membership including all socio-economic classes, although minority groups and families in the lowest economic stratum are under-represented. In general, the study population comprises white, married, employed men, many of whom have small children. The study was restricted to men in just four 5-year age groups, so as to reduce the number of independent variables.

This study population forms the basis for the three phases of the Smoking Project: 1) the Mail Questionnaire Survey; 2) the Treatment Methods; and 3) the Wives' Study.

THE MAIL QUESTIONNAIRE SURVEY

To identify smokers willing and able to participate in smoking control methods and to determine the characteristics of the entire population from which they came, we used as our principal instrument an eight-page survey questionnaire. We also used it to study characteristics of smokers, ex-smokers, and never-smokers, since it was administered to all classes of the population. Included are items relating to personal history; sociological and psychological variables; health status and use of medical care; and attitude toward accepting professional help with personal problems. Smoking habits and attitudes are examined in detail, including satisfaction with and concern over smoking, and willingness to stop.

The survey questionnaire contains part of the Personal Security Inventory developed by Knutson (1952), and nationally used attitude-toward-smoking items developed by Horn and Waingrow.[2] Both the mail questionnaire and instruments used among treatment subjects include items to test the validity of "typology of smokers" classifications proposed by Silvan Tomkins (1965).

The eight-page questionnaire was mailed to a one-in-seven (N=1203) random sample of the total study population. In addition, a four-page questionnaire was mailed to the remainder (N=7081) for the purpose of identifying smokers willing to quit smoking. The two survey questionnaires were developed after two pre-tests among randomly selected members of the same population for which the survey was intended.

---

[2] "Study of Behavior and Attitudes," PHS-T278, Study #1-466, October, 1964.

Questionnaire Returns

Pre-test experience had demonstrated the effectiveness of repeated contacts with subjects in eliciting the highest returns possible. Therefore, at least two follow-up letters were sent to all non-respondents. Those who still had not answered were telephoned. Even people who had at first refused, later agreed to cooperate when telephoned by a staff member. Subjects who did not have telephone numbers were visited personally to elicit their cooperation.

The random-sample survey yielded eight pages of detail information about the following three groups: smokers who were later assigned to a control group; smokers *unwilling* to participate in smoking clinic methods; and smokers who were later assigned to the various treatment groups.

THE TREATMENT METHODS

The treatment phase of the project is devoted mainly to an evaluation of three methods of helping people to stop smoking: 1) Prescription; 2) Individual Counseling; and 3) Group Counseling. The three treatments differ along dimensions of social and professional support, although all three are designed to allay anxiety caused by abstention from cigarette smoking. The prescription treatment reduces anxiety by means of medication alone; the counseling methods, by the additional factor of professional intervention. The group experience includes in addition, mutual involvement and cohesion among the members.

All smokers who answered either the four-page or the eight-page questionnaire and indicated at least minimal motivation to stop smoking were invited to participate in methods to help them quit smoking. Specifically they were asked to attend an *Intake* session, consisting of several socio-psychological tests and questionnaires. About 460 subjects completed Intake, and more than 400 of these also carried out the next step — a brief medical screening interview with an internist from the Permanente Medical Group. The doctor took basic physiological measurements and inquired as to current health status, previous use of tranquilizers, and other medication.

Our success in "recruiting" enough subjects to fill the requirements of the study may be attributed to the methods we employed, or to the growing popular awareness of the dangers of cigarette smoking, or both.

Structural Composition of the Treatment Methods

The study population was already homogeneous as to sex, and limited in age distribution. Since there is some evidence that factors associated with socio-economic status may affect the outcome of the various treatment methods, social class was controlled. First, all subjects were assigned to one of five social classes, according to the Hollingshead Two-Factor Index based on education and occupation (modified by taking income into account). Three main groupings emerged: I-II (the highest class); III; and IV-V (the lowest).

Next, to eliminate statistically the effect of social class on treatment outcome, subjects in the three social classes were assigned equally to each method: Prescription, Individual Counseling, and Group Counseling. Where counseling was provided, the various counselors also saw equal numbers from each social class, distributed evenly into tranquilizer and placebo groupings within the methods. The nine counseling groups are homogeneous with regard to social class, not only to control for that variable, but also to facilitate the development of cohesion and rapport (through similarity of backgrounds) among members of each group. Each counselor led three groups, one of each social class. (The no-pill group is composed of a different social class for each counselor.) Individual counselors also saw an equal number of persons in each social class.

Controls

Two groups of controls, I and II, (each one 36 in number) were selected, at different stages of the research. Table 1 shows the major differences among Con-

TABLE 1

Study Phases Completed by Controls and Treatment Subjects Smoking Control Research Project

	Control I	Control II	Treatment Subjects
Number	36	36	252
Detailed 8-page Questionnaire	X	X	X
Appointment for Intake (Willing to enter study)	X	X	X
Complete Intake (Psychological test and other instruments)		X	X
Complete Medical (Medically approved and willing to enter treatment)		X	X
Enter Treatment			X

trols I and II, and the treatment subjects regarding their exposure to experimental procedures. The second control group more closely resembles the final study population.

The first control (Control I) was intended to measure the effect of the questionnaire alone. The group was purposely chosen from among smokers who had completed the eight-page questionnaire, to ensure a maximum amount of information. They were all telephoned and invited to participate in methods to stop smoking, in the same way as regular treatment subjects. Anyone

who accepted was given an Intake appointment. A few days before their scheduled appointments, Control I subjects were again telephoned and told that they could not be included in the study, after all, because there were already enough participants from their locality.[3] Thus, Control I individuals had been equally motivated to participate at the start (before Intake).

Control II subjects, on the other hand, were randomly chosen from all those who had completed *all* the steps preliminary to entering treatment, including the eight-page survey questionnaire and the Intake procedures. They had also shown up for their medical interview appointments, and had been approved by internists for participation in the study. As with Control I, they were telephoned and told that the study quotas were already filled and they could not participate. Both control groups (I and II) contain an equal number of persons from each of the three social-class groupings.

Assignment of Subjects to Treatment Methods

After intake and medical screening, about 400 prospective treatment subjects were left, all of whom were willing and able to enter the study. This number was adequate to fill the requirements of the research design (288 subjects). Subjects were *randomly* assigned to treatments, with the restriction that all methods had to contain an equal number of persons from each social class. Moreover, each treatment method contained an equal number of tranquilizer and placebo subjects *within* each social class. Subjects were assigned to tranquilizer or placebo sub-groups *after* being placed in one of the treatment methods. Since all study assignments were made by a statistical consultant *outside* the project staff, the procedure fulfills the requirements of a double-blind design: counselors did not know which clients were assigned placebos. Subjects were told that the pills being distributed were tranquilizers.

Description of Treatment Methods

The following is a brief description of the treatment methods employed in the present study. Table 2 shows the distribution of subjects to treatment methods by type of medication.

1. *Prescription Method* (P). Seventy-two subjects, 24 from each of the three social classes, were assigned randomly to this method. Half of the subjects in each social class received tranquilizers, while the other half received placebos identical in appearance.

[3] Note that Control subjects were told that they were *out of* the study, *not* that they were on a "waiting list" to be contacted later. The latter message might have influenced the subject to postpone his quitting effort until he could actually enter the study. (The frustration induced by eliminating a subject from the program at this late stage may in itself constitute a new variable, and we did not wish to complicate the matter further.)

TABLE 2

Distribution of Subjects to Controls and Treatment Methods by Type of Medication Smoking Control Research Project

		Control I Question- naire Only	Control II Intake & Medical	Prescription	Individual Counseling	Group Dynamics
Totals	324	36	36	72	72	108
Controls	72	36	36			
Tranquilizers	108			36	36	36
Placebo	108			36	36	36
No Prescription	36					36

As with the other two methods, the treatment period lasted eight weeks, starting with the date of the first prescription. The pill supplies were delivered in bottles labeled with the subject's name to the Kaiser Clinic Pharmacy, where subjects picked them up at two-week intervals. In addition, they received a letter containing "Tips" about how to stop smoking, and literature on the dangers of smoking. Unused pills were to be returned to the pharmacy every two weeks, along with the Daily Smoking and Pill Records for that period.

2. *Individual Counseling* (IC). Seventy-two subjects, again equally divided into the three social classes, participated in the individual counseling method. Their treatment was to meet privately with a trained counselor once a week for 20-minute sessions over the eight-week period. They also received medication; half of them receiving tranquilizers and half placebos, and the same "Tips" and other literature given to Prescription subjects were made available to these subjects.

IC subjects were assigned to one of four professionally trained counselors. Although each counselor saw equal numbers of people in each social class, half of whom were prescribed tranquilizers and the other half placebos, the four counselors did not see the same number of "clients." Pills were distributed each week by the counselor, directly to subjects. All sessions were recorded by Dictaphone.

The counseling sessions were originally intended merely to support the subject in his attempt to quit smoking. As the study developed, however, we decided to allow the counselors greater freedom in choosing an approach. Thus, the discussion did not have to be restricted to the smoking issue, but could include other areas of importance in the subject's life.

3. *Group Method.* In all, 108 subjects were assigned to the group counseling method. Nine separate groups were formed, six of them receiving medication and three receiving no pill. Half the members of each "pill group"

were given tranquilizers while the other half were given placebos. The groups were homogeneous as to social class, and divided equally among the three main classes. The groups were assigned equally to each of three experienced group counselors, all of whom had received training in psychology at the master's level or beyond. Each counselor thus had three groups, one of each social class, two with pills and one without. The no-pill group was composed of a different social class for each psychologist. Pills were distributed each week to group subjects by the psychologist.

The groups met once a week, for 90 minutes each time, during the eight-week treatment period. All sessions were tape-recorded. Over all, efforts were made to keep the subjects interested throughout the sessions by allowing a free range of discussion (as in the Individual Counseling). The "Tips" and literature were also offered. In general, the aim was to maximize the development of group cohesion, as the principal factor in facilitating behavior change. A conference was held with the project staff and all the group counselors early in the treatment to discuss the progress being made and to consider other possible approaches.

General Program

Although the methods differed in many ways, *all* subjects were exposed to certain general influences:

1. *Length of Treatment* — Each method lasted for eight weeks.

2. *Quitting Date* — All subjects were asked to select a date by which they would be entirely off cigarettes. Prescription subjects chose this date by themselves; Individual Counseling subjects with their counselors; and Group subjects did it with the other group members.

3. *Progress Records* — All subjects were required to keep detailed daily records showing the number of cigarettes, cigars, and pipes smoked at different times. Those receiving medication also noted the number of pills taken each day. These daily smoking and pill record cards were intended as aids to quitting as well as progress records for the research project.

4. *Educational Materials* — Pamphlets and bulletins were offered to all subjects, at regular intervals during the treatment period. The project committee also sponsored a program of films about smoking, to which subjects and their families and friends were invited. All subjects, whether or not they developed weight problems in the course of trying to stop smoking, were offered consultation with a trained nutritionist. The literature was not a requirement, but was made available to subjects if they wanted to read it. It was not intended to "scare" smokers, but rather to present some facts (e.g., "A Summary of the Surgeon General's Report") or to help them quit (diets, "tips," etc.).

Research Instruments

Before the treatment program, all subjects had completed the eight-page survey questionnaire and Intake materials described above. Upon entering treatment, all subjects filled out a special intake form, providing information about recent changes in smoking habits and other data of importance. The medication-only group filled out no further forms until the end of the treatment period. The Individual and Group Counseling subjects, however, completed a variety of instruments at regular intervals, having to do with smoking habits and attitudes, self-esteem, feelings about the method, and so forth. These tests, most of them already administered at Intake, were designed to measure various aspects of the change process during the treatment period. At the end of the final week, a new set of forms was distributed to subjects in all three methods. These included the personality-and-attitude change instruments, plus detailed questions about present smoking status.

Analysis

Data from the survey and intake instruments will be analyzed in detail. Treatment data will be analyzed mainly to investigate the following factors:

1. Dropout rate in each method.
2. Rate and extent of success in giving up cigarette smoking.
3. Validity of success-predictive measures.
4. Psycho-social factors associated with behavior change.

Follow-ups

The first follow-up is scheduled for four months after the end of the eight-week treatment period. A second and final follow-up will occur eight months later (one year after the treatment ends). This last follow-up may be conducted by telephone or personal interview instead of by mail questionnaire. An attempt will be made to contact subjects who have *succeeded* in quitting and remaining off cigarettes, to explore the process of resistance to recidivism.

THE WIVES STUDY

Early in the study the project committee became aware of the need to investigate the influence of marital and family relationships on the subject's attempt to give up smoking.

The project committee, in collaboration with a team of twelve social work graduate students from the School of Social Welfare, University of California, undertook to study the wives of treatment subjects. The wives of *all* treatment subjects were included, rather than a subsample, to avoid introducing another uncontrolled variable into the main study.

This auxiliary study consists of two steps: a survey questionnaire and a home interview. First, a specially constructed mail questionnaire was sent to the wives of all the subjects in the three methods. (All but two per cent of the 252 subjects were married.) The questionnaire inquired into the wife's smoking habits and attitudes; her education, health and work status; and other factors.

Next, all wives willing to participate were interviewed in their homes. The interview schedule probes more deeply into the wife's influence on her husband's smoking patterns; and her estimate of how, if at all, the project has changed him. Questions are also asked regarding the marital relationship and possible environmental stresses affecting her husband.

SUMMARY

The Smoking Control Research Project was an attempt to compare three methods designed to help people stop smoking. In addition, the study includes two other parts: the Survey, and the Wives Study.

The study population comprised 8284 men (aged 25-44), all members of the Kaiser Foundation Health Plan, living in Contra Costa County, California. From this total group, a one-in-seven random sample was chosen to receive an eight-page mail survey questionnaire. Shorter forms were sent to the remainder. Responses of the random sample constituted the survey phase of the study, which aimed to characterize the population from which treatment participants were drawn.

The principal aim of the study is to make a definitive evaluation of certain smoking control methods, but there are other very important considerations. We realize, for example, that not all methods work equally well for all smokers. The present study attempts to reveal the dynamics underlying the smoking habit, and thereby to "diagnose" types of smokers and prescribe appropriate treatments. Social class, problems of motivation, and environmental conditions are also taken into account.

The selection of the present treatment methods was governed more by custom than by conviction. Although other methods exist, tranquilizers are prescribed so frequently by doctors, and counseling is used so extensively to change behavior, that it seemed most worthwhile to investigate these instead of less well-known, possibly more effective treatments. No definitive study has been made of the effectiveness of these devices in helping people to stop smoking. Hopefully, the results of the present study will provide a much-needed empirical basis for the choice of smoking control programs — a choice which has hitherto been governed largely by tradition.

Of the questionnaire respondents who were minimally motivated to quit smoking, those who completed intake instruments and medical screening were randomly assigned to treatment and control groups (N=324). The three methods — Prescription, Individual Counseling (with medication), and Group Counseling (with and without medication) — varied along the dimension of professional support, but all were designed to allay the anxiety that usually results from the attempt to give up cigarettes. Social class was controlled in each method. A double-blind design was followed in distributing tranquilizers and placebos to subjects. Special forms were administered to assess the subjects' progress, the nature of the change process, and the socio-psychological factors which influence the ability to give up smoking and resist recidivism.

The Wives Study employed mail surveys and home interviews to determine the effect of the wife and the home environment on a man's attempt to stop smoking.

In addition to evaluating certain specified smoking control methods, the study further attempted to investigate the dynamics underlying the smoking habit in order to "diagnose" types of smokers and prescribe appropriate treatments.

REFERENCES

Group for the Advancement of Psychiatry: *Some Observations on Controls in Psychiatric Research*, Report No. 42, The Group Publication Office, New York (May, 1959), 537–624.

Kish, Leslie. "Some Statistical Problems in Research Design," *American Sociological Review*, 24, 3 (June, 1959), 328–338.

Knutson, Andie L. "Personal Security as Related to Station in Life," *Psychological Monographs*, 66, 4: 1–31, American Psychological Association, Washington, D. C., 1952.

Mainland, Donald. "Notes on the Planning and Evaluation of Research, with Examples from Cardiovascular Investigations, Part 1," *American Heart Journal*, 55, 5 (May, 1958), 644–655.

Mausner, Bernard, and Platt, Ellen S. *Proceedings of the Conference on Behavioral Aspects of Smoking.* Glenside, Pa.: Beaver College (September, 1965).

Tomkins, Silvan S. "Psychological Model for Smoking Behavior." Paper presented at the Annual Meeting of the American Public Health Association, Chicago, Ill., Oct. 20, 1965.

DISCUSSION

Jerome Schwartz: Our preliminary data on quitting were based on the first 50 per cent return and I believe these rates will go down when other questionnaire data are analyzed. We first made a percentage reduction table and made a somewhat arbitrary definition of success: 85 per cent or more reduction in cigarette smoking. We thought perhaps we could get some help here at the Conference about different alternatives to this procedure. At any rate, there were 47 per cent who quit totally;

three per cent reduced their smoking by 85 to 99 per cent; another 11 per cent reduced by two-thirds to 84 per cent; 14 per cent reduced by one-half to two-thirds, meaning that 75 per cent of the people reduced their smoking by at least half. Then there were another six per cent who reduced by 33 to 49 per cent; six per cent more reduced by 16 to 32 per cent; and a final ten per cent reduced 15 per cent or less. When we left Berkeley, there were approximately 30 in each of the two control groups who had been telephoned, and there were four so far in each of the controls who had quit, which would be about 13 per cent.

After we heard Mr. Allen speak yesterday, Mildred Dubitzky and I figured out what happened to our people from the time they were selected for the study. We have those data, if anyone is interested in how you get from 8200 people down to 300. Where do they fall out?

Howard Leventhal: Did the control groups know they were control subjects?

Jerome Schwartz: No, they didn't.

Howard Leventhal: They didn't think that they were *expected* to stop smoking?

Jerome Schwartz: That's right, they did not. They might even have thought that they would come in some other time, although we didn't tell them that. We told them that we had too many people volunteering for the study and that we were very sorry but they could not participate in the study then or at a later date. I should think most of them felt very badly about not being accepted, because it was kind of a dirty trick to make them go through all the things they went through and then not include them.

Daniel Horn: Do you think they stopped smoking just to spite the research project?

Jerome Schwartz: I again appeal for some people who are interested in the criterion-of-success problem to get together, if it's possible, because if we used 50 per cent reduction as a criterion, as some of the other studies do, we'd be getting a 75 per cent success rate.

Daniel Horn: I can't help but feel that you are creating an artificial problem if you just want to get a definition of success and failure. I think that, just as a methodological consideration, your problem is that of what you can do with the data. How many cases do you have? What kind of categories can you define and get an adequate distinction? You have people who abstained completely, people who dropped off sharply, people who dropped off moderately, and people who dropped off only slightly. You may have to throw them together just to get adequate numbers. I'm sure you can't set up one set of criteria for success versus failure that everybody will follow because I don't think this is the problem. You're bound by the kind of data you have and the number of cases you have.

SYMPOSIUM:
Cessation Processes — Theoretical and Practical Implications of Reported Research

Moderator
DANIEL HORN

Discussants

FRANK BARRON   PERCY TANNENBAUM

BERNARD MAUSNER   SILVAN TOMKINS

DOROTHY NYSWANDER

SUMMARY

Frank Barron compares the success ratio in smoking treatment programs with that in psychotherapy and related treatment programs. Ego strength is seen as a unifying concept in the success of treatment. Sexual differences in ego strength are related to sexual differences in treatment success. Barron proposes that variables used to predict success in psychotherapy be used in smoking clinic programs; recommends that criterion-specific prediction scales be evolved through item-analyses of currently existing scales. Howard Leventhal urges a further consideration of the concept of motivation in treatment programs. Other parallels are drawn between the aims of psychotherapeutic programs and those of smoking programs. The problem of sampling in determining the effectiveness of treatment programs is examined. Sex differences are compared for a variety of treatment programs. The importance to the cessation process of ego strength, which Frank Barron has demonstrated to be a multi-dimensional variable, is questioned by Silvan Tomkins, who prefers to relate success and failure in treatment programs to achievement striving and the need for (social) affiliation. Sex (and personality) differences are related to situational factors in smoking behavior and treatment. Richard Jones relates smoking to conformity to group norms and discusses the concept of "norm-sensitive" behavior. The need for the study of personality differences between smokers and non-smokers. The question of addiction. Silvan Tomkins distinguishes between psychological and physiological addiction. The reliability and validity of self-reports in cessation studies is discussed.

The role of the physician is agreed to be a potentially crucial one in cessation programs. But the pressures of time, and his lack of specific information on the consequences of smoking are seen as serious deterrents to his willingness to participate in a cessation program. Research on action programs with physicians' cooperation was urged. Programmed instruction is suggested as a means of overcoming the problem of expense in treatment programs but is believed to have limited usefulness. Alternative methods to encourage cessation are reviewed: the effects of filling out questionnaires; government-sponsored educational television; demonstration projects; the traditional "lecture and slide technique." Mass screening programs are proposed to uncover preliminary signs of physiological dysfunction attributable to smoking.

Overview: *Frank Barron summarizes the panel's views on the link between the success ratio of smoking treatment programs and that of psychotherapy, with emphasis on the sex and ego strength variables. Silvan Tomkins reiterates his preference for "achievement orientation" and "sociophilia" as predictive variables. Percy Tannenbaum argues against conducting more post hoc studies in favor of experiments soundly based in theory which would enable prediction of success or failure. Dorothy Nyswander draws a parallel between smoking research and family-planning research in India: the costs of implementation are prohibitive. Jerome Schwartz counters with evidence from his own (ISPR) Project. Daniel Horn summarizes problems of research on cessation processes: the frequently temporary nature of cessation; the need for a research shift from the relative success of intervention methods to the dynamics of the cessation process itself: "What happens to people when they give up smoking?" The question of pay-off: level of success of cessation processes, and the number influenced; the potential help from mass media, physicians, and all others in the health professions. Finally, the overriding problem of logistics.*

Frank Barron: What has impressed me in these papers on Cessation Processes was the fair consistency in reports of the number of cases that improved and the considerable agreement between those average figures and the figures one finds over many years of research with psychotherapy in general. One finds improvement in psychotherapy in about 66 per cent of the cases, where 50 per cent would be expected by chance. This applies not only in psychotherapy for problems where the presenting symptoms are simple distress in interpersonal relations, but also in treatment programs for conditions such as obesity, where the motive is to reduce one's weight.

Dr. Ross has observed that the more stable subjects were the more successful in quitting. Perhaps the important variable is the one we found most significant in the psychotherapy studies — namely, *ego strength at the beginning of the program of treatment.* It appears that the higher the ego strength to begin with, the more likely the patient will be to make use of the therapeutic process to improve or to solve his problems.

Further, there is a sex difference similar to that reported by Dr. Guilford: men with high ego strength are much more likely to reject the therapeutic treatment itself after the first few initial interviews, but when they are tested again at the end of six months, they show equal success. For example, in reduction of scores on scales measuring psychoneurotic tendencies equal to that of the male patients who stay in treatment. This is not true of women. The women patients who stay in treatment are those with higher ego strength to begin with, and, further, they show improvement; those who drop out do not. I am suggesting that in programs designed to reduce cigarette smoking among persons who indicate some desire to quit, the processes involved may be very similar to those involved in psychotherapy.

If one half the patients who apply for psychotherapy are assigned to treatment and the other half to a waiting list, those on the waiting list usually show some improvement even without treatment. Merely having decided to seek treatment may itself have a good effect.

The kinds of tests that have been successful in predicting response to psychotherapy should be employed in some of these smoking-clinic programs. Further, I think the most important thing is that specific predictors in the form of personality scales should be developed against the criterion of quitting. That is, one should do initial testing, determine the outcome six months later, and then go back and item-analyze the original test responses. Not only should currently existing scales be item-analyzed, but new scales should be created which embody all the knowledge that one gains from looking at persons trying to quit smoking. From these, criterion-specific prediction scales can be evolved.

Howard Leventhal: Since I have never smoked, smoking has always seemed to me like a simple response. Isn't it conceivable that in the process of trying to stop smoking we bring into play a set of motives that require "psychotherapy" for the change to occur? If we didn't introduce these motives into the change situation, it might not become an issue of personality change. It might simply be an issue of modifying a single response. If this could be done, then the predictive variables, the factors that would count, would not necessarily be things like ego strength.

Frank Barron: Some of the evidence suggests that the psychotherapeutic process itself may not be the crucial factor. As far as those patients simply on a waiting list are concerned, one can say, "Well, it initiated a process." Maybe all it really involved was making a decision that they wanted to change, and thereafter those with higher ego strength tended to change. Once the process was thus started they didn't need the other kind of psychodynamic interpretations. Dr. Guilford's paper suggested that will power was one of the reasons given by the men who succeeded. Perhaps ego strength as a character variable would tend to predict who would be able to quit without psychotherapeutic aid.

Howard Leventhal: Even with respect to the will-power variable, that might be because the subject is blind to the fact that it controls the response. Individual differences in will power are irrelevant to learning to tie a shoe lace, and if the determinants of the response are made so clear to everyone that in fact they can't then manipulate the determinants themselves, it may cease to be an issue of will power.

Percy Tannenbaum: Indeed, whether it is true or not, if we can convince them that it has nothing to do with the ego to begin with, but that it's a simple conditioned response, thus merely a matter of *unconditioning,* this may be a form of therapy in getting them to stop smoking. That is to say that people come into the situation believing that it depends upon their ego strength. If they have some doubts about their ego strength to begin with, they won't be too prone to treatment.

Frank Barron: It is not a matter of self-perception; it is a matter of the actual facts of their character strength. There are two ways of looking at it. Persons of higher ego strength may be more able to quit smoking in any case. Even if that were so, it might still be true that a psychotherapeutic-type program which aims at increasing ego strength would be a good strategy where the final goal is changing smoking behavior.

Selwyn Waingrow: The current findings may simply be part of the current social scene, reflected by the fact that those who do go to clinics are such a small percentage of the total population. What happens when you start moving in the direction of making more clinics available, and if there is a greater movement toward acceptability of this kind of behavior? There is a large self-selective factor involved in attendance at clinics. How do such persons currently differ from those people who do not go to clinics, and what sort of scales currently get developed as a consequence? Social and personal acceptance of clinics changes in other words, as it becomes a little bit less deviant to go to a clinic. What will this mean in terms of differences between those who come and those who do not?

Joan Guilford: Dr. Barron referred to the differential effects of psychotherapy on men and women and pointed out that the differential effects we found in treatment of the sexes in the Five-Day Program might be analogous — that is, it seems that men can improve without the treatment, but women are much less likely to do so. He then said that this might be a function of ego strength. Well, this might explain the success of the men we studied, but not the women who, if anything, seemed to need the support of the group.

Percy Tannenbaum: There is a sex difference, which influences the data one way sometimes and another way at other times. Has anyone concerned himself with the question *why,* other than simply because it's there? Dr. Barron suggests that ego strength is differentially distributed between men and women, at least in determining how they react to therapy. But this means in terms of ego strength, and not in the genetic determinism of males and females. Several of the studies here have resulted in consistent sex differences. *(It was pointed out that these differences would not show up in scores on the ego strength scale, because it was developed in such a way as to control for sex differences.)*

Percy Tannenbaum: Is ego strength a constant characteristic? I can see that a person's ego strength is something that he is aware of and something that is partially created and shaped by his smoking behavior. If he finds he can't give up smoking, he may indeed see himself as having low ego strength, or he may succumb to begin with.

Edgar Borgatta: Further, can ego strength be used in a test sense? Perhaps you are using something much narrower than this very delicate ego strength kind of notion. There are many ego strength scales you could use that yield fairly stable response characteristics.

Someone then asked whether the difference in results of smoking cessation treatments might not indicate a multi-dimensional quality of ego strength. Dr. Barron affirmed that his own experiments had indicated some six or seven clusters on an ego strength scale.

Percy Tannenbaum: Whatever constitutes ego strength is secondary to finding some explanations. Looking at the research results with cessation clinics, one finds some successes, some failures. What differentiates them? Dr. Guilford's research (pp. 95–101), for example, dealt with something like 2,000 characteristics, which means that 4,000 more could probably be created. The point is that when differences turn up, they should be interpreted theoretically in terms of whatever underlying characteristics may be responsible for them. Male-female differences, for example, may obscure more fundamental factors. This is when one starts closing in to determine whether smoking or not smoking is a function of such variables as ego strength or dependence relationships, or something else.

Edgar Borgatta: Two aspects are involved here. One is status-description, which means an examination of selective factors that have operated in the past. After finding their concomitants (using as criteria smoking, not-smoking, etc.), one can examine whether ego strength is related to them. The other is that if you are now trying to alter behavior, differential characteristics of the subjects under treatment can be introduced. Along the lines of the first aspect, I think we are developing a number of large sample studies which will evidence certain signs that go along with personality differences associated with smoking.

Joan Guilford: Our study showed that men who were successful in quitting were more dependent than the men who were not. They were the kind who wanted to please their wives, and who, when they had personal problems, would go to their wives for help and so forth; the women's smoking behavior rarely depended on their husbands' opinions. This was true for both groups. Whether or not a man lived with a smoker made some difference, but this was of no consequence to a woman. The women seemed unaffected by those in their environment — except children. If a child disapproved of her smoking, women significantly more often failed than succeeded quitting. Can somebody explain that?

Selwyn Waingrow: That was also suggested by the results of a national study.

Silvan Tomkins: The sex-difference finding is one of the most reliable and substantial findings in the personality literature. Asexual hypotheses have been tested in at least two hundred studies, with the resulting data applicable to one sex and not to another. The results were as many times predicted as they were unpredicted. As a possible explanation for these results, let us consider the following problem, related somewhat to the concept of ego strength. What kinds of characteristics distinguish those who are helped by therapy from those who are not? (Put the problem that way, because that's your finding.) One obvious possibility is that the difference in personalities who are governed primarily by achievement striving, for example, would be helped differentially as compared with the personality organized primarily around affiliation and sociophilia. I'm not speaking of dependence necessarily, but simply a desire to be with people. Now, if we make the further assumption that in the female population there is a much higher proportion of people who are sociophilically oriented than achievement-oriented (which I think is not too gross an assumption), then that would account for this finding. If only those who are achievement-oriented can help themselves, and the sociophilic people need support and aid, then it would follow that women would more often show a differential response to aid and men less often. That's one possibility.

Leonard Berkowitz: A different line of reasoning can

be traced in Jerome Frank's book on *Persuasion and Healing.* He points out that sometimes the more dependent patient, the person who doesn't try to assert his independence, is more likely to take on the assumptive system, as he called it, of the psychotherapist; the dependent individual accepts the psychotherapist's view of life as the correct view. This would suggest that women perhaps might be more susceptible because they are more dependent or more submissive; they are more willing to take on the assumptive system of the change agent. If they are high in ego strength, they can then carry on the necessary act. This is also their role in life. But males, because of *their* culturally induced roles, and being high in ego-strength, may be less inclined to take on the assumptive system of the change agent.

Silvan Tomkins: This is an explanation not essentially different from the one I was offering except in the extent to which you assumed that the sociophilic or affiliation motive necessarily had within it submissive or dependency tendencies. In a test I have developed, there are measures which differentiate these two. I have no systematic evidence, actually, for a difference in sociophilia between men and women on a national sample of about 1500, so that this is evidence against what I'm saying. But it might be that a more sensitive measure would reveal it.

Bruce Straits: Let us suppose that smoking behavior can be explained solely in terms of certain personality characteristics and social environmental differences. If both of these factors are present in the right direction, the probability that a person will become a smoker is greater than if one or both factors are absent, and so forth. If this model holds true, then the reported sex-difference findings may be due not only to psychological differences between men and women but also to environmental differences associated with each of the sexes; men may be in social environments conducive to smoking more often than women. And the personality characteristics of male smokers may be more like males in general than female smokers will resemble the female population since smoking is much more prevalent among men than among women.

Richard Jones: Among the Indian high-school students the females and the Mexican-Americans had the same proportion of smokers as did the Anglo-American group. They were more passive, group-oriented, present-oriented in the Rosen scale; and the same ratio maintains itself in both cases. While this comparison is not related to sex differences in effectiveness of help programs, the interesting point is that the sexual differences (submissiveness, etc.) extend cross-culturally — at least as far as the Arizona data go.

Howard Leventhal: But shouldn't we consider situational, as well as personality variables? Women are at home; men are at work. Someone has commented about smoking behavior being more changeable in people who smoke for internal, personal reasons and less changeable for people who smoke for social reasons. If men do a great deal of smoking on the job, at business meetings and so forth, then the changeability of the behavior may be different because of some differences in what sustained the performance afterwards. It may have little to do with the taking of the change, the intervening process in the acceptance of the information itself and the willingness to change, but be more a matter of the environmental conditions that later support the behavior.

Selwyn Waingrow: I wonder about the concept of normative — in the case of the females it's still minority behavior, but more than half of the males smoke. It's a norm for males, but it isn't for females.

Richard Jones: In the Arizona study, it seemed that those females in the three groups (Anglo-, Mexican-, and Indian-Americans) who did not smoke were most characteristic of the values held by that group; that is, they were more norm-sensitive than any others of the group. The smokers were most norm *non-sensitive;* that is, they seemed to deviate somewhat from their respective non-smoking peers; the males in the study did not show the same tendencies *away from* the value orientations and health attitudes held by their respective groups.

Percy Tannenbaum (Responding to an observation by Frank Barron that it would be worthwhile to study characteristics of non-smokers): Smoker and non-smoker comparisons can be made on personality characteristics but not on treatment effects, of course, unless we make smokers out of non-smokers to serve as controls. Match the same characteristics and see if they are as receptive to the induction of smoking behavior as to the reduction of smoking behavior.

Silvan Tomkins: Is it possible that those who have high ego strength would not become addicted smokers in the first instance so that in general they would find it much easier to give it up?

Frank Barron: Can one speak meaningfully of addiction in the case of cigarettes?

Silvan Tomkins: It's a semantic issue. I believe the term addiction may be used, especially in the sense of *psychological* addiction. I don't believe there's a physiological addiction to smoking. At least there's no evidence that it has anything of the kind of severity of withdrawal symptoms that one gets with, let's say, alcohol or heroin or any of the other so-called addictive drugs. As you know, taking a person off alcohol suddenly, even under hospital conditions, results in a 10 per cent mortality rate. Severe convulsions are possible, and so on. I've never known anyone taken off cigarettes to have anything approaching this, so I don't think we can speak meaningfully of a massive physiological addiction. Even if it is there I would guess it to be slight. Psychological addiction is a real phenomenon, very similar in its method of operation to physiological addiction, except that the punishments occurring under conditions of deprivation are negative affective punishments; that is, there is terror, there is shame, there is distress, and so on. And these can be quite as punishing as convulsions. I think one can speak of addiction in the sense that a person who responds to cigarette deprivation in this way feels he cannot tolerate this subjective state.

Percy Tannenbaum: The question was raised about the uniformity of measuring success or failure. Now in relating ego strength and dependency needs to success in therapy, isn't a serious contaminating factor accruing from the nature of how these two variables are measured? Moreover, there may be reason to be suspicious of self-reports by subjects of their experiences of success and failure in the amount they smoke, have been able to cut down, and so forth.

Edgar Borgatta: There is little evidence that self-report is not an effective measure. In terms of lying, people certainly *can* do so deliberately, since they can be told the different ways by which to answer scale items. If they *have* been lying, they have been doing so remarkably consistently; independent measures on different occasions yield rather consistent data.

Percy Tannenbaum: The tobacco industry has spent considerable sums of money comparing self-reports with non-self-reports.

Howard Leventhal: A person's initial report on his behavior (which is used as a basis for measuring change) may more nearly reflect factors in his personality than his "instinct" to be honest. As the individual becomes involved in the study, the accuracy of his reports may improve. But this means that any change in his smoking habits may reflect the consequences of being involved in the study, rather than reflecting any real change in his behavior. Or it may even work the other way around: his accuracy in reporting may decrease as a result, for instance, of his desire to have the experiment succeed.

Edgar Borgatta: We have an interesting measure of balance order built into our procedure (see pp. 3 ff.): we secure an initial self-reported assessment, followed by another assessment of the current situation seven months later, with a request for information concerning that time seven months previous. In this way, we can compare their retrospective reports with their early reports.

Selwyn Waingrow: This is also being done on a national reinterviewed group as well. Other new independent national samples are also being drawn at the same time. These studies may prove to be revealing in the matter of reliability of reports.

Percy Tannenbaum: This may be true, but such studies involve a comparison of two indices or people undergoing treatment. My point is to emphasize the possible danger of using self-reports as reliable measures of the effectiveness of treatment of smoking behavior.

Turning to the problem of the family physician as an intermediary between national health agencies and the individual, the question was asked (of Dr. Ross) how much help the physician could be expected to offer in programs at the national level.

Charles Ross: Several physicians have wanted to make specific referrals, but we can't take them because we're working with an in-patient hospital. Allergists seem to be particularly interested in this. A number of allergists and some cardiologists warn their patients, "Either you quit smoking or I won't be your physician." This tends to leave some of them in a rather difficult situation. They have been making specific referrals only to be turned down, but this would be an appropriate thing to know.

Dr. Ross was asked if the physicians want an outsider — a consultant — to take on this problem, or whether they could handle it in their own office, as described in the Mausner paper. He replied that they could; they were attempting to set up a hospital program, but were confronted with a problem of implementing it.

Bernard Mausner: Our program (pp. 103 ff.) differed from the medically oriented smoking-control programs in that our experimental physician talked not only to people who were already showing signs of pathology from smoking; he talked to *everybody*. The question is, how many doctors can be induced to face the ridicule and hostility of their patients? I asked a physician who is very active in smoking research and state programs whether he talks to every patient. He replied, "Of course not. I don't want them to think I'm some kind of a kook." If many physicians react this way, it seriously questions the feasibility of the so-called physician program.

Donn Mosser: To be practical and effective, the program must be carried out in stages. Obviously, one of the groups of physicians interested in doing this could be the non-smoking physician. The smoking population is down to about 35 per cent among doctors, making it about 70 per cent who probably would be interested. And I think among the smoking doctors there may be a group who would be quite happy to say to the patient, "I can't help you out this way — I haven't helped myself — but this group could."

The start could be made with a group of patients with a medical problem (since it was reported that people who have a medical reason for stopping are more likely to stop). This would provide the physician with the encouraging feedback that this may be a productive method for this kind of patient. In any case, the program should be carried out a step at a time, beginning with those who do have a medical indication for stopping.

Charles Ross: The physicians of New York State were polled as to their willingness to participate in medical education programs concerning smoking, and the response was quite poor. I don't think this is because of a lack of interest, rather because of a lack of time that they would have to devote.

Judith Mausner: But it would not be an additional task; rather, part of the course of an interaction that would be taking place in the physician's office in any case.

Daniel Rosenblatt: Physicians have so many programs that they are asked to participate in — glaucoma, the pap smears, smoking. If it were possible to reach people when they go to physicians' offices, it would be an excellent way of attacking a whole series of health problems. But even if the physicians agreed to participate, they would soon start dropping out, simply because they don't have that much time to spend with each patient.

Donn Mosser: Do you mean by "participation" that a physician is going to have to do something that takes a substantial amount of time? We have encountered this problem in trying to get physicians to speak on the subject of smoking. Most of them, even non-smokers, are unwilling to put themselves in the position of appearing poorly informed in the area.

Dorothy Nyswander: Private physicians have co-operated well with medical committees with other problems, when they're approached in person rather than with questionnaires. From my experience, the internists would be the proper group; I don't know an internist who doesn't give you the works about smoking.

Charles Ross: A prior step we have taken at the (Roswell Park) hospital, which incidentally provides service to the physician and to the patient, is simply to get a detailed smoking history for the doctor's chart. Information is provided for the patient if he inquires; in any case it tells the patient that this is a normal part of the examination procedure. We gather data in the process, and the doctor gets information of a detailed nature about the patient's smoking history. This may or may not be relevant, but the doctor can use it as he sees fit.

Dr. Mosser was asked what steps could be taken to provide physicians with more information so they could "properly use it." He indicated that the American Academy of General Practice is a very well organized group, having done an excellent job in comparable areas, such as the pap smear program. If one were to initiate a smoking program with a medical group, he said, the Academy would probably be the best place to start.

Edward Oppenheimer: If the physician became personally interested through some special program, you could get a very effective response. This is easy in a special project, but it would be difficult to do across the nation. In following up the idea of programmed education, a programmed booklet could be made up very easily with one or even two methods, and sold over the counter. In this way you could tell which method is more effective.

Bernard Mausner: One of the problems is that there already are a fair number of little books that try to tell you how to quit. After working with it for several years, it's my impression that there is no special magic to programming, especially for literate, well-educated people, and less well-educated people simply won't buy these programmed booklets.

Charles Ross: We're assuming that the patient will need a lot of information in order to follow the advice of the physician. It just takes 35 seconds to talk. It's a matter of giving *advice* on the subject, not giving a lot of information. For instance, in the pap-smear program, we found that the main reason women take the smear test is that the doctor recommends it; the main reason that they *don't* take it is that the doctor does not mention it. It is not necessarily a matter of providing much technical information; many people simply do what the doctor advises.

The comment was made that the pap-smear parallel is not a good one because the number of women who get pap smears is so small compared to the whole female population, that the women who agree to take the test are usually health-oriented and already going to doctors anyway.

Donn Mosser: It is a more profound problem than one of providing information. In the first place, I despair of being able to intercede through the physician; if you can get him to make referrals to a group already set up for this purpose, you will have made your major effort. Another point is that of the willingness of the physician to put himself in the position of being challenged by someone who may have read a lot of particulars and wants to put him at a disadvantage. The public image of the doctor is that he is supposed to know everything about everything. The lawyer takes time to look up cases, but the physician must have the information at hand immediately. The problem is indeed a complex one.

Bernard Mausner: Until some fairly active research has been done, we simply can't answer the question as to how much doctors would be willing to break their chain of habits. On the question of time, all Dr. Rial spent with his patients on smoking was about 35 seconds, perhaps 40. He simply said, "Are you still smoking? You really ought to do something about it. Here's something to read." If they wanted something to help them stop or cut down, he gave them a pastille. He is a very busy practitioner with an enormous patient load, but it was something he was able to work in without too much strain.

Dorothy Nyswander: We may be discussing two different approaches here. The first is some research on the feelings of private physicians toward what they will include within their practice. The other is that of action: simply to get to work with private physicians and start the program. This is the way we often have to start, otherwise we would have no program going on at all if we had to wait for studies to be done at every step. This hunch about the importance of the private physician seems to me to be enough for an action program to be started, then strengthened by further research, followed by another modification of the action program. The plan could build a procedure of evaluation into the action program, so that research could be conducted simultaneously.

The problem of the expense involved in treatment was considered, as when groups of 1500 end up with as few as 27. The expense of maintaining a clinic staff — even for purely research purposes — was seen by some to be prohibitive. Daniel Rosenblatt suggested a cheaper way out: the use of programmed instruction. If a program were made for people who wanted to stop smoking, much of the attrition might be avoided. He felt that programmed instruction was worth the try despite the fact that social scientists are interpersonally oriented, and would probably not look upon the method with favor.

Bernard Mausner: Actually our own work on programmed instruction has been a failure. The "physician" part of our experiment included using a pamphlet put out by the Nicoban people, which has some of the character of programmed instruction — that is, it deals step by step with altering pieces of behavior. The people who were given the pamphlet probably read it. We did not have any direct evidence that reading the pamphlet made any difference, but it certainly is something to be tried, especially in line with Dr. Leventhal's (pp. 17 ff.) work suggesting that setting up a very carefully structured sequence of behaviors that people can learn and try to follow might have an effect.

The discussion turned to alternative methods aimed at getting people to quit, such as the act of filling out a smoking questionnaire, which Jerome Schwartz indicated was a control device built into his study. How many people would be influenced by Government-sponsored educational television programs? In attempting to determine what people were willing to go through to enable them to quit, Schwartz's group found that most would rather undergo electric shock treatment than read a book on how to quit smoking. The implication was that people seem to need an external agent; they feel that they cannot or prefer not to do it on their own.

Bernard Mausner again stressed the importance of distinguishing between samples of people that are program targets in gauging the effectiveness of the program. The Schwartz study, he stated, worked with people who have already indicated a willingness to quit, whereas the Mausner "Physician Influence" study involved all smokers visiting a given physician. Mausner contended that a smaller number of people are willing to take steps to quit than seems indicated by questionnaire data — that the act of going to a clinic is something quite different from saying on a questionnaire, "I would love to be able to stop." From the viewpoint of personal effort, this is an inexpensive thing to do, and has become socially acceptable. Only a tiny minority of the smokers will not tell you with a rueful sigh, "Gee, I wish I could quit!"

A mass-screening program was suggested. Mausner indicated that his project has plans along these lines: to set up a mass screening program in a community, report the results to the physicians of the persons involved, and use the physician as a vehicle for change with a message such as, "You're beginning to show some danger signs," or "You aren't yet." This screening program would be aimed at uncovering any preliminary sign of physiological dysfunction which has been associated with smoking, such as abnormal cells, altered vital function, increased heart rate or blood pressure on exercise, etc.

Charles Althafer: Our local Museum of Science and Industry sponsored a one-month inter-agency demonstration during which it presented whatever it felt related to the public on smoking. A pulmonary-function test was included, with a demonstration of how the efficiency of the lung was measured. It was not intended for diagnosis, merely for demonstration, but every person who took the test (we limited it to people roughly over age 35) was given a pamphlet on shortness of breath. It was surprising to note how effective this was; people who had quit came back after a year with the same pamphlet in their hand, wanting another test to check their improvement.

Edward Oppenheimer: In contrast to treating people who already have the disease, whether it's clinically symptomatic or not, you might let people see how the air-way resistance score, which is an indicator of lung function, changes after a cigarette, so that people can see that this is something that affects everyone, and not just the sick.

Bernard Mausner: I have to report something of a failure in one of my health classes at Beaver College. Seeing that the traditional lecture-and-slide technique was not going over, I tried to demonstrate the agonies of emphysema by simply getting the girls winded with running-in-place-exercises. This impressed them so that when they returned to their dormitories and lighted up their cigarettes, they did so with a little embarrassment. But the experience made one girl quit as of that moment. Her father is a doctor who tried for years to persuade her to stop smoking. On that day she finally made her decision.

Donn Mosser: I think the demonstration would have been more effective if you had asked them to breathe through their hands afterwards so that they had pressure against their breathing out. It's the expiration phase that's a real struggle for an emphysemic patient.

Frank Barron: One of the things suggested by the papers in this section is the resemblance between the statistics for success in programs designed to help people to stop smoking and the statistics in treatment programs of a more general sort, such as brief psychotherapy for conditions that could be described as psychoneurotic. The figure of about 15 to 20 per cent success, over and above chance fluctuations, has been reported fairly consistenly in such treatment programs.

Furthermore, some research reports suggested that individuals who are able to stop smoking have somewhat more ego strength, expressed as will power to begin with, or perhaps they are more achievement-oriented. These things, in turn, may reflect something about the sex differences that have been found where, for example, women who stayed in the treatment program were much more likely to be successes than those who dropped out of it, while for men the proportions were about equal.

We have considered the general problem of ego strength in relation to response to such treatment programs and the need for differentiating on both the criterion side and on the prediction side of variables that might be related to success in different kinds of treatment regimes. The burden of our discussion was that there is a very considerable interdependence among such so-called single dimensions, social roles as well as chosen social situations in general. One way of conceiving it would be that single variables might themselves predict, but in addition, a process which involves general personality change might be most relevant to a change of particular behavior patterns of this sort.

Silvan Tomkins: There is a rather sprited difference of opinion among us as to sexual differences in personality factors which make men respond no differently to help (i.e., therapy) than to non-help as compared to women. Women are helped by help, and hindered by *not* being helped. What could that difference hang on? Frank Barron has suggested it may be understood in terms of ego strength. My quarrel with that was that ego strength includes within its definition the very thing it attempts to account for. Let's say one of the prerequisites in ego

strength is that one can resist temptation; one can control himself; if one gets in a bind he can get out of it, and so on. I suggested the alternative interpretation, namely that if one were primarily achievement-oriented and used to doing things on one's own, outside assistance would not help any more or less than giving oneself the instruction apart from the clinic. But if one were sociophilic or affiliative in motivation, the support and help of other human beings would produce differential help, and being without that kind of support one would be less able to change a difficult behavior pattern. So, these are two rather different but related notions of why this very stable sex difference finding has been found. It is the single most reliable finding in all the personality literature that I know of; an unintended, usually unwelcome finding in the testing of almost any hypothesis. The women do it, but the men don't, or the other way around: rarely predicted but always found. I suggest that our finding represents a special case of a general theoretical problem.

Percy Tannenbaum: I think we now realize that we should conduct fewer *post hoc* analyses, such as those in which successes and failures are compared on a wide assortment of other characteristics. We must begin to build up samples having characteristics with which we have sufficient familiarity to enable us to predict success or failure according to the theoretical position with which we approach the problem. For example, we could form experimental groups including people with different types of high and low ego strength, high and low affiliatory behavior, etc. This seems to be a much more promising avenue for research than performing more and more *post hoc* studies.

Dorothy Nyswander: The question was raised, "If the private physician and the authority of the physician in working with his patients seem to be as important as the data would show, then should some national agency undertake to work with private physicians to get them to incorporate more of this personal teaching along with their work?"

Practitioners are aware that county medical societies usually include committees or individual physicians ready to help with working and planning. But we must not lose sight of the fact that they like to participate in the planning and the decision-making; they don't like to carry out plans which other people have made for them.

It was pointed out that although physicians are informed about smoking, it probably is only partial information. Two questions were related to the possibility of co-operative research which would include theoretical research and action research.

The suggestion of programmed instruction was considered. There are many ways that we practitioners have been working with programmed instruction; I hope that if those working on smoking use it, they look at some ways in which it can be most effectively combined with other methods. The health educator in a community does not usually work with just one method. Every feasible method and combination of methods is brought to bear for a solution to the problem. Certainly programmed instruction can be combined with other procedures. We need some experimental work with television that will provide measurable results. We made loose evaluations in the old days with radio-listening forums that we were able to get some measurements from. We should experiment freely with *all* techniques, to determine their effectiveness, being continually alert, I hope, to the ethnical implications of all methods.

In terms of the expense of applying programs at the individual and community levels, I believe the community approach would be a prohibitively expensive one to apply, although not necessarily an expensive one for research. It is somewhat reminiscent of family planning research in India, where we found that the case (clinical) approach was costing 34 American dollars (a considerable amount for India), for a person whom you *thought* was continuing to use the contraceptives. You couldn't prove it; you *thought* they were continuing. Imagine instituting a national program for family planning for a country as populous as India where each case would cost $34.00, and the outcome would still be only a supposition!

Jerome Schwartz: Regarding the practical costs, our eight-week group counseling method would cost about half the price of a package of cigarettes a day, so it's very practical. People can afford this; half of the amount that they spend for cigarettes they would have to pay in and this would take care of that method. In the individual counseling method they would have to pay twice the cost of what they are paying for cigarettes if they smoked about a pack a day. We made a profit of about $150.00 by actually getting a fee from one of our subject groups.

Daniel Horn: But the problem of cost is not so much in terms of dollars that go into one particular procedure for a given group as it is the cost of providing the technical competence and the personnel to operate a broad program. If, for example, half of the current 55 million cigarette smokers in this country express some interest in giving up smoking, and another quarter express some interest in considering the *possibility* of doing so, that amounts to about 40 million people. Where would you get enough therapists, group-discussion leaders, and so on, to work with 40 million people? Especially since they would have to give up smoking before they could be very effective.

Certain problems exist in research on cessation processes. There is the problem of the differences between the factors which enable people to go off smoking and the factors that enable people to *stay* off smoking. The cost problem that has been referred to here is very largely the problem of the reinforcements necessary to keep people off smoking. I suspect we are moving into a social problem in this connection, because in a sense, we almost have to change the world around us in order to make it the kind of place in which it is easier to stay off smoking compared with one in which it is easy to go back to smoking. Perhaps the challenge of creating a social climate in which it is easier to stay off smoking will be met most effectively by organizing community action programs.

Reinforcing what Dr. Tannenbaum has said, I would make a plea for an emphasis on investigations, not so much on whether a particular method is a success or a failure, or whether this method is more successful than that method, or even whether this technique is more successful with this kind of person and that technique more successful with that kind of person, but more on an understanding of the processes — the dynamics — that are involved in the cessation process. What happens to people when they try to give up smoking? What kinds of dynamics are involved, and what are the forces that come into play, both in the initial stages and in its continuation? If we can develop out of this research an understanding of these processes, then we ought to be in a position to develop control procedures that make use of an understanding of these processes and solve the logistic problems of the cost. It doesn't bother me if it's very expensive to carry out a cessation procedure in the research stage. But if we have any intention of applying it to millions of people, then the cost factor does come into play. Certainly, when it comes to reaching people in groups of 30 or 40 at a time with a 16 per cent reduction rate it would mean starting something like 250,000 clinics to reduce smoking by one half of one per cent. That's a rather small reward for a tremendous amount of investment. There's something impractical about that.

The question arises as to whether more is achieved in the long run by reaching a larger number of people with a somewhat lower level of success. Of course, the first thing one tends to think of is utilization. On one hand, it's the utilization of mass-media procedures. It is possible to use television, radio, and so on, to accomplish certain ends, but I don't think we have reached a level of competence to create effective cessation processes through this kind of stimulation. But perhaps we can learn something out of the experiences of both mass communications and mental-health clinics, and perhaps it is possible to develop techniques for doing this. Again, if it is possible to do it with smoking, we may have paved the way for the development of this kind of technique for helping people with a good many of their problems using mass media.

Moving to the other extreme, certainly the physicians, and not just the physicians but other health workers, seem to be another efficient, relatively economical means of using the personalized approach by making use of an existing structure, an existing relationship. It isn't very expensive for the physician to devote 30 seconds of his time to trying to help his patients give up smoking. If he can apply this to enough people, even with a relatively low success rate, again we have the multiplication of the 150,000 first-line physicians and the other 75,000 back-up physicians. But physicians see people with their initial complaints, and they can have an effect on their patients.

There are also the dentists. (Somebody once said that in working with teenagers, the dentist has a great advantage because it is the only situation in which the teenager can't talk back: he has a fist in his mouth.) Dentists comprise a professional group 100,000 strong who are concerned with health. The hundreds of thousands of nurses, the people who work in health departments, the occupational therapists — there is an entire range of professional workers with some responsibility for health and health maintenance who could add the smoking problem as one of their responsibilities and here, simply by the multiplication of the half-million, three-quarter-million, or million people who are already working in the field, it might be possible to add some influences that could have an effect.

The economic or logistic problem is the one we must come to grips with. And this is how I see the interplay between the kind of research activities that are very impractical, so far as wide-scale application is concerned, and the necessity for going beyond the structure of the individual experiment and building the experiment so that it answers some basic questions on the nature of the process and the dynamics involved in it. Otherwise, our experiments result only in our saying, "Well, this is a good method to apply," or, "It isn't a good method to apply." There we denegrate the role of research and turn it into what appears to be a practical testing method, whereas in terms of the kinds of results we get, it turns out to be a very impractical one.

PART IV

PERSONAL CHARACTERISTICS
OF SMOKER

Research Strategy in the Investigation Of Personality Correlates

RICHARD W. COAN
University of Arizona

The recognition that tobacco consumption constitutes a major public health problem in this country has led to a growing interest in finding some means of control that would reduce the hazard. The mere publication of scientific information has had a limited effect on tobacco consumption, and it seems clear that if we are to be effective in encouraging people to stop smoking or to smoke less we must have a clearer understanding of the habit. It is possible to seek understanding in terms of various sets of variables — some social, some personal, some cultural, some biological — to which smoking may be related. Effective control is most likely to be achieved if we can start with the combined knowledge of many facets of the problem. One major facet is the relationship of smoking habits and changes therein to various other enduring behavioral and experiential characteristics of individuals — in short, the personality correlates of smoking habits.

This paper is concerned with methodological issues that arise when we seek to study personality correlates of smoking. Since these are essentially the issues that arise when we attempt to understand any social or psychological phenomenon from the standpoint of individual personality, much of the thinking presented here would apply with equal force to research on numerous phenomena outside the realm of smoking. Some attention will be given, however, to personality variables that seem particularly relevant to this realm.

In seeking personality correlates of smoking, we are confronted with complexity on both sides of the relationship. With respect to smoking, it is obvious that much more is involved than the mere presence or absence of the habit. In fact, we can expect personality variables to be more markedly related to such things as the type of smoking indulged in, success in eliminating the habit, the social context in which the habit develops, and the situations that tend to arouse a desire to smoke.

On the personality side, the picture is far more complex, for here we are confronted with a vast territory that is still very poorly defined and for which measuring techniques remain at a crude level. In much research not focused primarily on personality theory, it is a common practice to include a few casually selected personality variables, relying on extant instruments, on the chance that something valuable may emerge. Very little useful information can be obtained, however, as long as we depend too heavily on currently available instruments and engage in a piecemeal pursuit of a few variables which idle speculation suggests may be important.

A prerequisite to major advance in any area that involves personality variables is a far clearer understanding of the overall organization of personality and a more precise definition of its components. To this end, the author would like to advance a few methodological prescriptions that seem particularly relevant, if not indispensable, to the quest for an organized overall conception of personality structure. While certain kinds of research strategy seem essential, however, it is not the aim of this paper to dictate research strategy. The ultimate achievement of an adequately comprehensive picture is bound to depend on the integration of knowledge derived through many different approaches. Perhaps many valuable fragments of this knowledge will come from researches of the sort that will be criticized in the pages that follow. Furthermore, the author is not so presumptuous as to contend that many of the theses he will endorse here are novel. It is evident, however, that they need reiteration, for they have been generally ignored.

THE SEARCH FOR OVERALL ORGANIZATION

Before we proceed to examine the means of gaining an understanding of personality organization, it must be recognized that the problem is not a purely empirical one. Whatever the state of our knowledge, the picture we possess of this organization will always be as much a product of theoretical construction as one of factual discovery. The scientific pursuit of insight has always combined the gathering of information with the creation of conceptual models, or schemes of interpretation, and the superimposing of these on the realm of observation. If we wish to proceed intelligently, it seems essential, on the one hand, that we acknowledge our need for models and, on the other hand, that we acknowledge our models for what they are once we have adopted them. To fail to do either leads to stagnation — in the one case, through conceptual poverty; in the other, through perpetuation of dogma.

Thus far, the structural model that has proven most fruitful in the personality realm is the dimensional, or factor, model. There is little doubt that we stand to gain much through more widespread application of both the model and the techniques of factor analysis.[1] At the same time, we should be alert to the possibilities of constructing and applying alternative models, as Lorr (Lorr, Klett and McNair, 1963), for example, has done in the realm of psychopathology. Unfortunately, most of the current advocates of alternative models do not seem to be tuned in to the theoretical needs of psychology.

In employing the factor model, we need to bear in mind two notes of caution: (1) the mere application of factor analysis on a wholesale basis does not guarantee fruitful use of the model, and (2) the model is a limited one and does not by itself meet all of our needs. Factor analysis may be flexibly applied to introduce structure into many kinds of data for many purposes. It is most likely to yield something worthwhile, however, if we begin by defining as clearly as possible the territory to be charted and then endeavor to sample it as adequately as current knowledge permits. The factor analysis of those odd bits of information that we just happen to have accumulated in our files is most often a waste of time.

In going from the products of factor analysis to a theory of personality structure, we have to skip over a few evidential gaps. Any theorist should be willing to reach beyond his data, for he would not otherwise devise theories, but he should not be blind to the gaps he blithely crosses. If our aim is to discern structural relationships within the personality or mental organization, the most serious deficiency of the R-technique[2] data we typically obtain is that they cannot reveal anything directly about these relationships. We must make inferences about intra-individual organization from what are at best dimensions of individual difference — i.e., variance components of covariation across a population of persons. Hence, there is an obvious need for checking the results of R-tech-nique factor analysis with other covariation techniques, such as P-technique, and with non-factorial methods. P-technique is often promoted as an ideal solution to this problem, but it is certainly only a partial one by itself, since its application is limited to certain variables whose interrelationships are manifested in temporal covaria-tion.

With respect to the limitations of the factor model, it is easy to show that it is not designed to handle every important kind of functional relationship. What is the relationship, for example, between anxiety and neuroti-cism? Some of Cattell's research indicates that these are essentially independent dimensions of comparable status. This is a useful finding as far as it goes, but there may be a rather complex interaction underlying the statistical independence. Indeed, the actual factorial data bear on this interaction and provide a basis for allowing for it in description and prediction. The point is simply that the factor model alone may not provide an adequate way of conceptualizing this interaction.

Some of the limitations of a coordinate dimensional model can be overcome by supplementing it with a hier-archical model, and we see increasing use in personality theory of a four-level pyramidal hierarchy first applied to factors by Burt (1941, 1949). In this model, factors of coordinate status are regarded as lying at a common level, while elevation within the hierarchy represents generality of influence or manifestation. The notion of four levels originated with a logical analysis of trait distribution and was equated by Burt with the four types of factors known as general, group, specific, and error. The relevance of orders of analysis in an oblique factor system to these levels is obvious.[3]

The need for dealing with dimensions in terms of a hierarchical system or something equivalent to this is obvious when we realize that the same characteristics will be represented by a single factor in the context of one factor study and by several factors in another study (depending on mode of sampling variables and subjects and on the manner in which the analysis is conducted).

---

[1] Factor analysis is a method of correlational analysis designed to identify the basic components that underlie a set of measured variables. It assumes that variables correlate to the extent that they contain common components and that the nature and relative contribution of various components will be reflected in the over-all pattern of correlations. The dimensional model employed in conjunction with factor analysis is one in which variables are represented as vectors radiating from a common point of origin in a space composed of as many dimensions as there are factors. The factors themselves are represented by coordinate axes running through this space. The position of any given test vector is a function of the extent to which the various factors contribute to the variable that it represents.

[2] *R-technique* refers to the most common type of correlational study — one in which we are concerned with the co-variation between tests over a sample of persons. There are many other forms of co-variation to which we might apply correlational techniques and associated forms of statistical analysis. *P-tech-nique* is a research design concerned with co-variation over time between tests given to a single individual.

---

[3] An oblique factor system is one in which the factors are permitted to correlate with one another, just as the variables from which they are extracted do. Once these factors (the original or first-order factors) are obtained, it is possible to analyze their intercorrelations in turn and extract a set of *second-order* factors. Thus, a set of ability factors derived from a large battery of intellectual measures may yield a broader second-order factor of general intelligence. A set of physique factors derived from bodily measurements might yield a second-order factor of over-all size. Under some circumstances a set of second-order factors will yield one or more third-order factors. Crucial to the present argument is the fact that what can appear as a factor of any given order depends on a variety of conditions, including the homogeneity of the sample of subjects, the density of sampling and generality level of the variables used, the number of factors one decides to extract, etc. What emerges as a first-order factor in one study may be a second-order factor in another study.

What we need for theoretical purposes, however, is a hierarchy in which elevation corresponds to generality of expression within the total system of behavior and experience that we call personality. For reasons discussed elsewhere (Coan, 1964a), generality in this sense (which the author has previously called referent generality) is related to the level of generality statistically manifested in a given factor-study context, but the correspondence is not of a simple one-to-one character. Furthermore, the notion of four fixed levels, however sensible it may be from a logical or mathematical standpoint, seems an arbitrary and pointless restriction in a model in which elevation is interpreted psychologically. Thus, the author has argued that for the present it would be more fruitful to adopt a hierarchical model in which the vertical continuum is actually treated as continuous.

In supplementing the factor model with this one, we must once again recognize that our scientific task involves more than blindly employing a certain research procedure and then feeding data into the model. There is no fixed place in our hierarchy for group factors and general factors or for first-order factors and second-order factors. We must assume the responsibility for constructing lucid theoretical interpretations that will integrate the products of various investigations.

If our aim is to develop a comprehensive picture of personality structure that deals effectively with the generality continuum, we must also prepare to handle research methodology in novel ways. In the vast majority of factor studies that have been done, no attention has been given to the generality issue in the assembling of test variables, the analysis of data, or in the interpretation of results. The typical result is a set of first-order factors varying widely in generality level. Most obviously, we shall need to employ first-order and higher-order factor analyses flexibly, along with other forms of multivariate analysis.[4] More subtle but probably more important is the need to work with varied batteries differing both in overall density of variable sampling and in overall generality of component variables.[5] The impossibility of precisely pre-defining the generality and density of a set of variables poses an ever-present problem in the interpretation of factors, though many factor analysts seem

unaware of the existence of this problem. But this difficulty can be offset in the long run by the flexible approach suggested here, in which we deliberately explore both aspects of variable sampling by attempting to employ very specific variables at one time and variables of broad scope at another, and by sampling over a broad behavioral realm at one time and focusing an entire battery on a narrow realm at another. By pooling data from such varied studies, we can hope by successive approximations to move toward a theoretical system in which all important variables are ordered most appropriately with respect to both their relative generality and their dimensional composition.

It would be difficult to predict the ultimate fate of the dimensional and hierarchical models. Surely, we must be prepared to abandon them if we can devise other structural models that will do a more satisfactory job of handling all observed relationships economically. One prediction that the author will venture to make, however, is that with the aid of whatever models we may choose to employ, personality theorists over the course of the decades and generations to come will attempt to establish order within an increasingly comprehensive set of variables. Within the context of a single network of constructs, they will attempt to handle a greater variety of behavioral, phenomenal, physiological and anthropometric variables than we now envision. It becomes increasingly evident that we are missing something vital when we confine all our attention to one kind of variable. It may or may not be strategic for us to aim immediately at a grandly comprehensive scheme and proceed to worry about the relationship of a host of undiscovered biochemical factors to the variables with which we are more familiar. There is one line of endeavor, however, that appears particularly urgent at the present stage of development of personality theory. We must seek to handle behavioral and phenomenal, or experiential, variables jointly in a more effective and comprehensive way, for we seriously limit current progress by neglecting either set of variables. Thus far, of course, it is the phenomenal variables that have suffered more from neglect in organized personality research. If we take seriously the basic task of science to make orderly sense of all of the contents of human experience, we shall be hampered neither by the naive metaphysical assumptions of the radical behaviorist nor by a misplaced emphasis on "objective" methodology.[6]

---

[4] Though several specific meanings have been assigned to the term *multivariate method,* we refer here generally to any research design dealing with a multiplicity of either dependent or independent variables and to any method of statistical analysis designed to elucidate data stemming from such research. A variety of clustering and grouping techniques have been devised to accomplish aims related to those of factor analysis.

[5] *Density* in this context refers to the concentration of a set of variables in a given content area; it is reflected in the intercorrelations among them. The generality of a variable or factor is the extent to which it relates to a broad range of behavioral and experimental manifestations.

[6] There is an obvious need for objective methodology in some sense. A danger arises only when methodological bias becomes a basis for prescribing and proscribing subject matter. A more detailed treatment of the above issues is presented in Coan, 1964b.

The main thesis advanced by the author so far is that our main hope for an increased understanding of personality structure in the years ahead lies in a judicious use of the dimensional and hierarchical models in conjunction with multivariate methods of investigation and analysis. Though this is not the place for an extensive review, it should not be assumed that no significant research of the required kind has yet been done. A great deal of factorial information about personality structure has already been amassed, particularly through the work of Cattell (cf. Cattell, 1957, 1965), whose investigations have been the most comprehensive to date as to both psychological content and measurement operations. It can be argued, however, that our knowledge is still very scanty with respect to relationships along the generality continuum and with respect to phenomenal structure and its relationship to behavioral structure. The clearest needs for the immediate future are for investigations aimed at clarification in these two realms of inquiry.

COMMON FAILINGS IN PERSONALITY RESEARCH

Perhaps it will be generally agreed that we can better understand the relationship between personality traits and anything else when we have a better grasp of personality structure as a whole. Somewhat less obvious are the various traps into which we readily tumble as we grope about in our present state of relative ignorance. One of the oldest hazards in personality research lies in the casual selection of concepts which, on the basis of common sense and fortuitous observation, seem to be variables of major importance. There is a stage in early research exploration, to be sure, when we must pursue every idle whim and fancy in seeking clues that will lead to later more systematic work. To this no reasonable scientist can object. The problem is that too often the early whim becomes an object of devotion, and much valuable research time is wasted on a variable that we assume possesses a certain functional coherence that it does not in fact possess. We adopt some simple measuring device which obviously assesses our favorite variable — "rigidity," let's say — and then proceed to an organized series of experiments calculated to contribute substantially to the advance of science. Meanwhile, several other investigators are doing similar things but employing other obvious measures of rigidity. Ultimately, of course, the inevitable step is taken, and we discover that their measures do not measure what our measures measure. While a certain amount of theoretical construction enters into every personality trait concept, this variable that has for so long guided our thinking displays an unnecessarily loose fit to the trends we should have been observing.

In the past, the practice of creating personality variables by fiat has flourished most openly in the questionnaire realm, where the traditional method of construction was to assemble scales of items manifesting face validity for variables selected a priori. As this method wanes, it becomes increasingly evident that the underlying problem is not confined to the questionnaire form of measurement, nor, within the questionnaire realm, is it confined to the traditional method of scale construction. Two tempering notes might be added to this general criticism. First, there is little ground for objecting to any kind of metric concoction that is not proclaimed to serve any purpose beyond exploration. Second, the a priori concept in which we invest our faith is not always nonsense, and the device we construct to tap it occasionally yields a rich harvest. Even when we succeed in aiming at variables that are fundamentally important, of course, the a priori approach hardly guarantees maximal efficiency. The soundest objection to constructing a questionnaire scale of introversion-extraversion or masculinity-femininity by the traditional method — or for that matter, by the "empirical" method — is not that we are trying to measure a trivial or non-existent variable or even that the resulting scale will not be fruitful. Our major failing, rather, is that we are blithely ignoring the complexity of our variable and losing a great deal of vital information by attempting to accomplish too much with a single score.

Fixation on poorly chosen concepts, however, is only one way in which we restrict our vision. We miss another large part of the landscape by sighting exclusively by means of certain extant measuring instruments, measurement operations, and methods of test construction. Most large-scale personality researches of recent years have suffered from insufficient inventiveness with regard to needed measurement operations. If one desires general personality information and is not prepared to devote much time to the task of personality assessment, dependence on an extant standard instrument recommends itself as a convenient and possibly unavoidable recourse. The assumption that one can obtain very comprehensive information with any current instrument is questionable, but the widespread use of such instruments is certainly understandable.

It is more difficult to understand why a researcher who is willing to expend the necessary time and effort to seek comprehensive information about personality or some aspect of it would confine himself to a single restricted type of test performance, whether it consists of conceptual associations to inkblots, figure drawings, copying designs, telling stories in response to pictures, or responding to questionnaire items. Lest the author suddenly arouse a fresh crop of enemies at this point, it may be said that this kind of methodological restriction is not always a mistake, but there is a vital issue here that needs to be aired.

In considering this issue, we must grant at the outset that there is no *a priori* reason to assume that any given bit or aspect of behavior cannot serve as a basis for global assessment. Thus, it is at least semi-plausible that every major facet of an individual's personality will somehow enter in and be expressed in the things he sees in an ink-blot, in his preferences for photographs of faces, his handwriting, and the way he wiggles his toes. It is at least conceivable, furthermore, that the individual will express himself most amply when compelled to perform some outlandish task that would not otherwise occur in the ongoing stream of behavior.

If we are interested in useful measurement, however, the important question is whether it is possible reliably to infer all those interesting features of the personality from the response in which they are expressed. This depends on the semantic invariance of the response characteristic that is being measured — statistically speaking, the extent to which it covaries over a given population of individuals with any characteristic that we wish to infer. If we equate meaning with covariation, it seems obvious that a given test-response characteristic is likely to have various levels of meaningfulness for various aspects of the personality. As a general rule, we might expect a given test result to be most revealing of characteristics that closely resemble the responses elicited by the test or are directly related functionally to those responses. How reasonable is it to expect one kind of test behavior to illuminate the complex essence of a creature who possesses such an elaborate response repertoire, who often displays marked shifts in behavior pattern from one social context to another, and who even more characteristically displays a great discrepancy between what he does and what he feels inclined to do?

The questionnaire item probably deserves some special attention, since it is the most widely used measuring device in the personality field. Because of its ease of construction and the enormous range of its potential content, it is certainly the most versatile extant measurement operation, and it undoubtedly deserves its wide use. It has obvious shortcomings, which arise chiefly from its transparency, and these have long been generally recognized. These shortcomings are most serious when questionnaire scales are constructed by the traditional *a priori* method of item selection. They are less troublesome in empirical and factor scales, where items are selected on the basis of the correlations they display rather than their verbal content. It should be noted, however, that highly valid items — those that correlate substantially with a factor or with an external criterion — are nearly always

face valid.[7] In any case, it is difficult to see how an item that works well could fail to be face valid to a psychologist with moderate insight. To this extent, the notion of a "subtle" scale is destined to remain chimerical.

It could be argued that every questionnaire item is valid for something in so far as it measures something. In the worst possible instance, it measures only a transitory impulse to mark an *a* or a *b* when confronted by an incomprehensible series of words. In the most fortunate case, it might be said to measure a variety of stable characteristics with which it co-varies. In view of the widespread use of questionnaire items, it is imperative that we gain a clearer understanding of the range of characteristics that can be effectively tapped by this measurement operation. This mode of measurement surely has inherent limits, and we may expect to reach a point of inconsequential returns as we attempt to infer characteristics less and less directly related to the verbal operation performed in responding to items.

The issue is one that can only be resolved as we approach a more comprehensive grasp of personality structure through multivariate research in which many types of measurement are jointly used. The author has long suspected that questionnaire items generally possess greater semantic invariance for phenomenal variables than for overt behavorial variables. Suppose, for example, that a subject marks the *a* answer to the question "Would you rather (a) go to a party or (b) read a book?" Assuming that the response is a function of the verbal content of the item and that it possesses a certain stability, we now know that the subject indicates a preference for going to parties when filling out questionnaire forms. There are two obvious low-level inferences that might be drawn from this: (1) he thinks of himself as a person who prefers going to parties, and (2) he actually does ordinarily go to parties when confronted with the choice. Both inferences may be correct, but the former is probably the safer bet. If we are going to make much use of the item, we shall expect it to co-vary and provide a basis for reliably predicting many other features of the subject. We should not be surprised if it proved to have generally higher correlations with other components of the self-concept than with other features of overt behavior. If questionnaire items should prove invariably to work this way, then they have a very important role to play, but they need to to be supplemented with other forms of measurement.

Closely related to the question of what can be measured by questionnaire items is the question of how best

---

[7] The converse does not follow. Face valid items frequently fail to measure what we expect.

to construct scales so as to extract this information efficiently. Perhaps scales can be constructed profitably in many ways for many purposes. If we face squarely our present relative ignorance of overall personality structure and yet aim at global measurement, it is evident that we can proceed most effectively with the method of factor-scale construction or at least something comparable in methodological rationale. Only this method is designed to insure the expression of maximal information in a conveniently small number of scores, whether applied to questionnaire items in general or to those of a specific form and content. To be sure, the specific details of factor-scale construction could stand considerable refinement, and it is to be hoped that the basic aim of the method will be implemented more efficiently in the foreseeable future. It is also likely that we shall see more flexible use of the method in future multivariate research on personality structure where questionnaire items will be used in conjunction with other forms of measurement.

Perhaps there would be no need to make a pitch for the factor-scale method if certain other techniques — particularly that of empirical scaling — had not been so drastically oversold in recent years. It is difficult to see how any collection of empirical scales, as currently devised, could be reasonably expected to provide a satisfactory basis for global personality assessment. The method of empirical scaling, in which items are selected on the basis of their correlations with a criterion, is a technique *par excellence* for constructing a scale for a specific practical selection purpose. Even for this purpose, if a scale is to be applied to many subjects over a long period, the method must be considered incomplete, for the systematic alteration of item content required for the highest level of efficiency demands more insight into the nature of the predictor variable than the method by itself affords.

No serious problem arises, however, until we attempt to use an empirical scale for a purpose much different from the criterion prediction for which it was assembled. If this second purpose is again a very specific prediction, the problem is minimal. The scale either works or it does not. If we seek a generalized kind of prediction or personality-trait evaluation, there is a more serious problem, for this requires a psychological understanding of what the scale measures. Our insight into the scale is hampered by the fact that it is complex, since the criterion was almost certainly complex. Hence, even the most extreme score on the scale may be subject to a dozen different interpretations. A judicious choice of criteria may improve the picture, but the best criteria are still likely to be complex, and their selection, in our current state of knowledge, is hazardous. When we combine several scales into a battery or derive several scales from a common battery of items, we may succeed in reducing some of the deficiencies of each individual scale. We shall also find, however, that our complex scales overlap in complex ways, so that with ten or twelve scales we may be securing what amounts to three or four distinct pieces of information. In view of these shortcomings of empirical batteries, it is very hard to comprehend the popularity of a test like the MMPI which combines them with such additional peculiarities as faulty item formulation and linear conversion of highly skewed scale scores. Future historians of psychology will doubtless look back on the great amount of research devoted to this test as a staggering demonstration of shortsightedness.

It would be inconsistent with the whole tenor of the foregoing discussion for the author to champion some specific instrument in place of the MMPI, though it is clear that the questionnaire batteries of Cattell and of Guilford must be held to represent an advance in methodological conception. A fundamental thesis of the present paper, however, is that we have come only a short distance and have yet a long way to go. We shall make varied use of available instruments, but to become unduly fixated on any one in its present form might be a mistake.

PERSONALITY VARIABLES OF PARTICULAR RELEVANCE TO SMOKING

Thus far we have been concerned with broad issues that are central to all research on personality structure. Some of the main points that have been made can be illustrated well by a consideration of two areas of personality in which a clarification of structure through multivariate research is likely to contribute significantly to our understanding of the habit regulation involved in such behaviors as smoking. The two areas are the broad and complex one of personality integration and the somewhat more specific and partially overlapping one of the experience of control. In each case there are bits of evidence from various sources that suggest a bearing of the area on smoking behavior.

The realm of personality integration, or successful personality organization, is one of obvious major importance, and the widespread concern with it is reflected in the proliferation of overlapping concepts of maturity, self-actualization, ego strength, positive mental health, etc. It would be difficult for any investigator engaged in large-scale multivariate studies of personality to avoid this realm, and it is hardly surprising that relevant factors have been turned up by such researchers as Cattell and Eysenck. Several fair-sized studies have been devoted specifically to the problem of personality integration. Yet research to date has barely begun to illuminate this area, for most investigators have proceeded with rather narrow conceptions of integration and have introduced very few of the novel measuring devices required to provide fresh information.

It may be entertaining to postulate a single dimension of integration or self-actualization — and this may even be in partial agreement with the facts — but surely our real concern is with a host of behavioral, experiential, and psycho-biological manifestations that covary quite imperfectly. We have as yet a murky picture of the behavioral and experiential effects that are most crucial, of the interrelationships among these effects and their relationship to physiological variables, and of the processes and mechanisms underlying these effects. It is a reasonable expectation that a more penetrating analysis will reveal several distinct dimensions of integration.

A prime requisite for such an analysis is the development of measures — tests, biographical indices, etc. — that will provide the information we need to arrive at a comprehensive picture of structure. Among the many classes of variables for which a clear need and possibility exist for further test development are the following:

1. Crystallization — the achievement of organized behavioral-experiential structures which will be evidenced in such things as:
   a. a well ordered, consistent system of values,
   b. a well defined interest pattern,
   c. behavior reflecting consistent striving toward well defined goals.
2. Self-consistency — This is closely related to crystallization, and it might prove on analysis to be indistinguishable, but the emphasis is on complementarity or noncontradiction of component ideas, attitudes, behaviors, etc., rather than mere clarity of direction. It would be manifested in:
   a. the logical consistency of ideas and attitudes,
   b. the complementarity of efforts displayed in various behaviors,
   c. a consistency of motives manifested at various levels of expression or recognition (in overt behavior, fantasy productions, verbal self-report, etc.),
   d. consistency of self-perception with ideals.
3. Scope of awareness — The focus here is on the relative accessibility of all the contents of experience to conscious recognition and differentiation. The total contents would include what Mason (1961) calls the external environment, cognitive activity, and noncognitive inner experience. Within each realm, relative accessibility implies a relative absence of what might be called repression, perceptual defense, or selective inattention. In theoretical formulations that stress the achievement of self-direction or "will," this accessibility is often treated, at least implicitly, as a prerequisite condition, since intelligent choice depends on clear recognition of the full nature of the alternatives. Logically related to this are various concepts that relate to a willingness to admit diversity or contradiction into conscious experience ("tolerance of ambiguity," Barron's "complexity," etc.). Implicit in such concepts is a desirable phenomenal inconsistency which must be differentiated in research analysis from those forms of inconsistency that represent a failure or inability to integrate.

4. Reality contact — This is related to scope of awareness, but it differs in that the emphasis is not on mere accessibility to conscious differentiation but rather on the veridical nature of the resulting perception and cognition. This implies not so much freedom from repression as a freedom from perceptual distortion (e.g., via projection). It is convenient to make a logical distinction between contact with reality in general and accuracy of self-assessment, but it remains to be seen to what extent these two aspects of reality contact are functionally separable.

5. Flexibility — This is also related to scope of awareness, but the emphasis is on the capacity for shifting from one mode of experience to another, rather than on consciously entertaining various contents. The need for flexibility is especially apparent with respect to certain widely discussed polarities. With respect to each of the following dichotomies, it could be argued that either pole is more appropriate than the other at some point in life and that optimal functioning at either pole depends on a capacity for alternative functioning in the opposite mode:
   a. understanding via abstraction vs. knowledge via immediate experience,
   b. experience of differentiated, individualized selfhood vs. deemphasis of individuality, experience of one's self as part of a more inclusive whole,
   c. experience of individual will vs. recognition of determination, inevitability of fate,
   d. ascendance vs. subordination, dependence,
   e. affirmation of life vs. acceptance of death, loss of individual existence,
   f. detached, "objective" experience of self and others as "objects" vs. relatedness, experience of self as "subject," experience of other as "thou" rather than "it,"
   g. accepting faith, commitment vs. doubt, skepticism, uncertainty,
   h. sobriety, seriousness vs. levity, humorous detachment,
   i. involvement vs. aloof detachment,
   j. optimism vs. pessimism.

In considering this suggestive list of overlapping phenomenal variables, we may note that here too is a broad realm that could stand multivariate exploration. We have only a limited understanding either of the dimensions of immediate experience represented by the above variables or of the dimensions of general crystallized attitudes (or

Weltanschauung) to which the immediate experiences are related.

6. Psycho-physiological (psycho-somatic) integrity—an organic self-consistent organization manifested in:

   a. appropriately adjustive response in behavior and perception to proprioceptive stimulation — appropriate attention to basic organic needs, capacity for relaxation, exertion guided by sensitivity to current physiological capacity, etc.,

   b. accurate perception on the basis of whatever sensory input is available (as shown, for example, in Witkin's tests),

   c. appropriate physiological response (changes in autonomic balance serving to enhance adjustment potential rather than interfering, etc.).

A number of additional concepts can be found in Jahoda's (1958) review. The list above is not intended to be exhaustive. It does embrace a variety of variables which are obviously pertinent to integration and for which some obvious psychometric possibilities exist. The author has made some preliminary attempts at devising tests for several of these variables, and it is quite likely that the Zeitgeist has by now led a number of other researchers independently to work on many of them. Once we have developed means of assessing these and a number of related variables, we can hope through multivariate research to obtain a clear picture of the basic dimensions of integrative processes and integrated functioning.

The experience of control — i.e., the experience of oneself as a person who actively chooses and successfully wills, as opposed to the experience of being governed by forces beyond personal control — is clearly one of the most fundamental features of human experience. Some of the more salient recent formulations of this variable have been reviewed by Rotter (1966), who himself conceptualizes a dimension of control in terms of the extent to which an individual regards reinforcements as contingent on his own behavior. Rotter's review makes no pretense of being exhaustive, and one could list a great number of phenomenological and existential theorists not mentioned by Rotter for whom the experience of control is of focal concern. The longstanding interest in the experience and its implications is reflected in the perennial debate over such metaphysical positions as voluntarism and determinism, since the experience of active choice is commonly regarded as the prime evidence of a free will. A concern with experienced will as a phenomenal variable, of course, really presupposes no necessary position with respect to the metaphysical issue.

To date several scales have been constructed to measure internal vs. external locus of experienced control, most of them outgrowths of a scale originally constructed by Phares (1957). Much of the evidence obtained with these scales suggests that individual differences in control can be largely accounted for in terms of a single dimension, although Liverant attempted to devise sub-scales to fit several different content areas. The areas, which included academic recognition, social recognition, love and affection, dominance, social-political orientation, and general philosophy, proved to yield highly inter-correlated scores.

From the evidence that has appeared thus far, the author is by no means convinced that the experience of control can be satisfactorily regarded as a single dimension. Casual clinical evidence would seem to run counter to such a conclusion, since an experienced loss of control seems frequently to operate in a selective fashion. A generalized loss, of course, is common in psychotics. It is not clear whether social learning theory, which has guided much of the scale construction so far, is really concerned with only one facet of phenomenal control. It is apparent, however, that the realm of phenomenal control has not been adequately explored psychometrically as yet. There are three broad content areas for which items need to be constructed: (1) external events (both social and physical); (2) personal habits, traits, goals, life style, etc.; (3) the body (including both long-term development and physiological processes). Most work to date has been concentrated in the first area. Items must also be varied systematically with respect to various aspects of external forces — particularly with respect to whether they are social, physical, or indeterminate and whether they are benevolent, malevolent, or indifferent. They need also to cover both the subject's personal experience and his perception of control on the part of people in general. Some of the variations in item construction noted here are apparent in extant scales and have not yet been shown to be particularly important. Whether they will reveal important individual differences when extended to other content areas remains to be seen.

Questionnaire items alone may not be sufficient to tap all major aspects of experienced control, and they need to be studied in combination with other kinds of test materials. Picture-interpretation and story-completion tests yielding scores for internal control as against both benevolent and malevolent external control have been used by the author in research with children (cf. Cattell and Coan, 1959). Adams-Webber (1963) has also employed a story-completion test, and Battle and Rotter (1963) have used a test modeled on the Rosenzweig picture-frustration approach. There is a clear present need for analysis of the experience of control in various areas and on various levels of expression. In the course of time, we shall also wish to gain a better understanding of the relationship between this experience and all other major facets of behavior and experience.

SUMMARY

A thorough knowledge of the personality correlates of smoking is possible only to the extent that we possess an understanding of over-all personality structure. Structural models are useful, if not indispensable, aids in the search for this general understanding, and the factor and hierarchical models have much to offer at the present stage of research. Ultimately multivariate research with all major classes of variables will be necessary. Increased attention to phenomenal variables seems currently vital. Common failings in personality research stem from fixation on haphazardly chosen concepts, preoccupation with particular forms of measurement, and over-dependence on available instruments. Personality integration and the experience of control serve as examples of areas in which multivariate research may extend our understanding and effective prediction.

REFERENCES

Adams-Webber, J. Perceived locus of control of moral sanctions. Unpublished master's thesis, The Ohio State University, 1963.

Battle, Esther S., and Rotter, J. B. Children's feelings of personal control as related to social class and ethnic group. *J. Pers.*, 1963, 31, 482–490.

Burt, C. *The factors of the mind.* New York: Macmillan, 1941.

———. The structure of the mind: a review of the results of factor analysis. *Brit. J. Educ. Psychol.*, 1949, 19 100–111, 176–199.

Cattell, R. B. *Personality and motivation structure and measurement.* Yonkers-on-Hudson: World Book, 1957.

———. *The scientific analysis of personality.* Baltimore: Penguin Books, 1965.

———, and Coan, R. W. Objective assessment of the primary personality dimensions in middle childhood. *Brit. J. Psychol.*, 1959, 50, 235–252.

Coan, R. W. Facts, factors, and artifacts: the quest for psychological meaning. *Psychol. Rev.*, 1964, 71, 123–140. (a)

———. Theoretical concepts in psychology. *Brit. J. Statist. Psychol.*, 1964, 17, 161–176. (b)

Jahoda, Marie. *Current concepts of positive mental health.* New York: Basic Books, 1958.

Lorr, M., Klett, C. J., and McNair, D. M. *Syndromes of psychosis.* New York: Macmillan, 1963.

Mason, R. E. *Internal perception and bodily functioning.* New York: International Universities Press, 1961.

Phares, E. J. Expectancy changes in skill and chance situations. *J. Abnorm. Soc. Psychol.*, 1957, 54, 339–342.

Rotter, J. B. Generalized expectancies for internal versus external control of reinforcement. *Psychol. Monogr.*, 1966, 80, No. 1 (Whole No. 609).

Smoking in Medical Students: A Survey of Attitudes, Information, and Smoking Habits

JUDITH S. MAUSNER
Women's Medical College of Pennsylvania

Because of the widespread cigarette smoking in this country, which persists despite the many anti-smoking campaigns, it seems important to enlist the active co-operation of all individuals who might influence the smoking of others. This survey of the attitudes and smoking habits of medical students arose from a belief, later tested in another study, that physicians could exert a significant impact on smoking behavior and from a curiosity as to whether physicians are prepared to be activists in the control of smoking. Included also was the hope of estimating the significance of a medical education on student smoking habits and attitudes, as opposed to another area of professional training where the students are comparable in age and level of achievement.

In September, 1964, approximately eight months after the release of the Surgeon General's Report, written questionnaires were distributed to 1057 students in four of the medical schools and 343 students in one of the law schools in Philadelphia. We received a 70 per cent response representing 1000 medical students and 343 law students. There was some follow-up on the non-respondents, since each student had also been given a letter to sign and return to the dean's office separately from his anonymous questionnaire.

The questionnaire consisted of items of personal identification followed by questions related to attitudes about smoking, the students' opinions of whether or not various diseases are associated with smoking and the students' own smoking habits. It also listed fourteen diseases as associated or not associated with smoking. (Ten of them actually were, and four were not.) The medical students showed significant variation by class as to information about diseases associated with smoking for 7 of the 10 entities listed: lip cancer, oral cancer, cancer of the lung, chronic bronchitis, emphysema, coronary artery disease, peptic ulcer, and, to a lesser extent, cancer of the larynx. The freshman students in both groups responded similarly to all of the items. By their second year, the law students seemed to indicate no increased knowledge, but the medical students showed definite evidence of learning. For all four diseases not associated with smoking, the medical students had a greater proportion of correct responses with increasing

professional education, a trend not found in law students. The only two conditions where the medical students showed no up-trend were in carcinoma of the esophagus and carcinoma of the bladder in males.

Over the next three months we sent two follow-up mailings to non-respondents. Because of financial limitations, the staff was too small to follow each individual in the medical schools. Since third- and fourth-year students are often away on assignments in other institutions, the Junior class was dropped in one school and the Senior class in another, permitting follow-up efforts to be concentrated on a smaller number of individuals. Usable replies were received from 1057 medical students and 343 law students. The response rate for the medical students was 79 per cent, for the law students 66 per cent. For individual classes the response rates varied from 59 per cent to 97 per cent. The percentage of females among the medical and law students was similar, 6 per cent for the former and 4 per cent for the latter.

Respondents were classified as current smokers, "changed smokers" or non-smokers. Non-smokers included persons who had never smoked and those who had smoked only briefly in their early teens. The term "changed smokers" was used to designate persons who had either stopped smoking completely, shifted away from cigarettes to cigars or pipes, or markedly decreased their cigarette consumption, e.g., from one pack per day to occasional. Comparison of law students with medical students was carried out for the major variables, although since they were of primary interest, most internal analyses were performed on the medical group alone.

Our results indicated that the proportion of smokers in the two groups of students were similar with one third in each currently smoking. There were some differences in smoking behavior: the medical students had a much smaller proportion of heavy cigarette smokers than the law students and a larger number of them (40 per cent for medical students versus 30 per cent for the lawyers) had never smoked; also, the mean age of starting to smoke was somewhat older in the medical group.

The difference in smoking between the groups did not appear to be correlated with attendance at medical school; moreover, we could not find any trend for a change in smoking behavior by class in school for either the medical or the law students. The difference in the number of non-smokers in the two groups may be related at least in part to differences in their parents' smoking habits. Students' smoking was found to be associated with parents' smoking for both medical and law students. A higher proportion of medical students had parents who did not smoke: twenty-six per cent of both parents of the medical student group were non-smokers compared with 18 per cent for the law students. A higher proportion of the medical students (28 per cent versus 18 per cent for law students) lived at home during college and a higher proportion had fathers who were physicians — who may possibly have been influential in regard to smoking habits.

Although 16 per cent of both medical and law students were following their father's professions, about the same per cent of medical students had fathers who were lawyers as law students had fathers who were physicians (2 per cent in the former group and 4 per cent in the latter). More law students, 43 per cent as compared to 29 per cent among the medical students, were children of fathers in managerial positions. Conversely, more medical students, 12 per cent as compared with 4 per cent for the law students, reported that their fathers were craftsmen or in service positions. No significant differences were noted between the two groups in regard to marital status; 72 per cent of the medical students and 69 per cent of the law students were single.

When the smokers among medical and law students were compared for the amount they currently smoked, it was found that the medical students smoke less than the law students. There was also a difference between medical and law students in regard to the age at which they started to smoke. The medical students started smoking at 16.9 years and the law students at 16.0 years. There were no important differences between the two groups to indicate when smoking was discontinued or reduced or why one or the other had taken place. Almost half of those in both groups changed from smokers to non-smokers prior to 1963; approximately 10 per cent changed immediately after publication of the Surgeon General's Report, and the rest changed sometime during the remainder of 1963 and 1964. There was a slight tendency for medical students to be more hostile to smoking than the law students, although the difference was small compared to the difference between smokers and non-smokers.

When asked about their opinion of the evidence linking smoking and disease, 75 per cent of the medical students and 69 per cent of the law students regarded the evidence as strongly or incontrovertibly convincing. Virtually no one in either group (3 per cent of the medical

students and 2 per cent of the law students) found the evidence completely unconvincing. When this item was analyzed by class in medical school, no variation among classes was found. The medical students were also more in favor of restrictions on the social controls over smoking than were the law students. (The differences, interestingly enough, were more marked about a medically based situation such as whether hospitals should permit vending machines on the premises than for a more general problem such as whether there should be restrictions on cigarette advertising for television and radio.)

In response to questions about how doctors should advise four hypothetical types of patients on smoking, a large majority of the medical students said that a doctor should advise strongly against smoking for a man with coronary disease or one with chronic bronchitis. Forty-two per cent of both the medical and the law students thought that smoking should be actively discouraged for the pregnant female and 26 per cent of the medical students and 22 per cent of the law students thought it should be discouraged among healthy young men. For all four types of patients, the medical students showed a trend toward stronger recommendations with increasing years in school; there was no such trend for the law students. The medical and law students resembled each other on their recommendations for the two healthy patients, but they differed on the two sick patients with the medical students urging stronger recommendations against smoking for the sick patients. Approximately one third of both medical and law students responded positively to the question about smoking as a health hazard. Significantly, more of the non-smokers (79 per cent) and "changed smokers" (82 per cent) found the evidence more strongly convincing than did the current smokers (66 per cent). Among those who answered the final question about smoking as a health hazard, a somewhat higher proportion of replies from non-smokers indicated that they considered smoking to be a serious health hazard.

The differences between male and female medical students did not significantly affect the comparison between medical and law students since the proportion of smokers was similar among males and females with 33 per cent of the males and 31 per cent of the females currently smoking. In terms of the level of smoking there were more light and more heavy smokers among the men; the women tended to cluster more in the middle. Men and women did not differ at all on the level of information; they were very much the same. On attitudes there was a slight difference indicating that women were slightly less hostile to smoking and somewhat less accepting of the evidence. A smaller proportion of them would urge stronger recommendations for patients.

The over-all findings, particularly in terms of the recommendations for individual patients, suggested that although the medical students successfully learned the facts about smoking as an etiological factor in disease, they were not prepared to act fully on the implications of these facts.

The choice of law students as the group to be compared with medical students was probably sound in view of their similarity in background and level of information. Despite the fact that differences between the two groups were noted and that law students from only one school may not be representative of law students in general, the law students surveyed in this study are probably as typical of any group entering a professional school as could be found. The knowledge of freshman students in both groups was remarkably similar, though the medical and not the law students showed increasing information about smoking hazards with increased years of training. However, the level of knowledge was not associated with demonstrable differences in attitudes and personal smoking behavior. There was no trend toward decreased smoking by class in medical school.

An important aspect of smoking, relative to physicians and medical students, is whether attitude or behavior is the more important. If it is attitude change then it would be important to create antipathy toward smoking in medical students and physicians in the expectation that this would lead them to stop smoking. If behavioral change is primary, then the most important approach would be to influence those in the medical profession to stop smoking, assuming that changes in their attitudes would follow from their changed behavior.

Surely there would be a greater ultimate impact on morbidity and mortality if healthy young people could be dissuaded from smoking than if smoking were successfully reduced among people who are already ill. There seemed to be a general lack of appreciation of the preventive potential of medicine as opposed to its curative function. By and large preventive medicine can be applied on a mass basis, but curative medicine generally requires a one-to-one interaction with an individual patient.

Assuming for the moment that smoking is a kind of disease, it would be very surprising if mass methods could provide the total answer to the control of smoking. On the other hand, prevention in terms of mass programs among the young cannot be relied upon exclusively, in view of all the pressures that exist in our society to favor the continuation of smoking. It seems relevant that interactions of patients and physicians should be considered further in programs of smoking control; and that medical schools should work further to prepare doctors for utilizing fully the potential of preventive medicine in this regard.

While there is a great deal of smoking information in the curriculum of every medical school and it is introduced in a number of courses, apparently the full implications of it are not being tested. Our findings suggest that the medical students who participated in this study were making judgments in terms of the presence or absence of disease in individual patients rather than viewing smoking as an etiologic factor capable of damaging healthy as well as sick individuals. Since cessation of smoking is considered by many to be the greatest single factor which could contribute to the prevention of disease, the need is urgent for intensified efforts in inculcating the preventive approach to medicine. Faculties of medical schools are in a position to influence their students by precept and example, and they should probably be encouraged to do so in the area of smoking.

SUMMARY

A survey of information and attitudes concerning smoking and health conducted among 1057 medical students and 343 law students in Philadelphia revealed that approximately one-third in each group currently smoked. A larger proportion of medical than law students had never smoked although a sizeable proportion of this group did not fully accept the evidence linking smoking and disease. The results call for intensified efforts to disseminate information on the preventive role the medical profession could play in regard to smoking.

Student Attitudes Toward Smoking[1]

LAWRENCE N. MOYER[2]
University of Toledo

The purpose of the present study was threefold: 1) to describe the smoking behavior of the students of the University of North Dakota and point up the relationships between that behavior and certain selected background variables; 2) to describe the attitudes and beliefs which these students have toward smoking and to show the relationship of these attitudes and beliefs to selected characteristics of the student body; and, 3) to investigate the possible changes in these behaviors, attitudes, and beliefs following the students' exposure to information regarding the probably deleterious effects of smoking.

This purpose was accomplished by administering an inventory-type questionnaire to a randomly selected sample of the student population at two points in time. In the interim between the first and second surveys, information in the form of a lecture, printed pamphlets, and a movie were made available to the student body. These were developed principally from educational materials available on campus. The program continued for several weeks and included a convocation by Senator Maurine Neuberger of Oregon, a series of pamphlets on the effects of smoking, and a movie entitled "One in Twenty Thousand." A week after termination of the program, the post-test questionnaire was administered, following the same procedure as the pre-test, except the sample included only those who returned adequately completed questionnaires during the pre-test. This was 667, or 85 per cent of the original useable questionnaires. The post-test questionnaire consisted of the pre-test questionnaire plus an additional page to ascertain the degree of exposure to the various materials that had been made available.

The analysis included three major control variables — sex, college class, and smoking habits. These were cross-tabulated with the various items: beliefs, behavior, attitudes, and so on. Finally, the response changes from pre-test to post-test were cross-tabulated with the post-test responses, which indicated the degree of exposure to the various educational materials. The questionnaire on the second survey, part of which was identical to the first, was also designed to discover how much of the information contained in the program was experienced by each student.

A summary of the major findings follows:

SMOKING BEHAVIOR

Most of the findings on smoking behavior could easily have been predicted from the general patterns found throughout the country.

There were more male students who smoked than females, but a larger per cent of men had quit than had women. Smoking was found to be related to number of years in college, with fewest smokers among freshmen and most among seniors. To some extent this was probably an age-related phenomenon. The exception to this trend was graduate students whose smoking habits were similar to those of freshmen. Marital status was found to be related to smoking behavior in that more married students smoked than did single students, but this finding was no doubt also influenced by the age factor. There also appeared to be more married students who had quit smoking. Fraternity and sorority members were more inclined to smoke than were non-members. Length of time smoking seemed to be related to amount consumed and inhaling habits, with those students who had smoked longest disposed to smoke more cigarettes and be more apt to inhale smoke regularly. The heavy smokers more often than the light smokers smoked plain rather than filtered cigarettes. As expected, students' smoking habits were found to be closely related to those of their parents, but comparisons indicated that second generation males were more likely to be non-smokers in spite of the fathers' smoking habits, while second generation females smoked considerably more than did their mothers. The student respondents' smoking patterns were also found to be associated with the smoking habits of roommates, steady dates, and spouses. The higher the percentage of these close associates who smoked, the higher the corresponding per cent of students who were smokers.

[1] This research was supported by funds from the U.S. Public Health Service. Cancer Research, U.S. Department of Health, Education, and Welfare.

[2] At the time this study was carried out, the principal investigator was a member of the Department of Sociology and Anthropology, University of North Dakota.

ATTITUDES AND BELIEFS

The analysis of student attitudes and beliefs was accomplished by using three control variables: sex, college class, and smoking habits.

Attitudes

Male students tended to be more favorably disposed toward smoking than females. Men checked more of the attitude items reflecting favorable attitudes toward smoking than did females, but this may have resulted from the fact that proportionately more smokers were found among males. This similarity in distributions between responses for males and responses for smokers was particularly noted when the preponderance of favorable male responses was reversed for the item, "If parents smoke they should allow their children to smoke" where fewer males than females and fewer smokers than non-smokers agreed.

Although it is difficult to make summary generalizations about distributions by college class, there does appear to be a tendency for these comparisons to be strongly influenced by smoking habits. Seniors had the largest percentage of favorable responses on more items than their classmates, and they also were more inclined to smoke. At the other extreme, freshmen and graduate students gave smaller per cents of favorable responses than did their classmates and also contributed more non-smokers to the sample.

There were some minor differences between students who had quit smoking for at least one year prior to the first survey and those who had quit for less than one year, but the frequencies were too small to allow for any solid affirmations about the discrepancies.

Beliefs

The comparisons between findings on attitudes and findings on beliefs give strong support to the notion that cognitive evidence has only minimal influence on attitudes held. Although males, generally, had more favorable attitudes toward smoking than did females, the reverse is true for their belief patterns. Of the sixteen belief items, thirteen were found to have higher per cents of "correct" responses for males than for females. Although males are apparently more aware of the possible harmful effects of smoking than their female counterparts, they persist in smoking more and maintaining more favorable attitudes toward smoking.

However, this distribution pattern does not hold for comparisons by class. Graduate students who were found to have the greatest percentage of non-smokers also had the largest percentage of "correct" responses to the belief items. On ten of the sixteen items the graduate group had the largest percentage of responses which reflected awareness of the evidence compiled on the effects of smoking.

Comparisons by smoking habits revealed the expected: those who had quit smoking were generally more aware of the evidence, as reflected in their greater percentage of "correct" responses, than were those who presently smoke or those who had never smoked. Of the latter two groups, those who presently smoke tended to be more unaware of the evidence on smoking than those who had never done so. The differences were not great, however, and the findings were not easy to interpret.

A comparison between pre-test responses and the post-test responses was not made for the three control variables (sex, class, and smoking habits); however, data from the second survey are presented with the reminder that they may not be comparable because of the differences in the total number of students responding to each of the two surveys.

CHANGES IN SMOKING BEHAVIOR, ATTITUDES, AND BELIEFS

Smoking Behavior

Changes in smoking behavior were slight for the student body as a whole during the interim between the pre-test and post-test. More students who attended the lecture quit smoking than those who did not attend; more students who read the pamphlets cut down on their smoking than those who did not read them; and a considerably larger per cent of students who saw the movie on smoking quit smoking than those who did not see it. Only thirteen subjects attended the movie, however, and the differences in changes in smoking behavior generally between the students who were exposed to the various types of information and those who were not, were not great.

Attitudes

Overall, there were a considerable number of students who changed in their attitudes toward smoking and, contrary to expectations, most of the changes were in the positive direction, more favorable toward smoking.

The only clear-cut relationship found between attitude changes and exposure to the available information was the slightly greater per cent of change in the direction of unfavorable attitudes on a larger number of items for those who attended the convocation when compared with the respondents who did not attend.

Beliefs

Contrary to the findings for changes in attitudes, the largest per cent of changes in beliefs were in the direction of "correct" responses. This was true generally for all of the students whether they had participated in the information program or not. Nevertheless, those students who attended the lecture, as well as those who read one or more of the pamphlets, had an excess of "correct" over "incorrect" changes in beliefs on more items than their non-attending, non-reading classmates. The latter groupings had more change excesses in the direction of "undecided" on more items than the attenders and readers.

CONCLUSIONS

Only one major conclusion can be made in terms of this gross preliminary analysis. Attitudes and their related behavior cannot easily be changed, particularly by exposure to information (as opposed to emotionally charged material). Beliefs are apparently easier to change, but they seem to have little effect on either attitudes or behavior, at least not in the area of cigarette smoking.

A note should be made on the shortcomings and problems of the present study.

a) As with all studies which utilize a mailed questionnaire, the returns were not as large as anticipated. This problem was compounded by the design of the project which required both a pre-test and post-test, thereby adding to the attrition.

b) Related to the above is the problem of small frequencies which appear when the cells are multiplied as in comparisons on smoking behavior. Often in the analysis, when discussions are based on percentage distributions, there appear to be important differences between grouping, but the frequencies upon which the percentages are based are too small to be meaningful. Caution should be exercised in making interpretations.

Because of the gross nature of the analysis, a recommendation is made for a future secondary analysis of these data. There is much information in this study which requires further analysis. For example, a comparison should be made between the pre-test and post-test utilizing the control variables for the sample that responded to both surveys. Other control variables could also be introduced, such as age, marital status, parents' smoking habits, etc. Comparisons could also be made between atti-

tudes and belief items to discover their possible interrelationships. Also, some of the findings on the group who had given up smoking indicate that it might be fruitful to do a major study of individuals who have quit to determine which factors were operating in their decision to stop smoking. It is apparent that information programs such as the one included in the present research are not very effective, yet some people do quit. Why?

Finally, a follow-up study of the sample used in this project could be undertaken to determine whether there is a real difference between freshmen and seniors in their attitudes and beliefs, or whether these are age-related responses which change during the course of four years of college.

SUMMARY

The purpose of this study was to investigate attitudes, beliefs, and behavioral changes among students exposed to materials describing the known and suspected physiological consequences of smoking.

On two separate occasions, a twenty per cent probability sample of University of North Dakota students were given a modified questionnaire of the Public Health Service's "Survey on Health Behavior and Health Attitudes" (PHS-T278). Selected educational materials pertaining to the health hazards of smoking were made available to them before the second questionnaire was given.

Cross-tabulations, using smoking behavior, sex, and college class as control variables, were used in the analysis of results. These showed that smoking patterns were related to sex, class, age, and reference-group behavior and that male students were more aware of the health-related consequences of smoking than female students.

The preliminary analysis of the first and second tests revealed relatively little modification of behavior, attitudes, or beliefs by exposure to smoking materials. Smoking behavior remained about the same; and although changes in beliefs were predominantly in the "correct" direction, the general direction of change in attitudes seemed to be positive or more favorable toward smoking.

Male Student Perceptions of Smokers

JOHN M. WEIR
California Department of Public Health

The research project from which the data reported here are drawn is based on the idea that cigarettes have expressive value and that student smoking behavior is often sustained because of its ability to serve a self-expressive function.

Specifically, the project was designed to demonstrate that cigarettes are useful, meaningful, descriptive cues to teenagers. Thus, subjects who are exposed to a stimulus person who is smoking will give descriptions of that stimulus person which will differ from the descriptions given by matched subjects who are exposed to the same stimulus person minus the smoking cues. The difference between these two sets of descriptions is indicative of the specific expressive value possessed by cigarettes.

One major impetus for undertaking our research came from talking to a California high-school counselor who was concerned about the kind of smoking information that was being taught in the school system, where teaching on the subject is required by a state law. He understood that cigarettes do cause increased morbidity and mortality in the adult population; but he was also convinced that students do not smoke in order to be numbered among the victims.

If this is not the case, then what do they get from smoking? What are their reasons for smoking? He rejected the fairly popular view of many elementary teachers that students really smoke to punish their teachers, to rebel, or to try being "big." An interesting possibility is that cigarette smoking might be like the many other kinds of behavior available to an adolescent for the first time — behavior that reflects economic independence, personal choice in grooming, operation and possession of automobiles, and so on. It seemed meaningful to examine the extent to which curiosity plays a role when an adolescent begins to smoke regularly and how much of it is a testing kind of behavior that fits his perception of himself and the reactions he gets from people around him. This study was designed to demonstrate that cigarettes are useful, meaningful, and descriptive cues to teenagers, that they are used to interpret the kinds of responses they can expect from other people who smoke and also as a vehicle for projecting the kind of image of themselves which they would like other teenagers to see.

It has often been noted that when teenagers are questioned about any area where there has been some moral concern on the part of adults they often anticipate what is expected of them and respond almost automatically with stereotyped, socially acceptable answers. Thus, if we ask them why they smoke, they give us the kind of answers they think we want to hear.

To avoid this, the purpose of the study was kept from the subjects until after it was over, and an indirect method was used in questioning.

Two instruments were used in the testing. One was a booklet of four photographs and four copies of an 80-item adjective check list (ACL) which was made up of words selected from Sarbin's Personality Word Card (Sarbin, 1965). The other was a short questionnaire about smoking habits and related information. The two were not given simultaneously.

The booklets were especially created for this project. Four young models, two males and two females, were photographed individually in candid situations presenting a maximum of information about the model, e.g., dress, posture, facial expression. Cigarettes were used in each scene. Each print was then retouched with all cigarette cues removed, thus resulting in two prints for each model. Four prints depict the models as smokers and four identical copies have all smoking cues removed. These eight prints were used to form two booklets.

Booklet A was presented to the subjects in Control Group A, Booklet B to Experimental Group B. Each booklet form was in the above order. Both include one smoking and one non-smoking male, one smoking and one non-smoking female. The order of presentation is the same in both forms: male, female; male, female.

The open booklet showed a photograph on the left-hand page and a copy of the adjective check list on the right-hand page. The same check list appeared facing each of the four photographs.

Our actual subject sample comprised 808 16- and 17-year-old science students from a generally upper-middle-class community near Berkeley. The number was divided evenly into a control group and an experimental group on the basis of academic achievement and the type of class in which they were enrolled.

Harvey, smoking — Booklet A

Janet, not smoking — Booklet A

Joe, not smoking — Booklet A

Gail, smoking — Booklet A

Harvey, not smoking — Booklet B

Janet, smoking — Booklet B

Joe, smoking — Booklet B

Gail, not smoking — Booklet B

TABLE 1
Combined Cluster Analysis Results
All Male Subjects

Nervous	Timid	Immature-Unpleasant
emotional	shy	irresponsible
high-strung	quiet	rebellious
nervous	meek	reckless
tense	timid	show-off
sensitive	awkward	interests narrow
touchy	gentle	irritable
		temperamental
None	**Pleasant**	unstable
artistic	friendly	immature
dignified	sociable	restless
infantile	pleasant	self-pitying
inhibited	good-natured	unfriendly
weak	warm	pleasure-seeking
unemotional	active	sulky
neurotic	relaxed	hasty
poised	eager	moody
submissive	easy-going	
moralistic	generous	**Adventurous**
feminine	calm	aggressive
uninhibited	self-confident	masculine
enthusiastic		rugged
suggestible	**Mature**	adventurous
formal	responsible	daring
dynamic	mature	informal
sophisticated	interests wide	energetic
anxious	broad-minded	individualistic
dominant	efficient	
sexy	frank	
unexcitable	curious	
conventional	self-controlled	
religious	independent	

TABLE 2
Common (p > .30) Descriptive Adjectives
Used By Male Subjects

Harvey, Not Smoking		Harvey, Smoking	
restless	relaxed	restless	relaxed
immature	easy-going	immature	easy-going
interests narrow	sociable	unstable	sociable
irresponsible	good-natured	irresponsible	good-natured
pleasure-seeking	interests wide*	pleasure-seeking	self-confident*
friendly	curious	friendly	independent*
calm	informal	calm	curious
			informal

Joe, Not Smoking		Joe, Smoking	
restless	independent	restless	irritable*
moody	interests wide*	moody	show-off*
rebellious	touchy	rebellious	curious*
mature*	individualistic	immature*	independent
frank*	masculine	irresponsible*	nervous
		unstable*	touchy
		interests narrow*	individualistic
		pleasure-seeking*	aggressive*
		temperamental*	informal*
		reckless*	masculine
			rugged*
			adventurous*

*Differentiates between the smoking stereotype and the not-smoking stereotype.

Classroom unit assignments to the control Group A or the experimental Group were made to match the number of subjects for both groups, the distribution of high, low, and middle stanine levels, and the class subject. It was hoped that this matching procedure would result in matched groups for such other variables as sex and smoking status, whose values were unknown at the time the subjects were assigned to a group.

The photo booklet was presented to two or three classes each period. Coverage of all thirty-seven classes took the better part of three days. The examiner entered each room and the teacher was instructed to say: "Today we are going to participate in a special project. This is Mr. ——, a psychologist from the University of California, who will explain the details." No institutional affiliation with the California Department of Public Health was mentioned.

About one week after presentation of the photographs, smoking information about the subjects was obtained by a five-minute, self-administered questionnaire. This sheet included smoking status, amount smoked, how long a smoker, sex, and name. Instructions were printed at the top of each questionnaire.

When the smoking questionnaire was complete, each teacher explained the research to his class and showed them both forms of the booklet. Most teachers reported that the subjects showed interest in the difference they saw between the two forms of the same photo. There were no spontaneous claims to having known all along what the research had been about. Two or three students did claim to have had some suspicion that cigarettes were more important than they were being told, and undoubtedly others shared this suspicion, but they were probably very few in number.

It was believed that the nature of the task they had been given would stimulate projection effects, and that interaction would result between the sex and smoking status of the subjects and the sex-smoking status of the four stimulus persons; therefore, separate analyses were carried out for each stimulus person by sex-smoking status of the subjects. The first task of analysis was to reduce the 80 adjectives to a more manageable number of concepts. The BC TRY system tapes for a Tryon system cluster and factor analysis (Tryon, R. C. and Bailey, D. E., 1965) were used, yielding six clusters of adjectives which hung together fairly well. For example, *timid* included shy, quiet, and meek; *adventurous* included aggressive, masculine, rugged, adventurous, daring, formal, and individualistic. The assumption was that the analysis of smoking effect on perception depends upon a variation of the stimulus object (i.e., the photograph) in smoking, not-smoking conditions; while the two groups of matched students are as nearly identical as experimental conditions allow.

Insofar as these data show a smoking effect for both Joe and Harvey, the reduction of the TIMID quality is the most striking result. Results for the ADVENTUROUS cluster are also interesting, especially in relation to the flavor of much of today's cigarette advertising. For one of the boys, Joe, a great increase in this quality ensued as a result of smoking. However, there seemed to be a slight decrease for Harvey as a result of smoking. Future investigations would do well to pay close attention to these qualities. To the extent to which these data reflect qualities of self which may be expressed by cigarette smoking, an increase in the quality ADVENTUROUS and a decrease in the quality TIMID could be important social gains for many teenagers. It is easy to imagine that some teenagers (and some adults as well!) would like to project this image of a person who lives a life of excitement, energetically and boldly.

Those who wish to project such an image are more likely to begin smoking regularly if they perceive smoking as a behavior which will assist them in accomplishing this goal and do not seem to be able to project these qualities in other ways. This research demonstrates that smoking does, for some students, express these qualities. Alternative behaviors for such expression are few, for it is not an easy image to project in this society even for adults. Consider the possible behaviors available to a teenager who wishes to be known as daring, rugged, masculine, adventurous, etc. Reckless driving, contact sports, petty crime, after-school fights, deviant classroom behavior, are some possibilities that come first to mind. Smoking, as a behavior for such expression, is somewhat milder and less deviant than most in such a list of behaviors.

This research has demonstrated that cigarette smoking is a psychologically meaningful behavior which serves a useful and meaningful purpose for the expression of psychological traits and qualities. Additionally, it has been seen that the effect of smoking on perceived personality is not independent of the specific personality being described. Smoking is a cue which, when added to one's behavioral matrix, does more than simply add one or another group of traits. Rather, the presence of smoking seems to require the perceiver to reorganize and reassess the total, inter-related impact of the stimulus person. The content of this reorganization is dependent on other qualities of the stimulus person and on characteristics of the subject group itself. The effect of smoking then is the result of perceiver-perceived characteristics. Future research in this area must not fail to take both sets of variables fully into account.

SUMMARY

A sample of 347 male high school students were exposed to photographs of some students shown smoking and others shown not smoking, and asked to describe each by use of an adjective check list. Differences between the smoking-non-smoking descriptions are interpreted as indications of the self-expressive value cigarette smoking behavior has in the view of students. Results are reported by the achievement level and smoking practice of the subjects. Empirically defined qualities of personality, ADVENTUROUS and TIMID, are proposed as especially relevant to investigations of the functional basis of teenage smoking.

REFERENCES

Sarbin, T. R. Personality Word Card. University of California, Berkeley, 1965.

Tryon, R. C., and Bailey, D. E. User's Manual of the BC TRY System of Cluster and Factor Analysis. 1965.

Psycho-Social Correlates of Smoking Behavior and Attitudes for a Sample of Anglo-American, Mexican-American, and Indian-American High School Students[1]

SALVATORE V. ZAGONA
University of Arizona

How to develop health education programs that will "reach" as many young people as possible — as effectively as possible — has long been a matter of concern to educators, public health people and others. The problem is becoming increasingly complicated by the growing number of competing demands for the attention of our youth. The ease with which messages can be flashed to them by radio, television, popular magazines, and other mass media — of exciting things, couched in the familiar jargon of adolescence — presents even a greater challenge to the health message to make its point. In the past (and, unfortunately, too often even now), educational programs have been developed without regard to the values, needs, and attitudes of those for whom they are intended. The language has reflected the language of the stern school teacher; the message has reflected the frame of reference of the "enlightened" adult. We seem to assume that information which reaches the middle-aged female school teacher with some sense of urgency will similarly influence the seventeen-year-old boy — a part and product of an alien and mysterious social world. The demands of age-mates, conflicts with parental values, frustrated attempts at being accepted by adults, and the agonizing rejection associated with minority group membership make the motivational structure of the adolescent a complex of contradictions.

A knowledge of the frame of reference of the adolescent is required so that lines of communication with him remain open. We are obliged, however, to bear in mind that adolescents do not exist as an abstraction, but as specific young persons from different families and communities, and from different ethnic groups, each with its own values, beliefs, and customs.

Data on individual and group differences must be uncovered and educational programs tailored to these differences. We would not expect, for example, a film on the dangers of drugs to have the same effect on an audience of Mexican-American females as on a group of Indian-American males. Similarly, the place that the act of smoking a cigarette has in the value structure of the Indian-American male may be quite different from its place in the value structure of the "middle class" Anglo-American female.

The assumptions which underlie the present research are that: (1) smoking behavior develops and is enacted within specific social contexts, and as such is subject to the same kinds of socio-cultural influences as are other socially relevant behaviors, and (2) attitudes and values related to smoking behavior, as well as other behaviors, such as drinking, are in large part culturally determined, and differ in a number of important ways from ethnic group to ethnic group.

This project was designed to explore the extent to which variables generally thought to be important in the development of smoking attitudes and behavior persist in their effect over ethnic lines. We attempted to determine how members of three ethnic groups compared with regard to:

1. attitudes and behaviors related to smoking;
2. extent to which parents and other adult models help to shape smoking attitudes and behavior;
3. extent to which peers influence the development of smoking attitudes and behavior;
4. certain "life values";
5. attitudes and behavior related to maintaining health.

Finally, we sought to order the resulting data into some theoretical framework by which we hope to clarify the observed relationships.

Mexican-Americans and Indian-Americans were selected as ethnic groups for comparison, owing to their importance as sub-cultures in Arizona. Data for these groups were to be compared with those of a relatively homogeneous sample of "Anglos" also included in the study. (In a correlative study, experimental and control

[1] This research, financed by USPHS Contract PH 108-65-14, is the product of the efforts of the entire staff of the Center for Research at Arizona on Smoking and Health (CRASH), of which Dr. Zagona is Project Director. Important contributions to the preparation of this manuscript were made by Dr. Louis A. Zurcher, Jr., now research psychologist for The Menninger Foundation; Frederick F. Ikard, now research psychologist for National Clearinghouse for Smoking and Health; Robert W. Lawrence, now at the University of New Mexico Medical School; Anthropologist Richard D. Jones; Sociologist Jean A. Johnson; and Research Assistants Roger Honomichl, Charles Christiano and Norla Antinoro.

groups were formed from each of the three ethnic groups; the experimental groups were provided with a series of communications on smoking as a hazard to health, and both groups were re-tested to determine the influence of the communications "package" on smoking behavior and attitudes. The results of this phase of the project will be reported later.)

During the spring semester of 1965, 6,346 questionnaires were filled out by students in eight high schools in southern Arizona. Of these, 440 (7.0 per cent) were later discarded because respondents had failed to indicate such necessary information as sex, grade level, smoking behavior or because they were members of ethnic groups which were not well enough represented in the sample to warrant analysis.

Ethnic identification was made on the basis of response to the following questionnaire item: "To which of the following groups of people do you belong?" (1) American Negro, (2) Anglo-American, (3) Mexican-American, (4) Chinese-American, (5) Japanese-American, (6) American-Indian (if so, what tribe?), and (7) other. Where a subject checked two or more groups he was asked to write in the *one* group to which he felt strongest identification.

The respondents were classified into the three ethnic categories:

Anglo-American (3,809: 64.5 per cent). In the Southwest, "Anglo-American" is a term widely used to distinguish those of general European background from Indian-Americans, Mexican-Americans, Negroes, and Orientals. An immigrant from southern Europe, for example, may be referred to as an "Anglo," for he is *not* a member of an otherwise physically distinguishable ethnic group. The Anglo-Americans were drawn mainly from three schools in the Tucson area, although some came from two schools in the rural communities of Casa Grande and Coolidge.

Mexican-Americans (1,112: 18.8 per cent). This group is a mixture of Spanish and Indian descent and because of the proximity to Mexico constitutes a sizeable proportion of the southern Arizona population. Nogales High School, near the border between the two countries, supplied most of Mexican-Americans, with an additional number coming from one of the Tucson high schools.

Indian-Americans (985: 16.7 per cent). This group was obtained from two boarding schools in the Phoenix area, and was made up predominantly (91.7 per cent) of members from five tribes: Papago (23.4 per cent), Navajo (23.2 per cent), Hopi (20.5 per cent), Pima (17.5 per cent), and Apache (7.1 per cent). Of course, no attempt is made to represent these tribes as forming one homogeneous cultural group; each tribe constitutes a cultural entity, but the consideration of an "Indian-American" ethnic group seems justified for the purpose of this exploratory study.

Grades nine through twelve were drawn upon for each group, breaking down to 28.1 per cent freshmen, 26.4 per cent sophomores, 24.3 per cent juniors, and 21.1 per cent seniors. Approximately half the sample were males (2,942) and half were females (2,964).

The questionnaire consisted of five sections. All subjects were asked to complete sections one and five, which were concerned with basic information and measures of attitudes. Other sections were answered according to the smoking category of the respondent: a "smoker" was one who smoked, whether daily or only occasionally; a "non-smoker" was one who had either smoked only a few experimental cigarettes or none at all. The questionnaire also included an "ex-smoker" category — one who had smoked at one time, occasionally or regularly, but did not then smoke. (Since the validity of this category among high-school students is doubtful, it will be omitted in the following discussion.)

I. INCIDENCE DATA

Incidence data by sex and school grade for Anglo-Americans, Mexican-Americans and Indian-Americans are shown in Tables 1, 2, and 3 respectively.

Smoking Category. In general, the percentage of *regular* and *occasional* smokers shows an increase for both sexes during the four years of high school for all three groups. The percentage of non-smokers decreases in both Anglo and Mexican groups, but shows little change over the four years for the Indian students. This difference may be attributed to the fact that, on the average, Indian students are older in their respective grades. Freshman students 14 years old or younger constitute 52.6 per cent of the Anglo group, but only 19.7 per cent of the

Mexicans, and 14.7 per cent of the Indian group. At the senior level, 46.0 per cent of the Anglos, 60.0 per cent of the Mexicans and 84.0 per cent of the Indian students are aged 18 years or older. Such age-in-grade differences are even more clearly shown for the female student groups within the ethnic classifications.

Sex Differences. Males, whether Anglo, Mexican or Indian, all include a higher proportion of regular smokers than do females, averaging for the four classes 14.7 per cent compared to 6.4 per cent for the girls. The proportions of occasional smokers (those who ". . . now smoke cigarettes once in a while but not every day") are roughly similar: twice as many boys smoke (14.0 per cent) as do

TABLE 1

Percentage Distribution of Cigarette Smoking Habits by Sex, School Grade, and Ethnic Group (Anglo-American: N=3809)

	Males					Females					Total
	Freshmen	Sophomores	Juniors	Seniors	Total	Freshmen	Sophomores	Juniors	Seniors	Total	
Never Smoked	26.2	23.6	19.0	17.0	21.5	47.8	44.5	37.1	37.5	41.9	
Experimental	42.4	41.1	38.6	34.1	39.2	38.6	39.3	40.4	33.8	38.1	
Ex-Occasional	14.3	10.9	11.2	11.7	12.0	6.5	4.7	7.0	8.3	6.6	
Ex-Regular	3.7	4.0	4.5	6.2	4.6	1.3	2.0	3.1	2.1	2.1	
Current Occasional	7.1	7.5	6.6	5.5	6.7	4.2	4.7	6.4	7.6	5.7	
Current Regular	6.3	12.8	20.0	25.6	16.1	1.5	4.7	6.0	10.6	5.5	
No. of Students	462	530	484	454	1930	521	443	483	432	1879	3809

girls (7.0 per cent). Almost corollary to these findings is the fact that females, whether Anglo, Mexican or Indian, all include a higher percentage of non-smokers at every grade level, averaging 36.6 per cent for all grades compared to 15.2 per cent for the boys.

Anglo-Americans (Table 1)

Males. A steady increase over the four years is noted in the proportion of regular smokers among Anglo males, but the percentage of boys who only smoke occasionally declines during the third and fourth years. The percentage of students who never attempted cigarette smoking decreases from 26.2 per cent in the freshman class to 17.0 per cent for the senior group. Also, the percentage of non-smoking experimentalists claiming "I have just tried cigarettes a few times to see what they were like," follows the same decline, from 42.4 per cent for the first year, to 34.1 per cent in the senior year.

Females. For girls, a steady increase is also noted in the proportion of regular smokers during the four years, but the proportion of occasional smokers does not drop during the last two years. Considering a 4.0 per cent increase in the percentage of regular smokers occurring between the junior and senior years, the overall proportion of smokers rises dramatically. Yet, this proportion is still lower throughout the grades than it is for Anglo males.

The proportion of females who have never smoked decreases during the first three years, but then remains stable for the senior year. Following this trend, experimental smoking also increases during the first three years

and then drops to the lowest point in the senior year. Although the percentage of girls who have never smoked is greater than that of the boys, the Anglo experimental groups reach a similar proportion in both sexes.

Mexican-Americans (Table 2)

Males. Following Anglo patterns, the proportion of regular smokers increases steadily from a low of 8.6 per cent in the first year to a high of 26.4 per cent in the senior year. But the proportion of occasional smokers, instead of dropping after the sophomore year as it does with Anglos, increases by 7.7 per cent among Mexican-Americans. The expected drop in the proportion of occasional smokers does not occur until the senior year.

Just as do their Anglo-American classmates, Mexican-American boys exhibit a steady decrease in the percentage of non-smokers, dropping from 27.6 per cent in the first year to 19.6 per cent in the last. Significantly, however, Mexican freshman boys are 6.0 per cent behind their Anglo classmates in the proportion of those who have actually tried a cigarette or two (experimentalists).

Females. Mexican-American high school girls show a gradual increase in the proportion of regular smokers among them, but this proportion is quite low, varying from 1.4 per cent of freshmen to 4.8 per cent of seniors. In contrast to Anglo females, Mexican-American girls show no tendency toward increase or decrease in the proportion of those who have smoked occasionally. In the senior year, proportionally half as many Mexican-American girls smoke as do Anglo-American girls.

Half of the Mexican-American freshman girls claimed

TABLE 2

Percentage of Cigarette Smoking Habits by Sex, School Grade, and Ethnic Group (Mexican-American: N=1112)

	Males					Females					Total
	Freshmen	Sophomores	Juniors	Seniors	Total	Freshmen	Sophomores	Juniors	Seniors	Total	
Never Smoked	27.6	19.2	13.7	12.6	19.6	50.2	46.7	33.9	35.2	43.5	
Experimental	36.8	33.6	34.7	35.6	35.2	36.9	45.3	51.4	43.8	43.0	
Ex-Occasional	17.2	19.2	13.7	11.5	16.0	5.1	3.3	5.5	7.6	5.2	
Ex-Regular	2.3	4.8	2.4	3.4	3.2	0.0	0.0	0.0	3.8	0.7	
Current Occasional	7.5	11.0	17.7	10.3	11.3	6.5	2.7	4.6	4.8	4.8	
Current Regular	8.6	12.3	17.7	26.4	14.7	1.4	2.0	4.6	4.8	2.8	
No. of Students	174	146	124	87	531	217	150	109	105	581	1112

TABLE 3

Percentage of Cigarette Smoking Habits by Sex, School Grade, and Ethnic Group (Indian-American: N = 985)

	Males					Females					Total
	Freshmen	Sophomores	Juniors	Seniors	Total	Freshmen	Sophomores	Juniors	Seniors	Total	
Never Smoked	5.8	6.3	4.3	7.8	6.0	37.8	20.0	20.0	20.7	24.8	
Experimental	26.3	21.8	15.1	25.6	22.7	46.2	49.3	47.5	41.6	46.8	
Ex-Occasional	20.4	19.0	21.5	14.4	19.1	9.1	17.3	14.5	22.1	15.1	
Ex-Regular	6.4	7.0	5.4	6.6	6.4	0.8	2.0	3.5	0.0	1.8	
Current Occasional	32.1	33.1	40.8	30.0	33.7	6.1	10.0	14.5	15.6	11.1	
Current Regular	9.0	12.7	12.9	15.6	12.1	0.0	1.3	0.0	0.0	0.4	
No. of Students	156	142	93	90	481	132	150	145	77	504	985

they had never smoked, while a slightly lower percentage (47.8 per cent) of their Anglo female classmates responded in that category. Again, just as among the Anglo girls, the proportion of non-smokers also decreases during the first three years, and then rises at a slightly lower proportion (35.2 per cent vs. 37.5 per cent) in the senior year.

Among Mexican females, the non-smoking experimental group increases in proportion much more sharply than it does among their Anglo classmates. This interest in "trying out cigarettes" occurs in the first three years in average increments of 7.1 per cent, compared to an average increment of 0.9 per cent for the Anglo girls. Even so, at the end of four years, Mexican-American girls show a non-smoker proportion of 43.8 per cent as compared to 33.8 per cent for the senior Anglo-American girls.

Indian-Americans (Table 3)

Males. Only 5.8 per cent of the Indian-American freshmen are non-smokers, but 26.2 per cent of the Anglo boys, and 27.6 per cent of the Mexican-American boys are in that category. Indian boys also differ in that the proportion of non-smokers among them does not show a general trend of increase or decrease; among both the Anglo- and Mexican-American groups there is a general decrease in the percentage of non-smokers.

At the freshman level, 26.3 per cent of the Indian-American males are experimental smokers, but 36.8 per cent of the Mexican-Americans and 42.4 per cent of the Anglo-American students are in that category. On the whole, Indian-American proportions of experimental smokers also decrease until the senior year. Thus, the major difference lies in the significantly fewer number of Indian students who have only experimented with cigarette smoking.

Approximately 9 per cent of both Indian- and Mexican-American freshmen males are regular smokers, compared to 6.3 per cent of Anglos.

The general four-year pattern in the incidence of occasional smoking follows a two- or three-year increase in proportion for all three groups, then an abrupt levelling off, as in the case of Anglo-American boys in the junior year, and finally, a reduction in the proportion of occasional smoking in the senior year. The three groups, however, start and end with different proportions of occasional smokers. (1) Anglo-American boys begin with a proportion of 7.1 per cent occasional smokers in the freshman year compared to 5.5 per cent in their senior year. (2) Mexican-American boys begin with a proportion of 7.5 per cent occasional smokers, reach a high of 17.7 per cent in the third year, followed by 10.2 per cent in the senior year. (3) 32.1 per cent of Indian-American boys are occasional smokers, followed by 40.8 per cent of the juniors and 30.0 per cent of the seniors. Thus, for Indian-Americans, and to some extent Mexican-Americans, occasional smoking seems to be the normative kind of smoking. The sharp rise in the proportion of this kind of smoking behavior occurs between the sophomore and junior years for both the Indian and the Mexican-American students.

Females. Very few Indian-American girls smoke regularly. In fact, they show the lowest percentage of regular smokers of any group, averaging 0.4 per cent for the four years, compared to 2.8 per cent for the Mexican-American girls, and 5.5 per cent for the Anglo-American girls. The major increase in proportion of regular smoking is seen among girls in the Anglo-American group. However, the percentage of occasional smokers among Indian girls is significantly higher, averaging 11.1 per cent compared with 5.7 per cent for Anglo-Americans and 4.8 per cent for Mexican-American girls.

Non-smoking females are proportionally fewer among Indian-Americans. On the four-year average only 24.8 per cent are non-smokers, compared to 41.9 per cent and 43.5 per cent for Anglo- and Mexican-American girls, respectively. Also, the general trend toward a decreasing proportion of non-smokers is not maintained by the Indian-American girls after the sophomore year.

In the first and second years, a higher proportion of Indian-American girls are experimental smokers, but during their junior and senior years Mexican-American

TABLE 4

Percentages of Current Smokers as Found in Three Independent Studies

Subject Group	Males				Females			
	Freshmen	Sophomores	Juniors	Seniors	Freshmen	Sophomores	Juniors	Seniors
Portland								
Regular	14.5	25.2	31.1	35.4	4.6	10.6	16.2	26.2
Occasional	3.8	4.5	4.4	4.3	1.7	2.4	3.9	4.4
Total	18.3	29.7	35.5	39.7	6.3	13.0	20.1	30.6
Rock Island								
Regular	13.0	19.0	26.0	31.8	4.8	5.8	10.0	17.0
Occasional	6.0	4.8	6.6	5.8	2.9	3.2	5.4	6.6
Total	19.0	23.8	32.6	37.6	7.7	9.0	15.4	23.6
(Rural) Regular	8.2	13.9	16.8	27.3	4.0	5.8	7.8	11.4
Southern Arizona (Anglo-Americans)								
Regular	6.3	13.4	20.5	25.7	1.7	4.7	6.0	10.6
Occasional	7.2	8.1	6.6	5.8	4.6	5.2	6.3	7.6
Total	13.5	21.5	27.1	31.5	6.3	9.9	12.3	18.2
(Mexican-Americans)								
Regular	9.0	12.2	16.9	26.1	1.4	2.6	4.6	4.8
Occasional	7.3	10.8	18.5	10.2	6.4	2.6	4.6	4.8
Total	16.3	23.0	35.4	36.3	7.8	5.2	9.2	9.6
(Indian-Americans)								
Regular	9.0	12.6	12.9	15.6	0.0	1.3	0.0	0.0
Occasional	32.1	33.6	40.8	30.0	6.1	11.2	14.5	15.6
Total	41.1	46.2	53.7	45.6	6.1	12.5	14.5	15.6

girls become outstanding as cigarette "testers." The total proportion of "experimenters" for each group, irrespective of school year, is 38.1 per cent for the Anglo-Americans, 43.0 per cent for the Mexican-American girls, and 46.8 per cent for the Indian-American girls.

Table 4 shows a comparative percentage distribution of current smokers as reported by three recent studies: the Portland study (Horn, *et al.*, 1959); the Rock Island County (Illinois) study (Ward, 1964), and the present data, drawn from three ethnic groups in southern Arizona. The sample studied by Horn and his associates in Portland was drawn principally from an urban population, and those by the other two studies (Rock Island County and southern Arizona) were from both urban and rural populations.

It will be noted that both the Portland and Rock Island urban samples show consistently larger proportions of current smokers than does the Anglo-American sample from the present study. It should also be noted, however, that the Arizona Anglo-American sample represented principally rural populations. A much closer correspondence of percentage distributions is found when the Rock Island *rural* samples are compared to our Anglo samples.

Indian-Americans show a larger percentage of current smokers (occasional plus regular) than do samples

from either of the other studies. However, fewer of these are in the current-regular smoker category than for any of the other samples. (An economic factor may be operating here, rather than any culture-specific prohibition.)

Table 5 shows the percentage distribution of current smokers by amount smoked and sex for the three studies. It should be noted that the Portland and Rock Island studies included only current-regular smokers. In the present study, all smokers (including occasional) are represented. Although it was shown that the Portland and Rock Island samples contributed a larger percentage of current smokers than the Anglos of the present study, a larger percentage of the current smokers in the Anglo sample are heavy smokers.

The same cross-cultural comparisons can be drawn between the Mexican-Americans and Indian-Americans of the present study and the Anglos of all three groups. The Indian group shows a larger percentage of their current smokers smoking less than one cigarette a day than do the other groups. The Mexican-American females show the same trend, while Mexican-American males show a smaller percentage in the higher smoking categories than is shown by the Anglos. There may be an economic factor at work here in all three instances. In the case of the Mexican females the cultural taboo against women smoking may also be a factor.

TABLE 5

Percentage Distribution of Current Cigarette Smokers by Average Amount Smoked Daily, Sex and Ethnic Group for 3 Studies

| | Southern Arizona Sample | | | | | | Rock Island Co. Sample | | Portland Sample | |
| | Anglo-Amer. | | Mex.-Amer. | | Ind.-Amer. | | | | | |
	Males	Females	Males	Females	Males	Females	Males	Females	Males	Females
Less than 1-6 per week	15.2	31.8	26.1	45.4	54.1	67.2	20.6	34.0	20.5	26.8
1-4 per day	24.5	29.4	34.1	34.1	34.1	19.0	25.5	28.4	25.6	32.4
5-10 per day	25.9	23.2	19.6	6.8	2.3	3.4	25.3	20.8	25.7	25.3
11-19 per day	12.5	6.2	6.5	4.5	.5	1.7	17.0	11.6	19.4	10.9
20 or more per day	19.5	6.6	8.0	9.1	1.8	1.7	11.5	5.1	8.9	4.5
Specific amount not stated	2.3	2.8	5.8	0.0	7.3	6.9	*	*	*	*
Number of Students	440	211	138	44	220	58	*	*	*	*

*Not available

SUMMARY AND DISCUSSION

The High School Pattern

The general increase each year in the percentage of high school smokers constitutes the salient finding of this study, as well as others which are not inter-ethnic in design. The pattern indicates a gradual increase in regular smokers, almost paralleling the increase in occasional smokers (every year except in the senior year in which there is a levelling-off or decline). Among the boys, particularly, whatever slight decrease does appear in the proportion of occasional smokers is matched by an increase in the proportion of regular smokers. Assuming a general inverse relation between the frequency of smokers and non-smokers, this senior-year relation may be an indication (1) that regular smokers are principally recruited from the ranks of occasional smokers, and (2) that the smoking habit diffused as far as it could among the inexperienced non-smoker group. By the junior and senior years smoking "hangouts" are well known; the custom is practiced or avoided by certain groups in which it encounters the resistance of non-smoker norms. In further support of this "saturation" theory is the fact that high school senior girls rank among the highest in percentage of non-smokers. Furthermore, among the class of senior girls, norm-sensitive and less affluent Mexican-Americans rank highest (43.5 per cent) in the percentage of non-smokers. Next are the Anglo-Americans at 41.9 per cent, and finally, the Indian-American girls with 24.8 per cent of their class reporting to be non-smokers.

Variations. Differences within this general pattern seem to relate to the different habits of males and females. For instance, for the senior girls, there is no such drop in the percentage of occasional smoking as there is among the boys. The average increment of increase continues, although it is much smaller than it is with the boys. Since all kinds of smoking (regular, occasional and even experimental) continue to increase among the girls, there is a rather sharp decline in the numbers of girls who had no smoking experience at all. A noticeable decrease takes place between the freshman and sophomore years, with a 17.1 per cent decline for female Indian-American non-smokers. Between the sophomore and junior years there is a 12.8 per cent and 7.4 per cent decline respectively, for Mexican-American and Anglo-American female non-smokers.

Continuing the analysis of differences in the ratio of non-smokers to smokers in the four-year pattern, some ethnic differences may be observed. Anglo-Americans are the most numerous in the sample, and they set the high-school pattern. Anglo boys begin high school with the lowest proportion of regular smokers, but four years later they are *highest* in this category. Mexican-Americans are close behind in following the same trend. An increase in the frequency of the regular smoking habit, however, means an increase in the social and economic opportunity for cigarette smoking. It means having money to buy them, having cigarettes at hand to satisfy requests of girl friends and buddies who offer, in return, acceptance and status. In some cases it also means being accepted as an adult by parents.

The greater percentage of occasional (compared to regular) smokers among Mexican boys may mean simply that such boys have not had the money and/or the social need to buy and keep cigarettes. This difference is particularly notable in the case of the Indian-American students who were questioned in the boarding school environment. Indian students are generally older; they are usually less homogeneous culturally, and they are less affluent than either Anglo- or Mexican-Americans.

The boarding school faculty not only plans the academic calendar but also arranges the daily round of activities for the students, from breakfast to bedtime. Opportunities to have part-time jobs, to own cars, to associate with youngsters from other cultures are decidedly limited. As a result, smoking becomes occasional smoking, taking place when cigarettes are offered or when special occasions warrant the opening of a sequestered pack.

II. PARENTAL INFLUENCES

One of the findings of the widely cited study by Horn, Courts, Taylor, and Solomon (1959) was that the amount of cigarette-smoking by high-school students is significantly related to that of their parents: most among children whose parents both smoked, intermediate where only one parent smoked, and lowest where neither parent smoked. Horn and his colleagues also observed that the smoking behavior of boys tends to conform more closely with that of their fathers; girls' smoking behavior is more nearly comparable to that of their mothers. Morison and Medovy (1961) confirmed the correlation between the smoking behavior of girls and that of their mothers; but no real link was found between boys' smoking behavior and that of either parent. Data by Salber and MacMahon (1961) indicate that whether the child and the parent are of the same sex is not important to the similarity of their smoking behavior.

It has been suggested that the parallel between parents' and children's smoking behavior may be a consequence of the attitudes toward smoking that parents reveal to their children, rather than whether (or how much) they smoke. The parent with an attitude against (or for) smoking will likely communicate that attitude to the child. The "wish-you-would-not" aspect of the attitude may be a more effective deterrent to the child than the parent's behavior itself.

Ward's (1964) attitude study of pupils in grades seven through twelve revealed a high correlation between children's smoking behavior and the attitudes of their parents. As might be expected, parental approval of smoking was reported far more frequently by smokers than by non-smokers, and disapproval was perceived more by non-smokers than by smokers. Ward also noted that when it comes to respecting parents' wishes regarding smoking, boys are clearly more rebellious than girls (p. 34). In the same study referred to above, Salber and MacMahon used father's occupation as a means of assigning social class, and found the percentage of smokers significantly greater for lower socio-economic (occupational) groups. Conversely, the proportion of non-smokers was found to be greatest among higher socio-economic categories.

The purpose of this part of the present study is to investigate the differences among ethnic groups in the influences that parents exert on the smoking behavior of their children of high-school age. Among the variables examined were parental smoking behavior and attitudes, circumstances of child-rearing within the family (whether the respondent was raised under the influence of one parent, both parents, or none) and father's occupation.

Student Smoking Related to Incidence of Parental Smoking

Confirming the findings of Horn *et al.* in the study noted above, the smoking behavior of children of both sexes — for all three ethnic groups — reflects that of his parents. Although for Anglo-American boys, there is not a significantly larger percentage of smokers in families with both parents smoking than in families where only one parent smoked, the difference between the proportions of smokers when one parent smokes and when neither parent smokes is a significant one (P<.001). Conversely, no significant differences are found among Anglo-American girls between the proportions of smokers when neither parent smokes and when only one parent smokes; but there is a significant difference (P<.01) in percentages when one parent smokes and when both parents smoke. Thus, the likelihood of an

TABLE 6

Students' Smoking Behavior as Related to Parents' Smoking Behavior
(By Percentages)

	Proportion of Students Who Smoke					
	Anglo-Amer.		Mex.-Amer.		Indian-Amer.	
Parents' Smoking Behavior	Males	Females	Males	Females	Males	Females
Both Parents Smoke	27.6 (192/ 695)	15.7 (97/ 617)	31.6 (49/ 155)	9.5 (16/ 169)	50.0 (34/ 68)	15.8 (12/ 76)
Only Mother Smokes	26.7 (31/ 116)	10.8 (11/ 102)	31.2 (10/ 32)	9.7 (3/ 31)	25.0 (3/ 12)	23.1 (3/ 13)
Only Father Smokes	24.8 (136/ 549)	10.1 (63/ 626)	23.4 (40/ 171)	6.2 (13/ 210)	46.4 (84/ 181)	9.7 (19/ 196)
Neither Parent Smokes	13.4 (60/ 447)	7.1 (30/ 425)	20.5 (24/ 117)	6.9 (8/ 116)	44.2 (57/ 129)	7.4 (9/ 122)
TOTAL	23.2 (419/1807)	11.4 (201/1770)	25.9 (123/ 475)	7.6 (40/ 526)	45.6 (178/ 390)	10.6 (43/ 407)
One or Both Not Given	(123)	(109)	(56)	(55)	(91)	(97)

Anglo-American boy's becoming a smoker seems considerably increased even when only one of his parents smokes but the probability of an Anglo-American girl's becoming a smoker increases appreciably only when *both* of her parents are smokers. It has been suggested that relationships may be accounted for by the fact that the child tends to follow the smoking example of the parent of the same sex; that the greater tendency for a boy to become a smoker when only one of his parents smokes merely reflects the fact that this smoker is far more likely to be the father than the mother. However (confirming the findings by Salber and McMahon noted above), the data in Table 6 indicate that the Anglo student does not tend to model his smoking behavior after that of a particular parent.

Mexican-American responses follow the same general pattern: the proportion of smokers is directly related to whether neither, one, or both parents smoke. The data suggest that the mother's example is followed more closely than the father's, although the difference fails to reach statistical significance. The difficulty in drawing meaningful comparisons lies in the small number of cases in which the mother smokes while the father does not. Analyses of data from a larger sample may be required to clarify these comparisons.

The same general trend is also found for the Indian-Americans, although no significant differences are noted. This may be caused partially by the heterogeneity of the Indian sample and partially by the absence of direct parental influence on the Indian children, who were living in a boarding school away from their parents. Again, the small cell sizes in some instances make it difficult to make meaningful statistical comparisons.

Children of parents who smoke were asked, "How much does your father (mother) smoke?" Interesting differences in responses are noted among the three ethnic groups. Anglo-American boys and girls who smoke report their mothers and fathers as smoking more while the non-smokers report their parents as smoking less. It should be noted, however, that these responses represent only the students' perceptions of how many cigarettes their parents smoke daily — an estimate which may be quite erroneous and could itself be the subject of further research. One might conclude either that the Anglo student's smoking behavior tends to conform to that of his parents or that he simply perceives his parents' smoking behavior to resemble his own; indeed, both these interpretations may apply.

A slightly different sex-influenced relationship appeared among Mexican-Americans. The non-smoking boy reports his father as smoking less than does the smoker; but both the smoker and non-smoker responded almost identically regarding the amount smoked by their mothers. The girls' responses form a mirror image of this trend: the non-smoker sees her mother as smoking less

than does the smoker; but both groups have very similar perceptions of the number of cigarettes smoked by their fathers. Superficially interpreted, the data suggest that Mexican-American students' smoking behavior is a function of the smoking behavior of the parent of the same sex.

No significant relationship was found between the Indian-American respondent's smoking behavior and the number of cigarettes he reports smoked daily by either parent. The absence of such a relationship may stem from the fact that the Indian-Americans were questioned in a boarding-school setting, away from parental influence.

Student Smoking Related to Attitudes of Parents Toward Student Smoking

When non-smoking students were asked who would be most upset if they were to begin smoking, a substantial majority indicated one or both of their parents. No significant differences by sex are observed within the Mexican- or Indian-American groups, but distinctions appeared among the responses of the Anglo-Americans. While the Anglo boys more often cited one parent or the other, a greater percentage of the girls reported that *both* parents would be upset if they started to smoke (P < .001), suggesting that girls expect to meet more united parental opposition to their taking up the cigarette habit.

More Mexican-Americans think one or both of their parents would be upset if they started to smoke; fewest "parental objection" responses came from the Indian-Americans. (Probability values for these differences were .001 for the males and .02 for the females.) To determine whether these differences result from the fact that the Indian-American children were questioned in a boarding school away from their parents, children from all groups were asked whether they thought their parents knew they smoked. About three-fourths of the Indian youngsters responded affirmatively, indicating a parental awareness of their smoking equal to that of the Anglo parents and greater than that of the Mexican parents. A comparatively large percentage of Anglo girls report their parents do not know they smoke. Responses by girls differ significantly from those of the boys for all three groups, the P value reaching .001 for Anglos and Indians, and .05 for Mexicans.

Non-smoking students were questioned about their main reason for not engaging in the habit. In response, the objection of one or both parents is second only to health considerations as a reason given for not smoking. Girls of all three ethnic groups cited the objection of both parents more often than did boys, but this distinction attained significance only among the Anglo-Americans (P < .001) and Mexican-Americans (P < .01). Also, Anglo girls more often report objections by the mother as their main reason for not smoking, although they do not differ significantly from the boys in reporting objections by the father. These results may be accounted for by any combination of four possible factors: (1) girls see more parental resistance to their starting to smoke than do boys; (2) girls are more compliant, and boys are more rebellious to parental objections concerning smoking; (3) an alternative questionnaire response, "Not good for you — sports," is more applicable to boys than girls, hence drawing responses away from the parental-objection choice; and (4) boys may be more reluctant than girls to admit, even on an anonymous questionnaire, that they don't smoke "because my folks would object."

The question of parental opinion toward student smoking behavior was broached directly for both smokers and non-smokers by the question: "How does or would your father (mother) feel about your smoking?" Anglo children are significantly more aware of their father's attitude toward smoking than are Mexican-Americans or Indian-Americans, whose fathers also show significantly less objection to the practice. As expected, in all cases objections to a daughter's smoking is significantly greater than to a son's.

Among Anglo-Americans, the father is perceived as disapproving the habit more often by non-smokers than by smokers (P < .001 for both males and females). He is seen as "not minding" more often by smokers than non-smokers (P < .001 for boys, P < .001 for girls). More boy non-smokers than smokers report that they do not know how their fathers do or would feel about their smoking. This is as expected, since the habit would seem to be less likely to become an issue when the child does not smoke. For the girls, an opposite trend appeared (perhaps pointing toward a tendency of girls to deny paternal objections toward their smoking behavior). To substantiate this, a comparison of responses from male and female smokers shows that the latter claim ignorance of their father's feelings about their smoking significantly more than do the boys (P < .001). A similar comparison between the non-smoking boys and girls shows no such difference, suggesting that the smoking girl has greater motivation to suppress this kind of knowledge than does her non-smoking counterpart.

The data on Mexican-Americans reveal a trend approaching that of the Anglos; smokers perceive more approval and less disapproval by their fathers than do non-smokers.

The percentage of Indian-Americans responding that their father approves of their smoking was extremely small; but significant relationships were found in some of the other categories: far more non-smokers than smokers see their fathers as disapproving (P < .001 for males, P < .01 for females), and considerably more smokers than non-smokers answered that they do not know how their father would feel about the matter (P < .001 for males, P < .05 for females).

Comparisons by sex yield information consistent with findings reported above. In every case where differences are found to be statistically significant, the girls of all ethnic groups report less approval and more disapproval, and they state more often that they do not know how their father would feel.

An equivalent question concerning how the mother does or would feel about her child's smoking reveals answers almost identical to the above. These results are in agreement with those obtained by Ward (1964) and may be explained by a combination of two factors: (1) high-school students are probably more likely to smoke if their parents approve of (or "don't mind") the practice; (2) the figures very likely represent the tendency of smokers to minimize any effects of cognitive dissonance by denying parental disapproval or by claiming that they don't know how their parents feel.

Student Smoking Related to Occupation of Father

Fathers' occupations were classified as follows: Group 1 — professional and managerial; Group 2 — sales and clerical; Group 3 — operatives (skilled laborers); Group 4 — private household, services, non-commissioned officers, and laborers. Not counted in the tabulation were responses that the father was deceased, unemployed, or retired. Virtually no differences are revealed between smokers and non-smokers according to the occupational classification of their father. The only exception is for the Anglo-American girls whose fathers are in Group 1. Here there are significantly more non-smokers than smokers. The failure to substantiate the findings of Salber and MacMahon (1961) (see p. 163 above), in this connection may very well be attributed to the different methods of classifying occupational groups. A need for further research seems to be indicated, but it would be hindered, in this type of cross-cultural study, by the relatively few Mexican- and Indian-American fathers identified with higher occupation groups.

Student Smoking Related to Being Raised by One, Both, or Neither of the Parents

For the Anglo- and Mexican-Americans, significantly more non-smoking students than smoking students answer that they they were raised by both parents. (P < .001 for Anglo males, P < .01 for Anglo females, P < .02 for Mexican males, P < .001 for Mexican females.) The trend for Indian-Americans is in the same direction, but does not reach statistical significance.

For the Anglo- and Mexican-Americans the tendency to smoke also shows a significant increase among children who perceive themselves as having been raised primarily by their mother. The trend is stronger for boys (P < .001 for the Anglos, P < .001 for the Mexicans), than for girls whose P value approaches .05 for both groups. For Indian-Americans, the relationship does not hold.

In none of the ethnic groups is there a significantly

greater tendency to smoke associated with being raised primarily by the father. Considered in conjunction with the raised-by-the-mother smoking relationship just discussed, this seems to indicate that a mother alone does not, perhaps *cannot,* provide the same degree of control over student smoking behavior as does a father.

Another point of interest is derived from a comparison by sex of those who report themselves as having been raised by someone other than either parent. While smoking and non-smoking boys do not differ significantly in this regard, significance levels for Anglo- and Mexican-American girls reached .05 and .001, respectively. This seems in accord with the relatively high degree of parental opposition to female smoking discussed above: when the girl is raised by someone other than her parents, she is likely to take up cigarette smoking as well, no doubt, as other deviant behaviors associated with lack of parental control. (The trend is seen for the Indian-Americans as well, although it does not reach statistical significance.)

The question "With whom do you currently live?" was meant to approach more directly and objectively the subject of broken homes. It was expected that a lower incidence of smoking would be associated with the response, "I *live with* both parents" than for "I *was raised by* both parents," which could include parental deaths, separations, divorces, or changes in residence by the students. (The Indian-Americans were instructed to answer the question as though they lived at their regular home instead of at a boarding school.) This was indeed true in most cases, although 72 per cent of the Mexican-American girls who smoke responded that they *lived with* both parents and only 58 per cent claimed to have been *raised by* both parents. Since this difference did not hold for the corresponding non-smokers (81 per cent currently lived with both parents, 82 per cent were raised by both), it would seem that the female Mexican-American smoker perceived herself as receiving considerably less parental guidance than does her non-smoking counterpart. Further substantiating this was the report by 14 per cent of the Mexican-American girl smokers that they were raised mostly by someone other than one or both of their parents, with only 7 per cent responding that they they lived with neither parent. A case can be made here for "uncertain" parental guidance leading to an increased tendency among these students to smoke.

It was also evident that smokers, contrasted with non-smokers, are less frequently found living with both parents than with only one or neither parent. This is readily understood in terms of parental objection and control, and found to apply to all three ethnic groups to varying degrees. For Anglo-Americans, significantly more non-smokers than smokers live with both parents (P < .001 for boys; P < .001 for girls); more smokers than non-smokers live with their mothers only (P < .001 for boys, P < .05 for girls), more smokers than non-smokers live with their father only (P = .02 for boys; not significant for girls), and more smokers than non-smokers live with neither parent (P < .001 for girls; not significant for boys).

The Mexican-American ethnic group reveals the same trend, but only two comparisons of boys reach statistical significance: more-non-smokers than smokers live with both parents (P < .02), and more smokers than non-smokers live only with their mother (the probability level approaches .05). The remaining differences are in the expected direction, but fail to attain significance.

The same relationships apply for the Indian-American sample, but to a still lesser extent; the only meaningful difference is that more of the girls who did not smoke than those who did lived with both parents (P < .05). As has often been the case, the Indian-Americans' boarding-school environment has evidently reduced the influence of the parents over their offspring's smoking behavior.

SUMMARY

The findings of Horn *et al.* (1959), Salber and MacMahon (1961), and Morison and Medovy (1961) received further support from this study, particularly in terms of the proportion of student smokers which increased directly with the number of parents (neither, one or both) that smoked. Further confirming data by Salber and MacMahon, but contrary to findings by other investigators, no significant relationship was found linking the smoking of boys and girls to that of either parent. Anglo-American smokers report heavier smoking by their parents than do non-smokers; Mexican-American smokers answer similarly, but only for the parent of the same sex. No significant parental correlation was revealed for the Indian-Americans, as was fairly consistently found to be the case in this study, although the absence of observable parental influence may be attributable to the boarding-house environment of this sample.

The smoking behavior of children seems closely associated with the attitudes of their parents toward it. To a significant extent, girls perceive their parents as being more opposed to their smoking than do boys, and, perhaps in compliance with this perceived opposition, smoke considerably less.

In agreement with Ward (1964), the data for the Anglo-Americans show that adolescent smokers tend to view their parents as approving of the habit more than do non-smokers. Little or no relationship was seen between the occupation of the father and his child's smoking habits. There was also a higher incidence of smoking among students who were raised by one or neither parent than those raised by both parents.

III. PEER GROUP INFLUENCES

Of the many forces directing the behavior of high school youth, one of the most important is the tendency to conform to peer group standards. Such peer groups, often with overlapping memberships, have their own sets of norms and expectations. By subtle forms of communication and social control, members quickly become aware of *general* and *unusual* standards of behavior, attitudes and opinions and respond to them. Salber *et al.* (1963b), investigating the development of smoking behavior among youth, found conformity to the peer group to be a major influencing factor. She found conformity expressed in such statements as "follow the crowd," "be fashionable," "be one of the gang," "because my friends do," and "because others smoke." Her data show that high school students tend to have friends with similar interests, values, and habits. Thus, smokers tend to have friends who smoke, and non-smokers tend to have non-smoking friends. As further evidence of the influence of friends on the development of smoking behavior, Horn and his associates (1959) found that while students acquire most of their cigarettes from stores or machines, some are acquired from friends — an indication, perhaps, of the importance of smoking as a shared experience.

An analysis of the differences among the ethnic groups with respect to the influence of friends on the respondents' smoking behavior was made chiefly from responses to the following questionnaire items:

A) *How do you think most girls feel when they see boys smoking cigarettes?* For the Anglo-American group, differences between males and females responding "do not care" were found to be statistically significant. Of the girls who smoke, 67 per cent claim they "do not care" if boys smoke. Boys who smoke were evenly divided in their opinions as to whether girls "don't care" or "disapprove" of boys smoking. Only 4.2 per cent of the boys who smoke think that girls "approve." By almost two to one Anglo-American boys and girls who don't smoke believe that girls "disapprove" of boys smoking cigarettes. Data for Mexican-American smokers parallel those for the Anglo-Americans; however, a significantly lower proportion of the non-smokers (of both sexes) believe that girls disapprove of boys smoking. Mexican-American non-smoking boys and girls provide strikingly similar responses to this query, as, indeed, did the Anglo-American non-smokers. The notable sexual differences in responding to this question came from the smokers, where males saw "disapproval" twice as frequently as did females. Among Indian smokers, these differences between males and females are not significant, but most girls see members of their own sex as not caring whether

boys smoke cigarettes or not. Among Indian non-smokers differences in response between males and females were also not significant, but they, too, indicated they did not care whether boys smoked cigarettes or not.

Indian boys and girls — smokers as well as non-smokers — see girls as not caring whether boys smoke; in neither case is the difference between the sexes a statistically significant one.

TABLE 7

How Do You Think Most Girls Feel When They See Boys Smoking Cigarettes?[1]

	per cent Smokers		per cent Non-smokers	
	Males	Females	Males	Females
Anglo-Americans				
Approve	4.2	8.4	5.4	3.9
"Do not care"	47.5	67.4	27.8	30.2
Disapprove	48.2	24.2	66.9	64.1
Total N	425	178	1138	1478
Mexican-Americans				
Approve	8.4	6.8	11.4	10.5
"Do not care"	45.0	70.5	40.6	41.2
Disapprove	46.6	22.7	48.0	48.4
Total N	131	44	281	488
Indian-Americans				
Approve	7.0	11.1	15.6	9.5
"Do not care"	56.0	63.0	47.5	53.8
Disapprove	37.0	25.9	36.9	36.7
Total N	200	54	122	346

[1] Data for "Quitters" have been eliminated from this and following tables for reasons noted earlier (see p. 158).

TABLE 8

How Do You Think Most Boys Feel When They See Girls Smoking Cigarettees?

	per cent Smokers		per cent Non-smokers	
	Males	Females	Males	Females
Anglo-Americans				
Approve	9.7	6.4	7.4	5.4
"Do not care"	28.8	18.2	15.5	7.9
Disapprove	61.6	75.4	77.1	86.7
Total N	424	203	1142	1479
Mexican-Americans				
Approve	9.9	4.6	11.7	10.2
"Do not care"	24.4	13.6	14.5	7.6
Disapprove	65.6	81.8	73.8	82.2
Total N	131	44	282	488
Indian-Americans				
Approve	13.9	7.3	14.3	15.1
"Do not care"	36.1	18.2	28.6	18.3
Disapprove	50.0	74.5	66.1	66.7
Total N	202	55	112	345

B) *How do you think most boys feel when they see girls smoking cigarettes?* Approximately three-fourths of our entire subject sample — regardless of sex, ethnic affiliation or smoking category — believe that boys disapprove of girls smoking cigarettes. For almost all groups (except the non-smoking Indian sample) girls saw this masculine disapproval to be more pronounced than the boys themselves did.

C) *How would you describe the smoking habits of your male friends?* As would be expected, the data for all groups show that smokers tend to associate with smokers, and non-smokers to associate with non-smokers. This trend is somewhat more marked for males, with females tending to associate about equally with smokers and non-smokers.

TABLE 9
How Would You Describe the Smoking Habits of Your Male Friends?
(By Percentages)

	Smokers		Non-smokers	
	Males	Females	Males	Females
Anglo-Americans				
All smoke	55.9	70.1	8.8	21.3
About half smoke	27.3	19.4	13.5	18.1
None smoke	16.9	9.5	77.7	60.7
Total N	433	211	1157	1488
Mexican-Americans				
All smoke	73.1	87.8	21.5	47.2
About half smoke	17.2	9.8	15.8	10.1
None smoke	9.7	2.4	62.7	42.7
Total N	134	41	284	485
Indian-Americans				
All smoke	74.4	71.9	24.2	44.2
About half smoke	9.3	14.0	12.9	11.3
None smoke	16.3	14.0	62.9	44.5
Total N	215	57	124	337

D) *How would you describe the smoking habits of your female friends?* Significant (P < .01) differences were obtained for Anglo-American male and female smokers on this item. Male smokers tend to associate with female smokers, and female smokers with other female smokers. Non-smoking males and females associate with, and seem to be influenced by, the non-smoking peer group to which they belong. Mexican-American male-female comparisons show a comparable difference (P < .01). Of the smoking males, 77.4 per cent indicated that *most* of their female associates are non-smokers, but the majority of smoking females associate with girls who are also smokers.

Indian-American smokers, males and females, differed significantly in the frequency of association with female smokers. Females claimed an equal number of smoking and non-smoking female friends. Non-smoking

males showed a significantly greater tendency (P < .01) than females to exclude smoking females from their circle of friends (93 per cent vs. 74 per cent).

TABLE 10
How Would You Describe The Smoking Habits of Your Female Friends?
(By Percentages)

	Smokers		Non-smokers	
	Males	Females	Males	Females
Anglo-Americans				
All smoke	10.9	33.8	1.3	2.1
About half smoke	14.2	30.9	2.2	5.4
None smoke	74.9	35.3	96.4	92.5
Total N	422	207	1123	1478
Mexican-Americans				
All smoke	7.5	30.2	1.1	2.5
About half smoke	15.0	23.3	1.8	4.9
None smoke	77.4	46.5	97.1	92.6
Total N	133	43	275	485
Indian-Americans				
All smoke	8.6	36.2	5.0	10.2
About half smoke	6.7	25.7	1.7	15.7
None smoke	84.7	37.9	93.3	74.1
Total N	209	58	120	343

E) *Which of the following people might be most upset if you were to begin smoking?* This item, answered by non-smokers only, distinguished between the best girl-friend or boy-friend as the one who might be the most upset if a non-smoker were to start smoking. While the influence of boy friends or girl friends on their smoking or non-smoking partners seemed to be rather small, the opposite-sex friend was invariably perceived to be more upset by the possibility of the respondent's taking up the habit. All these differences were significant beyond the .01 level. (These data should be compared with the respondents' perception of parental concern over their taking on the habit; see p. 164.)

TABLE 11
Which of the Following People Might Be Most Upset If You Were to Begin Smoking? (Non-Smokers: N = 3967)
(By Percentages)

	Best Girl Friend	Best Boy Friend	Total Subjects
Anglo-Americans			
Males	4.6	0.3	1171
Females	1.2	6.4	1503
Mexican-Americans			
Males	4.5	0.3	291
Females	0.6	4.6	503
Indian-Americans			
Males	7.3	0.7	138
Females	0.8	4.4	361

TABLE 12

Where Do You Get Your Cigarettes?

(Percentage of smokers who claim "friends" as a major source of cigarette supply)

	Males					Females					
	Freshmen	Sophomores	Juniors	Seniors	Total	Freshmen	Sophomores	Juniors	Seniors	Total	Total
Anglo-Americans	12.9	11.1	5.4	2.8	7.0	36.7	11.9	11.7	19.0	18.0	
Total Subjects	62	108	129	141	440	30	42	60	79	211	651
Mexican-Americans	17.9	23.5	11.4	9.4	15.2	23.5	28.6	40.0	30.0	29.5	
Total Subjects	28	34	44	32	138	17	7	10	10	44	182
Indian-Americans	23.4	18.5	24.0	9.8	19.5	75.0	47.1	28.6	16.7	37.9	
Total Subjects	64	65	50	41	220	8	17	21	12	58	278

F) *Where do you get your cigarettes?* (Asked of smokers only.) The percentage of friends supplying cigarettes to friends is rather small. Freshmen of all ethnic groups receive cigarettes from friends, but this source becomes less important as the student progresses through high school. More females than males receive cigarettes from their friends, and only a small proportion of Anglo-American males and females, as a group, get their cigarettes from pals. While Mexican-American males showed about the same pattern as Anglo-American males, the Mexican-American females, however, instead of dropping in their rate of receiving cigarettes from friends, increased this rate until the junior year. Results from Indian males and females correspond to those obtained for Anglo-Americans, except that friends were a much more important source of supply of cigarettes when they were freshmen.

DISCUSSION

The data indicated that the behavior and attitudes of age-mates, particularly of the same sex, are strong influences in the smoking habits and attitudes of high school students, confirming (on a somewhat broader base) findings reported by Salber *et al.* (1963).

Non-smoking students are seen to be most emphatic in their disapproval of smokers, and exclude themselves from such smoker groups. Whether this is a matter of the selectivity resulting from co-membership in non-smoking athletic or religious groups is a matter of conjecture. Perhaps the parents do not smoke and disapprove as well. The attitudes of non-smoking females toward boys' smoking are not significantly different from those of non-smoking males.

According to the judgments of their peers, Mexican-American males correspond in attitudes and associations with both the Anglo-American males who smoke and those who do not smoke. Mexican-American female smokers resemble Anglo-American female smokers in that they both have similar attitudes and association patterns, and both groups are "unconcerned" if boys smoke.

This attitude may reflect similar dating procedures in the two groups. However, the Mexican-American female non-smoker is more liberal than her non-smoking Anglo counterpart. Some disapprove while others just do not care if boys smoke. Indian-Americans do not differ from the other two groups in their approval (or disapproval) of boys smoking.

There is a definite change from one of permissiveness to one of disapproval among all ethnic divisions when they are confronted with the idea of females smoking. Among the Anglo-American males 61.1 per cent of the smokers and 77.1 per cent of the non-smokers definitely disapprove of the idea of girls smoking cigarettes. Males may feel that cigarette smoking is a masculine activity, for Mexican-American males are seen to disapprove just as strongly as Anglo-American males. Indian-Americans, however, seem to be undecided as to the idea, with equal percentages reporting approval, not caring or disapproval.

It would be interesting to determine the female motivation for taking on a behavior that meets with the (claimed) disapproval of all groups. In all ethnic groups studied, smokers characterize their friends as smokers, and non-smokers describe their friends as non-smokers.

Most high school students, when first starting to smoke, acquire cigarettes from their friends, an indication that peers contribute (as suppliers, at any rate) to the development of the cigarette habit. The trend is for freshmen to acquire cigarettes from friends, and then, as they progress through high school, to furnish an increasingly larger proportion of their own cigarette supply.

SUMMARY

There is strong evidence that the behavior and attitudes of peers influence smoking by high school students. Similarities of attitudes toward smoking are accompanied by similarities in smoking behavior among peers: smokers tend to associate with smokers, and non-smokers tend to associate with non-smokers. Non-smoking males apparently influenced at different times by different norms have both smoking and non-smoking male and female friends. The indications are, however, that smoking behavior is consistent within particular student peer groups and that it may be a factor in barring or admitting individuals to membership.

This consistency in smoking behavior and attitudes among peers is either a consequence of the need to alter behavior toward conformity, or an expression of the factor of selection, i.e., the youngsters seek out acquaintances who both act and feel as they do with regard to smoking. This conformity to the smoking behavior of associates is most strikingly seen for male smokers and female non-smokers.

IV. VALUE ORIENTATIONS

This section deals with some basic value orientations assumed to be related to smoking attitudes and behavior of the three ethnic divisions included in the study. Measures of value orientations were derived from scores on a scale developed by Rosen (1956, 1959), which was included in the questionnaire filled out by our subject sample.

In studies leading to the development of his scale, Rosen demonstrated that social classes and ethnic groups can be distinguished with respect to certain value orientations. To measure motives, values and aspirations of different racial groups, he divided "the individual's psychological and cultural orientation toward achievement" into three groups: (1) Activistic-Passivistic Orientation, (2) Individualistic-Collectivistic Orientation, and (3) Present-Future Orientation. Rosen described these three orientations as follows:

1. *Activistic-Passivistic Orientation* concerns the extent to which the culture of a group encourages the individual to believe in the possibility of his manipulating the physical and social environment to his advantage. An activistic culture encourages the individual to believe that it is both possible and necessary for him to improve his status; a passivistic culture promotes the acceptance of the notion that individual efforts to achieve mobility are relatively futile.

2. *Individualistic-Collectivistic Orientation* refers to the extent to which the individual is expected to subordinate his needs to the group. Rosen's study was specifically concerned with the degree to which the society expects the individual to maintain close physical proximity to his family, or orientation, even at the risk of limiting vocational opportunities; and the degree to which the society emphasizes group incentives rather than personal rewards. The collectivistic society places a greater stress than the individualistic on group ties and group incentives.

3. *Present-Future Orientation* concerns the society's attitude toward time and its impact on behavior. A present-orientated society stresses the merit of living in the present, emphasizing immediate gratifications; a future-orientated society encourages the belief that planning and present sacrifices are worthwhile, or morally obligatory, in order to insure future gains (Rosen, 1959, pp. 80–81).

Rosen found significant differences among six racial and ethnic groups in his study: (1) social class level was more significantly related to achievement motivation than ethnicity, (2) social class was significantly related to achievement values, (3) social class was significantly related to vocational aspiration.

In another study, Rosen (1959) found that Italian and French-Canadian subjects were more passivistic, collectivistic, and present-oriented, in contrast to the Jews, Protestants, and Greeks who participated in the study. Bronson (1966) found a significant relationship between scores on the Rosen Scale and the number of years of schooling for a sample of Mexican-Americans. Persons with less schooling tended to respond to value items in a pattern expressing a passive, collectivistic, and present orientation.

The purposes of the present study are (1) to determine gross value orientations as measured by the Rosen Scale of a sample of Anglo-, Mexican-, and Indian-American high school students in southern Arizona; (2) to compare value orientations of each group with their smoking behavior; and (3) to compare value scores of male and female smokers and non-smokers.

RESULTS AND CONCLUSIONS

Confirming Rosen's previous finding of differences for other ethnic samples, significant differences were found in value orientations of Anglo-, Mexican-, and Indian-American high school students. Moreover, significant relationships were found between the value orientations of each group and their smoking behavior. In general, female non-smokers tended to contrast most with other groups, being the most activistic, individualistic and future-oriented of all those in the sample.

Significant differences in Rosen Scale responses were found among Anglo-, Mexican-, and Indian-Americans in 60 of 77 chi square comparisons made. Of the 60, 56 reached a P value of .001 or better. Fourteen of the 17 comparisons failing to reach significance were intra-ethnic, between-sex comparisons.

Anglo-American subjects tended to be significantly more activistic, individualistic, and future oriented. Mexican- and Indian-Americans tended toward a more passivistic, collectivistic, and present orientation. A greater difference was found between Anglo-Americans and Indian-Americans than between Anglo-Americans and Mexican-Americans, i.e., Indian-Americans were the most passivistic, collectivistic, and present-oriented of all three ethnic divisions.

A. Ethnic Group Comparisons (By Sex)

Response frequencies for the various subgroups shown in Table 1 are termed activistic or passivistic, individualistic or collectivistic, and future- or present-tending. More specifically, the dominant trends are summarized in the following categories:

The Active-Passive Polarity

Q 1. All a man should want out of life is a secure, not too difficult job, with enough pay to afford a decent car, and some day, a home of his own.

A greater percentage (P < .001) of Anglo-American females (58.5 per cent) disagreed with the statement than the Anglo-American males (50.4 per cent), indicating comparatively more activism on the part of the Anglo-American females. Also, a higher percentage of the Mexican-American males (60.5 per cent) and the Indian-American males (59.5 per cent)agreed with the statement than did their female counterparts (female Mexican-American 53.8 per cent), female Indian-American (50.5 per cent) indicating that they too showed a more passive orientation than their female classmates.

Q 2. When a man is born, the success or failure he is going to have is already in the cards, and there is not much he can really do to change it.

Once again, a higher percentage of the Anglo-American females (87.5 per cent) disagreed with the statement, indicating a more activistic attitude than their male counterparts (82.3 per cent). Seventy-four and seven-tenths per cent of the Mexican-American females disagreed, vs. 69.0 per cent of the males.

Indian-American males and females revealed a more passivistic orientation with 53.8 per cent of the females and only 49.9 per cent of the males disagreeing with this statement.

Q 3 The secret of happiness is not expecting too much out of life and being content with what comes your way.

The Anglo-American males and females scored toward activism on this question, as contrasted with Mexican- and Indian-American males and females, whose responses tended toward passivism.

The Individualistic-Collectivistic Polarity

Q 1. Moving away from one's parents is the most difficult thing for a person to do.

TABLE 13

Value Orientations for Three Ethnic Groups: Male-Female Comparisons (By Percentages)

A. Activistic-Passivistic Orientation

1) All a man should want out of life is a secure, not too difficult job, with enough pay to afford a decent car, and someday, a home of his own.

	Males			Females		
	Agree	Disagree	Neither	Agree	Disagree	Neither
Anglo-Americans	37.0	50.4	12.6	29.4	58.5	12.1
Mexican-Americans	60.5	28.1	11.4	53.8	32.7	13.5
Indian-Americans	59.5	20.5	20.0	50.5	27.6	21.9

2) When a man is born, the success or failure he is going to have is already in the cards, and there is not much he can really do to change it.

	Males			Females		
	Agree	Disagree	Neither	Agree	Disagree	Neither
Anglo-Americans	9.3	82.3	8.4	6.2	87.5	6.2
Mexican-Americans	16.9	69.0	14.1	11.9	74.7	13.4
Indian-Americans	29.3	49.9	20.9	23.1	53.8	23.1

3) The secret of happiness is not expecting too much out of life and being content with what comes your way.

	Males			Females		
	Agree	Disagree	Neither	Agree	Disagree	Neither
Anglo-Americans	38.1	46.1	15.7	40.2	46.7	13.1
Mexican-Americans	51.8	30.6	17.6	55.4	27.3	17.3
Indian-Americans	51.2	19.7	29.2	58.2	19.5	22.3

B. Individualistic-Collectivistic Orientation

1) Moving away from one's parents is the most difficult thing for a person to do.

	Males			Females		
	Agree	Disagree	Neither	Agree	Disagree	Neither
Anglo-Americans	47.6	28.0	24.4	47.0	31.0	22.0
Mexican-Americans	67.2	14.4	18.4	66.3	18.3	15.4
Indian-Americans	60.1	18.4	21.4	63.7	18.2	18.2

2) The best kind of job to have is one where you are part of an organization all working together even if you don't get any credit.

	Males			Females		
	Agree	Disagree	Neither	Agree	Disagree	Neither
Anglo-Americans	35.3	37.5	27.2	33.6	41.5	25.0
Mexican-Americans	42.8	33.7	23.5	32.3	39.6	28.1
Indian-Americans	46.3	24.4	29.3	43.9	30.4	25.7

C. Present-Future Orientation

1) Planning for the future only makes a person unhappy since your plans hardly ever work out anyway.

	Males			Females		
	Agree	Disagree	Neither	Agree	Disagree	Neither
Anglo-Americans	14.6	71.6	13.7	7.5	84.4	8.1
Mexican-Americans	21.6	61.3	17.1	17.3	61.9	20.8
Indian-Americans	28.5	43.0	28.5	25.8	48.1	26.0

2) Nowadays, with the world conditions the way they are, the smart person lives for today and lets tomorrow take care of itself.

	Males			Females		
	Agree	Disagree	Neither	Agree	Disagree	Neither
Anglo-Americans	20.1	63.7	16.2	19.2	67.2	13.6
Mexican-Americans	26.0	52.6	21.4	26.4	51.7	21.9
Indian-Americans	36.7	34.3	29.0	36.2	35.6	28.2

Q 2. The best kind of job to have is one where you are part of an organization all working together even if you don't get any credit.

Anglo-American males and females revealed a more individualistic orientation than Mexican- and Indian-Americans. Mexican-American males and females scored highest in the direction of a collectivistic orientation. Significant differences were noted in response to question No. 1 in all comparisons except the following: 1) Anglo- and Mexican-American females, and 2) male and female Indian-Americans.

The Present-Future Polarity

Q 1. Planning for the future only makes a person unhappy since your plans hardly ever work out anyway.

Q 2. Nowadays, with the world conditions the way they are, the smart person lives for today and lets tomorrow take care of itself.

Anglo-American females disagreed more frequently with both items than any other group, including Anglo-American males. Mexican-Americans did not differ significantly from Indian-Americans on this scale. There were, however, significant differences in every other case, especially between Anglo-American and Mexican-American males.

B. Smokers vs. Non-Smokers

An analysis of the data to determine significant differences of orientation between smokers and non-smokers revealed the following:

The Active-Passive Polarity

With but one exception there were no notable differences in responses between smokers and non-smokers. Mexican- and Indian-Americans were generally passive and Anglos were active. Anglo female *non-smokers* were most active of all, but Anglo female *smokers,* curiously, registered a "passive" response to Statement No. 3 "The secret of happiness is not expecting too much out of life . . ."

Non-smokers generally tended to intensify the values toward which their group was tending, that is, non-smoking Anglos were most active and non-smoking Mexicans and Indians were most passive. Significant differences were found between Anglo- and Mexican-American non-smokers in two out of three cases. Also, Indian-Americans registered the most passive responses to this set of statements.

The Individualistic-Collectivistic Polarity

Again, with but one exception, no differences were noted in the responses of smokers and non-smokers. Generally, on Q 1. all respondents tended to be more "collec-

tive" oriented with the exception of Anglo female *smokers* who registered the only "individualistic" response in the series. On Q 2. Anglo-Americans and Mexican-American females were individualistic; Mexican-American males and Indian-American males were collectivistic. Their non-smokers' responses only tended to emphasize this contrast. As might be expected, non-smoking Anglo-Americans differed most from non-smoking Indian-Americans. Perhaps the most curious contrast is between the Mexican-American males and females, a contrast revealed in response to Q 2. of this section, "The best kind of job . . . where you are part of an organization . . ." More Mexican boys agreed with this item than disagreed; but more Mexican girls tended to disagree, with the smokers among them emphasizing the contrast.

The Present-Future Polarity

Generally all groups — smokers and non-smokers — tended toward future orientation, yet Indian-American males were mixed in their response to the first item with about half of the smokers agreeing and half disagreeing. The non-smokers, however, registered a definite *future* oriented response. On Q 2, Indian males and females showed present orientation, yet there was no real difference between Indian smokers and non-smokers on this statement.

Anglo-Americans differed from both Mexican- and Indian-Americans on this scale, and the non-smokers intensified all differences. In short, significant differences were found in the value orientations of Anglo-, Mexican-, and Indian-American high school students. Anglo-Americans were activistic, individualistic and future oriented, while the Mexican- and Indian-Americans were more passive, collectivistic, and present oriented.

Significant relationships were found also between the value orientations of the groups and their smoking behavior. That is, non-smokers tended more to adhere to whatever dominant mode was expressed by their group as a whole. Finally, the data tend to confirm the usefulness of the Rosen Scale as a means of comparing ethnic groups by contrasting basic attitudes expressed by individuals with different cultural backgrounds.

SUMMARY

The smoking habits and some value orientations of Anglo-, Mexican-, and Indian-American high school students were compared. Significant group differences were found in value orientations, in value orientations and smoking behavior, and between the value orientations of the smokers and non-smokers (males and females) of the groups. Data confirmed the Rosen Scale as a valid measure of inter-ethnic differences in certain value orientations.

TABLE 14

Value Orientations for Three Ethnic Groups: Percentage Comparisons by Sex and Smoking Category

A = agree   D = disagree   N = neither agree nor disagree

A Activistic-Passivistic Orientation

1) All a man should want out of life is a secure, not too difficult job, with enough pay to afford a decent car, and someday, a home of his own.

	Males						Females					
	Smokers			Non-Smokers			Smokers			Non-Smokers		
	A	D	N	A	D	N	A	D	N	A	D	N
Anglo-Americans	40.2	44.2	15.6	35.7	53.7	10.6	30.9	54.4	14.7	37.0	59.2	11.3
Mexican-Americans	62.8	25.6	11.6	58.0	29.3	12.7	52.3	36.4	11.4	54.6	31.8	13.6
Indian-Americans	57.3	23.1	19.6	56.5	20.2	23.4	48.2	26.8	25.0	49.6	27.9	22.6

2) When a man is born, the success or failure he is going to have is already in the cards, and there is not much he can really do to change it.

	Males						Females					
	Smokers			Non-Smokers			Smokers			Non-Smokers		
	A	D	N	A	D	N	A	D	N	A	D	N
Anglo-Americans	13.0	74.9	12.1	8.1	84.8	7.1	9.3	81.4	9.3	5.6	88.4	6.0
Mexican-Americans	18.1	72.4	9.4	15.3	68.7	16.0	11.4	77.3	11.4	11.8	74.9	13.3
Indian-Americans	30.3	44.4	25.3	26.4	57.6	16.0	14.3	60.7	25.0	24.1	52.8	23.2

3) The secret of happiness is not expecting too much out of life and being content with what comes your way.

	Males						Females					
	Smokers			Non-Smokers			Smokers			Non-Smokers		
	A	D	N	A	D	N	A	D	N	A	D	N
Anglo-Americans	37.4	42.4	20.2	38.9	47.6	13.5	46.1	40.7	13.2	39.5	47.9	12.6
Mexican-Americans	43.0	35.9	21.1	56.7	27.3	16.0	52.3	27.2	20.5	56.1	27.5	16.4
Indian-Americans	48.7	19.7	31.6	57.4	17.3	25.4	48.1	27.8	24.1	58.5	19.1	22.4

B Individualistic-Collectivistic Orientation

1) Moving away from one's parents is the most difficult thing for a person to do.

	Males						Females					
	Smokers			Non-Smokers			Smokers			Non-Smokers		
	A	D	N	A	D	N	A	D	N	A	D	N
Anglo-Americans	44.9	27.8	27.3	49.4	27.3	23.3	33.8	44.8	21.4	49.8	27.9	22.3
Mexican-Americans	69.8	17.5	12.7	65.9	14.0	20.1	45.5	36.4	18.2	68.5	16.3	15.2
Indian-Americans	57.8	18.8	23.4	61.4	20.2	18.4	50.9	25.5	23.6	68.8	12.5	18.8

2) The best kind of job to have is one you are part of an organization all working together even if you don't get any credit.

	Males						Females					
	Smokers			Non-Smokers			Smokers			Non-Smokers		
	A	D	N	A	D	N	A	D	N	A	D	N
Anglo-Americans	33.2	36.9	29.9	36.8	37.7	25.5	28.6	40.4	31.0	33.9	42.1	24.0
Mexican-Americans	41.4	31.3	27.3	43.0	35.7	21.3	32.6	44.2	23.3	32.4	39.8	27.7
Indian-Americans	45.1	24.1	30.8	46.3	25.2	28.5	41.8	23.6	34.5	44.8	31.2	24.0

C Present-Future Orientation

1) Planning for the future only makes a person unhappy since your plans hardly ever work out anyway.

	Males						Females					
	Smokers			Non-Smokers			Smokers			Non-Smokers		
	A	D	N	A	D	N	A	D	N	A	D	N
Anglo-Americans	23.4	59.6	17.1	11.6	76.6	11.8	14.8	75.4	9.9	6.4	85.9	7.7
Mexican-Americans	22.8	57.5	19.7	20.3	64.8	14.9	25.6	53.5	20.9	16.7	62.9	20.4
Indian-Americans	35.2	35.8	29.0	28.7	45.1	26.2	21.4	46.4	32.1	26.2	48.5	25.3

2) Nowadays, with the world conditions the way they are, the smart person lives for today and lets tomorrow take care of itself.

	Males						Females					
	Smokers			Non-Smokers			Smokers			Non-Smokers		
	A	D	N	A	D	N	A	D	N	A	D	N
Anglo-Americans	24.0	54.9	21.2	18.5	67.3	14.2	26.2	59.4	14.4	18.0	68.2	13.7
Mexican-Americans	24.2	59.4	16.4	26.2	50.9	22.9	36.4	45.5	18.2	25.5	52.2	22.4
Indian-Americans	38.2	33.0	28.8	37.9	33.9	28.2	33.9	35.7	30.4	35.9	37.0	27.1

V. HEALTH ATTITUDES AND PRACTICES

The following discussion deals with the health attitudes and practices of the students of the three ethnic groups and relates these to their cigarette-smoking behavior. Also briefly summarized is the development of health values for each of the groups from a historical perspective. Three general questions were considered:

1. How aware — or interested — are high school students in the state of their health? What are the differences among the ethnic groups and between smokers and non-smokers in this awareness?

2. Are there differences among the ethnic groups and between smokers and non-smokers with respect to the amount of "control" they believe they can exercise over the state of their health? How is the deterministic, "role of fate" philosophy related to health practices and attitudes among these high school groups?

3. What relationship exists between high-school students' expressions of concern about the effects of smoking on health and their actual smoking behavior?

Anglo-American Attitudes Toward Health

Anglo-American attitudes toward health do not of course exclusively belong to this ethnic group, since Mexican- and Indian-American students are continually in contact with these through the generally Anglo-dominated society in which they live. This is especially true in the schools. At the risk of over-generalizing, one might characterize the contemporary Anglo-American as being 1) health conscious, 2) progress or activity oriented toward a solution to health problems, 3) specialist oriented for treatment, and 4) materialistic in considering what leads to good health practices.

The Anglo-American consciousness of health is related to a number of factors: a high level of prosperity, the rapid advance of medical knowledge, increased attention to nutrition both at home and in the school, mass media campaigns, and so on. Anglo-Americans have been given objective standards for the best physical performances of their bodies, and the eight-hour day is considered a normal work-performance period. Increased conformity, the presence of school nurses, factory clinics, military hospitals, Medicare, and other governmental and private health insurance programs reflect the importance placed upon good health by society.

Americans most commonly meet health problems with the positive attitude of doing something about them. The common phrase "Help stamp out ——" well reflects the view that with sufficient concern and attention even the most difficult of diseases can be eliminated. The public expects control of epidemics. Whatever mystery remains in death is vitiated by statistics and research reports. No Anglo-American is going to meet death passively.

The Anglo-American sees disease as the product of numerous causes; accordingly, heart disease, tuberculosis, and ulcers are all separate and distinct in their manifestations and causes, and each needs to be treated separately and distinctly.

Proper health care is tabulated in terms of money, men, and materials. Health is normal, sickness abnormal, and problems of health become problems of serving people properly, communicating the values of the services tendered, and convincing people to practice good health habits.

Indian- and Mexican-American Folk Medicine and Attitudes Toward Health

The health attitudes of present-day Mexican-Americans tend to reflect early Spanish medical practices and theories. Indian-American attitudes toward health vary considerably among the different tribes (as do other aspects of culture) and may be linked to aboriginal concepts.

The cultures of the various tribes include curing practices which are consistently passed on from generation to generation, also serving to integrate the members of small tribal communities. Health practices receive differential emphasis depending upon what culture is under discussion. The Papago tribe seems to emphasize group singing as a curing method; the Zuni have special curing societies and kivas; and the Navajos stress both singing and dancing. All of these Indian cultures, however, have at least some of their beliefs and practices based on the early Spanish conquerors.

The Spanish brought to the Western world a system of medicine that had its roots in the writings of Hippocrates. Basically it was the system of humors authoritatively held during the Renaissance coupled with an additional set of superstitions learned during the Arab occupation of Spain. Sound health is seen as resulting from a balance of the four humors, and sickness as imbalance which might be rectified by purges, internal medicine, bleeding, diet, cupping, or some combination of these methods.

Spanish theories of medicine and health penetrated the health notions of the Indians whose use of herbs in turn influenced Spanish concepts and practices. Certain treatments — such as massage, blood sucking, and emetics — had already been practiced by the Indians before the arrival of the Spanish; but Spanish and Indian cultures shared certain superstitions concerning loss of soul, infusion of evil spirits, and witchcraft. The mixture of all these practices has become what is now the holistic folk medicine of cultures descendant of Spanish-Indian amalgamation (Foster, 1953, pp. 201–204).

In classifying Mexican-American folk diseases, Holland (1963, pp. 92–93) called them diseases of dislocation of internal organs, diseases of emotional origins, and diseases of magical origins. They are treated by women known as *curanderas,* who have a broad role in Mexican-American and urban Indian cultures. The woman, usually Spanish-speaking and a close friend of the family, advises patients in simple terms, using concepts they understand. Families will first seek out a *curandera,* yet many will also seek help from a sympathetic specialist — even one who does not speak Spanish — if he fulfills the role of a curer. For example, chiropractors are popular because they advertise in Spanish, show respect to the beliefs and cures of the people, and charge reasonable fees.

Standards of health are well established in the family, which is the center of the health program. Since an illness will affect them all because of the time, effort, and money spent, relatives are very concerned about symptoms. All family members are consulted in making medical decisions, and older persons have the greatest influence. The authority of the family is above that of any attending medical practitioner (Clark, 1959, pp. 206–208).

Holland says that traditional medicine, unlike modern scientific medicine, is the creation of the common people, the end product of knowledge of herbal cures and magico-religious assumptions which they share. It is the wisdom of the forefathers handed down from generation to generation through which the layman perceives and interprets experience related to illness (1963, p. 90).

While the folk-medicine beliefs of the Mexican-Americans and Indian-Americans have much in common, the health attitudes of the two ethnic groups are subject to different cultural influences. The Indian-Americans to a large extent retain their tribal affinities which serve to perpetuate beliefs and practices of healing. The Mexican-Americans have become more urbanized and, in the process, more "Anglo-Americanized" so that, according to Madsen, "through education and other contacts with the Anglo world," the younger generation of all classes has become increasingly skeptical of supernatural beliefs derived from Mexican folk medicine (1964, p. 68).

Folk Attitudes and Health Practices

Returning to our high-school students with their different experiences, one may now understand the conflict between the two medical approaches. Across the United States the doctor by virtue of his training is permitted to issue orders, and he expects to have them obeyed. In contrast, the folk curer (*curandera*) is not authoritarian and only advises. Also the more objective, clinical approach common nationally is not warm nor does it show enough interest in the patients to suit folk believers. Finally, the Anglo-American doctor's no-time-to-waste efficiency seems unduly discourteous to a Mexican- or Indian-American. He demands more time and attention in the treatment of his illness. In short, doctors and hospitals are too cold, too hurried, and too expensive for those with folk beliefs.

Contrasting Mexican- or Indian-American folk medicine to Anglo-American secular medicine, it will be observed that instead of being health conscious, Mexican-Americans and Indian-Americans are soul conscious. Their attention is focused on how to adjust to infirmities and to soothe the anguish of the spirit. Faced with death and disease, they are fatalistically oriented, rather than activity-oriented. As Chance has commented, this fatalism is a result of facing up to realities in the past:

The acceptance of illness as a normal part of the life cycle has its roots in the traditional culture pattern where attitudes of fatalism, patience, and endurance were basic to the process of survival (1962, p. 414).

This is not to say that folk-believers do not do anything about illness. On the contrary, in their view everything possible is done, but most of their activity is of a personal and religious nature.

Instead of recognizing different etiologies, they view all or most diseases as being caused by just two or three major maladjustments. For example, besides the idea of the four humors, the principle of harmony is common among Indian curing beliefs. Navajo, Hopi, and Papago all maintain formally a belief in the curing power of good thoughts and a harmonious relationship with the world around them.

Finally, instead of viewing health problems materialistically simply as a public problem in logistics requiring bigger and better national programs, folk-believers tend to view illness and misfortune personally or on a family basis. Illness and accidents are often envisioned as punishments for sin. In order to get well, the afflicted person must confess his sin. Illness becomes a mysterious challenge sent either by God or something evil to test the faith or will of a person to survive. The idea of health among folk-believers is the idea of life, and life includes a certain amount of disease; but if fate intends it, nothing can interfere with death.

Implications for Cross-Cultural Health Programs

The following data explore attitudes toward health among Anglo-American, Mexican-American, and Indian-American students. While for these different cultural groups the relationship between these attitudes and smoking behavior may vary, they may also have enough in common to suggest to investigators that anti-smoking information be approached in ways which reflect the dual cultural environment of Mexican- and Indian-American students.

Responses to four questionnaire items were analyzed to determine the relationship between student attitudes toward their own health and smoking behavior. The items and the summaries of response patterns follow:

Item 1. *How would you rate your present state of health?*

    (good)   (fair)   (poor)

This query was intended to reveal whether or not smokers had a higher opinion of their health than non-smokers; whether males, who as a group contribute the higher proportion of regular smokers, had a higher frequency of "good" health appraisals, and whether or not there were any differences among the ethnic divisions in the types of appraisals. The student was asked implicitly to define good or poor health and compare his own to this abstract notion.

In the resulting data, the non-smokers generally ranked themselves in better health than did the smokers. Among smokers and non-smokers alike, there was little difference found between boys and girls in either the Anglo- or Indian-American groups. However, the Mexican-American boys usually had a vastly higher opinion of the condition of their health than did their female counterparts.

Cross-culturally, the Anglo-American group appraised themselves more frequently in good health than did either the Mexican- or the Indian-Americans, with the latter responding least frequently that they were in good health.

Item 2. *How concerned are you about the effects of smoking on your health?*

    a. Very concerned

    b. Fairly concerned

    c. Only slightly concerned

    d. Not at all concerned

The intention here was to ascertain whether the group which claimed the greatest concern about the effects of smoking would be the group including fewest smokers. Ultimately this question posed the prospect of having to give up smoking in the interest of good health. When an individual's smoking habit is regular and established, he may feel that he is being asked to become uncomfortable and nonsociable if he gives it up. But to an experimental or occasional smoker, the prospect of quitting merely means refusing a proffered cigarette or two.

Smokers proved to be definitely less concerned than the non-smokers about the effects of smoking on their health. The boys generally appeared more concerned than the girls, but this difference attained significance only in the Indian-American group. (The Anglos were the least concerned, and the Indians were the most concerned; the Mexicans were in between.)

Item 3. *Trying to stay healthy is pretty much a waste of time because when your time comes there is nothing you can do about it.*

    a. Agree

    b. Neither agree nor disagree

    c. Disagree

This statement and the one following were used to uncover those who had "fatalistic" attitudes toward their health. There was also the hope of discovering whether such attitudes were more common among smokers or non-smokers, among the boys or the girls and in which ethnic group the view was most prevalent.

All those who smoked were more fatalistic than those who did not; the boys were more fatalistic than the girls in the Anglo- and Indian-American groups, but the Mexican-American girls were more fatalistic than their male counterparts. The Indians were more fatalistic than the Mexicans, who in turn were more fatalistic than the Anglos.

Item 4. *Which of the following best describes how you feel about health and illness?*

    a. If I take care of myself, I can avoid all or most illnesses.

    b. If I take care of myself, I can avoid some illnesses.

    c. It does not matter how I take care of myself, because if I am going to get sick, I am going to get sick.

As would be expected, the smokers were significantly more fatalistic than non-smokers, but no reliable difference appeared between the sexes. The Indian-Americans were the most fatalistic, however, followed by the Mexicans and then the Anglos. Indian boys were significantly more concerned than were Indian girls.

SUMMARY

It is recognized that health attitudes and values are often strongly influenced by the family and other primary groups. To present health information in the schools to children in the hope that this information influences attitudes, values and behaviors that are strongly entrenched culturally may be unrealistic. There is evidence, principally drawn from interviews with these children, that they do "accept" this information, are able to learn its details and recite them if necessary in the classroom. But in the familiar surroundings of the home, age-old customs, values and beliefs prevail; the learning is left in the classroom, and behavior remains uninfluenced. To deal with the problem of modifying attitudes and behavior in terms of their social contexts, the health educator should have the advantage of at least some awareness of ethnic group differences and their socio-cultural determinants.

We have briefly described a few health beliefs, customs, and attitudes peculiar to the three ethnic groups in our sample. Obviously, these have implications for the preparation of education programs, particularly as these may relate to health practices.

The health attitudes of the three groups used in the study appeared to be related to the following variables:

1. *Sex.* In responding to the second question about fate's role and health measures, the boys were more fatalistic in both the Anglo- and Indian-American groups. The girls, however, were more fatalistic in the Mexican-American group.

2. *Smoking Behavior.* The non-smokers appraised themselves as being in better health, more volitional and less fatalistic, and more concerned about the effects of smoking on their health. There seemed to be a relationship between contemporary Anglo-American secular health attitudes and the incidence of non-smoking behavior among all three ethnic groups.

3. The data from the third question revealed no significant difference between boys and girls in their responses. If anything, the girls were slightly more fatalistic than the boys.

VI. AN INTERPRETATION OF SOME DOMINANT TRENDS

A practical question serves to unite the aims of the Southern Arizona Project: "How may we best communicate the hazards of smoking to high school students so they will not smoke?" Stated this way, the question implies a certain audience homogeneity. But teachers and school administrators with whom our staff members discussed the problems of developing smoking education programs consistently complained of problems in organizing materials that would be uniformly effective for their intended audiences. In populations representing widely divergent socio-economic levels, ethnic backgrounds, and rural-urban identification, for example, appeals that would prove effective for one group may, for another, fall on deaf ears. Thus it soon became apparent that one of the first problems of designing effective educational materials is to determine the ways in which groups would be expected to differ in their reactions to these programs.

Previous studies have adequately revealed the strong influence of peer groups and parents on the behavior of high school students. But how do these types of influences vary with ethnic differences? How do cultural differences in health views and attitudes serve to resist or favor the "pitch" against smoking? Are the differences great enough to justify several tailor-made approaches designed to reach the insulated groups? These questions have stimulated this five-part analysis of audience-centered research. In the first section, we described the "facts" of smoking in our sample — the quantity of cigarettes consumed and the frequency of various kinds of smoking, whether *regular, occasional* or *experimental,* among student grades and ethnic groups. The second and third sections explored the influence of certain social relations on smoking behavior. What ethnic differences are revealed in the relationships of parental smoking behavior and attitudes to those of their children? How great an influence do peers have in either discouraging or recruiting new smokers? The next two sections then focused on different value orientations and attitudes toward health that were related, possibly, to different frequencies of smoking behavior. How do the ethnic groups vary with respect to certain basic value orientations, and how do these values vary with the attributes of smoking? Do heavy smokers, for example, have a more deterministic view of life and good health? The fifth section analyzed student health attitudes and practices, and related these to their ethnic identification and smoking behavior.

These analyses of audience variation might better be drawn together and interpreted within the concepts of *enculturation,* the process of learning a cultural tradition, and *acculturation,* the modification of one culture through more or less continuous contact with another. Since outstanding differences have appeared mainly not between one ethnic group and another, but between smokers and non-smokers and between males and females, we will first discuss smoking and enculturation processes.

Throughout American and Canadian society the custom of smoking is generally accepted; that is to say, the rules governing the context of the custom do not prescribe that one *should* smoke, rather it is more economical to say that at a given place and time one should *not* smoke. As far as we know, there are no national, state or local sanctions against smoking. Instead, prohibitions against smoking take the form of norms or mores adhering to particular groups, in this way resembling the process of enculturation — largely a process of first learning the contexts of acceptable behavior: how and when to drive a car, when one may swear aloud or offer a lady a Tiparillo.

Studies of smoking behavior have largely been focused upon high school or college students, despite the fact that the adult normative patterns and frequencies serving as models and contextual influences in the society at large are still being examined. Many excellent reasons may be offered for picking on high school students. They are generally available, they are docile, we may easily acquire volumes of figures about them, and, most importantly, they are not all smokers at this age. But students have adult reference groups and models of a highly various sort. By asking them for responses while they are at work — so to speak — we are assuming a greater homogeneity than may be justified.

In addition to describing more completely the great smoking, non-smoking groups in our society at large, we might do another thing that most young people do unconsciously. We might take particular note of our own culture heroes. We speak not only of smokers such as the late President Roosevelt, who enjoyed his cigarettes, but of the number of serious professional non-smokers whom we hold in esteem. In short, non-smoking and non-smokers are neither fashionable nor unfashionable in our society.

Smoking as an Enculturation Mechanism

Broadly speaking, *enculturation* is another word for education, yet it emphasizes the informal learning of general knowledge and traditions of a culture. In employing the word *mechanism* instead of *aspect* or *feature* of enculturation, we wish only to convey the notion that through smoking behavior numerous other cues for independence, maturity, and adult acceptance are unconsciously expressed by the young smoker. By lighting up in various human environments, a youth also tests his own predictions of expectant behavior — some environments are hostile, some indifferent, and some are accepting.

The evidence for smoking behavior as a mechanism of enculturation is suggested by the close relation of the smoking behavior of parents to that of children. For both sexes of all three ethnic groups, a definite trend was seen relating the smoking behavior of the student to that of his parents. For boys the likelihood of becoming a smoker is considerably increased when only one of the parents smokes. But for girls this probability increases only when both parents smoke. Non-smoking children thus tend to have non-smoking parents. In such non-smoking home environments the innovation of smoking behavior by any member of the family is likely to be quickly perceived as a matter of concern, especially in Anglo and Mexican groups.

The introduction of smoking into the home by the children is likely to be seen as a challenge to the norms of the sub-culture of the home. But if a parent smokes, the other parent and children merely view the behavior as "carrying over" from the normative behavior of groups outside the home. A child is not expected to belong to groups outside the home in which smoking is a normal trait. Thus, we have the "Don't-do-as-I-do, do-as-I-say" challenge to this imitative behavior which merely indicates to the youthful smoker that he is not yet accepted as a member of the same outside group as his smoking parent. Across the sex divisions, mothers may prevail upon sons, and fathers may ask their daughters not to smoke, but in the adult world husbands and wives rarely respond to similar mutual requests. Also, very few adult hosts in their homes request other adult guests not to smoke. Viewing such inconsistencies, the boy or girl can only conclude that norms against smoking are somewhat arbitrary and when such prohibitions are directed at them, it is merely because they have not become adult enough in the eyes of their parents.

Even in homes in which smoking behavior is common with both parents and offspring there are implicit rules about when, where, and how to smoke. The custom of smoking, this piece of neutral behavior, is something which invites comment, and every native American group in the Southwest has had some rules and formal expectations about when and where smoking is appropriate.

Insofar as youth are concerned, boys and girls had to "grow up" before they could smoke, but girls were generally not expected to smoke; only old women did that. More specifically, in the living memory of Southwestern Indians, the use of tobacco by youngsters was of special concern in the Navajo, Apache, Papago and Zuni tribes. All of these people were more or less serious about the effects of smoking on the condition of runners and warriors. Usually young men were told that they first had to run down and capture a coyote before they could smoke. Among the Eastern Navajo the coyote symbolized the wife and the "capture" was marriage — thus only married men were allowed to smoke. The Southern Tonto Apache men were not allowed to smoke until they were 20 or 21 years old because it made them short of breath and made their hearts pound too hard. In Zuni, only warriors were allowed to smoke. Besides telling the fictitious coyote capture story, they claimed a man could only smoke after he had first killed a Navajo.

Thus we see that regardless of the particular structure offered, youth in Southwestern cultures were generally not expected to smoke until they had achieved adult status in other ways. Smoking behavior in these cultures was also a mechanism for displaying adult status.

Smoking and Acculturation

Taking the historical view of the custom, our national use of tobacco has been but one item in the general process of Indianization of the Europeans. From the long list of cultivated plants used by the native Americans, the Europeans selected one particular weed, adapted it to their highly various cultures and are now seen passing the custom back as a culture-trait of their own to the native Americans. Needless to say, it is not the same thing. Along with a more developed leaf and other technical refinements in wrappers and packaging there are entirely different norms governing its use and establishing its contextual propriety. Southwestern Indians mixed tobacco with many other weeds, some of which were piñon needles, juniper foliage, sage leaves and deer or buffalo fat. In addition every one of these Southwestern groups had social restrictions and rules defining who should smoke, when he should smoke and just how smoking was to be done. Much of the tobacco consumed was in ceremonial contexts of healing and religious worship. Today, we have re-interpreted these usages more broadly and have now reached the point where we offer only functional rationalizations for prohibiting its use in certain contexts. We observe no-smoking regulations, for example, in hospitals, in airplanes, trains, around gasoline stations and in certain places on-the-job. But most Americans of the national tradition who readily obey such signs feel quite upset when other kinds of reasons, such as courtesy or respect, for instance, are advanced to explain the prohibitions. Thus, cigarette smoking is treated as a social "necessity" (perhaps World War II had someting to do with it) and we as a nation of smokers seem to be unconcerned about all but the most functional restrictions against it.

Returning now to our data, there are trends indicating that Indian-, Mexican-, and even Anglo-American youngsters do not become more Indian, Mexican or Anglo when they take up the custom, but as smokers become less characteristic of their groups.

1.) With the penetration of the smoking habit into each group there seems to be a levelling-off of the extremes in ideal norms, or differences contrasting the groups. In other words, the active-individualistic-future-oriented Anglos become less so and the passive-collectivistic and present-oriented Indians and Mexican-Americans also become less so when they take up smoking.

2.) Also, as smoking became more characteristic of each group, the smokers most frequently appraised themselves as being in poorer health, most fatalistic about the condition of their health, and least concerned about the effects of smoking. In this respect Anglo-American smokers tended to imitate the basic attitudes shared generally by the Mexican- and Indian-American students.

3.) In all three groups females were expected to be non-smokers, yet the only combination of attributes found to limit that social scope of interaction was being both a female and a non-smoker. There seems to be no general limitation, however, on the combinations open to female smokers.

4.) Since there is a much greater percentage of Anglo-American parents who smoke, it would appear that the model for smoking belongs primarily to the Anglo-American adults.

SUMMARY

Responses to the questionnaire administered to Anglo-American, Mexican-American and Indian-American students revealed that with the penetration of the smoking habit into the three divisions there was a concomitant levelling off of extreme values and attitudinal differences descriptive of each group. With this levelling-off there was also a tendency for Indian- and Mexican-American students in high school to imitate the value-norms of their Anglo-American school mates. Yet, the response frequencies describing the dominant attitudes toward health and disease revealed that Anglo-American students tended to imitate the attitudes of Mexican- and Indian-Americans when they took up smoking. Such apparently conflicting tendencies plus the clear relationship demonstrated between parental smoking behavior and that of their offspring are here interpreted in the light of two concepts borrowed from anthropology, the concepts of *acculturation* and *enculturation*. In the complex processes of acculturation the early Europeans selected and changed the form of smoking behavior, re-interpreted its function, and broadened the norms governing its use. This modified form has been taken over today as a national custom and through the different processes of learning the national culture, all three groups of students imitate, in their own way, this manner of smoking. The revised custom of smoking is associated with "adult" attitudes and values which differ from those of each ethnic group, yet there is some evidence to support the idea that the custom with its "adult" attributes reflects an Anglo-American image.

REFERENCES

Bronson, Louise, Changes in Personality Needs and Values Following Conversion to Protestantism in a Traditionally Roman Catholic Ethnic Group, Unpublished Doctoral Dissertation, University of Arizona, 1966.

Chance, N. A., "Conceptual and Methodological Problems in Cross-Cultural Health Research," *American Journal of Public Health*, March 1962: Vol. 42, No. 3, pp. 410–417.

Clark, M., *Health in the Mexican-American Culture*, Berkeley and Los Angeles, University of California Press, 1959. pp. 206–208.

Foster, G. M., "Relationship Between Spanish and Spanish-American Folk Medicine," *Journal of American Folklore*, 1953, 66: pp. 201–208.

Holland, W. R., "Mexican-American Medical Beliefs: Science or Magic?" *Arizona Medicine*, May, 1963, 20: pp. 89–102.

180

Horn, D., Courts, F. A., Taylor, R. M., and Solomon, E. S., "Cigarette Smoking Among High School Students," *American Journal of Public Health,* 1959, 49, pp. 1497–1511.

Madsen, W., *The Mexican-Americans of South Texas,* New York: Holt, Rinehart, and Winston, 1964. pp. 68.

Morison, J. B., and Medovy, H., "Smoking Habits of Winnipeg School Children," *Canadian Medical Association Journal,* 1961, 84, p. 1006.

Rosen, B. C., "The Achievement Syndrome: A Psychocultural Dimension of Social Stratification," *The American Sociological Review,* 21, April 1956, pp. 203–211.

Rosen, B. C., "Race, Ethnicity, and The Achievement Syndrome," *The American Sociological Review,* Vol. 24, No. 1, Feb. 1959. pp. 47–60. In Mack, R. W., *Race, Class and Power,* New York: American Book Co., 1963, pp. 71–90.

Salber, Eva. J., and MacMahon, B., "Cigarette Smoking Among High School Students Related to Social Class and Parental Smoking Habits," *American Journal of Public Health,* 1961, 51, pp. 1780–1789.

Salber, Eva J., Welsh, Barbara, and Taylor, S. V., "Reasons for Smoking Given by Secondary School Children," *Journal of Health and Human Behavior,* Summer, 1963, Vol. 4, No. 2.

Ward, W., *Cigarette Smoking Among Pupils in Rock Island County Schools, Grades 7 through 12.* (A Joint Project of the Rock Island County Unit of the American Cancer Society and the Department of Sociology of Augustana College, Rock Island, Illinois), August, 1964.

SYMPOSIUM:
Personal Characteristics of Smokers — Theoretical and Practical Implications of Reported Research

Moderator
FRANK BARRON

Discussants
DOROTHY NYSWANDER   SILVAN TOMKINS
PERCY TANNENBAUM   GERHART WIEBE

SUMMARY

The need for sound longitudinal studies of personality among smokers is emphasized. Daniel Horn and Nevitt Sanford see the Grant study (Harvard) sample as a promising one, data having already been obtained for drinkers. This would also provide clues as to temporal changes in stereotypes associated with smoking. Silvan Tomkins leads a discussion on the difficulties of interpreting responses from modified TAT pictures as measures of "perception of smokers." The question of the significance of smoking as a role-defining-self-expressing behavior. Stereotypes of smokers. Leonard Berkowitz cites the behavior-modification approach to therapy, which contends that the genesis of a disorder is irrelevant to treatment; infers that research preoccupation with the determinants and correlates of smoking behavior may be unnecessary for development of change programs.

Before summarizing the panel's discussion of the implications of this section's reported research, Frank Barron discusses the question of heritability of tendencies related to the adoption of the smoking habit, cites data from twin studies and "home environment" studies. Recommends that traditional "foster home" and life history study methods be applied to shed further light on the matter. Discusses the question of addiction and the "habit facilitating role" of nicotine. Believes decay function studies could shed light on the addictive potency of nicotine. Proposes a multivariate discriminant function analysis for matched pairs in studying determinants of pathological conditions. Argues for more and better longitudinal studies; warns against stereotypy of studies that may lead to redundancy of data. Strongly supports Richard Coan's recommendations, especially re factor strategy; discusses the role of factor analysis in research on personality correlates of smoking behavior. Recommends inclusion of biographical items in large-scale testing programs. In discussing "language of exhortation" used in smoking programs, suggests avoiding the term "quitting smoking" ("no one wants to be a quitter"). Calls for more research on potential influence of peers, parents, and physicians on smoking adoption and discontinuance. Discusses the question of financial commitment as a motivating influence in treatment programs.

The absence of sound longitudinal studies in research on the development of smoking behavior was commented on by Dr. Tannenbaum; Dr. Horn indicated that while several longitudinal studies have been attempted, they were somewhat lacking in the sophistication of their measures, that they were concerned simply with the development of the smoking habit, without reference to relevant psycho-social variables. He indicated that in view of the emphasis on personality factors in smoking research (such as those related to accepting the smoking habit, rather than changing to non-smoking) it would appear that this kind of study would be appropriate.

Daniel Horn: I have been thinking about the value of going back to some of the early child-study groups like the Berkeley studies in the 1930's and picking that up for later information. To some extent, this has already been done, as MacArthur has done with the Grant study. We have some long-term material on Harvard undergraduates, but the difficulty — especially with those of the early 1940's — is that they are not typical of anybody, not even themselves.

Nevitt Sanford: That could be done. These people, who are now about 45 years old, were studied intensively from the ages of 12 to 17. Mary Jones has recently interviewed them with respect to their drinking behavior, and found that people who differ in their current drinking behavior had already differed in personality and backgrounds when they were 12. While these findings don't confirm any particular hypotheses she had made, they do provide meaningful relationships. The same thing could be done by someone interested in variations in smoking behavior.

Daniel Horn: It's called a *retroprospective* study.

Percy Tannenbaum: I was referring more to a short-term longitudinal study of students in a high-school setting just before the critical age when they tend to acquire the smoking habit. We could follow them for several years.

Daniel Horn: But there may be some very significant factors in what has intervened during the last few years. Nor am I sure that the changes in the views of what smoking means would give you quite different factors.

John Weir's report (pp. 151 ff.) on the adventurousness of the person who smokes a cigarette habitually provides a good example. It is true that the smoker is adventurous; after all, he is taking a real risk. This is indeed risk behavior, and apparently the health factors are fairly well known. They change our perception of what the individual is doing. When we did this type of study ten years ago, the resulting picture was mostly one of antisocial behavior, rather than risk-taking behavior. We used six TAT pictures, which we had re-drawn, showing people smoking cigarettes. We were familiar with the standard responses to the pictures, and sensed a considerable shift in stereotypes. For example, the girl leaning in a doorway is usually seen as just having had a fight with someone; but given a cigarette, she was perceived as having just discovered that she was going to have an illegitimate baby. An older man and a young man (smoking cigarettes) were both seen as criminals. These interpretations were by high-school students.

The difficulty of drawing inferences from responses to semi-projective devices was discussed: a cigarette dangling from the lips of a female, for example, may be too suggestive. Someone proposed that using motion pictures instead of photographs would make for greater flexibility. John Weir noted that for his subjects, the cigarette served to emphasize — or enhance — a trait observed without the cigarette. For example, a figure perceived to be "sexy" without a cigarette was seen to be sexier in the photo which included the cigarette. The same held true for other traits, such as adventuresomeness; if the figure was seen as having some, the cigarette gave him more. But if he is not seen as having the trait in question without the cigarette, smoking doesn't change the picture. In Weir's words, "If one is not sexy without a cigarette, smoking doesn't help." Silvan Tomkins then described the difficulties of interpreting data from projective materials under these circumstances:

Silvan Tomkins: This seems to be a special case of a larger problem. In the assessment of the impact of anything that one introduces to a picture, the crucial difficulty is in estimating how much weight should be given to that which is introduced differently in two pictures as a function of the original picture. It is the kind of problem that cannot be solved with a sampling of the kind that you have. Take the picture, let's say, of a boy who looks as though he could not possibly be adventuresome, and portray him with a cigarette. Assuming that the cigarette means the same thing to everybody, one of at least two possibilities should apply: 1) that it has no effect — it is discounted because the bulk of the meaning is given by other parts of the picture; and 2) that the cigarette is so conspicuous — such an extreme thing — that the rest of the picture is transformed by just changing its display

a little. This makes for a labile interpretive task dependent upon the weight given to different parts, a relationship that is itself somewhat labile. If, for example, your subjects firmly believe that a cigarette means adventure, then this mousey character is suddenly going to be interpreted as being out of his mind, drunk, or taking a terrible risk; or, the subject may not see the cigarette at all. For example, I didn't notice the cigarette in some of these pictures. An adult, I'm sure, will simply not see the cigarette or the ashtray because they will have much less meaning for him. It will vary, of course, as a function of the extent to which cigarettes *per se* are salient for the subject. If he is struggling with that problem, then the weight will shift considerably. It's an intriguing technique but not without its problems.

John Weir: Of course, it is important to emphasize that adding the cigarette does not create a singular effect. A child shown smoking changes the entire context in which he is viewed. One can't say that a cigarette by itself is this or is that; it's this *in relationship* to this person, and the perceiver too.

Silvan Tomkins: May I object slightly to that formulation? If the subject is particularly concerned at that moment with the question of whether to take up smoking, and if there is great pressure being brought to bear, let's say by peers, then I would not necessarily agree that the interpretation of cigarette smoking is contextual. Rather, the relationship between any part and the rest of the stimulus display is itself a critical question. One cannot say that the cigarette *per se* is necessarily a function of the rest of the picture, because what is a function of what is itself a variable phenomenon, depending on a great many other things.

Percy Tannenbaum: There is a substantial amount of research in the area of personality impression formation with adjectives that may be relevant here. This research has tended to indicate that the whole is not the sum of its parts — it may be greater or less — and each component doesn't maintain its respective contribution in different contexts. This is a fairly consistent finding. The order in which it is presented changes it, for example. Obviously there are a number of factors involved, but the methodology is an intriguing one.

Frank Barron: It is interesting that the cigarette companies have been pounding for many years through their advertisements at the idea that cigarette smoking is associated with virility, while right after the Civil War the association was quite the opposite. In some of the old Westerns to smoke a cigarette was the sign of a dude, since a real man smoked a cigar. This is still true in some parts of the country. A real man chews or smokes a cigar, but certainly won't smoke a cigarette.

Daniel Horn: A curious situation actually occurred recently along these lines: in an attempt to encourage more men to smoke a cigarette which already enjoyed a fairly substantial female market, a "virility campaign" was launched. It did not succeed in attracting more male smokers, but the female market increased so much that the virility theme was continued. It is now definitely a woman's cigarette; 90 per cent of its smokers are women. With the constant repetition of commercials showing a man with a tattoo in Such-and-Such country, a very large female following results. What can this mean?

Leonard Berkowitz: From the point of view of changing smoking habits, it may well be largely irrelevant what stereotypes people associate with smoking. To return to the analogy with psychotherapy made by Dr. Barron earlier, the behavior-modification approach to psychotherapy contends that the genesis of a particular behavior disorder is really irrelevant. Various techniques can be used to modify a behavior, regardless of its source. It may not at all matter what the young boys associate with cigarette smoking, or what women think about tattooed cowboys.

Bernard Mausner: Nevertheless, in behavior therapy one cannot ignore the sources of support of the behavior. When one wants to change a behavior, he wants to know what is continuing to reinforce it. For instance, if cigarette smoking is partly reinforced because it is self-defining, it helps the smoker to know who he is and to play that role to others. Here is a good example of the value of John Weir's study. His results provided some clues to how the self-defining behavior was operating and to whom it was important.

Research is needed to determine the significance of self-defining, role-determining, behavior; to determine whether in responding to these pictures, people are merely reflecting all the propaganda to which they have been exposed. The question of role defining behavior arose during the 1965 (Beaver College)[1] Conference. It was then considered a trivial issue, since what appears to be role-defining behavior may merely be a reaction to advertising and propaganda. This may indeed be the case, but it is something to be determined empirically. The Weir study does provide us with some tools that may help us to arrive at an answer.

Bruce Straits: Many of us would like to have a disguised instrument for measuring individual differences in perceptions of smoking as a self-expressive behavior. One approach might be the use of attitude scaling techniques to form a perception-of-smoking scale from a series of pictures similar to those employed by Mr. Weir.

Bernard Mausner: In the stereotypes of the role-defining, all this will vary with the individual. A college girl who smokes is defining one role, and the middle-aged

truck driver who smokes is defining another role. The response content will be determined by the nature of the subject sample. It will require insight, of course, in examining the response content to determine the extent to which it is merely a superficial reflection of what people have been told about smoking or whether it is really significant. Many of my smoking respondents have claimed that smoking provides them with a sense of identity. They say, "If I don't smoke, I won't know who I am."

Silvan Tomkins: They've been reading too much social psychology.

Frank Barron: I will try to summarize some of the ideas that emerged on the discussion of the implications of research on personal characteristics of the smoker. Let me begin with a couple of thoughts that I have had that I won't attribute to the panel because I doubt that many members of it would agree with the interpretation or at least suggestion that I am going to put forward. I should also emphasize that I have very little experience in the field of smoking research.

First of all, there has been a repeated observation that children who come from homes where neither parent smokes are much less likely to be smokers, probability about 0.5 rather than unity. I think in all these cases the implicit interpretation was that this showed the strong effect of home environment on smoking habits. However, there was another possible relevant observation. In studies using the classical twin method, monozygotic twins showed a much higher concordance of smoking behavior than dizygotic twins did. Ordinarily, considering almost any other behavorial attributes, if you put these two sets of facts together, you would at least be inclined to investigate further the possibility that the behavior in question is the result of some inherited tendency. A study of the smoking behavior of adopted children may provide additional data on the matter of heritability. Of course, there are other ways. One could study the further life history of the children from homes where parents don't smoke to see whether indeed the home environment is the effective variable.

Another thought: I have been told by several people that it seems unlikely that cigarette smoking is an addiction. The word *addiction* may be misleading; it is one of those categorical words that often obscure things. A substance may be instrumental in the development of a habit, where the mediating variable in the substance's effect is the reaction of the body to it, without its being addicting physiologically in the ordinary sense of the term. I am suggesting that there may be a habit-facilitating role of nicotine. Various physiological effects of nicotine have been mentioned, all the way from temperature changes while smoking cigarettes to the effect on fetal size and fetal heartbeat when the mother smokes.

---

[1] National Conference on Behavioral Aspects of Smoking, Beaver College, Glenside, Pennsylvania, 1965.

I feel there is a need for certain kinds of relatively basic and simply developed information which might shed some light on this, for example, the development of a decay function for the addictive potency of nicotine, if that is a relevant variable. One could take a group of smokers who have been smoking for the same number of years and have smoked about the same number of cigarettes, all of whom undertake to quit smoking. The frequency of resumption for each day thereafter can easily be established. Such a curve might give a clue as to the decay function of the addictive potency of nicotine.

Dr. Coan's paper deserves much discussion which I won't be able to give to it. I will simply say that my own preference is for the multivariate discriminant function type of analysis. I can think of a number of studies that would be important and would yield results rather readily. For example, when an individual develops a pathological condition, whatever it might be — lung cancer, a cardiac disability, something of this sort — find a matching case in terms of age, length of time having smoked, and smoking pattern, and then for those two classes of individuals do a discriminant function analysis in terms of both the psychological and physiological variables.

Longitudinal studies are definitely needed. Here we can make use of existing data such as the MMPI (Minnesota Multiphasic Personality Inventory) data pool. Go back to the subjects who in 1938 served as part of the original standardization group. Find those cases which since then have developed some sort of pathology relevant to smoking, and then item-analyze the 1938 responses against this later criterion.

Another simple technique is certainly necessary. This is to test a population of non-smokers, all of whom have not yet had the chance to start smoking, such as junior high-school students; take a wide variety of techniques from adjective check lists through psychiatric-type tests through the projective-type material Weir (pp. 151 ff.) was using; then wait until they have developed the criterion behavior, smoking or not smoking; then do the same kind of discriminant function analysis. You then have a basis for experimentation. Once you have good prediction equations you can put people into experimental situations and see whether you can produce behavior modifications by some techniques that come from general personality theory or from theory of psychotherapy.

I would like to make the general comment (without attaching any judgment to it) that there seems to be a certain amount of stereotypy developing in the kinds of studies reported here. There may be some usefulness in having a brain-storming kind of session centered around research methodology and research approaches with the view of broadening our approaches. I think part of the redundancy is necessary to establish facts in what is so new an area; you have to replicate and so on, and things

go on slowly. I am well aware of that, having participated in the development of information in the area of creativity, and I know that it took us many years before we began to be fairly sure of some of the basic facts. But, even so, it would be fruitful to address oneself consciously to the question, "What other kinds of studies besides those that we have been doing might by useful?"

I have been interested in the things that this section is devoted to, namely the personality attributes of smokers. It seems that there are very few studies that demonstrate personality differences of a substantial sort, an established sort, between smokers and non-smokers. So, in thinking about Dr. Coan's paper, I found myself agreeing very much with certain of his methodological recommendations, especially, for example, the factor strategy. The key point about the factor strategy is that you have to find the right variables to include in your initial matrix. And you find the right variables in part, in my judgment, by dealing with behavior outcomes or socially visible kinds of performance which have found their way into the folkway of thinking about things. That is why the empirically developed scales have a certain merit; they are attached to social reality, and they're not impervious to subsequent factor analysis or reinterpretation in the light of their relationship to other variables and the communities of variance that they share. The question that I ask — a clarifying-type question as to whether the factor-analysis approach has a unique contribution to make to research on smoking behavior — is this: "Would the factorial structure of personality among smokers be different from that among non-smokers?" Professor Coan gave an answer which I believe is a correct one, namely, "Probably not." Then the question becomes "Does smoking behavior occupy some position in a clearly defined personality factor, where its location would cast light upon its origins in personality?" We don't quite know the answer to that. It would be very interesting and valuable to include this kind of item in surveys where the data are later to be subjected to factor analysis.

I might add another research strategy suggestion: many of the large-scale testing projects, such as Project Talent and the National Merit Scholarship Program, might be asked to include biographical items on smoking behavior. Then one could correlate all the rest of the data with the responses on that. One might also include ways of describing patterns within the smoking behavior. I think you would then immediately get a lot of light shed on correlates of smoking, all the way from socio-economic-class variables through intellectual aptitude variables. You would even be able to get a more comprehensive set of evidence on the twin relationships.

If twins are given special study, there is one other important control which could be added. In recent National Merit twin studies, the author of the studies,

Robert Nichols, realized that it would be too expensive to do zygosity diagnoses using blood tests. He therefore developed a physical-similarity index in the form of a brief questionnaire, which he sent out to a limited sample (about 200 pairs) and then did blood tests for these. He achieved 93 per cent accuracy of diagnosis with the physical-similarity index. He proceeded to study the 93 per cent who were accurately diagnosed, but not those who were misdiagnosed. It would be interesting to study those dizygotic twins who were mistaken for monozygotic twins on the basis of physical similarity.

Other suggestions developed from the panel discussions, particularly that dealing with prediction studies from theory. Studies of non-smokers would be very important. If you wish to find out which race horses win regularly the most obvious thing to study would be the attributes of the winners. It might be just as valuable to study the attributes of the losers, however. Why do some people not smoke?

This leads to the question of the language of exhortation used in smoking cessation programs. If it can be done without appearing artificial, it may be worth considering other kinds of words we could use besides "quitting smoking." No one wants to be a quitter. I am not being facetious, for I think this points to something more important than just those words, namely the whole question of associated imagery. And here you have a formidable opponent indeed in the tobacco advertising companies, since they are pushing hard, in a very professional way, a certain kind of image. Whether or not it could actually be countered at this point, I don't know.

Another question that should be studied is the role of persuasion by peers as well as by authority figures. I was impressed by some of the data recorded on the role of the physician. In Judith Mausner's study (pp. 143 ff.) in which in some cases the physician exhorted his patients to give up smoking and in other cases he did not, the important point might be whether the patient came back to that physician. For example, to avoid being scolded he might change his behavior in regard to smoking, but he also might change doctors. The effect of peer groups upon behavior is very important, of course. Studies of the effect of peer judgment, and especially the role of the most respected member or leader, particularly in the adolescent community, would be most important to do.

Dr. Barron was asked if he had had any experience with the tri-patient therapy group. How would he estimate its effects in a cessation program?

Frank Barron: Few psychoanalysts would allow a patient psychoanalytic therapy without a fairly good financial commitment to make sure that he is serious. I don't know if people would pay to quit smoking, but if they would — and I think many probably would — some arrangement whereby it costs them something for the course of treatment would be an important motivating variable itself. Certainly in all these things *motive* is most important.

Someone cited the studies of a Dr. Harris in Sweden as an example of this method; he initially charged them about $30, payable in advance, returned only to those persons who couldn't tolerate the course of treatment, which was sub-cutaneous injections of Lobeline and some other kinds of procedures. No data were available as to the effectiveness of the course of treatment.

PART V

EVALUATION AND SUMMARY

SYMPOSIUM I

Practical and Ethical Implications of Smoking Research — The Role of the Social Sciences and of Government in Promoting and Utilizing Research on Smoking and Health

Moderator
WARD EDWARDS

Discussants
GEORGE BEAL   NEVITT SANFORD
LEONARD BERKOWITZ   GERHART D. WIEBE
DANIEL HORN

Ward Edwards: There seems to be a general agreement among us on the need to examine the question of just how far it is appropriate for the social scientist to go in using his presumed special knowledges and skills to modify the behavior of the rest of the world. By what right can he say, "Let's get people to stop smoking"? How far do his specific skills entitle him to go in imposing his standards on everybody else? Daniel Horn seems to be in a particularly vulnerable position on that question, since he is spending a great deal of time and effort and money in doing this, not only as a social scientist, but also as an administrator of a government department. Would you like to begin our discussion, Dr. Horn?

Daniel Horn: Those are questions I have been wrestling with for some time. As I look back on it, I think the answers were relatively simple when my activities were restricted to epidemiological research. I was simply directing my scientific curiosity to the relationship of smoking and disease processes. I was motivated (in common with many others working in the field) largely by the hope that somehow I would uncover data that would permit me to keep on smoking. Unfortunately, the results came out the way they should have. I did not influence them, but they influenced me. In 1957 when the question arose of developing programs for school children, I began to worry about this business of influencing behavior and whether or not I had a right to do that. Although I have never engaged in clinical practice, my training was in the clinical field, and I see this as a problem that practitioners must face very early in the game, because everything they do is an attempt to influence the behavior of their clients. Those of us who are engaged in research activities are one step removed from the client, so we feel somewhat more detached about the responsibility of making decisions for change. It seems much easier to get money for research on why children smoke and for attempting to influence their behavior than it is to get money to find out why adults smoke and what might be done to influence their behavior, for it's adults who make the decisions as to where the money goes. I recall the occasion in which a speaker, addressing the New York Academy of Medicine, criticized the nature of epidemiological data. He finally said, in effect, "With all the res-

ervations I have about the data, I still think it's a good idea to teach youngsters not to smoke. But don't try to do anything about me!"

The situation can be viewed somewhat like this: Suppose a new product — a cigarette — were being proposed for marketing, and a government regulatory agency required testing the effects of this product and its potential harm. If it were to be learned that under certain conditions it could be harmful, but that under other conditions it might not be so very harmful, then providing people with just this information might be enough. But we are faced with a situation with a background of fifty or sixty years in which a habit has taken hold in a large portion of the population — more than half of the males and over a third of the adult females. And during this period this hold developed with little awareness that this was a serious health hazard. One has heard people say, "Well, of course it isn't good to take all this stuff into your lungs. It isn't natural, and probably does you some harm." But basically we looked at it as a minor vice that did not pose a serious threat to health — one of those minor risks that we are willing to expose ourselves to and we can tolerate. Then swiftly, beginning about 1950, ominous data started to be reported. Over a period of fifteen years, we have come to learn that we are indeed faced with a very serious health problem, one that affects millions of people each year, and causes annually the premature deaths of some three hundred thousand people in our country alone. We are talking about something that has enormous economic and health consequences — not only in terms of the number of people involved, but also in the magnitude of their involvement. Its cost to the country as a whole is tremendous. We are dealing with what has appeared to be a perfectly acceptable habit, but one which we rather suddenly learn is a real monkey on our back — a most urgent problem. It is a national habit that has grown to involve the expenditure of a quarter of a billion dollars a year for promoting the sale and use of its product.

I recall the debate that took place in the House of Lords in England shortly after the Royal College of Physicians' report in 1962. Lord Hailsham, then minister of science, said, "All of us have the feeling that somehow every man has an inalienable right to go to hell in his own way, and we resist putting restrictions on this right." And yet, in facing the knowledge of the hazards involved, we have the feeling that somehow the balance is one-sided. Someone must assume the responsibility for restoring that balance, and who is going to do it if it is not government? This seems to be the real issue here.

Nevitt Sanford: Is all smoking damaging to all individuals who smoke?

Daniel Horn: No. I'm sure some people who smoke get away with it. (Of course, one way to get away with it is to be run over by an automobile before smoking has had a chance to have taken effect!) But seriously, not enough data are available to identify what proportion of the population is uninjured by its smoking. Certainly there is a proportion that is, but it cannot be estimated because adequate measures of a threshold below which no damage is done are not available. It is known that even among men who smoke a half pack a day or less a measurable and significant amount of damage results. That doesn't mean that each person in this group is hurt by it, but there is a significant elevation of the rates of death and disability in men at that level.

The data reported recently in the National Cancer Institute monograph of Hammond's study of women suggest that there is a threshold below which smoking is not seriously harmful to them. Women smoke in a way quite different from the way men smoke, and for those who smoke less than half a pack a day, the total effect on mortality appears to be negligible. Women don't smoke cigarettes as far down as do men; they use lower-nicotine, lower-tar cigarettes; they don't inhale as deeply, they don't inhale as frequently, and they do a lot more "puffing" on the cigarette. This seems to indicate that there is a way of smoking a kind of cigarette at a level in which large numbers of people can smoke so that it does not affect their overall mortality rate. This also suggests a further exploration of the nature of this threshold. It is quite obvious that this threshold must be quite low, because even what we consider very light smoking, which is less than half a pack a day, results in a serious health hazard among men.

Nevitt Sanford: This point is rather important, I think, for a consideration of ethical or value questions. In the case of alcohol, for example, it would be extremely difficult today to take the position that nobody should drink at all. We who are concerned with the problem have given up the idea of making a pitch for no drinking at all. We try to distinguish among kinds of drinking, conditions of drinking, motives for drinking, meanings of drinking, and so on, and then argue that some kinds are less harmful than others. People will accept this kind of discussion. I think the country has demonstrated that it will not accept prohibition again as far as drinking is

concerned. I expect that they are not going to accept total prohibition of smoking either; there will be too many people who will claim — and present evidence to confirm the claim — that it's more harmful for some people than it is for other people, that there are some ways of smoking which are harmful and other ways which are not so harmful. There's bound to be more research on which kinds are which.

Daniel Horn: Let me make some rough guesses as to the proportion of people involved. I'll restrict this to men, because we have more adequate data for them than for women. (The figures on women now appear to be somewhat lower, although not a great deal so.) Overall, about one person in five or six who smokes cigarettes has his life appreciably shortened by his smoking; possibly twice that proportion have some measurable disability induced by their smoking. (Let me emphasize that these figures represent rough estimates.) The proportion of people affected obviously increases with the dosage that people get out of smoking, although the only measure that has been used in most of the studies has been *numbers* of cigarettes, which we know is a very crude measure. Among people who smoke half a pack a day, about ten per cent are affected by their smoking in terms of mortality and perhaps fifteen to twenty per cent in terms of disability. Among the two-packs-a-day smokers, the rate may go as high as one out of three or four affected in terms of premature death, and a somewhat higher proportion in terms of measurable disability and reduction of function. We are talking about a substantial portion of the population. Now, what is striking about this in contrast with alcohol consumption is that it is the individual who misuses alcohol by our normal conception of moderate usage of alcohol who suffers from its use. But it is the *average* consumer of cigarettes and the person who consumes cigarettes in a way which we normally consider to be *average* who is injured, not the individual who obviously misuses it or is an excessive user by whatever definition.

Nevitt Sanford: Much could be gained if one could say to young people, "If you are going to smoke, smoke in a lady-like fashion" — that is to say, in the shallow, not-inhaling kind of way. Then we come to another issue: consider the people who are really heavy smokers, who inhale deeply, feel a great need for it, and derive enormous satisfaction from it and perhaps even have something like withdrawal symptoms when they give it up. If they were to stop smoking, what then? There is a suggestion that smoking may involve some fairly basic, complex needs of the person, and if one says just don't smoke, and leaves it at that, he may be creating other health hazards that could be equally serious in their implications.

Daniel Horn: There have been a number of investigations and follow-ups of people who have given up smoking. The individuals themselves may be sensitive as to whether or not they can tolerate giving it up. Some people try and try and are unsuccessful and finally stop trying. This may be good judgment on their part; maybe they simply are unable to give it up without hurting themselves. Certainly in every study I know of, those who have been able to give it up show practically nothing but benefits in terms of health, a sense of well-being, better ability to function, and so on. The positive benefits of giving up smoking seem marked and self-evident to the individual who experiences it. I don't know of any contrary data to this point.

Bernard Mausner: This is a pseudo issue, if I may say so. No one has proposed prohibition; no one has discovered a technique which will compel people to give up smoking without their knowing it when the technique is used, nor is the discovery of such a technique of "manipulating" people anywhere near at hand. If we were to use isolation chambers and water torture, we could in an unethical manner get people to quit smoking. But within the range of techniques for informing and trying to persuade people, and for assisting them if they have made a decision to quit, the methods that have been proposed and that are on trial do not seem to involve questions of ethics.

It would be more to the point not to talk in general about the possible ethical issues, but raise ethical issues about specific techniques which have been used and applied. Now, Professor Sanford's point about the potential harm to someone who might give up smoking and go into a schizophrenic breakdown is well taken. There is no question that disturbed people would need medical supervision if they gave up smoking and many of them would need psychiatric attention. But we do outlaw things which are probably less dangerous than smoking — like LSD, for example — which can also drive certain unstable people over the edge. Every society, if it is to stay organized, requires the authority to set boundaries to people's behavior, not only in terms of social harm but also in terms of harm to the self.

Leonard Berkowitz: One of the specific ethical questions is, by what standards shall we judge the techniques we use to obtain our data? This is a matter that particularly concerns Howard Leventhal (pp. 17 ff.) and people like me who sometimes try to frighten or anger subjects deliberately. A number of social psychologists are now beginning to ask whether this kind of treatment given to our poor volunteer subjects is not unethical behavior. It may be that only one person in ten thousand will be adversely affected by the fear arousal, by the anger arousal, or what have you. The question is, what limits shall we impose upon our investigations? This is an issue that is relevant not only to smoking

research, but more generally to all social-psychological problems.

Bernard Mausner: But these are not issues that specifically relate to smoking research. If we were to use some sub-lethal shocks which might put people into cardiac arrest as a way of de-conditioning them from the smoking habit, then this would raise some ethical problems. All behavioral research with human subjects bears potential for harm; the question is one for setting limits, and these have to be set in terms of the specific possibilities for harm and the specific social goals. I make a plea to restrict the discussion here to specific terms — to techniques which have been applied — rather than to a continued general query about the ethical propriety of changing people's ideas and feelings about smoking.

Nevitt Sanford: I think the issue is plainly an ethical one; we can't avoid it by saying that so far social scientists have not been very competent in changing people's behavior. As a matter of fact, I'm surprised that the taxpayers are willing to support Dr. Horn's work.

Daniel Horn: They have guilty consciences.

Nevitt Sanford: Yes, they have guilty consciences, and also they are quite sure that it's not going to affect their behavior.

In comparing smoking to alcohol consumption, there is much more reason for control in the case of alcohol, because drinking affects other people. Clearly, drunkenness and the behavior consequent to it have a big impact on other people.

Daniel Horn: But it can be argued that smoking also has a big impact on other people. Don't economic problems result when a man dies at the age of forty-eight from a heart attack that he probably wouldn't have had if he weren't a smoker, leaving four children without a father? He has affected his family, certainly — and possibly also the Department of Welfare. Another instance: suppose a man who is very prominent in Public Health Service research goes on television and chain-smokes before an audience of four or five million people while talking about a new vaccine. As a top representative of a government organization that is responsible for the health of the nation, he can influence a great many people, and his smoking can have an effect on them. Many other instances can be found in which smoking does affect other people, from the point of view of health, from the point of view of influencing other people's behavior, and from the point of view of simply polluting the air that non-smokers have to breathe.

Ward Edwards: It is certainly clear that not smoking would influence other people, for example, tobacco farmers. Arguments exist on both sides of this particular question, which seems analogous to that of the establishment of traffic laws. In Paris, for example, a *laissez faire* approach to traffic regulation is accompanied by a high traffic death rate. The real issue seems to involve that of limits. Where lies the point at which one is willing to say, "So far we will attempt to influence, and beyond we will not attempt to dictate?"

Daniel Horn: Two different problems are involved: one is the problem for the social scientist in general. And I must say I think it's rather silly for the social scientist to be concerned with how and why people behave but refuse to accept the responsibility of applying his knowledge at some point. One cannot back away and say, "I will find these things out; I will give my findings to the world and let those who want to apply them do so as they wish, but I will take no responsibility for their application." This is being irresponsible. The other problem is the question of whether or not there is a special problem for government, simply because government is big, it's influential, it's Big Brother. A kind of philosophy is reflected here on the relationship between government and the people being governed.

Gerhart Wiebe: From what we have seen so far, it doesn't worry me on the basis of ethics that the social scientists might get across the line of propriety in influencing people in their smoking behavior. In fact, the general conclusion of the studies is that we don't influence people; they go right on smoking. Perhaps we may be coming toward the time when we'll have to face the possibility of an ethical problem arising on the other side, i.e., how long do we take the government's money, dragoon subjects and have them fill out long questionnaires within the rationale of doing something about smoking behavior when we have thick volumes in well replicated variety testifying that we are having little effect? There is also the possibility that if somebody said, "I know how to do it," we would only open up a different set of complications, because apparently the methodology toward which we are moving is vaguely related to depth therapy. We study the dynamics of personality structure and so on to see how it may relate to our purposes.

If something equivalent to a short psychoanalysis could be found to relieve the person of the smoking habit, then we would still be in the same box that the mental-health people are in. We could not afford the treatment and there aren't enough therapists. So even if depth treatment were found to be effective, it could not be applied. We, as social scientists, as people concerned with the welfare of society, have got to look the problem straight in the eye and ask, "Are we doing or are we encouraging other people to do the kinds of things that would be most likely to alleviate the thing that we consider unfortunate?" I don't think that we have been doing that. Let me suggest several reasons why I don't think so.

For one thing, the government is putting peanuts and pennies into anti-smoking activities of all kinds, com-

pared with the money it is putting into subsidizing the tobacco crop. If this is true, maybe we ought to be using what skills we have in convincing these government people that they are encouraging in a very substantial way the kind of behavior that we and they have good reason to think should not be encouraged. A reasonable way to start would be to stop subsidizing something that we think is unfortunate.

Another way in which someone might address himself to this problem is by trying to improve the product itself — that is, by trying to make the cigarette less harmful. Maybe this is being done, and because such work falls under a different discipline we simply aren't hearing about it. We hear a bit from time to time about filters, about oxidation, combustion temperatures, the dilution of smoke; but I haven't seen any summarizing of those data, nor have I seen any plans for using them in devising ways to present the public with substitute gratifications. We hear practically no talk about substitute gratifications. Has anyone mentioned trying to cultivate pipe smokers or cigar smokers? Are there systematic studies of filter holders and the promotion of their use? I recall Franklin Roosevelt using a very long cigarette holder. Do such holders make an important difference in the temperature of the smoke when it gets to the mouth? Having established a base line with studies that are now available, we may be rather soon coming to a time when we will be ethically obligated to diversify our approaches to the problem.

Daniel Rosenblatt: I'd like to say something in support of Dr. Mausner about the ethical issue not being accurately defined. He has already pointed out that by its nature society is coercive. As social scientists rather than as philosophers, we must determine the point at which intervention is appropriate. This means examining our own value orientations, some of which have been referred to implicitly, without being formalized. One of these values concerns the sacredness of human life. Whenever this is threatened, then we permit some kind of intervention. Traffic regulations, for example, are enforced to reduce the risk of highway accidents. The data gathered on the effects of cigarette smoking also indicate a threat to human life.

Now, when we make the analogy with the use of alcohol, another value is involved — that a person should be in control of himself and not a threat to others. Otherwise, speedy social intervention materializes; the police pick them up and put them away, and they may be sent to a drying-out institution for some kind of treatment. The cigarette "addict" presents a different problem. He is not seen as a person who is out of control and a potential danger to himself. If we define what would constitute cigarette addiction, we may, at that point, accept the fact that society has the right to intervene, to try and dry somebody out, in a sense, if he's an addict. Health is another of our values that isn't as explicitly raised, but one might think in terms of the immunizations that are legally mandatory, in the sense that every child who is born must be immunized. We actually don't get this rate of immunization, but society attempts to employ it as a kind of sanction. These are three of the values that I think permit us ethically to intervene: sacredness of human life, general well-being in terms of health, and lack of personal control, which may result as a threat to the well being of others.

Nevitt Sanford: The value that I wanted to accent was the value of the individual's freedom to decide things for himself. This is what worried me about a government agency set up to prevent people from doing what they want to do in the belief that it's not harmful to them. Now, I would say that Dr. Horn is within his rights as a citizen and social scientist to do everything possible to make clear to people the facts about the dangers of smoking. But just to take the flat position that nobody should smoke at all without making any distinctions among kinds of smoking, for example, might easily deprive the individual of the right to make his own decision in the matter.

I made a note also when we were told (pp. 57 ff.) about the kind of teaching in which the committed teacher influences the pupils as best she can to be the way she is. This is a slightly questionable goal because it might very well be that both parents of half the children in that class are smoking cigarettes. She is not saying only that each child should be fully informed about the dangers of smoking or that each child should be brought up to make his own decisions in important matters of this kind. She is saying, in effect, "You be the way I am, rather than the way your parents are." The question should be whether we can win the participation of the individual in making the decision about smoking. If we talk to school children and make the decision for them, we are, in a way, depriving them of a certain freedom. It's about this, I think, that we have to be particularly careful.

Edgar Borgatta: But other people are telling them the same thing and they get paid for it. These are the people on the other side — who do smoke and say, "Be like me!" *That's* called business!

Daniel Rosenblatt: We call them corrupt, sold out, and so on. But I do want to answer your point because you are raising the value of individualism — an eighteenth-century conception of it — which has recently become more clearly enunciated, and to which we in America are most sensitive. We hold to the idea that the individual is above everything in a sense. Now I would uphold this value, and indeed treasure it highly, but I think it has to be measured against other values. Dr.

Rosenstock has mentioned fluoridation and other public health areas where intervention has been quite successful. In these cases, the individual was not made to cede his autonomy, or his individual rights. One also thinks of malaria control, or TB control, or a whole series of other aspects in which public health has been most successful. It has been the government which has recognized a need and has taken action and made planned efforts to control the situation. And this has been at the expense of the individual. But we accept it in these other areas. The question is, is cigarette smoking a behavior that is so important that the individual aspects of it are worth keeping?

Nevitt Sanford: Of course, it's not analogous. Vaccination and other public-health procedures are not the same as regulating the decision-making process of the individual.

Daniel Rosenblatt: People who are against fluoridation of water see it that way.

Nevitt Sanford: Anyway, I'd rather lead a short, autonomous life than a long, healthy, supine one in the hands of a group of behavioral scientists.

Daniel Horn: That's just because you don't trust the behavioral scientists.

Edgar Borgatta: There is another consideration, however, if one moves beyond the medical problems that are involved. The children are in school whether their parents want them there or not. The individual's freedom has been inhibited in this area and in many other areas where we have tested behavior, licensed behavior, or required that certain criteria be met. The matter of individual freedom is an issue which is related to many areas and must be continually examined. But this need not interfere with the rights of the majority or of government to enter into other areas in a regulatory manner.

It's a matter of some concern that a clear distinction has not been made between the role of the scientist in smoking research and the implementation of government policy. If government policy tends in both directions, the ethical issue may be automatically resolved. In this particular era, I don't have any qualms about trying to change behavior in the direction of not smoking (which is the direction of control for which the government provides support). I would feel *considerably* uneasy about conducting an experiment aimed at inducing people to smoke. I would have this uneasiness simply because I know that tobacco companies and a few other organizations have been involved in personal suits where people are trying to claim money for damage done to them. Isn't this an issue that is not involved in the pro-smoking direction? We have at the level of experimentation another set of criteria which are associated with the ethical issue of a person's liability as he undertakes the research. In the government's circumstances, I think that one may have an even easier solution or set of solutions available.

Donn Mosser: There is certainly ample precedent for governmental agencies imposing things on us where we don't have a free choice; an example of which is suggested by the date April fifteenth. But one thing from the medical side puzzles me, where an analogy of the cardiac surgical experience in the last twenty-five years is pertinent. For quite a while many of the studies were more or less academic from the viewpoint of anatomy, with no real prospects of practical application. When we progressed to experiment with heart pumps, we were dealing with patients who had the potential for longer life, but who would not live a full life if they were left with the cardiac defect they had. In this case, the people who were doing the surgery took the bull by the horns. They accepted the possibility of death — quick death — in many patients. For instance, constriction of the aorta is what I think cost the lives of the first six or seven patients. From then on the technical problems were corrected. The same type of experience has occurrred in many other areas of organic medicine. But the reluctance of people in the behavioral areas to become involved somewhat implies that there are things that are worse than death, and one of them may be the attempt to control behavior. One might lose a few people to the equanimity of their present status. But I think one must have the courage of his convictions. I quite agree with Dr. Mausner; the ethical problem here is quite clear. It is a matter of deciding whether this effort is worth taking, and if it is, to get on with it.

Leonard Berkowitz: The problem is not quite that simple. As an experimental social psychologist, I'm discovering that the decision is not entirely up to the behavioral scientist. More and more educational institutions are setting limits, restrictions, and barriers to the use of human subjects in experiments. For that matter, I understand the National Institute of Health has now become so concerned that it requires a statement from researchers as to what committees have supervised the preparation of procedures for the use of human subjects in their particular experiments. The responsibility does not rest entirely with the behavioral scientist.

Donn Mosser: That's part of the problem. In medical research, we have anti-vivisectionists to deal with: so it may very well be that the sacrosanct attitude toward the control of behavior is just about as unrealistic for real progress as that of the anti-vivisectionists, although the anti-vivisectionist says, "Do your experimentation on people, but don't do it on dogs. Do it on rats or mice or guinea pigs, but not dogs."

Jerome Schwartz: It has been claimed here that no methods are currently being used that violate the ethics of behavioral science, but I wonder about the methods in our own study (pp. 115 ff.). We get smokers who say they want to quit and invite them in and give them a battery of tests which include all kinds of personal questions. After that, we give them a physical examination, and they keep coming and coming. Finally we make random assignments, and some wind up being placed in the placebo method group — even though they really want to quit. Are we going too far in this? Perhaps the use of placebos is unethical, especially if there is another method that really is more effective. If these subjects fail to stop smoking, do they fail because we have put them into the placebo group? They may become shattered because they made the attempt to quit. And perhaps later they find out they were taking placebos, and that upsets them — because they feel they were manipulated.

Donn Mosser: The Veterans Administration did a project on five hundred patients with cancer of the lung. They set up a control group, a placebo group, and four other groups. It turned out that the placebo group did the best of the whole lot! You may very well find this to happen with your group.

Bernard Mausner: Two problems are at issue that need separating. One is the effect of our researches on people, which, as I have indicated before, is not an issue specific to smoking research. But the issue that Professor Sanford raises is a different one; it's the issue of compulsion in smoking control programs, and no one has proposed that the government compel people to stop smoking. Perhaps Professor Sanford is implying that somehow Dr. Horn and others among us are sneakily getting people to do something they don't intend to do, which I submit is nonsense. The fact is that we have come into a situation in which we know that people make continuing chains of decisions about smoking, some of them realistically, others not.

We've discovered that just giving people information does not seem to make much difference in the way they make these decisions. We're looking for ways of getting people to face up to the consequences of their behavior. If you insist that there's something immoral about that, then I'm a little depressed. But none of the techniques that have been discussed at this conference or anywhere else that I know of consist of anything other than an attempt to get people to understand the possible consequences of their smoking behavior.

Now, if one of the ways of doing this is to show them a gory picture, fine. While it's true that an occasional subject may have such a sensitive cardiovascular system that he will go into shock or might even die, I don't think there are ethical problems raised here, merely realistic problems of control over who does or doesn't participate in the experiment. But I don't think that anything that has been proposed includes an element of compulsion. Before we even start a discussion of ethics, then, someone should point to a specific technique that has been proposed and say, "This is unethical, because it compels people." I don't think Dr. Sanford in his sort of general fear that individual rights will be invaded has succeeded in doing this.

Mildred Dubitzky: Dr. Mausner has defined the issue of ethics too specifically by limiting it only to compulsion of people to behave in a certain way — including entering research projects on smoking. Even if people volunteer to be experimental subjects, it still behooves social scientists to be ethical about the way they investigate them. I would agree that most of the studies are done with volunteers and not people who are forced to participate.

But the invasion of privacy is often involved in the process of gathering information. There is also the deception — if you want to go so far as to call it that — of telling people they're receiving tranquilizers when they really are not. Then there is the problem of handling control groups. The control situation is even worse than the placebo problem in a certain way, unless one really tells people they are controls. A person volunteers only in order to let someone help him stop smoking or find out his attitudes in various areas. Frequently, he doesn't know what he may be revealing about himself, nor what he's submitted himself to.

John Weir: I'm disturbed by Dr. Mausner's protestations that the research techniques and designs used to date in the smoking field do not raise ethical issues. I might be willing to agree that they are marginal or easily resolved, but I cannot agree that they are non-existent. Consider, for example, any person who served in one of the experiments which have been reported at this conference. With our purposes unknown to him, a subject is brought into a laboratory situation where we induce experimental anxiety about his smoking, an anxiety which could be reduced by reducing or quitting smoking. Unfortunately, some subjects are unable or unwilling to do this. In addition, after the experiment is finished, the experimenter makes no attempt to reduce the subject's anxiety, unlike experiments in social psychology where anxiety has been removed upon the conclusion of the experiment. This kind of smoking research deserves attention as an ethical issue because we want the subject's anxiety to continue until he does the thing we want him to do — stop smoking. If he cannot or will not quit, he is stuck with the anxiety induced by the experimenter.

George Beal: We seem to be searching for that marginal case involving an ethical issue that requires a decision. While I am not sure of the complete accuracy of my data, I have an empirical case which can serve as an example. Is it compulsion when all psychology students are required to participate in experiments, when they are not made aware of the nature of the experiments, and when they are assigned to them randomly? It was a requirement of all psychology majors in a Midwestern university to participate as subjects in such experiments or have their grades lowered. Is this not a major sanction? Isn't this getting into the area of compulsion, with ethical implications?

Bernard Mausner: May I only repeat that unethical behavior on the part of investigators is something I do not sanction. I am not in favor of sin. I agree that creating anxieties that cannot be allayed is bad, and I would agree that forcing people to serve as experimental subjects is bad. But the questions Dr. Sanford raised were not about that; they concerned the ethics of smoking-control investigations: how far should we go in controlling smoking and whether we have a right to persuade people to stop smoking. These constitute a different set of questions which should be discussed separately.

Frank Barron: It might be better to avoid the term "ethics," which is a befuddling one in this context. The real problem is that social control of the individual is increasing exponentially, and behavioral science is assisting in this increase. The question for us, individually and collectively, is how close an eye we should keep on the practices of those persons, in government and elsewhere, who now have new techniques available to them for the control of society.

The American College Testing Service, which is sensitive to the problem of the future use of its records, is said to be considering destroying all tapes of scores made by individuals on their aptitude tests for admission to college. The problem in organizations like the Peace Corps and the Civil Service Commission is even more difficult, because they have information of a highly intimate and confidential sort, which they gain by asking questions of persons close to the individual being investigated. The techniques of social control are reaching a frightening stage of efficiency, and the machine itself cares nothing for the individual.

In the case of smoking, of course, we are motivated to get people not to do things that harm them. In order to do that, we have to develop and promote certain techniques of control; so the behavioral scientist is actually caught in a dilemma which is quite clearly a dilemma in terms of utilitarian values. One can think of it ethically, but only in the sense in which ethical responsibility arises out of our ability to forecast the future. It is basically a practical problem; at least, I prefer to look at it that way. Our interest is involved at the moment in keeping our personal freedom and individuality.

Selwyn Waingrow: Two questions might be raised which are either complementary or act as counterpoint to these considerations. The first is, "social science for what?" The second is, "what are the ethics of non-intervention?" — that is, what are the ethical or professional justifications of merely noting or studying pathology without attempting to do something about it?

Ward Edwards: Perhaps it is worth mentioning that there are somewhat similar moral dilemmas in other sciences. For example, a physical scientist concerned with weapons development may chew his fingernails over somewhat related issues, but not to the extent of not developing weapons. I rather imagine social scientists are not going to stop figuring out how to achieve higher levels of social control, either.

Daniel Horn: The problem may seem worse than it is because people derive pleasure from their smoking and the knowledge that we intend to do something that denies individual pleasure creates the feeling that we are being puritanical, that we are doing something that is not in the best interests of the individual. If we were going to do the same sort of thing on behaviors that are not pleasurable, we might not have the same restrictions on our methods.

Selwyn Waingrow: Dr. Horn's reference to the concept of pleasure suggests another dilemma. One way of evaluating our decision is to weigh the consequences of alternative courses of action. For example, how would one equate losses caused by premature death with losses caused by abstinence from a particular form of pleasure over a lifetime? That is, compare the loss in the quantity of life with the loss in the quality of life.

Which kind of "mistake" is more tolerable? Persuading a person to forgo pleasurable behavior that may end in his death, only to discover in retrospect that this particular person would not have died because of this behavior, and that he was unnecessarily deprived of a lifetime of some form of pleasure? Or deciding *not* to persuade someone to stop something that he enjoys and that may result in premature death? How does one meaningfully compare the quality of life with the quantity of life? But once death is a *fait accompli,* it is irrelevant to worry about life's quality. Errors involving pleasure are often rectifiable; errors involving death rarely are.

Daniel Horn: I have known personally some people who have developed a fatal illness, like lung cancer, because of their smoking. I have never made it a practice to try to persuade any individuals to give up smoking. But people have asked me, after it was too late, "Why didn't you persuade me to give up smoking?" Was I at fault in not making the effort to do this since I knew what the effects were? They did not know, and were resistant to whatever facts were available.

Nevitt Sanford: People are often willing to surrender their decision-making powers to other people. That's one of the great dangers of our time. It's hard to be a decision-maker. I suppose one way to put it would be this: all I'm asking you, Dr. Horn, is that the things you and your colleagues do in the interest of getting people to stop smoking be, insofar as possible, things in which they themselves will participate with their own free will.

Dr. Mausner seems to think that because I tried to define an ethical issue I immediately accused you and him of being unethical. I'm merely trying to say what would be unethical in my view, and this would be that if in the pursuit of one particular value, which is to get people to stop smoking, one were to ignore all other aspects of human welfare, including the most precious of all, which is the autonomy of the individual personality. I would ask you, why have healthy people if they are going to sacrifice their will in the process?

Daniel Horn: Your question implies that one is a necessary condition for the other.

Nevitt Sanford: No, I'm merely trying to indicate where the limits have to be drawn and what one has to watch out for.

Daniel Horn: If one had a choice, I think I would agree with you. Every person has a right to decide for himself whether or not he wishes to smoke, but he should understand the possible consequences of his action. I think the problem stems from the present social acceptance of smoking and the influences that are brought to bear by vested interests which profit from the sale of cigarettes. The weight of fifty years of acceptable smoking habits, with the consequent psychological and physiological addiction, make it very difficult for people to accept a clear understanding of the possible consequences of smoking. The question involves how far one goes, what kinds of activities one can engage in legitimately to try to bring people to this realization of what it is they're exposing themselves to. With that knowledge, they could then make their own decisions.

Leonard Berkowitz: You are saying they are not free to make use of the information.

Daniel Horn: They are not, for their autonomy has already been invaded by other interests. It has been invaded by social pressures, and it has been invaded by the world as it exists when the problem has been identified. What one is trying to do is to redress the balance, to put them in a position where in a sense one is almost freeing them to be autonomous and to make an individual decision, rather than to deprive them of their autonomy. They do not have the autonomy to make a decision for themselves if their smoking is based on a variety of pressures that instigated the habit in the first place.

Nevitt Sanford: I think you are quite right there. Many people have never really made any decision about smoking. They do it willy-nilly, because it's part of the culture in which they grow up. And you are quite right in bringing the other side to their attention so that there is something to make a decision about. But I think we will all agree that in the process one should not use the same techniques that the industry uses.

Daniel Horn: Someone has raised the question here of the ethics of certain kinds of experiments. Around 1955 we were considering a controlled withdrawal experiment. It would have required getting about 100,000 smokers to cooperate, assigning them randomly to two groups, persuading half of them as best we could to quit smoking for the duration of the experiment, and persuading the other half to continue smoking for that period. I felt that I could not participate in this experiment because at that time I was convinced that if I were to impose the pressures of an experimental procedure on a group of individuals in an attempt to make them continue smoking I was subjecting them to a potential damage to which they might not otherwise be exposed. I could not ask subjects to engage in this experiment. This experiment has never been conducted, and this was a large part of the reason. One simply cannot put the pressure of being a good experimental subject on the side of putting someone in the position where he would be hurting himself.

Michael Garity: It has been claimed here that Dr. Sanford has mentioned no specific techniques currently used which would raise a specific ethical question. Now it seems rather odd to me that the social scientist, with the perspective that he presumably has, need not look ahead to the eventual consequences of his intervention. It has also been claimed that most of us do not see any specific ethical issues arising. But shouldn't the social scientist be particularly sensitive to these kinds of issues? It was also stated that social scientists have a vested interest, since so many other areas of science are promoting and developing their capacity for controls, and that we must push forward with our own controls. It seems that Dr. Sanford is suggesting the possibility that we may go into this blindly, as it were, and get involved in things that we're not fully aware of and become nothing more than highly expert technologists or at least expert counselors directing the technology of changing behaviors. I would like to pose a question to those making these statements: When would be a better time to consider ethical questions than at the beginning of such investigations?

Bernard Mausner: The burden of the discussion has been that we need rules to determine the proper techniques to be used in manipulating the behavior of human beings. I don't think any of us would disagree with the notion that rules of this kind should be discussed, and that once they are established, any procedure that we propose should be judged in terms of those standards. Developing rules of this kind is extremely difficult. For one thing, it's very hard to know exactly what a good ethical rule is, what ethical behavior is.

In a recent lecture on problems of ethics in medicine, Dr. Louis Lasagna raised a question concerning the assignment of patients to control groups. He proposed a rule of thumb: if one is trying out a new drug and doesn't have any really good reason to believe that it's going to work, then it's ethical to give some patients placebos. If one is trying out an old drug and pretty sure that it would help the patient, then withholding it is probably not ethical. I asked him if he accepted the idea of a universal ethical standard or was he merely applying utilitarian standards. He replied that he hadn't really worked that one out. And I don't think any of us have really worked that one out.

I believe Dr. Sanford has implied a universal value for autonomy, but he didn't react negatively to the proposal that a society requires the surrendering of a certain amount of autonomy. He said rather ruefully that people are willing to do this. Then this is no longer a universal. If we are to make more progress in this discussion, it seems to me that we should cope with specific issues raised by specific problems in research actually under way, rather than try to solve general, hypothetical ethical issues.

Louis Zurcher: How secure we are in the role of laboratory social scientists on the one hand and of citizens on the other hand! But when we talk in the newly emerging social role of citizen-social-scientist, we seem to lose this confidence. I think we are seeing the beginnings of a role conflict here, and perhaps an emerging social role for the citizen-social-scientist. By the time of our next annual conference, perhaps that social role will have been learned. Social scientists are now at the crossroads — that junction between the "theoretical" and the "practical" — and we are standing there in great dissonance, not knowing really which way to go, because components of both have been internalized at the same time. It looks as though what we're observing here is actually the birth pains of a new social role that of, say, the applied social scientist.

John Weir: I'd like to try again to respond to Dr. Mausner's plea for a specific problem. Many of us have used smoking only as a vehicle for studying social-psychological principles and theory. In so doing, we have induced threat and anxiety in the subject's mind about his personal susceptibility to death and disease. Then, within some theoretical framework, we compare his reactions to those of subjects who received a more balanced, or neutral, treatment of the relation between smoking and health. This subject came in willing to serve in an experiment but he expressed no intention of quitting smoking or any desire to be "persuaded" to quit. We induced anxiety in order to examine some experimental manipulations but, when the measurements are made and the subject is ready to leave, no attempt is made to reduce anxiety. I'll admit there are experiments conducted which induce a much higher level of anxiety; those, for example, which induce the fear of latent homosexuality, which has been used in some recent dissonance research, or, as another example, recent cases in the East where subjects believed they were personally delivering very painful electric shocks to other persons. In those instances, however, the experimenter ends the experimental sessions with attempts to reduce the anxiety he had induced. In the case of smoking, we make no such attempts. Now is that a specific enough example?

Bernard Mausner: You'd be telling a lie if you told a subject, "It's really all right for you to keep smoking."

John Weir: Certainly there is no evidence that would lead one to say, "It is safe to smoke." But slanted presentations are used to induce threat in the experimental situation. We may, for instance, neglect to mention that a very large proportion of those who smoke half a pack a day do not shorten their life span to any discernible degree. But we present the facts about smoking and health in a manner designed to imply that everyone is in great risk if he smokes. This is not in fact true.

Bernard Mausner: I would agree that if one tells his subjects lies during the course of the experiment as a way of inducing anxiety, he ought to give them an account of what he did when the experiment is over. But if one raises their anxiety by subjecting them to a film in which they see a lung being cut out in full bloody color, then it seems to me one has done something which probably any smoker in the population wouldn't be harmed by, unless he were someone who needed psychiatric care. If a psychologist is not sufficiently in command of his discipline so that he cannot recognize people who are severely upset; if he does not have resources to call upon to help someone who is thrown out of balance, then he shouldn't be doing the research. If there is a long-range effect that he couldn't recognize, then I suppose he is exposing the subject to serious disability, and I guess one has to re-evaluate his experiment in this light. I suppose this is the kind of thing that Dr. Berkowitz was talking about and the kind of thing that N.I.H. is forcing us all to re-examine.

Selwyn Waingrow: I would like to raise a different kind of question. Dr. Horn, would you please estimate for us how many deaths attributable to smoking have occurred during this discussion of ethical problems involved in what can or should be done by social scientists and government to promote and utilize research on smoking and health?

Daniel Horn: In this country alone, one death every one hundred and five seconds.

George Beal: Have there been — not on the experimental side, not on the research side, but on the "education" side — any decisions not to use a technique or strategy based on *ethical* grounds, rather than public relations and political grounds? I think sometimes decis-

ions are made in terms of "Well, we couldn't get away with this because we would jeopardize funding." But have there been policy decisions made in terms of program strategies based on ethical grounds? Have there been any cases that you know of?

Daniel Horn: I don't know of any in the area of smoking education.

George Beal: Has there been concern about fear arousal?

Daniel Horn: One might criticize techniques which arouse a great deal of anxiety. I know I've been critical of some of the techniques used in withdrawal clinics that so emphasize the importance of quitting that if a subject fails he is completely shattered by his failure. I've seen a few people being put through this experience who express this feeling of great denigration and loss of self-confidence because they've been unable to do what has been made to seem terribly, terribly important to them. But I can't think of any procedures that haven't been used because somebody thought they were unethical.

Jerome Schwartz: I can think of a possible example. Somebody mentioned today that the smoking-education programs are being presented to lower and lower grade levels — which I think is probably a good thing. But when you begin reaching children in the fourth grade or younger, you run the risk of arousing their anxiety about their own parents, who might happen to be smokers. You show them films and tell them frightening things, and they worry that their mother and father will die, or something like that. What about this? These school programs are starting to pick up; more and more materials are being prepared for these children in the lower grades. What are the ethical implications of these programs?

Daniel Horn: Our advisory committee has dealt with grant applications where this matter was of concern. In both cases the discussion included the stipulation that some attempt be made by the investigators to anticipate the likelihood of this happening and take steps to prevent it. So in fact ethical problems like these are a concern of the granting committee when reviewing proposals for funding.

I'm sure Dr. Tomkins, who has also been concerned with these matters in the past, would like to comment. Dr. Tomkins?

Silvan Tomkins: I'm a renegade moral philosopher. I took my degree in the theory of value. One of the reasons that I left the field to go into this easier one of the behavioral sciences was the apparently insoluble nature of many of the basic ethical dilemmas. There seems to be a feeling in this group that we can somehow reach a consensus on the resolution of serious moral problems. I would rather define a moral problem as one which involves a very serious conflict between fundamental values — frequently those values that are held in common by the individual and by his society. When that occurs, that is to say, when something that one wants to do or someone else wants to do necessarily violates one or another of at least two values, then there is moral conflict. The assumption that at any given moment this conflict may be empirically resolved seems to me to be extraordinarily optimistic. That is not to say that we cannot solve *any* moral problems. However, when one puts the wish to understand and to control nature and human nature — a desire which we here all highly value — into conflict with the wish for everyone to be as happy, as dignified, as free as he can be; for everyone to suffer no control, no invasion of his privacy; then we are in the domain of moral conflict. These are fundamental values.

But there happen to be specific circumstances where these ideals may come into severe conflict. This can happen quite easily. I should like to give a personal example, an experience which I will never forget. It was on the night my father lay dying of cancer. Hovered around him were a group of very inquisitive doctors and interns, for whom he was an interesting cancer case. They wanted to find out what cancer really was and could hardly wait to ask my mother for permission to do an autopsy. (To my great surprise my mother gave that permission in the midst of her grief. I'm not sure I would have.) To me he was uniquely valuable, because he was my father. Now I did not, at that moment, surrender my interest in truth or my interest in understanding nature and the human body; I recognized that these people in a sense were behaving the way they should behave. They were concerned with a larger, long-term goal, perfectly appropriate for the research physician, but not at all appropriate for the physician who is taking care of someone when he and his family are undergoing acute stress. Here two fundamental values came into conflict, as values so often do. One may think there is a solution to satisfy these conditions, but I don't see how it's possible. This is not to say that we cannot progress toward arranging the world to meet these head-on confrontations, but it is most unlikely that we will ever have enough control over the world to resolve them.

For example, we are coming to know a great deal about the genetic code. If it ever comes to the point where someone must decide what kinds of people should be produced in the future (which is an extraordinary amount of control), it is unlikely that we would ever all agree on the ideal kind of human being that ought to be produced. Here again the truth value would come into very serious conflict with other fundamental values. It is one of the tragic circumstances of humanity that the world was not designed for maximizing all our values. We can work towards that goal but success in specific cases is never guaranteed.

Take the dispute here between Nevitt Sanford and Daniel Horn on the issue of freedom: they're both concerned with freedom. But Daniel says freedom has been violated by this whole apparatus of the tobacco industry which dominates the individual so that in this area he no longer really has freedom of choice and we ought to enlarge that freedom of choice. And Nevitt Sanford says, "A human being has got the right to have the freedom to kill himself if he wants to. That's the human thing." Here is a case where two people are really basically agreeing on the same value, as I see it; and the value is human freedom. Yet in this particular condition these two versions, even of the same value, can in fact come into head-long conflict. I don't mean this to be a pessimistic tract on the nature of resolution of moral problems, but simply a stricture against the assumption that there are easy solutions. We ought to remind ourselves that many fundamental moral problems trouble people principally because such problems have no easy solution and, indeed, they may not have any solution. In particular confrontations one or another of two fundamental values must give way. Then we have to decide on the hierarchy of our values — that when value A comes into conflict with value B, as in a traffic rule, it will give way to B whenever they come into collision. We may want to minimize that type of compromise, but if we must make a choice — as, for example, whether we should or should not have a control group in an experiment involving therapy — then we're putting one very fundamental value into confrontation with another, and there is usually more than one reasonable answer.

SYMPOSIUM II
The Influence of Social-Personality Theory on Research in Smoking Behavior

Moderator
NEVITT SANFORD

Discussants

FRANK BARRON   DANIEL HORN
LEONARD BERKOWITZ   PERCY TANNENBAUM
EDGAR BORGATTA   SILVAN TOMKINS

Nevitt Sanford: This discussion plan calls for people who have not had much to do with investigations of smoking behavior, but who have been identified with personality theory and research, or with social theory and research, to say what they believe they can learn (or how their disciplines might be advanced) through association with people on the firing lines, where smoking behavior research is concerned, or by their examining closely such behavior. At the same time, those members of the panel or others here who are particularly concerned with smoking behavior research might take this opportunity to put questions to the personality and social theorists, making them justify their existence, as it were. Also, the theorists will have a chance to say what particular messages they would like to leave with people who are involved on the action front.

I will presently ask each of the people here engaged in personality or social research to address himself to the question of what he thinks he can learn, or how his discipline might be advanced through the study of smoking behavior. One great advantage to any investigator of a subject such as smoking behavior is that he is almost bound to begin asking questions which traditionally belong in a diversity of scientific domains. This will bring him into contact with members of other disciplines, whom he doesn't ordinarily see in the normal course of his work, particularly in this age of specialization. For example, the Arizona Project suggests that one way for an anthropologist to learn about a culture is by examining its smoking habits, which study is in the domain of the psychologist, as well as other social scientists. American Indians, for example, seem to have been very wise in their methods of managing smoking. This suggests that there may be ways and means of constructing a culture which could handle smoking in as favorable a way as did the Navajo or other Indian groups. This raises another question for which I hope someone has the answer: What are the rates of lung cancer among these Indian tribes? I would predict that the rates are lower than in our culture, where smoking is a fairly meaningless act and there is little culture built around it. When the Indians passed the pipe, it had special significance; there were initiation rites for smokers, smoking was sometimes a reward for

socially constructive behavior, it was postponed in the interests of various other kinds of social benefits, and so on. We apparently learned nothing from the Indians except that this weed could be used for various personal reasons.

The scientist can learn a good deal about a culture by examining the phenomena associated with behaviors such as smoking. Actually, smoking has only recently been perceived as a problem. Accordingly, it has not been investigated very much. This means that the scientist examining smoking behavior is bound to encounter empirical phenomena that he has not seen before. Only if he is lucky will these new phenomena fall within the conceptual scheme that he has already worked up for himself. He can try that scheme if he likes, but I think he would be better advised to pursue new empirical phenomena with an open mind and see whether these require new concepts or formulations somewhat different from those he has used before. In the study of alcoholism and the treatment of alcoholics, for example, it has been painful for people in the psychoanalytic tradition to learn that one cannot treat alcoholic patients in the traditional psychoanalytic way, or even in the traditional passive psychotherapeutic way. Here the psychotherapist is dealing with phenomena different from neuroses. He must adapt not only his methods but his conceptualization of problems to the new kind of phenomena.

I should like to ask Dr. Berkowitz what he thinks that psychologists like himself can learn, or how the discipline can be advanced, by the study of smoking-related phenomena.

Leonard Berkowitz: I'm rather pessimistic about what our respective disciplines can learn, although I agree that they *should* learn. All of us are probably first going to sift new data accumulated through our own particular biases. It's going to be a very, very slow and arduous process correcting our preconceptions in terms of the very meaningful and important data that will be accumulated. I think that the area of smoking research is an exceedingly important one, not only practically but theoretically. It should make us come face to face with many problems of an important conceptual-theoretical nature. I wonder how quickly we will do that.

Let me reflect on some of my own biases. I see the field of motivation changing radically. The motivational concepts being advanced by experimental psychologists today differ in many ways from the ideas of the 1950's and earlier. Many of us in the fields of social and personality psychology and in the various practical fields are still tied to the motivational conceptions of these earlier periods. In a sense, we are still laboring under somewhat outmoded conceptions of what makes people act as they do. For example, it seems that a good deal of the data already gained from the smoking research reported at this Conference indicate that people are not uniformly controlled by simple positive and negative incentives as we ordinarily assume they are — at least not constantly and not always completely. There are other determinants of behavior than these simple incentives. I'm not sure that we have really come to grips with this concept in our research.

Another difficulty is that smoking has been considered mainly from an experimental-psychology framework, and not adequately interpreted from a sociological point of view. It may be argued, for example, that one of the reasons many youngsters start to smoke involves their alienation from their particular segment of society. *Alienation* has not been mentioned at all in connection with the research reported here. Yet it is an exceedingly important concept which has been very fruitful in many sociological investigations and probably has important implications for the study of smoking. What this means is that smoking may not be a behavior to be understood only in itself but has to be tied to various other forms of deviant behavior. It has been reported at this Conference, for example, that students who develop venereal diseases are also likely to start smoking early in life. Smoking here is not a deviant behavior carried out in isolation but appears to be just one facet of a general behavior pattern, possibly involving some sort of alienation.

My observation, then, is that as an ivory-tower psychologist I hope to be able to learn. I think all of us should be able to learn. I have a feeling, however, that it's going to be a slow learning process. The applied researchers also have much to learn from the ivory tower. They have to learn more about what's going on in experimental psychology and theoretical sociology as well.

Nevitt Sanford: It is interesting that the sociologists seem to be somewhat under-represented at this conference. I, too, noted the absence of reference to sociological concepts, even in places where they seem to be called for. But Dr. Borgatta will come to that, probably.

Frank Barron: Your reference to Indian culture set my mind adrift, and I'm back there with the Navajo and the smoke rising from their ceremonial pipes. Smoking really did begin with the Indians, of course, but they invested it with a philosophical significance rather foreign to us. With them it was part of a way of life and a tradition; it was a means for invoking the higher powers, a ceremonial that had considerable import for the resolution of life crises, such as wars between tribes. At least in my imagery, the smoking ceremony was an occasion for meditation and philosophic detachment. Tobacco and other plants were smoked by pipe. There wasn't any burning paper in the picture, and no nervous fidgeting. One imagines the smoke going up slowly and quietly. Perhaps it's important to remember that there was often something other than tobacco, or *more* than tobacco, in those pipes. It is a fact that in the world at large, the substance smoked by more people than any other is opium. If one wanted to broaden one's way of viewing smoking behavior, he should look at it in terms of the historical development of smoking. Ordinarily, as one looks at it now, he thinks in terms of a process which leads to disease, something that's undesirable, an end product which we in our society would like to find ways of avoiding, and so on. Perhaps we're missing some of the deeper, mythical significance or motives in smoking.

Nevitt Sanford: What Dr. Barron says about smoking reminds me of that episode in *Sweet Bird of Youth,* when the broken-down actress asked the young man to give her a cigarette. He offered her one from the package he had in his pocket. "Oh, not that kind," she said, "they cause cancer!" . . . May we hear from you now, Dr. Borgatta. Be more sociological — and not so social-psychological as you've been thus far, will you?

Edgar Borgatta: I have what we call "self-hatred" or something similar associated with my occupation. This is part of my problem when responding as a sociologist. One thing I will not speak about, however, is alienation, because that's the kind of concept with which I have a great deal of difficulty. Conceptually it's an appealing notion but empirically it just doesn't correspond to measures of values and the like, which when ordered into well-defined clusters, appear to have reasonably defined structures. Alienation just does *not* occur as a well-defined concept in any analysis of values or orientations toward life, although it may break up into several other concepts and therefore be slightly difficult to handle. If one is concerned with building theories that have some direct empirical reference to measures he is going to utilize when he does research, there is something appealing about a concept like alienation. Yet, I would have to say that it arises not out of theory but out of *ad hoc* speculation; that is, I would take the more hard-nosed approach and say that theory, in a scientific sense, is generalization which is drawn from empirical experience, and there are some requirements implied about the ways in which data are collected when the empirical experience is judged relevant.

But as a sociologist, let me remark that there is a

large area of sociology which is called "social-problems," or the "analysis of deviant behavior." If we conceive smoking as a social problem in society, it can be found to be analogous to many other problems in which we have some experience. I won't say that it's a happy experience, because the science has to be characterized as a descriptive science, very often a descriptive science based on intuitions and impressions, rather than a formal gathering of data. I would go just a little further and say that I have had the unfortunate experience, having taught mostly graduate work, of thinking that I would enjoy teaching an undergraduate course sometime as an introduction to sociology. I proposed to build the course around what we would call the cumulative science, that is, those areas in which there is an accumulation of research in sociology, and where essentially some empirical theory might be drawn and would be susceptible to systematic presentation at a reasonably descriptive level. I encountered no such area in sociology, which made the task rather difficult. But there were some areas in which there were indications that this may be a process that is going on, and these areas are of some interest. They all focused around selected variables that are of enumerative or a registration type, such as the kind of statistics which are drawn from the census, death registrations, marriages — things of this sort. Theories and information are organized and accumulated, are refined in time relative to the prediction of such events. Smoking falls in this category. On this basis, we should have some expectations about what should develop as knowledge about smoking behavior. I would not expect large amounts of variance to be predicted in terms of changes up and down on the statistics of these things; social trends would have to be characterized as being associated with historical periods, rather than with long variations of cyclical types or seasonal types, although there may be such variations. We have the same problem in predicting juvenile delinquency. We predict it very well as long as we are predicting for a short-term trend. It is a problem which is not unique to sociology or even to the social-psychological sciences.

Nor are social problems ever clear-cut in a society. They always arise because of a system of values which is not monolithic in any sense; it's one in which there are conflicts at various levels. There are conflicting sources of values in a society involving values on one side which claim, for example, that society should be gravitating toward more unity and uniformity, and on the other side defend the tendency of maintaining segregated groups. The values are highly complex, endless in number, and often poorly defined. They may be able to exist together quite nicely as long as no one forces a confrontation of one value with another.

The study of smoking behavior is no different from the study of any other social problem, except that it is an area where a change in values is occurring. We certainly can chart this change and anticipate that it will continue. This, I think, is an important kind of sociological study to which we have had very little reference. But it is a kind of global description that is possible and that we ought to anticipate. The study of smoking behavior would then proceed toward the prediction of its occurrence as an individual phenomenon. By prediction, I refer essentially to its occurrence among individuals in particular classes or groups.

One of the rather disheartening aspects of study of a number of our interesting problems (such as academic performance or dropout rates) is that we ordinarily begin with some interesting and complex theories of motivation and personality, only to find them insufficient for the prediction of the behavior, particularly in the field situation. For example, predicting who is going to go on to college is a rather humbling experience. The best predictor here is the answer to the question gained by asking high school students whether they are going to go on to college. That one question accumulates practically all of the variance of all of the other predictors, and one can move away from asking that question into other concepts which may appear essentially to add information. For example, one can split that question into less direct questions in terms of performance. "How well have you performed?" or "How interested are you in performing?" If one asks the question, "How important is it for you to get ahead?" essentially he may be asking the question "How important has it been in the past for you to get ahead?"

So we get into the kinds of questions posed here by Dr. Leventhal about the circularity of prediction involved in concepts that we order. The fact is that when we deal with the motivational concepts we often find, if we have taken into account some of the more gross sociological or background variables and the so-called experience variables, that there is very little left to predict. There is very little left in the sense that there is very little that we *can* predict.

Certainly we are not going to cope with this situation by avoiding it; I'm sure that we are going to have to move ahead in the slow and tedious way of refining instruments, both at the level of criteria and at the level of measurement. This does imply, to some extent, a multi-disciplinary approach, because one really cannot be purely a sociologist or psychologist, as he proceeds here; he has, in effect, to bring in predictors from both levels or from these levels and others in predicting such a phenomenon.

Silvan Tomkins: In reflecting on our discussion here, I am impressed again by the problem of what smoking behavior research can do for psychological science — although the obvious question is the reverse one. As I view it, sciences develop just as human beings develop, performing differently at different stages of development: infancy, adolescence and maturity. Problems that can be solved in a jiffy at maturity are stumbled over and cause a great waste of time in the earlier stages. A critical question arises: should any science concern itself with a particular problem or set of problems at a particular stage of its development? Is there any kind of optimal match between the stage of development of a science and the nature of the problem to which it is addressing itself? It is entirely possible for one of three things to happen here.

One: The attempt to solve the problem slows down and curtails the development of the science, wastes its time, discourages it, gets nothing done; the field to which it is addressing itself is not helped in any way. Progress can become stalled in striving for a kind of theoretical approach or a kind of technique or whatever, if they are inappropriate at that particular stage of the science's development. Some of my mathematician friends, for example, pure mathematicians, take a very jaundiced view of the present-day interest of some psychologists in mathematical models in psychology. This is not because they dislike psychology or love mathematics less; but they say, "At your present stage of development this is an absurdity. Mathematics was useful, for example, to physics only when it had attained a certain level of development. You are trying to rush it too much!" This may be a mistaken judgment, but it is the judgment of some very competent mathematicians. If the problem posed isn't optimally matched to the science's advance, it can set that science back, and also do it harm. And since the science that is thus harmed is essential for the solution of that problem, the harm is not just to the science, it is also to the problem.

Two: The attempt to solve a particular problem may produce little positive effect. The problem won't be solved; the science won't be set back, but left as it was.

The third is a possibility which I think is particularly relevant to the smoking problem. That is the possibility that the focus of scientific attention to a particular problem, such as smoking, or to the application of a particular technique, such as, for example, the use of tracer studies in biochemistry after the Second World War, could be timed well enough to accelerate enormously the development of that science. There are numerous instances in which science has taken on a new problem, thereby providing impetus to its growth and at the same time promoting the development of related disciplines. From the point of view of abstract possibility, we should entertain these three possibilities concerning the relationship between personality theory and smoking behavior.

I tend to favor the third of these possibilities. I believe that most of the models that held sway in general psychology and personality theory in the last fifty years or

so remain in a state of slight to severe disrepute — so that posing a problem which embarrasses us a little in terms of our present knowledge will in all probability accelerate the development of psychological science. In this regard, I would agree with Dr. Berkowitz, who has commented here about the unstable state of theoretical and methodological development in which psychology finds itself today. I may be mistaken, but this appears to be an optimal situation for radical and quick transformation of thinking.

If the problem of the study of smoking behavior had been posed to psychology in the days of Titchener, damage would have resulted — not only to Titchenerian psychology, but to the development of the problem area itself. What an extraordinary fantasy to entertain — the great wealth of detail that would have come out of the analyses of all the sensations involved in smoking! They would have had a field day. But I am convinced the yield from this toward an understanding and control of smoking behavior would have been about zero. It also might have simply confirmed Titchener in his folly. If smoking behavior had become a problem when Pavlov and the conditioned reflex were at the peak of their influence, it probably would have been equally disastrous. There is very little in conditioning theory that could have been of any use in the understanding of the smoking problem. If there is anything that lighting up and puffing a cigarette is not, it is not a reflex. We forget that there was a very subtle switch from the concept of reflex to response and from conditioned response to instrumental learning. These were all big leaps which evolved without any explicit acknowledgment that the theory was changing radically. Had the smoking problem been investigated when the only concepts that we really had at our disposal were something like the salivary reflex, we'd have been in trouble.

Frank Barron: I must disagree with you. I think the Pavlovian theory has great possibilities for the study of smoking behavior.

Silvan Tomkins: Pavlovian theory? In the sense in which that was a conditioned reflex theory? I'm not talking about modern conditioning.

Frank Barron: I was thinking about the possibility of there actually being some physiological role played by nicotine in the development of the habit. A big factor in smoking in terms of the experience of the person may be the physiological changes produced by nicotine. Though not addictive in the strong sense of the term, it may encourage the habit. Also, I wouldn't throw out Titchenerian introspection.

Silvan Tomkins: I do not equate all introspection with Titchenerian introspection. I was talking about what went on in Titchener's lab, which was far from the way we use the word introspection now. You know that set of categories? I mean it was pretty esoteric: light pressure, dull pressure, and so on.

Frank Barron: On one of the eighteen occasions on which I quit smoking, I managed to do it by serious introspection on the act of smoking itself. I realized I had in my hand a small bunch of weeds with wrapping paper around it, and I was putting it in my mouth and lighting a fire. Then I was breathing the products of the combustion of the paper and weeds into my delicate pink bronchioles, and I could see all the horrible pieces of grit, the size of rocks by comparison with the bronchioles rolling around down there. I threw the cigarette away in horror. That's what I call a Titchenerian approach.

Silvan Tomkins: That's not a Titchenerian approach, that's a more modern introspective approach. Regarding the reflex theory, there is a definite importance of innate biological structures and mechanisms, and programs and responses. I believe that there is an innate affective basis for some of the rewards and punishments of smoking, but I don't think of them as reflexes. They sound very much like reflexes, but there are some fundamental differences. The major one is that the inborn affect programs, as I understand them, are triggered by a wide variety of circumstances, which is not true of reflexes. The patellar tendon and the salivary glands have very restricted sets of activators. One must tap the patellar tendon somewhere near it, for example, to get a reflex response.

Jerome Schwartz: What does a secretary do when she knows a coffee break has come, or someone else when he works in an oil plant where he can't smoke, and then he goes on his break? Could this be compared with the ringing of Pavlov's bell?

Silvan Tomkins: I believe you are equating conditioning theory, as we presently understand it, with Pavlovian theory. I was trying to say that introspection and conditioning principles as such are useless for understanding smoking. I was being historic in my comments about a particular psychological theory which is distinct from the meaning of introspection in general, as we understand it today, and about a particular learning theory as Pavlov developed it which differs from the modern definition of conditioning. As I said earlier, had smoking become a problem in the early days of psychology it would in all probability have helped neither to solve the smoking problem nor to help the science. For example, if we had tried to solve the cancer problem a hundred years ago, my guess is that we wouldn't have had a prayer. Without the rapid advancement of molecular biology, the causes of cancer probably never would be found. One never knows for sure whether the problem that he is trying to solve is in fact solvable at that particular stage of scientific development, or whether the challenge is going to help the science or crush it. I disagree with Nevitt Sanford, who believes that concentrating the energies of psychology on the study of human problems will enrich psychology and help society at the same time — a perfectly reasonable position in the abstract. I'm disputing it here by saying that there probably are some problems which will greatly accelerate the science, and others that will harm it and not lead to any solutions. In part it's an article of faith and a gamble deciding whether a particular problem is appropriate for study. It is always possible for any science to go up a blind alley in the pursuit of a will-o'-the-wisp. The fact that we are men of good will and would like to prevent people from dying of cancer from smoking is neither here nor there. The question, as I see it, is an intellectual one and one of adequacy, involving the distance between where the science is now and where it will be if it addresses itself to this problem. Again — will it accelerate the development of the science and the solution of the problem or will it hurt the science and fail to solve the problem?

Selwyn Waingrow: How does one decide when to take up the challenge and when not to do so?

Silvan Tomkins: There are no clear guideposts. In the last war, for example, there was a question raised at one point about what it was profitable to try to develop to win the war. Should we go into the atom-bomb development or not? Should we go into biological warfare or not? There were numerous options raised at various times during the progress of that war. But theorists and others were sought out in each of these fields and opinion canvassed, and action was based on their opinions. Einstein's support was sought to help persuade Roosevelt that it was worth putting great time and energy into the development of the atomic bomb. But nobody knew at that time for sure.

Percy Tannenbaum: Well, it took that critical event in Stagg Field to demonstrate the feasibility of building the bomb. Once they could show the reaction, they could start thinking about the technical matters involved.

Frank Barron: With the exception of a very few radically divergent theoretical developments, the whole history of science is the response of science to human problems. The scientist brings to bear all that he knows at that point about the way the world works and the way he works, in an effort to solve a particular problem. This is the process by which theory advances.

Selwyn Waingrow: But whose responsibility is it to decide the proper time for involving a science in a problem so that neither is a solution to the problem delayed nor is the science destroyed? What are the criteria to be used by a scientist in deciding when to "bail out" or when to continue studying a "problem"? In the absence of criteria, what alternative does one have?

Silvan Tomkins: It's a question in risk behavior. People make bets. If one takes the race track as a paradigm here, some people like to bet on horses "to show," with the payoff at ten cents on the dollar, and they do this with a high degree of regularity. Others find this a bad bet. They want a one-hundred-to-one, even though it comes rarely. There are wide individual differences among scientists as to what they think is an appropriate risk.

Mildred Dubitzky: Why, Dr. Tomkins, do you consider this a propitious era or moment in time for psychology and other social scientists to investigate the smoking problem?

Silvan Tomkins: Because, as I said, I believe psychological theory is today in a state of ferment; that is to say, psychologists are very uncertain about what they think. While the theories of Freud, Pavlov, Titchener or Hull have captured the imagination of psychologists for many decades, they probably would not have been capable of handling a problem of this magnitude. This is not to imply, of course, that any new theories are now available which would be more helpful, but I do believe that psychology is in a state where it is prepared to entertain alternative models, some of which might be appropriate to the solution of this problem.

Percy Tannenbaum: The decision to probe a new problem is usually an individual one. Even during the war when there was a mobilization of physicists and engineers on the Manhattan project not all physicists devoted their time to it. If we could declare a state of national emergency on the smoking problem, we might be able to mobilize all available talent in the social sciences. Whether social science is ready to take up the challenge is questionable. I don't think we have reached a degree of development where we can say, "Here is a problem we can start looking at for technical applications." We may want to try it, and I think many of us do feel a personal challenge. We have spent a good part of a year at the Center for Advanced Study[1] working on what we call "the consistency theory," which is probably one of the more significant recent developments in social psychology. It involves about six different theories, such as dissonance theory, balance theory, and so on. Our concern is with consistencies or balances among an individual's cognitions; or among and within his attitudes and cognitions; among and within his attitudes and behavior, etc. Within this consistency model, our predictions seem to be borne out. But along comes smoking behavior! Is this just another kind of general behavior or a special case? It is a *very* special case, it turns out; it has some specific, even unique, characteristics that no other behavior we have studied has. The consistency model has not yet been found to apply in this case. Perhaps we have to make changes in the model. Or perhaps the special characteris-

tics of the smoking problem take it outside the realm of the theory's applicability altogether. If it is a case of addiction, for example, then a physiological basis is involved, rather than merely a cognitive one. This study presents a challenge — a personal challenge, as well as a challenge to theory in psychology.

Leonard Berkowitz: It is not only in the area of smoking that the consistency theories have not worked out. For example, they have had trouble generally with the problem of reactions to fear arousal. As a matter of fact, there are *many* places in which consistency theories haven't worked out.

Percy Tannenbaum: And there will be many more, I'm sure. But the point I'm trying to make is that the smoking problem, which should fit the model, has aroused the interest of some scientists who are concerned with certain theoretical formulations. They are trying to see if the fit is possible, and if so, what kinds of manipulations are necessary. You are quite right, Len, when you say that the problem of smoking behavior is not the only one that the consistency theories can't seem to handle. But it has recently been found to be a particularly embarrassing one for them.

Frank Barron: Why does smoking catch on so fast and last so long once it's started? It was unknown to Europe until relatively recently; yet it caught on very quickly and it has lasted a long time.

Selwyn Waingrow: There must be *something* right about it.

Percy Tannenbaum: Obviously it serves certain needs. But I'd like to change the subject and discuss communication, a term that is being used and bandied about much too generally. Communication is an *indirect* exposure to the outside world, as opposed to direct exposure, such as the reaction of the sense organs to a set of stimuli. I think this is an important distinction, because the smoking-behavior field compares with others which study behavior that threatens the individual's well-being. The individual cannot afford to learn by direct exposure because he may die as a result. We *try* to teach our children a lot of behaviors indirectly. Once they learn the language and code that represent actual events we can teach them how to behave accordingly. I think that basically the purpose of smoking behavior research — at any rate, that with which the National Clearinghouse is concerned — revolves about the mobilization of communications on smoking.

Generally we speak of communication on three levels: how information is received, how it is processed, and how it finally develops in some form of behavior. The capacity to communicate freely is a uniquely human achievement, which man— also a social animal — uses to interact with other men. At this level — that of indi-

---

[1] Center for Advanced Study in the Behavioral Sciences, Stanford, California.

vidual behavior — definite problems are encountered such as the problem of interpersonal influence.

The greater challenge here lies in prevention rather than cure; to try to discourage youngsters from smoking to begin with. I think we can be more successful here than at the level where we would be attempting to change existing behavioral patterns. The third level of interest in communication is in the area of mass media. Whether caused by the growth of industry itself, the kinds of societies that industrial growth produces, or a combination of these, most industrial societies have institutions whose function and interest it is to produce information and entertainment. Particularly in our commercial system, their objective is persuasion. Recently there has been some rather interesting research on immunization against it which may have some application in the area of stopping youngsters from starting to smoke. It is my belief that the role of the mass media will be very minimal in any program designed to change smokers into non-smokers. The mass media aren't ready to do these things for us. They are much too *broadcast,* too impersonal, in the literal sense. Perhaps mass-media messages can hit the right people who will then (to use the Lazarsfeld-Katz model, if it still holds) influence other people. But these means are indirect indicators of what might happen to one if he continues to engage in this behavior.

Selwyn Waingrow: Smoking presents specific communications problems. First there is the problem of trying to get somebody not to do something. Second is the question of which aspects of communications are applicable in the absence of a precise threshold for defining risk. We still don't know how many cigarettes over how long a period of time will kill a person. We are forced to sell a generalized risk concept coupling it with proposals for avoidance behavior rather than suggesting an alternative.

Percy Tannenbaum: I believe we must examine further the assumption that cigarettes are so bad for people that we have to do something about them. Despite all the statistics, there is still a higher probability that one won't be killed by lung cancer from smoking than that one will be — a factor in any individual's risk judgment. In a consideration of the mass media, if I may continue in that vein, scholars are interested in how mass media form policy decisions, how they prepare their messages, and why. The media entrepreneurs themselves are often in conflict. They are in private business with profits to consider. There is also the public interest, and here broadcast media in particular are under some government regulations. The U. S. Government hasn't debated the cigarette issue although other countries have. By law, there is no advertising on English television, for example. This was a governmental policy decision that affected the

media because the media are under more control there. More regulation may occur in this country soon, also; it would be interesting to see how the media respond to it. Again these define a set of problems that communication research people might get interested in, vis-a-vis the cigarette-smoking issue. Smoking — stopping people from starting and stopping them after they have started — becomes a rather special case, where we might examine how the media function, how people are influenced by them, and so on. The problem is to start defining the special characteristics of the cigarette-smoking situation, which we have only skirted. For example, what kinds of needs does smoking indeed serve, and can we overcome or compensate for them?

Frank Barron: What kind of information is *genuinely* relevant to the individual smoker? We do know that for the population as a whole there is a certain risk attached to smoking cigarettes over a given period of time. Why doesn't knowledge of this fact make people nervous about smoking and make them want to stop? I think the reason is that in most cases it's not *personally relevant* information. Recall the kind of experiment that I proposed here today: I suggested that every time any individual develops lung cancer as a result of smoking we should try to find another individual of similar age and smoking habits. We then assign him to a control group. When we have enough cases in both groups, we compare them on a host of variables. I mentioned as an example of a potential resource the MMPI item pool of 1938. We should try to get historical data and also make concurrent studies of the characteristics of those who get the disease and those who do not. Out of that we might be able to gather evidence which would be *personally* relevant.

Again, let's consider the matter of risk. Let's say that the risk itself is actually normally distributed in the population of smokers, so that there is some cutting point, fairly far from the mean of the distribution, where the risk becomes something that indeed one *ought realistically* to worry about. Now, the problem becomes one of predicting at what point an individual, given his known personality characteristics, or his physical and physiological make-up, or his life situation, or his history of smoking, has reached the real danger point *for him.* That's the research strategy I would adopt.

Selwyn Waingrow: Assign a weight to each one and get a cumulative score of risk, and tell someone he is not a high risk?

Frank Barron: Yes, enable the risk for the given individual to be specified. One might find a large number of relevant factors that could be assigned unit weights. Once one has a list of indicators that can be used by the individual to figure his own risk, given the kind of person he is, then one can communicate something that might affect behavior in the sense that rationality enters in and a person says, *"Yes,* I have had enough, I can see by what he has told me that I'm going to get lung cancer if I don't quit, so I'll quit."

Percy Tannenbaum: But this may well be wishful pipe-smoking. The MMPI contains many items, and it's marvelous, but it may not include those relevant items, or there may be only a few of them instead of the one hundred that may be critical here.

Frank Barron: That may be true, of course. We don't know. I mention the MMPI because it does contain a large number of items and there are many cases with records intact as of 1938.

Percy Tannenbaum: One might argue that we ought to let 1938 lie with other decadent techniques and start with new concepts that might be even better.

Frank Barron: The conceptual scheme on which the MMPI rests is not what I am urging here. As an alternative I'll suggest getting all the one-hundred-yard sprinters of 1938 and taking them as a sample. My general point is that there are records from recent history that may prove immediately useful: one may not need to wait for the future to amass suitable criterion cases.

Edgar Filbey: Although those who suffer the physical effects of smoking are probably the best prospects and the most successful at quitting, there are a number of persons in our hospital study, for example, who have the highest risk. That is, they *have* a cardiac problem, chronic bronchitis, or emphysema, and they still don't quit. They are in the high-risk group because they either cannot accept or cannot act upon their knowledge of the effects of smoking. While personal information is of interest and would probably influence a good number, it would not sway others.

Frank Barron: Again I say that I am not trying to suggest hypotheses. I have no idea what the results of such studies would be. I do say, however, that adopting strategies like this, regardless of the particular set of facts in the records, is one possibly fruitful way of approaching the problem.

Daniel Horn: A number of things have been said here that make me feel that more bits of information at this point may be helpful. The picture of the Indian smoking a ceremonial pipe has been discussed as has the question of the needs satisfied by smoking. Perhaps a little excursion into history may be helpful. Tobacco smoking by Indians in the fifteenth century had quite a different effect from tobacco as we know it today. Botanically it was different; and the descriptions of the experiences sound much more like the experience recorded for the use of drugs like LSD or peyote. Some of the religious ceremonial drugs with consciousness expansions, high degrees of fantasy, states of unconsciousness, etc., were very unlike the kinds of experiences that most of us have had from tobacco. So we are talking about something that has changed over the years.

I would like to point out that the problem today is cigarette smoking, which is a relatively new problem. In Western civilization the use of tobacco only goes back to the end of the fifteenth century; but the use of the cigarette in its problem form only goes back about fifty years. During this short period of time many changes have taken place in the consumption of tobacco. There have been periods in which pipes were the primary form; periods in which cigars were the primary form. A graph of the consumption of chewing tobacco in the United States through the years shows a very interesting curve which reached a peak figure in 1894 of four and a quarter pounds of chewing tobacco per person over the age of fifteen. After that time, it has dropped — down, down, down; it is practically off the chart now at the level of under one quarter of a pound per person. The point is that here is a use of tobacco — once very widespread — which has changed. There are a number of reasons why that change took place; one reason was the development and widespread use of an alternative, the modern cigarette, which really got started sometime between 1910 and 1915. All these different uses of tobacco (including snuff, for example, which is still used by one adult out of fifty) serve a purpose for the numbers of people who use them. Our concern is with one specific form of tobacco, because this is the one that does damage to the individual. If one looks at the history of fashions, the changes in tobacco may make the smoking problem look a little bit different from what it is. If one simply thinks of this as a drug with effects which people *must* have one has to remember that the effects have changed and usage has changed. The problem exists solely in a particular form.

I would also like to comment on the concept of alienation, because there is some evidence that it is indeed identifiable. A set of conditions that could fit this rubric has been identified as an important factor in the taking up of smoking. Certainly the taking up of smoking is common among delinquent youth. One observation was reported to me which has many fascinating implications, and I wish somebody would verify it. I was told by a New York City junior high school principal who was invariably assigned to areas with problem populations, that when he had a school of roughly eighty-five per cent Negro and fifteen per cent Puerto Rican, the only youngsters who smoked were Puerto Ricans. "But," he said, "two blocks away in a school of eighty-five per cent Puerto Rican and fifteen per cent Negroes, the smokers were the Negroes, the delinquent and problem children." The implication is that for some reason smoking becomes a symbol, a substitute for certain kinds of relationships.

I can't resist commenting also on Dr. Tannenbaum's suggestion that we might do a lot better concentrating on keeping youngsters from starting to smoke and giving up on adults. This is indeed tempting. In the first place, I think we have fewer guilt feelings about interfering with children. What disturbs me about this is that if we are dealing with a habit where a large part of the attraction is its symbol of adulthood, smoking remains attractive to the child looking for a symbol of maturity. Therefore, unless we can curb adult consumption, we are sowing the seeds of our own failure with children. I think it becomes almost essential to work both ends of this problem at the same time.

Frankly, I think the solution to the health problem of cigarettes is inevitable, for unless something gives, such a large portion of the population will start dropping dead of heart attacks, be disabled by emphysema, develop lung cancer, and so on, that it will become an obvious national catastrophe. Things are already happening. The nature of the cigarette is changing. The nature of the way people smoke is changing — and the proportion of those who smoke is changing, simply because of the number of people who are becoming aware of its effects. Once a problem reaches a certain point, certain counteracting forces begin to act. I see our role not as agents for a change that would not otherwise take place, but possibly simply as activators to speed up the social process and enable a few million people to benefit earlier.

Nevitt Sanford: Is there any possibility that cigarette smoking will be replaced by some other use of tobacco, the way snuff and cigar smoking had their day and passed on? That's a rather encouraging thought.

Daniel Horn: Many people are working on that. Someone recently asked me if I had found a good substitute for the cigarette. I replied that if I had I'd be busy manufacturing it, not working at this job.

Nevitt Sanford: You remind us of the enormous extent to which culture determines not only what drugs or substances are used, but how they are responded to. It is interesting that one can give the same kind of history about alcohol. According to historians, when wine was first produced, it was regarded as a gift from the gods. It assumed various forms of symbolic value and was used mainly on ceremonial occasions for a very long time. Similarly, when the process of distillation was invented, a great reaction followed. There was even more excitement about alcohol than there is about LSD today. In fact, similar types of psychological, mind-altering kinds of reactions were in vogue then. The same was true of coffee. In Switzerland it was once a crime punishable by death to have coffee in one's possession, because it was considered a mind-altering drug. I think it is well to remember the degree to which our responses are learned

and shaped by the culture of the time. It seems to me that those who would prevent cigarette smoking have a good chance to act in concert with forces that are already changing this habit. We definitely have the impression, for example, that the consumption of alcohol is changing in the direction of greater moderation, that the most destructive patterns of drinking have rather gone by, and that adolescent drinking is being replaced by a kind of adolescent drug culture.

Selwyn Waingrow: Dr. Sanford has talked about sociological concepts that might be used and have not been; and Dr. Berkowitz has talked about advances made since the 1950's in psychology and social psychology that have not been considered. What are some of the concepts implied in these statements?

Edgar Borgatta: I should like to elaborate somewhat on the concept of alienation as Dr. Horn has used it. He probably did exactly what I object to. In providing an example he described a man's impression of what was happening in a high school down the street. I just question that man's observation.

Daniel Horn: Well, we have a much more solid background of data than that. It was just that this observation happened to fit into it and it was a little more of a dramatic kind of story.

Leonard Berkowitz: I'm not as negativistic as Dr. Borgatta in this matter, perhaps because I'm not a sociologist. I think the concept of "alienation" can be very useful empirically, although it certainly has been used in an overly gross and overly diffuse and imprecise manner. Although it involves a fairly complex syndrome or cluster of feelings and attitudes, it seems to me that people who have a sense of purposelessness or a feeling of isolation from their fellows, and so forth, may well be more prone to practice deviant behaviors, including smoking. So that's one seemingly obvious place where social-science theory has not contributed to smoking research. In regard to psychological theorizing, motivational theorizing, I think much of the survey research on smoking behavior has been guided by a fairly simple-minded incentive theory or hedonistic conception which means that people will do what they enjoy and avoid acts which will result in unpleasant or adverse consequences. I suggest that classic motivational theorizing is being found to be over-simplified, because there are many other stimulus determinants of behavior, and it is among these, I think, that smoking should be studied.

Perhaps what we should do is separate the reasons for starting smoking from the reasons for the persistence of the smoking habit and those that result in its cessation. Actually, there may be three very separate sets of phenomena here. The reason a person starts to smoke may come from certain gratifications or needs that are thereby satisfied. But the frequency of his smoking may not be determined by hedonistic principles at all, or at least not exclusively.

Selwyn Waingrow: It appears as though there is an element of functional autonomy in the continuance behavior of some smokers.

Leonard Berkowitz: There may be many stimulus determinants influencing how often an individual smokes which may have nothing to do with any needs that are gratified. Similarly, the factors that may produce a change in smoking habits may be independent of the reasons the individual started smoking.

Selwyn Waingrow: Do you think the study of smoking behavior has anything to contribute to theory in this area?

Leonard Berkowitz: Well, I should hope so, but I think it's going to be a long and arduous process.

Selwyn Waingrow: Dr. Sanford, you intimated that there were certain sociological concepts that you felt weren't being exploited in this problem area, and I wondered what you had in mind.

Nevitt Sanford: My remark was that I thought sociologists were under-represented in our group. I'd like to hear them discuss the question of how young people begin smoking, because I'm sure it would be quite different from a discussion among personality psychologists. I think sociologists would pay attention to the structure of the youth group involved and they would look for the functions smoking serves for the group. They wouldn't pay any particular attention to individuals but would try to find out what problems are shared by all the individuals in the group, what the group's problems are and whether smoking provides some sort of solution to the group's problems. I imagine they would look at drinking among teenagers in somewhat the same way. They might suggest that smoking, drinking and other youthful activities be looked at in the same terms. In fact, teenage activities might well be grouped in some fashion, and what we learn about one might be applicable to the others.

Bernard Mausner: One of the most generally supported conclusions drawn after studying a raft of data on the personality characteristics of smokers is that different people smoke for different reasons. For example, we queried about fifty smokers in a junior high school population and received various reasons for their current smoking. But the most important impetus for beginning to smoke was, as has been suggested, social support. They smoked because an older brother smoked or because a parent smoked or because friends smoked. Very shortly after, they discovered that smoking was fun. And at the time when we interviewed them about sixty per cent said they smoked for some kind of affective reason, mostly to relieve tension. Others gave social reasons for their smoking, and still others said they smoked simply for enjoyment. For them it was rather a solitary exercise. These smokers also had a significantly lower I.Q. and grade status than a random sample of non-smokers. An *F* test showed that there were significant differences among the three kinds of smokers (tension relief, social and individual) in grades but not in I.Q. Smokers who smoked for tension release — these were fourteen-year-olds, some of whom said there are times when they must have a cigarette — had grades that were almost as high as the average grades of non-smokers. These are not, incidentally, trivial differences. The non-smokers' grades were in the neighborhood of 80, while the average for the smokers was around 74. The tension-release smokers averaged about 77, with social smokers down around 70. It seems to me we demonstrated, even in a small group, a number of different mechanisms and functions behind smoking. The tension-releasing youngsters may be bucking some inadequacy; they just need those cigarettes. For the other smokers inadequacies were not being bucked, and for them cigarettes had a completely different significance. If we accept the idea that different people smoke for different reasons, then I'm afraid the sort of study that Dr. Barron suggested would be very hard to do. If all smokers risk contracting lung cancer from smoking and not from their temperament (which, I suppose, is an open question) then unless we can sort out the reasons for smoking, it would be a little futile to look for differences between smokers and non-smokers in the thirty-year-old MMPI. In fact, I suspect one of the reasons studies which have tried to find some correlation between psychological characteristics and smoking habits are largely unsuccessful is that there are too many variables to consider. The variety of reasons for smoking suggests no one personality factor is predominant among smokers. As a result of this, no one kind of variable is predominant unless there happens to be some kind of sampling variation that stresses a particular motive for a group. It is an extremely complex problem.

Frank Barron: But your finding argues for just the kind of study I would do. When one has located the sets of variables which have predictive validity in multiple-discriminant function analysis, then he should factor those sets.

Bernard Mausner: While I agree with you that multiple-discriminant analyses provide an excellent approach, it is a kind of *data* which we must stress — data on the function that smoking plays in the ecology of the smoker's life.

Frank Barron: At this point I am willing to forget about 1938. Let's start with 1966 and let's wait until the year 2000 for our criterion groups to develop. It will just take a little longer.

John Weir: Dr. Barron has suggested the possible

value of research designed to calculate the "risk of ruin" for any single individual, given his personality characteristics, physiological characteristics, health, age he began smoking, and so on. A Scot, David Kissen, has reported studies of hospitalized smokers and non-smokers who had either lung cancer or, in the case of his controls, a disease unrelated to smoking practice. He found that smokers without lung cancer when compared with smoker and non-smoker cancer cases were emotionally labile, non-tension binding kinds of people. Studies like this one, which search for characteristics other than smoking that are related to disease development, would go a long way toward specifying the risks an individual takes in becoming a smoker.

Richard Jones: I'd like to ask Dr. Horn whether the non-smokers' geographic and stratificational distribution in the population has been worked out very carefully within the United States.

Daniel Horn: The biggest collection of data is the 1955 survey of 40,000 households. More recently The National Health Survey conducted from July 1, 1964 to July 1, 1965 has studied samples large enough to provide a basis for more detailed analyses. With the exception of highly concentrated ethnic or religious sub-groups — such as Amish, Mormons, Seventh-day Adventists — or areas of concentrated poverty such as the deep South, the survey doesn't indicate much variation in smoking habits.

OVERVIEW I

NEVITT SANFORD

The study of smoking behavior is not as far behind alcohol studies, in which I have been involved, as some people have suggested. I am particularly interested in the possible relationship of research in these two areas. The study of drinking, having only just begun, is at about the same stage as the study of smoking. While much research has been done on alcoholism, drinking as a form of behavior has actually had little study.

My other chief interest is to see whether smoking studies could contribute to the study of drinking. While I have favored the "human problems" approach, I could argue on the side of pure science if forced to it, as I did thirty-five year ago. My Ph.D. thesis was entitled, "The Effects of Abstinence from Food Upon Imaginal Processes." When friends asked about the subject of my research, Mrs. Sanford would say, "He showed that when you're hungry, you think of food." The amused reaction forced me to go into a defense of pure science as a tool-sharpening operation, pointing out that we need to re-learn what we already know to develop tools and concepts that eventually can be used in the study of less familiar material.

Of course, in advocating the human-problems approach, I do not argue that all scientists ought to throw themselves wholeheartedly into it, neglecting everything else. I am saying that *some* scientists should, which would have the effect of counterbalancing what I regard as an over-accent on specialized, pure-science inquiry today. The field of psychology is almost dominated by those who are primarily interested in the purest aspects of the science. My view is that in order to advance the science it is necessary to refresh ourselves from time to time by looking at problems in their natural state or in their totality; looking at problems as they exist for people in general (which is what is meant by a "human problem"). Ordinarily there is a tendency for scientists to confine themselves to the laboratory and to occupy themselves with more and more specialized aspects of their discipline, getting them too far away from relevance to general problems.

Psychologists need to go back to the clinic or to the streets occasionally in order to be challenged by new ranges of phenomena. I'm still under the influence of Freud's model of interaction in the psychoanalytic situa-tion, in which inquiry and action were parts of the same enterprise. I want to see if we can apply this model to social processes or to social structures, with a view to changing something in some favorable way. It would require trying to see whether this, that, or the other procedure, not damaging to the individual, might be effective. We would then be in a position to profit from failures as well as successes. I should add that this approach is broader than merely applied science. It is, rather, a kind of involvement which puts just as much accent on advancing science as it does on solving problems.

Further, in this approach the scientist participates in the definition of the problem, and this is fundamentally important. Usually when laymen ask the scientist to address himself to some problem, it turns out that they don't know the best way to formulate the problem. One of the best things the scientist can do is to set in motion a set of processes for defining the problem in a different way. Sometimes, of course, the scientist can define it out of existence, although I rather doubt that this could be done to the smoking problem.

The values that might accrue to science from direct attacks on human problems could be important. I don't believe it is possible to persuade many social scientists to neglect their present research and address themselves to problems that worry other people. They would say their greatest contribution lies in developing the science first and later, perhaps, in applying it. Perhaps one way to persuade them to involve themselves in solving problems related to our society is by showing them that such studies can be connected with work they are already interested in. This would be an important step, because the neglect in some of these areas is rather sad. Alcohol problems, for example, are still a terribly neglected area of inquiry, both in terms of coping with the problems and in terms of what scientists can learn from them. Of the 1,065 papers presented at a recent annual meeting of the American Psychological Association, only two (by my own count) were concerned with alcohol. A count for smoking research, I expect, would yield a somewhat higher number. But there is genuine neglect, and it means, and has meant in the case of alcohol problems, that knowledge is not far advanced.

After some work with us on alcohol problems,

Howard Becker, a sociologist and the author of a paper titled "Becoming a Marijuana Smoker," said that there was no adequate sociological study of drinking practices. He meant that while there were many studies which correlated variables with drinking, there were no studies that took into account and actually explained the whole system of drinking practices. I didn't believe that, but when I reviewed the research on personality in relation to drinking, I had to admit that there were no adequate studies in this field either.

Note how we forget or overlook some of these problems. In all of the intense personality studies nobody has remembered to ask the subjects about their drinking. When I first noticed this I became a little moralistic, wondering why the researchers — Frank Barron and associates [at the Institute of Personality Assessment, Berkeley] for example — didn't remember to ask just a few questions about drinking when they were making these thorough assessments of people. Obviously, if we are going to understand personality and drinking, we must have differentiated pictures of the drinking, and, of course, we need very full information on personality. The questions had not been asked, and I was about to accuse my colleagues of some sort of motivated neglect, when I realized that in our own studies of drinking among Stanford students we had forgotten to ask them about smoking. So it goes. There is something about the psychologist that causes him to become narrowly focused in his work.

I also suspect that this neglect of drinking and smoking is partly motivated by our unwillingness to become involved in problems that are quite close to home. It can be a bit embarrassing to be involved in the study of alcohol problems. Friends assume that one must be either an alcoholic or a teetotaler. I don't know what students of smoking have experienced in this respect, but there are some indications that the observation "once a smoker always a smoker" may be a valid one. Perhaps we shouldn't say "ex-smokers" but "arrested smokers"; there is a kind of personal interest in this topic among the "ex-smokers," as well as among the "arrested alcoholics."

We have been considering the ways in which we might advance the social sciences by the human problems approach to inquiry. In this connection I was struck by how soon we found ourselves discussing one of the most persistent problems in all psychology. I refer to the dispute between Howard Leventhal and Silvan Tomkins (pp. 40–42) on the question of the role of fear in shaping behavior.

After seventy years or so, we are still debating what makes people afraid or how people react to danger. Indeed, I thought for a time that we were going to review the James-Lange theory of emotion, — "do you act because you are afraid, or are you afraid because you act?" What is the relationship between the action in response to danger and the effect of fear? For at least seventy years psychology has been trying to come up with general laws governing the relationships between stimuli and responses by studying samples of forty subjects in experimental situations. Year after year, different psychologists do the same kinds of experiments with somewhat different groups of subjects, and we still ask ourselves what general law can be stated concerning fear in relation to danger. It is a persisting problem because some psychologists, including me, make the claim that we never will discover general laws in that fashion. As soon as we use different subjects — for example, women instead of men, sophomores instead of freshmen, Mexican-Americans instead of Anglo-Americans — we get a different result. It may be, as Raymond Cattell and others have claimed, that the only general laws in psychology will turn out to be organismic laws, that is to say, relationships between some particular bit of behavior or performance and some kind of dynamic structure within the person. This will be debated back and forth. But the point is that we can confront the danger-fear issue just as well — perhaps better — by studying smoking as we can by studying anything else. If a student of personality is interested in showing that some kind of durable structure in the person is expressed in a great diversity of behavior patterns — that there is an oral complex, let's say — he must go back and forth between his hypothetical construct and his observations of behavior. He can do this in the case of smoking and drinking as well as with any other kind of behavior.

The study of human problems continually forces the scientist to address himself to new empirical observations. For example, present-day concern about youth will compel someone to determine the extent to which they are changing by examining their behavior itself. It won't do just to keep on using the MMPI method of sorting out people. Sooner or later we shall have to think up some new items based upon knowledge of what young people actually are today.

New problems also require exploratory methods of investigation. It won't do to apply immediately the conventional designs used to test hypotheses; new problems need new hypotheses. There must be a kind of inquiry that favors their generation. I would like to see, for example, more case studies of how people learn to smoke and of how people succeed in giving up smoking. I would like an enormous collection of personal vignettes, and I would like to think about them in relation to some kind of general theoretical formulation. Frank Barron has emphasized the phenomenological aspect of smoking of which I have heard too little. I would like to know what it is really like to be this, that, or the other type of smoker or to be in varying situations with respect to giving it up. This is how we arrive at the meanings of things. If one learns anything from psychoanalysis, it is that behavior has a diversity of meanings and that the same observed behavior can have different meanings in different people. We cannot discover the meaning unless we examine very closely both the behavior and the kinds of experience that accompany it.

This confronts us with the question of how we get support for exploratory work. I don't know just what the fund-granting structure is at the moment, but it appears we need a kind of "Royal Commission on Smoking" — a group of people who make policy with respect to all aspects of the subject and who have funds at their disposal to support research. My hope would be that such a group would recognize that new problem areas require exploratory research. One cannot throw the whole thing into the hands of a study committee for a granting agency which typically consists of people who did some research n years ago and who are now mainly concerned with demonstrating to all that they are really sophisticated in research methodology. We need people big enough and free enough not to feel that their scientific reputations are at stake when they support exploratory inquiries. This would mean supporting case studies, supporting purely clinical research, supporting program research which doesn't require the researcher's defining each of his projects, but allows him freedom to design his second project on the basis of what he learns in the first one — all of which does not seem to be too much to ask. But I would put this as almost the first order of business when it comes to promoting and organizing research in this area. Many research projects on smoking are a little bit lacking sometimes in respect to imagination and significance, because the mechanism of research support is well calculated to keep out imagination and significance.

Another factor in the human-problems approach that seems very important is that it can counter-balance the over-accents on specialization and the purely analytic methods of pure science, since human problems require phenomena to be looked at in context. When one talks about smoking and what to do about it one ranges over a whole set of concepts that are no respecters of disciplines. This is how it should be. Disciplines, after all, have grown up more or less accidentally in response to circumstances of particular times, and now they have become institutionalized. There is little reason to believe that real problems require the precise delineation of disciplines that we have in our universities today. Why can't there be some new disciplines as new problems present themselves?

Taking things in context means looking at genuine problems and taking some responsibility for change. To avoid the risk of doing more harm than good one is com-

pelled to look at the whole person. If one takes action with a view to changing a particular function and does not look at the whole person, one will have unanticipated consequences to deal with. One must design a particular change activity with some attention to whether this is favorable or unfavorable to the overall functioning of the person.

This is where value orientation comes in. The general well-being of people is certainly a value, and whatever we do ought to be geared to promoting that well-being. Concern about it means being forced to try out conceptions of what good functioning in people actually is. In the case of treatment, we should always plan what we do after assessing the person to be treated.

In alcohol work the situation has typically been egregious. Somebody has *a* method of treatment he believes in — such as conditioned-response therapy — so he gives this treatment to all comers. I know one place, for example, where patients are examined carefully for heart condition, or for some other physiological defect which would make the use of emetics dangerous, but that is all. Presumably all alcoholics coming there for treatment are regarded alike and given the same treatment. I would not even call this treatment without first giving some attention to what condition one wants to affect. It is obvious that at this particular hospital, and I am sure there are others, a whole range of conditions have been labeled alcoholic, and the same strategy is applied to them all. I don't think this will do it all; and I am afraid that something of the same state of affairs still exists with respect to smoking. I would say that the person who undertakes to change an addicted smoker is under quite an obligation to make a fairly thoroughgoing assessment of that individual — not just in an effort to say precisely what kind of smoker he is (in terms of the Tomkins typology), but with attention to numerous other factors too, on the theory that any one of them may be relevant.

Coming to research leads, I think there is a difference between studies using mass statistics in correlating one variable with another and studies accenting the mutual dependence of multiple variables. Dr. Borgatta has called for investigations that tell us something about the systems aspects of this — the kinds of totalities and patterns observed as interactions among diverse particular variables — which can be shown to have some relationship to the phenomena in question. He suggested what might be done if one were to use a large enough sample. Frank Barron pointed out that the conventional study affords basic preliminary information. I suppose with respect to smoking and drinking, we can't do without it. It is of some importance to know that (1) young people's smoking in general has to do with the smoking habits of their parents and that (2) women in general respond somewhat differently to a given form of therapy than do men;

but the trouble is that when we deal with a particular individual the chances are very good that he will be an exception to any rule. If I am a therapist and I say, "Aha! women are more accepting of help than men," it may be just my luck that a particular woman whom I want to treat has a large male component, and her behavior is more characteristic of men than women. Similarly, if I assume because of a correlation between smoking by parents and by offspring, that the latter will stop smoking if their parents do, it is very likely to turn out that a youngster whom I am concerned with is rebelling against his parents and likely to do the opposite of what they do. Generalized relationships between two variables are numerous, and yet rarely strong enough to enable us to predict for individuals; one has to make quite a study to figure out whether a given individual is a case in point or not. I think this means that we have to have models like those Professor Coan has recommended to us for the whole structure of the person — models that permit us to define variables that are significant, in the sense that there is theory that relates them to other variables. We must fit the numerous variables that we measure into some sort of scheme. The irony is that Professor Coan offered us a conceptual approach to personality, but he didn't offer us any data. A number of other investigators presented a great deal of data, but they didn't offer us any theoretical organization of it, and some who did apologized by saying they were going to offer us some wild speculations. We must, sooner or later, narrow the gap between some sort of legitimate conceptualizing of the person and these empirical inquiries. Professor Coan has shown us one way in which that can be done: the factorial approach to personality. He made it quite clear that he was not urging this approach for everybody — that he was willing to be reasonably tolerant of other conceptual approaches to personality. But he would not give up the point that if one is going to make sense in personality inquiry one must have some kind of conceptual scheme at the very beginning. And if one is going to make empirical investigations that matter and that will be cumulative, one must somehow order them to a general formulation of the person.

Silvan Tomkins' scheme of types of smokers ought to be confirmed or disconfirmed by investigation. I would suppose on clinical grounds that there are enormous differences among smokers, and that the differences between those who derive pleasure from it and those who do it in some automatic way would seem to be enormously significant. There is no longer much point in our using smoking as opposed to not smoking as a major variable.

I see little point in an investigation that doesn't take into account variations in respect to the smoking itself. This is the kind of error that has dogged alcohol studies for forty years and still does. In a typical research somebody compares a sample of so-called alcoholics with another patient sample or with a sample of so-called normal drinkers, thereby throwing into his sample of so-called alcoholics an enormous diversity of conditions. We know enough now about alcoholics to know that they differ almost categorically with respect to certain major variables, which in almost all previous researches have been thrown together for comparison. The result is that one comes up with a correlation of, say, .32 (significant at the 5 per cent level) between "the alcoholic" and some diagnostic category on the Rorschach or the TAT. All of which is one of the most useless pieces of information that can be thought of. There is no longer any excuse for doing this kind of thing in respect to smoking. If smokers vary, then start with the variations among the smokers and correlate those variations with personality or situational variables.

I admit, however, that some general information about variables is not to be despised. I think it was made clear in the discussion on communications that if one addresses himself to the mass of the population with a finding based on mass statistics, he can use that; particularly if it is harmless. If it is generally true, for example, that fears of more immediate consequences are more effective than fears of remote consequences, then anti-smoking propaganda could be guided by this fact, even though the correlation was not very high. All advertising is based on this kind of correlational knowledge — general notions about what are the appeals that can be made to people in order to get them to smoke. If we are to have counter-propaganda, the same kind of general knowledge would be entirely relevant.

Personality studies are fundamental to treatment. We must treat in accordance with some conception of the whole person and work similarly for prevention, including preventing people from starting to smoke or preventing people who are going to smoke from smoking in the most harmful ways. Personality theory is here fundamental. Silvan Tomkins told us that people who get the most pleasure from smoking are actually those who find it easiest to stop. I have the same impression about alcoholism. The people who know how to enjoy drinking are not typically those who become alcoholics. One form of treatment for alcoholics, then, might be some measures that would teach them to enjoy drinking. This might be a means of getting them off the addictive process, by which they must drink in order to relieve some unpleasant affective state.

The point about this may not be completely obvious perhaps, but to me it is fundamentally significant. I have distinguished "integrated" drinking from "facilitative" and "escapist" drinking. In the first type the pleasure in drinking is had by a highly developed person who has very good ego strength. This means that his pleasure is not followed by regret, but is greater because this particular pleasurable act correlates with a variety of needs that happen to be more or less operative at the time. Through a single act he can satisfy a diversity of needs because of the flexibility and communication among the different parts of personality.

If this formulation is correct, it follows that the kind of person who really enjoys smoking has a well-developed ego; he has no fears with respect to pleasure; he knows how to get pleasure; and he knows how to do without pleasure. One reason why it would be easier for him to give up smoking is his access to a whole range of other pleasures; he can more easily find substitutes for this particular one than can people who have actually been addicted to smoking.

In respect to drinking, we have something that we *can* promote — the idea of "integrated" drinking, and we of the Cooperative Commission on the Study of Alcoholism are doing this. We are in favor of drinking that is integrated with the ego; we are against drinking that is not integrated. I don't want to force this conception upon smoking, but there is something to it. When we study the developmental aspects of young people we should look at smoking or non-smoking in relation to what is going on in respect to the development of the ego. I would not regard non-smoking as a virtue, if the individual himself didn't enter into the decision affecting him. If he is not smoking because of some automatic adherence to family values or some unrecognized fear, he is not as virtuous as he would be had his decision been made with the full participation of his conscious ego.

This way of looking at smoking and drinking is based in theory and suggests interesting hypotheses. For example, if we were to make longitudinal studies of drinking nowadays, we would pay special attention to the conditions under which the person first started to drink. We could well be guided by the work of a doctoral candidate at Stanford, who studied diagnosed "alcoholics" with special reference to their religious backgrounds. He found that people who for religious reasons had taken oaths never, never to touch liquor, were more often alcoholics than people who were free of that kind of restriction. You can see why. If one decides that he will never do something and doing it becomes deviltry itself, he creates an enormous temptation to do precisely that; he practically *must* in order to demonstrate that he can do it and still live. This is the kind of theory that should guide longitudinal studies of smoking, as well as of drinking. When we of the Commission have considered the question of prevention of alcoholism, it seemed to us that a way should be found to remove drinking from the context of emotionalism, guilt, and rebelliousness in which it so often begins.

This same general framework might be used in approaching an addiction to smoking; something may very well be learned. At the same time, there is a strategic reason for doing this: it might be more appealing to scientists to have centers for the study of addiction — which is a respectable psychological phenomenon to study — than to have centers for the study of alcoholism. The scientist doesn't like getting himself identified with a particular practical problem. He wants to be identified as a systems man, a communications man, a learning man, or perhaps an addiction man. We might as well take advantage of this state of affairs.

The prospect of studying the personality characteristics of non-smokers and ex-smokers is also interesting. We had exactly the same idea about non-drinkers and ex-alcoholics. It is quite interesting that ex-alcoholics — arrested alcoholics — play a very important role both in treatment and in promotion of public attitudes toward alcoholism. I suppose ex-smokers and non-smokers tend to take a somewhat similar type of role regarding smoking. There are probably both gains and losses from this. Ex-alcoholics insist that it takes an alcoholic to understand an alcoholic, which makes it difficult for the psychiatrist to know where *he* fits in. (The psychiatrist disagrees, for the most part.) But there is something to be gained if the ex-alcoholic can throw some light upon the phenomenology of being an alcoholic and being an ex-alcoholic — if he can put himself forward as a *case* rather than as an authority. He can give special insight — although we court the danger of getting a special kind of bias. We get zeal, which sometimes has the value of focusing attention on something important, but may involve the danger of neglecting other important circumstances that might not so far have entered the picture. In respect to smoking, something of the same kind may very well be at work.

Of course, from studying abstainers and ex-smokers and ex-alcoholics, we may get the benefit of learning the kinds of processes that might be started in people whom we want to change. In problems of alcohol, there are some people who are protected from becoming alcoholics because of the effects on them of alcohol. It upsets the stomach, puts them to sleep, makes them dizzy, creates unpleasant sensations, etc. These people will never become alcoholics. There are other people who are affected by alcohol as though it were their "cup of tea." I wonder if the same sort of thing isn't true of smoking? If there are some people who just don't get anything out of smoking and we can discover *why,* we may be able to generate this condition in other people.

The problems of prevention are, of course, fairly obvious: treating people is difficult and expensive. But if we can find the means of preventing smoking from starting in the first place, we are that much better off. I think it would be interesting, in this regard, to consider what it is that we are trying to prevent. Are we trying to prevent lung cancer or are we trying to prevent smoking? Is it some kinds of smoking or all smoking? Are we trying to prevent smoking or are we trying to prevent some underlying condition, such as the alienation and demoralization of youth, which underlie in many cases premature and harmful smoking as well as premature drinking and sexuality?

It makes a considerable difference how we define our specific objective, but rather than dwelling upon that now, I would like to point out that the same general strategies apply in all cases. Some of these strategies we learn from the public health people: altering the host, altering the agent, altering the environment. I was very much interested in what Dr. Wiebe (p. 192) said about the possibilities of altering the agent. In the alcohol field there is a lot of talk about the possibility of adding things to alcohol — or removing them — that would permit people to drink without getting drunk or permit them to get drunk without its having any deleterious effects upon physiological functioning. I suppose that the tobacco people and the AMA are giving sufficient attention to the possibilities of modifying tobacco so that people will have the same kind of satisfaction that they get from smoking now without causing them to become addicted.

Incidentally, anthropologists claim that addiction doesn't exist in all cultures; indeed, there are some cultures in which the *concept* of addiction doesn't exist. There are people who will drink whenever there is anything to drink available, and they might drink for weeks on end, then the liquor runs out, and they feel no particular loss. This seems to be the same with smoking, as has been pointed out in the case of the Indians, for whom the concept of addiction to smoking probably never existed. I would suggest that the concept of addiction might be a product of Anglo-Saxon culture; the same culture that invented habit theory is the culture that invented the idea that once one starts something that is pleasurable but proscribed, one is lost. There is a lively possibility that in addiction the belief system of a person is enormously important. I have a strong hunch that those alcoholic people who can't stop once they take one drink are governed in considerable part by a belief that has been reinforced a thousand times by their membership in alcoholic groups — "one drink and you are lost."

Altering the agent is quite an interesting possibility. We might well borrow another leaf from the book of public health and pay some attention to what is sometimes called secondary prevention. What are the possibilities of examining people with attention to their particular susceptibilities to smoking, or particular susceptibilities to various kinds of diseases, such as lung cancer and emphysema? If there are young people who have already begun to smoke or to drink and there are signs that this is going

badly with them — that their smoking, for example, is already beginning to take a form suggestive of pathology — it might be possible then to counsel them in a more effective way than would be possible later on, after the difficulty had become deep-seated. Early case-finding, then, may have a place in this field, as it does in many others.

Much of our discussion about smoking has concerned *specific prevention,* rather than *non-specific.* Teaching about smoking is specific prevention. I can't think of any possible objection to giving young people all possible knowledge about the dangers of smoking. The more knowledge they have about everything the better. I would say, however, that they need much more knowledge than that about the dangers. They need knowledge about motives for drinking, about the way our culture operates in this respect. They need knowledge about how to criticize smoking advertisements, and much more. This would be non-specific prevention, i.e., activity where benefits would go beyond changing a particular behavior pattern. Giving young people knowledge about smoking or drinking ought to be done in a clinical way or in a counseling setting; just giving them literature or just presenting facts in the classroom can hardly suffice. Group discussion is a method *par excellence* for this kind of instruction — group discussion in which most time is spent listening to the young people tell about their problems. We will find that they instruct each other, and if the discussion is led by an adult in whom young people have confidence, they will talk about their smoking problems, their drinking problems, their problems relating to their parents, and their problems relating to sex, all at the same time. One will see their smoking in this context, and one can be helpful in a general way, not only with respect to smoking, but with respect to the other problems of young people.

Finally, non-specific prevention includes building strengths and resistances in the individual, and building supports in societies. Whether it is a case of preventing people's starting smoking or preventing their going to harmful lengths in their smoking, there is a lot to be said for the non-specific technique of building strengths in individuals. It seems that the safest, most important thing that we can do with young people is not so much to focus on particular weaknesses, susceptibilities, and dangers, but to develop a program for promoting ego development. If we do this, we not only create a situation in which they are better able to deal with smoking, but we benefit them in numerous other ways at the same time. This is where value orientation comes in again. As Silvan Tomkins indicated (pp. 198 ff.) we are bound to have conflicts with respect to values in society and among ourselves. There are times when there is nothing but to state our value position, and to stay with it, acknowledging that others have different values. I think, however, that we can work using our heads as well as empirical science to arrange things so that as many values as possible are realized at the same time, achieving a particular value at no more expense to another value than is necessary. Practical work considerations of this kind should enter the picture at all stages. When we treat people or try to change their behavior we do well to avoid those techniques which make the individual less autonomous — techniques like hypnosis or pure conditioning, in which the individual's self doesn't participate.

I urge that insofar as possible we choose therapeutic techniques which enlarge the personality and call upon the full participation of the individual self. We are used to the fact that in medicine anything goes, as long as it can be regarded as a means to save life. Psychologists by and large have resisted this; they have resisted the application to psychological and social problems of that medical model which invites one to put himself in the doctor's hands and to sacrifice his autonomy in the interests of a cure. Psychologists traditionally have said that this is rarely necessary and in all stages of the treatment process the individual's autonomy should be fully protected, insofar as possible. If we take it away from him now, we immediately think of how we can reconstruct it as soon

as this becomes possible. We weigh values and sacrifice no more of the good than we have to.

We have to work to develop our children and our young people as best we may, so that they have the ego strength to get well once they become ill or to confront an issue like smoking in a way that is maximally favorable to personality development. But I hasten to add that we need not wait until we have done everything; we need not wait until we have learned how to develop good personalities before we can do anything about smoking. We may go at it the other way 'round. Probably as good a way as any to get busy making the most of people and helping people realize their potential is to start in on their smoking behavior. If we know how to persuade teenagers not to smoke in ways that are unfavorable to their further development, then we have a way, at the same time, of further developing them as personalities. If we start talking about their smoking with a view to putting this in the larger context of making them maximally aware of themselves and of social processes, we would not only be preventing their smoking, or smoking in the wrong way, but also at the same time favorably developing their learning about many other things and developing them in a more general way.

OVERVIEW II

GEORGE BEAL

The discussant at a symposium of research has a number of alternative courses open to him: if he is truly knowledgeable, he can discuss and criticize the research head on; if he is not very knowledgeable, or if the research is really good, he can criticize the authors for what they *didn't* do (which the authors may already have indicated was not within the scope of their objectives). When the discussant becomes desperate, he talks about his own research, instead of talking about that which is under discussion. Perhaps I shall use each of these approaches. Since I have had no previous experience with smoking research, and since I am not a psychologist, my remarks may be characterized by social psychologists as coming from a "low credibility source." But I would like to make some very generalized reactions to the research that has been reported here. Obviously, there is a wide range of research being conducted, in terms of objectives, conceptual level, methodology, populations, and sophistication of analysis. There seems to be a high degree of consistency in the results among certain populations for given categorical concepts. Is further replication necessary? Or should we move into other, more significant research areas, at a different conceptual level? If psychology is in "ferment," let the ferment lead to more innovative-type studies!

The plea has been made for the involvement of other disciplines on a single or multi-discipline basis. This has been a meeting of psychologists, mainly, with some people from other fields invited. What would have been the reactions of a better representation of people from such fields as psychiatry, sociology, economics, communications, and anthropology? It was interesting to note, for example, the impact made on the group by the presentation of several ideas from anthropology (pp. 177 ff.). An economist would have been interested in our dicussion of alternative educational approaches and costs, because this relates to the economics of education: input-output relationships.

Help and insights sometimes come from very interesting places. I was recently privileged to be a member of a UNESCO team whose purpose was to help develop an evaluation guide for measuring the effectiveness of functional literacy training. The economist in the group (Professor Zamin from Russia) was by far the most sophisticated and made the most important contributions. Why? Because in a planned economy there is concern about allocation of resources between sectors of the economy, of which education is one. Decisions are made in terms of marginal returns from dollars invested in education, as opposed to investments in heavy industry, agriculture, dam-building, and so on. In our system, we accept education as being "good," and go fumbling along. We find help for answering some of our questions in areas where we might least expect it.

I have mentioned some fields of study or disciplines which can contribute to research in smoking. I wonder if health educators have been adequately represented in this research? Have the policy-makers and operations people been represented to the extent they should be? A crucial issue for debate is the question of the appropriate links and chains of responsibilities among the researcher, the policy maker, and the operations person. This has some ethical overtones of academic freedom and also of the responsibilities that a researcher owes to his grantor or contracting agency. Those of us who have not been involved in research in this area probably tend to take most of our research cues from other research workers. It may be argued that this is not necessarily the best place from which to take research cues. It may, in fact, lead to doing over and over again the same type of study, because one knows the definition of the problem only as other researchers have defined it. This in a sense is a plea for a more effective communication among the policy makers, the operations people, and the research workers.

I have been involved enough in research not to be so naive as to think that operations people always recognize their problems, or conceive their problems the way *we* might conceive them. Yet this interaction in the real world with operations people, it seems to me, would provide a basic fund of data from which research ideas would come for tackling more significant problems. It might be argued that we are interested in basic human behavior which is so generic we do not have to know what operational problems are. Because we are interested in something as generic as human behavior does not mean that it is too early to start worrying about the administrative operational strategy of implementation and involvement. Experience leads me to believe that the definition of an operational problem that gets to the federal level has gone through a lot of filtering screens. One has to go down to the regional, state, county, community, or local-agency level to know what the operational problems are. From this vantage point can be developed some manageable yet important research objectives that have theoretical meaning as well as the potential for solving real-world problems.

Some researchers could not care less whether their research at a given time has real-world application. We have room for and a need for this type of scientist. However, there are other researchers who like to be just as theoretical, just as antiseptic, in their research as they possibly can but who also derive tremendous satisfaction in seeing the findings of their research tested and applied under real-world conditions. It is to this latter group that I am addressing my remarks.

A wide variety of research has been reported here, ranging through what might be called the bushel-basket, the shot-gun, the salt-shaker, down to the rifle-type studies. Basically, the approach I call the "bushel-basket" comes from the researcher who doesn't know quite what is relevant but gathers everything that *might* be, dumps it into a bushel basket, and decides what he is going to do with it when he gets it back from the field.

The "shot-gun" approach is similar. Here there is a very general theoretical orientation, without a middle-range theory or propositional statement. Percy Tannenbaum has commented that he begins to worry about data when they "include the kitchen sink," because they require a great deal of interpretive "plumbing." But at the beginning of an attack on a problem area, there may be a need for a very broad-based approach. When we move into a new research area, in most cases we are trying to answer what may be called the *what* question. *What* is the real world like? How many smoke, and how many don't smoke? How many have quit smoking? What are the knowledge and attitude levels and some 1600 other items that we have? I am not deprecating this kind of research. Properly conceived, it certainly helps to quantify various dimensions of a problem. But the basic question is, how much insight is obtained from these data?

At another level is research which attempts to answer *how* questions. "How are things different?" What are the differences among categories of smokers and nonsmokers, ethnic groups, males and females, those with high or low knowledge, and so on? In most cases, these are tests of simple differences — chi squares, t-tests, etc. Or at most they tend to use a simple zero-order of correlations of two-variable relationships.

While this can be important, in many cases the most significant question is not answered — namely, the *why*

question. Before the data-collection stage, *why* should we include any given variable? *Why* would we expect x to be related to y? In asking the *why* questions, which are frequently not asked even after the data are in, we force ourselves to some type of existing theory or explanatory statement that accounts for relationships. *Why* or why might we *not* expect a relationship to attend? It forces us to use existing models or to create new ones, to turn to past related research using similar concepts; and we are compelled to develop new statements of relationships and to move to a different conceptual level.

To illustrate what I mean, it was said that the sex variable is related to or predictive of certain outcomes — therapy, and so forth. But there is a difference between the predictive statement and other kinds of logical, explanatory statements. It is interesting to observe discussions when the statement is made that sex is a differentiating variable. The *why* question is asked, and explanations using other concepts are given that women are more dependent, for example. Dependency is at a different conceptual level from sex. It can be applied to both sexes. There is a tremendous amount of data on hand where this approach could be used, where these questions could be asked, and where we could develop and test *post factum* data and certain kinds of propositions within some theoretical framework.

In many studies there is a need for a more careful selection and definition of concepts, because we use concepts very differently. Concepts often remain undefined, and in the papers given here very few concepts are defined. Others are defined in terms of what I would call extensive or example definitions, rather than intensive. When one starts moving toward hypothesis-testing, it may mean facing up to problems of conceptual definition and relationships. I am not talking about any grand theory or closed-system theory but what Merton has termed middle-range theory. I am making a plea for more of the propositional-type exploration.

Multivariate analysis has been emphasized rather than single zero-order correlations for predictive purposes. It might be argued that this would allow us to determine the predictive power of a number of variables in combination, or the predictive power of a given variable when the other variables are controlled, and to determine the predictive "weights" of variables. I should like to illustrate the possibilities of this method with an example from my own research.

We are involved in predicting the role performance of civil-defense directors, starting with a social-system model comprising some twenty concepts. We have tried to put these concepts into practice, and, within the logic of the system, to predict outcome relations — for example, that a person who understands the goals of the system (namely civil defense) and believes in them would enact his role more effectively than he would without this understanding. Using this approach in a multivariate analysis we can predict about sixty-two per cent of the variance in role performance. Beta weights will help reveal which are the most powerful predictors. The highest predictor, interestingly enough, is a sociological variable — systemic linkage, the degree to which a local civil-defense director establishes relationships and liaison with other organizations and agencies in that community. Because the civil-defense director is in many cases a volunteer or only partly paid, he doesn't have the resources to get the job done. He has to capture resources, and one way to do so is by establishing a systemic linkage. For a given input of training to help civil-defense directors establish effective systemic linkages, we may be able to predict x amount of increase in role performance. The above input-output statement assumes a linearity of function. The point is that thinking and doing research in logical predictive terms open up new dimensions for problem definition and solution. It does, then, appear that there is a possibility of logical-proposition building through multivariate analysis with existing data. Certainly we should be able to include these elements in more studies in the future.

Howard Leventhal's paper (pp. 17 ff.) represents the "rifle" in the "shotgun to rifle" continuum. He started with a very simple relationship, and developed a rationale for it. He has tested that relationship under varying conditions, with varying degrees of input. Finding other relationships, he has introduced additional variables into his matrix. The argument can be made that his approach has been experimental, contrived, sterile. But some of his findings do relate to the real world.

Perhaps the hedge solution is that we need both kinds of research, the shot-gun and the specific conceptual scheme. We start to make headway some place in the middle ground, which we can approach from both ends. Are we using the most sophisticated analysis possible with the available data? Have we thought through the possible analyses that we might make with the data before we conceive and design field instruments?

In terms of needed research, it seems there is an area on which there is general agreement: personality correlates. I think Richard Coan's paper (pp. 133 ff.) is to be highly commended. It raises a great number of problems but also provides some positive suggestions. Another area is that under which might be subsumed the rubrics "social interaction," "peer group," "referent group relations," "influentials," and so on. We have some inferential data from studies in this area. However, so far the researcher has just asked people if they associate with other people who smoke, if other people smoke where they work, etc. We don't really have any data on the importance of the norm, its attendant attitudes among

work groups, and so forth. Here also are indicated important areas for future study.

It is not too early to think about the process and strategy of involvement. Percy Tannenbaum has told us not to depend on mass media to do the whole job. It seems, also, that impersonal communication will not do the job either. It probably has to be done by some type of personal communication from a formal or informal organizational structure as part of an ongoing program. But how does one get messages down through the bureaucracy? How does one mobilize resources at the community level? How does one get the professionals to understand the objectives and articulate them into an action program? This is a very fascinating area. Some of the data available show how from a start with an immense population, the screening process ends up with fifty people for a clinic (see Allen-Fackler study, pp. 63 ff.). Knowledge of the characteristics of some of these people who "fell out" at various points is available. Can we begin to construct a strategy of action based on some of these data? Do we really know what the treatment was, what was communicated to these people? What were their interpretations of the messages? This would provide a very interesting area of study. With the data already available such an analysis could give insights into the strategy of change and the strategy of involvement.

Another intriguing research area stems from the statement, "The world around us apparently makes it easy for many to smoke." And the world around us apparently makes it difficult to stop! How does one change the world to make it easy to stop? A sociological approach would use the concepts of *norms* and the process of *norming*. How do social systems — and by "social systems" I mean the generic term which includes families, formal and informal groups, institutions, communities, and subcultures and society — how do *they* norm? How do they prescribe rules by which people behave? It would be useful to research the norming process in existing or newly formed groups. The anti-smoking club referred to here is an example of this, where a system is created with a norm structure which makes it easy to quit smoking. Daniel Horn has referred to schools in which there is apparently a different norm structure in terms of what gives status, what is acceptable and unacceptable behavior.

Another way of using the norming process would be working with selected religious groups to set certain norm structures which they presently don't have or encouraging people to be comfortable not smoking. Is there a norm structure built into the functioning of government agencies working on smoking behavior? If not, would it be possible to build in a norm structure? Perhaps this is already being done. Perhaps the American Cancer Society has already tried this. There are many organizations which include health committees. Is it possible to motivate them to go through a norming process that will make it "comfortable" for their people to quit or cut down on smoking? One can find allies in very interesting places. It is very interesting, for example, that the Junior Chambers of Commerce are presently making a major effort in the problem of mental retardation.

The need for longitudinal studies has been cited a number of times. But what do we really mean by longitudinal studies? Do we mean still shots, two or four years apart over x number of years, and then, from these still shots trying to reconstruct the intervening time between studies? Or, do we mean process studies? Deciding to smoke, deciding to continue smoking, and deciding to stop smoking are very complex processes. Yet we tend to ask people why they started smoking, when this may have occurred over a three- or four-year period of time. An interesting point in terms of the cessation of smoking is that one is literally faced with thousands of decisions — every time someone lights a cigarette, every time one is offered a cigarette, every time one gets the yen. It is a process that goes on over time. What is the solution? I think that in our attempt to be sophisticated we have discarded some still acceptable techniques, namely the case-study and the participant-observer methods. Is it not possible to observe the dynamics of change and the decision-making processes as they develop?

I am currently engaged in a research project which involves problems somewhat similar to those in the study of smoking behavior. But there are also striking differences. Our project deals with farm and urban consumer behavior related to the use of pesticides. Here is a product with a high danger potential to the user (in this case the farmer), to livestock, to crops, to wildlife, and to the ultimate consumer through milk, meat, and other products marketed. Yet we find many farmers have little knowledge, mixed attitudes, and a relatively low level of concern about the potential danger. Instances have been reported of the misuse of agricultural chemicals with negative consequences. In a sense there are some similarities between this kind of behavior and smoking behavior. Smoking represents a danger to the user; there are also many instances where the improper use of chemicals is a danger to the user also. Consumers are not trying to get farmers to stop using chemicals; they are trying to get them to use chemicals "properly," with the proper recognition of safety, in terms of application rates, timing, etc. Apparently one strategy in smoking behavior is not getting smokers to stop smoking, but getting them to use cigarettes "properly." The use or non-use of both products has tremendous economic implications.

Our approach to the study of pesticide use has been basically similar to that reported for tobacco use. If we know the person's past experience with it, and how he views these past experiences; if we know the extent of his knowledge, and something about his attitude structure, we think we might be able to predict his behavior in terms of use and misuse. I am now *less* sure, because of the difficulty smoking research is experiencing in predicting behavior changes from these same variables.

But our research includes additional variables. We have attempted to get at the salience of attitudes related to pesticides by asking a series of questions about how concerned the respondent is about the possible harm of chemicals to milk, eggs, livestock, and various aspects of health, such as skin and eye irritation, nausea, headache, heart conditions. This provides us with a [salience of attitude] dimension I have not heard discussed with regard to smoking research — one that may allow us to predict behavior a little better.

Turning to the problem of experiments with clinical procedures, it seems that when we subject people to experimental treatment, the effort is so complex in terms of treatment and effect, and what we are trying to measure is so much a part of the treatment, that perhaps all we get out of it is confusion. A rather intriguing idea has been suggested: is there a simple, rational decision-making model that can be used? Are we really trying to make these phenomena too complex, as social-scientists are sometimes suspected of doing? If only we could require people to be introspective about their own behavior; if we could come up with some kind of confrontation (not necessarily fear) to compel them to place their values and their knowledge in some kind of rational framework, might they change their behavior?

I am reminded of an educational program that may provide an analogy. In Iowa, through our Co-operative Extension Service, we have been involved for many years in what is called public-affairs education, ranging from international policy to farm policy. By way of example, two years ago we provided a series of education programs on public services and taxation, a topic that is heavily value-laden. Considering the existing tax structure, the present quantity and quality of public services, and the population growth, an increase in taxes is necessary. By means of an educational program, people were encouraged to work their way through a decision-making matrix. The teaching method used was the self-administered discussion group. In its simplest form this entailed four or five couples meeting four times in a home. Each person was provided with a fact sheet which attempted to provide the facts as objectively as possible, taking them through a logical series of confrontations, in this case public services and taxation. What is meant by confrontation? Taxation, like cigarette-smoking, has a high emotional connotation. Almost everyone who came to the first meeting was certain he wanted no more taxes. But the logic of presentation and confrontation was somewhat as follows: At first were listed the public services that are paid for out of public monies — how the taxpayer's money is spent.

The second step involved projections of population growth: if we continue to provide existing public services at the present level of quality, so much more money will be needed in future years. With the present tax structure, there will be this much increase in property taxes, sales tax, income tax, etc. Questions were then raised. Which of these services do you want to increase? Which do you want to decrease? It soon became apparent that there was little the taxpayer wanted to give up. A great majority of the groups came to the conclusion that not only were "natural forces" (population increase, increasing costs in wages, etc.) working toward increased expense for public service, but that in reality they want more and better quality services. The individual was not "trapped" in the fact sheets. He could have made the decision to cut off everything if he wanted to. But the fact-sheet data and the decision-making matrix act to compel rational decision-making. If one wants more services, then he is obliged to decide through what tax structure he is going to pay for the services. Most groups found themselves taxing themselves more by the end of the discussion meetings.

This is what is meant by logical confrontation, data and decision matrices with consequences. The technique requires a relatively low input in terms of professional workers and can be extended to many groups. I don't know whether it would work with the problem of smoking behavior. But it may be possible to confront people with this kind of decision-making matrix, after which they have to live with the consequences of their decisions. There is still a question: will it change behavior? Perhaps it is worth a trial. To me it is an intriguing idea that involves some of the things about which we have been talking, both on the operational and theoretical levels. Maybe there is a simpler device of confrontation, or reality testing, to move people to rational behavior. It is not "forced" learning, as in learning with correct answers. Rather, it emphasizes the fact that once a person has made a decision he has to live within the consistency of that decision and recognize some of the consequences of it.

REFERENCE MATERIALS

BIBLIOGRAPHY

Abelin, T. Smoking habits and survival of lung cancer patients. Application of the temporary expectation of life as a measure of survival. *Amer. J. Epidem.* 84: 110–19, July 1966.

Action on cigarette smoking. [Editorial] *Amer. J. Public Health* 52: 1330–1, 1962.

Adams, J. R., and Williams, E. B. The association between smoking and accidents: overdependency as an influencing variable. Unpublished manuscript, Safety Res. and Ed. Proj., Teachers College, Columbia Univ.

Advertising of tobacco. [Correspondence] *New Zeal. Med. J.* 61: 423, 1962.

Aegerter, E. That cigarette again. *Arch Environ. Hlth.* (Chicago) 11:1 July 1965.

AHA approved educational program to discourage cigarette smoking. *Med. Rec. Ann.* (Houston) 56:180, 1964.

Albert, R. E., and Nelson, N. Special report to the Surgeon General's Advisory Committee on Smoking and Health. Washington, D.C., Government Printing Office, 1964.

Allen, B. V. An investigation of the relationship between smoking and personality. Unpublished MA thesis, Univ. of Portland, 1958.

Almoslino, J. Das Rauchen: Wie man es einschränkt und wie man es sich ganz abgewohnt. (Smoking: how to limit it and how to give it up entirely.) Vienna: Kommissionsverlag Wiener Volksbuchhandlung, 1931. p. 35.

American Cancer Society. Lung cancer prevention and the physician. Pamphlet No. 3417, 1960.

———, Rock Island County Unit. *Annual Report,* 1963–1964, June, 1964.

Analysis of tobacco advertising. [Annotations] *Lancet* 1: 846, 1962.

Anderson, C. L., and Caviness, L. H. Orality and the smoking habit. (Unpublished manuscript sent by Dr. Anderson, 120 N. Oak St., Hinsdale, Ill., April, 1966.)

Anderson, D. D., Culling, C., Parnell, J. L., and Vassar, P. Nurses' smoking. *Canad. Med. Assn. J.* 92: 579–580, 1965.

Anderson, J. The dangers of smoking. *Nurs. Times* 58: 424–6, 1962.

Anderson, J. M., and Brown, C. W. A study of the effects of smoking upon grip strength and recuperation from muscular fatigue. *Research Quarterly* 22: 102–108, 1951.

Andersen, K., and Clevenger, T. A summary of experimental research in ethos. *Speech Monogr.* 30: 59–78, 1963.

Andosca, J. B. The incidence of smoking and smoking habits in 5000 registrants for military service. *Conn. Med.* 30: 322–5, May, 1966.

Andrews, P, B. B. The cigarette market, past and future. *Advertising and Selling,* p. 27, January 16, 1936.

———. What happened to cigarettes in 1945. *Advertising and Selling,* p. 37, Feb., 1946.

Andrus, L. H., Hyde, D. F., and Fisher, E. Smoking by high school students. Failure of a campaign to persuade adolescents not to smoke. *Calif. Med.* 101: 246–47, 1964.

Angus, M. Stop. *Canad. Nurse* 59: 653–5, 1963.

Anonymous. Behind the cigarette curtain. *Transaction* 2: 3–8, 1965.

Anonymous. Nurses and cigarettes, Oh! Oh! Oh! What a smoke! *Inform. Canad.* 8: 53, 1966.

Anticancer league of Israel. Smoking and air pollution as causes of bronchogenic carcinoma. *Harefuah* (Hebrew), 66: 209–10, March, 1964.

Anti-cigarette League of America, Woman's Temple. 108 S. La Salle St., Chicago.
 1 Why the cigarette is deadly (D. H. Kress).
 2 Maxim, Burbank, Edison, and Hamilton attack the cigarette.
 3 A warning to boys (David Paulson).
 4 The boy who quit smoking (Ben Lindsey).

The anti-smoking clinic. [Editorial] *Lancet* 2: 353–4, 1964.

Anti-smoking posters. [Public Health] *Lancet* 2: 88, 1963.

Arfmann, B., and Chapanis, N. P. The relative sensitivities of taste and smell in smokers and nonsmokers. *J. Gen. Psychol.* 66: 315–20, 1962.

Arkin, H. Relationship between human smoking habits and death rates. *Current Med. Digest* 22: 37–44, 1955.

Arnett, J. H. Youth confronts the cigarette. *J. Amer. Coll. Health Ass.* 11: 159–61, 1962.

Askevold, F. Why do we smoke? *J. Norsk Laigeforen* 84: 159–163, 1964.

Aspects of the cigarette problem. I. Smoking habits of school children. *Canad. Med. Ass. J.* 88: 326–7, February 9, 1963.

Aspects of the cigarette problem. II. Misleading advertising. *Canad. Med. Ass. J.* 88: 626–7, March 23, 1963.

Aspects of the cigarette problem. III. Nicotine addiction. *Canad. Med. Ass. J.* 88: 1120–1, June 1, 1963.

Aubry, F., Collins, J. P., and Dufour, B. A study of the smoking habit in relation to occupation. *Canad. J. Public Health* 57: 335–42, August, 1946.

Austin, F. A., and Eales, H. T. Medicosocial history of snuff. *St. Barth. Hosp. J.* 48: 44–47, April, 1944.

Bachman, D. S. Group smoking deterrent therapy. *G.P.,* 86–89, 1964.

Backett, E. M. Advances in preventive medicine. *Practitioner* 181: 494–502, 1958.

Badenhop, M. B. A survey of smokers in Italy. *J. Marketing* 24: 66–8, Oct., 1959.

Baer, D. J. Smoking attitude, behavior, and beliefs of college males. *J. Soc. Psychol.* 68: 65–78, 1966.

Bajda, B. A survey of the smoking habits of students of Newton High School — a cooperative project. *Amer. J. Pub. Hlth.* 54 (3): 441–446, 1964.

Bales, R. F. Social therapy for a social disorder — compulsive drinking. *J. Soc. Issues* 23: 1–9, 1945.

Ball, K. P. First year's experience in anti-smoking clinic. *Brit. Med. J.* 5451: 1651–3, June 26, 1965.

Banerjee, R. N. Prevalence of habit-forming drugs and smoking among the college students — a survey. *Indian Med. J.* 57: 193–6, Aug., 1963.

Barckley, V. The adolescent who smokes. *Nurs. Outlook* 12: 25–7, Feb., 1964.

Baronchelli, A. Sull'azione stressante del fumo di sigaretta. [Stressing effect of cigarette smoke.] *Bull. Soc. Ital. Biol. Sper.*, (Italy) 28: 1423–25, 1952.

Barrett, K. A. High school students' smoking habits. *Canad. Jour. Pub. Hlth.* 53: 12, 500–506, 1962. (ref. *Excerpta Medica*, Vol. 9, no. 7: section XVII, 492), July, 1963.

———. High school students' smoking habits. *J. Irish Med. Ass.* 51: 150–5, 1962.

Barry, M. J. Psychologic aspects of smoking. *Proc. Mayo Clin.* 35: 386–389, 1960.

Bartlett, W. A., and Whitehead, R. W. The effectiveness of meprobamate and lobeline as smoking deterrents. *J. Lab. Clin. Med.* 50: 278–281, 1957.

Bates, R. L. The effects of cigar and cigarette smoking on certain psychological and physiological functions. *J. Comp. Psychol.* 3: 1923.

Bauer, W. W. Don't let tobacco trap your teenager. *P.T.A. Magazine* 4–7, March, 1961.

Baumgartner, L. The facts on teenage smoking. *Parents Magazine* 22, 1960.

Beck, F. Stopping smoking. *Lancet* (London) 2: 392–397, 1953.

Beckerman, S. C. Report of an educational program regarding cigarette smoking among high school students. *J. Maine Med. Ass.* 54: 60, *passim*, 1963.

Beebe, G. W. Lung cancer in World War I veterans. Possible relation to mustard-gas injury and 1918 influenza epidemic. *J. Nat. Cancer Inst.*, 25: 1231–52, 1960.

Beliaev II, The fight against tobacco smoking — a current social and health problem. *Gig Sanit.* (Russia) 30: 85–8, February, 1965.

Bell, G. When habit gets out of hand. *Smoke Signals* XII (12): December, 1966.

Bell, R. G. Tobacco withdrawal symptoms. *Appl. Ther.* 4: 1028, 1962.

Berelson, B., and Steiner, G. A. *Human Behavior.* New York: Harcourt Brace, 1964.

Berfenstam, R., and Billes, B. S. Smoking during pregnancy and nursing: some viewpoints on a current problem. *Nord. Med.* (Sw) 62: 1294–6, August 27, 1959.

Bergen, B. J., and Olesen, E. Some evidence for a peer-group hypothesis about adolescent smoking. *Hlth. Educ. Journ.* 21: 113, 1963.

Bergler, E. Cigarette neurotics. *Dis. Nerv. Syst.* 19: 305–6, 1958.

———. Psychopathology of compulsive smoking. *Psychiat. Quart.* 20: 297–321, 1946.

———. Smoking and its infantile precursors. *Int. J. Sexol.* 6: 214–220, 1953.

Beritic, T. Smoking, diseases, and health education. *Lijecn Vjesn* (Ser) 86: 1409–11, November, 1964.

Berkson, J. Smoking and lung cancer: Some observations on two recent reports. *J. Amer. Stat. Ass.* 53: 28–38, 1958.

———. Statistics and tobacco. [Correspondence] *J.A.M.A.* 172: 967–9, 1960.

———. The statistical investigation of smoking and cancer of the lung. *Proc. Mayo Clin.* 34: 206–24a, 1959.

———. The statistical study of association between smoking and lung cancer. *Proc. Mayo Clin.* 30: 319–48, 1955.

Berlo, D., and Gulley, H. E. Some determinants of the effect of oral communication in producing attitude change and learning. *Speech Monogr.* 24: 10–20, 1957.

Bernhard, P. On tobacco addiction. *Med. Mschr.* 18: 344–8, August, 1964.

Berry, C. S. Effects of smoking on adding. *Psychol. Bull.* 14: 25, 1917.

Best, E. W. A Canadian study of smoking and health — second report. *Canad. J. Public Hlth.* 55: 1–11, January, 1964.

———, Josie, G. H., and Walker, C. B. A Canadian study of mortality in relation to smoking habits. A preliminary report. *Canad. J. Public Health* 52: 99–106, 1961.

Bettinghaus, E. P. The operation of congruity in an oral communication situation. *Speech Monogr.* 28: 131–142, 1961.

Beumer, H. M. Smoking and health. *Nederl. Milit. Geneesk. T.* (Dut) 16: 11–4, January, 1963.

Biener, K. Tobacco and school children. *Ther Gagenw* 104: 631–44, May, 1965.

Birath, G. Hypotheses and facts concerning smoking and health. *Svensk Lakartindn* 61: 3968–75, December 16, 1964.

Bishop, R. Smoking in front of children. [Letters to the editor] *Lancet* 2: 934, 1962.

Bjurielf, C. Commentary on the American expert committee's report on "smoking and health." *Svensk. Lakartidn* 61: 2659–66, Sept. 9, 1964.

Bjurulf, P. On health propaganda against smoking. I. The medical debates on smoking and disease. *Socialmed T* (Sw) 40: 280–5, Sept., 1963. (43 ref.)

———, On health propaganda against smoking. II. Smoking habits in relation to age, income, and education *Socialmed T* (Sw) 40: 344–52, Oct., 1963.

———, On health propaganda against smoking. III. Knowledge of health information concerning the relation of smoking to cancer. *Socialmed T* (Sw) 40: 385–96, Nov., 1963.

———. On health propaganda against smoking. IV. Reactions to health information on the relation between smoking and cancer. *Socialmed T* (Sw) 41: 64–78, Feb., 1964.

Blair, W. M. Huge tobacco industry again on defensive. *New York Times,* July 21, 1957.

Blakeslee, A. L. It's not too late to stop smoking cigarettes. New York, Public Affairs Pamphlets, 1966.

Boatman, R. H. How can we change attitudes and action on smoking? *Conn. Med.* 27: 16, 1963.

Bocker, D. Bibliography on smoking and health, 1959–1963. (prep. for Surg. Gen. Adv. Comm. Smok. and Hlth.) Washington, D.C.: Dept. Hlth., Educ. and Welf., Oct., 1963.

Bogen, E. Composition of cigarettes and cigarette smoke. *J.A.M.A.* 93: 1110, October 12, 1929.

Bohne, G. The effect of smoking on sensory functions of the eye of special significance to the motor vehicle driver. *Klin. Mbl. Augenheilk.* (Ger.) 140: 717–729, 1962.

Bonnevie, P. On tobacco consumption. *Ugeskr Laig.* 126: 180–2, February, 1964.

———. Smoking habits of the population. *Ugeskr Laig* (Dan.) 126: 1433–5. Oct. 15, 1964.

Bonnell-Lewis, M. H. B. The smoking habits of women students in a teachers training college: a pilot survey. *Hlth. Educ. J.* 31 (1): 4–11, 1963.

Bothwell, P. W. The epidemiology of cigarette smoking in rural school children. *Med. Offr.* 102: 125–132, 1959.

Boucot, K. R. and others. Smoking and the health of older men. 1. Smoking and chronic cough. *Arch. Environ. Health* (Chicago) 4: 59–72, 1962.

Bourke, G. J. The opinions of some medical students on smoking, cancer and fluoridation. *J. Irish. Med. Ass.* 53: 154–6, Nov., 1963.

Boutwell, W. D. What's happening to dissuade youngsters from smoking? *Nat'l Parent Teach.* 54, 1959.

Boyd, H. W., and Levy, S. Cigarette smoking and the public interest: Opportunity for business leadership. *Bus. Horizons* 6: (3) 37–44, 1963.

Brandes, L. G. Policies with regard to smoking. *Sch. Prin. Bull.* 45, 1961.

Brannan, J. H. Smoking and health . . . has the report been accepted? *J. Sch. Hlth.* 35: 362–366, 1965.

Brean, H. *How To Stop Smoking.* New York: World's Work Press, 1951.

———. *How To Stop Smoking* (rev. ed.). Vanguard, 1958.

———. *How To Stop Smoking.* Pocket Books, 1963.

Brecher, Edward. Smoking and lung cancer. We are living in an epidemic; the statistical evidence; the experimental evidence; summing up. *Consumer Repts.* 28: 265–80. June, 1963.

Brecher, Ruth. Smoking, the great dilemma. New York: Public Affairs Committee, 1964.

———, and E., Herzog, A., Goodman, W. and Walker, G., editors of Consumer Reports, *The Consumers Union Report on Smoking and the Public Interest.* Mt. Vernon, New York: Consumers Union, 1963.

Brehm, J. W. Motivational effects of cognitive dissonance. In Jones, M. R. (ed.). *Nebraska Symposium on Motivation.* University of Nebraska Press, 1962.

———, and Cohen, A. R. *Explorations in Cognitive Dissonance.* New York: John Wiley & Sons, Inc., 1962.

Brenner, M. M. How a teen-age cancer club operates. *J. Sch. Health.* 35: 73–4, February, 1965.

Breslow, and others. Occupational and cigarette smoking as factors in lung cancer. *American J. Pbl. Hlth.* 171–181, Feb., 1954.

Briggs, J. F. To smoke or not to smoke. [Editorial] *Geriatrics* 17: 624, 1962.

Brill, A. A. Tobacco and the individual. *Int. J. Psychoanalysis.* 3: 430–444, 1922.

British cigarette makers claim cancer risk in smoking may be reduced. *Printers Ink* 264: 9–10, July 18, 1958.

British Tuberculosis Association. Smoking deterrent study. *Br. Med. J.* 486–487, 1963.

Brock, T. C. Commitment to exposure as a determinant of information receptivity. *J. Pers. Soc. Psychol.* 2: 10–19, 1965.

Bronson, Louise. Changes in personality needs and values following conversion to protestantism in a traditionally Roman Catholic ethnic group. Unpublished dissertation, University of Arizona, 1966.

Brown, C. T. Tobacco addiction: A further inquiry. *Milit. Med.* 129: 637–640, 1964.

———. Tobacco addiction (Suggested Remedy). *Texas J. Med.* 50: 35–36, January, 1954.

Brown, J. A. C. The nature and treatment of smoking. *Med. World (London)* 98: 187–92, 1963.

Brozek, J. and Keys, A. Changes of body weight in normal men who stop smoking cigarettes. *Science* 125: 1203, 1957.

Bruggen, P., and MacKeith, S. Development of the habit of cigarette smoking. [Letters] *Lancet* 1: 450, 1963.

Bulletin on tobacco. *New England J. Med.* 268: 1087, May 9, 1963.

Burney, L. E. Excessive cigarette smoking. *Public Health Reports,* 72 (9): 786, Sept., 1956.

Butler, N. R. The problems of low birthweight and early delivery. *J. Obstet. Gynaec. Brit. Comm.* 72: 1001–1003, 1965.

Cain, A. H. *The Cigarette Habit: An Easy Cure.* New York: Doubleday & Company, 1964.

———. *Young People and Smoking.* New York: John Day Co., 1965.

Caldwell, E. *How You Can Stop Smoking Permanently.* Alhambra, Calif.: Borden, 1960.

Can Cigarettes Be Made Safe? *U.S. News and World Report,* July 2, 1954.

Canadian Cancer Society: *Cancer Newsletter* 13: 1, Feb. 1960.

Canadian Public Health Association: *Canad. J. Pub. Hlth.* 50: 483, 1959.

Cancer of the Lung. *New England J. of Med.,* 465, 1953.

Cancer of the Lung in Physicians, *New England J. of Med.,* 441–444, March, 1953.

Cannell, C. F., and MacDonald, J. D. The impact of health news on attitudes and behavior. *Journalism Quarterly,* 33: 315–323, 1956.

Carney, R. E. Research with a recently developed measure of achievement motivation. *Percept. and Motor Skills.* 21: 438, 1965.

Carr, A. J. Smoking in teenage boys. *Nurs. Times,* 1093–1095, 1963.

———. Smoking in teenage girls. *Nurs. Times.* 61: 225–7, Feb. 12, 1965.

Carr, D. T. One physician's philosophy about smoking. *New Physician,* 11; 298–9, Sept., 1962.

Carthew, A. John Bull Keeps Right on Smoking. *New York Times Magazine,* Jan. 19, 1964.

Cartwright, A., Martin, F. M., and Thompson, J. G. Distribution and development of smoking habits. *Lancet,* 2: 725–727, 1959.

———, ———, and ———. Efficacy of an anti-smoking campaign. *Lancet* 1: 327–329, February, 1960.

———, and others. Health hazards of cigarette smoking. Current popular beliefs. *Brit. J. Prev. Soc. Med.* 14: 160–6, 1960.

———, and Thompson, J. G. Young smokers: An attitude study among schoolchildren, touching also on parental influence. *Brit. J. Prev. Soc. Med.,* 14: 28–34, 1960.

Carver, N. J. The immediate psychological effects of tobacco smoking. *J. Comp. Psychol.* 2: 279–302, 1922.

Case, R. A. M. Smoking habits and mortality among workers in cigarette factories. *Nature* (London) 181: 84–86, 1958.

Castillo, J. J. *Lung Cancer and Cigarette Smoking.* New York: Carlton Press, Inc.

Cauffman, J. G. Advantages in teaching health education by television. *J. Sch. Hlth.* 32, 1962.

———. Experimenting with the direct teaching of health education by television in the Columbus public schools. *J. Sch. Hlth.* 30, 1960.

Cautela, J. R. Treatment of compulsive behavior by covert sensitization. *Psychol. Rec.* 16: 33–41, 1966.

Cederlof, R., Friberg, L., and Johnson, E. Morbidity among monozygotic twins. *Arch. Env. Hlth.* 10: 346–350, 1965.

———, and others. Morbidity in uniovular twins in relation to smoking habits and residence. A preliminary report. *Nord Hyg. T.* 45: 71–5, 1964.

———. Register of twins (preliminary report). *Nord. Hyg. I,* 45: 63–70, 1964.

———, Friberg, L., Jonsson, E., and Kaij, L. Studies on similarity diagnosis in twins with the aid of mailed questionnaires. *Acta Genet.* 11: 338–62, 1961.

Cesio, F. R. Psicoanálisis del hábito de fumar (Psychoanalysis of smoking habits.) *Rev. Psicoanal.* (Buenos Aires) 14: 368–374, 1957.

Chalke, H. D. Smoking. *Royal Social Hlth. J.* 84: 271–276, 1964.

Chance, N. A. Conceptual and methodological problems in cross-cultural health research. *Amer. J. Pub. Hlth.* 52 (3): 411–417, March, 1962.

———. Culture change and integration: an Eskimo example. *American Anthro.* 62: 1028–1044, 1960.

Chave, S. P. W., and Schilling, R. S. F. The smoking habits of school children. *Brit. J. Prev. Soc. Med.* 13: 1–4, 1959.

Chesser, Eustace. *When and How To Quit Smoking.* Emerson, 1964.

Chessick, R. D. The problem of tobacco habituation. *J.A.M.A.* 188: 932–3, June, 1964.

Chicago University Committee on Communication. *Studies in public communication.* pp. 47–60. Summer, 1959.

Childish habit. *J.A.M.A.* 189: 850, Sept., 1964.

Chisholm, J. An anti-smoking experiment... *International J. Health Ed.* 7: 35–41, 1964.

Choo, T. H. Communicator credibility and communication discrepancy as determinants of opinion change. *J. Soc. Psychol.* 64: 65–76, 1964.

A cigarette advertising code. *Canad. Med. Assn. J.* 92: 134–5, Jan. 16, 1965.

Cigarette advertising. *Med. J. Aust.,* 1: 998, 1964.

Cigarettes anonymous. *Penn. Med. J.* 67: 57–8, 1964.

Cigarette figures: A nine-year record of volume by brands; also advertising in newspapers, magazines, and radio. *Printers Ink* 55–58, May 26, 1938.

Cigarette industry changes its mind. *Reader's Digest,* July, 1958.

Cigarette industry grows rapidly as tobacco consumption increases in United States. *Am. Trust R. of the Pac.* 16: 5–8, Jan., 1927.

Cigarette scare: what'll the trade do? *Business Week,* p. 58, Dec. 5, 1953.

Cigarette smoking. [Editorial] *Public Health,* 76: 194–7, 1962.

Cigarette smoking and disease. *The American Biology Teacher,* Nov., 1959.

Cigarette smoking and health. *Amer. J. Pbl. Hlth.* 54: 322–4, February, 1964.

Cigarette smoking and health, a statement of public health officials. *T. Norsk Laegeforen* (Nor) 84: 300–4, Feb. 1964.

Cigarette smoking and health; a summary of opinion; a proposal for action. *California Dept. of Public Health,* 1963.

Cigarette smoking in Canada. II. *Monetary Times* 58–60, July, 1955.

Cigarette smoking, lung cancer, the medical profession's responsibility. *Canad. Med. Assn. J.* 84: 1006–1012, May 6, 1961.

Cigarette smoking: the tough decisions ahead. *Consumer Reports* 29: 464–8, Oct., 1964.

Cigarette warning: the aftermath, reaction of smokers, congressmen, stock market. *U.S. News* 56: 38–9, Jan. 1964.

Cigarettes, *Consumer Reports,* 13–21, January, 1960.

Cigarettes: are the facts being filtered? *Redbook,* June, 1960.

Cigarettes: Notes on the industry, cigarette consumption and smoking habits. A report from the Marketing Research Department, Redbook Magazine. *Market Reports — Redbook Magazine,* April, 1956, p. 41.

Cigarettes: Their Role and Function. Chicago: Social Research, Inc., 1952.

Cigarettes: their use and sale; a digest of the laws of the various states of the United States. Wis. leg. ref. dept. July 10, 1915.

Cohart, E. M. Socioeconomic distribution of cancer of the lung in New Haven. *Cancer* 8: 1126–9, 1955.

Cohen, J., and Heimann, R. K. Heavy smokers with low mortality. *Industr. Med. Surg.* 31: 115–20, 1962.

Comparative study of smoking habits of physicians. *New England J. Med.* 252: 619–696, 1955.

Comroe, J. H., and Nadel, J. The effect of smoking and nicotine on respiration. In James, G., and Rosenthal, T. (Eds.). *Tobacco and Health.* Springfield: Thomas, 1962, 233–43.

Conterio, F., Charelli, B. Study of the inheritance of some daily-life habits. *Heredity* 17: 347–59, 1962.

Cook, B. A. Survey on smoking. *Med. J. Aust.* 1: 363–5, Feb. 26, 1966.

Cope, V. Z. The economic aspects of tobacco addiction. *Brit. J. Addict.* 45: 81–92, 1948.

Cordaro, M. Consultation center for smokers in Czechoslovakia. *Dia. Med.* 33: 1633–4, 1961.

Corridan, J. P. A smoking survey of Cork City children. *J. Irish Med. Ass.* 53: 147–53, Nov., 1963.

Corsini, R. *Methods of Group Psychotherapy.* New York: Blakiston, 1957, 79 pp.

Corti, E. C. *A History of Smoking.* New York: Harcourt Brace, 1932, 295 pp.

Cousin, M. Tobacco: what should one think about it? *Concours Med.* 84: 3977–86, June 30, 1962.

Cramer, T. Anti-schoolchild-smoking campaign in Denmark. *Acta Un. Int. Canor.* 19: 935–6, 1963.

Crampton, C. W. Cigarette, soldier, and physician. *Mil. Surgeon.* 89: 1–13, July, 1941.

Croog, S. H. Ethnic origins, educational level, and responses to a health questionnaire. *Human Organization,* 20: 65–69, 1961.

Cross, K. W., and others. Current smoking habits in 1957 based on mass radiography surveys in the Midlands. *Brit. Med. J.*, 1: 862–5, 1958.

Cruickshank, A. Smokers' advisory clinic. *Monthly Bull. Minist. Hlth.* (London), 110–116, 1963.

———. Smokers advisory clinic: Ministry of health final report on the initial clinic. *Monthly Bull. Minist. Hlth.* (London), 22: 163–194, 1963.

———. Smoking and health. *Monthly Bull. Minist. Health* (London), 23: 64–7, Apr., 1964.

Culling, C., Vassar, P., and Saunders, A. M. Smoking patterns of university students in Canada. *Canad. Med. Assn. J.* 83: 630–632, 1960.

Cutler, S. J., and Loveland, D. D. Risk of developing lung cancer and its relation to smoking. *J. Natl. Cancer Institute* 20: 201–211, 1954.

Dale, C. L. A report on the 5-day plan to help adult smokers stop smoking. In *Helping the Adult Smoker to Stop Smoking.* Illinois: American Cancer Society, 1964, pp. 18–23.

Dalzell-Ward, A. J. The development of anti-smoking clinics in the United Kingdom. In *Helping the Adult Smoker to Stop Smoking.* Illinois: American Cancer Society, 1964, pp. 18–23.

Dam, C. Tobacco among the Indians. *Amer. Mercury* 16: 74, 1929.

Dammann, C. J. *How To Stop Smoking Cigarettes the ABC Way.* Fell, 1963.

Damon, A. Constitution and smoking. *Science* 134: 339–340, 1961.

———, and others. Tobacco smoke as a possible genetic mutagen. *Amer. J. Epidem.* 83: 530–6, Sept., 1966.

Darrow and Hill, Lung cancer and other causes of death in relation to smoking. *Brit. Med. J.,* Nov. 10, 1956.

David, J. C. Cigarette smoking — a deadly habit. *J. Christ. Med. Assn. India* 37: 334–6, July, 1962.

Davidson, H. A. Rationalizations for continued smoking. *N.Y. J. Med.,* 2993–3001, 1964.

Davies, C. N. Dangers of cigarette smoking. [Letter] *Brit. Med. J.* 1957, ii, 410.

Davies, D. F. A review of the evidence on the relationship between smoking and lung cancer. *J. Chron. Dis.* 11 (6): 579–614, June, 1960.

Davis, H. F. Teen-age problems on cigarette smoking and lung cancer. *Sch. & Com.,* 47, 1961.

Davis, R. L. Progress in smoking education — one year after establishment of the National Clearinghouse for Smoking and Health. Paper presented at the 94th annual meeting of the American Public Health Association in San Francisco, California, November 1, 1966.

Dawber, T. R., Kannel, W. B., Revotskie, N., Stokes, J., Kagen, A., and Gordon, T. Some factors associated with the development of coronary heart disease. *Amer. J. Pub. Hlth.* 49: 1349–1356, 1959.

Day, C. W. Fear-reduction and cigarette marketing. *Stud. Publ. Commun.,* Committee on Communication, The University of Chicago, 48–53, 1959.

Day, Cameron. Six weeks after the cigarette report: a lot of smoke but — *Sales Mgt* 92: 30–1, F 21, 1964.

De Takats, G. Smoking withdrawal: the physician's role. *Illinois Med. J.* 127: 141–6, Feb., 1965.

Delarue, N. C. Cigarette smoking: a clinical and public health challenge. I. The clinical challenge. *Canad. Med. Assn. J.* 87: 961–9, Nov. 3, 1962.

———. Cigarette smoking: a clinical and public health challenge. II. The public health challenge. *Canad. Med. Assn. J.* 87: 1018–22, Nov. 10, 1962.

Dept. of Agric., Agric. Marketing Service. Quarterly Report. *Agricultural Economics Research,* 8 (1): 1959.

Department of National Health and Welfare. (Can.) Research concerning smoking habits and hazards. Draft, May 19, 1964.

———. *Smoking and Health Bibliography.* May, 1965.

Dickson, Sarah A. *Panacea or Precious Bane.* New York Public Library, 1954.

Diehl, H. S. The physique of smokers as compared to non-smokers: A study of university freshmen. *Minn. Med.* 12: 424–427, 1929.

Dimond, S. J. Smoking habits of delinquent boys. *B. J. Prev. & Soc. Med.* 18: 52–54, 1964.

Dixit, R. C. A socio-psychological study of tobacco smoking. *J. Indian Acad. Appl. Psychol.,* 1: 49–54, 1964.

Do as we do? [Editorial] *Arch. Environ. Health* (Chicago). 6: 694–5, 1963.

Doctors have changed their smoking habits. [Editorial] *Resident Physician* 3: 50–63, 1957.

Doggart, J. H. Smoking as a factor in visual disturbance. *Practitioner* 182: 204–211, 1959.

Doll, R., and Hill, A. B. Lung cancer and other causes of death in relation to smoking. A second report on the mortality of British doctors. *Brit. Med. J.* 2: 1071–81, 1956.

———, and ———. The mortality of doctors in relation to their smoking habits; a preliminary report. *Brit. Med. J.* 1: 1451–5, 1954.

———, and ———. Smoking and carcinoma of the lung. *Brit. Med. J.* 2: 648–739, Sept., 1950.

———, ———, Gray, P. G., and Parr, E. A. Lung cancer mortality and the length of cigarette ends: an international comparison. *Brit. Med. J.,* 1: 322–5, 1959.

Dominion Bureau of Statistics. *The Smoking Habits of Canadians, August, 1964.* Ottawa: Department of National Health and Welfare, 1965.

Dorcus, R. M. The effect of suggestion and tobacco on pulse rate and blood pressure, *J. Exp. Psychol.* 8: 297–309, 1925.

Dorn, H. F. Note on cigarette smoking and lung cancer. *Public Health Rep.* 75: 582, 1960.

———. The mortality of smokers and non-smokers. *Amer. Stat. Assn. Proc. Soc. Stat. Sec.* 33–71, 1958.

———. Tobacco consumption and mortality from cancer and other diseases. *Publ. Hlth. Report.* 74: 581–593, July, 1959.

Dorsey, J. L. Control of the tobacco habit. *Ann. Int. Med.* 10: 628–631, 1936.

Douyon, E. The psychology of the smoker. Paper read at Canad. Youth Conf. Smokg. and Hlth. (Ottawa) May, 1965.

Downing, J. A. A study of brand images: An experiment approach to attitude measurement. *Attitude Scaling* (London) Market Research Society, 57–67, 1960.

———. What is a brand image? *Advertising Quarterly.* in press.

Drehl, H. S. The physique of smokers as compared to non-smokers. *Minn. Med.* 12, 1929.

Drogendijk, A. C. Is the current anti-smoking campaign socio-medically justified? *I. Soc. Geneesk* 43: 249–52, April 2, 1965.

Duffy, W. An eighteen-month study into the patterns of smoking among ten thousand children attending thirty schools in Staffordshire. Unpublished paper. Stafford: Health Education Office, 1963.

Dunn, J. E. Jr., Linden, G., and Breslow, L. California State Dept. of Public Health. *Special Report to the Surgeon General's Advisory Committee on Smoking and Health.*

Dunhill, R. What's the situation in cigarettes? *Advertising and Selling,* p. 62, Jan., 1945.

Earle, R. W. Nicotine and smoking. *Calif. Clin.* 57: 219–25, 1961.

Earp, J. R. The smoking habit and mental efficiency. *Lancet,* 1927.

———. *The Student Who Smokes: An Original Statistical Investigation.* Yellow Springs, Ohio: The Antioch Press, 1926.

———. Tobacco and scholarship. *Scient. Mon.,* 1928.

Education to discourage cigarette smoking. [Editorial] *Am. J. Pub. Health.* 53: 1133–4, 1963.

Edwards, A. S. The effect of smoking on tremor. *J. Appl. Psychol.* 32: 150–158, 1948.

Edwards, F., McKeown, T., and Whitfield, A. G. W. Association between smoking and disease in men over sixty. *Lancet* 1: 196, 1959.

Edwards, G. Hypnosis and lobeline in an anti-smoking clinic. *Med. Off.,* 111: 239–243, 1964.

Effect of smoking on appetite and on peripheral vascular disease. (Queries and minor notes) *J.A.M.A.* 119: 534, 1942.

Effect of smoking on visual search performance. *J.A.M.A* 196: 1048–52, June 20, 1966.

Effler, D. B. One surgeon's attitude toward cigarette smoking. *Surg. Gynec. Obstet.* 111: 232–3, August, 1960.

Ejrup, B. A proposed medical regimen to stop smoking: the follow-up results. *Swedish Cancer Soc. Yearbook,* 3: 468–473, 1963.

———. Breaking the cigarette habit. *CA.* 13, 1963.

———. Follow-up of the material of smokers difficult to treat. (Sw) *Svensk Lakartian* 56: 2254–62, August 14, 1959.

———. Proposals for treatment for smokers with severe clinical symptoms brought about by their smoking habit. *Brit. Columbia Med. J.* 2: 441–53, 1960.

———. The role of nicotine in smoking pleasure. In *Helping the Adult Smoker to Stop Smoking.* Illinois: American Cancer Society, pp. 63–69, 1964.

———. Treatment of smoking addicts. *Svenska Lakartidningen,* August, 1959. (Quoted from summary that appeared in the Foreign Letters Section, *J.A.M.A.* 12: 1727, November 21, 1959.)

———. Treatment of tobacco addiction: experiences in tobacco withdrawal clinics. In *Helping the Adult Smoker to Stop Smoking.* Illinois: American Cancer Society, 1964, pp. 3–17.

Ejrup, F. Experience in smoking withdrawal clinics. Science Writers Seminar, La Jolla, California. (Sponsored by the American Cancer Society, April 5–10, 1963.)

Elementary school children in state are target for smoking and health project this fall. [Editorial] *Med. Assn. State of Alabama.* 2(30): 1–4, 1966.

Elia, J. C. The suicidal weed. *Western Med.,* 5: 131–2, April, 1964.

Erickson, M. H. The burden of responsibility in effective psychotherapy. *Amer. J. Clin. Hypn.,* 6: 269–271, 1964.

Erskine, Hazel Gaudet. The polls: smoking. *Pub. Opinion Quarterly* 30: 140–152, 1966.

Essenberg, J. M. The deterioration of intelligence of albino rats chronically poisoned by nicotine. *J. Psychol.* 40: 209–213, 1955.

———. The effect of nicotine on maze learning ability of albino rats. *Fed. Proc.* 7: 31 (Abstract) 1948.

———. The effect of nicotine on maze behavior of albino rats. *J. Psychol.,* 37: 291–295, 1954.

Estrin, E. R. & Querry, D. L. A "no-smoking" project for ninth and tenth grades. *J. Sch. Hlth.* 35: 381–382, 1965.

Evans, P. A. Smoking and health. *Cent. Afr. J. Med.* 8: 234–6, 1962.

Excerpts from report on smoking, health. *Wall Street Journal,* Jan. 13, 1964, p. 6.

Eysenck, H. J. Personality and cigarette smoking. *Life Sci.,* 3: 777–792. 1964.

———. *Personality Factors and Smoking.* London: Mass-Observation, 1959.

———. *A Report on Personality Factors and Smoking.* Part 2. London: Mass-Observation, 1962.

———. Smoking and personality and lung cancer. *Family Doctor* 11: 420–422, 1961.

———. *Smoking, Health, and Personality.* New York: Basic Books, 1965, 166 p.

———. Smoking, personality and psychosomatic disorders. *J. Psychoso. Res.,* 7: 107–130, 1963.

———. The verdict on smoking. *Encounter* 23: 11–16, 1964.

———. Tarrant, M., Woolf, M., and England, L. Smoking and personality. *Brit. Med. J.,* 1: 1456–1460, 1960.

Faber, A. D. *Smokers, Segars and Slickers.* Watkins Glen, N. Y.: Century House, 1949.

Fabre, R., and Perdreau, H. Risk of nicotine impregnation in rooms where smoking occurs. *Bull. Acad. de Med.* (Paris). 126: 627, 1952.

"Facts about smoking." A Swedish medical team endorses a recent pamphlet. *Epione* 58: 265–6, October, 1965.

Facts for Teenagers: Smoking, Health, and You. Children's Bureau. HEW Dept., 1964.

Facts on teen-age smoking. *Parent's Magazine,* October, 1960.

Farrell, H. The billion-dollar smoke. A working truth in reference to cigarettes and cigarette smoking. *Nebraska Med. J.,* 18: 226–8, 1933.

Feather, N. T. Cigarette smoking and lung cancer: A study of cognitive dissonance. *Aust. J. Psychol.* 14: 55–64, 1962.

———. Cognitive dissonance, sensitivity, and evaluation. *J. Abnorm. Soc. Psychol.* 66: 157–163, 1963.

Ferris, B. G., Jr., and Anderson, D. O. The prevalence of chronic respiratory disease in a New Hampshire town. *Amer. Rev. Resp. Dis.* 86: 165–77, 1962.

Festinger, L. *A Theory of Cognitive Dissonance.* Evanston: Row, Peterson and Company, 1957.

The fight against tobacco smoking — a current social and health problem. Beliaev II *Gig. Sanit.* 30: 85–8, February, 1965.

Filters Win, Going Away. Tables. *Business Week,* pp. 47-8 Dec. 31, 1955.

Fine, B. J., Marchesani, M., and Sweeney, D. R. A bibliography on the psychological aspects of smoking. *Psych. Rep.* 18: 783–787, 1966.

Finker, A. L., Horvitz, D. G., Foradori, G. T., Fleischer, J., and Monroe, J. An investigation on the measurement of current smoking by individuals. *Univ. N. Carolina Inst. Stat. Mimeo. Series* No. 177, 1957.

Finnegan, J. K., Larson, P. S., and Haag, H. B. The role of nicotine in the cigarette habit. *Science* 102: 84–96, 1945.

Fisher, R. A. Cancer and smoking. *Nature,* 182: 596, 1958.

——. Cigarettes, cancer, and statistics. *Centennial Rev. Arts and Sci.,* 2: 151–66, 1958.

——. Dangers of cigarette-smoking. *Brit. Med. J.,* 2: 297–8, 1957.

——. Lung cancer and cigarettes. *Nature* 182: 108, 1958.

——. *Smoking — The Cancer Controversy.* Edinburgh, Scotland: Oliver and Boyd, 1959.

Flamant, R., Lassarre, O., & Lazar, P. Differences in sex ratio according to cancer site and possible relationship with use of tobacco and alcohol; review of 65,000 cases. *J. Nat. Cancer Inst.,* 32: 1309–1316, 1964.

Flick, A. L., and Paten, R. R. Obstructive emphysema and cigarette smoking. *A.M.A. Archives of Internal Med.* 104: 518, Oct., 1959.

Flick, J. B. The cigarette smoking problem. *Delaware Med. J.,* pp. 51–53, March, 1964.

Ford, A. S. *Tobacco Poisoning and Your Health.* New York: Carlton Press, Inc.

Ford, A. S., and Ederer, F. Breaking the cigarette habit. *J. Amer. Med. Ass.* 194: 139–142, 1965.

Forrest, D. W. Attitudes of undergraduate women toward smoking. *Psychol. Reports* 19: 83–7, August, 1966.

Forrester, A. H. *Few Words About Pipes, Smoking, and Tobacco.* New York Public Library, 1947.

Forsgren, E. Is nicotinism an incurable popular disease? *Svensk Lakartidn* (Sw) 57: 398–406, Feb. 5, 1960.

——. Nikotinforgifning och litterar angest. (Nicotine poisoning and literary anxiety.) *Sven. lak. Tidn.* (Sw), 56: 983–986, 1959.

Foster, D., and Gassney, H. An investigation of the retention of smoke particulate matter by inhaling and non-inhaling type of cigarette smoker. Presented at the Tobacco Chemists Conference, Hoboken, N. J., Oct., 1958.

Fraser, J. G. Cigarette smoking: causes and effects. *Addict.,* 10: 49–56, 1963.

Freedman, A. M., and Wilson, E. A. Childhood and adolescent addictive disorders. *Pediatrics.* 34: 283–292, 1964.

Freeman, Jean T. Who said we couldn't stop smoking? *Ladies Home J.,* Nov., 1961.

Freud, S. *Inhibitions, Symptoms and Anxiety.* J. Strachey (Ed.). London: Hogarth Press and Institute of Psycho-Analysis, 1961.

Freudenberg, K. Smoking and health. *Med. Welt.* 52: 2805–9, December 26, 1964.

Friberg, L., and others. Smoking habits of monozygotic and dizygotic twins. *British Medical Journal,* 1: 1090–1092, 1959.

Friedman, S. H. I choose not to smoke. *Nur. Outlk.* 40–42, 1964.

Frizelle, G. M. Tobacco, cigarettes, and ill health. *J. Roy. Institute Public Health* 27: 201–3, July, 1963.

Frumkes, G. A depression which recurred annually. *Psychoanal. Quart.* 351–364, 1946.

Gadourek, I. Evaluation of public education on smoking. *J. Soc. Genusk.* (Dutch) 43: 827–30, November 19, 1965.

——. Drinking and smoking habits and the feeling of well being. *Sociologia Neerlandica* (Dutch), 3(1): 28–43, Winter, 1965–1966.

Galarneaux, A. F., and Thompson, C. W. The selection, development, and evaluation of tobacco smoking concepts. *Research Quarterly,* 30: (2) 144–154, 1959.

Gardiner, C. E., Taylor, C. D. Derek, and Roberts, L. D. Smoking habits of schoolchildren. A survey of the smoking habits of New Zealand schoolchildren. New Zealand Department of Health, Medical Statistical Branch, 1961.

Garland, L. H. Smoking and health. (Correspondence) *New Eng. J. Med.* 267: 627–8, 1962.

Garner, L. L., Carl, E. F., and Grossman, E. E. Effect of cigarette smoking on flicker fusion threshold. *Amer. Med Assn. Ophthalmology* 51: 642–655, 1954.

Gedalia, I., and others. The effectiveness of filtertips on Israeli cigarettes. *Harefuah* 56: 110–1, 1959.

Gendreau, P. E., and Dodwell, P. C. An escape-learning treatment for addicted cigarette smokers. Submitted for publication: *Canad. Psychol.,* 1966.

Gesheidt, A. and Jacobs, F. *30 Ways To Stop Smoking.* Pocket Books, n. d.

Giving up the habit. *Newsweek,* p. 52, January 25, 1965.

Glenn, W. J. An approach to smoking deterrence in adolescence. *South Nud. J.,* 58: 1549–53, December, 1965.

Goldstein, K. M. (Staten Island Mental Health Society, New York) Note: A comparison of self- and peer-reports of smoking and drinking behavior. *Psychological Reports,* 18(3): 702, 1966.

Golland, E. B. On the hazards of smoking (topics for conversation *Feldsh Akush* (Israeli), 11: 10–4, 1965.

Good, R. Tobacco smoking *Lancet* 265: 676–677, 1953.

Gordon, H. L., and Atoman, D. Cigarette smoking in a psychiatric hospital. Unpublished research report, Veterans Administration Hospital, Fort Lyon, Colorado, 1966.

Gordon, R. Smoke abatement. *Punch,* Feb. 24, 1954. (copied in *J. Amer. Med. Ass.,* 159: 511, 1955.

Gould, W. L. Use of lozenge to curb smoking appeal. *G. P.* 7: 53–54, February, 1953.

Gowen, H. G. The smoking habit: a cancer control problem. Division of Chronic Diseases, Washington, D.C., 20201 — Mimeographed manuscript.

Graff, H., Hammett, Van Buren, O., Bash, N., and others. Results of four anti-smoking therapy methods. *Penn. Med. J.,* 69, 39–43, 1966.

Graham, H. Smoking — the facts. *Brit. Med. Assn.* (London), 1961, 32 pp. (A Family Doctor Booklet)

Grant, Marjorie. The group therapeutic approach for weight control. *Group Psychother.* 4: 156–165, 1951.

Graybiel, A., and others. Electrocardiographic changes following the inhalation of tobacco smoke. *American Heart Journal,* p. 89, 1938.

Green, G. H. Some notes on smoking. *Int. J. Psychol. Anal.,* 4: 323–328, 1923.

Greenberg, D. S. Tobacco: administration showing little enthusiasm for follow-up on Public Health Service report. *Science* 143: 1417–9, March, 1964.

Greene, R. J. The modification of smoking behavior by free operant conditioning methods. *Psychol. Rec.,* 14: 171–178, 1964.

Gridgeman, N. T. Psst! Cigarettes may not be coffin nails (the differences in risk are small, except perhaps at the extremes). *Saturday Night* 77: 44–5, May 12, 1962.

Grushka, T. Support of the American report "Smoking and Health." *Oncologia* (Basel) 19: 495–507, 1965.

Gsell, O. Smoking habits among students of the University of Basel. *Z. Praeventivmed*, 3: 221–37, 1958.

———. Smoking habits in a rural community in Switzerland. *Schweiz. Med. Wschr.* 88: 349–53, 1958.

———. Tabakrauchen und Krankheit. Hamburg, Neuland, 52 pp., 1959.

Guilford, Joan. Factors related to successful abstinence from smoking: An interim report of results of three-month follow-up of the clinic group. Los Angeles: American Institute of Research, 1965.

Gunn, W. T. An approach to smoking deterrence in adolescence. *Southern Med. J.* 58: 1549–53, December, 1965.

Guthjonsson, H. Exploration of smoking habits of middle and upper class students in Reykjavik. *Laeknabladid* 45: 1–7, 1961.

Guthrie, E. H. Smoking and health . . . one year later. *J. Sch. Health.* 35: 53–7, Feb. 1965.

Haag, H. B., and Hanmer, H. R. Smoking habits and mortality among workers in cigarette factories. *Industr. Med. Surg.* 26: 559–62, 1957.

Haag, J. H. and Garcia, N. Smoking habits of secondary school pupils. *Hlth. Ed. J.*, 25, 1962.

Hadley, E. D. Psychiatrists trace excessive smoking to interruptions in feeding as an infant. *New York Times.* Section 7. October 28, 1936.

Hadley, H. C. History of tobacco. *M. Ann. Dist. Colum.*, 46: 49–65, 1949. (Cross-reference)

Haefner, D. Use of fear arousal in dental health education. Paper read at the 92nd Annual Meeting of the American Public Health Association Dental Health Section, October 7, 1964.

Haenszel, W. Cancer mortality among the foreign-born in the United States. *J. Nat. Cancer Inst.*, 26: 37–132, 1961.

———, Loveland, D. B., and Sirkin, M. G. Lung-cancer mortality as related to residence and smoking histories. 1. White males. *J. Nat. Cancer Inst.* 28: 947–1001, 1962.

———, Marcus, S. C., and Zimmerer, E. C. Cancer morbidity in urban and rural Iowa. *Pub. Health Monogr.* 37: 1–85, 1956.

———, and Shimkin, M. B. Smoking patterns and epidemiology of lung cancer in the United States. Are they compatible? *J. Nat. Cancer Inst.* 16: 1417–41, 1956.

———, ———, and Miller, H. P. Tobacco smoking patterns in the United States, *Pub. Hlth. Monogr.*, 45, 1956. (Public Health Service Publication, No. 463, 1956.)

Hall, A. R., and Blakeslee, A. F. Effect of smoking on taste thresholds for phenyl-thiocarbamide (PTC). *Proc. Nat. Acad. Sci.* 31: 390–396, 1945.

Hamilton, A. E. *This Smoking World.* New York, London: The Century Co., 1927.

Hamilton, J. D., Sepp, A., Brown, T. C., and MacDonald, F. W. Morphological changes in smokers' lungs. *Canad. Med. Ass. J.*, 77: 177–82, 1957.

Hammett, V. B., and others. Therapy of smoking. *Curr. Psychiat. Ther.* 6: 70–5, 1966.

Hammond, E. C. Air pollution, smoking, and health. *Texas J. Med.*, 58: 639–47, 1962.

———. Evidence on the effects of giving up cigarette smoking. *Amer. J. Public Hlth.*, 55: 682–91, May, 1965.

———, and others. Influence of health on smoking habits. *Nat. Cancer Inst. Monogr.* 19: 269–85, Jan., 66.

———. Inhalation in relation to type and amount of smoking. *J. Amer. Statist. Assn.*, 54: 35–49, 1959.

———. Lung cancer death rates in England and Wales compared with those in the United States. *Brit. Med. J.*, 2: 649–54, 1958.

———. Prospective study of 1,085,000 men and women in 25 of the United States aged 35–89. Unpublished data.

———. *Report to the Surgeon General's Advisory Committee on Smoking and Health*, 1963.

———. Smoking and death rates: A riddle in cause and effect. *Sci. Progr.* 11: 239–267, 1960.

———, and others. Smoking habits and health in Georgia and other Southern states. *J. Med. Assn. Georgia* 54: 278–81, August, 1965.

———. Smoking habits and disease in Illinois. *Illinois Med. J.*, 126: 661–5, Dec., 1964.

———. Smoking habits and health in Indiana and neighboring states. *J. Indiana Med. Assn.* 58: 945–50, September, 1965.

———, and others. Smoking habits and health in Iowa and neighboring states. *J. Iowa Med. Soc.* 54: 563–7, October, 1964.

———, and others. Smoking habits and health in Kansas and other central states. *J. Kansas Med. Soc.* 65: 586–90, December, 1964.

———. Smoking habits and health in Maryland and neighboring states. *Maryland Med. J.* 13: 45–9, November, 1964.

———, and others. Smoking habits and disease in Minnesota. *Minnesota Med.* 48: 44–9 Jan. 1965.

———, and others. Smoking habits and disease in Missouri. *Missouri Med.* 62: 109–12, Feb., 1965.

———, Van Griethuysen, T. H., and Dibeler, J. B. Smoking habits and disease in New York state. *New York J. Med.* 65: 2557–61, Oct. 15, 1965.

———, and others. Smoking habits and disease in Ohio. *Ohio Med. J.* 61: 134–7, Feb., 1965.

———. Smoking in relation to lung cancer. *Conn. Med. J.* 18: 3–9, 1954.

———. Smoking in relation to physical complaints, *Archives of Environmental Health*, August 1961, Veumen 3, pp. 146–64.

———. The association between smoking habits and death rates. *J. Pub. Hlth.* 48: 1460–8, November, 1958.

———. The effects of smoking. *Sci. Amer.*, 207 (1): 1–15, 1962.

———. The influence of health on smoking habits. *Nat. Cancer Inst. Monogr.* 19: 269–85, 1966.

———, and Garfinkel, L. Changes in cigarette smoking. *J. Nat'l Cancer Instit.*, 33 (1): July, 1964.

———, and Garfinkel, L. Smoking habits of men and women. *J. Nat'l Cancer Instit.*, 27, 1961.

———, and Horn, D. Smoking and death rates — report on forty-four months of follow-up of 187,783 men. Part I (Total mortality), Part 2 (Death rates by cause). *J. Amer. Med. Ass.* 166: 1159–1294, 1958.

———, and ———. The relationship between human smoking habits and death rates. A follow-up study of 187,766 men. *J. Amer. Med. Ass.*, 155: 1316, 1954.

————, and Percy, Constance. Ex-smokers. *N. Y. State J. Med.* 2956–2959, Sept., 1958.

Haneveld, G. I. A curious smoking habit in the Caribbean region. *Trop. Geogr. Nud.* 17: 186–7, June, 1965.

Hardy, W. For teen-age smokers. *Health.* 48 (4): 5–6, 1962.

Harnett, A. L. How we do it. *J. Sch. Hlth.*, 35: 64–66, 1965.

Harper, A. *It's Easy to Quit Smoking.* Alhambra, Calif.: Borden Publishing Co. n.d.

Harvey, T. G. Is this the negligent physician? *J. Maine Med. Ass.* 53: 246–7, Oct. 1962.

Has the smoking scare ended? Chart. *U.S. News.* 50: 132, p. 18, 1965.

Hauser, H., Schwarz, B. E., Roth, G., and Bickford, R. G. Electroencephalographic changes related to smoking. *Electroenceph. Clin. Neurophysio.* 10: 576, 1958.

Hawkins, C. H. Legal restrictions on minors' smoking. *Amer. J. Public Hlth.* 54: 1741–4, Oct., 1964.

Haynes, W. F., Jr., Krstulovic, F. J., and Loomis Bell, A. I. Smoking habit and incidence of respiratory tract infections in a group of adolescent males. *Amer. Review on Resp. Disease.* 93 (5): May, 1966.

Head, J. R. The effects of smoking. *Illinois Med. J.* 76: 83–287, 1939.

Health vs Cigarette Smoking. A report of the Governor's Advisory Committee on cigarette smoking and health. California State Department of Public Health, 1964.

Hearings Before A Subcommittee of Committee on Government Operations, House of Representatives. 85th Congress, First Session: *False and Misleading Advertising.* (Filter-tip cigarettes) July, 1957.

Heath, C. W. Differences between smokers and nonsmokers. *A.M.A. Arch. Intern. Med.* 101: 377–388, 1958.

Heinzl, Z., Hroch, V., Janouskova, N., and Utrata, R. (Cz) Our experience with anti-smoking campaigns. *Activ. Nerv. Sup (Praha)* 3: 223–4, May, 1961.

Heise, J. G. *The Painless Way to Stop Smoking.* Manhasset, New York: Channel Press, 1962.

Higgens, I. T. T. Tobacco smoking, respiratory symptoms, and ventilatory capacity. Studies in random samples of the population. *Brit. Med. J.* 1: 325–9, 1959.

————. Length of cigarette-ends and inhaling. *Brit. J. Industr. Med.* 21: 321–3, October, 1964.

Hilding, A. C. On cigarette smoking, bronchial carcinoma, and ciliary action: II. Experimental study on the filtering action of cows' lungs, the disposition of tar in the bronchial tree, and removal of ciliary action. *The New England J. of Med.*, June 21, 1956.

Hilton, M. E. Teaching them young. *Med. Officer* 109: 111, 1963.

Hinkle, L. E., and Wolff, H. G. Health and the social environment: Experimental investigations. In A. H. Leighton, J. A. Clausen, and R. N. Wilson (eds.). *Explorations in Social Psychiatry.* New York: Basic Books, pp. 105–137, 1957.

Hirvonen, L., and others. Servicemen's smoking habits. Preliminary report. *Sotilaslaak Aikak* (Fin.), 35: 220–7, 1960.

————, Paavilainen, T., and Peltonen, T. Smoking and the flicker fusion threshold. *Sotilasaak Aikak* (Fin.) 36: 62–68, 1961.

————, and others. Smoking habits of Finnish conscripts. *Sotilaslaak Aikak* (Fin.), 40: 35–36, 1965.

Hobbs, P. Susceptibility of teenagers to anti-smoking propaganda. *Hlth. Ed. J.*, 33: 41–46, 1965.

Hobsen, J., and Henry, H. (eds.). Patterns of smoking habits. In *Hulton Research Studies of the British Social Pattern.* London: Hulton Press, 1948.

Hochbaum, G. M. A critique of psychological research on smoking. *Symposium Amer. Psychol. Assn. Convention,* Sept., 1964.

————. Psychosocial aspects of smoking with special reference to cessation. *Amer. J. Pub. Hlth.* 55 (5): 692–697, 1965.

————. *Public Participation in Medical Screening Programs: a Socio-Psychological Study.* Washington, D.C. Public Health Service Publication No. 572, Washington, D.C.: Govt Printing Office, 1958.

————. The vice of smoking. *Maryland Med. J.* 14: 21–26, 1965.

————. What they believe and how they behave. *International J. Hlth. Ed.*, XI p. 43, Jan. 1959.

Hoffstaedt, E. G. W. The treatment of the unwilling smoker. *Practitioner* 195: 794–8, Dec., 1965.

————. The use of lobeline in the treatment of smokers. *Med. J. Austral.* 288, 1964.

————. Anti-smoking campaign. *Med. Off.*, 59–60, 1964.

Hojer, J. Reversal of physicians' opinions on tobacco. *Svensk. Lakartidn.* 58: 3253–71, Nov. 9, 1961.

Holmes, J. K. Smokeless hospitals. [Correspondence] *New Eng. J. Med.* 269: 377–8, 1963.

Horn, D. An analysis of the educational problems of controlling cigarette smoking. Paper presented at the 9th International Cancer Congress, Tokyo, Japan, October 26, 1966.

————. An experimental course for the control of personal cigarette smoking. Paper read at annual meeting of the Amer. Publ. Hlth. Ass., New York, 1964.

————. Behavioral aspects of cigarette smoking. *J. Chronic Dis.* 16: 383–395, 1963.

————. Modifying smoking habits in high school students. *Children* 7: 63–65, 1960.

————. Patterns of teenage smoking. *Public Hlth. News,* 41: 6, 1960.

————. Teenage smoking patterns. An address presented at Los Angeles, California, May 19, 1960. Distributed by the Am. Cancer Society in multilith form, 11 pp., Jan., 1961.

————. Teenage smoking patterns. Presented at the First Illinois Cancer Congress, Springfield, Illinois, March 9, 1960.

————, Cameron, C. S., and Kipnis, D. Survey of medical opinion towards smoking. The American Cancer Society, 1955.

————, Courts, F. A., Taylor, R. M., and Solomon, E. S. Cigarette-smoking among high school students. *Am. J. Pub. Hlth.*, 49: 1497–1511, 1959.

————, and Waingrow, S. Questionnaire: Study of behavior and attitudes, Public Health Service — T278, Study #1–466, October, 1964.

————, ————. *Some Dimensions of a Model for Smoking Behavior Change.* Paper presented at the 93rd Annual Meeting of the American Public Health Association in Chicago, Illinois, pp. 1–10, Oct. 20, 1965.

————, ————. What changes are occurring in public opinion toward cancer: National public opinion survey. *Amer. J. Pub. Health,* 54 (3): 431–440, March, 1960.

Horne, T. Smoking and health. The activities of a high school student committee. *J. Sch. Health,* 33: 451–6, Dec., 1963.

Horner, J. S. Cigarette smoking and health education. *Med. Officer,* 108: 305–308, 1962.

Horowitz, E. V. Civilian cigarette prospects *Conference B. Bus. Rec.* 2: 21–2, Dec., 1944, Jan., 1945.

Horowitz, M. J. Psychological aspects of education related to smoking. *J. Sch. Health* 36: 281–8, June, 1966.

Horton, P. B., and Leslie, G. R. *The Sociology of Social Problems,* 2nd ed. New York: Appleton-Century-Crofts, Inc., 1960.

Hovland, C. I., Janis, I. L., and Kelley, H. H. *Communication and Persuasion.* New Haven: Yale University Press, 1963.

How I quit smoking . . . and why. *Texas Health Bulletin,* State Dept. of Hlth., Vol. 2, pp. 3–6, Nov., 1958.

How much did you smoke? *Lancet* 1: 648–9, March, 1966.

How to stop smoking. *Brit. Med. J.* 2: 1235, 1950.

How to Stop Smoking. [News from the field] *Amer. J. Public Health* 53: 1168–9, 1963.

Hruskoric, J., and others. Research on the beginning and causes of smoking in juveniles from 14 to 16 years. *Cesk. Pediat.* (Cz) 21: 363-4, April, 1966.

Hueper, W. C. A quest into the environmental causes of cancer of the lung. *Public Health Monogr.,* 36: 45, 1955.

Hull, C. L. The effects of tobacco smoking on mental and motor efficiency. *Psychol. Monogr.,* 33 (3 Whole No. 150), 1924.

Husband, R. W., and Geoffrey, J. An experimental study of cigarette identification. *Journal of Applied Psychology,* 18: 220–223, 1934.

Huttunen, J., and others. The smoking habit among schoolchildren. *Duodecim* 76: 487–92, 1960.

Ikard, F. F. Smoking bibliography: Selected references. Mimeo. National Clearinghouse for Smoking and Health, 1966.

Increased penalties for supplying tobacco to children. *Monthly Bull. Minist. Health* (London) 23: 67–8, 1964.

Ingalls, A. G. If you smoke. *Scient. Amer.,* 154: 310–13, 1936.

Insko, Chester A., Arkoff, A., and Insko, Verla M. Effects of high and low fear-arousing communications upon opinions toward smoking. *Journal of Experimental Social Psychology* 1 (3): 256–266, 1965.

International Medical Abstracting Service. *Excerpta Medica,* 9(7): Section XVII, July, 1963.

Interview with Dr. E. Cuyler Hammond: Does smoking shorten life? *U.S. News and World Report,* pp. 54–64, July 2, 1954.

Jacobs, Martin A., and others. Relationship of oral frustration factors with heavy cigarette smoking in males. *Journal of Nervous and Mental Disease,* 141 (2): 161–171, 1965.

Jacobson, E. Muscular tension and the smoking of cigarettes. *Amer. J. Psychol.* 56: 559–574, 1943.

James I, King of Great Britain 1566-1625. *A Counter-Blast to Tobacco.* Edmund Goldsmith (Ed.) Edinburgh: Priv. Print., 1884.

James I of England. Counterblast to tobacco (1604) *Cancer Bull.* (Texas) 16: 52–4, May–June, 1964.

James, G. A "stop smoking" program. *Amer. J. Nurs.* 64: 122–5, June, 1964.

————, Rosenthal, T. (Ed.) *Tobacco and Health,* Springfield, Ill.: Thomas, 1962. 408 pp.

James, W. H., Woodruff, A. B., and Werner, W. Effect of internal and external control upon changes in smoking behavior. *J. Consult. Psychol.,* 29: 184–186, 1965.

Janis, I. L. Factors influencing tolerance for deprivation. Unpublished research progress report, Yale Univ., 1965.

————, and Mann. L. Effectiveness of emotional role-playing in modifying smoking habits and attitudes. *J. Exp. Res. Pers.,* 1: 84–90, 1965.

————, and Terwilliger, R. F. An experimental study of psychological resistances to fear-arousing communications. *J. Abnor. Soc. Psychol.,* 65: 403–410, 1962.

————, ————. Psychological resistance evoked by fear-arousing communications. In Janis, I. L. and collaborators. *Fear and Adjustment Mechanisms.* New York: Wiley and Sons, 1959.

Jeffereys, Margot. Smoking amongst school children. An assessment of the effect on school children of a television programme and of recent publicity on the ill effects of smoking. *Med. Officer,* 109: 91–4, 1963.

————, and Westway. W. C. Catch them before they start. *Health Education Journal,* XIX, 3–17, 1961.

Jensen, L. M., and others. Report of 1965 smoking survey — Lincoln Public Schools — Senior High Schools. *J. Sch. Health,* 35: 366–73, October, 1965.

Jochum, K., and Jost, F. Nicotine addiction and its treatment. *München. Med. Wschr.* (Ger.) 103: 618–22, 1961.

Johansson, G., and Jansson, G. Smoking and night driving. *Scand. J. Psychol.* 6: 124–128, 1965.

Johnson, D. Pros and cons of teenage smoking. *Texas Health Bull.* 14 (4): 3–4, 1962.

Johnston, D. M. A preliminary report of the effect of smoking on size of visual fields. *Life Sci.* 4: 2215–21, November, 1965.

————. Effect of smoking on visual search performance. *Percept. Motor Skills.* 22: 619–22, April, 1966.

Johnston, L. Cure of tobacco smoking. *Lancet,* 2: 480–482, 1952.

————. Tobacco-smoking. [Letters to the editor] *Lancet.* 1: 218, 1958.

Johnston, L. M. Tobacco smoking and nicotine. *Lancet.* 2, 742, 1942.

Jones, H. A report on the national interagency council on smoking and health. *J. Sch. Hlth.* 35: 214–216, 1965.

————. A report on the national interagency council on smoking and health. *J. Sch. Health,* 36, 1966.

Jost, F., and others. Experiences and practical implications in breaking the nicotine habit. *Folia. Clin. Int. (Barc)* 12: 303–14, 1962.

————, Jochum, K., and Tuba, J. Rauchergewohnheiten und Nikotinentwohnung — prakische nervenarztliche Grundlagen und Erfahrungen. [Smokers habits and nicotine withdrawal — practical neurological bases and experiences.] *Wien. Med. Wschr.* (Ger.) 111: 727–735, 1961.

————, ————. Breaking the tobacco habit. *Clin. Ter.* 23: 432–50, 1962.

Joyner, R. E. Effect of cigarette smoking on olfactory acuity. *Arch. Otolaryng.,* 80: 576–579, 1964.

Kahn, E., and Guldea, E. F. How to overcome the smoking habit. *Conn. State Med.* 5: 886–888, 1941.

Kahn, H. A. The Dorn study of smoking and mortality among U.S. veterans; report on eight and one half years of observation. *Nat. Cancer Inst. Monogr.* 19: 1–125, Jan., 1966.

Kaiser, E. R. Psychology of the thrill. *Pedagog. Sem. J. Genet. Psychol.* 27: 243–280, 1920.

Kallner, Gertrude. Smoking habits of the population. *Statist. Bull. Israel,* in press. (English translation of a mimeographed report, Central Bureau of Statistics, State of Israel, Nov. 1958).

Kampmeier, R. H. On the smoking of cigarettes. *Southern Med. J.,* 56: 79–80, Jan., 1963.

Kane, D. A., Hospitals give de facto endorsement to a health hazard. *Hosp. Managr.* 101: 32–3, April, 1966.

Kassarjian, H. J., and Cohen, J. B. Bibl. Cognitive dissonance and consumer behavior. Tables. *Cal. Mgt. R.,* 8: 55–64, Fall, 1965.

Katz, E., and Lazarsfeld, P. *Personal Influence.* Glencoe, Ill.: Free Press, 1955, 400 pp.

Kaufmann, H., and Bensimon, L. Breaking the tobacco habit. *Vie. Med.,* 41: 1139–50, 1960.

Keays, J. The smoking enigma. *Canad. J. Public Hlth.* 56: 105–8, March, 1965.

Kegeles, S. S. Some motives for seeking preventive dental care, *J. Amer. Dent. Asoc.* 67: 110, 1963.

Kesic, B. Smoking and health, *Lijecn. Vjesn.* 86: 1325–40, 1964.

Kimeldorf, C., and Gerwitz, P. J. Smoking and the blacky orality factors. *J. Project. Tech. and Person Access,* 30: 167–168, 1966.

Kingsley, H. J. Unusual way of smoking. Adda Poga or Candela Pa Den reverse smoking. *Cent. Afr. J. Med.* 12: 56, March, 1966.

Kirchoff, Helen, and Rigdon, R. H. Smoking habits of college students in Texas. *Tex. Rep. Biol. Med.,* 12, 292–299, 1954.

——, ——. Smoking habits of 21,612 individuals in Texas. *J. Nat. Cancer Inst.,* 16: 1287–1304, 1956.

Kissen, D. M. Aspects of personality of men with lung cancer. *Acta. Psychother.,* 11: 200–210, 1963.

——. Emotional factors, cigarette smoking and relapse in pulmonary tuberculosis. *Hlth Bul.,* 18: 38–44, 1960.

——. Personality and lung cancer. [Correspondence] *Brit. Med. J.* 1: 1107, 1961.

——. Personality characteristics in males conducive to lung cancer. *Brit. J. Med. Psychology,* 36, 27–36, 1963.

——. Psychosocial factors in cigarette-smoking motivation. *Med. Officer,* 104, 365–372, 1960.

——. Relationship between lung cancer, cigarette smoking, inhalation, and personality. *Brit. J. Med. Psychol.,* 37: 203–216, 1964.

——, and Eysenck, H. J. Personality in male lung cancer patients. *J. Psychosom. Res.* 6: 123–7, 1962.

Kistner, R. W. Hazards of obstetrical and gynecological drugs. *Ohio Med. J.,* 60: 1125–1129, 1964.

Klein, D. C., Ayling, R. I., and Skirmuntas, Daina. Contract for development of training for community smoking and health problems. Unpublished research report, Boston Univ. Human Relations Center, June, 1965.

Knapp, P. H., Bliss, C. M., and Wells, Harriet. Addictive aspects in heavy cigarette smoking. *Amer. J. Psychiat.,* 119, 10, 966–972, 1963.

Kneist, W. Smoking and drinking habits in 14- to 18-year-old boys and girls. *Z. Ges. Hyg.* (Ger.) 10: 937–48, October, 1964.

Knutson, A. L. Personal security as related to station in life. *Psychol. Monogr.,* Amer. Psychol. Assn., Washington, D.C., 1952. 4, 1–31, 1966.

Koenig, K. P., and Masters, J. Experimental treatment of habitual smoking. *Behav. Res. Ther.,* 3: 235–243, 1965.

Korteweg, R. The significance of selection in prospective investigations into an association between smoking and lung cancer. *Brit. J. Cancer* 10: 282–91, 1956.

Koskowski, W. *The Habit of Tobacco Smoking.* London: Staples Press Ltd., 1955.

Kosonen, T. Smoking and health. *Suom Laak* (Fin.), 19: 386–7, Feb., 1964.

Kress, D. H. Cigarette or tobacco smoke inhalation and its influence on civilized races; is the habit curable? Anti-cigarette League, 108 S. La Salle, St., Chicago.

Krut, L. H., Perrin, M. J., and Bronte-Stewart, B. Taste perception in smokers and nonsmokers. *Brit. Med. J.,* 1: 384–387, 1961.

Kune, K. P. Smoking habits and attitudes of 3057 public school students and their families. *J. Sch. Hlth.* 35: 458-9, December, 1965.

Kuvin, S. F. The smoking habits of school children. *J. Med. Soc. New Jersey,* 60: 415–6, Sept., 1963.

Lampert, K. J., and others. The effectiveness of anti-smoking campaigns: moralistic or scientific approach? *J. Sch. Health* 36: 34–40, Jan., 1966.

Lane, J. P. Smokers' reactions to a television program about lung cancer: A study of dissonance. Unpublished doctoral dissertation, Stanford Univ., 1960.

Langer, M. Sobre un detalle insignificante: el fumar durante el análisis. [On an insignificant detail: Smoking during the analysis.] *Rev. Pers., Buenos Aires,* 4: 220–223, 1946.

Larsen, O. Smoking habits among 19-yr. old males in Ostfold. *I Norsk Laegeforen* 85: 443–8, Mar. 1, 1965.

Larson, P. S., Finnegan, J. K., and Haag, H. B. Observations on the effect of cigarette smoking on the fusion frequency of flicker. *J. Clin. Invest.,* 29: 483–485, 1950.

——, Haag, H. B., and Silvette, H. Measurement of tobacco smoking. *Med. Times,* 88: 417–29, April, 1960.

——, ——, and ——. *Tobacco Experimental and Clinical Studies.* Baltimore: Williams & Wilkins, pp. 27–81, 526–547, 565–574, 1961.

Laufer, B. *Introduction of Tobacco into Europe.* Chicago: Field Museum of Natural History (Anthropology Leaflet No. 19), 1924.

——. *Tobacco and Its Use in Africa.* Chicago: Field Museum of Natural History (Anthropology Leaflet No. 29), 1930.

——. *Tobacco and its Use in Asia.* Chicago: Field Museum of Natural History (Anthropology Leaflet No. 18), 1924.

Lawton, M. P. A group therapeutic approach to giving up smoking. *Appl. Ther.* 4: 1025–1028, 1962.

——. Psychological processes in the cessation of smoking. (Paper presented to the American Psychological Association, Los Angeles, Calif. Sept. 8, 1964.)

——. Psychosocial aspects of cigarette smoking. *J. Hlth. Hum. Behav.* 3: 163–170, 1962.

——. The psychology of adolescent anti-smoking education. *J. Sch. Hlth.* 33: 337–345, 1963.

——, and Goldman, A. E. Cigarette smoking and attitude toward the etiology of lung cancer. *J. Soc. Psychol.* 54: 235–248, 1961.

Lawton, M. P., and Goldman, A. E. Cigarette smoking and attitude toward the etiology of lung cancer. *Amer. Psychol.* 13: 342, 1958.

———, and Phillips, R. W. The relationship between excessive cigarette smoking and psychological tension. *Amer. J. Med. Sci.* 232: 397–402, 1956.

Le Cron, L. M. *How To Stop Smoking Through Self-Hypnosis.* Prentice-Hall, 1964.

Le Mer, C. Results obtained with an anti-smoking agent on a group of 45 smokers. *Clinique* (Paris) 56: 643, 1961.

Ledermann, S. Cancers, Tabac, Vin. et Alcool. *Concours Med.* 77: 1107, 1109–11, 1113–4, 1955.

Lefcourt, H. M. *Personality Correlates of Cigarette Smoking.* Ottawa: Dept. of National Health and Welfare, 1965.

Lemere, F. Effects of smoking. *J.A.M.A.,* 189: 382, Aug., 1964.

Leton, D. A. Report of survey on adolescent smoking behavior. Conducted for the Hawaii Dept. of Public Health, Cancer Control Division. Honolulu, Hawaii, Sept., 1964. (Unpublished)

———. Survey of adolescent smoking behavior. Supplementary report: survey of parents' attitudes and behavior as related to adolescent smoking. Conducted for the Hawaii Dept. of Public Health, Cancer Control Division, December, 1964. (Unpublished)

Let's urge youngsters not to smoke. [Editorial] *J. Iowa Med. Soc.,* 53: 167–8, 1963.

Letton, A. H. Teen age program on cigarettes and lung cancer. *J. Med. Assn. Georgia* 49: 329, 1960.

Leventhal, H., and Niles, P. A field experiment on fear arousal with data on the validity of questionnaire measures. *J. Pers.* 32: 459–479, 1964.

———, and Watts, J. C. Sources of resistance to fear-arousing communication on smoking and lung cancer. *J. Personality* 34: 155–75, June, 1966.

Leverenz, I. W. Evaluation of cancer education programmes directed to young people. *Acta. Un. Int. Cancr.* 19: 961–3, 1963.

Levin, M. Perceived risk in smoking: an exploratory investigation. *Stud. Publ. Commun.,* Committee on Communication, The University of Chicago, 54–60, 1959.

Levine, M. L. Clinics for breaking the adult cigarette smoking habit. Paper presented before the American Public Health Association meeting, October 7, 1964, New York.

Lewis, A. B. *Use of Tobacco in New Guinea and Neighboring Regions.* Chicago: Field Museum of Natural History (Anthropology Leaflet No. 17), 1924.

Lewis, D. J. Expectation and resistance to extinction under partial reinforcement and risk-taking. *Amer. J. Psychol.* 75 (1): 79–84, 1962.

Liebeschuetz, H. J. Respiratory signs and symptoms in young soldiers and their relationship to smoking. *J. Roy. Army Med. Corps.* 105: 76–81, 1959.

Lilienfeld, A. M. Emotional and other selected characteristics of cigarette smokers and nonsmokers as related to epidemiological studies of lung cancer and other diseases. *J. Nat. Can. Inst.* 22: 259–282, 1959.

———. Smoking and other habits. *Proc. Nat. Cancer Conf.* 4: 120–34, 1960.

Link, H. D. Significance of change in cigarette preference. *Advertising and Selling,* p. 27, June 6, 1935.

Lister, J. The hidden persuaders. *New Eng. J. Med.* 265: 1107–8, 1961.

Little, C. C. *Report of the Scientific Director. Tobacco Industry Research Committee.* New York: 1–62, 1957.

———. The public and smoking: Fear or calm deliberation? *Atlantic,* 200: 74–76, 1957. (Reprinted: Ca: *Bul. Cancer Progress,* 49–52, 1958.)

Littman, R. A., and Manning, H. M. Methodological study of cigarettes; brand discrimination. *J. Appl. Psychol.* 38: 185–190, 1954.

Lokander, S. Weaning moderate smokers from tobacco. *Svenok Lakartidr* 56: 2080–9, 1959.

London, S. J. Clinical evaluation of a new lobeline smoking deterrent. *Current Therapu. Res.* 5 (4): 167–175, 1963.

London School of Hygiene and Tropical Medicine, Public Health Department, *Brit. J. Prev. & Social Med.* 13: 1, 1959.

Long, P. H. Doctor, can you stop smoking? *Med. Times,* 92: 407–8, 1964.

———. The problem of smoking. *Med. Times,* 92: 411–2, 1964.

Lowe, C. R. Effect of mother's smoking habits on birthweight of their children. *Brit. Med. J. No.* 5153: 673–6, Oct. 10, 1959.

———. Smoking habits related to injury and absenteeism in industry. *Brit. J. Prev. Soc. Med.* 14: 57–63, April, 1960.

Luban-Plozza, B. Maniacal smoking or dry-drunkeness *Folio Clin. Int.* (Sp.) 16: 150–9, March, 1966.

———. On Smoking. *Ther. Umsch.* 21: 456–65, November, 1964.

Lundberg, A. Cigarette smoking among schoolgirls. *Svensk Lakartidn* 57: 1568–79, 1960.

Lundman, I. Smoking in relation to coronary heart disease and lung function in twins. *Acta. Med. Scand.* 180: Suppl. 455: 1–75, 1966.

Lung cancer and cigarettes. *Reader's Digest,* June, 1962.

Lung cancer and smoking. *Lancet,* 1: 1374–5, 1964.

Lynch, G. W. Smoking habits of medical and non-medical university staff. Changes since R.C.P. report. *Brit. Med. J.* 5334: 852–5, 1963.

Lynn, R. M. A study of smokers and nonsmokers as related to achievement and various personal characteristics. *UNC Rec. Res. Progr.,* No. 464, 164, (Grad. Sch. Series no. 56.), Abstract and M.A. thesis, 1948.

McArthur, C. C. Subculture and personality during college years. *J. Educ. Sociol.,* 33: 260–268, 1960.

———. The personal and social psychology of smoking. *Proc. 7th Int. Cancer Congr.* (London), 6–12, pp. 291–299, July, 1958.

———. The personal and social psychology of smoking. In: James, G., and Rosenthal, T. (Eds.) *Tobacco and Health.* Springfield, Ill.: Thomas, 1961.

McArthur, C., Waldron, E., and Dickinson, J. Smoking and personality: a progress report, Harvard Univ., *J. Consult. Psychol.* 1956.

———, ———, and ———. The psychology of smoking. *J. Abnorm. Soc. Psychol.* 56: 267–275, 1958.

McCall, C. B. Tobacco and health. *Memphis Med. J.* 38: 481–2, Dec., 1963.

McCord, H. Preventing "teen-age smoking" *J. Amer. Soc. Psychosom. Den. Meet.* 12: 31, Jan., 1965.

McDonald, R. L. Personality characteristics, cigarette smoking, and obstetric complications. *J. Psychol,* 60: 129–134, 1965.

McFarland, J. W. Lifeline for ex-smokers. *Nur. Out.* 500–502, 1964.

———. Physical measures used in breaking the smoking habit. *Arch. Phys. Med. Rehab.*, 64: 4, 323–327, 1965.

———, Gimbel, H. W., and Donald, W. A. J. The five-day program to help individuals stop smoking: A preliminary report. *Conn. Med.* 28: 885–890, 1960.

McGrady, Pat. *Cigarettes and Health.* 20 p. il. charts. Public Affairs Pam. No. 220 a, 25 c, Public Affairs Com., March, 1960.

McGuire, J. D. *Pipes and Smoking Customs of the American Aborigines Based on Material in the U.S. National Museum.* (U.S. National Museum Annual report 1897, Washington, 1899, pt. 1 pp. 351–645.)

McGuire, R. J., and Vallance, M. Aversion therapy by electric shock: a simple technique. *Brit. Med. J.* 1: 151–153, 1964.

———, and ———. Aversion therapy by electric shock: A simple technique. In Franks, C. M. (Ed.). *Conditioning Techniques in Clinical Practice and Research.* New York: Springer, 1964, pp. 178–185.

McMillen, Sim I. *Cancer By the Carton.* New Jersey: Fleming H. Revell Co., 1963.

MacDonald, I. A new brand of prohibitionism. *Surg. Gynec. Obstet.* 116: 239–40, Feb., 1963.

Macek, T. K. A status report on smoking. *J. Am. Pharm. Assn.* 6: 15–6, January, 1966.

Machen, A. *The Anatomy of Tobacco.* London: A. A. Knopf, 1926.

MacLaine, A. G. Smoking and young people: An analysis of research and recommendations for remedial educative action. *Med. J. Aust.* 2: 388–390, 1964.

MacMahon, B., Alpert, M., and Salber, E. J. Infant weight and parental smoking habits. *Amer. J. Epidem.* 82: 247–261, 1965.

Maddison, D. The positive side of smoking. *Appl. Ther.* 4: 938, *passim* 1961.

Madis, G. *Smoking, Life, and Health.* Lancaster, Texas: American Book Publishing Co., 1964.

Maljkovic, J. Further observations on smoking and health. *Lijecn. Vjesn* (Ser.) 87: 1272–9, Nov., 1965.

Mann, Leon. The effects of emotional role-playing on smoking attitudes and habits. *Dissertation Abstracts* 26 (7): 4104–4105, 1966.

Manuel, H. T. Is the college "smoker" a worthy social institution? *School and Soc.* 4: 699–705, November 4, 1916.

Markiewitz, K. History of smoking. *Pol. Tyg. Lek.* (Polish), 18: 1040–1, July, 1963.

Marks, Sylvia, L. *Smoking Is For Suckers.* New York: Exposition Press, 1964.

Markush, R. E., and Schaaf, W. E. Cigarette smoking and medical attendance prior to death. *Arch. Environ. Health* (Chicago) 13: 66–71, July, 1966.

Marshall, M. V. *Teaching About Tobacco in Canadian Schools* (general summary). A report prepared for the Department of National Health and Welfare. August 15, 1964.

Matarazzo, J. D., and Saslow, G. Psychological and related characteristics of smokers and nonsmokers. *Psychol. Bul.*, 57: 493–513, 1960.

Maucorps, P. H. Tabagisme et travail. (Nicotinism and work.) *Travail et Methodes* (Fr.), 19: 38–39, 1949.

Mausner, B. A decisional model for the study of the interrelation of attitudinal and behavioral change. Unpub-

lished research report, Beaver College, Glenside, Pa., April, 1966.

———. Report on a smoking clinic. *Amer. Psychol.*, 21: 251–255, 1966.

———, and others. Change in a salient attitude: cigarette smoking and lung cancer. Pittsburgh: Graduate School of Public Health, University of Pittsburgh, 1962 (Mimeographed).

———, and Platt, Ellen. *Changing attitudes toward cigarettes and lung cancer,* Glenside, Pa.: Beaver College, 1964.

———, and ———. *Proceedings of the Conference on Behavioral Aspects of Smoking.* Glenside, Pa.: Beaver College, September, 1965.

———, and ———. Smoking: A behavioral analysis. Unpublished research report, Glenside, Pa.: Beaver College, 1966.

———, and ———. Behavioral Aspects of Smoking: A Conference Report. *Health Education Monographs,* Supplement 2, 1966.

Mausner, J. S. Smoking in medical students. A survey of attitudes, information, and smoking habits. *Arch. Environ. Health* (Chicago) 13: 51–60, July, 1966.

Maxwell, J. C. Cigarette Special. ill. tables. *Printers Ink.* 291: 13–16, Dec. 10, 1965.

Maxwell, J. C., Jr., Cigarettes: Still bouncing back. [with table entitled] How the cigarette brands ranked in 1964 and 1963. *Printer's Ink.* 289: 21–2, December, 18–25, 1964.

———. Smokers light up less but habit bounces back. *Business Week.* p. 88–9, Dec. 12, 1964.

Medicine Section, *Time Magazine,* p. 17, April 23, 1956.

Medovy, H. Cigarettes, school children, and lung cancer. *J. Pediat.,* 63: 1060–1062, 1963.

Meigham, S. S., and others. Smoking: habits and beliefs of Oregon physicians. *J. Nat. Cancer Inst.* 35: 893–8, November, 1965.

Meiklejohn, A. Smoking and health. *Brit. Med. J.* 5292: 1618–9, June 9, 1962.

Melick, D. W. Please pass the cigarettes. *Arizona Med.* 23: 405–6, May, 1966.

Merry, J., and Preston, G. The effect of buffered lobeline sulfate on cigarette smoking. *Practitioner,* 190: 628–631, 1963.

Meylan, G. L. The effects of smoking on college students. *Pop. Science Monthly.* 77: 171, 1910.

———. The effects of tobacco on boys. *Med. Times,* Manhasset, 42: 171, 1914.

Migasham, J. Smoking: clinico-social problem. *Practitioner,* 168: 282–288, 1952.

Miley, R. A., and White, W. G. Giving up smoking. *Brit. Med. J.,* 1: 101, 1958.

Miller, Lois. The dilemma of the problem smoker. *Reader's Digest,* 63–68, May, 1965.

Miller, M. M. Benzedrine sulphate in the treatment of nicotinism. *Medical Rec.* 153: 137, 1941.

Miller, N. E. Fear as an acquirable drive. *J. Exp. Psychol.* 38: 89, 1948.

Mills, C. A. *This Air We Breathe.* Boston: Christopher, 1962.

———. Tobacco smoking: Some hints of its biologic hazards. *Ohio Med. J.,* 46: 1165–70, 1950.

———, and Porter, M. M. Tobacco-smoking habits and cancer of the mouth and respiratory system. *Cancer Res.* 10: 539–42, 1950.

Mills, C. A., and Porter, M. M. Tobacco-smoking habits in an American city. *J. Nat. Cancer Inst.,* 13: 1283–1297, 1953.

———, and ———. Tobacco smoking, motor exhaust fumes, and general air pollution in relation to lung cancer incidence. *Cancer Res.* 17: 981–90, 1957.

Milmore, B. K., and Conover, A. G. Tobacco consumption in the United States, 1880–1955. *Public Health Monogr.,* 45: 1–111, 1956.

Mitchell, R. S. Cigarette smoking, cigarette advertising, and health. *J. Sch. Hlth.* 251–259, Sept., 1960.

Mohr, W. D. Is smoking a process? *Control Eng.* 11: 83–5, April, 1964.

Monk, M., Tayback, M., and Gordon, J. Evaluation of an anti-smoking program among high school students. *Amer. J. Pub. Hlth.,* 55: 994–1004, 1965.

Moodie, W. Smoking, drinking, and nervousness. *Lancet* 2: 188–189, 1957.

Moore, G. E., and Vincent, R. G. Where do we go from here in research? Paper presented at the 94th Annual Meeting, American Public Health Association, San Francisco, California, November 2–4, 1966.

Morgan, A. C. Tobacco and scholarship. *Indus. Fd.,* 27: 276, 1926.

Morgan, W. K. The pernicious weed. *Maryland Med. J.* 12: 576–7, Nov., 1963.

Moring, G. Are the British ahead of us in research, recognition, and prevention of the hazards of smoking? *München Med. Wschr.* 104: 1837–9, 1962.

Morison, J. B. Cigarette smoking: Surveys and health education program in Winnipeg, Manitoba. *Canad. J. Pub. Hlth.,* 55: 16–22, 1964.

———, and Medovy, H. Smoking habits of Winnipeg school children. *Canad. Med. Assn. J.,* 84: 1006–1012, 1961.

———, ———, and MacDonnel, G. T. Health education and cigarette smoking: A report on a three-year program in the Winnipeg school division, 1960–1963. *Canad. Med. Assn. J.,* 91 (2): 49–56, July 11, 1964.

Mortality of doctors in relation to their smoking habits. *British Med. J.,* June, 1954.

Moses, F. M. Treating smoking habit by discussion and hypnosis. *Dis. Ner. Syst.,* 25: 184–188, 1964.

Moss, G. W. Smoking and health — the association and you. *Canad. J. Public Hlth.,* 46: 34–6, Jan., 1965.

Moyer, L. M., and others. A study of student attitudes toward smoking. Unpublished research report, Univ. of North Dakota, August, 1965.

Mulcahy, R., Hickey, N., and McDonald, M. A note on a quantitative method of recording cigarette smoking experience. *Irish J. Med. Sci.* 6: 301–4, July 1966.

———, and others. Cigarette smoking habits of patients with coronary heart disease. *Arch. Derm.* (Chicago) 94: 62–3, July, 1966.

———, and others. Public health aspects of cigarette smoking, with a note on public and professional attitudes. *J. Irish Med. Assn.* 58: 82–8, March, 1966.

Mulhall, J. C. Cigarette habit. *Ann. Otol. Rhin. and Laryng.,* 52: 714–721, Sept. 1943. This is a reprint of the original article that appeared in the Transactions of the American Laryngological Association, XVII, 192, 1895.

Murphy, T. H. Current status of cigarette smoking among Rhode Island physicians. *Rhode Island Med. J.* 46: 655–7, Dec., 1963.

Nagylucskay, S. The incidence of smoking. *Nepegeszsegugy* 42: 345–50. Nov., 1961.

Nahum, L. H. Breaking the cigarette habit. *Cancer Res.* 26: 575–9, April, 1966.

Nahum, L. H. Breaking the cigarette habit. *Conn. Med.* 30: 322–5, May, 1966.

Napolitano, L. Physiological and pathological effects of smoke. *Progr. Med.* (Nap.) 16: 734–6, Nov. 15, 1960.

Neuberger, M. B. *Smoke Screen: Tobacco and the Public Welfare.* New Jersey: Prentice-Hall, 1963.

New York (State) Senate. Special Committee on smoking and health report, pp. 22–7 (processed) bibl. Albany, N. Y., 1964.

Newman, Clarence, Breaking the habit: cigaret health furor spurs demand for items to help curb smoking. *Wall St. J.,* 162–1 + n12, 1963.

———. Tobacco in court: cigarette makers fear US report will spur smokers' damage suits. *Wall St. J.* 163: 1 Jan. 10, 1964.

Nicholls, A. G. Herba Panacea. *Canad. M.A.J.* 46: 277–281, March, 1942.

Nicotine and Tar Effects. *Science World,* March 28, 1962.

Nilson, E. Smoking habits among school children in Norway. *Brit. J. Prev. Soc. Med.,* 13: 5–13, 1959.

No immediate anti-smoking campaign ahead. *Chem. and Eng. N.,* 42: 24, Jan. 20, 1964.

Norgaard, A. Tobacco consumption in Denmark. The Danish National Morbidity Survey of 1950. Communication No. 15. *Dan. Med. Bull.,* 6: 54–8, 1959.

Northington, J. M. Cigarettes and lung cancer. [Editorial] *Clin. Med.,* 8: 1845–6, 1961.

Northrup, D. W. What to tell your young people about alcohol and narcotics. *W. Virginia Med. J.,* 59: 374–7, December, 1963.

Northrup, E. *Science Looks at Smoking: A New Inquiry Into the Effects of Smoking on Your Health.* New York: Coward-McCann, 1957.

Noshpitz, J. D. A smoking episode in a residential treatment unit. *Amer. J. Orthopsychiat.* 32: 69–81, 1962.

Nugent, S. M., and O'Keeffe, K. A. The treatment of addictive smokers. *Brit. J. Addict.,* 1965, 61: 125–128.

Observations on smoking. *New Eng. J. Med.,* 268: 54, Jan. 1963.

Ochsner, A. Comments of the surgeon. *Surg. Proceedings* 2 (3): 11–12, 1965.

———. *Smoking and Cancer: A Doctor's Report.* New York: J. Messner, 1954, 86 pp.

———. *Smoking and Health.* New York: J. Messner: 1959, 106 pp.

———. *Smoking and Your Life.* New York: J. Messner, 1964.

O'Donnell, L. G. Cigarettes fight back. *Wall Street Journal,* July 22, 1959.

Offord, D. R. The orbiting teenager — a seminar in problems with smoking, alcohol, and drug abuse. *Med. Times,* 93: 207–8, February, 1965.

Old salts or young lovers. Although there is an apparent lull in the cigarette market it will not last long. *Director* (Great Britain), 13: 226–9, February, 1961.

On smoking habits. Evaluation of a survey of 35,000 citizens of a municipal and rural county. *Deutsch Gesundh* 16: 2479–83, Dec. 28, 1961.

On taking snuff. *Brit. Med. J.* 1: 1155, 1950.

Open letter from a physician to his son. *Today's Health,* Nov., 1958.

Oppers, V. M., and others. Smoking habits in the Army. *Nederl. Milit. Geneisk.* I, 18: 115–9, April, 1965.

Osborne, R., and Benton, F. W. *Dying to Smoke.* Houghton Mifflin, 1964.

Otterland, A. Juvenile workers in Sweden. *Industr. Med. Surg.,* 33: 201–8, April, 1964.

Overholt, R. H. The physician's obligation in the smoking issue. *New York J. Med.,* 64: 1287–1300, 1964.

Owen, M. Smoking and smokers, and doctors in hospital (with a brief reference to nurses). Point of view, *Med. J. Aust.,* 1: 710, 1963.

Palmer, J. W. Smoking, caning, and delinquency in a secondary modern school. *Brit. J. Prev. Soc. Med.,* 19: 18–23, 1965.

Parnell, R. W. Smoking and cancer. *Lancet* 1: 963, 1951.

Parr, D. Smoking and psychiatric patients. [Correspondence] *Brit. Med. J.,* 1: 1611–2, 1963.

Parry, W. H. That smoking habit. *Nurs. Times,* 61: 964–967, 1965.

Peacock, P. R. Cigarette smoking experiments. *Brit Emp. Cancer Campaign,* 35th Ann. Rep., Part 2, 303 pp., 1957.

Pearl, R. Tobacco smoking and longevity. *Science,* pp. 216–217, 1938.

Peeples, W. A. A survey of smoking practices among employees of the California State Department of Public Health. *California's Health,* 22: 6: 41–44, Sept. 14, 1964.

Pel, P. K. Eine Tabakpsychoso bei oinom 13-jahrigen Knaben. *Berl. klin. Wschr.,* 48: 241, 1911.

Pell, S., and D'Alonso, C. A. Blood pressure, body weight, serum cholesterol, and smoking habits among executives and nonexecutives. *J. Occup. Med.* 3: 467–70, October, 1961.

Penn, W. G. Health education and smoking. *Chest Heart Bull.* 25: 101–3, 1962.

Perlstein, I. B. An approach to smoking deterrence in adolescence. *Southern Med. J.* 58: 1549–1553, December, 1965.

————. Smoking and its deterrence: a medical problem, presented as a scientific exhibit at the American Heart Association meeting (privately printed). New York: M. R. Thompson, 1963.

Perrin, M., and Bronte-Stewart, B. Taste perception in smokers and non-smokers. *Brit. Med. J.* 1: 384–386, 1961.

Perrin, M. J., and others. Smoking and food preferences. *Brit. Med. J.* 1: 387–8, 1961.

Pervin, L. A., and Dalrymple, W. Undergraduate smoking habits and related behavior. II. Attitudes toward the smoking-cancer relationship and personality traits. *J. Amer. Coll. Hlth. Assn.,* 13: 379–389, 1965.

Pervin, Lawrence and Yatko, R. Cigarette smoking and alternative methods of reducing dissonance. *J. Pers. & Soc. Psychol.* 2 (1): 30–36, 1965.

Peterson, W. F., and others. Smoking and prematurity. *Obstet. Gyn.* 26: 775–9, December, 1965.

Petmecky, B. *Confessions of a Tobacco Addict.* New York: Doubleday, 1962.

Petrie, C. R. Informative speaking: a summary and bibliography of related research. *Speech. Monogr.,* 30: 79–91, 1963.

Pezer, V. Teachers' habits and attitudes toward smoking (unpublished manuscript). A report prepared for the Department of National Health and Welfare. University of Saskatchewan. Sept., 1964.

Pflaum, J. H. Smoking behavior: a critical review of research. *J. Appl. Behav. Sci.,* 1: 195–209, 1965.

Pflaum, J. H. The psychology of smoking. *Psychol.,* 2: 44–58, 1965.

Phanishayi, R. A. Causes of smoking. *J. Educ. Psychol.,* Baroda, 9: 29–37, 1951.

Phillips, A. J. The relationship between smoking and health — a review of the evidence. *Canad. J. Public Health.* 55: 12–5, January, 1964.

Physique and smoking. *Brit. Med. J.* 5355: 456–7, August 24, 1963.

Pinto, Edward H. *Wooden Bygones of Smoking and Snuff Taking.* Newton Centre, Mass.: 1961.

Plakun, A. L., Ambur, J., and Bross, I. Clinical factors in smoking withdrawal: preliminary report. *Amer. J. Public Health.* 56: 434–41, 1966.

Platt, R. Smoking and Health. [Editorial] *J. Chronic Dis.* 15: 1001–2, 1962.

Plomp, N. A. C. ten Have and his anti-smoking campaign. *Nederl Milit Geneesk* I., 18: 111, April, 1965.

Porter, E. O. Cigarettes in the United States. *Southwestern Soc. Science Quarterly* 28: 64–75, 1947.

Porter, Muriel N. *Pipas precortesianas. Introd. de Chita de la Calle.* Mexico 1948. (Acta antropológica U. 3 No. 2).

Poussaint, A. F., Bergman, S. H., and Lichtenstein, E. The effects of physician's smoking on the treatment of smokers. *Dis. Nerv. Syst.* 27: 539–43, Aug., 1966.

Povorinsky, Y. A. Psychotherapy of smoking. In R. B. Winn (ed.), *Psychotherapy in the Soviet Union.* New York: Philosophical Library, 1961. pp. 144–152.

Powell, E. Breaking the defensive mechanisms. *Med. Officer.* 107: 228, 1962.

Premack, D. Toward empirical behavior laws: I. positive reinforcement. *Psychol. Rev.,* 66: 219–233, 1959.

Prescott, F. The smoking problem in Britain. *Appl. Ther.* 4: 1018–22, Nov., 1962.

Proosdij, C. Van. Smoking: its influence on the individual and its role in social medicine. Amsterdam: Elsevier Publishing Co., 1960.

Prothro, E. T. Identification of American, British, and Lebanese cigarettes. *J. Appl. Psychol.* 37: 54, 1953.

Psychological aspects of education related to smoking. *J. Consult. Psych.,* 30: 225–9, June, 1966.

Public persuasion in health matters with particular reference to smoking. *Proc. Roy. Soc. Med.* 57: 449–58, June, 1964.

Pygott, F. Changes in smoking habits, *Brit. J. Prev. Soc. Med.,* 18, 163–165, 1959-1963-1964.

Pyke, S., Agnew, N. M., and Kopperud, H. Modification of an overlearned maladaptive response through a learning program: A pilot study on smoking. *Bhav. Res. Ther.,* 4: 197–203, August, 1966.

Quick reference guide to report, smoking and health. Report of Advisory Committee to Surgeon General of Public Health Service. Public Health Service. HEW Dept. March, 1965.

Quigley, L. F., Cobb, C. M. and Hunt, E. E., Sr. Reverse smoking and its oral consequences in Caribbean and South American peoples. *J. Amer. Dent. Assn.* 69: 426–442, 1964.

Quinn, R. P. Cranberries, cigarettes, cancer, and cognitive dissonance. *Amer. Psychologist,* 16: 409, 1961.

Raaschou-Nielsen, E. Smoking habits in twins. *Danish Med. Bull.* 7: 82–8, 1960.

Ramond, C. K., Rachal, L. H., and Marks, M. R. Brand discrimination among cigarette smokers. *J. Appl. Psychol.* 34: 282–284, 1950.

The rapid increase of cigarette consumption in the United States. *Econ. World* 28: 515, Oct. 11, 1924.

Rapp, C. W., Dusza, B. T., and Blanchet, L. Absorption and utility of lobeline as a smoking deterrent. *Amer. J. Med. Sci.*, 237, 287, 1959.

———, and Olen, A. A. A critical evaluation of a lobeline-based smoking deterrent. *Amer. J. Med. Sci.* 230: 9, 1955.

———. Lobeline and nicotine. *Amer. J. Med. Sci.*, 230: 9, 1955.

Ravdon, I. S. Opinion and reason. *Surg. Gynec. Obstet.* 117: 497–8, October, 1963.

Raven, R. W. Smoking habits of schoolboys. *Lancet,* 1139–1141, June, 1957.

Ravenel, M. P. Tobacco and mental efficiency. *Amer. J. Pub. Health* 13: 763–776, 1923.

Ravenholt, R. T. Cigarette smoking: magnitude of the hazard. *Amer. J. Public Hlth.* 54: 1923–6, November, 1964.

———, and Applegate, J. R. Measurement of smoking experience. *New Eng. J. Med.,* 272: 789–790, Apr. 15, 1965.

Read, J., and Selby, T. Tobacco smoking and ventilatory function of the lungs. *Brit. Med. J.,* 2: 1104–8, 1961.

Reeves, W. E., and Morehouse, L. E. The acute effects of smoking upon the physical performance of habitual smokers. *Research Quarterly* 21: 245–248, 1950.

Registrar General for England and Wales. *Decennial Supplement on Occupational Mortality,* Part II, Vol. I., H. M. Stationery Office. (1958).

Reid, F. P. Tobacco habit (medical aspects). *South African J. Clinic. Sc.* 4: 106–110 June, 1953.

Reitynbarg, D. I. Smoking and health. *Soviet Zdravookhr.* 24: 78–80, 1965.

Rele, J. R. Demographic approach to the problem of the connexion between lung cancer and smoking. *Brit. J. Prev. Soc. Med.* 14: 181–4, 1960.

Rice, J. R. *Tobacco: Is Its Use a Sin?* Murfreesboro, Tennessee: Sword of the Lord, n.d.

Richards, H. J., and Crowdy, J. P. Smoking habits of young soldiers. *Brit. J. Prev. Soc. Med.* 15: 84–8, 1961.

Riess, B. J. Whither Ortho- or Ortho withers: The mental health of the mental health professions and professionals. *Amer. J. Orthopsychiat.,* 36: 591–594, 1966.

Rigdon, R. H. Consideration of the relationship of smoking to lung cancer: With a review of the literature. *Southern Med. J.* 50: 524–32, 1957.

———. The smoking controversy. *J.A.M.A.* 173: 293–5, May 21, 1960.

———, and Kirchoff, H. Smoking and disease: a study based on 12,050 individuals. *Texas Rep. Biol. Med.* 16: 116–32, 1958.

Rizk, A. M. Smoking among adolescents: an objective study. *Egypt. J. Psychol.* 3, 1947.

Robert, J. C. *Story of Tobacco in America.* Durham, N.C.: Duke University Press, 1938.

Robicsek, M. U. H. Eine neue Therapie der Nikotinsucht oder die Kunst, das Rauchen zu lassen. *Fortschr. Med.* (Ger.) 50: 1014–5, 1932.

Rogers, K. D., and Reese, G. Smoking and high-school performance. *Amer. J. Dis. Child.* 108: 117–121, 1964.

Rosenberg, A. An attempt to break the smoking habit. *Appl. Ther.* 4: 1029–33, Nov., 1962.

———. Attempt at stopping the tobacco habit. *Ugeskr Laig* 122: 714–8, 1960.

Rosenblatt, M. B. Sex distribution, longevity, smoking and lung cancer. *J. Amer. Geriat. Soc.* 14: 711–5, July, 1966.

Roth, Grace M. *Tobacco and the Cardiovascular System.* Springfield, Ill.: Charles C. Thomas, 1951.

———, McDonald, J. B., and Sheard, C. Effect of smoking cigarets and of intravenous administration of nicotine on electrocardiogram, basal metabolic rate, cutaneous temperature, blood pressure and pulse rate of normal persons. *J.A.M.A.* 125: 761–67, July 15, 1944.

Roussel, J. M. Alcoholism, the tobacco habit, and drug addiction. *Am. Med. Canada.* (Fr.) 89: 489–92, April, 1960.

Rowland, J. F. Tobacco and health. *J. Roy. Inst. Public Health* 26: 251–65, Oct., 1963.

Royal College of Physicians. *Smoking and Health.* London: Pitman Medical Publ. Co., 1962.

Ruesch, J. Social technique, social status, and social change, in illness. In Kluckhohn, C. & Murray, H. A. (Eds.), *Personality in Nature, Society, and Culture.* New York: Alfred A. Knopf, 1956. 2nd ed., pp. 123–36.

Rukeyser, W. S. European cigaret sales climb despite 'ad bans, anti-smoking drives. Foreign trends may give clue to impact of newly issued U.S. Surgeon General study. *Wall St. J.* 163: 1+, Jan. 13, 1964.

Russ, S. *Smoking and Its Effects.* New York: MacMillan, 1956.

———. Smoking and its effects: with special reference to lung cancer. *Hutchinson's Scientific & Technical Publications* (London), p. 141, 1955.

Russek, H. J. Stress, tobacco and coronary disease in North American professional groups. *J. Amer. Med. Assn.* 189–94, 1965.

———. Tobacco consumption and emotional stress in the etiology of coronary heart disease. *Geriatrics* 19 (6): 425–33, 1964.

Russell, R. J. Are health educators "warriors against pleasure"? *J. Sch. Health* 33: 201–4, 1963.

Rutstein, D. D. An open letter to Dr. Clarence Cook Little. *Atlantic,* 200, 41–3, 1957. (Reprinted *Can. Bull. Cancer Progress,* 8: 46–8, 1958.)

———, and Conover, A. G. Tobacco smoking in the U.S. in relation to income. *U.S.D.A. Market. Res. Rpt.* 189: 1957.

Sackrin, S. M. Factors affecting demand for cigarettes. Economic Research Service, Agr. Dept. Agriculture Economic Report, August, 1962.

Salber, Eva J. Infant orality and smoking. *J. Amer. Med. Assn.* 187: 368–69, 1964.

———. Smoking among school children. *Amer. J. Publ. Hlth.* 52: 1017–18, 1962.

———, and Abelin, T. Smoking by Newton High School students: follow-up study. Paper presented at a meeting of the Epidemiology and School Health Sections, American Public Health Association, San Francisco, November 2, 1966.

————, Goldman, E., Buka, M., and Welsh, B. Smoking habits of high-scool students in Newton, Mass. *New Eng. J. Med.* 265: 969–74, 1961.

————, and MacMahon, B. Cigarette smoking among high-school students related to social class and parental smoking habits. *Amer. J. Pub. Hlth.* 51: 1780–89, 1961.

————, ————, and Harrison, Sarah V. Influence of siblings on student smoking patterns. *Pediatrics* 31: 569–72, 1963.

————, ————, and Welsh, Barbara. Smoking habits of high school students related to intelligence and achievement. *Pediatrics* 29: 780–787, 1962.

————, Reed, R. B., Harrison, S. V., and Green, J. H. Smoking behavior, recreational activities, and attitudes toward smoking among Newton secondary school children. *Pediatrics* 32: 911–918, 1963.

————, and Rochman, J. E. Personality differences between smokers and nonsmokers. *Arch. Environmental Hlth.* 8: 459–465, 1964.

————, Welsh, B., and Taylor. S. U. Reasons for smoking given by secondary school children. *J. Hlth. Hum. Behavior* 4 (2): 118–129, 1963.

————, and Worcester, Jane. Change in women's smoking patterns. *Cancer* 17: 32–36, 1964.

Sallak, V. J. A study of smoking practices of selected groups of junior and senior high school students in public schools in Erie County, New York. *J. Sch. Hlth.* 31: 307–314, 1961.

Salter, A. The addictions. In: *Conditioned Reflex Therapy.* New York: Creative Age Press, 1949. pp. 188–219.

Samp, R. J. Wisconsin physicians and cigarette smoking. *Wisconsin Med. J.* 62: 229, May, 1963.

Schmidt, F. Cigarettes, the most important single cause of death. *Aerztl Forsch* (Ger.) 19: 421–32, August 10, 1965.

Schneider, Elsa. Surgeon General's Report on smoking: Call for action; What part will schools play? Education Office. HEW Dept. 1964. Reprint from *School Life* Aug., 1964.

Schneider, J. A., and Sundermann, E. Smoking habits of Berlin physicians. *Aerztl. Wschr.* 15: 118–23, 1960.

Schoenberg, E. H. The demand curve for cigarettes. *J. Bus.* 6: 15–35, January, 1933.

Schrumpf, Pierron, P. *Tobacco and Physical Efficiency: a Digest of Clinical Data.* N. Y.: Hoeber, 1927.

Schubert, D. S. P. Arousal seeking as a central factor in tobacco smoking among college students. *Int. J. Soc. Psychiat.,* 221–225, 1965 (Summer).

————. Arousal seeking as a motivation for volunteering: MMPI scores and central-nervous-system-stimulant use as suggestive of a trait. *J. Proj. Tech. & Pers. Assess.* 28: 337–340, 1964.

————. Personality implications of cigarette smoking among college students. *J. Consult. Psychol.* 23: 376, 1959.

Scott, G. W., Cox, A. G. C., Maclean, K. S., Price, T. M. L., and Southwell, N. Buffered lobeline as a smoking deterrent. *Lancet* 1: 54–5, 1962.

Sehnert, K. W. Profile of a smoker. *CA.* 14: 88, 1964.

Seltzer, C. Masculinity and smoking. *Science* 130: 1706–1707, 1959.

————. Morphologic constitution and smoking. *J. Amer. Med. Assn.* 183: 639–645, 1963.

————. Occupation and smoking in college graduates. *J. Appl. Psychol.* 48: 1–6, 1964.

————. Why people smoke. *Appl. Therap.,* 4: 1023–1024, 1962.

————. Why people smoke. *Atlantic. Mon.* 41–44, July, 1962.

Senator Ribicoff attacks smoking report. *Chem. and Eng. N.* 42: 37, March 2, 1964.

Shaffer, Helen B. Smoking and health. *Editorial Research Repts.* 815–31, November 14, 1962.

Sheard, C. The effects of smoking on the dark adaptation of rods and cones. *Fed. Proc.* 5: 94, 1946.

Shift in cigarette preferences: how cigarette brands did in 1949. *Business Week* p. 60, Jan. 21, 1950.

Short, J. J., Johnson, H. J. and Ley, H. A., Jr. The effects of toabcco smoking on health. A study of 2,031 medical records. *J. Lab. Clin. Med.* 24: 586–9, 1939.

Signorini, L. F. Smoking habits among students of secondary schools in Florence. *Ann. Sanit. Pubblica.* (Italian) 24: 45–91, Jan.-Feb., 1964.

Silvette, H., Larson, P. S., and Haag, H. B. Medical uses of tobacco past and present. *Virginia Med. Monthly* 85: 472–84, 1958.

Simon. D. L., and Iglauer, A. The acute effect of chewing tobacco and smoking in habitual users. *Ann. N. Y. Acad. Sci.* 90: 119–132, 1960.

————, ————, and Braunstein, Jr. The immediate effect of cigarettes on the circulation of healthy and habitual male smokers. *American Heart Journal* 48: 185, 1954.

Simon, W., and Lucero, R. J. Consumption of mentholated cigarettes by alcoholics. *Dis. Nerv. Syst.* 21: 313–4, 1960.

Sinnot, J. J., and Rauth, J. E. Effect of smoking on taste threshold. *J. Gen. Psychol.* 17: 151–53, 1937.

Skinner, B. F. Contingencies of reinforcement in the design of a culture. *Behavioral Science* 11 (3): 159–166, 1966.

Slinin, S. N. Smoking and health (Result of a survey). *Klin. Med.* (Mosk.) 38: 105–9, October, 1960.

————. Smoking and health, USSR. *Joint Publications Research Service* Dec. 20, 1964.

Slough, H. H. The dentist's role in the five-day plan. *J. Nat. Assoc. Seventh Day Advent. Dent.* 8: 8 *passim,* Spring, 1966.

Smith, G. M. Personality correlates of cigarette smoking in students of college age. Presented at the N. Y. Academy of Sciences Conf. on "The Effects of Nicotine and Smoking on the Central Nervous System." Unpublished manuscript received May, 1966.

Smith, L. W. Smoking and your health. A review of the filtration concept in its practical applications. *New York Physician* 56(5): 42–7, 1961.

Smith, N. GSR measures of cigarette smokers' temporal approach and avoidance gradients. *Psychol. Rec.* 15: 261–268, 1965.

Smith, S., Thakurdas, H., and Lawes, T. G. Perceptual isolation and schizophrenia. *J. Ment. Sci.* 107: 839–844, 1961.

Smoking among school children. [Editorial] *Am. J. Pub. Health* 52: 1017–19, June, 1962.

Smoking and death rates. *American Scientist* (Nor.) December, 1958.

Smoking and health. *T. Norsk. Laegeforen* (Nor.) 84: 938–40, June, 1964.

Smoking and Health: Report of the Advisory Committee to the Surgeon General of the Public Health Service. Washington, D.C.: U.S. Dept. Hlth., Educ. and Welf., 1964. (Publ. Health Serv. Publ. No. 1103).

Smoking and health research. Report from Committee on Agriculture to accompany H. J. Res. 915. House Reports on public bills. Feb. 7, 1964.

Smoking and Health: The report of the Royal College of Physicians. Some comments. *Med. Proc.* (Johannesb.) 8: 145–51, April 21, 1962.

Smoking and lung cancer: recent evidence and a discussion of some questions. *Journal of the National Cancer Institute* January, 1959.

Smoking and mortality. *Med. J. Aust.* 2: 423–4, September 12, 1964.

Smoking and news: coverage of a decade of controversy, has American journalism given a full, fair, and intelligent account of the complex debate over the effects of smoking on health? The staff of the Review inspects evidence since 1953 and offers preliminary answers. *Columbia Journalism R.* 2: 6–12, Summer, 1963.

Smoking and sense. *New York J. Med.* 64: 1174–5, May, 1964.

Smoking deterrent study. A report from the Research Committee of the British Tuberculosis Association. *Brit. Med. J.* 2: 486–7, 1963.

Smoking Habits of Canadians. Report of a survey carried out by the Dominion Bureau of Statistics for the Department of National Health and Welfare, Aug., 1964.

Smoking habits of college students. *Univ. Chicago Sch. Bus. N. Bul.* 3: 35–7, March 26, 1940.

The smoking habits of school children. Group study of the Public Health Department, London School of Hygiene and Tropical Medicine. *Brit. J. Prev. Soc. Med.* 13: 1–4, 1959.

Smoking habits of young soldiers. *Brit. J. Prev. Soc. Med.* 15: 84–8, April, 1961.

Smoking, health, and a giant industry. *US News* 55: 84–6, D. 2, 1963.

Smoking on the rise again. *U.S. News* p. 30, Oct. 14, 1965.

Smoking report. *Scientific American* 210: 66–7, 1964.

Smoking scare? What's happened to it. [Editorial] *U.S. News and World Report* 58: 38–41, 1965.

Smoking: urgent need for combined action. [Points of view] *Lancet* 1: 530–2, 1962.

Smyth, D. A. Experience with an anti-smoking clinic. *J. Coll. Ten Pract.* 11: Suppl. 2: 8–16, March, 1966.

Snegireff, L. S., and Lombard, O. M. Comparative study of smoking habits of physicians. *New Eng. J. Med.* 252: 691–696, 1955.

———, and ———. Smoking habits of Massachusetts physicians. *New Eng. J. Med.* 261: 603–604, 1959.

———, and ———. Survival of Massachusetts physicians according to smoking habits. *Cancer* 16: 212-7, 1963.

Sorensen, B. F. Possibility of breaking the tobacco habit. *Ugeskr Laig* 126: 1277–8, Sept. 10, 1964.

Spence, P., and Ehrenberg, B. Effects of oral deprivation on responses to subliminal and supraliminal verbal food stimuli. *J. Abnorm. Soc. Psychol.* 69: 10–18, 1964.

Sprague, H. B. Environment in relation to coronary artery disease. *Arch. Environ. Health* (Chicago) 13: 4–12, July, 1966.

———. What I tell my patients about smoking *Mod. Conc. Cardiov. Dis.* 33: 881–4, Oct., 1964.

Sramkova, J. and others. Smoking and mental hygiene. *Activ. Nerv. Sup.* (Praha) 6: 109–10, 1964.

———, and others. Smoking as a factor of mental hygiene in relation to prevention, origin, and therapy of neuroses. *Activ. Nerv. Sup.* (Praha) 7: 204, 1965.

Stanton, T. Tobacco's troubled road. *Wall Street Journal* 165: 20, Jan. 8, 1965.

Stapleton, J. E. The anti-cigarette campaign — A wholesome effort? *Nova Scotia Med. Bull.* 42: 166–8, 1963.

Starkie, C. Can we stop smoking? [Correspondence] *Med. Officer* 107: 43, 1962.

Staszevski, J. Is the hazard of cancer increased by smoking? *Wiad Lek.* (Polish) 18: 1333–4, August 15, 1965.

———. Smoking and cancer in Poland. *Brit. J. Cancer* 14: 419–36, 1960.

Statement of the American Cancer Society on cigarette smoking and lung cancer, *J. A. M. A.* Vol. 172: 13, 1960.

Statement on cigarette smoking and health. Minutes of the Board of Directors Meeting, Nat'l Tuberculosis Assn., Feb. 27, 1960.

Steinbart, H. Historical note on tobacco smoking *Med. Klin.* 56: 26–7, Jan., 1961.

Stern, G. S., Lana, R. E., and Pauling, F. J. Fear arousal and order of presentation of persuasive communications, Part I. *Psychological Reports* 16 (3): 789–795, 1965.

Stewart, L., and Levison, N. Smoking and rebelliousness: A longitudinal study from childhood to maturity. *J. Consulting Psychol.* 30 (3): 225–229, 1966.

Stocker, R. B. Smoking and restless young men. [Correspondence] *Lancet* 1: 797, 1958.

Stocks, P. Town-dwelling, smoking, and cancer. [Annotations] *Brit. Med. J.* 1: 33–4, 1958.

Stop smoking! *Brit. Med. J.* 5338: 1106, Apr., 1963.

Stouffer, S. A., Guttman, L., and Suchman, E. A. *Studies in Social Psychology in World War II. IV. Measurement and Prediction.* Princeton, N.J.: Princeton Univ. Press, 1950, p. 121.

Strahlmann, E. Scandaniavian physicians against smoking. *Landarzt* 40: 161, Feb. 10, 1964.

———. The dangers of cigarette smoking for the female sex, *Landarzt* (Ger.) 41: 688, June 10, 1965.

Straits, B. C. *Sociological and Psychological Correlates of Adoption and Discontinuation of Cigarette Smoking: A Report to the Council for Tobacco Research U.S.A.* Chicago: The University of Chicago, 1965.

———, and Sechrest, L. Further support of some findings about the characteristics of smokers and nonsmokers. *J. Consult. Psychol.* 27: 282, 1963.

Strecker, H. P. Review of 1949/50 literature of addiction. *Brit. J. Addict.* 48: 3–119 (January-July) 1951.

Streit, W. K. Motivating motivators. *The Phys. Ed.* 23: 74–76, 1966.

Strnad, L., Fingerland, A., and Novakova, H. Some sociological and medical aspects of smoking. *Cesk. Zdrav.* 14: 89–95, 1966.

Study group on smoking and health. Smoking and health: Joint report on the study group on smoking and health. *Science* 125: 1129–1133, 1957.

Stunart, L. and others. Smoking and rebelliousness, *J. Call. Gen. Pract.* 11: Suppl. 2: 57–8 Mar. 1966.

Success in cancer education. *Canad. Med. Assn. J.* 89: 1294–5 December 21, 1963.

Swinehart, J. W. and Kirscht, John P. Smoking: A panel study of beliefs and behavior following the PHS report. *Psychological Reports* 18 (2): 519–528, 1966.

Swinford, O., Jr., and Ochota, L. Smoking and chronic respiratory disorders. Results of abstinence. *Ann. Allerg.* 16: 455–8, 1958.

Tackling the smoker — a health problem for local authorities; a ban in public places? *Munic. J.* (Great Britain) 70: 1227–8, April 27, 1962.

Tacon, P. H. B. *A Comparison of Attitudes Toward The Effects of Smoking and Personality Variables of Smokers and Non-Smokers in a Population of University Students.* Summary, Conclusions, and Bibliography. Canada: University of New Brunswick.

Tate, E. I., and others. Seventy per cent of Florida physicians are nonsmokers. *J. Florida Med. Assn.* 52: 47–8 Jan., 1965.

Taylor, G. B. A survey of health education and smoking. *Med. Officer* 156–157, March 15, 1963.

Taylor, H. C., Jr. Physicians and cigarette smoking. *J.A.M.A.* 181: 777–8, Sept. 1, 1962.

Taylor, R. Who should lead fight-against-the-killer-week? *Appl. Ther.* 5: 597–8, July, 1963.

Teen-age antismoking campaign in Denmark. *CA* 11: 56–7, 1961.

Teenagers and cigarettes. [Editorial] *Kiplinger Magazine,* March, 1962.

Teenagers and cigarets. Educational campaign to inform adolescents and young adults of the dangers and to give them facts upon which they can base a decision about whether or not they are going to smoke. *Changing Times,* March, 1962.

Terry, L. L. Smoking and Health. *Progr. Clin. Cancer* 1: 538–42, 1965.

———. Where do we go from here with smoking control programs? Paper presented at the 94th Annual Meeting of the American Public Health Association in San Francisco, California, November 2, 1966.

Text of findings on smoking, health risks, text of the "Summaries and conclusions" chapter on smoking and health of the report of the advisory committee to the Surgeon General released Jan. 11, 1964. *Cong. Q. W. Report* 22: 125–30, January 17, 1964.

Thakurdas, H. Smoking and psychiatric patients. [Correspondence] *Brit. Med. J.* 2: 388, 1963.

There ought to be a law. *Rocky Mountain Med. J.* 60: 23–4, Oct., 1963.

Thomas, C. B. Characteristics of smokers compared with nonsmokers in a population of healthy young adults including observations on family history, blood pressure, heart rate, bodyweight, cholesterol and certain psychological traits. *Ann. Intern. Med.* 53: 697–718, 1960.

———, and Cohen, B. H. Comparison of smokers and nonsmokers. *Bull. Johns Hopkins Hosp.* 106: 205–14. April, 1960.

Thompson, C. W. Cigarette smoking and lung cancer, *Journal of Health, Physical Education and Recreation* pp. 29–32, Dec. 1957.

———. Let's teach the real facts about smoking. *J. of Amer. Assn. for Hlth., Phy. Ed. and Rec.,* pp. 19–21, Jan. 1954.

———. Thompson smoking and tobacco knowledge test. *Res. Quarterly* 35 (1): 60–68, 1964.

———, and Johnson, D. Thompson smoking and tobacco knowledge and test results. *Minnesota State Assoc. Health, Phys. Ed. and Rec. Newsletter* May, 1961.

Thompson, D. S. Survey of college health directors regarding smoking. *J. Amer. Coll. Health Ass.* 11: 312–25, 1963.

———, and Wilson, T. R. Discontinuance of cigarette smoking: "natural" and with "therapy." *J.A.M.A.* 196: 1048–1052, 1966.

Tobacco and Health. *Bull. N. Y. Acad. Med.* 41: 404–5, April, 1965.

Tobacco and teenagers. [Editorial] *Rhode Island Med. J.* 46: 155, 1963.

Tobacco situation. Dept. of Agriculture, Economic Research Service, 1965.

Todd, G. Statistics of smoking. Research paper No. 1. London: Tobacco Manufacturers' Standing Committee, 1959.

———, and Laws, J. T. The reliability of statements about smoking habits. Research paper No. 2. London: Tobacco Manufacturers' Standing Committee, 1959.

———, and Mason, J. L. Concordance of smoking habits in monozygotic and dizygotic twins. *Heredity,* 13: 417, 1959.

Tokukata, G. K. Familial factors in human lung cancer and smoking. *Amer. J. Pub. Hlth.* 54: 24–32, 1964.

Tomkins, S. S. Psychological model for smoking behavior. Presented at the 93rd Annual Meeting of the American Public Health Association in Chicago, Illinois, October, 20, 1965. Unpublished paper.

———. Theoretical implications and guidelines to future research. In Mausner, B., and Platt, Ellen (eds.). Behavioral Aspects of Smoking: A Conference Report. *Health Education Monographs,* Supplement 2, 1966.

Tompkins, R. K., and Samovar, L. A. An experimental study of the effects of credibility on the comprehension of content. *Speech Monogr.* 31: 120–123, 1964.

Tooley, R. W. Survey of opinions and actions concerning smoking and health among medical officers and nursing sisters of the Canadian Forces Medical Service. *Med. Service J. Canad.* 21: 113–6, February, 1965.

Trahair, R. C. Cigarette Smoking in Melbourne. *Med. J. Aust.* 2: 741–6 October 30, 1965.

Trask, Rev. Thoughts and stories for American lads or Uncle Toby's antitobacco advice to his nephew Billy Bruce, 1852. In: Van Proosdij, C. *Smoking: Its Influence on the Individual and Its role in Social Medicine.* New York: Elsevier, 1960.

Trcala, J. Pathophysiology and psychopathology of smoking. *Casopis lekaru Ceskych.* (Czech.) 102: 977–980, 1963. Trans. Div. Foreign Techn. Div., Wright-Patterson AFB, Ohio, FTD-TT 64–264.

Troemel, R. G., Davis, R. T., and Hedley, C. D. Dark adaption as a function of caffeine and nicotine administration. *Proc. S. Dak. Acad. Sci.* 30: 79–84, 1951.

Truex, E. H. Letter to the editor: Teenage smoking. *Conn Med.* 27: 219, Apr., 1963.

Turle, G. C. An investigation into the therapeutic action of hydroxyzine (atarax) in the teatment of nervous disorders and the control of the tobacco habit. *J. Mental Sci.* 104: 826–833, 1958.

Underhill, R. M. *Singing for Power.* Berkeley, Calif.: University of California Press, 1938.

Underwood, P. B., Kesler, K. F., O'Lane, J. M., and Callagan, D. A. Parental smoking empirically related to pregnancy outcome. Unpublished manuscript sent to Dr. Clarke by Dr. Underwood, National Naval Med. Center, Bethesda, Md. June, 1966.

Ungar, S. D. *Anyone Can Stop Smoking.* Santa Monica, California: Goodwin Co., 1964.

U.S. Department of Commerce, Bureau of the Census. Tobacco consumption per capita, 15 years and over, in the United States by calendar years. *State. Abstr. of the U.S.,* Washington, D.C.: U.S. Government Printing Office, p. 796, 1962.

U.S. House Committee on Agriculture. *Smoking and Health Research: Report.* Feb. 7, 1964 (to accompany H.R. res. 915) (88th congress 2nd session) H. rept. no. 1135, 1964.

U.S. House Committee on Agriculture subcommittee on tobacco. Tobacco research laboratory hearings, Jan. 29-31, 1964 on H.J. res. 885, H.S. res. 891 H.J. res 894. (88th Congress 2nd session.) The economics of the American tobacco industry and the possibility of instituting a program of research into the health factors involved in smoking.

U.S. leads in cigarette smoking. *Mid-Mo. R. Bus.* p. 6, Nov. 17, 1927.

U.S. Public Health Service. Note on report of continuing statistical survey of smoking as reported at the Seventh International Cancer Congress, London, July 8, 1958. *Public Health Rep.* 73: 714, 1958.

The U.S. sums it up: quit smoking: report of the surgeon general offers little in new research material, but its conclusions are tough: smoking is a major cause of lung cancer and other diseases. *Bus. Week* pp. 42 ff. January 18, 1964.

United States House Committee on Govt. operations. False and misleading advertising (filter cigarettes): 20th report, 1958. iii + 25 pp. tables (85th congress 2nd session H. report no. 1372) (Union calendar no. 539).

Vallance, T. R. Suggestibility of smokers and nonsmokers. *Psychol. Rec.* 4: 138–144, 1940.

Van Dellen, T. R. The tobacco problem. *Illinois Med. J.* 125: 129–32, Feb., 1964.

Van Meurs, J. H. Significance of smoking and opposition to it. *T. Soc. Geneesk.* (Dutch) 42: 440–2, June, 1964.

Van Proosdij, C., and others. An inquiry into the smoking habits in 24 primary schools of Amsterdam. *Nederl. T. Geneesk.* 102: 902–5, 1958.

———. *Smoking: Its Influence on the Individual and Its Role in Social Medicine.* Amsterdam: Elsevier, 1960.

———. Tobacco habit and health. *Nederl. T. Geneesk.* 102: 1808–12; 1958-63, 1958.

Verde, J. C. L., and Folco, J. A. A. Frecuencia de los hábitos tóxicos según el sexo y su coincidencia con alteraciones patológicas. [Incidence of toxic habits according to sex and its coincidence with pathological changes.] *Dia Med., Buenos Aires* 31: 115–116, 1959.

Vincent, R. G. Smoking among students. *J. Amer. Coll. Hlth. Assn.* 13: 235–41, Dec., 1964.

Vitz, P. C. and Johnson, D. Masculinity of smokers and the masculinity of cigarette images. *J. Appl. Psychol.* 49: 155–159, 1965.

Von Dedenroth, T. E. Further help for the "tobaccomaniac." *Amer. J. Clin. Hypn.* 6: 332–336, 1964.

———. The use of hypnosis with "tobaccomaniacs." *Amer. J. Clin. Hypn.* 6: 326–331, 1964.

Von Verschuer, F. Twin research from the time of Francis Galton to the present day. *Proc. Roy. Soc. B.* 128: 68–81, 1939.

Voorst, Vader P. J. Van. Relations between smoking and mortality in the Netherlands during 1963. *Nederl. T. Geneesk.* (Dut.) 109: 601–8, March 27, 1965.

Wake, F. R., Moore, R. J., and Boothe, B. S. Socio-psychological aspects of cigarette smoking. Report to the Dept. of National Health and Welfare, Canadian Smoking and Health program, Dept. of National Health and Welfare, Ottawa, January, 1966. (Unpublished manuscript)

Wakefield, J. The organization of public education about cancer. *Monthly Bull. Minist. Health* (London) 21: 82–8, 1962.

Wakerlin, G. Cigarette smoking and the role of the physician. *Circulation* 29: 651–6, May, 1964.

Walster, Elaine, and Festinger, L. The effectiveness of "overhead" persuasive communications. *J. Abnorm. Soc. Psychol.* 65: 395–402, 1962.

Ward, W. Cigarette smoking among pupils in Rock Island County schools, grade 7 through 12. A joint Project of the Rock Island County Unit of the American Cancer Society and the Department of Sociology of Augustana College, Rock Island, Ill., 1964.

Ware, E. W. How to stop smoking and why. *Maryland Med. J.* 11: 290–3, June, 1962.

Warwick, K. M. An experimental study of the effects of nicotine on certain psychological functions. Unpublished Ph.D. thesis, Univer. of London, 1963.

———, and Eysenck, H. J. The effect of smoking on the DFF threshold. *Life Sci.* 4: 219–225, 1963.

———, and ———. The effects of smoking on the CF threshold. *Life Science* 4: 219–225, 1963.

Watkins, S. C. *Pleasures of Smoking.* New York: Abelard-Schuman, Ltd., 1948.

Watne, A. L. A cigarette information program. *J.A.M.A.,* 188: 872–4, Jun., 1964.

Weatherley, D. Some personality correlates of the ability to stop smoking cigarettes. *Journal of Consulting Psychology* 29 (5): 483–485, 1965.

Weaver, J. D. Capsule history of tobacco. *Holiday* 31: 76–77, 1962.

Weber, C. *Pleasures of Pipe Smoking.* Camden, N. J.: Nelson and Sons, 1965.

Weber's Guide to Pipes and Pipe Smoking. New York: Cornerstone Library, Inc.

Wechsler, R. L. Effects of cigarette smoking and intravenous nicotine on the human brain. *Fed. Proc.* 17: 169 (Abstract), 1958.

Wegener, H. Smoking as the expression of the claim of importance in young people. *Aesthet. Med.* (Berlin) 14: 338–43, December, 1965.

Wegman, R. A. Cigarettes and health. Tables. *Cornell Law.* 2 (51): 678–759. Summer, 1966.

Weiss, R. F., Buchanan, W., and Pasamanick, B. Social consensus in persuasive communication. *Psychol. Rep.* 14: 95–98, 1964.

Weiss, W. A "sleeper" effect in opinion change. *J. Abnorm. Soc. Psychol.* 48: 173–180, 1953.

Wellmann, K. F. Smoking and health. On the report of the Advisory Committee to the Surgeon General of the Public Health Service. *Deutsch. Med. Wschr.* (Ger.) 98: 1085–6, May, 1964.

Wenusch, A., and Scholler, R. Uber den Einflus des Rauchens auf die Reizschwelle des Drucksinnes. *Med. Klinik.* 32: 356–358, 1936.

Werner, E. Smoking habits. Evaluation of a survey of 35,-000 citizens of a municipal and rural county. *Deutsch Gesundh.* 16: 2479–83, 1961.

West, G. A. Tobacco, pipes, and smoking customs of the American Indians. Milwaukee, Wis., Pub. by order of the Board of Trustees 1934 (Bulletin of the Public Museum of the city of Milwaukee. Vol. XVII, June 11, 1934.)

What should smokers do now? *Med. Mschr.* (Ger.) 18: 49–50, Feb., 1964.

Wheller, E. *Tested Ways to Stop Smoking.* Ernstrom, 1964.

Whiskin, F. E., Dibner, A. S., and Rhudick, P. J. Psychological, cultural, and health characteristics of aging smokers and nonsmokers. *J. of Gerontology* 17: 69–74, 1961.

White, M. E. Cigarette smoking. *Med. World* (London) 97: 489–90, Dec., 1962.

Whitlow, C. M. The prevalence of smoking and drinking among high school pupils. *Sch. & Soc.* 36: 177–178, 1932.

Why is the smoking public changing its cigarette preferences? *Sales Management* 38: 830–1, June 1, 1936.

Why people smoke. [Annotations] *Lancet* 2: 250–1, 1958.

Wiggersen and Kohan, Relationship of smoking to respiratory complaints, *Canadian Medical Association Journal pp.* 585–587, Sept. 10, 1960.

Wilde, G. Behavior therapy for addicted cigarette smokers: A preliminary investigation. *Behav. Res. Ther.* 1964.

William-Olsson, L. Experiences in breaking the smoking habit. *Svensk Lakartidn* (Sw.) 61: 1547–9, May, 1964.

———. On breaking the smoking habit, some experiences. *Svensk. Farm. T.,* (Sw.) 68: 475–7, June, 1964.

Winsor, A. L., and Richards, S. J. The development of tolerance for cigarettes. *J. Exp. Psychol.* 18: 113–120, 1935.

Winstanley, D. P. Smoking and health. *Deutsch. Med. Wschr.* 87: 1210, June 8, 1962.

Wishik, S. D. Should our children pay for cigarette commercials? *Ped.* 31, 1963.

With filters, record cigarette sales [1957 and 1958 estimates]. *Business Week* pp. 49–50, Dec. 27, 1958.

Wolfe, P. O. Sobre el tobaco y la costumbre de fumar. (Tobacco and the custom of smoking) *An. Soc. Cient Argent.* 143: 25–48, 1947.

Wolman, I. J. Smoking and the pediatrician. *Clin. Pediat.* (Phila.) 3: 255–6, May, 1964.

Wolman, W. A. A study of cigarettes, cigarette smoke, and filters. *J. Amer. Med. Ass.* 917, 1953.

Woodruff, A. B., James, W. H., and Werber, W. The effect of internal and external control upon changes in smoking behavior following the government report on smoking. Paper presented at Midwestern Psychological Assoc., 1964.

Wootten, H. M. Cigarettes' high ceiling. *Printers Ink. Mo.* pp. 5–8, Feb., 1941.

Wrather, S. E. *Cigarette Outlook.* Production and Marketing Administration. Agri. Dept. (before National Tobacco Tax Assoc.) Sept. 14, 1953.

———. *Outlook for Cigarette Consumption.* Agriculture Marketing Service. Agri. Dept. (before National Tobacco Tax Assoc.) Sept. 10, 1956.

Wright, I. S., and Littauer, D. Lobeline sulfate, its pharmacology and use in treatment of the tobacco habit. *J.A.M.A.* 109: 649–654, 1937.

Wyckoff, V. J. *Tobacco Regulation in Colonial Maryland.* Baltimore: Johns Hopkins Press, 1936.

Yllo, A. Cures in breaking the smoking habit. *Svensk Lapartidn* (Sw.) 56: 2139–44, July 31, 1959.

You can quit smoking; young smokers aren't really hooked. Children's Bureau: HEW Dept., 1966.

Young, M. DiCicco, L., Paul, A., and Skiff, A. Methods and materials in health education (communication). Section 3 in: Review of research related to health education practice, *Hlth. Educ. Monog., suppl. No. 1,* 1963.

Your teenage children and smoking. Children's Bureau, HEW Dept., 1964.

Zagona, S. V. Studies and issues in smoking behavior research: summary of a conference. *The American Journal of Public Health* (in press).

———, and Harter, M. R. Credibility of source and recipient's attitude: factors in the perception and retention of information on smoking behavior. *Perceptual and Motor Skills,* 23: 155–168, 1966.

———, and Zurcher, L. A., Jr. An analysis of some psychosocial variables associated with smoking behavior in a college sample. *Psychol. Rep.* 17: 967–978, 1965.

Zalla, A., and Palazzuolli, M. On the probable correlations between the smoking habit and some depressive states. *Rass Stud. Psichiat.* 51: 117–23, 1962.

Zukel, W. J., and others. Smokers and double non-smokers in heart disease. *Public Health Rep.* 74: 241–2, 1959.

Zulliger, H. Psychoanalytic experiences in public school practice. II. (Trans. by G. U. Swackhamer). *Amer. J. Orthopsychiat.* 10: 595–609, 1940.

MATERIALS ON SMOKING FOR POPULAR USE

SOME BOOKS ABOUT SMOKING FOR THE LAYMAN

Allen, W. A., Angermann, G., & Fackler, W. A., *Learning to Live Without Cigarettes*, 1967, Health Dept., Room 540 Municipal Service Bldg., Philadelphia, Pa. 19107

Barclay, S. G., *Smoke Your Way to Health!* Vantage Press, Inc., New York, 1956. $2.00.

Blakeslee, A. L., *It's Not Too Late to Stop Smoking Cigarettes!* Public Affairs Pamphlet #386, New York, 1966. 20 pp., illustrated.

Brean, H., *How to Stop Smoking*, Vanguard Press, Inc., New York, 1958. $3.50.

Cain, A. H., *The Cigarette Habit*, Doubleday & Co., Inc., Dolphin, New York, 1964. $.95.

Caldwell, E., *How You Can Stop Smoking*, Plaza Book Co., New York, 1954. $1.98.

Chesser, E., *When and How to Quit Smoking*, Emerson Books, Inc., New York, 1964. $2.95.

Consumer Reports. *Consumers Union Report on Smoking and the Public Interest,* by the Editors of Consumer Reports, Simon and Schuster, Inc., New York, 1963. $3.50; $1.50 (paperback).

Dammann, C. J., *How to Stop Smoking Cigarettes the ABC Way,* Frederick Fell, Inc., New York, 1964. $1.00 (paperback).

Dunhill, A. H., *Gentle Art of Smoking*, G. P. Putnam & Sons, New York, 1954. $3.75.

Eysenck, H. J., *Smoking, Health and Personality*, Basic Books Inc., New York, 1965. $4.95.

Harper, A., *It's Easy to Quit Smoking*, Borden Publishing Co., Alhambra, California. $.60.

Heise, J. G., *The Painless Way to Stop Smoking,* Appleton-Century, New York, 1962. $2.95.

King, A., *The Cigarette Habit: a Scientific Cure*, Doubleday & Co., Inc., New York, 1959. $2.00.

Kushner, A. S., *Stop Smoking, Live Longer*, Vantage Press, Inc., New York, 1956. $2.75.

Le Cron, L. M., *How to Stop Smoking Through Self-Hypnosis*, Parker Publishing Co., New York, 1964. $4.95.

Lehrer, J. M., *How You Can Stop Smoking Permanently,* Wilshire Book Co., Hollywood, 1960. $1.00 (paperback).

Lieb, C. W., *Safer Smoking*, Exposition Press, Inc., New York, 1953. $2.50.

McFarland, J. W. & Folkenberg, E. J., *How to Stop Smoking in Five Days*, Prentice-Hall, 1964. $3.95.

McMillan, S. I., *Cancer by the Carton*, Fleming H. Revell Co., New Jersey, 1964. $.60.

Marks, S. L., *Smoking Is for Suckers,* Exposition Press, Inc., New York, 1964. $3.00; $1.00 (paperback).

Northrup, E., *Science Looks at Smoking,* Coward-McCann, Inc., New York, 1957. $3.00.

Ochsner, A., *Smoking and Health,* Julian Messner, Inc., New York, 1959. $3.00.

Osborn, R. C. & Benton, F. W., *Dying to Smoke,* Houghton Mifflin Co., Boston, 1964. $4.95.

Ostrow, A. A., *Why Stop Smoking?* E. P. Dutton & Co., New York, 1955. $1.75.

Salzer, K., *13 Ways to Break the Smoking Habit,* Sterling Publishing Co., New York, 1958. $1.00 (paperback).

Shryock, H., *Mind If I Smoke?* 2nd ed., Narcotics Educ., Inc., Washington, D.C., 1963. $2.50; $.50 (paperback).

Smoking and Health: Report of the Advisory Committee to the Surgeon General of the Public Health Service. U.S. Department of Health, Education, & Welfare, No. 1103, 1964. $1.25 (paperback).

Smoking and Health: Summary and Report of the Royal College of Physicians of London on Smoking in Relation to Cancer of the Lung and Other Diseases. Pitman Publishing Co., New York, 1962. $1.00 (paperback).

Ungar, S. D., *Anyone Can Stop Smoking,* Goodwin Co., Santa Monica, California, 1964. $1.00.

AMERICAN CANCER SOCIETY

All American Cancer Society material is available free by contacting local ACS chapters or writing directly to the American Cancer Society, 219 East 42nd Street, New York, New York 10017.

Pamphlets

I'll Choose the High Road. Folder on cigarette smoking and health related to the filmstrip of the same title. 6-page cartoon fold-out. Upper elementary grades.

Shall I Smoke? Presents basic facts about the risks of smoking that will help students to make their own decision. 4-page fold-out. High school.

Statement of the American Cancer Society on Cigarette Smoking and Lung Cancer. 4-page fold-out. High school.

To Smoke Or Not to Smoke. General information on smokings hazards. 6-page, 3"x9" fold-out. Adults.

Who, Me — Why? Stresses the health advantages of quitting cigarettes even after years of smoking. Emphasizes that "the time to stop smoking cigarettes is now." 4-page flyer; short answers to health questions. High school.

Your Health and Cigarettes. Outlines the health hazards of cigarette smoking, stressing the health benefits of ending the habit. 6-page fold-out. Adults.

Booklets

Answering the Most Often Asked Question About Cigarette Smoking and Lung Cancer. 10 pages, 8"x10". High school and general public.

Cigarette Smoking and Cancer. Presenting the research evidence upon which the ACS's position and programs are based. 32 pages. General public.

Cigarettes and Health. Public Affairs Pamphlet #220 A. 20 pages, 6"x6". Adults.

It's Not Too Late to Stop Smoking Cigarettes. This Public Affairs Pamphlet #386 discusses the evidence that cigarette smoking is a hazard to health and then describes the beneficial results of stopping cigarettes, with reference to some actions to help cigarette smokers to stop smoking. 20 pages, 6"x6". Adults.

Smoking and Health. Report of the Advisory Committee to the Surgeon General. Reprint of Chapter 4, Summaries and Conclusions. 40 pages. Adults.

Smoking — the Great Dilemma. Presents the facts and the paradox of the smoking situation, and discusses constructively and provocatively the problems faced by responsible citizens — smokers and non-smokers — the taxpayer and the Government. Public Affairs Pamphlet #361. 28 pages, cartoon illustrated, 6"x6". High school and Adults.

Where There's Smoke. Cartoon booklet presentation on cigarette smoking and health addressed chiefly to secondary school students. (Spanish version available.) 15 pages.

Filmstrips

Cigarettes and Health — a Challenge to Educators. Produced by National Interagency Council on Smoking and Health; presented to encourage teacher interest in classroom methods and approaches. 17 minutes, 93 frames, color, 1966.

I'll Choose the High Road. Relates cigarette smoking to health complications, stressing importance of fitness through development of wholesome habits. Most suitable for upper elementary grades. 15 minutes, 59 frames, color, recording, 1963. Teacher's Guide including text.

The Cancer Challenge to Youth. Covers the nature and history of cancer, normal and abnormal cell behavior, diagnosis and treatment; the importance of individual responsibility for self-protection, and the hope found in various fields of cancer research. 15 minutes, 65 frames, color, sound, 1959. Grades 7 through 12.

To Smoke or Not to Smoke? Describes causal relationship between cigarette smoking and lung cancer. Teacher's Guide including text, and reference booklet. 15 minutes, 84 frames, color, 1960.

Films

Breaking the Habit. Humorous cartoon emphasizing the strong hold of the cigarette smoking habit and difficulties experienced in trying to stop. 16 mm., 6 minutes, color, 1964. Adults.

Is Smoking Worth It? Discussion of lung cancer-cigarette link. Teenagers are featured. Approach is factual, not moralistic or authoritarian. 16mm., 16 minutes, color, 1962. Youth.

From One Cell. Describes the growth of cancer and cancer's relation to smoking. 16 mm., 14 minutes, color, 1950. Youth.

Man Alive. General information on smoking and health. 16 mm., 12 minutes, color, 1952. Adults and youth.

The Huffless, Puffless Dragon. Animated cartoon film particularly effective as an introduction to subject of cigarette smoking and health. 16 mm., 8 minutes, color, 1964. Upper elementary and junior high.

The Time to Stop Is Now. Emphasis for cigarette smokers: ending the cigarette habit checks further health damage, permits gradual repair of damage by years of cigarette smoking. 16 mm., 4½ minutes, color. 1965. Adults and youth.

Time For Decision. Cigarette smoking as a special as well as an individual problem. Presents concept of community action, seeking the support of opinion leaders e.g., physicians, clergymen, teachers, and business leaders. 16 mm., 18 minutes, color, 1967. Adults.

Who, Me? Role of parents in discouraging cigarette smoking of children. Intended primarily for adults. 16 mm., 19½ minutes, color, 1965. Adults and high school.

Display Materials

Best Tip Yet, Don't Start! Paper bulletin board poster addressed chiefly to young people and non-smokers. 12"x16" color (similar bookmarks also available).

Congress Has Acted, the Next Step Is Yours. Paper poster featuring the warning on cigarette packages. 12"x16", color.

I Don't Smoke Cigarettes. Series of bulletin board posters stressing that "winners" are non-smokers and good examples to follow. Pictured are: Bob Mathias, Bobby Richardson, Pat Boone, Murray Rose, Bart Starr, Bill Russell. 8¾"x11", color, paper.

If You Figure It's Too Late to Quit . . . This is a display for table-top use. Art work differs from the poster, also offers the pamphlet, Who, Me — Why? 4'x7', color.

If You Figure It's Too Late to Quit . . . We've Got News For You. This poster offers the pamphlet Who, Me — Why? Emphasizes the advantages of ending cigarette habit. 12"x16", color.

More Cigarettes, More Lung Cancer. Bulletin board poster. Graphic relationship between lung cancer and number of cigarettes smoked. 11"x17", color, paper.

Smoking Is Very Debonair. Series of 5, separately titled, illustrate degenerates smoking. 8½"x11", black and white, paper.

To Smoke or Not To Smoke? Table-top display presenting facts on smoking, 3'x5' cardboard, black and white, paper.

Miscellaneous

Bookmark. With same art work as poster, Best Tip Yet, Don't Start!

Photos. Still pictures relating to the comic book, *Where There's Smoke There's Danger* and to these ACS films: *Who Me; Is Smoking Worth It; Breaking The Habit; Huffless, Puffless Dragon.*

Record: containing several spot announcements of various lengths.

Television. Two slides and three 60-second spot announcements.

1967 Wallet-Size Calendar. Chart featuring theme "stopping cigarettes means longer life." Color, plastic.

Filmstrip Kit

To Smoke Or Not To Smoke? Complete in cardboard box 12½"x12½" containing: Filmstrip: 84 frames, color, 35 mm. Record: 10" disc, 1 side. 15 minutes. Teacher's Guide: 24 pages (Code No. 2387.01) Pamphlet (sample): *Shall I Smoke?* (Code #2042) Bulletin board poster (sample): *More Cigarettes, More Lung Cancer* (Code #2100) Reprint, *Smoking and Lung Cancer* (Code #2387.03).

AMERICAN HEART ASSOCIATION

Single copies of all American Heart Association material are available without charge from local Heart Association. For quantity orders please query local Heart Associations. Films or exhibits are generally available on loan. (44 East 23rd Street, New York City.)

Reprints

Cigarettes: Are the Facts Being Filtered? Reprint from *Redbook* magazine.
Cigarette Smoking and Cardiovascular Diseases. Report of AHA Committees reviewing scientific evidence concerning the relationship of smoking and CV diseases. 4 pages, 8½"x11", 1963. Adults.
Cigarette Smoking and the Role of the Physician. By Dr. G. Wakerlin. Background information for physicians. Reprint from *Circulation.* Adults.
What I Tell My Patients About Smoking. A reprint by Howard Sprague, M.D., former president, American Heart Association. Advice to patients regarding smoking. Reprint from *Modern Concepts.* 4 pages, Oct. 1964. Dissuasion techniques a doctor can use.

Leaflets

Cigarette Quiz. Questions and answers about smoking. Teenagers and general public.
What Everyone Should Know About Smoking and Heart Disease. A four-panel leaflet pointing out studies showing a statistical association between heavy cigarette smoking and death or illness from coronary heart disease. A statement by the Board of Directors of the American Heart Association in 1960 included. 2½"x4½", color. General public.
What To Tell Your Parents About Smoking. Leaflet to be taken home by youngsters who want their parents to stop smoking. Children.
Where There's Smoke, There's Danger from Heart Disease. Envelope stuffer with 3 good reasons for not smoking. Flyer, color. General public.
Cartoon Leaflet: "Enjoy the Pleasures of Not Smoking."

Display Materials

Don't Smoke Posters. Set of four in color, 11"x14".
Smoking and Heart Disease. Set of two posters in two colors, two sizes, with slogans: "Why Risk Heart Disease — Don't Smoke," and "Be Smart, Save Your Heart."
Transparency for Use with Shadow Box Flasher Display. One of the set of five transparencies is on smoking.

Miscellaneous

Educational Radio Script Packet: Smoking and Heart Disease. Fifteen spot announcements.
Educational TV Film Kit: Smoking and Heart Disease. Three live-action spots on risks of smoking.
Newspaper cartoons: Sets to be ordered in mats or repros. Proofs will be sent with order blanks.
Live TV Program: Outline for a half-hour panel-quiz show, with film clips supplied from Wexler film.

Films

Too Tough To Care. Film satire to deglamorize cigarette advertising. Available on loan from most Heart Associations. 16 mm., 18 minutes, color, sound, 1966. Upper elementary grades, college, general public.
Barney Butt: The animated cartoon color film, produced in Germany with adaptation for American audiences in the open and close narration. About 12 minutes. With promotion leaflet and discussion guide.
Smoking and Coronary Heart Disease (Wexler) About 8 minutes. Animated color film depicting effects of cigarette smoke on various functions of the body; presents the statistical evidence that smoking cigarettes increases the risk of heart attack, and that stopping smoking diminishes the risk. With promotion leaflet and discussion guide.

Exhibits

Where There's Smoke — There's Danger From Heart Disease. Table-top display made of cardboard, in black, red, gray, and white. Stands 27" high, 36" wide and 12" deep. Pocket has space for display of leaflet. Packs flat in its own self-mailer (24"x24"). Available from local Heart Associations. $6.00.

Bibliographies

Audio-Visual Aids on Smoking. AHA School Health Section. Mimeographed sheet listing resource units for use with school and college youth.
Health for Youth. Heart Association of S. E. Penn. 26-page inter-agency booklet listing resource materials.
Selected References on Smoking. AHA School Health Section. Mimeographed sheets.

Guidance for Teachers

Florida Smoking Materials. Guidelines recommended by Florida Comm. on Smoking and Health with bibliography of basic materials.
Resource Guide on Smoking and Health (Elementary Grades V & VI). Maryland Committee on Smoking and Health. Guidelines for local programs and suggested activities for grades 5 & 6.
Smoking and Health. Idaho Dept. of Health and Idaho Heart Association. Printed guide for teachers with list of resource materials.
Smoking and Health (Teacher Resource Kit). Illinois Dept. of Health and Illinois Office of Public Instruction. Kit with selected references.
Smoking and Health Resource Kit. Tulsa County Heart Association. Chapter survey and educational program in the schools.

Smoking and Health — Resource Unit for Teachers. Heart Association of Southeastern Penn. Printed guide for teaching secondary school students.

Smoking and Its Relationship to Health and Disease (A Resource Guide for Michigan Teachers of Grades 5 to 12). Michigan Council on Smoking and Health. 28-page booklet.

Smoking and Your Health. 4th, 5th, 6th grade teaching materials.

Teachers Resource Kit on Smoking and Health (Grades 5 through 8 in Elementary Schools). California Heart Association. Teachers guide, summary of research, review of studies in California and list of resource materials.

Teachers Resource Kit on Smoking and Health (Grades 7 through 12 in Jr. High Schools and High Schools). California Heart Association. Teachers guide, summary of research, review of studies in California, and list of resource materials.

Teaching Aids on Smoking and Health. New Mexico Heart Association. Kit of pamphlets and memoranda from agencies in New Mexico.

Upper Elementary Smoking Education. American Heart Association School Health Section. Mimeographed sheets suggesting approaches at three grade levels.

Workshops, Conferences, etc.

Advisory Sessions on Health. Chicago Heart Association. 2-page outline for four sessions.

Cigarettes In and Out of School. Cleveland Health Museum. 22-page mimeographed booklet, a summary of a workshop with list of reference materials. Loan only.

Delaware Conference on Smoking and Health. Delaware Heart Association. Kit with agenda and materials used at one-day inter-agency conference.

No Ifs . . . Ands . . . Or Butts. Rhode Island Interagency Council on Smoking. Program outline of one-day conference for youth.

Proceedings: Maryland Conference on Smoking and Health. Maryland State Dept. of Education and Health. Proceedings of one-day conference.

Report on Smoking — 1964. Penn. Heart Association. History of AHA concern and program of Pennsylvania Heart Association.

Second Annual Delaware Conference on Smoking. Delaware Heart Association. Program outline for high school conference.

Summary Proceedings — National Interagency Conference on Cigarette Smoking and Youth. American Cancer Society. Complete proceedings of a two-day conference. Loan only.

Summary Report — Conference on Smoking and the Health of Youth. Penn. Heart Association. Background of the entire program.

Tobacco Education Workshop. Brigham Young University. For teachers.

Cigarette Smoking and Your Health. California Interagency Council on Cigarette Smoking and Health. Part of a Speakers' Kit available from AHA School Health Section.

The Effectiveness of Education and Small Group Interaction in Modifying the Cigarette Smoking Habits of Parents of Philadelphia Elementary School Children.

Report of an inter-agency study. Heart Association of S. E. Penn. participated.

Facts in the Cigarette Case Packet. Heart & Torch free offer.

Health Hazards of Smoking. Roswell Park Memorial Institute for Cancer Research, N. Y. State Dept. of Health. 15-page booklet.

Health vs. Cigarette Smoking. California Heart Association. Printed report of Governor's Advisory Committee on Cigarette Smoking and Health with recommendations.

Information on Smoking and the Health of Youth, for School Programming. Penn. Dept. of Public Instructions and Penn. Dept. of Health. Packet of materials for students and teachers. Loan only.

What School Children Think about Smoking. California Heart Association. Anti-smoking poster and essay contest. Illustrated with children's posters.

What about Smoking and Heart Disease. Printed folder for general distribution and for use in programs for youth.

Will Your Students Smoke? Ohio State Heart Association. Summary of current knowledge, psychological aspects, and resources. 14-page booklet.

AMERICAN TEMPERANCE SOCIETY

All American Temperance Society material is available by writing directly to them (640 Eastern Avenue, Washington, D.C.) or to Narcotics Education, Inc., 6830 Laurel Street, N.W., Washington, D.C.

Books

Don't Let Smoking Kill You! Clarence W. Liebe, M.D. Sifts out real truth from welter of material on smoking and health. $1.95 (hard cover), $.75 (paperback).

Dying to Smoke. An artist and a doctor present a graphic statement against smoking. $4.95. Young people.

How to Stop Smoking in Five Days. Step by step routines of daily living shaped to help break the smoking habit. $3.95.

Mind If I Smoke. Scientifically discusses how smoking affects the health, $2.50 (hard cover), $.75 (paperback).

Smoking and Your Life. Alton Ochsner, M.D. Summarizes all accumulated evidence on the effects of smoking. $3.00.

Smoking or Health? Study made by Advisory Committee is summarized. $.50 (paperback).

The Tobacco-Health Problem. Presents factual information on tobacco and health in a readable text and aids the teacher in presenting these facts in a clear manner. Junior and senior high school.

Leaflets

How to Stop Smoking. Wayne McFarland, M.D., Ten steps to eliminate smoking. $1.25 per 100; $10.00 per 1,000.

Lung Cancer and Its Relation to Smoking. Alton Ochsner, M.D. $5.50 per 100; $50.00 per 1,000.

Should a Boy Smoke? Harold Shryock, M.D. $5.50 per 100; $50.00 per 1,000.

Should a Girl Smoke? Harold Shryock, M.D. $5.50 per 100; $50.00 per 1,000.

Will One Million Really Die? Refers to denials by cigarette companies that they are seducing young people through ads.

Reprints

When Habit Gets Out of Hand. R. Gordon Bell, M.D. Physician, specializing in treating addictions, looks at his own habit of smoking. *Smoke Signals.* Dec. 1966.

Why Quit Smoking? Paul Harvey, ABC News Analyst. 16 pages. $5.50 per 100; $50.00 per 1,000.

Periodicals

Smoke Signals. Interprets the extensive tobacco research of today, focusing attention on latest findings. Six issues each semester, 4-page monthly, single copy $.10; Subscription $1.00 per year; special prices: $3.50 per 100, $30.00 per 1,000.

The Winner. Two-color periodical for students in grades 1-6. $1.00 per year.

Filmstrip

Nature's Filter. Richard H. Overholt, M.D., Tufts University, shows effect of smoking upon respiratory system. Complete with script. 55 frames, color, 30 min., $6.75.

Films

Beyond Reasonable Doubt. Presents questions on the issues of smoking and health. 16 mm., 25 min., color, 1964. $197.50 or $7.50 rental per day. General public.

Cancer by the Carton. Features four noted doctors in Boston. Shows relationship between smoking and lung cancer. 16 mm., 30 min., color, 1958, $265.00 or $7.50 rental per day. Teenagers.

One in 20,000. Shows relationship between smoking and lung cancer. Dr. Alton Ochsner in actual lung cancer operation. 16 mm., 30 min., color, 1956. $265.00 or $7.50 rental per day.

Time Pulls the Trigger. Features relationship of smoking to various aspects of health. 16 mm., 23 min., color, animated. 1960, $197.50 or $7.50 rental per day. General public.

Up in Smoke. Shows half-truths and deceptive claims are forced upon the public to protect economic interests of tobacco industry. 16 mm., 23 min., color, 1961.

Display

Smoking Sam. Smoking manikin, size of a 12-year-old boy, with side zippers for viewing from the rear. $136.50.

The Other Side of the Coin. Compelling pictorial presentation of facts on smoking. 7'x7', simulated coin 14" in diameter, motor operated, 2 color blowups 20"x28". Use at county fairs, film presentations, schools, churches, service organizations.

NATIONAL TUBERCULOSIS ASSOCIATION

All National Tuberculosis Association material is available from local NTA chapters or by writing to them at 1790 Broadway, New York, New York.

Leaflets

Chronic Bronchitis, the Facts. Discussion of the disease with reference to the importance of not smoking. 6 page fold-out, 1963, color. Adults.

Cigarette Smoking, the Facts. Excellent factual presentation of the hazards of smoking. 6 page fold-out, color. High school/Adults.

Emphysema, the Facts. Questions and answers relating smoking and this little-known disease killing over 10,-000 Americans yearly. 6 page fold-out, color. High school/Adults. 1963.

Here Is the Evidence, You Be The Judge. Cartoon type, briefly defines hazards of smoking. 4 page fold-out, color. Teenagers/Adults.

My Dear, This'll Kill You! Very brief factual presentation on smoking hazards. 4 page flyer. color, illustrated. Adolescents/Adults.

No Ifs, No Maybes, No Butts. Very brief factual presentation on smoking hazards. 4 page flyer, color, illustrated. Adolescents/Adults.

Too Many Cigarettes? Why Damage Your Health? Answers static and brief. 4 page flyer, color, illustrated. Adolescents/Adults.

What's the Score? Quiz on cigarette smoking. 2 page flyer, color, illustrated. Adolescents/Adults.

U.S. Government Wants You to Know. Relates to the warning on cigarette packages. 6 page fold-out. Adolescents/Adults.

Filmstrip

Cigarettes & Health. For teachers & school administrators (not students) to stimulate anti-cigarette smoking education. (Produced by National Interagency Council.) Needs filmstrip projector with turntable. Sound on record. 93 frames, color, 1966. Adults.

Films

Point of View. Directed at young people to expose cigarette smoking and what it really is. 16 mm. and 35 mm., 19 minutes, 7 seconds. Black & white. Sound. Loan arranged by local or state tuberculosis associations. 1965. Adolescents/Adults.

Miscellaneous

U.S. Government Warns! Poster, 11"x14", two colors. Adolescents/Adults.

Cigarettes Shorten Lives, Poster (matches leaflet — No Ifs, No Maybes, No Butts), 8½x11", two colors. Adolescents/Adults.

Booklets

Problems of Changing Attitudes and Actions on Smoking. Informative, sophisticated analysis for presenting smoking and health to teenage children. 15 pages, 5"x8". Adults.

What Is It About Cigarettes? How cigarette smoking affects the cleansing system of the breathing passages. Charles F. Tate, Jr., M.D. Reprint from National Tuberculosis Association, Feb., 1964.

PENNSYLVANIA
TUBERCULOSIS AND HEALTH ASSOCIATION

All Pennsylvania Tuberculosis and Health Association material is available from local Tuberculosis and Health Associations or by writing directly to them (311 S. Juniper St., Philadelphia, Pa. 19107).

Leaflets

Don't Let Your Health Go Up in Smoke. 5 pages, August, 1960. Teenagers.

Filter the Facts Before the Smoke. A mass of statistical evidence indicating that smoking is harmful. 6 pages, January, 1963. Adults.

Let's Face It Pal. Aimed at hospital and other patients with respiratory disease. Points out that smoking does a well person no good and can be deadly to patients with respiratory diseases. 4 panel leaflet.

Reprints

Cigarette Smoking, Cigarette Advertising and Health. A review concerning tobacco and the health facts, Roger S. Mitchell, M.D. Reprint from the *Journal of School Health,* 10 pages.

Modifying Smoking Habits of High School Students. Discusses the problem of smoking withdrawal by high school youngsters, Dr. Daniel Horn. Reprint from *Children,* March-April, 1960, Vol. 7, #2. 24 pages.

The Effect of Smoking. Discusses effects of smoking on health. Dr. E. Cuyler Hammond. Reprint from *Scientific American,* July, 1962. 16 pages. Brighter high school students.

Films

Tobacco and the Human Body. Analyzes the contents of tobacco smoke; demonstrates some of the physiological effects of smoking, and sums up the factors to be considered in deciding whether or not to smoke. 15 minutes, black and white, sound.

PUBLIC AFFAIRS PAMPHLETS

All Public Affairs Pamphlets are available at $.25 a copy; special quantity rates as low as $.10 apiece on large orders. Subscription rates: $3.00 for 15 pamphlets; $5.00 for 30 pamphlets; $7.00 for 45 pamphlets (381 Park Ave. South, New York 10016).

Cigarettes and Health. Public Affairs Pamphlet #220 A. 6"x6", 20 pages. Adults.

It's Not Too Late To Stop Smoking Cigarettes. Discusses the evidence that cigarette smoking is a hazard to health and then describes the beneficial results to stopping cigarettes, with reference to some actions to help cigarette smokers to stop smoking. Public Affairs Pamphlet #386. 6"x6", 20 pages. Research information. Adults.

Smoking — The Great Dilemma. Presents the facts and paradox of the smoking situation, and discusses constructively and provocatively the problem faced by responsible citizens — smokers and non-smokers — the taxpayer and the Government. Public Affairs Pamphlet #361. 6"x6", 28 pages, cartoon illustrated. High school/Adults.

ROSWELL PARK MEMORIAL INSTITUTE

All Roswell Park Memorial Institute material is available from them (666 Elm Street, Buffalo, New York 14203).

Educational Materials on Smoking. Produced by New York State Department of Health. March, 1965. Contains posters, matchbooks, leaflets, pamphlets, kits, and auto plates. Price list included.

En-Garde. Curriculum on Smoking and Health. Produced by Cigarette Cancer Committee of Roswell Park. Contains outlines for grades 5 thru 12 and adults; resource materials; experiments for science classes; and class survey form.

Filmstrip Kit. Presents facts about smoking, lung cancer, and other smoking-related diseases. Includes a written script for easy reference. 52 frames, 28 minutes, with descriptive lecture recorded on tape. Young people.

Lecture Slide Kit. Lecture outline is included. 40 color slides. 2"x2", 35 mm. Physicians, teachers, nurses and science students.

U.S. DEPARTMENT OF HEALTH PUBLICATIONS

All U.S. Department of Health, Education, and Welfare material is available from the National Clearinghouse for Smoking and Health, Division of Chronic Diseases, 4040 N. Fairfax Avenue, Arlington, Virginia 22203.

Cigarette Smoking — Chronic Bronchitis and Emphysema. States some facts and what you should do. Public Health Service Publication #1103-E. 6 pages. Adults.

Smoking and Health. Report by Advisory Committee to the Surgeon General confirms cigarette hazards. Reprint by Public Health Service.

Smoking and Lung Cancer. Discusses in detail the relationship of smoking and lung cancer. Also answers some common questions asked by the general public. 26 page booklet. Adults.

Smoking and the Heart. Related to Smoking and Health. Report of the Advisory Committee to the Surgeon General. Publication #1103-b. Designed to give facts about smoking to adults. 4 page leaflet. $.05 each or $2.00/100 copies. Adults.

Smoking, Health, and You. Facts on smoking and health for teenagers. Children's Bureau Publication #424. 22 page booklet. $.15 each. 1964. Teenagers.

Summary of the Report of the Surgeon General's Advisory Committee on Smoking and Health. Public Health Service Publication #1103-D.

Your Teenage Children and Smoking. Contains ideas and opinions expressed by teenagers; geared toward parents. Children's Bureau, Publication #423. 14 page booklet, $.15. 1964. Adults.

MISCELLANEOUS MATERIALS AVAILABLE

Cigarettes and the School. 8 page fold-out, 3"x8", 35 for $1.00. General public. American Association for Health, Physical Education and Recreation, 1201 Sixteenth Street., N.W., Washington, D.C. 20036.

Smoking Facts You Should Know. Gives facts on the smoking and health problem as related to the individual smoker. 8 page leaflet, $.05 per copy with discount for larger purchase. American Medical Association, 535 N. Dearborn Street, Chicago, Illinois.

Should We Believe Everything We Are Told About Tobacco? 58 Medical authorities answer questions. 32 page booklet, 5"x8" Adults. Anti-Tobacco Center of America, Inc., 366 Fifth Avenue, New York, New York.

Smoke Anyone? Film. 16 mm., color, 9 minutes, $100 per print. Junior and senior high school students. Center for Mass Communication, Columbia University, 1125 Amsterdam Ave., New York, New York.

Teenagers and Cigarettes. Discussion answering some questions relating to the teenager and the smoking habit. 4 pages. Reprint. Teenagers. Changing Times, The Kiplinger Magazine, 1729 H Street, N.W., Washington, D.C.

Teenage Cigarette Purchasing and Smoking Habits in the USA — 1963. 19 page booklet. 1963. Teenagers. Gilbert Marketing Group, Inc., 235 East 42nd Street, New York, New York.

His First Cigarette May Be A MATTER OF LIFE OR DEATH. 8 page pamphlet, 9"x3", free. Parents. National Congress of Parents and Teachers, 700 North Rush Street, Chicago, Illinois 60611.

Smoking: the School's Responsibility. 8 pages, 35 for $1.00. General Public. National Education Association, 1201 16th Street, N.W., Washington, D.C. 20036.

Cigarettes and Health: a Challenge to Educators. Filmstrip. 93 frames, color, 33⅓ record, 17 minutes. $2.25/copy in lots of 1-99, plus $.75 mailing and handling each copy. Teachers. Also display material. 10' length, 3' deep, 6' high. Available on loan. Focuses attention on the scientific evidence of the hazards of cigarette smoking and on the cigarette package warning label and presents information about the organization and programs of the Council. National Interagency Council on Smoking & Health, P. O. Box 3654 Central Station, Arlington, Virginia 22203.

Smoking and Health 1966. Teaching Reference Guide. New Jersey State Department of Health; New Jersey State Department of Education. Trenton, New Jersey.

Smoking — It's Up to You. Leaflet for young people to look at the facts and decide what they can do. 1960. Teenagers. New York State Department of Health, Albany, New York.

The Facts on Teenage Smoking. Leona Baumgartner, M.D. Reprint from *Parents' Magazine,* October 1960. Parents' Institute, 52 Vanderbilt Ave., New York, New York.

The Man Who Wrote His Own Obituary. Mark Waters. Reprint from *Reader's Digest,* July 1966. Reader's Digest Association, Inc., Pleasantville, New York 10570.

Ten Little Smokers. Cartoons showing how smoking is harmful to health. Leaflet. Free. Teenagers and Adults. Smoking and Health Research Project, Castor & Lycoming Avenues, Philadelphia, Pennsylvania 19124.

Cigarette Smoking and Health; a review of studies by the California State Department of Public Health; a summary of opinion and a proposal for action. 1963. Booklet. State of California, Department of Public Health, 2151 Berkeley Way, Berkeley, California.

INDEX